T0338312

Extreme Events in Finance

Wiley Handbooks in
FINANCIAL ENGINEERING AND ECONOMETRICS

Advisory Editor
Ruey S. Tsay
The University of Chicago Booth School of Business, USA

A complete list of the titles in this series appears at the end of this volume.

Extreme Events in Finance

A Handbook of Extreme Value
Theory and its Applications

Edited by

FRANÇOIS LONGIN
Department of Finance,
ESSEC Business School,
Paris, France

Published by John Wiley & Sons, Inc., Hoboken, New Jersey
Published simultaneously in Canada

For general information on our other products and services or for technical support, please contact
our Customer Care Department within the United States at (800) 762-2974, outside the United States
at (317) 572-3993 or fax (317) 572-4002.

Wiley also publishes its books in a variety of electronic formats. Some content that appears in print
may not be available in electronic formats. For more information about Wiley products, visit our web
site at www.wiley.com.

Library of Congress Cataloging-in-Publication Data:

Names: Longin, François Michel, 1968- editor.
Title: Extreme events in finance : a handbook of extreme value theory and its
    applications / edited by François Longin.
Description: Hoboken : Wiley, 2017. | Series: Wiley handbooks in financial
    engineering and econometrics | Includes bibliographical references and
    index.
Identifiers: LCCN 2016004187| ISBN 9781118650196 (hardback) | ISBN
    9781118650202 (epub)
Subjects: LCSH: Finance–Mathematical models. | Extreme value
    theory–Mathematical models. | BISAC: BUSINESS & ECONOMICS / Insurance /
    Risk Assessment & Management.
Classification: LCC HG106 .E98 2016 | DDC 332.01/5195–dc23 LC record available at
    http://lccn.loc.gov/2016004187

Cover image courtesy of iStockphoto © Nikada

Typeset in 10/12pt TimesLTStd by SPi Global, Chennai, India

Printed in the United States of America

10 9 8 7 6 5 4 3 2 1

1 2017

Contents

François Longin (ESSEC Business School)

 François Longin graduated from the French engineering school Ecole Nationale des Ponts et Chaussées in 1990, and received the PhD degree in finance from HEC Paris in 1993 for his thesis "Volatility and extreme price movements in equity markets." He then conducted research on financial markets at New York University and the London Business School. He is now Professor of Finance at ESSEC Business School and a consultant to several financial institutions and firms. He is an active member of CREAR (Center of Research in Econo-finance and Actuarial sciences on Risk) at ESSEC. His current research interests include extreme events in finance, as well as financial applications of extreme value theory in risk management and portfolio management. His works have been published in international scientific journals such as the *Journal of Finance, Journal of Business, Review of Financial Studies, Journal of Banking and Finance,* and the *Journal of Derivatives.* He is Associate Editor of the *Journal of Banking and Finance* and the *Journal of Risk.* His domains of expertise include risk management for banks, portfolio management for fund management firms, financial management for firms, and wealth management for individuals. (More information can be found on www.longin.fr.) He is also a participant in the SimTrade project, which is a pedagogical tool to help understand how financial markets work and to learn to act in financial markets, and a simulation-based research program to improve the behavior of individuals and the statistical characteristics of financial markets. More information can be had from www.simtrade.fr.

About the Contributors

Jan Beirlant (KU Leuven University)

 Jan Beirlant obtained a PhD in statistics from KU Leuven in 1984. He is currently a Professor with the Department of Mathematics, KU Leuven University. Presently, he is chairing LRisk, a center for research, training, and advice in insurance and financial risk analysis, combining all relevant KU Leuven expertise. His main research interests include extreme value methodology with emphasis on applications in insurance and finance. He has published over 100 papers in statistical research journals and has published the following books: *Statistics of Extremes: Theory and Applications*, with Y. Goegebeur, J. Segers, and J.L. Teugels (2004), and *Reinsurance: Actuarial and Statistical Aspects*, with H. Albrecher and J.L. Teugels (2016).

Chapter: Estimation of the Extreme Value Index

Patrice Bertail (University of Paris-Ouest-Nanterre la Défense)

 Patrice Bertail is Professor of applied mathematics (statistics and probabilities) at the University of Paris-Ouest-Nanterre la Défense. He has been in charge of the Master's ISIFAR (Ingénierie Statistique et Informatique de la Finance, l'Assurance et du Risque) program. He is also a researcher with the MODAL'X laboratory and CREST-ENSAE. His research interests include resampling methods for dependent data, survey sampling, empirical processes and extremes, especially for Markovian data (with applications toward food risks assessment).

Chapter: Extreme Values Statistics for Markov Chains with Applications to Finance and Insurance

Philippe Bertrand (IAE Aix-en Provence)

Philippe Bertrand obtained a PhD in mathematical economics from Ecole des Hautes Etudes en Sciences Sociales and the Habilitation à diriger des recherches (HDR) from University Paris-Dauphine. He is currently a Full Professor of finance with IAE Aix-en Provence. He is also a member of the CERGAM Research Center and a member of Aix-Marseille School of Economics. He joined IAE in 2011, from the Faculté d'Economie of Aix-Marseille, where he was Professor of finance. He was formerly the head of Financial Engineering, CCF Capital Management. His research interests include portfolio management, risk and performance evaluation, and portfolio insurance, as well as financial structured products. He has published numerous articles in scientific journals such as the *Journal of Banking and Finance*, *Finance, Geneva Risk and Insurance Review*, *Financial Analysts Journal*, and the *Journal of Asset Management*. He is currently the executive president of the French Finance Association (AFFI). He has served as an associate editor of the review *Bankers, Markets & Investors*. He chaired the 31st Spring International Conference of the French Finance Association, held at IAE AIX, May 20–21, 2014.

Chapter: Portfolio Insurance: The Extreme Value Approach Applied to the CPPI Method

Laurent Bibard (ESSEC Business School)

Laurent Bibard has been a Professor with ESSEC Business School since 1991. He was Dean of the MBA Programs (2005–2009), and is currently a Full Professor, Management Department, and Head of the Edgar Morin Chair on Complexity. His current research interests include organizational vigilance interpreted as the organizational conditions favoring collective as well as individual mindfulness. He has been invited to many prestigious universities in Germany (Mannheim), Canada (UQAM), Japan (Keio Business School, Keio University), and others. His publications include "Management and Philosophy : What is at Stake?" (*Keio Business Forum*, March 2011, Vol. 28, no 1, pp. 227–243) and *Sexuality and Globalization* (Palgrave Macmillan, New York, 2014). His book *La sagesse et le féminin* (*Wisdom and Feminity*) was republished in Japan, at the end of 2014.

Chapter: Bounded Rationalities, Routines, and Practical as well as Theoretical Blindness: On the Discrepancy Between Markets and Corporations

Jean-François Boulier (Aviva Investors France)

Jean-François Boulier graduated from the Polytechnique and obtained a PhD in fluid mechanics. He was a researcher with CNRS in Grenoble. He started his career in finance in 1987 with Credit Commercial de France, where he headed the Research and Innovation Department, then the Market Risk Department, and subsequently became CIO of Sinopia asset management and deputy CEO. He is currently the CEO of Aviva Investors France. He joined Aviva Investors in 2008 and has held several positions: CIO in Paris, then CEO in Europe, and Global CIO for Fixed Income. Between 2002 and 2008, he was heading Euro FI at Credit Agricole Asset Management.

Chapter: EVT Seen by a Vet: A Practitioner's Experience on Extreme Value Theory

Henri Bourguinat (University of Bordeaux IV)

Henri Bourguinat is Emeritus Professor of Economics, University of Bordeaux IV. In 1974, he founded LAREFI, a research laboratory dedicated to monetary and financial economics (http://lare-efi.u-bordeaux4.fr/spip.php?article36). He is a former research director at CNRS. He is the author of sixty articles published in various journals, such as *Revue Economique, Economie Appliquée*, and others. He has (co)-authored eighteen books on international economics and finance. His book, *Finance Internationale*, has been a best seller since it was first published.

Chapter: Credo Ut Intelligam

Geoffrey Booth (Michigan State University)

Geoffrey Booth holds the Frederick S. Addy Distinguished Chair in Finance, Michigan State University. He has published more than 150 journal articles, monographs, and professional papers. Booth's work has appeared in the *Journal of Finance*, *Review of Economics and Statistics*, and *Review of Financial Studies*, to name but a few. His current research interests include the behavior of financial markets with special emphasis on market microstructure issues and asset allocation decisions of financial institutions.

Chapter: The Sortino Ratio and Extreme Value Theory: An Application to Asset Allocation

Eric Briys (Cyberlibris)

Eric Briys is the co-founder of www.cyberlibris.com, and a former Managing Director, Deutsche Bank Global Markets Division, London, where he headed the European Insurance Coverage Group. Prior to joining Deutsche Bank, he worked with Merrill Lynch, Lehman Brothers, Tillinghast, and The World Bank. He has held academic positions at CERAM, Concordia University, University of Montreal, and HEC Paris. He has published articles in *American Economic Review*, *Journal of Finance*, *Journal of Financial and Quantitative Analysis*, *Journal of Risk and Insurance*, *Geneva Papers on Risk and Insurance Theory*, the *Southern Economic Journal*, *Journal of Risk and Uncertainty*, *Journal of International Money and Finance*, *European Economic Review*, and others. He is a former Editor of *Finance*, the *Journal of the French Finance Association*, and Founding Editor of the *Review of Derivatives Research*. He has also (co)-authored 11 books on economics and finance.

Chapter: Credo Ut Intelligam

John Paul Broussard (Rutgers University)

John Paul Broussard is an Associate Professor of finance at Rutgers University, Camden, NJ, where he teaches investments and corporate finance courses. His research papers have been published in the *Journal of Financial Economics, Financial Management, Management Science, Journal of Financial Services Research, Quarterly Review of Economics and Finance,* and the *European Journal of Operational Research,* as well as in other journals and monographs. His current financial market research interests include extreme value applications to portfolio decision making and high-frequency trading.

Chapter: The Sortino Ratio and Extreme Value Theory: An Application to Asset Allocation

Frederico Caeiro (Nova University of Lisbon)

Frederico Caeiro received a MSc in probability and statistics in 2001, and a PhD in statistics in 2006, from the Faculty of Science, Lisbon University. He is currently an Auxiliary Professor with the Mathematics Department, Faculty of Science and Technology, Nova University of Lisbon, and a member of the Center for Mathematics and Applications. His current research interests include statistics of extremes, extreme value theory, nonparametric statistics, and computational statistical methods.

Chapter: Bootstrap Methods in Statistics of Extremes

Kam Fong Chan (University of Queensland Business School)

Kam Fong is currently a Senior Lecturer in finance with the University of Queensland Business School, University of Queensland, Australia. He has previously worked for several years as a quant at the Risk Analytics Division of the Risk Management Department, United Overseas Bank (UOB), Singapore. His research interests include modeling asset prices using various state-of-the-art econometric techniques, derivatives pricing, and risk management. He has published in various journals of international repute, including the *Journal of Banking and Finance*, *International Journal of Forecasting*, *Pacific Basin Finance Journal*, and the *Journal of International Financial Markets, Institutions & Money*.

Chapter: Extreme Value Theory and Risk Management in Electricity Markets

Stephen Chan (University of Manchester)

Stephen Chan is currently working toward the PhD degree at the University of Manchester, UK. He is the winner of an EPSRC Doctoral Prize Fellowship. His research interests include extreme value analysis, financial theory, and distribution theory. His publications include an R package and papers in *Quantitative Finance*.

Chapter: Estimation Methods for Value at Risk

Jean-Marie Choffray (ESSEC Business School and University of Liège)

Dr. Jean-Marie Choffray was, until recently, Senior Lecturer at ESSEC (France) and Chair Professor of Management Science at the Graduate School of Business, University of Liège (Belgium). He is the author of several books and a frequent contributor to scientific and professional journals, which includes over 70 articles. He is the recipient of a number of distinguished research awards and sits on the boards of several companies that he co-founded.

Chapter: Protecting Assets Under Non-Parametric Market Conditions

Stéphan Clémençon (Telecom ParisTech)

Stéphan Clémençon received a PhD in applied mathematics from the University Denis Diderot, Paris, France, in 2000. In October 2001, he joined the faculty of the University Paris X as an Associate Professor and successfully defended his habilitation thesis in 2006. Since October 2007, he has been a Professor and Researcher with Telecom ParisTech, the leading school in the field of information technologies in France, holding the Chair in Machine Learning. His research interests include machine learning, Markov processes, computational harmonic analysis, and nonparametric statistics.

Chapter: Extreme Values Statistics for Markov Chains with Applications to Finance and Insurance

John Cotter (University College Dublin)

John Cotter is Professor of Finance and the Chair in quantitative finance, University College, Dublin. He is also a Research Fellow with the UCLA Ziman Research Center for Real Estate. His recent professional papers include those in the *Review of Financial Studies, Journal of Banking and Finance*, and *Journal of International Money and Finance*. He is an associate editor of the *Journal of Banking and Finance, Journal of International Financial Markets, Institutions and Money*, and *European Journal of Finance*.

Chapter: Margin Setting and Extreme Value Theory

Miguel de Carvalho (Pontificia Universidad Católica de Chile)

Miguel de Carvalho is an Associate Professor of applied statistics, Pontificia Universidad Católica de Chile. Before moving to Chile, he was a postdoctoral fellow with the Swiss Federal Institute of Technology (EPFL). He is an applied mathematical statistician with a variety of interdisciplinary interests, inter alia, biostatistics, econometrics, and statistics of extremes. In addition to serving at the university, he is also a regular academic consultant of Banco de Portugal (Portuguese Central Bank). He has been on the editorial board of the *Annals of Applied Statistics* (IMS) and *Statistics and Public Policy* (ASA).

Chapter: Statistics of Extremes: Challenges and Opportunities

Thanh Thi Huyen Dinh (De Lage Landen Group)

Thanh Thi Huyen Dinh studied at Maastricht University, the Netherlands. She obtained a PhD based on her research on collateralization and credit scoring in the Vietnamese loan market and on tail risk and systemic risk of different types of financial institutions, the topic of this handbook contribution. She is currently a Global Analytics Consultant at the US division of the De Lage Landen Group (DLL), a Dutch insurance company.

Chapter: Comparing Tail Risk and Systemic Risk Profiles for Different Types of U.S. Financial Institutions

Kevin Dowd (Durham University)

Kevin Dowd is Professor of finance and economics at Durham University, UK. He has written extensively on the history and theory of free banking, central banking, financial regulation and monetary systems, financial risk management, pensions, and mortality modeling. His books include *Private Money: The Path to Monetary Stability*, *The State and the Monetary System*, *Laissez-Faire Banking*, *Competition and Finance: A New Interpretation of Financial and Monetary Economics*, *Money and the Market: Essays on Free Banking*, and *Measuring Market Risk*. He is also the co-author with Martin Hutchinson of *Alchemists of Loss: How Modern Finance and Government Intervention Crashed the Financial System* (Wiley, 2010).

Chapter: Margin Setting and Extreme Value Theory

Isabel Fraga Alves (University of Lisbon)

Isabel Fraga Alves obtained a PhD in statistics and computation in 1992 for her thesis "Statistical Inference in Extreme Value Models," and the Habilitation degree in statistics and operations research in 2004, both from the University of Lisbon. She is currently an Associate Professor with the Department of Statistics and Operations Research, Faculty of Sciences, University of Lisbon. She is a past Coordinator of the Center of Statistics and Applications, University of Lisbon (2006–2009), an elected member of International Statistical Institute, and a member of the Bernoulli Society for Mathematical Statistics and Probability, Portuguese Statistical Society, and Portuguese Mathematical Society.

Chapter: Extreme Value Theory: An Introductory Overview

Ivette Gomes (University of Lisbon)

Ivette Gomes obtained a PhD in statistics from the University of Sheffield, UK, in 1978, and the Habilitation degree in applied mathematics from the University of Lisbon in 1982. She was a Full Professor with the Department of Statistics and Operations Research, Faculty of Sciences, University of Lisbon (1988–2011), and is now a Principal Researcher with the Centre for Statistics and Applications, University of Lisbon (CEAUL). Her current research interests include statistics of extremes. She is a founding member of the

Portuguese Statistical Society and member of several scientific associations. She has been involved in the organization of several international conferences, including the 56th Session of ISI, 2007. Among other editorial duties, she has been the chief editor of *Revstat*, since 2003, and associate editor of *Extremes* since 2007. She is currently Vice-President of the International Statistical Institute (ISI) for the period 2015–2019.

Chapter: Bootstrap Methods in Statistics of Extremes

Philip Gray (Monash Business School)

Philip Gray is a Professor of finance with the Monash Business School, Monash University, Melbourne, Australia. His research interests include asset pricing, empirical finance, and capital markets. He also applies quantitative techniques in derivative valuation and risk management. His research has been published in journals including the *Journal of Finance*, *Journal of Futures Markets*, *Journal of Banking and Finance*, *Journal of Business*, *Finance & Accounting*, *International Review of Finance*, and *International Journal of Forecasting*.

Chapter: Extreme Value Theory and Risk Management in Electricity Markets

Lígia Henriques-Rodrigues (University of São Paulo)

Lígia Henriques-Rodrigues received a degree in applied mathematics and computation (probability and statistics) from the Instituto Superior Técnico (Technical University) of Lisbon in 1996, a Master's in applied mathematics (probability and statistics) from the University of Évora in 2000, and a PhD in statistics and operational research in the field of probability and statistics from the Faculty of Sciences, University of Lisbon in 2009. She was as a postdoctoral fellow with the Faculty of Sciences, University of Lisbon, in 2014. She is currently an Assistant Professor with the Institute of Mathematics and Statistics, University of São Paulo, Brazil, and a Researcher at the Center of Statistics and Applications, University of Lisbon. Her research interests include extreme value theory, reduced-bias semiparametric estimation, location- and scale-invariant estimation, and resampling methodologies in statistics of extremes, with applications to life sciences, environment, risk, insurance, and finance.

Chapter: Bootstrap Methods in Statistics of Extremes

Klaus Herrmann (KU Leuven University)

Klaus Herrmann obtained a PhD in science from KU Leuven in 2015 under the supervision of Professor Irène Gijbels. He completed a research stay at the ETH Zurich RiskLab with Professor Paul Embrechts in the same year. He is currently with the Department of Mathematics, KU Leuven, as a postdoctoral researcher. His research interests include statistical and probabilistic dependence concepts and their application to financial and actuarial mathematics.

Chapter: Estimation of the Extreme Value Index

Marie Kratz (ESSEC Business School Paris – Singapore, Center of Research in Econo-finance and Actuarial Sciences on Risk – CREAR)

Marie Kratz is Professor at ESSEC Business School and Director of its risk research center, CREAR. She holds a Doctorate in Applied Mathematics (UPMC, Paris 6; carried out to a great extent at the Center for Stochastic Processes, Chapel Hill, North Carolina) & Habilitation (HDR), did a post-doc at Cornell University. Her research addresses a broad range of topics in probability and statistics, and actuarial mathematics, with a focus on extreme value theory, risk analysis and Gaussian processes. These fields find natural applications in Finance and Actuarial Sciences that she is developing at ESSEC. Marie is a Fellow (Actuaire Agrégée) of the French Institute of Actuaries. She coordinates the ESSEC-ISUP (Paris 6) Actuarial Track, as well as organizes since 2009 a fortnightly Working Group on Risk Analysis at ESSEC – Paris La Défense with Academics and Professionals. Marie is also the President of the Group 'Banque Finance Assurance' of SFdS (French Society of Statistics).

Chapter: On the Estimation of the Distribution of Aggregated Heavy-Tailed Risks: Application to Risk Measures

Maxime Laot (European Central Bank)

Maxime Laot obtained a MBA with a major in applied economics from the ESSEC Business School. He is a practitioner in the field of banking supervision. He has spent several years working as an internal auditor for Groupe BPCE, one of the largest French banks, assessing the level and risk management of financial, credit, and operational risks in various retail and wholesale banking institutions in France and abroad. He recently joined the new regulatory body of the European Central Bank, and is responsible for the direct supervision of the Eurozone's largest banks.

Chapter: Managing Operational Risk in the Banking Business – An Internal Auditor Point of View

Ross Leadbetter (University of North Carolina)

Ross Leadbetter received a MSc from the University of New Zealand in 1954, a MA from Cambridge University in 1962, and a PhD (1963) from the University of North Carolina (UNC), Chapel Hill. He has also received honorary Doctorates from Lund University, Sweden (1991), and Lisbon University, Portugal (2013). He is currently Professor of statistics at UNC. Before joining UNC in 1966, he worked with the New Zealand Applied Mathematics Laboratory, Wellington, the Naval Research Laboratory, Auckland, and the Research Triangle Institute, North Carolina. His research interests include probability and statistics, stochastic processes, extremal theory, and statistical communication theory in engineering, oceanographic, and environmental applications. He has written many articles and books including *Stationary and Related Stochastic Processes* (with Harald Cramer) and *Extremes and Related Properties of Random Sequences and Processes* (with Georg Lindgren and Holger Rootzen).

Chapter: Extremes Under Dependence—Historical Development and Parallels with Central Limit Theory

Olivier Le Courtois (EMLyon Business School)

Olivier Le Courtois is a Professor of finance and insurance with the EMLyon Business School. He is also the head of the CEFRA research center of this institution. He has published articles in academic journals such as *Quantitative Finance, Mathematical Finance, Journal of Mathematical Economics, Insurance: Mathematics and Economics*, and the *North American Actuarial Journal*. His book, published by Imperial College Press, examines the application of Lévy processes in both risk management and portfolio management. He is currently writing a new book on the Solvency II regulation and its requirements.

Chapter: Lévy Processes and Extreme Value Theory

B G Manjunath (Dell)

B G Manjunath was born in Bangalore, India, and has lived in Siegen (Germany), Lisbon (Portgual), and Delhi (India). He received a Bachelor's and Master's degrees from Bangalore University. From April 2007 to October 2010, he pursued his doctoral degree on "Extremal discriminant analysis" under the supervision of Prof. R.-D. Reiss at the University of Siegen, Germany. Later, he spent a year at ISI, Delhi, as a Visiting Scientist. Further, from December 2011 to February 2014, he was a postdoctoral fellow working with Prof. MI Gomes, at the University of Lisbon, with financial aid from FCT. Currently, he is working with Dell, India, and also pursuing collaborative and independent research. His research interests include generalized Pareto distributions, extreme value index inference, distribution theory, characterization of distributions, and statistical inference.

Chapter: Bootstrap Methods in Statistics of Extremes

Saralees Nadarajah (University of Manchester)

Saralees Nadarajah is a Senior Lecturer with the School of Mathematics, University of Manchester, UK. His research interests include climate modeling, extreme value theory, distribution theory, information theory, sampling and experimental designs, and reliability. He is an author/co-author of four books, and has over 600 papers published or accepted. He has held positions in Florida, California, and Nebraska.

Chapter: Estimation Methods for Value at Risk

Cláudia Neves (University of Reading)

Cláudia Neves received a PhD in statistics and operational research from the Faculty of Science, University of Lisbon, Portugal, in 2006. She is currently a Lecturer with the Department of Mathematics and Statistics, University of Reading, UK. Her research interests include extreme value theory, theory of regular variation, semiparametric inference, spatiotemporal modeling, risk assessment and large sample theory. Dr Neves is a member of the Institute of Mathematical Statistics, the Portuguese Statistical Society, and the Royal Statistical Society.

Chapter: Extreme Value Theory: An Introductory Overview

Jacques Ninet (La Française)

Jacques Ninet graduated from ESCP-Europe and also from the Institut Technique de Banque. He is a consultant and Senior Research Advisor with La Française Group and Convictions AM. He shares his professional life between financial markets and academics. He has been head of the Financial Markets Department, CEPME, and led teams of fund managers in various asset management companies, such as Fimagest, Barclays, and Sarasin, France. Throughout his career, he has been constantly active in the academic field, teaching finance-oriented Master's degree students. His research interests include responsible finance and sustainable development, as well as risk management.

Chapter: Two Tales of Liquidity Stress

Serguei Novak (Middlesex University, London)

Serguei Novak holds a MSc, PhD, and Dr Sc degrees. He teaches the postgraduate modules "Portfolios and Risk" and "Risk Measurement" at Middlesex University, London. His areas of expertise include extreme value theory, sums of random variables, nonparametric lower bounds, methods of nonparametric estimation of value at risk and expected shortfall, and others. His current research interests include probability theory, statistics, and quantitative finance.

Chapter: Measures of Financial Risk

Charles Pahud de Mortanges (University of Liège)

Charles Pahud de Mortanges is Professor Emeritus with the University of Liège, Belgium, and an active investor. He has contributed to several books, and has published in numerous scientific journals and conference proceedings. Prior to his academic career, he has held executive positions with two international trading firms. Through his own consulting firm, he has carried out brand valuation projects for several multinational companies.

Chapter: Protecting Assets Under Non-Parametric Market Conditions

Wesley Phoa (Capital Group)

Wesley K.-S. Phoa obtained a Bachelor's degree with honors from the Australian National University, and a PhD in pure mathematics from Trinity College, University of Cambridge, UK. He is currently a fixed-income portfolio manager and economist with Capital Group. Prior to joining Capital, he was director of research with Capital Management Sciences and a quantitative analyst with Deutsche Bank in Australia. He is an elected member of the Conference of Business Economists and the International Conference of Commercial Bank Economists, and a member of the Editorial Board of the *Journal of Portfolio Management*.

Chapter: Extreme Value Theory and Credit Spreads

Jean-Luc Prigent (University of Cergy-Pontoise)

Jean-Luc Prigent obtained a PhD in mathematics from the University of Rennes I, and two Habilitations à Diriger des Recherches (HDR) degrees, in management from the University of Paris and in Economics from the University of Cergy-Pontoise. He is currently a Full Professor of economics and finance with the University of Cergy-Pontoise. He is also a member of the ThEMA Research Center and a member of Labex MME-DII. His research interests include portfolio optimization, performance measurement, asset pricing and hedging, financial econometrics, risk management, and decision theory. He is the author of five books and of about 70 papers published, for example, in the *Journal of Banking and Finance*, *European Journal of Operational Research*, *Journal of Economic Dynamics and Control*, and the *Geneva Risk and Insurance Review*. Since 1995, he has presented his research papers in about 80 international conferences. He has been a scientific consultant for many financial institutions.

Chapter: Portfolio Insurance: The Extreme Value Approach Applied to the CPPI Method

Hubert Rodarie (Groupe SMA)

Hubert Rodarie graduated from the Ecole Centrale de Paris in 1979 and Institut d'Etudes Politiques de Paris in 1981. He started his career as an Engineer with Commissariat à l'Énergie Atomique (CEA) and Electricité de France (EDF). He then worked in the financial sector as a Financial Engineer with EDF, as CEO at Union de Garantie et de Placement, then with the asset management firm BTP Investissements, and finally deputy CEO with Groupe SMA, where he is responsible for finance, investments, and life insurance. He has written several articles, book chapters, and two books: *Dettes et Monnaie de Singe*, published by Salvator (2011), and *La Pente Despotique de L'économie Mondiale* published by Salvator (2015) (Prix 2016 Directeur financiers DFCG-TURGOT). Since 2008, he has been organizing, biennially, a scientific conference on the basis of norms in finance.

Chapter: The Robotization of Financial Activities: A Cybernetic Perspective

Stefan Straetmans (Maastricht University)

Stefan Straetmans is an Associate Professor of finance at Maastricht University, the Netherlands. His research includes, inter alia, the modeling and measurement of systemic risk, financial risk management and contagion, market linkages, and financial integration. Parts of his work have been published in international academic journals like the *Review of Economics and Statistics*, *Journal of Applied Econometrics*, *Oxford Bulletin of Economics and Statistics*, *Journal of International Money and Finance*, and *Journal of Banking and Finance*.

Chapter: Comparing Tail Risk and Systemic Risk Profiles for Different Types of U.S. Financial Institutions

Jozef Teugels (Catholic University of Leuven)

J(oz)ef Teugels obtained a PhD from Purdue University, USA, in 1967. Subsequently, he was appointed at the Catholic University of Leuven, Belgium, where he stayed until his retirement in 2004 as Professor of statistics. His interest in actuarial sciences emerged from experience with extreme value statistics. Among the topics that he dealt with in some 200 publications are stochastic processes (queuing theory, renewal theory, random walks, ruin theory), actuarial mathematics (especially reinsurance and catastrophic events), multivariate discrete data, and extreme value theory (probabilistic and statistical aspects plus applications).

Chapter: Estimation of the Extreme Value Index

Charles Tillier (University Paris-Ouest)

Charles Tillier graduated in fundamental mathematics and obtained the Master's degree in applied mathematics (data sciences) from the University of Reims. He is currently pursuing a PhD, working on extensions of ruin models and multivariate regular variations, under the supervision of Patrice Bertail (University Paris-Ouest) and Olivier Wintenberger (University Paris 6 and University of Copenhagen). His works have applications in finance, insurance, and food risk assessment.

Chapter: Extreme Values Statistics for Markov Chains with Applications to Finance and Insurance

Christian Walter (Fondation Maison des Sciences de l'Homme)

Christian Walter obtained a PhD in economics in management science from ESSEC and Habilitation à diriger des recherches (HDR). He is an Actuary (Fellow of the French Institute of Actuaries). He currently holds the Chair "Ethics and Finance" at the Collège d'études mondiales of the Fondation Maison des sciences de l'homme (FMSH), Paris. He specializes in financial-market-related issues (mathematical, economic, philosophical, and historical) with interplays between the history of science, modern financial approaches to pricing, and ethical perspectives. He has had 30 years of experience in the financial industry, in various areas covering asset allocation, risk management, performance measurement and analysis, quantitative products, and others. He launched, in 1996, the research program "History and epistemology of finance" at the FMSH, devoted to the investigation of nonfinancial roots of financial theory as applied in the financial industry, and the critical analysis of theoretical foundations of finance. His main articles cover in-depth analysis of the market efficiency concept, Lévy modeling of the behavior of stock market prices and asset pricing, the history of financial thought, and critical analysis of financial mathematical concepts. His last book: *Extreme Financial Risks and Asset Allocation* (with Olivier Le Courtois), Series in Quantitative Finance, was published by Imperial College Press, London, in 2014.

Chapter: Lévy Processes and Extreme Value Theory; The Extreme Value Problem in Finance: Comparing the Pragmatic Program with the Mandelbrot Program

Chapter One

Introduction

François Longin
Department of Finance, ESSEC Business School, Paris, France

1.1 EXTREMES

When I started to study extreme events in finance just after the stock market crash of October 1987, academic studies considered such events as outliers. It meant that the data associated with extreme events in financial markets were considered as abnormal and were discarded in empirical works. A few decades later, I am more than happy to edit a collective book about extreme events in finance.

Over the past decades, extreme value theory (EVT) has shown that we are gaining a better understanding of the statistical behavior of extreme movements of financial asset prices. Moreover, the understanding of the behavior of the market during extreme events is also useful for understanding the whole behavior of the market, both under ordinary and extraordinary conditions. In other words, it is a mistake to separate extreme events from other events. In fact, this could be a universal truth touching many aspects of society including business, politics, and religion.

This book is a *collective* work: it gathers 25 chapters written by more than 40 contributors from all over the world. This book is *diverse* in terms of contributors: it includes academics and practitioners from banks, fund management firms, insurance companies, and central banks. This book is also *open minded* in terms of areas: while most of the chapters deal with EVT and its applications in finance and insurance, it also includes professional expressions, reflection on modeling issues, and time.

This book is about extreme events in finance with an emphasis on EVT. It gives all the necessary information (theoretical results and estimation methods) to apply the techniques to financial problems. It also provides useful information about financial problems where extremes matter from different points of view: academics who applied EVT in finance (mainly risk management and portfolio

Extreme Events in Finance: A Handbook of Extreme Value Theory and its Applications,
First Edition. Edited by François Longin.
© 2017 John Wiley & Sons, Inc. Published 2017 by John Wiley & Sons, Inc.

management) and also practitioners who experienced extreme events in their working life. The objective of this book is to offer a comprehensive overview in terms of both methods and problems.

I would also like to mention the website that has been created to support this book: http://extreme-events-finance.net/ where you will find additional resources: information about events such as workshops and conferences, an interactive blog, a community open to academics, practitioners, and investors.

The book is organized as follows: history, EVT, statistical estimation of extremes, applications in finance, practitioners' points of view, and a broader view on modeling.

1.2   HISTORY

The book starts with two chapters about history.

Ross Leadbetter (University of North Carolina at Chapel Hill) in his chapter "Extremes Under Dependence: Historical Development and Parallels with Central Limit Theory," looks back at the theoretical developments of EVT, beyond well-known results for the independent identically distributed case. Ross shares with us the secrets of the development of all these results that are so useful today in applications of EVT in finance. Very interestingly, you will learn the relation of EVT with another fundamental field in statistics: central limit theory (CLT).

Christian Walter (Ethics and Finance Chair at Fondation Maison des Sciences de l'Homme) will, in the third chapter, "The Extreme Value Problem in Finance: Comparing the Pragmatic Program with the Mandelbrot Program," bring you back to the history of financial modeling. Should we use a diffusion process, a jump process, or a mixed diffusion process to describe the behavior of financial asset prices?

1.3   EXTREME VALUE THEORY

After these historical developments in statistics and financial modeling, Isabel Fraga Alves (CEAUL & University of Lisbon) and Cláudia Neves (University of Reading), in their chapter "Extreme Value Theory: An Introductory Overview," lay down in a very clear and well-illustrated way the fundamental results of EVT, both in the univariate case and the multivariate case. They start from the first results found in the middle of the twentieth century by Gumbel, Fréchet, Weibull, Gnedenko, and others, and finish with references for further reading about the most recent research in the field.

1.4   STATISTICAL ESTIMATION OF EXTREMES

From the theoretical results presented in the chapter by Isabel Fraga Alves and Claudia Neves, we learned that the behavior of extremes is well known and can be modeled by the extreme value distribution. The key parameter of this distribution is the tail index, also called the extreme value index. Jan Beirlant, K. Herrmann and Jozef Teugels (KU Leuven), in their chapter "The Estimation of the Extreme Value Index" address the statistical estimation techniques for the tail index. This is a "must read" if you want to apply EVT to data.

Following this general presentation of the statistical issues in estimating the central parameter of the extreme value distribution (the tail index), Ivette Gomes (Universidade de Lisboa, FCUL, DEIO, and CEAUL), Frederico Caeiro (Universidade Nova de Lisboa, FCT and CMA), Lígia Henriques-Rodrigues (Instituto Politecnico de Tomar and CEAUL), and B.G. Manjunath (Universidade de Lisboa and CEAUL) present, in their chapter "Bootstrap Methods in Statistics of Extremes," the promising bootstrap approach. In particular, they address the critical issue of bias in the estimator with small samples.

In finance, the modeling of asset prices in continuous time has provided plenty of models. A critical choice is whether to model the path of an asset price as continuous or to introduce jumps. Olivier Le Courtois (EM Lyon Business School) and Christian Walter (Ethics and Finance Chair at Fondation Maison des Sciences de l'Homme) make the link, in their chapter "Lévy Processes and Extreme Value Theory," between Lévy processes and EVT. Some models proposed in the finance literature will belong to the domain of attraction of the Gumbel distribution (thin and semiheavy-tailed distributions), while other models will belong to the domain of attraction of the Fréchet distribution (fat-tailed distributions).

Patrice Bertail (modal X, Université Paris Ouest Nanterre La Défense et CREST), Stéphan Clémençon (Telecom ParisTech), and Charles Tillier (Université Paris Ouest Nanterre La Défense), in their chapter "Extreme Values Statistics for Markov Chains with Applications to Finance and Insurance," are interested in extremes for dependent processes. Such processes are important in finance because it is well known that volatility of financial asset prices is changing over time. The dependence in extremes (clustering) is modeled by an additional parameter called the extremal index.

Miguel de Carvalho (Pontificia Universidad Católica de Chile), in his chapter "Statistics of Extremes: Challenges and Opportunities," provides a personal overview of some recent concepts and methods for the statistics of extremes. Measure-dependent measures are presented as a natural probabilistic concept for modeling bivariate extreme values, and predictor-dependent spectral measures are introduced as a natural concept for modeling extremal dependence structures that vary according to a covariate. Families of g-tilted measures are presented as a unifying device connecting some recently proposed approaches. En passant, Miguel discusses a new estimator for the so-called scedasis density function.

Serguei Novak (Middlesex University, London), overviews available measures of financial risk in his chapter "Dynamic Measure of Financial Risk," and investigates a new risk measure. Traditional risk measures such as value-at-risk (VaR) and expected shortfall are rather static as they change slowly over time and do not necessarily take into account current market conditions. Using concepts related to technical analysis, Dr Novak proposes a dynamic risk measure that takes into account current market conditions.

Marie Kratz (ESSEC Business School, CREAR), in her chapter "On the Estimation of the Distribution of Aggregated Heavy Tailed Risks," proposes a sharp approximation of the entire distribution of independent aggregate risks. It is obtained by distinguishing two parts: a trimmed sum (taking away a small number of extremes) modeled by a normal distribution, and a Pareto distribution for the sum of extremes. When working on financial or insurance data under the presence of fat tails, it allows one to obtain the most accurate evaluations of risk measures, whatever the aggregation size. A direct application is for the sum of returns of different assets of a portfolio, when moving from daily to yearly returns.

Saralees Nadarajah and Stephen Chan (University of Manchester) provide a comprehensive review of estimation methods for VaR, in their chapter "Estimation Methods for Value at Risk." The properties of this well-used risk measure in finance are presented in detail: ordering properties, upper comonotonicity, aggregation of risks, risk concentration, and various inequalities. Furthermore, the authors provide an impressive list of useful references about VaR.

1.5 APPLICATIONS IN FINANCE

Wesley Phoa (Capital Group), in his chapter "Extreme Value Theory and Credit Spreads," gives a practical introduction to the use of EVT in modeling and managing credit portfolios. Using both univariate and multivariate EVT, Wesley computes VaR for credit portfolios using CDS.

Kam Fong Chan (The University of Queensland Business School) and Philip Gray (Monash University), in their chapter "Extreme Value Theory and Risk Management in Electricity Markets," emphasize the importance of risk management in financial markets and especially for nontraditional securities such as electricity markets. Such markets present episodes of extreme volatility rarely observed in equity markets, which make trading and hedging challenging issues. The authors show that EVT can then be a very useful tool in risk management.

Stefan Straetmans (Maastricht University) and Thanh Thi Huyen Dinh (Group de Lage Landen), in their chapter "Comparing Tail Risk and Systemic Risk Profiles for Different Types of US Financial Institutions," use EVT to propose innovative ways to measure risk in the banking sector. While risk is usually measured by variance or covariance, Stefan and Thanh use tail VaR to measure individual bank risk and a measure of extreme systematic risk (tail β) to capture systemic risk. Their approach allows one to answer various relevant questions: which institutions are the most sensitive to tail risk or systemic risk – deposit banks, broker-dealers, or insurance companies? Is there a relation between extreme risks and institutional size?

John Cotter (University College Dublin School of Business) and Kevin Dowd (Durham University Business School) explain in their chapter "Margin Setting and Extreme Value Theory" that extreme price movements are central to the setting of margins in futures markets and that EVT can play a very important role in setting margins at the appropriate level. Margin setting by the clearinghouse for each counterparty is one of the mechanisms to mitigate default risk. How should margin levels be set in practice? From a quantitative view, the margin level can be interpreted as a quantile of the distribution of price movements in futures contracts. The authors emphasize that the use of a normal distribution would lead to an underestimation of margin levels but that the use of the extreme value distribution would adequately estimate margin levels.

Geoffrey Booth (Eli Broad Graduate School of Management at Michigan State University) and John Paul Broussard (School of Business at Camden Rutgers, The State University of New Jersey) use EVT in their chapter "The Sortino Ratio and Extreme Value Theory: An Application to Asset Allocation," to improve the measure of performance of financial assets portfolios. They focus especially on the Sortino ratio, which considers the downside risk of portfolios.

Philippe Bertrand (University of Aix-en-Provence and Kedge Business School) and Jean-Luc Prigent (University of Cergy-Pontoise) propose, in their chapter "Portfolio Insurance: The Extreme Value Approach Applied to the CPPI Method," a straight-forward application of EVT to a well-known asset allocation method: portfolio insurance. Such a method allows one to provide a capital-guarantee for portfolios. When market prices are assumed to follow a continuous path and returns are normally distributed, portfolio insurance techniques work fine; the fund management firm that manages this product will succeed in delivering the guarantee. But in real markets characterized by jumps and fat-tailed distributions, portfolio insurance techniques may fail as the fund value may be below the guarantee level because of a market crash. Using the EVT allows a better risk management of such financial portfolios.

François Longin (ESSEC Business School), in his chapter "The Choice of the Distribution of Asset Returns: How Extreme Value Theory Can Help?" explains that one of the issues of risk management is the choice of the distribution of asset returns. Academics and practitioners have assumed for a long time that the distribution of asset returns is a Gaussian distribution. Such an assumption has been used in many fields of finance: building optimal portfolio, pricing and hedging derivatives, and managing risks. However, real financial data tend to exhibit extreme price changes such as stock market crashes that seem incompatible with the assumption of normality. This chapter shows how EVT can be useful to know more precisely the characteristics of the distribution of asset returns and finally help to choose a better model by focusing on the tails of the distribution. An empirical analysis using equity data of the US market is provided to illustrate this point.

Jean-Marie Choffray (ESSEC Business School and University of Liège) and Charles Pahud de Mortanges (University of Liège), in their chapter "Protecting Assets Under Nonparametric Market Conditions," share their experience as both academics and individual investors. They propose a concise set of heuristics aimed at conceptualizing response to the unknown, at connecting proven facts, and at identifying profitable investment opportunities when market states and events are not generated by continuous models – or probabilistic processes – that would render them amenable to mathematical analysis.

1.6   PRACTITIONERS' POINTS OF VIEW

Jean-François Boulier (Aviva) shares his experience in his chapter "EVT Seen by a Vet: A Practitioner's Experience on Extreme Value Theory," of applying statistical models to financial data: the Gaussian distribution, ARCH processes, and EVT. Jean-François situates the development of quantitative finance with the development of financial regulation and internal risk management in financial institutions. Related to extreme events, he discusses the concept of "stress scenarios," which complements the VaR measure. He argues that while models based on normality do their job of computing the VaR (associated with market shocks appearing every four years on average), EVT adds value for designing "stress scenarios" (associated with extreme market shocks appearing every 20 or 50 years on average). Finally, Jean-François asks the question: what could EVT additionally bring to the party?

Hubert Rodarie (SMA), in his chapter "The Robotization of Financial Activities: A Cybernetic Perspective," shares his thoughts about the trend toward the use of robots in finance (a trend that seems to apply to every sector, and finance is no exception). The author uses the framework of cybernetics to analyze the finance machine. Is automation going in the right direction? What is its impact on financial markets in terms of volatility and extreme events? What can be done to improve the financial sector?

Jacques Ninet (La Française) addresses an important issue in finance, liquidity, in his chapter "Two Tales of Liquidity Stress." Jacques shares his long experience as an asset manager. He explains in detail the forex exchange crisis of 1992–1993 and the recent financial crisis of 2007–2008. Such episodes, lived "from the inside," remind us that "those who cannot remember the past are condemned to repeat it." What is the meaning of an extreme situation in financial markets? What can we learn from historical extreme events?

Maxime Laot (European Central bank), in his chapter "Managing Operational Risk in the Banking Business: An Internal Auditor Point of View," shares his thoughts and experience of operational risk, which has only recently been studied and considered by financial regulation (as compared with market risk and credit risk). Maxime details the types of operational risk and the different approaches to measure operational risk and provides data on bank losses due to the realization of operational risk.

1.7   A BROADER VIEW ON MODELING EXTREMES

Henri Bourguinat (University of Bordeaux) and Eric Briys (Cyberlibris) offer a critical view of modern finance in their chapter "Credo Ut Intelligam," characterized by the extensive use of models with the hypothesis of normality for asset prices and the hypothesis of an average individual (*homo economicus*) driven by rationality. What is the role of models? Should the world of finance deviate from traditional assumptions? Do we believe in models to understand them or do we try to understand models to believe them?

Laurent Bibard (ESSEC Business School), in his chapter "Bounded Rationality, Routines, and Practical as well as Theoretical Blindness: On the Discrepancy between Markets and Corporations," discusses the behavior of individuals, firms, and markets. The consideration of time (short-term vs long-term) is especially important.

1.8 FINAL WORDS

The French mathematician, physicist, and philosopher Henri Poincaré (1854–1912) once noted that "All the world believes it (the normal distribution) firmly, because the mathematicians imagine that it is a fact of observation and the observers that it is a theorem of mathematics." It seems that more than a century later, the world, especially in finance, has not changed much as the Laplace–Gauss distribution is still considered as *normal*. While the normal distribution tends to underestimate the weight of extreme events in finance, and therefore risk, an objective of this book is to show that EVT with its strong theoretical results, extensive empirical evidence, and new applications in risk management can be an alternative to the current paradigm of the normal distribution.

The German mathematician Emil Gumbel (1891–1966), who was a pioneer in the application of EVT to engineering problems, in particular to hydrological phenomena such as annual flood flows, once wrote: "It seems that the rivers know the theory. It *only* remains to convince engineers of the validity of this analysis." Considering the world of finance, we can paraphrase Gumbel words by saying:

> It seems that financial markets know the theory.
>
> It only remains to convince traders, investors, financial engineers, risk managers, asset managers, bankers, central bankers, regulators, and professors of the validity of this analysis.

Together with the contributors to this handbook, I hope that this collective work will help to open up wider consideration of this direction.

1.9 THANK YOU NOTE

I would like to thank all the contributors to this collective book for their willingness to provide the best of their work. I would like to thank the Wiley team for its excellent work: Jon Gurstelle, Sari Friedman, Kathleen Pagliaro, Allison McGinniss, Steve Quigley, Vishnu Priya R, and Anitha Jasmine Stanley.

This handbook also benefited from the ESSEC Conference *Extreme Events in Finance* that I organized at Royaumont Abbey, France, in December 2014. It was a peaceful place to discuss extreme events and to exchange ideas. This conference benefited from the financial support of the Labex MME-DII

(ANR11-LBX-0023-01), the CERESSEC, ACE Finance & Conseil, SMA, and La Française and from media support by CREAR, Pôle Finance Innovation, SimTrade, and ESSEC Chair Edgar Morin on complexity. Beyond institutions, I would like to thank personally Gabriel Eschbach (ACE Finance & Conseil), Xavier Lépine, Jacques Ninet and Nicolas Duban (La Française), Hubert Rodarie (SMA); Maximilien Nayaradou (Pôle Finance Innovation); Patrick Ségalou (SimTrade); members of the scientific committee composed of Geoffrey Booth (Michigan State University), John Paul Broussard (Rutgers University), Ivette Gomes (Universidade de Lisboa), Hélyette Geman (Birkbeck University of London and Johns Hopkins University), and Marie Kratz (ESSEC Business School and CREAR); members of the organization committee led by Pauline Delécaut and composed of Dylan Blandel, Sangwon Lee, and Giovanni Pagliardi (ESSEC Business School) and, finally, Laurent Bibard, Jean-Michel Blanquer, Patricia Charléty, Jean-Marie Choffray, Vincenzo Esposito Vinzi, Jean-Pierre Indjehagopian, Jocelyn Martel, Patrice Poncet, and Radu Vranceanu (ESSEC Business School) and Ani Guerdjikova and Arnaud Lefranc (University of Cergy-Pontoise) who all supported the project. Finally, I also would like thank Ruey S. Tsay (The University of Chicago) who is the editor of the Wiley Handbook in Financial Engineering and Econometrics.

References

Alves Fraga I., Neves C. Extreme value theory: an introductory overview. In: Longin F., editor. *Extreme Events in Finance: A Handbook of Extreme Value Theory and Its Applications*. Wiley; 2017.

Beirlant J., Herrmann K., Teugels J.L. Estimation of the extreme value index. In: Longin F., editor. *Extreme Events in Finance: A Handbook of Extreme Value Theory and Its Applications*. Wiley; 2017.

Bertail P., S. Clémençon and C. Tiller Extreme values statistics for Markov chains with applications to finance and insurance published in *Extreme Events in Finance: A Handbook of Extreme Value Theory and Its Applications*. edited by F. Longin, Wiley; 2017.

Bertrand P., Prigent J.-L. Portfolio insurance: the extreme value approach applied to the CPPI method. In: Longin F., editor. *Extreme Events in Finance: A Handbook of Extreme Value Theory and Its Applications*. Wiley; 2017.

Bibard L. Bounded rationalities, routines, and practical as well theoretical blindness: on the discrepancy between markets and corporations. In: Longin F., editor. *Extreme Events in Finance: A Handbook of Extreme Value Theory and Its Applications*. Wiley; 2017.

Booth G.G., Broussard J.-P. The Sortino ratio and the generalized Pareto distribution: an application to asset allocation. In: Longin F., editor. *Extreme Events in Finance: A Handbook of Extreme Value Theory and Its Applications*. Wiley; 2017.

Boulier J.-F. EVT seen by a vet: a practitioner's experience of extreme value theory. In: Longin F., editor. *Extreme Events in Finance: A Handbook of Extreme Value Theory and Its Applications*. Wiley; 2017.

Bourguinat H., Bryis E. Credo Ut Intelligam. In: Longin F., editor. *Extreme Events in Finance: A Handbook of Extreme Value Theory and Its Applications*. Wiley; 2017.

Chan K.F., Gray P. Extreme value theory and risk management in electricity markets. In: Longin F., editor. *Extreme Events in Finance: A Handbook of Extreme Value Theory and Its Applications*. Wiley; 2017.

Choffray J.-M., Pahud de Mortanges C. Protecting assets under non-parametric market conditions. In: Longin F., editor. *Extreme Events in Finance: A Handbook of Extreme Value Theory and Its Applications*. Wiley; 2017.

Cotter J., Dowd K. Margin setting and extreme value theory. In: Longin F., editor. *Extreme Events in Finance: A Handbook of Extreme Value Theory and Its Applications*. Wiley; 2017.

de Carvalho M. Statistics of extremes: challenges and opportunities. In: Longin F., editor. *Extreme Events in Finance: A Handbook of Extreme Value Theory and Its Applications*. Wiley; 2017.

Gomes M.I., Caeiro F., Henriques-Rodrigues L., Manjunath B.G. Bootstrap methods in statistics of extremes. In: Longin F., editor. *Extreme Events in Finance: A Handbook of Extreme Value Theory and Its Applications*. Wiley; 2017.

Kratz M. On the estimation of the distribution of aggregated heavy tailed risk. In: Longin F., editor. *Extreme Events in Finance: A Handbook of Extreme Value Theory and Its Applications*. Wiley; 2017.

Laot M. Managing operational risk in the banking business – an internal auditor point of view. In: Longin F., editor. *Extreme Events in Finance: A Handbook of Extreme Value Theory and Its Applications*. Wiley; 2017.

Leadbetter R. Extremes under dependence: historical development and parallels with central limit theory. In: Longin F., editor. *Extreme Events in Finance: A Handbook of Extreme Value Theory and Its Applications*. Wiley; 2017.

Le Courtois O., Walter C. Lévy processes and extreme value theory. In: Longin F., editor. *Extreme Events in Finance: A Handbook of Extreme Value Theory and Its Applications*. Wiley; 2017.

Longin F. The choice of the distribution of asset returns: how extreme value theory can help? In: Longin F., editor. *Extreme Events in Finance: A Handbook of Extreme Value Theory and Its Applications*. Wiley; 2017.

Nadarajah S., Chan S. Estimation methods for value at risk. In: Longin F., editor. *Extreme Events in Finance: A Handbook of Extreme Value Theory and Its Applications*. Wiley; 2017.

Ninet J. Two tales of liquidity stress. In: Longin F., editor. *Extreme Events in Finance: A Handbook of Extreme Value Theory and Its Applications*. Wiley; 2017.

Novak S.Y. Measures of financial risk. In: Longin F, editor. *Extreme Events in Finance: A Handbook of Extreme Value Theory and Its Applications*. Wiley; 2017.

Phoa W. Extreme value theory and credit spreads. In: Longin F., editor. *Extreme Events in Finance: A Handbook of Extreme Value Theory and Its Applications*. Wiley; 2017.

Rodarie H. The robotisation of financial activities: a cybernetic perspective. In: Longin F., editor. *Extreme Events in Finance: A Handbook of Extreme Value Theory and Its Applications*. Wiley; 2017.

Straetmans S., Huyen Dinh T.T. Comparing tail risk and systematic risk profiles for different types of US financial institutions. In: Longin F., editor. *Extreme Events in Finance: A Handbook of Extreme Value Theory and Its Applications*. Wiley; 2017.

Walter C. In: Longin F., editor. *Extreme Events in Finance: A Handbook of Extreme Value Theory and Its Applications*. Vol. The extreme value problem in finance: comparing the pragmatic programme with the Mandelbrot programme. Wiley; 2017.

Extremes Under Dependence—Historical Development and Parallels with Central Limit Theory

M.R. Leadbetter
Department of Statistics and Operation Research, University of North Carolina, Chapel Hill, North Carolina

2.1 INTRODUCTION

I first encountered the field of extreme value theory (EVT) as a young mathematician when it had become an essentially complete and major discipline for independent, identically distributed (i.i.d.) random variables (r.v.'s) and widely used though often with seemingly little thought given to the validity of the i.i.d. assumptions. I was aware that sequential dependence of data was intrinsic to very many classic common time series situations (daily high temperatures, sea levels, stock prices) and found it fascinating that the i.i.d. theory of extreme values seemed to apply to such data without change. Interest was indeed developing in extension to dependence as a natural mathematical undertaking stimulated by corresponding central limit theory (CLT) results as I will indicate (e.g., Watson, 1954) and the landmark 1956 introduction of mixing conditions by Rosenblatt providing a general framework for discussion of long-range dependence.

In any case the time was ripe for a period of high activity by many researchers to investigate EVT under more general assumptions (particularly stationarity and Gaussian modeling). I was personally highly privileged to work with outstanding mentors and collaborators, among those seeking extension of the theory to provide greater realism in EVT applications. It turned out that under wide conditions, the same central results were found to apply to stationary series as if the data were

Extreme Events in Finance: A Handbook of Extreme Value Theory and its Applications,
First Edition. Edited by François Longin.
© 2017 John Wiley & Sons, Inc. Published 2017 by John Wiley & Sons, Inc.

i.i.d., requiring just a simple adjustment of constants in the limiting distributional results for maxima and explaining the early success of the classical theory when applied to non-i.i.d. data. This was also a precursor of some of the extremal problems in financial settings which have seen tremendous developments and which are the main concern of this volume.

Our plan in this short contribution is to recall personal impressions of the development of EVT for stochastic sequences and processes from the existing i.i.d. results already in a satisfying detailed form in the 1950s. Of course extreme values have been of concern since time immemorial, for example, as observed by Tiago de Oliveira—one of the champions of EVT development and use—biblical accounts of maximum age (Methuselah) and extreme floods (Noah's ark and issues of its structural safety relying on divine guidance rather than mathematics). But formal development of what we know as classical EVT took place in the first half of the twentieth century. This primarily focused on limiting results for the distribution of the maximum $M_n = \max(X_1, \dots, X_n)$ of n r.v.'s $X_1, \dots, X_n$ as $n \to \infty$, when the X_i are assumed to be i.i.d.

2.2 CLASSICAL (I.I.D.) CENTRAL LIMIT AND EXTREME VALUE THEORIES

The development of EVT is intertwined with that of CLT whose results motivated many of those of EVT. At the risk of possible appearance of some lack of continuity, we sketch a brief history of these two disciplines in parallel—typically alternating CLT with EVT results which they motivate. We first indicate some milestones in the early theories for i.i.d. sequences followed by the again parallel activity when dependence is introduced via stationarity. No attempt is made at completeness, and we focus only on the theory of EVT and not its applications—a reader wishing to learn both the structural theory of extremes and its use in application would be well advised to study one of a number of available excellent accounts such as the splendid volume of de Haan and Ferreira (2006).

A paper by Dodd (1923) is sometimes regarded as giving birth to EVT and primarily involves convergence in probability of $M_n - u_n$ for some sequence u_n and various classes of the distribution functions (d.f.'s) of the i.i.d. r.v.'s $\{X_i\}$. Its first result is that $M_n \to x_F$ in probability where x_F is the right end point of the d.f.'s F of each X_i (and hence also almost surely since its monotonicity implies the existence of a limit, finite or infinite). Thus M_n has the almost sure limit $x_F \leqslant \infty$. When $x_F = \infty$, limits in probability for $M_n - u_n$ are shown for several classes of d.f. F. For example, for a sequence of standard normal r.v.'s $\{X_i\}$, it is shown that $M_n - \sqrt{2 \log n} \to 0$ in probability. Also, for a sequence of Pareto r.v.'s $\{X_i\}$ with d.f. $F(x) = 1 - Kx^{-\alpha}, \alpha > 0, x > K^{1/\alpha}, M_n - n^{1/\alpha} \to 0$ in probability.

This is reminiscent of CLT where weak and strong laws of large numbers give the "degenerate" convergence of averages $S_n/n := n^{-1} \sum_{i=1}^{n} X_i$ to $EX_i = \mu$ with probability one. But it is found to be much more useful to consider distributional convergence of the normalized sums $(S_n - a_n)/b_n$ for appropriate constants a_n, b_n, where this is possible, and to determine what limits in distribution can occur and their domains of attraction.

The simplest example of such theory is of course the central limit theorem where $(S_n - n\mu)/\sigma\sqrt{n}$ is shown to have a standard normal distributional limit for (i.i.d.) r.v.'s $\{X_i\}$ having finite means μ and variances σ^2. This was greatly generalized (almost ad infinitum) in the study of a wide variety of "central limit" results for "array sums" $\sum_{i=1}^{k_n} X_{n,i}$ where $X_{n,i}$ are i.i.d. for each n in which the possible limits may be the class of self decomposable stable or infinitely divisible distributions.

It does not seem surprising, at least in hindsight, that the extensive CLT for sums should suggest the possibility of similar asymptotic distributional results for the maximum $M_n = \max\{X_1, \dots, X_n\}$ of i.i.d. $\{X_i\}$, that is, results of the form $P(a_n(M_n - b_n) \leqslant x) \to G(x)$ for some constants $a_n > 0, b_n$ and some distribution G. This probability is clearly $F^n(a_n^{-1}x + b_n)$ which is known exactly when the d.f. F of each X_i is known but changes with F and may be difficult to calculate.

Following the model of CLT, obviously there would be great practical utility if one G corresponded to many different F's aside from changes of normalizing constants. It was found in a series of papers (including Fréchet 1927; Fisher and Tippett 1928, and von Mises, 1936) that certain specific G could be limits and in fact that they must have one of three general forms (extreme value "types") to be limiting distributions for maxima in the sense given in the previous paragraph. These results were given a rigorous formulation and proof by Gnedenko (1943) and were refined by de Haan. This is the centerpiece of EVT and its application referred to by various names including Gnedenko's theorem, Fisher–Tippett–Gnedenko theorem, Gnedenko–de Haan theorem, and extremal types theorem (ETT). The theorem is stated as follows.

THEOREM 2.1 Extremal types theorem (ETT) *Let* $X_1, \dots, X_n$ *be i.i.d. with common d.f. F, and let* $M_n = \max\{X_1, \dots, X_n\}$. *If for some constants* $a_n > 0, b_n$

$$P(a_n(M_n - b_n) \leqslant x) \to G(x) \tag{2.1}$$

as $n \to \infty$ *where G is a nondegenerate d.f., then G must be one of three "types":*

Type I ("Gumbel"): $G(x) = \exp(-e^{-x}), \quad -\infty < x < \infty$

Type II ("Fréchet"): $G(x) = \exp(-x^{-\xi}), \quad x > 0,$ *some* $\xi > 0$

Type III("(reverse) Weibull"): $G(x) = \exp(-(-x)^{\xi}), \quad x \leqslant 0,$ *some* $\xi > 0$

In these x may be replaced by $ax + b$ for any $a > 0, b$. In other words, the specific expressions listed are representatives of the types. Also, types II and III are really families of types, one type for each $\xi > 0$.

For each G of one of these types, there will be a family of d.f.'s F for which this G applies as the limiting d.f. for (normalized) M_n—referred to as the domain of attraction ($D(G)$) for G. Not all d.f.'s F lead to a limiting distribution for a linearly normalized version of M_n, (e.g., if F is Poisson), that is, not all F's belong to any domain of attraction. However, most common continuous d.f.'s F do belong to the domain of attraction of one of the types.

Note that the limiting distribution (2.1) for M_n can be written as $P(M_n \leqslant u_n) \to e^{-\tau}$ where $\tau = -\log(G(x))$ and $u_n = a_n^{-1}x + b_n$. The following almost trivially proved result is basic for classical EVT and a cornerstone for the natural extension when dependence is introduced.

LEMMA 2.2 Basic EVT Lemma *Let $\{X_i\}$ be i.i.d. with d.f. F and $\{u_n\}$ be a sequence of constants. Then for any τ, $0 \leqslant \tau \leqslant \infty$*

$$P(M_n \leqslant u_n) \to e^{-\tau} \text{ if and only if } n(1 - F(u_n)) \to \tau. \tag{2.2}$$

It is seen at once from this that (2.1) holds for a given F, G (i.e., $F \in D(G)$) and constants $a_n > 0$, b_n if and only if

$$n(1 - F(a_n^{-1}x + b_n)) \to -\log(G(x))$$

for each x. In some cases for given F, the search among the three types for which the previous equation holds for some constants a_n, b_n (and hence $F \in D(G)$) is very simple. For example, for a uniform distribution F on $(0, 1)$, it is immediate that $P(M_n \leqslant 1 - \tau/n) = (1 - \tau/n)^n \to e^{-\tau}$ giving $P(n(M_n - 1) \leqslant x) \to e^x$, $x < 0$, a type III limit with $a_n = n$, $b_n = 1$. On the other hand the determination of which (if any) G applies for a given F can be an intricate matter facilitated by domain of attraction criteria which have been developed. Our purpose here is not to review the extensive theory now available for extremes of i.i.d. r.v.'s but to indicate and motivate the extension to dependent cases with personal observation on some of its history.

One convenient view of the i.i.d. theory is that it (i) first involves result (2.2) and (ii) allows the determination of constants a_n, b_n such that $u_n = a_n^{-1}x + b_n$ satisfies $n(1 - F(u_n)) \to \tau = -\log(G(x))$ some extremal d.f. G. As noted earlier success in this gives domain of attraction and much related detailed theory. Part (ii) of the activity is essentially unaltered under dependence assumptions, and hence the extension of the ETT to dependent cases depends on finding a modification to Lemma 2.1 for useful non-i.i.d. situations.

2.3 EXCEEDANCES OF LEVELS, kTH LARGEST VALUES

First we mention some interesting and useful implications of the choice of constants u_n to satisfy $n(1 - F(u_n)) \to \tau$. Regarding u_n as a "level," we say that X_i has an *exceedance* of u_n if $X_i > u_n$. This clearly implies that the mean number of exceedances converges to the value τ. Further if the X_i are i.i.d., then the events $X_i > u_n$ are independent in i and have probability $1 - F(u_n)$ so that the number of exceedances of u_n for $1 \leqslant i \leqslant n$ is binomial in distribution, $B(n, p_n = 1 - F(u_n))$, which converges as $n \to \infty$ to a Poisson r.v. with mean τ.

It is useful to regard the exceedance points as a point process: a series of events occurring in "time." For this it is more convenient to normalize by the factor n and consider the *exceedance point process* N_n to be the points i/n for which $\xi_i > u_n$, $1 \leqslant i \leqslant n$. The points of N_n all lie in the unit interval $[0, 1]$, and for any set $E \subset [0, 1]$, $N_n(E)$ is the number of normalized points in the set E, namely, the number of points $i/n \in E$, $1 \leqslant i \leqslant n$, for which $\xi_i > u_n$. This is a point process on the "space" $[0,1]$, consisting of (no more than n) normalized exceedance points and is simply shown to converge in distribution to a Poisson process N with intensity τ on $[0, 1]$ in the full sense of point process convergence. In particular this means that $N_n(E) \overset{d}{\to} N(E)$ for any Borel set $E \subset [0, 1]$ and corresponding joint distributional statements for $N_n(E_1), \dots, N_n(E_k)$ for Borel k subsets $E_1, \dots, E_k$ of $[0, 1]$. If the E_i are disjoint, then the limits $N(E_1), \dots, N(E_k)$ are independent Poisson r.v.'s with means $\tau m(E_1), \dots, \tau m(E_k)$ where $m(E_i)$ is the Lebesgue measure of E_i.

Note that the probability $P(M_n \leqslant u_n)$ may be written in terms of N_n as $P(N_n(0, 1) = 0)$. Similarly $P(N_n(0, 1) \leqslant k - 1)$ is just $P(M_n^{(k)} \leqslant u_n)$ where $M_n^{(k)}$ is the kth largest of X_i, $1 \leqslant i \leqslant n$ (the kth order statistic). The use of the previous Poisson convergence of $P(N_n(0, 1) < k)$ to $P(N(0, 1) < k)$ with $u_n = a_n^{-1}x + b_n$ immediately gives the limiting distribution for $M_n^{(k)}$, modifying (2.1) to read

$$P(a_n(M_n^{(k)} - b_n) \leqslant x) \to G(x) \sum_{s=0}^{k-1} (-\log G(x))^s/s!$$

with the same constants a_n, b_n, and d.f. G as in (2.1). This shows one of the many uses of the point process N_n in classical EVT. We will see later the interesting way this is modified to accommodate dependence.

2.4 CLT AND EVT FOR STATIONARY SEQUENCES, BERNSTEIN'S BLOCKS, AND STRONG MIXING

As indicated earlier, i.i.d. theory for maxima followed similar patterns to those established in CLT—replacing the convolution $F_n^* = F * F * \cdots * F$ for the d.f. of $S_n = \sum_{i=1}^n X_i$ by the power F^n for that of M_n. This potentially simplifies the theory for maxima, but the situation is reversed for transforms where, for example, the characteristic function for the sum S_n is the nth power of that for each X_i. In both cases one standard method of including dependence is to make use of the i.i.d. theory by restricting the dependence between two separated groups of X_i in some way. In describing the principles we assume strict stationarity of the sequence X_i—thus introducing dependence between the X_i but leaving them identically distributed.

This originated from a suggestion of Markov (discussed in Bernstein, 1927) to the effect that one expects a CLT to hold if the r.v.'s of the sequence behave more like independent r.v.'s the more they are separated. Specifically, Bernstein introduced the very useful device of dividing the integers $1, \dots, n$ into $k_n \to \infty$

alternating "big blocks" and "small blocks" of respective sizes r_n, ℓ_n such that $r_n = o(n)$ and $\ell_n = o(r_n)$. Under specific dependency conditions, he showed that the sums of the X_i over each big block are approximately independent giving a normal limit for their sum, whereas the sum over all small blocks is small by comparison and hence may be discarded in the limit. In this way it is shown (albeit under complex conditions) that the CLT can hold under dependence assumptions.

Later Hoeffding and Robbins (1948) showed that this result holds for m-dependent processes—a statistically useful class—under certain very simple conditions by using the block method with big blocks of length $[n^\alpha]$ - m alternating with small blocks of length m, for some $\alpha < 1/4$. Thus the groups of X_i in two different big blocks are independent, and the classical CLT may be applied to their sums. Then showing that the total normalized sum from small blocks tends to zero in probability gives the desired CLT. The proof is straightforward and even simpler if stationarity is assumed.

The previous method of Bernstein was given considerable generality by Rosenblatt (1956) with the formal introduction of a hierarchy of the so-called "mixing conditions" differing in the degrees of dependence restrictions. The most used of these is *strong mixing* satisfied by a sequence $X_1, X_2, \ldots$ if for some $g(k) \to 0$ as $k \to \infty$ $|P(A \cap B) - P(A)P(B)| < g(k)$ when $A \in \sigma(X_1, \ldots, X_p)$, $B \in \sigma(X_{p+k+1}, X_{p+k+2}, \ldots)$ (the σ-fields generated by past and future by the indicated r.v.'s for any p and k). That is, any event A based on the past up to time p is "nearly independent" of any event B based on the future from time $p + k + 1$ onwards.

Rosenblatt obtained a CLT using Bernstein's method and strong mixing as its dependence assumption, initiating significant activity in that area (see, e.g., Ibragimov and Linnik, 1971; Bradley, 2007). In some cases strong mixing can be readily checked, for example, a stationary Gaussian sequence with continuous spectral density having no zeros on the unit circle—Ibragimov and Linnik (1971), Theorem 17.3.3. But in general it may be very difficult or impossible, and it has been suggested by a Swedish colleague that to start a theorem with "Let X_n be a strongly mixing sequence" seems to be essentially assuming what one wants to prove! Nevertheless even if strong mixing cannot be fully verified, it may still be a reasonable assumption in useful cases.

We turn now from this tour of CLT history to the corresponding EVT it motivated. Perhaps the earliest result for dependent EVT was a paper by Watson (1954) generalizing the early paper of Dodd applicable to i.i.d. r.v.'s described earlier to m-dependent sequences. In this it is shown that the basic lemma 2.2 of the i.i.d. theory holds for stationary m-dependent sequences $X_1, X_2, \ldots$. This result was motivated by the paper of Hoeffding and Robbins (1948), showing the CLT under m-dependence as discussed earlier.

Watson's result was straightforward probability calculations with a simple form of Bernstein's method. He obtains the basic Lemma 2.2 but does not discuss detailed extremal forms under linear normalization. However, it is readily shown that the limits for the maximum in this case are the same as would apply if the X_i were independent with the same marginal d.f. F as the stationary m-dependent sequence. In fact this holds for any identically distributed sequence for which the basic lemma holds, regardless of the dependence structure as the following result holds. We term this a "proposition" at the risk of inflating its importance.

PROPOSITION 2.3 *Let* $\{X_i\}$ *be a sequence of r.v.'s with the same d.f. F but not necessarily independent but for which it is known that the basic lemma conclusion applies, that is, for any sequence* $\{u_n\}$ *of constants,* $P(M_n \leqslant u_n) \to e^{-\tau}$ *iff* $n(1 - F(u_n)) \to \tau$. *Then if* $F \in D(G)$ *for one of the extremal d.f.'s G, it follows that* $P(a_n(M_n - b_n) \leqslant x) \to G(x)$, *where* a_n, b_n *are the constants which will apply to i.i.d. sequences, that is,* $F^n(a_n^{-1}x + b_n) \to G(x)$. *Thus, the maximum* M_n *of the potentially dependent sequence has the same limiting distribution (with the same* a_n, b_n) *as if the* X_i *were i.i.d.*

PROOF If $F \in D(G)$, $F^n(a_n^{-1}x + b_n) \to G(x)$, some $a_n > 0, b_n$ so that $n(1 - F(u_n)) \to \tau = -\log G(x)$, $u_n = a_n^{-1}x + b_n$ by the basic lemma for i.i.d. r.v.'s. Since the conclusion of the basic lemma is assumed to hold for our potentially dependent sequence $\{X_i\}$, we have that $P(M_n \leqslant u_n) \to e^{-\tau}$ or $P(a_n(M_n - b_n) \leqslant x) \to G(x)$ as asserted. ∎

The basic lemma was proved for i.i.d. sequences, but as noted above it was shown by Watson to apply to stationary m-dependent sequences. It also applies to other cases with strongly restricted dependence—for example, stationary normal sequences with correlations r_n satisfying Berman's Condition $r_n \log n \to 0$ to be discussed next indicating low correlations at large separations. One may thus conjecture that the basic lemma applies to sequences which are in some sense "close to being i.i.d." One way of making this precise is to note that for i.i.d. sequences, exceedances of a high level tend to occur singly and not in clusters, whereas for significant (positive) dependence one high value will tend to be followed by another, initiating a cluster. For many stationary sequences the limiting mean number of exceedances in a cluster is a parameter which we denote by θ^{-1}, $0 \leqslant \theta \leqslant 1$ and $\theta = 1$ for i.i.d. sequences as well as "nearly i.i.d." sequences such as stationary normal sequences satisfying Berman's condition stated above.

Another special class of sequences is considered by Berman (1962) in which the r.v.'s X_i are assumed to be exchangeable and the possible limits for the maximum obtained. That paper also considers the classical i.i.d. framework but where a random number of terms are involved.

Berman is perhaps most recognized for his work on maxima of Gaussian sequences and continuous time processes. He shows (Berman, 1964) that for a standard stationary Gaussian sequence with correlation sequence $r_n = E[X_1 X_{n+1}]$ satisfying $r_n \log n \to 0$, the maximum M_n has a type I limit $P(a_n(M_n - b_n) \leqslant x) \to \exp\{-e^{-x}\}$ where $a_n = (2 \log n)^{\frac{1}{2}}, b_n = (2 \log n)^{\frac{1}{2}} - \frac{1}{2}(2 \log n)^{-\frac{1}{2}}$ (log log n + log 4π), the same constants that apply to i.i.d. standard normal r.v.'s. This condition gives a sufficient condition for the limit, and while not necessary, it is close to being so, and known weaker sufficient conditions only differ slightly from it. As indicated earlier stationary Gaussian sequence satisfying Berman's condition exhibits no clustering and satisfies the basic lemma even though not i.i.d.

For more general stationary processes as noted earlier, Rosenblatt (1956) introduced the concept of strong mixing and used it in discussion of the CLT. Loynes (1965) used the strong mixing (albeit referred to there as "uniform mixing") assumption in developing EVT for stationary sequences—including the ETT. He also gave a version of the extension of the basic i.i.d. result $P(M_n \leqslant u_n) \to e^{-\tau}$ iff $n(1 - F(u_n)) \to \tau$ in which under strong mixing the limit $e^{-\tau}$ is replaced by $e^{-\theta\tau}$ for some θ, $0 \leqslant \theta \leqslant 1$, the parameter referred to earlier in the context of clustering (θ^{-1} = mean cluster size). This foreshadowed the use of the parameter θ as the "extremal index" (EI) under weaker conditions than strong mixing. As discussed later, this provides a simple and natural link between the limiting distribution for maxima under i.i.d. assumptions and under stationarity.

2.5   WEAK DISTRIBUTIONAL MIXING FOR EVT, $D(u_n)$, EXTREMAL INDEX

In attempting to weaken the strong mixing condition for EVT, one notes that the events of interest for extremes are typically those of the form $\{\xi_i \leqslant u\}$ or their finite intersections. For example, the event $\{M_n \leqslant u\}$ is just $\cap_{i=1}^{n}\{\xi_i \leqslant u\}$. Hence it is natural to attempt to restrict the events A and B in strong mixing to have the form $A = \{X_i \leqslant u, i = i_1, \dots, i_p\}$, $B = \{X_j \leqslant u, j = j_1, \dots, j_q\}$ where the i indices are separated by some ℓ from the j's. For a level u, note that $P(A) = F_{i_1,\dots,i_p}(u)$, the joint d.f. of $X_{i_1}, \dots, X_{i_p}$ with all arguments equal to u and similarly for $P(B)$ and $P(A \cap B)$. This leads to the following weak dependence condition introduced in Leadbetter (1974) (see also Leadbetter et al., 1983). The stationary sequence $X_1, X_2, \dots$ is said to satisfy the condition $D(u_n)$ for a sequence $\{u_n\}$ if for any choice of integers $i_1 < \dots i_p < j_1 < \dots < j_q \leqslant n, j_1 - i_p \geqslant \ell$,

$$\left| F_{i_1,\dots,i_p,j_1,\dots,j_q}(u_n) - F_{i_1,\dots,i_p}(u_n)F_{j_1,\dots,j_q}(u_n) \right| \leqslant \alpha_{n,\ell}, \qquad (2.3)$$

where $\alpha_{n,\ell_n} \to 0$ as $n \to \infty$ for some $\ell_n = o(n)$.

The ETT holds for a stationary sequence $\{X_n\}$ satisfying $D(u_n)$ for appropriate u_n. Specifically if $P(a_n(M_n - b_n) \leqslant x)$ converges to a nondegenerate G and $D(u_n)$ holds for $u_n = x/a_n + b_n$, each real x, then G is one of the three extreme value types. This of course includes the result of Loynes under strong mixing which clearly implies $D(u_n)$.

The basic lemma however does not hold as stated under $D(u_n)$ but may be modified in a very simple and useful way to relate limits under $D(u_n)$ to those for i.i.d. sequences. Specifically, with a slight abuse of notation, write $u_n(\tau)$ to denote a sequence such that $n(1 - F(u_n(\tau))) \to \tau$ as $n \to \infty$ (which exists under wide conditions—certainly if F is continuous). Then if $P(M_n \leqslant u_n(\tau))$ converges for one $\tau > 0$, it may be shown to converge for all $\tau > 0$ (e.g., Leadbetter et al., 1983) and $P(M_n \leqslant u_n(\tau)) \to e^{-\theta\tau}$ for all τ and some fixed θ, $0 \leqslant \theta \leqslant 1$. We term θ the "Extremal Index (EI)". From the basic lemma it takes the value 1 for i.i.d. sequences and for some dependent sequences including m-dependent stationary sequences and stationary normal sequences under Berman's conditions.

If X_n is a stationary sequence, write $\hat{X}_n$ for a sequence of i.i.d. r.v.'s with the same marginal d.f. F as each X_n. $\{\hat{X}_n\}$ has been termed "the independent sequence associated with the stationary sequence $\{X_n\}$" (Loynes, 1965; Leadbetter et al., 1983). Now if $\hat{M}_n = \max\{\hat{X}_1, \dots, \hat{X}_n\}$, then by the basic lemma $P(\hat{M}_n \leqslant u_n) \to e^{-\tau}$ if $u_n = u_n(\tau)$. If $D(u_n)$ holds and $\{X_n\}$ has EI $\theta > 0$, then as earlier $P(M_n \leqslant u_n) \to e^{-\theta\tau}$.

In particular if $P(a_n(\hat{M}_n - b_n) \leqslant x) \to G(x)$, then $P(a_n(M_n - b_n) \leqslant x) \to G^\theta(x)$ if $D(u_n)$ holds for $u_n = a_n^{-1}x + b_n$ for each x. That is, if $\hat{M}_n$ has the normalized limit G, M_n has the limit G^θ with the same normalizing constants. For each extreme value d.f. G, G^θ is easily seen to be of the same extremal type as G, and indeed by a simple change of normalizing constants, it follows that $P(\alpha_n(M_n - \beta_n) \leqslant x) \to G(x)$ for some α_n, β_n. Hence under $D(u_n)$ assumptions the normalized maximum M_n for the stationary sequence $\{X_n\}$ has a limiting distribution if (and only if) it would if the X_i were independent, with the same distribution. Further, the form of the limit in the stationary case is trivially determined from the i.i.d. limit G, either as G^θ with the same normalizing constants or as G itself by a change of normalizers.

2.6 POINT PROCESS OF LEVEL EXCEEDANCES

Finally in our personal tour of the development of EVT under dependence, we return to the discussion of exceedances of a level u_n normalized to occur on the unit interval as the points i/n for which $X_i > u_n$. As already indicated these form a point process N_n on $(0, 1)$ which converge to a Poisson process with intensity $\tau = \lim_{n \to \infty} n(1 - F(u_n))$ if the X_i are i.i.d. When the X_i form a stationary sequence satisfying $D(u_n)$ with $n(1 - F(u_n)) \to \tau$ and having EI $\theta > 0$, the exceedance points tend to coalesce in groups to become clusters, the locations of which form a Poisson process with intensity $\theta\tau$ in the limit. The limiting cluster sizes cause multiple events in the point process N_n which converges to a "compound Poisson process" if the dependence restriction $D(u_n)$ is strengthened in a natural and modest way (see, e.g., Hsing, 1987). For $\theta = 1$ the limiting point process is Poisson as discussed earlier. Other related Poisson processes are of considerable interest in addition to that of exceedances and of their locations. For example, the point process of sums of values in a cluster or the maximum values in a cluster are of interest, the latter generalizing the popular "peaks over thresholds" notions used in classical i.i.d. theory, with typically compound Poisson limits.

We have focused in our tour on some milestones in the historical development of EVT in its classical results for i.i.d. sequences and the evolution of the natural extensions to dependent (stationary) cases. These are more realistic since, for example, temporal data is almost always correlated in time at least at some small spacing. We have not discussed statistical analysis at all—methods for which abound and are documented in many publications and books. But it should be noted that the recognition of the EI and the (extended) basic lemma can really facilitate the application of inference for i.i.d. situations to, for example, stationary sequences. As a simple example one traditional way of fitting an extremal distribution G from a series of observed maxima is to graphically compare the empirical distribution $\hat{G}$ with each EV type. For example, if G is type 1, $G(x) = \exp\{-e^{-(ax+b)}\}$, then $-\log-\log G(x) = ax + b$ and so a, b may be chosen by linear regression of $-\log-\log \hat{G}(x)$ on x. If the fit of G is good, one concludes that G is the appropriate choice of extremal type and can estimate the normalizing constants by linear regression. This procedure is valid for a stationary sequence with some EI θ (its extremal limit G^{θ} is of the same type as G). One cannot therefore differentiate between stationarity and independence but can in either case hope to determine the correct limiting type and use the regression to estimate the normalizing constants giving the limit in standard form. It is thus by no means a test for stationarity but makes the method of determination of extremal type (and constants) valid whether or not the data is i.i.d. or stationary. This may account for success in determining extremal types for data by applying i.i.d. methods to (perhaps clearly) correlated data before the advent of the dependent theory!

2.7 CONTINUOUS PARAMETER EXTREMES

In the foregoing we have focused on extremes in sequences (i.i.d. and stationary) which are traditionally basic for very many applications. However (stationary) processes in continuous time also have significant applications—for example, in continuous monitoring of values of a pollutant for environmental regulation. Some such cases may be approximated by high-frequency sampling to give a discrete series, but the consideration of continuous parameters can be natural and helpful.

In fact much of the continuous parameter theory parallels that for sequences at least under stationarity. For example, let $M(T) = \max\{X(t) : 0 \leqslant t \leqslant T\}$ where $X(t)$ is a stationary process on $t \geqslant 0$. Then under weak dependence restrictions (akin to $D(u_n)$), the ETT holds: If $M(T)$ has a limit $P\{a_T(M(T) - b_T) \leqslant x\} \to G(x)$ (for some $a_T > 0$, b_T and nondegenerate G), then G must be one of the EV types. If $X(t)$ is stationary and Gaussian with correlation function $r(\tau)$, then the previous limiting distribution $G(x)$ is of type 1, under the weak dependence restriction of Berman, $r(t)\log(t) \to 0$ as $t \to \infty$. This is entirely analogous to the sequence case described previously.

For a continuous parameter process $X(t)$, of course exceedances of a level u occur in ranges rather than discrete points and hence do not form a point process. However, the closely related "upcrossings" of u (points t at which $x(t) = u$), but $x(s) < u$ for $s < t$ and $x(s) > u$ for $s > t$ when s is sufficiently close to t, do form a useful point process.

Analogous (e.g., Poisson) results hold under appropriate conditions to those for exceedance in the sequence case described earlier with close connections to maxima. For example, $M(T) > u$ if and only if either $X(0) > u$ or $X(t)$ has at least one upcrossing of u in $0 \leqslant t \leqslant T$. A systematic study of upcrossings was initiated by the pioneering electrical engineer Rice (see, e.g., Rice, 1944) and is important for assisting with obtaining asymptotic distributional properties of $M(T)$ but also in many other engineering applications. For example, the intensity of upcrossings (expected number per unit time) of ozone levels is of real interest in environmental (tropospheric) ozone regulation. Discussions of issues regarding maxima and level crossings by stationary stochastic processes may be found, for example, in Cramér and Leadbetter (1967) and Leadbetter et al. (1983) as well as other references cited.

A well developed useful theory for a class of one-dimensional problems of any kind often attracts interest in extensions to higher dimensions. Sometimes such extensions are not obviously useful and done because they are "there for the taking" and sometimes are too intricate, requiring too much effort in calculation, but often can lead to new and interesting theories which are not just obvious extensions of the one-dimensional case.

For a stochastic process X_t or sequence X_n, there are two obvious forms of introducing multidimensional versions of results in one dimension. One is to consider a finite family (vector) $X_{1,n}, X_{2,n}, \ldots, X_{k,n}$, for example, if $k = 3$, and $X_{1,n}, X_{2,n}, X_{3,n}$ may be the gross national products of China, the United States and Russia in year $n = 1, 2, 3, \ldots$, to compare economies over a period of years.

There is a huge literature on the study of the vector of maxima $(\max_{1 \leqslant j \leqslant n} X_{1j}, \max_{1 \leqslant j \leqslant n} X_{2j}, \max_{1 \leqslant j \leqslant n} X_{kj})$ known as multivariate EVT (see, e.g., de Haan and Ferreira, 2006). This does not yield the simple classification of possible limit distributions into the three forms as in one dimension but does give useful and interesting classification methods regarding families of possible limits.

The other extension of the classical theory to higher dimensions is to consider r.v.'s indexed by multidimensional parameters, for example, $X_{s,t}$, a r.v. measured at a point of the plane with coordinates s, t for, for example, $s \geqslant 0, t \geqslant 0, 0 \leqslant s, t \leqslant T$ (a square area) or a discrete version $X_{n,m}$ for $1 \leqslant n, m \leqslant N$ say. Such an $X_{s,t}$ (or $X_{n,m}$) is termed a random field (r.f.). A simple example is where (s, t) is the coordinate location of a point on a map with x-coordinate $x = s$ and y-coordinate $y = t$. $X_{s,t}$ may be measured NO_x levels at that location at a specified time, and one is interested in $M_T = \max\{X_{s,t} : 0 \leqslant s, t \leqslant T\}$, that is, the maximum level at locations in the square area with x and y coordinates no more than T.

A regulating agency, for example, may be interested in modeling the distribution of this maximum in an area (e.g., a county) in which measurements are made to determine compliance with environmental standards. Trends over time may be assessed by introducing a further (time) parameter to define a "spatio temporal" r.f. X_{t_1, t_2, t_3} at spatial location (t_1, t_2) and time t_3.

In one dimension conditions such as $D(u_n)$ or strong mixing really assert a degree of independence between past and future of a sequence $X_n, n = 1, 2, \ldots$ or process X_t ($t \geqslant 0$). But in two dimensions there is no natural ordering of the pairs of points and so no natural definition of past and future. One can of course limit dependence between $X(s, t)$ in regions separated by large distances, but this is far too restrictive and can require the terms $X(s_1, t_1), X(s_2, t_2)$ to be almost independent for different (s, t) points.

A promising approach is to not seek a single condition based on some measure of separation of two sets but rather require a "$D(u_n)$" type of condition applied sequentially in each coordinate direction, taking advantage of each past–future structure. This is explored in Leadbetter and Rootzen (1998) where, for example, an ETT is shown.

It is interesting to note the continuing intertwining of EVT and CLT, for example, the CLT result of Bolthausen (1982).

There are also many structural results even for i.i.d. situations which are important for inference but not included in our sketch of development. For example, we have barely referred to order statistics (of any kind—"extremal," "central," "intermediate"), associated point processes (e.g., exceedances of several levels), exceedance, and related point processes as marked point processes in the plane. See also Hsing (1987) for general results relevant to a number of these topics. In this chapter there has been no attempt to review the growing literature involving specific models for economic extremes. But the general methodology described earlier complements these, as should be clear. Economic data is certainly dependent and if not stationary can often be split into periods of stationarity which can be separately studied. High exceedances are certainly of considerable interest and can potentially be used to test for reality of changes, for example, of stock price levels. Study of exceedance clustering may well give insight into underlying causative mechanisms.

Our selection of papers considered has not been on the basis of mathematical depth or topic importance though some are universally considered to be pathbreaking. Rather we have attempted to give sign posts in the development of EVT from its i.i.d. beginnings, its pathway to and through stationarity, and its parallels with CLT from our own personal perspective.

References

Berman, S.M. Limiting distribution of the maximum term in sequences of dependent random variables. Ann. Math. Stat. 1962;**33**:894–908.

Berman, S.M. Limit theorems for the maximum term of a stationary sequence. Ann. Math. Stat. 1964;**35**:502–516.

Bernstein, S. Sur l'extension du theoreme limite du calcul des probabilités aux sommes de qusntites dépendentes. Math. Ann. 1927;**97**:1–59.

Bolthausen, E. On the central limit theorem for stationary mixing fields. Annals Prob. 1982;**20**:1047–1050.

Bradley, R.C. Basic properties of strong mixing conditions. A survey and some open questions. Probability Surveys 2005;**2**:107–144.

Bradley, R.C. *Introduction to Strong Mixing Conditions*. Volumes **1-3**. Heber City (UT): Kendrick Press; 2007.

Cramér, H., Leadbetter, M.R. *Stationary and Related Stochastic Processes*. New York: John Wiley & Sons, Inc.; 1967.

de Haan, L., Ferreira, A. *Extreme Value Theory An Introduction*. New York: Springer-Verlag; 2006.

Dodd, E.L. The greatest and least variate under general laws of error. Trans. Am. Math. Soc. 1923;**25**:525–539.

Fisher, R.A., Tippett, LMC. Limiting forms of the frequency distribution of the largest and smallest member of a sample. Proc. Camb. Philol. Soc. 1928;**24**:180–190.

Fréchet, M. Sur la loi de probablité de l'écart maximum. Ann. Soc. Polon. Math. (Cracovie) 1927;**6**:93–116.

Gnedenko, B.V. Sur la distribution limite du terme maximum d'une série aléatoire. Ann. Math. 1943;**44**:423–453.

Hoeffding, W., Robbins, H. The central limit theorem for dependent random variables. Duke Math. J. 1948;**15**:773–780.

Hsing, T. Characterization of certain point processes. Stochastic Processes and their Applications 1987;**26**:297–316.

Ibragimov, I.A., Linnik, Yu. *Independent and Stationary Sequences of Random Variables*. Groningen: Walters-Noordhott; 1971.

Leadbetter, M.R. On extreme values in stationary sequences. Z. Wahrscheinlichkeitstheorie verw Geb 1974;**28**:289–303.

Leadbetter, M.R., Lindgren, G, Rootzén, H. *Extremes and Related Properties of Random Sequences and Processes*. New York, Heidelberg, Berlin: Springer-Verlag; 1983.

Leadbetter, M.R., Rootzen, H. On extreme values in stationary random fields. In: Rajput, B.S. et al., editors. *Stochastic Processes and Related Topics*. In Memory of Stamatis Cambanis 1943-1995. Birkäuser Boston. 1998;**1**:275–285.

Loynes, R.M. Extreme values in uniformly mixing stationary stochastic processes. Ann. Math. Statistics 1965;**36**:308–314.

Rice, S.O. Mathematical analysis of random noise. Bell Syst Tech J 1944;**23**:232–282, and **24**:46–156.

Rosenblatt, M. A central limit theorem and a strong mixing condition. Proc. Natl. Acad. Sci. USA 1956;**42**:43–47.

von Mises, R. La distribution de la plus grande de *n* valeurs. Rev. Math. Union. Interfalkanique. 1936;**1**:141–160.

Watson, G.S. Extreme values in samples from *m*-dependent stationary stochastic processes. Ann. Math. Stat. 1954;**25**:798–800.

Chapter Three

The Extreme Value Problem in Finance: Comparing the Pragmatic Program with the Mandelbrot Program

Christian Walter

Collège détudes mondiales, Fondation Maison des sciences de l'homme, Paris, France

3.1 THE EXTREME VALUE PUZZLE IN FINANCIAL MODELING

The extreme value puzzle in finance has a long history (Longin, 1993; Fraga Alves and Neves, 2017). As early as in the 1950s, one noticed that the price changes presented such a phenomenon. For example, in a landmark paper published in the *Journal of the Royal Statistical Society*, Maurice Kendall wrote that the results from price data between 1883 and 1934 are such that "[t]he distributions are accordingly rather leptokurtic" (Kendall, 1953, 13). Seven years after, in the *Food Research Institute Studies*, Arnold Larson noticed that "Examination of the pattern of occurrence of all price changes in excess of three standard deviations from zero ($\cdots$) indicated that [there is] presence in the data of an *excessive number of extreme values*" (Larson, 1960, 224, our italics).

The mainstream view of the extreme values of distributions considered these data as irrelevant for financial modeling. For example, Granger and Orr (1972) asserted that "[i]f the long tails of empirical distributions are of concern to the time-series analyst or econometrician, it is natural to consider reducing the importance of these tails. The most obvious approach is to truncate the data." On the contrary, Mandelbrot (1962) viewed these extreme values as something extremely important for the understanding of market behavior. But in the 1970s, the Gaussian

Extreme Events in Finance: A Handbook of Extreme Value Theory and its Applications,
First Edition. Edited by François Longin.
© 2017 John Wiley & Sons, Inc. Published 2017 by John Wiley & Sons, Inc.

distribution was the predominant tool used to describe the empirical distribution of returns, and Brownian motion was just rediscovered by the founders of the "modern" financial theory. Hence, at this time, it was not possible to take account of the tails of the distributions. I now elaborate this point, which is of a great importance for the history of financial thought, the origins of the multiple financial accidents since 1987, and the issue of extreme values I aim to address here.

I have argued that some of the key differences between the two approaches can be illuminated by reference to a familiar debate in philosophy over the principle of continuity (Le Courtois and Walter, 2014b). Although this philosophical debate may seem to be a scholastic preoccupation within a tight circle of specialists in philosophy of science, far from the financial stakes of modeling and with no impact on concrete financial practices, I argue, on the contrary, that the divergent positions about the mind-set behind the price changes implicate entirely different views of what it is important to capture and how to model it. Let us emphasize this point.

In physics, the principle of continuity states that change is continuous rather than discrete. Leibniz and Newton, the inventors of differential calculus, said, "*Natura non facit saltus*" (nature does not make jumps). This same principle underpinned the thoughts of Linné on the classification of species and later Charles Darwin's theory of evolution (1859). In 1890, Alfred Marshall's *Principles of Economics* assumed the principle of continuity, allowing the use of differential calculus in economics and the subsequent development of neoclassical economic theory. In 1900, Louis Bachelier defends his thesis *Theory of Speculation* in which price movements are modeled by Brownian motion (Bachelier, 1900). Modern financial theory grew out of neoclassical economics and naturally assumes the same principle of continuity. One of the great success stories of modern financial theory was the valuation of derivatives. Examples include the formulas of Black et al. (1973) for valuing options and the subsequent fundamental theorem of asset pricing that emerged from the work of Harrison, Kreps, and Pliska between 1979) and 1981. These success stories rest on the principle of continuity. In the twentieth century, both physics and genetics abrogated the principle of continuity. Quantum mechanics postulated discrete energy levels, while genetics took discontinuities into account. But economics—including modern financial theory—stood back from this intellectual revolution.

The crux of my argument about the extreme value puzzle in financial modeling can be summarized in the following statement. There are two fundamentally different ways of viewing price changes in finance. One side of the debate, "Leibnizian," takes the continuity as a cornerstone for financial modeling. In this view, following Bachelier's legacy, price movements are modeled by continuous diffusion processes. The contrary "anti-Leibnizian" position holds that discontinuity is crucial for grasping the true nature of price changes without intellectual cleavage. According to the second view, following Mandelbrot's legacy, price movements are modeled by discontinuous processes, as, for instance, Lévy processes. *Mandelbrot's pivotal move was to reconceptualize the discontinuity of price changes as an empirical problem for financial modeling.*

With the presence of extreme value in financial time series, the Mandelbrot view might have been expected to start a new way of modeling price changes.

But the early attempt by Mandelbrot to take explicit account of discontinuities on all scales in stock market prices led to huge controversies in the profession (Walter, 2009a). By the 1980s, the academic consensus reaffirmed the principle of continuity, despite the repeated financial crises following the 1987 stock market crash. The principle of continuity was still predominant in the 1990s despite the growing evidence of extreme values in the tails of empirical distribution (Longin, 1996) mainly with the high-frequency data. Many popular financial techniques, such as portfolio insurance or the calculation of capital requirements in the insurance industry, assumed that (financial) nature does not make jumps and therefore widely promoted continuity in the professional community (see however Bertrand and Prigent, 2017 for a recent account of the CPPI method and EVT approach). Most statistical descriptions of time series in top journals in the field of finance assumed continuity. The Brownian representation still underlies almost all prudential regulations worldwide: for instance, the so-called square-root-of-time rule underlying the regulatory requirements (Basle III and Solvency II) for calculating minimum capital is a very narrow subset of time scaling rule of risk and comes directly from the hypothesis that returns follow a Brownian motion. I termed this Brownian mind-set the "Brownian virus" (Walter, 2009b), a notion inspired by Durkheim's writing (*Le suicide*, 1930), for suggesting a cognitive bias: a "suicidogenic" school of thought creating an pathogenic environment (intellectual and social) that destroyed the prudent instincts of risk professionals and led to the financial meltdown of 2008.

In fact, one of the cognitive consequences of the Brownian virus is a negative spillover about the extreme value puzzle: the truncation of financial time series into "normal" periods (continuous market) and periods of "insanity" where markets are deemed "irrational" (extreme value periods). This dichotomy leaves the profession unable to explain the transition from one period to another. For example, in an editorial in the *Financial Times* (16.3.08), Alan Greenspan commented on the financial crisis of 2007–2008, "We can never anticipate all discontinuities in financial markets." For Greenspan, (financial) nature does not make jumps and extreme values are unpredictable outliers. This cognitive bias demonstrates the limits of risk management when considering the extreme value problem with a continuity Brownian-based framework completed with an extreme value approach and the need for a global discontinuous framework. If extreme value theory can efficiently help to choose a distribution for rare events (Longin, 2005), the problem of tackling discontinuities at all scales remains.

Brownian motion increments have the important property of being independent and identically distributed (hereafter IID). The processes with IID increments are called Lévy processes after the French mathematician Paul Lévy. Brownian motion is a specific Lévy process: it assumes continuity. Other Lévy processes do not. This chapter gives an overview of the financial modeling of extreme values and discontinuities in the behavior of stock market prices with Lévy processes. I present to the two main competitors for this stake: stable Lévy processes (Mandelbrot's first program) and the nonstable Lévy processes-based approach. I suggest that the nonstable Lévy-based approach of discontinuities can be viewed as a "pragmatic program" (PP) launched in the 1970s against the Mandelbrot's first program, which I term "radical program" (RP). I use Sato's classification to contrast the two programs. Next I present the two competitors from a historical perspective. The PP split into two branches: the heterodox financial modeling and the econophysics view. There are interesting parallels between them, which derive from their reliance on the RP.

The outline of the chapter is as follows. Section 3.2 introduces some fundamental notions from Lévy processes such as activity, variation, and Lévy measure. Next, I introduce Sato's classification to characterize the two programs. Section 3.3 presents the Mandelbrot program and discusses the related problems. Section 3.4 presents the PP with is three stages: Section 3.4.1 begins with mixed jump-diffusion processes in the 1970s; Section 3.4.2 follows with infinite activity finite variation processes and infinite activity infinite variation processes in the 1990s. Section 3.5 concludes.

3.2 THE SATO CLASSIFICATION AND THE TWO PROGRAMS

This section presents in the simplest and most intuitive way possible the main characteristics of Lévy processes. Many books present a comprehensive view of these processes, as, for example, Bertoin (1996) and Sato (1999), for more details.

3.2.1 Lévy Processes

To specify a Lévy process, there are two alternative routes: either to describe the marginal probability distribution of the process, that is, the shape of the probability density function of the law, which describes the morphology of market uncertainty, considered from a static standpoint, or to describe the Lévy measure, a mathematical object that captures the structure of the dynamics of jumps. The marginal probability distribution corresponds to a representation of uncertainty in the real world (here, the reality of the chance of the market, the reality of the stock price behavior, and the reality of the financial phenomenon), which can be used for real-world calibrations with market data, whereas the Lévy measure appears only in the transformed space of characteristic functions: the inverse Fourier transform of the probability density function. The characteristic functions can also be used as part of procedures for fitting probability distributions to samples of data. These two representations are equivalent for the specification of a Lévy process in the sense that knowing one of the functions always makes it possible to find the other. Both provide different insights for understanding the morphology of uncertainty in the financial world.

However, the two cannot be used indifferently. The probability density function does not always exist (closed-form expression is not available), whereas the characteristic function of any infinitely divisible distribution always exists. Thus, for reasons of mathematical convenience, one uses the characteristic function and the characteristic exponent (see Box 3.1) to define in a simple way an infinitely

▣ BOX 3.1 **Characteristic function and characteristic exponent**

> The characteristic function of a random variable Y is the Fourier transform of its density function:
>
> $$\Phi_Y(u) = E\left[e^{iuY}\right] = \underbrace{\sum_{k=0}^{\infty} e^{iuk} \Pr(Y = k)}_{\text{discrete r.v.}} = \underbrace{\int_{-\infty}^{+\infty} e^{iux} f_Y(x)dx}_{\text{continue r.v.}},$$
>
> where $f_Y(x)$ is the density function. The characteristic function can be written as
>
> $$\Phi_Y(u) = \exp(\Psi_Y(u)), \tag{3.1}$$
>
> where $\Psi_Y(u)$ is the characteristic exponent of Y.

divisible distribution and the Lévy processes corresponding to it. The characteristic function of a Lévy process has an equivalent meaning to the density function: it describes the *morphology of uncertainty* of the observed phenomenon.

The explicit form of the characteristic exponent of a stochastic process with IID increments was obtained in the most general case by Paul Lévy in 1934 and is the so-called Lévy–Khintchine formula (see Box 3.2). The Lévy measure was

▣ BOX 3.2 **Characteristic exponent and Lévy measure**

> The explicit form of the characteristic exponent of a random walk was obtained by Paul Lévy in 1934 for the processes with IID increments. This form is
>
> $$\Psi_{X_t}(u) = \underbrace{t\left(i\mu u - \frac{1}{2}\sigma^2 u^2\right)}_{\text{DIFFUSION}} + \underbrace{t\int_{\mathbb{R}^*}(e^{iux} - 1 - iux\,\mathbf{1}_{|x|<1}(x))\nu(dx)}_{\text{JUMPS}}.$$
>
> $$\tag{3.2}$$
>
> This is the Lévy–Khintchine formula, the interpretation of which is the following. The first term ("DIFFUSION") represents the normal distribution with the expectation μ and the standard deviation σ, the diffusive component of the stochastic process also termed the "volatility" of the markets. The second term ("JUMPS") is the jump component of the stochastic process, which contains the Lévy measure $\nu(dx)$.
>
> Heuristically, the Lévy measure provides the number of jumps per unit of time as a function of their size. It is the mathematical object that allows to quantify the jump arrival and the jump size. This is a key component of a Lévy process, which completely defines the structure of "erraticity" of the market behavior.

explicitly used in the models of the 1990s, whereas it was only implicit in those of the 1970s, with the exception of Mandelbrot's model (1962, 1963), in which it appeared in an integrated form of the characteristic exponent.

A very important property of Lévy processes due to the IID property is that the characteristic exponent is proportional to the time duration: the marginal distributions of these processes are infinitely divisible (see Box 3.3). This means that a random variable can be understood as the sum of identical random variables, at any order. When modeling market uncertainty on whatever scale, one uses this property. The characteristic exponent at a given time t (uncertainty at time t) is easily obtained from the characteristic exponent at time 1 (uncertainty at time 1) following (see Box 3.3) the rule (3.6). This is one of the main attractions of Lévy processes, making them preferable to other types of model where the IID property does not hold.

■ BOX 3.3 **Characteristic exponent and infinitely divisible distributions**

For any positive integer n, one has $X_n = X_1 + (X_2 - X_1) + \cdots + (X_n - X_{n-1})$ and therefore

$$\Phi_{X_n}(u) = E\left[e^{iuX_n}\right],$$

$$= E\left[e^{iu(X_1 + (X_2 - X_1) + \cdots + (X_n - X_{n-1}))}\right],$$

$$= E\left[e^{iuX_1} \times e^{iu(X_2 - X_1)} \times \cdots \times e^{iu(X_n - X_{n-1})}\right]. \qquad (3.3)$$

If X is a Lévy process, the increments are IID. From the independence of the increments, it follows that

$$\Phi_{X_n}(u) = E\left[e^{iuX_1}\right] \times E\left[e^{iu(X_2 - X_1)}\right] \times \cdots \times E\left[e^{iu(X_n - X_{n-1})}\right].$$

From the stationarity of the increments, it follows that

$$\Phi_{X_n}(u) = \underbrace{E\left[e^{iuX_1}\right] \times E\left[e^{iuX_1}\right] \times \cdots \times E\left[e^{iuX_1}\right]}_{n \quad \text{times}} = \left(E\left[e^{iuX_1}\right]\right)^n.$$

Finally one obtains

$$\Phi_{X_n}(u) = (\Phi_{X_1}(u))^n. \qquad (3.4)$$

This result can be generalized in the case of a continuous time t (real positive) to

$$\Phi_{X_t}(u) = (\Phi_{X_1}(u))^t. \qquad (3.5)$$

Now one considers the characteristic exponent. It follows from (3.5) that

$$\exp\left(\Psi_{X_t}(u)\right) = \left(\exp\left(\Psi_{X_1}(u)\right)\right)^t = \exp\left(t\Psi_{X_1}(u)\right).$$

Hence the relationship between the characteristic exponent of the process X at time 1 and at time t is

$$\Psi_{X_t}(u) = t \times \Psi_{X_1}(u). \tag{3.6}$$

This is the reason why the characteristic exponent of a Lévy process is equal to t times that of its underlying infinitely divisible distribution, which is in fact the distribution X_1.

3.2.2 Activity and Variation of Lévy Processes

One source of the extreme value puzzle is the interpretation of jumps in statistical descriptions.

3.2.2.1 Jumps? What jumps?

A stock price trajectory is by construction discontinuous, because it comprises jumps at all quote times. In the classic case of the Brownian representation of fluctuations, trajectories are continuous. The classic Brownian representation views quotes as points sampled in a continuous trajectory. In the case of a Brownian representation, quote jumps are proportional to the volatility of Brownian motion, and hence it is not necessary to change representation. This statement correctly addresses the puzzle of jumps. In a given representation, are the points separated by distances that are consistent with the postulated model for paths? In the Brownian representation, are the observed jumps consistent with the diffusive nature of Brownian motion, or are they too large?

Strange as it may seem, this issue had not been tackled in finance literature until very recently. While normality tests have been well known for many years, it was not until the contributions of Aït-Sahalia and Jacod (2009) that appropriate tests for the detection of jumps were constructed, adding discontinuity tests to the classical toolbox of financial statistics.

3.2.2.2 Shaping the path irregularity in an IID framework with the Lévy measure

With a Lévy process, each trajectory is by definition discontinuous everywhere. Intuitively, the greater the number of jumps per time unit, the more the trajectory of the stochastic process will have a high degree of irregularity and the more erratic the random walk will be. Hence a stochastic process will be highly erratic if the average number of jumps occurring per unit of time is very large. The average number of jumps per unit of time defines the so-called intensity of a Lévy process—also termed "activity" by analogy with turbulence. The activity can be finite or infinite.

📖 BOX 3.4 **The Lévy measure in simple cases with Poisson processes**

Let us consider a Poisson process with parameter λ: the average number of jumps per unit of time—the activity of the process—is simply λ. Let us continue with this simple example to get an intuitive idea of what the Lévy measure is. Whenever a jump in the Poisson process occurs, suppose that the magnitude Y of the jump is random with known density $f_Y(x)$. Let us note $v(x)$ the product:

$$v(x) = \lambda \times f_Y(x). \tag{3.7}$$

This product is the Lévy measure. One sees that the Lévy measure captures both the occurrence rate of discontinuities and their magnitude: the product (3.7) fully characterizes the jump structure of the process. One observes that the integral of the Lévy measure is equal to λ:

$$\int_{-\infty}^{+\infty} v(dx) = \lambda \times \underbrace{\int_{-\infty}^{+\infty} f_Y(x)dx}_{=1 \text{ (density)}} = \lambda = \text{activity}.$$

Hence the integral of the Lévy measure provides the activity of the process.

Suppose that the distribution of jumps is normal with a mean μ_Y being the average size of jumps and a standard deviation σ_Y being the volatility of the size of jumps (a compound Poisson process with a normal distribution or "compound Poisson-Normal" process). Hence, following (3.7), the Lévy measure is

$$v(x) = \lambda \times \frac{1}{\sigma_Y\sqrt{2\pi}} \exp\left(-\frac{(x - \mu_Y)^2}{2\sigma_Y^2}\right). \tag{3.8}$$

In the simple case of a compound Poisson process with any probability distribution Y with known density $f_Y(x)$, the Lévy measure is just the product:

$$\text{activity} \times \text{density}$$

The rudimentary example of Box 3.4 shows that, in order to "isolate" the activity of a Lévy process, it is sufficient to calculate the integral of the Lévy measure. This integral may be either finite or infinite. In all cases in which one constructs a compound Poisson process with another distribution, the number of jumps per unit of time (the occurrence rate of discontinuities) is finite and the resulting Lévy process is of finite activity. In this situation one can clearly separate the activity from the density. When the activity is finite, the product activity-density is the Lévy measure.

It makes sense to generalize this approach for moving from finite to infinite activity. Indeed there is no reason why the average number of small jumps per unit of time should stay finite. The advantage of generalizing in this way is that the very many small market movements can be taken into account. In the case of infinite activity, it is no longer possible to separate the activity λ from the density f. Both are "mixed" in the Lévy measure, which entirely shapes the morphology of the irregularity of the financial phenomenon. The activity is "isolated" in the same way as in the simple previous example.

Let us consider now the average distance between two points of the process. The average distance can be finite or infinite (the mean may or may not exist). This idea of average distance corresponds to what is called the variation of a Lévy process. The variation may be finite or infinite. The variation is another feature of the morphology of financial uncertainty.

Let us summarize what has been presented so far. A Lévy process is fully defined by the specification of three quantities: the mean of the diffusive component (the trend of the process), the diffusion coefficient (the *scale of fluctuations*), and the Lévy measure (the *morphology of uncertainty*). The role of the Lévy measure is decisive. It contains all the information needed to characterize the trajectory of a Lévy process, apart from its tendency and its diffusive fluctuation scale ("volatility"). It is the quantity that shapes the size of the tails of distribution and the patterns of jumpy fluctuations:

$$\text{Characteristic exponent} = \text{Trend} + \text{Scale} + \text{Morphology}$$

The significance of the new approach adopted in the 1990s came precisely from this possibility of defining any market dynamics with irregularities at all scales by direct specification of the Lévy measure. Thus, the dynamic of stock prices being any Lévy process, the representation of market fluctuations shifted, in the 1990s, from exponentials of Brownian motions to exponentials of Lévy processes.

Another consideration also favored Lévy processes. Lévy processes are semimartingales. The work of Ross, Harrison, and Pliska between 1976 and 1981 on arbitrage showed that the arbitraged prices of securities ought to be capable of being modeled by semimartingales. Thus for these reasons applying both to financial modeling and to the technique of stochastic calculus, the Lévy processes disinterred in the early 1990s, after a decade of growing maturity in financial thinking around the theory of arbitrage and the usefulness of intrinsic market temporality, and appeared extraordinarily well adapted to the new way of conceiving the modeling of arbitraged markets, whether in calendar time or market time. The match between the most modern finance (absence of arbitrage) and the development of working techniques on Lévy processes was pivotal for the introduction of these processes into financial research.

3.2.3   The Two Programs in the Light of Sato's Classification

In brief, three alternatives exist for shaping financial uncertainty with Lévy process: either the activity is finite or infinite, the variation is finite or infinite, or the

TABLE 3.1   The Sato classification, the variance issue, and the financial modeling programs

Activity	Variation	Variance	Financial modeling	Program
INFINITE	INFINITE	INFINITE	Mandelbrot (1962)	RADICAL
Finite	Finite	Finite	Press (1967), Merton (1976)	PRAGMATIC
			Cox and Ross (1976)	Stage 1
INFINITE	Finite	Finite	Madan and Seneta (1990)	PRAGMATIC
			Madan and Milne (1991)	Stage 2
INFINITE	INFINITE	Finite	Eberlein and Keller (1995)	
			Barndorff-Nielsen (1997)	
			Eberlein et al. (1998)	PRAGMATIC
			Madan et al. (1998)	Stage 3
			Prause (1999)	
			Carr et al. (2002, 2003)[a]	

[a]Depends on exponent.

variance can be finite or infinite. The Sato (1999) classification defines a process by its pair (activity and variation) according to the double criterion finite or infinite. In the PP, the variance is finite, and in the RP (Mandelbrot's view) the variance is infinite. It appears that there are four types of stochastic processes depending on whether their activity and their variation are finite or infinite and whether variance is finite or infinite. Table 3.1 exhibits the Lévy processes in financial modeling following this double criterion, the variation being that of the jump part of the stochastic process.

In general, the models of the late 1990s and early 2000s used processes with infinite activity and infinite variation but with finite variance. As an outlaw, the Mandelbrot model (1962) comprised infinite activity, infinite variation, and infinite variance.

3.3   MANDELBROT'S PROGRAM: A FRACTAL APPROACH

The initial idea of discontinuities at any scale of the observation of market behavior came from Mandelbrot (1962 and 1963). How to name financial markets that are "continually discontinuous"? Mandelbrot felt that the name should reflect the fractured nature of the paths representing price changes. He coined the term "fractal" (from the Latin *fractus*, meaning fractured) to characterize discontinuities at all scales.

He developed his main ideas in a series of significant papers published in French. Some of these texts are translated in English, modified, and reprinted in his 1997 *Fractals and Scaling in Finance*. In this chapter, I term "Mandelbrot's program" the research program described in these papers corresponding to Mandelbrot (1966, 1967, 1973a, 1973b, 1973c). The three main concepts of the first research program for financial modeling are summarized in Walter (2015): fat tails, long-range dependence, and intrinsic time. A second strand of papers came after his 1997 book, corresponding to Mandelbrot (2001a, 2001b, 2001c), which built on the generalized multifractal model put forward in 1997, outside the IID framework. This model was the result of Mandelbrot's coming back to finance after the 1987 crash. The three papers of 2001 echoed the three of 1973 and represent a second stage of the program, moving from unifractals to multifractals. Ultimately, multifractal modeling allows a comprehensive view of discontinuities with bypassing the limitations of the first approach.

The idea of discontinuity in price variations at any scale is closely related to the scaling view of price fluctuations (the "fractal description of markets"), a current of thought which is initially entangled with the "chartist" approach to markets, before being adequately mathematicized with fractals. I now elaborate this point.

3.3.1 The Fractal View of Price Behavior

Stock market charts representing changes in the stock prices over a given period of time look like irregular patterns that seem to be reproduced and repeated in all scales of analysis. Rising periods follow periods of decline and the rises are punctuated with intermediate falling phases and falls are interspersed with partial rises, and this goes on until the quotation scale limit is reached.

This mixture of repetitive patterns of rising and falling waves at all scales was Elliott's (1938) intuition, to whom this idea occurred while observing the ebb and flow of tides on the sands of the seashore. From this, he coined a financial symbolization known as "stock market waves" or "Elliott's waves," which he subdivided into huge tides, normal waves, and wavelets. In mathematical terms, the so-called Elliott wave principle presents a deterministic self-similar fractal description of stock markets with self-similar geometric patterns found on all scales of observations.

The fractals of Mandelbrot, though developed in a radically different intellectual context, fit in this understanding of stock market variations. It presents, like the common view with Elliott's waves, a method for disentangling the inextricable interlacing of stock market moves at all scales. Fractals represented an adequate conceptualization allowing the translation of intuitions of technical analysts into rigorous mathematical representation, because this mathematics deals with two financial stylized facts: *discontinuity* and *scaling*. The notion of "roughness" addresses these facts by creating a strange nexus between two seemingly disparate cases: discontinuity and scaling. Random fractal curves adequately mimic stock market charts. In the following section, I elaborate on this.

3.3.2 Fractal Modeling: Discontinuity and Scaling

Despite the promising results opened up with this new way of thinking financial modeling, the adventure of fractal modeling in finance does not display a smooth (continuous) history. It is more an eventful (discontinuous) progression of Mandelbrot's assumptions through the evolution of finance theory over 40 years, from 1960 to 2000. In a paper summarizing the Mandelbrot's state of research program in the 1980s, Mirowski (1995) observed that "the economics profession dropped the Mandelbrot hypothesis largely for reasons other than empirical adequacy and concise simplicity. [...] The only purpose of the negative studies was to refute Mandelbrot." In his admirable book about the development of financial economics, MacKenzie (2006) stressed this point by hypothesizing that Mandelbrot's model was viewed by the financial academic community as a probability "monster." Let us have a closer look on this point.

3.3.2.1 The extreme values and the stable model

At the origin of the fractal modeling in finance is the "leptokurtic phenomenon," that is, the presence of fat tails due to extreme values in the empirical distributions of returns. Mandelbrot's idea for suggesting the simplest generalization of Brownian motion that takes account of the extreme values was to put forward the simplest process, which was, in this sense, stable by addition, the alpha-stable motion. But the price to pay was the abandonment of finite variance because the variance of alpha-stable motion is infinite. This infiniteness of a crucial financial quantity which just arose in the new models for portfolio management (Markowitz, 1952, 1959) and option pricing (Black et al., 1973) was seen as horrific by the academic mainstream of the 1970s. For example, one can find in a textbook that "many researchers find the conclusion of infinite variance unacceptable" (Taylor, 1986).

On the other hand, there was a lack of statistical tools to tackle the estimation of the parameters of stable distributions. For example, Fama (1965) wrote that

> "economic models involving stable Paretian generating processes have developed more rapidly than the statistical theory of stable Paretian distributions. It is our hope that papers like this will arouse the interest of statisticians in exploring more fully the properties of these distributions."

In a reference textbook on one-dimensional stable distributions, Zolotarev (1986) echoes Fama by saying that "it can be said without exaggeration that the problem of constructing statistical estimators of stable laws entered into mathematical statistics due to the work of Mandelbrot."

An important point to be understood is the following. It is possible to tackle the extreme value puzzle with models other than alpha-stable motions, indeed an unlimited number of models. But if one wants to keep the IID hypothesis and have non-Gaussian tails with scaling property (Brownian motion), the only alternative is the alpha-stable motion. The controversies resulting from the leptokurtic phenomenon and extreme values of the distributions became entangled in the intrication of the static approach (Gaussian or non-Gaussian) and the dynamic approach (Brownian or non-Brownian). In the 1970s, the debates ignored the stochastic process issues and concentrated on the extreme values of the distributions.[1]

3.3.2.2 The Rejection of the Stable Model

A review over forty years of searching for scaling laws in distributional properties of price variations (Walter, 2009a) exhibits a turbulent story with fierce controversies that stirred up the academic community with regard to the continuous/discontinuous debate. So strong was the opposition to Mandelbrot's hypothesis that any kind of alternative model was preferred to the idea of infinite variance as embedded in the alpha-stable motion proposed by Mandelbrot. For example, in a paper devoted to the statistical properties of exchange rates, Elie et al. (1993) wrote that "ARCH models allowed us to solve largely this problem of heavy tails of distributions while keeping a Gaussian framework which turns out more tractable than that of stable laws" (our translation).

Underpinned by the desire to reject fractality ("anything but Mandelbrot" or "ABM" because Mandelbrot was working at IBM and was the watchword of the pro-continuity approach activists), the debates shifted to the testing of the alpha-stability-under-addition property. They ended with the empirical rejection of fractal modeling for distributional properties returns in the 1970s because the scale invariance principle was found too strong for adequately modeling price variations. The alpha-stable Lévy processes were abandoned by the mainstream.

3.3.2.3 The tempered stable family in econophysics

To remedy the inconvenience of not having any moments for the alpha-stable models of the Mandelbrot's program, other models were developed with a truncation principle. In the alpha-stable models, the Lévy measure displays a power law that produces Paretian tails (see Box 3.5). This power law is precisely the origin of the nonexistence of the moments when the Paretian exponent is less than 2. A simple way of avoiding this problem is to weight the Lévy measure by an exponential quantity in order to reduce large fluctuations and therefore recover the moments. This idea corresponds to a class of Lévy processes whose marginal distributions are truncated stable distributions, the so-called "tempered stable" models. The stable distributions are truncated by exponential functions, hence the term tempered stable processes. The distribution tails of these models, tempered by the truncation, are semilight.

In the 1990s, physicists began to propose such models combining truncated alpha-stable distributions with exponential tails (Mantegna and Stanley, 1994; Koponen, 1995; Bouchaud and Potters, 1997), and physicist research activity enters the financial modeling field. As Mantegna and Stanley (2000) noticed,

---

[1]It is worth noting that this intrication is sometimes a source of confusion in the existing literature of historical financial thought, based on an analysis that does not distinguish between the so-called Lévy distributions (actually stable distribution with Pareto tail) and Lévy processes (actually stochastic processes with IID increments). Here the semantics is misleading.

▣ BOX 3.5 **The Lévy measures of the radical and pragmatic programs**

The stable model/RP proposed by Mandelbrot (1962) has the characteristic exponent:

$$\Psi_{X_t}(u) = t \left(i\mu u + \int_{-\infty}^{0} \psi(u,x) \frac{C_-}{|x|^{1+\alpha}} dx + \int_{0}^{+\infty} \psi(u,x) \frac{C_+}{x^{1+\alpha}} dx \right)$$

(3.9)

with

$$\psi(u,x) = e^{iux} - 1 - iux \, \mathbf{1}_{|x|<1}(x).$$

From (3.2) and (3.9), it follows that the Lévy measure of the α-stable motion is

$$\nu(dx) = \frac{C_-}{|x|^{1+\alpha}} \mathbf{1}_{(-\infty,0)}(x)dx + \frac{C_+}{x^{1+\alpha}} \mathbf{1}_{(0,+\infty)}(x)dx$$

(3.10)

or in a more intuitive form

$$\nu(x) = \begin{cases} \dfrac{C_-}{|x|^{1+\alpha}} & \text{if } x < 0, \\[3mm] \dfrac{C_+}{x^{1+\alpha}} & \text{if } x > 0. \end{cases}$$

(3.11)

This last form (3.11) exhibits a power Paretian law in the Lévy measure. This precisely allows to understand Mandelbrot's intuition: *the search for Paretian tails for solving the extreme value issue*. A tale of fat tails, he named later "the power of power laws" (Mandelbrot, 2004, p. 13).

Model	Lévy measure for		Program	Field
	$x < 0$	$x > 0$		
Mandelbrot (1962)	$\dfrac{C_-}{|x|^{1+\alpha}}$	$\dfrac{C_+}{x^{1+\alpha}}$	Radical	Finance
Koponen (1995)	$\dfrac{C_-}{|x|^{1+\alpha}} e^{-a_- |x|}$	$\dfrac{C_+}{x^{1+\alpha}} e^{-a_+ x}$	Pragmatic	Econophysics
Carr et al. (2002)	$\dfrac{C}{|x|^{1+\alpha}} e^{-a_- |x|}$	$\dfrac{C}{x^{1+\alpha}} e^{-a_+ x}$	Pragmatic	Finance

In the Koponen (1995) and Carr et al. (2002) models, one sees that the stable distributions are truncated by exponential functions. These models are named tempered stable processes. The distribution tails of these models, because of tempered by the truncation, are semilight. The parametrization is asymmetric in the decay rate of large jumps.

"since 1990, a research community has begun to emerge." This new community baptized itself with the name "econophysics." Hence in the 1990s, research in financial modeling then split into two separate communities: that of financial academics—the mainstream—and that of physicists—the heterodox view known as "econophysics." Physicists continued along the way paved by Mandelbrot's model, working in particular with the scaling concept: as Mantegna and Stanley (2000) pointed out, financial academics were "trying to determine a characteristic scale for a problem that has no characteristic scale."

While physicists launched this new strand of research, mathematical financial academics then moved to the development of Lévy processes, following the first jump-diffusion-type models of the 1970s that were developed to tackle the discontinuity issue in the framework of the finiteness of the second moment. I term this mainstream strand of research the "PP." The PP opened the first period of model tinkering in financial modeling: a situation in which researchers, confronted with descriptive inadequacy, decide to "repair" existing models with a new data-driven approach. The story of jump processes represents an illustration of this data-driven model tinkering. I will now elaborate on the PP.

3.4 THE PRAGMATIC PROGRAM: A DATA-DRIVEN APPROACH

I begin this section with this excerpt from a paper by Applebaum (2004):

> "A sociologist investigating the behavior of the probability community during the early 1990s would surely report an interesting phenomenon. Many of the best minds of this (or any other) generation began concentrating their research in the area of mathematical finance. The main reason for this can be summed up in two words: option pricing."

The Black–Scholes model is based on the assumption that returns from the underlying assets follow a diffusion-type process, in particular a geometric Brownian motion. A large number of empirical studies showed that this model was inadequate, partly because of the continuity assumption. For example, Merton (1976) admitted that "there is a prima facie case for the existence of jumps" and Cox and Ross (1976) agreed that "exploring alternative forms is useful to construct them as jump processes." Ball and Torous (1985) pointed out that "empirical evidence confirms the systematic mispricing of the Black–Scholes call option pricing model" and "the Merton model which explicitly admits jumps in the underlying security return process may potentially eliminate theses biases." The goal of the PP was precisely to overcome these inadequacies by tackling the issue of discontinuities without accepting Mandelbrot's program. For example, Carr et al. (2002) said that they "seek to replace this process with one that enjoys all of the fundamental properties of Brownian motion, except for pathwise continuity and scaling, but that permits a richer array of variation in higher moment structure, especially at shorter horizons." This will be achieved with a "non-Gaussian

Merton–Black–Scholes Theory" (Boyarchenko and Levendorskii, 2002), which gained official recognition.

This section provides a brief overview of the PP by following the evolution of the modeling of jump processes, from the rediscovery of Poisson's law in finance by Press (1967) to the Lévy infinite activity processes of the 2000s. It came in two major stages. First, with the rediscovery of Poisson's law in the late 1960s, a jump component was added to the diffusion process (Brownian motion): this superposition of jump and diffusion processes opened the period of hybrid models known as jump-diffusion processes (1970–1990), which state that prices undergo large jumps followed by small continuous movements. These models were initiated by Press (1967) and Merton (1976). It is a simple case of Lévy process with finite activity and finite variation in the jump component. This is the first stage of the PP. Then, in the second period, the diffusive component was removed leaving only the jump component, moving to Lévy processes keeping finite variation in the jump component but with infinite activity. This is the second stage of the PP. The third stage of the PP corresponds to the infiniteness of the variation, itself divided into two subgroups, according to the finiteness of infiniteness of variance.

In contrast to these PPs, the RP proposed by Mandelbrot in 1962 had infinite activity, infinite variation in the jump component, and infinite variance. It was—for this reason—a heterodox view. A convenient way to grasp the conceptual difference between the framework of Mandelbrot's first representation (1962) and that of Press' (1967) successors is to consider the intuition underlying the modeling of trajectory discontinuities by jump-diffusion processes: the invalidation of the stability-under-addition property, one of the cornerstones of Mandelbrot's models, precisely the scaling view of markets (fractal nature) embedded in the stability-under-addition property.

This first approach to jump-diffusion processes, initially limited to Lévy processes with finite activity and finite variation, was generalized and fully developed only in the 1990s: the second life of Lévy processes belongs to the late twentieth century.

3.4.1   The Jump-Diffusion Models in the 1970s

The emergence of the PP was prepared for a long time by research around Poisson's law and process. At first, I present the rediscovery of this law in finance. Next, I present the two first stages of the PP.

3.4.1.1   The rediscovery of Poisson's law in financial modeling

The issue of the explicit modeling of jumps (discontinuities) was well known to insurance companies as early as 1903. In the context of managing their contracts, insurance companies had used the Poisson process to model the assessment of claims in non-life insurance. Lundberg's thesis of 1903 on insurance risk theory was the equivalent of Bachelier's theory of risk quantification in finance: Bachelier's (1900) Brownian model corresponded to Lundberg's (1903) Poisson model. Subsequently Harald Cramer and the Stockholm school introduced

Lundberg's ideas into the theory of random processes, resulting in the so-called Cramer–Lundberg actuarial model.

If the Gaussian and Brownian motion constituted the mathematical basis of classical financial modeling, Poisson's law and process were their counterparts in traditional actuarial models. Brownian motion and the Poisson process are two examples of simple Lévy processes. When researchers tried to model the discontinuity of stock paths with a nonstable approach, this law and these processes emerge as the most "natural" candidates for the production of heavy-tailed distributions, since Poisson's law precisely creates these tails. The Poisson framework appeared as the first response of financial economics mainstream to Mandelbrot's program.

Thus in 1967 the Cramer–Lundberg actuarial model made its entry into finance. In that year, five years after Mandelbrot, to tackle the jumpy nature of the price process, Press' proposition provided, for the first time in financial modeling, a nonstable generalization of Bachelier's model, by complementing the Brownian continuous diffusive component with a discontinuous Poisson component (Press, 1967). This innovation was able to produce a representation of the morphology of static uncertainty with a non-Gaussian distribution tail, a tail resulting from the introduction of the Poisson law.

Poisson's formula enables us to determine the probability of the occurrence of infrequent events (sometimes called rare events), provided that we know the constant average frequency at which these events occur. This frequency is described by the parameter of the Poisson distribution. Imagine, for example, that we consider a trajectory discontinuity as a jump. One easily sees to what extent the Poisson process is applicable in financial modeling: this process includes moments of jumps, the amplitude of which then simply has to be modeled. The combination of a Poisson process (for periods of jumps) and any law of distribution (for the size of jumps) produces what is called a compound Poisson process, that is to say, a process where the jumps occur at times coming from a simple Poisson process and have a determinate size. The choice of the probability law of the size fitting the possible values of this amplitude will then constitute the second stage of modeling.

If one chooses a Gaussian distribution to model the size of jumps, one will obtain a structure combining a Poisson process and a Gaussian distribution, also called the normal compound Poisson process. But it is possible to choose any probability law for the distribution of the size of jumps, such as a power law, a gamma distribution, and a Pareto law. Any distribution can be arbitrarily used for modeling the amplitude of discontinuities, coupled with the Poisson counting process. This linkage will then produce a compound Poisson process with these other laws (exponential Poisson, gamma Poisson, etc.). It is this insight that underlies the representation of market discontinuities by jump processes.

3.4.1.2 The mixed jump-diffusion processes

However, the Poisson component is not sufficient to model all market changes since, with this pure Poisson representation, nothing happens between two jumps: the market remains inert, except when it jumps. It is therefore necessary to supplement it with another model. In the 1960s and 1970s, the only way to model this change in the market, perceived as "smoother," between two jumps was to opt for a Brownian motion. That's why one added a Brownian component to the Poisson component, and this linear combination of a compound Poisson process and Brownian motion corresponds precisely to Press' (1967) model. This model is thus presented as a simple juxtaposition of a process producing a very large number of small stock market fluctuations (Brownian motion) and a process of producing a small number of market discontinuities (the normal compound Poisson process). These two basic building block processes are completely separate ("orthogonal"). Thus it is a mixed process involving diffusion and jumps, termed mixed jump-diffusion.

As the increments of the mixed jump-diffusion processes are IID, mixed jump-diffusion processes are Lévy processes. These are special cases of general nonstable Lévy process. The mixed Press model thus represents the first introduction of nonstable Lévy processes into finance. These processes had already been highlighted by Samuelson in 1965, echoing the work of Mandelbrot, but without giving rise to an explicit use, since Samuelson preferred returning to the usual Brownian motion model.

The values of the Poisson parameter λ (average number of jumps per unit of time) allow us to localize the mixed jump-diffusion processes in relation to the Bachelier and Mandelbrot models. By characterizing these two models by the number of jumps occurring during the evolution of market prices, that is, by the Poisson parameter, the value of $\lambda = 0$ (no jumps) leads back to the Bachelier model, and the value of $\lambda = \infty$ (infinite number of jumps) leads to the Mandelbrot model. Between these two values (0 and infinity), any finite value of λ results in a finite number of jumps between two given quotes. There are an infinite number of possible mixed jump-diffusion processes, all filling the range between the Bachelier and Mandelbrot representations. The Press model thus represented an intermediate solution between Bachelier and Mandelbrot.

In the first stage of the PP, the market dynamics of a given stock resulted simultaneously from frequent small movements, forming the continuous part of its trajectory and resulting from the Brownian diffusive component of the process, and from less frequent sudden movements forming the discontinuities of its trajectory, stemming from the Poisson component of the process. As Merton (1976) said, "the total change in the stock price is posited to be the composition of two types of changes: diffusion and jumps. The natural prototype process for the continuous component of the stock price change is a Wiener process, so the prototype for the jump component is a 'Poisson-driven' process." Again Cox and Ross (1976) stated that "in contrast to the diffusion process, the jump process [introduced] follows a deterministic movement upon which are superimposed discrete jumps."

From a financial standpoint, the mixed jump-diffusion processes modeled the fluctuation risk of any asset in terms of two dimensions: (classic) volatility risk corresponding to the Brownian diffusive component and a (new) jump risk corresponding to the Poisson component. This innovation was important because it indicated to professionals that usual risk diversification on the basis solely of the volatility dimension was not sufficient to protect against adverse stock market fluctuations. The market risk of any asset was therefore at least two-dimensional.

The second component of risk, or jump risk, was soon seen to be nondiversifiable, as became apparent from the work undertaken on the equity valuation models (Jarrow and Rosenfeld, 1984) and on the term structure of interest rates (Ahn and Thompson, 1988). This jump component creates a specific uncertainty as regards the risk usually measured by volatility (Box 3.6).

⬛ BOX 3.6 **Financial modeling with jump-diffusion processes (1967–1976)**

The classical models of market behavior implement the sole Brownian representation, that is, the diffusive part of the Lévy processes. Let X be the cumulative return of a given asset. In these first jump-diffusion processes, the cumulative return X results simultaneously from a large number of small variations (Brownian part) and a small number of large variations (Poissonian part). In these simple cases of Lévy processes, the activity and the variation remain finite.

The characteristic exponent of market dynamics in the classical Brownian models is

$$\Psi_{X_t}(u) = t\left(i\mu u - \frac{1}{2}\sigma^2 u^2\right). \tag{3.12}$$

Adding a Poissonian part to this Brownian component leads to

$$\Psi_{X_t}(u) = t\left(i\mu u - \frac{1}{2}\sigma^2 u^2\right) + t\,\lambda(\Phi_Y(u) - 1), \tag{3.13}$$

where λ is the Poisson parameter. The sizes of the jumps are independent and their stationary distribution Y has a characteristic function Φ_Y.

The impossibility of perfect hedging for this type of risk was no doubt an obstacle to the widespread use of these mixed jump-diffusion processes in financial engineering for some fifteen years. Note that the use of alpha-stable motions also implied the need to take into consideration a second dimension of risk, namely, jump risk. Because this second dimension of risk was not taken up in financial circles, it can be assumed that the professional community was not sufficiently mature in the 1970s to manage financial products with two risk dimensions.

3.4.2 Pure Jump Models in the 1990s

The rebirth of the random walk model in finance is due to the rediscovery of two important characteristics of Lévy processes. First, in order to describe the jumping behavior of various asset prices and interest rates, it became clear that the use of Lévy processes with infinite activity was sufficient. Hence, it was no longer necessary to build superpositions of jump and diffusion process (Brownian motion) in price dynamics equations, namely, what was called jump-diffusion processes (special case of very simple Lévy processes) in the 1970s. Second, it was redis-covered that any Lévy process has an interesting relation to the Brownian motion, considering the morphology of uncertainty. Using a subordinator process for mea-suring time that increases with a randomly varying speed, any Lévy process in calendar time (physical time) can be written as Brownian motion measured in a time distorted by the pace of trading. The randomly increasing time has been interpreted as an operational time or a trading time reflecting the market activity. The fact that a Lévy process can capture the time change of the markets opened a new strand of research about the nature of intrinsic time in markets. At the end, the random walk model is released from the prison of the Brownian representa-tion in calendar time in which it was trapped and becomes a powerful tool for financial modeling using these two characteristics that foster the understanding of market price behavior: infinite activity and the distortion of time. I now elaborate on this.

3.4.2.1   Financial modeling with infinite activity

The separation between the two sources of market movements—the Brownian source, forming the continuous part of the trajectories, and the Poisson source, creating discontinuities—was simple and convenient, but limited the possibilities for modeling. Moreover, as one has seen, even those changes perceived as con-tinuous (between two jumps) could be represented differently, since share quotes are by definition discontinuous, with the tick defining the smallest time interval between two quotes. The notion of discontinuity is essential for modeling stock market variations. In other words, the intrinsic bumpiness of the financial phe-nomenon did not require the diffusive Brownian part of models to be retained. It was necessary only to be able to account variously for a very large number of very small jumps (ticks), a large number of larger jumps, and a very small number of very large jumps (market discontinuities), to obtain a relevant model of stock market functioning. The probabilistic representation of market fluctuations did not ultimately entail the use of the Brownian diffusive component.

This idea slowly made its way into the academic community, up to the early 1990s. The diffusive part of probabilistic representations had been needed for the modeling of the small movements only in the case of finite activity: the finite activ-ity of the process required the addition of another component. But as soon as it was admitted that infinite activity was possible, the usefulness of the diffusive compo-nent disappeared, and a pure jump process seemed to be sufficient to represent the entire stock market phenomenon, that is, its bumpiness at all scales. The argument is well described in the paper by Carr et al. published in 2002:

> "The rationale usually given for describing asset returns as jump-diffusions is that diffusions capture frequent small moves, while jumps capture rare large moves. Given the ability of infinite activity jump processes to capture both frequent small moves and rare large moves, the question arises as to whether it is necessary to employ a diffusion component when modeling asset returns."

These studies and those that followed mark the turning point in the modeling of jump processes in finance, confirming their disembeddedness from Brownian representation, even if complemented by compound Poisson processes as in the case of the mixed jump-diffusion processes of the 1970s.

Let us summarize. By adopting a representation of market fluctuations using an infinite activity Lévy process, it appeared possible in the 2000s to manage without any diffusive component. The structure of trajectory discontinuities (the morphology of the bumpiness of the stock market phenomenon) is fully characterized by Lévy's measure. Compared to the mixed jump-diffusion processes that followed the path opened up by Press and Merton, this new representation of small market fluctuations was instead situated in the tradition of normal compound Poisson-type pure jump processes, as proposed by Cox and Ross in 1976 for evaluating options in markets with trajectory discontinuities. In jump-diffusion processes, jumps are considered as rare events. In Lévy processes with infinite activity, jumps are always present at any scale of the fluctuations.

3.4.2.2 The generalized hyperbolic family

The first studies focusing on general nonstable Lévy processes had been explored in a completely different context in Denmark and Germany, namely, studies of sandstorms. Geophysicists like Ole Barndorff-Nielsen and Ernst Eberlein worked on a family of distributions called hyperbolic distributions. One of the arguments given from the beginning in favor of applying these distributions to finance was they were not stable. In this vein, Eberlein and Keller (1995) wrote that "real stock-price paths change drastically if one looks at them on different time scales." The hyperbolic distributions are infinitely divisible and can therefore be used to construct Lévy processes by specifying the underlying marginal distribution. But the hyperbolic distributions are not stable. In other words, if the underlying distribution is hyperbolic at one given scale, then this does not imply that it will remain this way at any other scale. Hence a numerical computation will be useful for going from one scale to any other scale. The paper by Eberlein and Keller (1995), which introduces the class of hyperbolic distributions—and as a consequence hyperbolic Lévy motions as driving processes for financial modeling—was the first used for analyzing and modeling financial data. The hyperbolic model was the next intensively examined by Eberlein et al. (1998). Unlike previous work, the papers on these distributions aimed to fit the data; in other words, these distributions represent an "application-driven" approach, like an inflection point in the PP: "these distributions seem to be tailor-made to describe the statistical behavior of asset returns" (Eberlein and Prause, 1998).

An intuitive understanding of what motivated the term "hyperbolic" and its fruitfulness in finance is the following. Let us consider the graph of a Gaussian density in a semilogarithmic graph, that is, a graph where one axis is plotted on a logarithmic scale. One will find a parabola because of the square power of the variable. This parabola is characterized by a rapid fall of the distribution tails. But empirical semilog graphs of empirical returns at any scale exhibit a hyperbola, contrary to the parabola of the Gaussian density. This is the reason why these distributions are called hyperbolic. A heuristically bottom-up building of an hyperbolic distribution is given by Le Courtois and Walter (2014b). The usefulness for the modeling of price changes stems from the slower decrease of their tails. The hyperbola fits the empirical data better. Like alpha-stable distributions, hyperbolic distributions are defined by four parameters: localization, asymmetry, dispersion, and kurtosis of the distribution. Like alpha-stable distributions, hyperbolic distribution can characterize the risk of any stochastic change with two dimensions: their size (the parameter of dispersion or scale parameter) and their form (the fatness of the tails and asymmetry). But, unlike alpha-stable distributions, hyperbolic distributions have all their moments. Hence these distributions modeled both the skewness and leptokurtic features encountered in empirical distributions from the real financial world rather well, without running into the perceived inconvenience of alpha-stable distributions of Mandelbrot's program. The capacity of these processes to model in an extremely powerful way all trajectory irregularities, while not retaining the property of stability by addition, the cornerstone of the first stage of Mandelbrot's program, made the family of Lévy processes a serious candidate for the probabilistic representation of market fluctuations.

Another interesting feature of hyperbolic distributions is the limiting case, when the dispersion parameter takes values between 0 and infinity. The two limit cases correspond to the two Laplace laws: Gaussian (Laplace's second law, of 1778) and double exponential (Laplace's first law, of 1774). This shows Laplace's two laws as limit laws of hyperbolic distributions.

Hyperbolic distribution is a subclass of the generalized hyperbolic (GH) distribution introduced by Barndorff-Nielsen (1977) for the study of particle size in wind-blown sand deposits. The generalized version of the hyperbolic distributions allows other distributions to be obtained depending of the value of the generalization parameter λ. For example, the hyperbolic distribution corresponds to $\lambda = 1$. For $\lambda = 0.5$, one obtains the density of the normal inverse Gaussian (NIG) distribution. The NIG distribution is obtained by mixing normal and inverse Gaussian (IG) distributions. Barndorff-Nielsen moved into finance in 1995. In his papers, Barndorff-Nielsen (1995, 1997) used the NIG distributions. As for the hyperbolic distribution, the NIG is a subclass of the GH distributions. Next, the GH distribution, which generates the GH Lévy processes, was systematically analyzed by Eberlein and Prause (1998) and Prause (1999). The first applications to the valuation of derivatives appeared and the PP succeeded to price options.

3.4.2.3   The tempered stable family in finance and the link with econophysics

The symmetric variance gamma (VG) model was introduced by Madan and Seneta (1990) to generalize the Black–Scholes formula in the case of the evaluation of options. The main impetus for constructing this process concerned a practical market problem: finding a suitable model for the so-called volatility "smile" or "smirk" phenomenon. It was extended to incorporate skewness by Madan and Milne (1991) and Madan et al. (1998) to become the so-called VG model. The terminology is due to the fact that the variance follows a gamma distribution. The CGMY process

TABLE 3.2   **Examples of Lévy processes in financial modeling**

	Financial models	Type of Lévy process
1900	Bachelier	Brownian motion
1962	Mandelbrot	Stable motion
1976	Merton	Brownian motion and Poisson component
1995	Eberlein and Keller	Hyperbolic motion
1997	Barndorff-Nielsen	Generalized hyperbolic motion
1998	Madan et al.	Variance gamma process
2001	Kotz et al.	Laplace process
2002	Carr et al.	Generalized variance gamma process
2014	Le Courtois and Walter	Generalized Laplace process

of Carr et al. (2002) generalizes the VG process by adding a parameter permitting finite or infinite activity and finite or infinite variation.

The VG model of Madan et al. (1998) and the CGMY model of Carr et al. (2002) are special cases of the Koponen (1995) model. Here there is an overlap with the physicist's approach: the academic territory of financial modeling is complex and overlapping. The PP and the econophysics program (EP) develop similar readings of the Mandelbrot view they shared with the tempered stable family. Hence the financial field of modeling extreme values is not simply divided into two camps: mainstream finance (moving to PP) and econophysics. Despite their separate lines in the academic fields, the EP and the PP derive from their reliance on Mandelbrot's view: two offshoots of what I suggest to call the "discontinuous turn" in financial modeling, introduced by Mandelbrot in (1962).

3.5   CONCLUSION

In this chapter, I have presented the two competitive programs for solving the extreme value puzzle in financial modeling with Lévy processes: the RP (Mandelbrot) and the PP (see Table 3.2). Both programs investigate the ability of Lévy processes to capture the extreme values of price changes. The Mandelbrot program contributed to a better understanding of the discontinuous nature of price change, but the first Mandelbrot models initially based on stable motions were not accepted by the mainstream financial academics community. I have argued that some of the key points of the academic debates can be illuminated by reference to a familiar debate in philosophy over the principle of continuity. One side of the debate, "Leibnizian," takes the continuity as a cornerstone for financial modeling and hence splits the market regimes between "normal" periods and extreme values, seen as irrational periods. The contrary "anti-Leibnizian" position holds that Mandelbrot's view is crucial for grasping the true nature of price changes without intellectual cleavage. I have argued that in the 1970s, the mainstream view of price changes made specific assumptions to defend the mathematical tractability of the financial modeling based on continuous diffusion models, by using a compound *ad hoc* approach, which gained high recognition in the 1980s: the PP. I have explained the successes of the PP in the 1990s by showing that an inflection point appears due to a twofold phenomenon. Firstly, a reorientation of the mathematical financial research due to European academics who put forward the fruitfulness of infinite activity of the Lévy processes in case of pure jump models. Secondly, the emergence of a challenger for mathematical finance field: econophysics. At the end, although the PP (financial) and the EP can be traced through separate lines in the academic fields, the two programs derive from their reliance on Mandelbrot's view, and Mandelbrot can be regarded as the pivotal figure for a "discontinuous turn" in financial modeling.

Acknowledgments

I would like to thank, without implicating, Ernst Eberlein for helpful incisive comments on an earlier version of this document and many constructive criticisms. François Longin encouraged the project of writing down this history for the ESSEC Conference on Extreme Events in Finance. I also would like to thank Olivier le Courtois for stimulating and challenging discussions.

References

Ahn C., Thompson H. Jump-diffusion processes and the term structure of interest rates. J Finance 1988;**43**(1):155–174.

Aït-Sahalia Y., Jacod J. Testing for jumps in a discretely observed process. Ann Stat 2009;**37**(1):184–222.

Applebaum D. Lévy processes-from probability to finance and quantum groups. Not Am Math Soc 2004;**51**(11):1336–1347.

Bachelier L. Théorie de la spéculation. Annales de l'ecole normale supérieure 1900;**27**(3):21–86.

Ball C., Torous W. On jumps in common stock prices and their impact on call option pricing. The Journal of Finance 1985;**40**:155–173.

Barndorff-Nielsen O.E. Exponentially decreasing distributions for the logarithm of particle size. Proceedings of the Royal Society of London. Series A 1977;**353**:401–419.

Barndorff-Nielsen O.E. Normal inverse Gaussian processes and the modelling of stock returns. Research Report 300. Dept. Theor. Statistics, Aarhus University; 1995.

Barndorff-Nielsen O.E. Normal inverse Gaussian distributions and stochastic volatility modelling. Scandinavian Journal of Statistics 1997;**24**(1):1–14.

Black F., Scholes M. The pricing of options and corporate liabilities. Journal of Political Economy 1973;**81**(3):637–659.

Bertoin J. *Lévy Processes*. Volume **121**, Cambridge Tracts in Mathematics. Cambridge: Cambridge University Press; 1996.

Bertrand P., Prigent J-L. Portfolio insurance: the extreme value approach applied to the CPPI method. In: Longin F., editor. *Extreme Events in Finance: A Handbook of Extreme Value Theory and its Applications*. John Wiley & Sons; 2017.

Bouchaud J-P, Potters M. Théorie des risques financiers, Saclay, CEA (collection Aléa). English translation 2003, *Theory of Financial Risk and Derivative Pricing: From Statistical Physics to Risk Management*. Cambridge: Cambridge University Press; 1997.

Boyarchenko S., Levendorskii S. *Non-Gaussian Merton-Black-Scholes Theory*. Volume **9**, Advanced Series on Statistical Science and Applied Probability. Singapore: World Scientific; 2002.

Carr P., Geman H., Madan D., Yor M. The fine structure of asset returns: an empirical investigation. The Journal of Business 2002;**75**(2):305–332.

Carr P., Geman H., Madan D.B., Yor M. Stochastic volatility for Lévy processes. Math Finance 2003;**13**:345–382.

Cox J., Ross S. The valuation of options for alternative stochastic processes. Journal of Financial Economics 1976;**3**:145–166.

Eberlein E., Keller U. Hyperbolic distributions in finance. Bernoulli 1995;**1**(3): 281–299.

Eberlein E., Keller U., Prause K. New insights into smiles, mispricing and value at risk: the hyperbolic model. The Journal of Business 1998;**71**(3):371–405.

Eberlein E., Prause K. The generalized hyperbolic model: financial derivatives and risk structure. *Freiburg Data Center for Analysis and Modelling*. Volume **56**. University of Fribourg; 1998.

Elie L., El Karoui N., Jeantheau T., Pferzel A. Les modèles ARCH sur les cours de change. Actes du 3ecolloque international AFIR, Rome: Institut des actuaires italiens; 1993;**1**:91–101.

Elliott R. *The Wave Principle*. New York: Collins; 1938.

Fama E. Portfolio analysis in a stable paretian market. Manage Sci 1965;**11**(3): 404–419.

Fraga Alves I., Neves C. Extreme value theory: an introductory overview. In: Longin F, editor. *Extreme Events in Finance: A Handbook of Extreme Value Theory and its Applications*. John Wiley & Sons; 2017.

Granger C., Orr D. Infinite variance and research strategy in time series analysis. Journal of the American Statistical Association 1972;**67**(338):275–285.

Harrison M., Kreps D. Martingales and arbitrage in multiperiod securities markets. Journal of Economic Theory 1979;**20**:381–408.

Harrison M., Pliska S. Martingales and stochastic integrals in the theory of continuous trading. Stochastic Processes and Applications 1981;**11**(3):215–260.

Jarrow R., Rosenfeld E. Jump risks and intertemporal capital asset pricing. The Journal of Business 1984;**57**(3):337–351.

Kendall M. The analysis of economic time series-Part I: Prices. Journal of the Royal Statistical Society. Series A 1953;**96**:11–25, and discussion p. 25–34.

Koponen I. Analytic approach to the problem of convergence of truncated Lévy flights towards the Gaussian stochastic process. Physical Review E 1995;**52**(1):1197–1199.

Larson A. Measurement of a random process in future prices. Food Research Institute Studies 1960;**1**(3):313–324.

Le Courtois O., Walter C. *Extreme Financial Risks and Asset Allocation*. Volume **5**, Series in Quantitative Finance. Singapore: World Scientific; 2014b.

Longin F. Volatilité et mouvements extrêmes du marché boursier [thèse de doctorat]. HEC; 1993.

Longin F. The asymptotic distribution of extreme stock market returns. The Journal of Business 1996;**69**(3):383–408.

Longin F. The choice of the distribution of asset prices: how extreme value theory can help? Journal of Banking and Finance 2005;**29**(4):1017–1035.

MacKenzie D. *An Engine, Not a Camera. How Financial Models Shape Markets*. Cambridge (MA): MIT Press; 2006.

Madan D.B., Carr P., Chang E. The variance Gamma process and option pricing. European finance review 1998;**2**(1):79–105.

Madan D., Milne F. Option pricing with VG martingale components. Mathematical Finance 1991;**1**(4):39–55.

Madan D., Seneta E. The variance Gamma (V.G) model for share market returns. The Journal of Business 1990;**63**(4):511–524.

Mandelbrot B. Sur certains prix spéculatifs : faits empiriques et modèle basé sur les processus stables additifs non gaussiens de Paul Lévy. CRAS 1962;**254**:3968–3970.

Mandelbrot B. The variation of certain speculative prices. The Journal of Business 1963;**36**:394–419.

Mandelbrot B. Nouveaux modèles de la variation des prix (cycles lents et changements instantanés). Cahiers du Séminaire d'économétrie 1966;**9**:53–66.

Mandelbrot B. Sur l'épistémologie du hasard dans les sciences sociales. Invariance des lois et vérification des prédictions. In: Jean P (dir.), editor. *Logique et connaissance scientifique*, Volume **22**. Paris, Gallimard: Encyclopédie de La Pléiade; 1967. p 1097–1113.

Mandelbrot B. Formes nouvelles du hasard dans les sciences. Économie Appliquée 1973a;**26**:307–319.

Mandelbrot B. Le syndrome de la variance infinie et ses rapports avec la discontinuité des prix. Économie Appliquée 1973b;**26**:321–348.

Mandelbrot B. Le problème de la réalité des cycles lents et le syndrome de Joseph. Économie Appliquée 1973c;**26**:349–365.

Mandelbrot B. *Fractals and Scaling in Finance: Discontinuity, Concentration, Risk*. New York: Springer-Verlag; 1997.

Mandelbrot B. Scaling in financial prices, I: Tails and dependence. Quantitative Finance 2001a;**1**:113–123.

Mandelbrot B. Scaling in financial prices, II: Multifractals and the star equation. Quantitative Finance 2001b;**1**:124–130.

Mandelbrot B. Scaling in financial prices, III: Cartoon Brownian motions in multifractal time. Quantitative Finance 2001c;**1**:427–440.

Mandelbrot B., Hudson R. *The (mis) Behaviour of Markets: A Fractal View of Risk, Ruin and Reward*. New York: Basic Books; 2004.

Mantegna R., Stanley E. Stochastic process with ultraslow convergence to a Gaussian: the truncated Lévy fligh. Physical Review Letters 1994;**73**(22):2946–2949.

Mantegna R., Stanley E. *An Introduction to Econophysics: Correlations and Complexity in Finance*. Cambridge: Cambridge University Press; 2000.

Markowitz H.M. Portfolio selection. Journal of Finance 1952;**7**(1):77–91.

Markowitz H.M. *Portfolio Selection: Efficient Diversification of Investment*. 2nd ed. 1971. New Haven (CT): Yale University Press; 1959.

Merton R. Option pricing when underlying stock returns are discontinuous. Journal of Finance Econ 1976;**3**:125–144.

Mirowski P. Mandelbrot's economics after a quarter century. Fractals 1995;**3**(3): 581–600.

Prause K. The generalized hyperbolic model: estimation, financial derivatives, and risk measures. PhD thesis. University of Fribourg; 1999.

Press S. A compound events model for security prices. The Journal of Business 1967;**40**:317–335.

Sato K. *Lévy Processes and Infinitely Divisible Distributions*, Studies in Advanced Mathematics. Cambridge: Cambridge University Press; 1999.

Taylor S. *Modelling Financial Time Series*. New York: John Wiley & Sons, Inc.; 1986.

Walter C. Research of scaling laws on stock market variations. In: Abry P, Gonçalvés P, Lévy Vehel J, editors. *Scaling, Fractals and Wavelets*. London; John Wiley & Sons, Ltd; 2009a.

Walter C. Le virus brownien. La réduction brownienne de l'incertitude et la crise financiére de 2007-2008 [The Brownian virus. The Brownian reduction of uncertainty and the financial crisis of 2007-2008]. Communio 2009b;**34**(3–4):107–120.

Walter C. Benoît mandelbrot in finance. In: Frame M, Cohen N, editors. *Benoît Mandelbrot. A Life in Many Dimensions*. Singapore: World Scientific; 2015.

Zolotarev V. *One-Dimensional Stable Distributions*, Translations of Mathematical Monographs. Providence (RI): United states of America; 1986. p 65.

Chapter Four

Extreme Value Theory: An Introductory Overview

Isabel Fraga Alves[1] and Cláudia Neves[2]

[1]*CEAUL, University of Lisbon, Portugal*
[2]*CEAUL, Portugal and Department of Mathematics and Statistics, University of Reading, United Kingdom*

> *"It seems that the rivers know the theory. It only remains to convince the engineers of the validity of this analysis."*
>
> –Emil Julius Gumbel (1891–1966)

4.1 INTRODUCTION

In this chapter we give an introduction to the most important results in extreme value theory (EVT) with a flavor of how they can be applied in practice. EVT is the theory underpinning the study of the asymptotic distribution of extreme or those rare events, which can be considered huge relatively to the bulk of observations. Relying on well-founded theory on which parametric or semiparametric statistical models are built for handling with rare events, EVT is the adequate theory for modeling and measuring events which occur with a very small probability. EVT has proven to be a powerful and useful tool to describe atypical situations that may have a significant impact in many application areas, where knowledge of the behavior of the tail of the actual distribution is in demand. The main objective is to tackle the problem of modeling rare phenomena with large magnitude, hence lying outside the range of the available observations (*out-of-sample*).

Extreme Events in Finance: A Handbook of Extreme Value Theory and its Applications,
First Edition. Edited by François Longin.

The typical question we would like to answer is

If things go wrong, how wrong can they go?

which in a certain sense is the mitigation attitude to Murphy's law:

If anything can go wrong, it will!

In fact, the statistical analysis of extremes is the key step in the analysis of many risk management problems related not only to insurance, reinsurance, and finance in general but also in other fields as geophysics and environment, where the analysis of extremes is of primordial importance, as it happens with sea levels, river levels, snow avalanches, wind speeds, temperatures, rainfall, snow, air pollution, storms, hurricanes, earthquakes, or even other areas as Internet traffic, reliability, and athletics. One should not forget natural hazards with extreme consequences for the society, often entailing big fatalities with the loss of human lives. For instance, one learns from catastrophic events such as the 9 min of Lisbon earthquake and tsunami in 1755 (Figures 4.1 and 4.2).

AARDBEEVING TE LISSABON, IN DEN JAARE 1755.

FIGURE 4.1 A natural disaster: Lisbon earthquake in 1755 —engraving "Aardbeeving te Lissabon in den Jaare 1755" by Reinier Vinkeles and François Bohn at Biblioteca Nacional Digital de Portugal, open source. *Source:* **Nacional Digital de Portugal, http://purl.pt/13102. Public domain.**

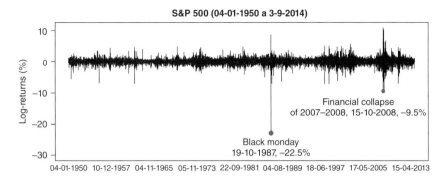

FIGURE 4.2 Financial disasters: Black Monday in 1987 and the financial collapse of 2007–2008.

When we are dealing with financial or even meteorological data, there are two situations which matter to differentiate: the case where the data highly concentrates around the average value, with none of these observed values being dominant, and the case where a few observations overpower the remainder of the sample by their large (or low) magnitude. Since the latter can have a very negative impact, it is important to quantify its occurrence. Typically, one is interested in the analysis of maximal (or minimal) observations and records over time, since these may entail the negative consequences. Reinsurance is also a good example of this: the reinsurance premium needs to be computed to withstand the extremal behavior of the claims process. Another problem concerns the so-called return period (or waiting time period) for high levels u, and $1/P[X > u]$ corresponds to average return period, for a random variable (r.v.) of interest X exceeds the high level u; close to this, the dual problem of return levels is also most important in applications. In hydrology, design levels typically correspond to return periods of 100 years or more; however, time series of 100 or more years are rare. A model for extrapolation is required and here intervenes the EVT. More precisely, suppose the problem consists in estimating the tail probability associated with an r.v. X with cumulative distribution function (c.d.f.) F:

$$p = P[X > x_p] = 1 - F(x_p),$$

with p being small, that is, a near-zero probability. This entails a large $(1 - p)$ quantile x_p, so that x_p is approaching the right endpoint of F defined as $x^F = \sup\{x : F(x) < 1\}$. On the other hand, and in the context of financial variables, for instance, a primary tool for assessment of financial risks is the value-at-risk, VaR(p), which is nothing more than a p-quantile for the distribution of returns for very small probability p of an adverse extreme price movement that is expected to occur. Bearing the previous estimation purpose in mind, suppose that $x_{1:n} \leq x_{2:n} \leq \cdots \leq x_{n:n}$ is an ordered sample of n observations from the distribution function F. One can use the empirical distribution function (e.d.f.), defined by

$$\hat{F}_n(x) = \frac{i}{n}, \quad \text{if} \quad x \in [x_{i:n}, x_{i+1:n}],$$

$i = 0, 1, \ldots, n$, where $x_{0:n} = -\infty$ and $x_{n+1:n} = \infty$. For small p, the e.d.f. $\hat{F}_n(x_{1-p})$, defined as the proportion of values $x_{i:n} \leq x_{1-p}$, can however lead us to a null estimated probability, and, clearly, we cannot assume that these extreme values x_{1-p} are simply "impossible"! With the purpose of VaR estimation, this is the same to say that the *historical simulation* fails. On the other hand, the classical theory allows a possibly inadequate methodology in such a way that a specific probabilistic model would be fitted to the whole sample, for instance, the normal $N(\mu, \sigma^2)$, and use that model to estimate tail probability as $\hat{p} = \hat{P}[X > x_p] = 1 - \Phi\left(\frac{x_p - \hat{\mu}}{\hat{\sigma}}\right)$ (notation: Φ is the c.d.f. of a $N(0, 1)$ r.v.), with estimated mean value μ and standard deviation $\sigma > 0$. But what if the variance $Var[X]$ or even the mean value $E[X]$ does not exist? Then the central limit theorem (CLT) does not apply, and the classical theory, dominated by the normal distribution, is no more pertinent. These types of problems associated with rare events are very important, since the consequences can be catastrophic. When we deal with log returns in finance, for instance, most of the observations are central, and a global fitted distribution will rely mainly in those central observations, while extreme observations will not play a very important role because of their scarcity (see Figure 4.3 for illustration); those extreme values are exactly the ones that constitute the focus for traders, investors, asset managers, risk managers, and regulators. Hence EVT reveals useful in modeling the impact of crashes or situations of extreme stress on investor portfolios. The classical result in EVT is Gnedenko's theorem (Gnedenko, 1943). It establishes that there are three types of possible limiting distributions (*max-stable*) for maxima of blocks of observations—annual maxima (AM) approach—which are unified in a single representation, the generalized extreme value (GEV) distribution. The second theorem in EVT is the so-called Pickands–Balkema–de Haan theorem (Balkema and de Haan, 1974 and Pickands, 1975). Loosely speaking, it allows us to approach the generalized Pareto (GP) distribution to the excesses of high thresholds—peaks-over-threshold (POT) approach—for distributions in the domain of a GEV distribution. Complementary to these parametric approaches, we also pick up a possible semiparametric approach, comparing it with the previous ones. In order to present some of the basic ideas underlying EVT, in the next section we discuss the most important results on the univariate case under the simplifying independent and identically distributed ("i.i.d.") assumption; for instance, in insurance context, losses will be i.i.d., as in risk models for aggregated claims, and most of the results can be extended to more general models.

4.2 UNIVARIATE CASE

4.2.1 Preliminaries

Extreme value analysis (EVA) can be broadly described as the branch of statistics that focuses on inference for a c.d.f., F, near the endpoint of its support. In the univariate case, one usually considers the upper tail, that is, the survival function $1 - F$, in the neighborhood of the right endpoint of the distribution, x^F. The most powerful feature of EVA results is the fact that the type of limiting distribution for

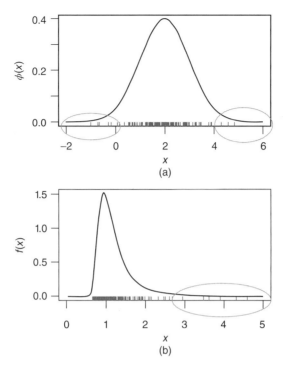

FIGURE 4.3 Densities of one normal distribution (ϕ) and one heavy-tailed distribution (f). Interest is on both tails (a) and on the right tail (b) In log returns in finance, for instance, most of the observations are central, but it is exactly those extreme values (extremely low and/or extremely high) that constitute the focus for risk managers.

extreme values does not depend on the exact common c.d.f. F, but depend only on the tail; this allows us to "neglect" the precise form of the unknown c.d.f. F and pay attention only to the tail. Then, a semiparametric approach enables inference for rare events. It is possible to apply large sample results in EVT by assuming the sample size toward infinity.

Let $(X_1, X_2, \ldots, X_n)$ be a sample of n i.i.d. r.v.'s, with c.d.f. F, and let the corresponding nondecreasing order statistics (o.s.'s) be $(X_{1:n}, X_{2:n}, \ldots, X_{n:n})$. In particular, $X_{1:n}$ and $X_{n:n}$ represent the *sample minimum* and the *sample maximum*, respectively. We will focus only on the results about the sample maximum, since analogous results for the sample minimum can be obtained from those of the sample maximum using the device

$$X_{1:n} = \min(X_1, X_2, \ldots, X_n) = -\max(-X_1, -X_2, \ldots, -X_n).$$

The exact distribution of $M_n = X_{n:n}$ can be obtained from the c.d.f. F, as follows:

$$F_{M_n}(x) = P(M_n \leq x) = \prod_{i=1}^{n} P(X_i \leq x) = (F(x))^n = F^n(x), \quad \text{for all } x \in \mathbb{R}.$$

Notice that, as $n \to \infty$, the c.d.f. of the partial maxima M_n converges to a degenerate distribution on the right endpoint x^F, that is,

$$F_{M_n}(x) = F^n(x) \xrightarrow[n \to \infty]{} \begin{cases} 0, & \text{if } x < x^F, \\ 1, & \text{if } x \geq x^F. \end{cases}$$

Figure 4.4 illustrates this behavior of the c.d.f. of the sample maximum F_{M_n} for several beta distributions. [1] From the two top rows of Figure 4.4, we clearly see that

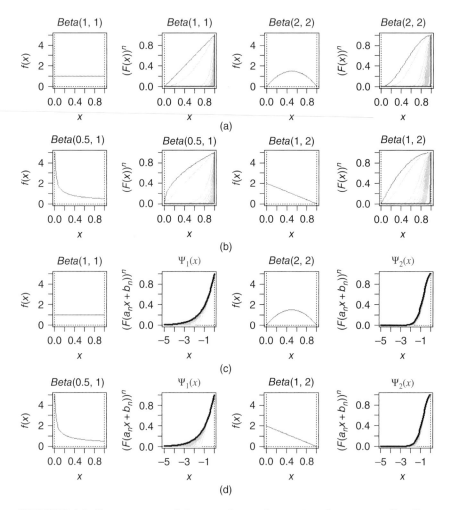

FIGURE 4.4 Convergence of the sample maximum to a degenerate distribution on the right endpoint (a and b) for $n = 1, 2(10)300, 10,000$; convergence of the normalized maximum to a nondegenerate distribution, max Weibull, for suitable constants $a_n > 0$ and b_n (c and d), for $n = 1(1)300$.

[1] We say that $X \frown Beta(a, b)$, with $a, b > 0$, if its p.d.f. is $f(x) = x^{a-1}(1-x)^{b-1}/B(a,b)$, for $0 < x < 1$, and with $B(a, b) := \int_0^1 t^{a-1}(1-t)^{b-1} dt$; the model $Beta(1, 1)$ corresponds to Uniform $\mathcal{U}_{(0,1)}$.

as the sample size increases, the c.d.f. of the maximum M_n approaches a degenerate distribution on the right endpoint x^F equal to one. The following theorem expounds this result in a slightly stronger statement.

THEOREM 4.1 *Let F be the underlying c.d.f. of a sequence of i.i.d. r.v.s and $x^F \leq \infty$ its right endpoint. Then*

$$M_n \xrightarrow[n \to \infty]{p} x^F,$$

where $\xrightarrow[n \to \infty]{p}$ denotes convergence in probability.

Moreover, the strong convergence $M_n \xrightarrow[n \to \infty]{a.s.} x^F$ also holds (notation: $\xrightarrow[n \to \infty]{a.s.}$ almost sure convergence). Since M_n has a degenerate asymptotic distribution, a suitable normalization for M_n is thus required in order to attain a real limiting distribution, which constitutes one key step for statistical inference on rare events. We henceforth consider a linear normalization for the partial maxima of the sequence $\{X_n\}_{n \geq 1}$ of i.i.d. r.v.'s, $(M_n - b_n)/a_n$, for real sequences a_n and b_n, with positive scale a_n, $n \in \mathbb{N}$]. Then

$$P[(M_n - b_n)/a_n \leq x = P[M_n \leq a_n x + b_n] = F^n(a_n x + b_n).$$

If we look at the two bottom rows of Figure 4.4, it is clear that for beta models with different shapes, it is possible that the linearized maximum has exactly the same asymptotic distribution. Indeed, what is determinant for that is the shape of the probability density function next to the right endpoint.

Example 4.1 Maximum of exponential r.v.'s

Consider $X_i \frown \text{Exp}(1)$, $i = 1, \dots, n$, i.i.d. with c.d.f. $F(x) = 1 - \exp(-x), x > 0$. If we choose normalizing sequences $a_n = 1$ and $b_n = \log n$, then

$$
\begin{aligned}
P[M_n - \log n \leq x] &= P[M_n \leq x + \log n] \\
&= \{F(x + \log n)\}^n \\
&= \{1 - \exp(-x)/n\}^n, \text{ for } x > -\log n \\
&\to \exp[-\exp(-x)], \text{ as } n \to \infty, \text{ for } x \in \mathbb{R}.
\end{aligned}
$$

4.2.2 Theoretical Framework on EVT

We now explore the possible limiting distributions for the linearized maxima. In this sequence, we assume there exist real constants $a_n > 0$ and b_n such that

$$\frac{M_n - b_n}{a_n} \xrightarrow[n \to \infty]{d} Z, \tag{4.1}$$

(notation: $\xrightarrow[n\to\infty]{d}$ convergence in distribution) where Z is a nongenerate r.v. with c.d.f. G, that is, we have that

$$\lim_{n\to\infty} P(M_n \le a_n x + b_n) = \lim_{n\to\infty} F^n(a_n x + b_n) = G(x),$$

for every continuity point x of G. The first problem is to determine which c.d.f.'s G may appear as the limit in (4.1)—*extreme value distributions (EVD)*. First, we introduce the notion of "type."

DEFINITION 4.2 (Distribution functions of the same type) *Two c.d.f.'s F_1 and F_2 are said to be of the same type if there exist constants $a > 0$ and $b \in \mathbb{R}$ such that*

$$F_2(ax + b) = F_1(x). \tag{4.2}$$

It means that F_1 and F_2 are the same, apart from location and scale parameters, that is, they belong to the same location/scale family. The class of EVD essentially involves three types of extreme value distributions, types I, II, and III, defined as follows.

DEFINITION 4.3 (Extreme value distributions *for maxima*) *The following are the standard extreme value distribution functions:*

(i) *Gumbel (type I):* $\Lambda(x) = \exp\{-\exp(-x)\}, x \in \mathbb{R};$

(ii) *Fréchet (type II):* $\Phi_\alpha(x) = \begin{cases} 0, & x \le 0; \\ \exp\{-x^{-\alpha}\}, & x > 0, \alpha > 0; \end{cases}$

(iii) *Weibull (type III):* $\Psi_\alpha(x) = \begin{cases} \exp\{-(-x)^\alpha\}, & x \le 0, \alpha > 0; \\ 1, & x > 0. \end{cases}$

The three types can be expressed by the corresponding location/scale families, with location λ and scale δ, with $\lambda \in \mathbb{R}, \delta > 0$:

$$\Lambda(x|\lambda, \delta) = \Lambda\left(\frac{x-\lambda}{\delta}\right); \quad \Phi_\alpha(x|\lambda, \delta) = \Phi_\alpha\left(\frac{x-\lambda}{\delta}\right); \quad \Psi_\alpha(x|\lambda, \delta) = \Psi_\alpha\left(\frac{x-\lambda}{\delta}\right).$$

Among these three families of distribution functions, the type I is the most commonly referred in discussions of extreme values (see also Figures 4.5 and 4.6). Indeed, the Gumbel distribution is often coined "*the*" extreme value distribution (see Figure 4.7).

The following short biographical notes are borrowed from an entry in International Encyclopedia of Statistical Science (Lovric, 2011).

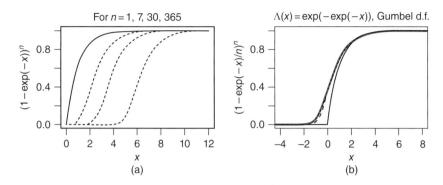

FIGURE 4.5 For r.v.'s **Exp(1)**, distribution of M_n (a) and of $\frac{M_n - b_n}{a_n}$ (b), $a_n =$ 1, $b_n = \log n$, for $n = 1$ (*daily*), 7 (*weekly*), 30 (*monthly*), 365 (*yearly*), comparatively to the limit law Gumbel (*fast convergence*).

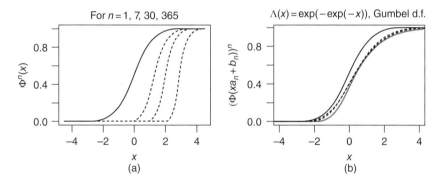

FIGURE 4.6 For r.v.'s $N(0, 1)$, distribution of M_n (a) and of $\frac{M_n - b_n}{a_n}$ (b), $a_n =$ $(2 \log n)^{-0.5}$, $b_n = (2 \log n)^{0.5} - 0.5(2 \log n)^{-0.5}(\log \log n + \log 4\pi)$, for $n =$ 1 (*daily*), 7 (*weekly*), 30 (*monthly*), 365 (*yearly*), comparatively to the limit law Gumbel (*very slow convergence*).

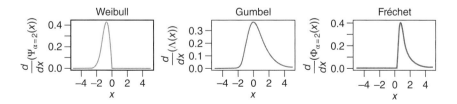

FIGURE 4.7 Max-stable distributions.

The Gumbel distribution, named after one of the pioneer scientists in practical applications of the EVT, the German mathematician Emil Gumbel (1891–1966), has been extensively used in various fields including hydrology for modeling extreme events. Gumbel applied EVT on real-world problems in engineering and in meteorological phenomena such as annual flood flows (Gumbel, 1958).

Emil Gumbel[2]

The EVD of type II was named after Maurice Fréchet (1878–1973), a French mathematician who devised one possible limiting distribution for a sequence of maxima, provided convenient scale normalization (Fréchet, 1927). In applications to finance, the Fréchet distribution has been of great use apropos the adequate modeling of market returns which are often heavy tailed.

Maurice Fréchet[3]

The EVD of type III was named after Waloddi Weibull (1887–1979), a Swedish engineer and scientist well known for his work on strength of materials and fatigue analysis (Weibull, 1939). Even though the Weibull distribution was originally developed to address the problems for minima arising in material sciences, it is widely used in many other areas thanks to its flexibility. If $\alpha = 1$, the Weibull distribution function for *minima*, Ψ_α^*, reduces to the exponential model, whereas for $\alpha = 2$ it mimics the Rayleigh distribution which is mainly used in the telecommunications field. Furthermore, Ψ_α^* resembles the normal distribution when $\alpha = 3.5$.

Waloddi Weibull[4]

DEFINITION 4.4 (Extreme value distributions *for minima*) *The standard converse EVD for minima are defined as* $\Lambda^*(x) = 1 - \Lambda(-x)$, $\Phi_\alpha^*(x) = 1 - \Phi_\alpha(-x)$ *and* $\Psi_\alpha^*(x) = 1 - \Psi_\alpha(-x)$.

PROPOSITION 4.5 (Moments and mode of EVD) *The mean, variance, and mode of the EVD as in Definition 4.3 are, respectively,*

(i) *Gumbel*—Λ: $E[X] = -\Gamma'(1) = \gamma = 0.5772 \ldots = Euler's\ constant;$
     $Var[X] = \pi^2/6;\ Mode = 0;$

---

[2]Source: http://www.ub.uni-heidelberg.de/helios/fachinfo/www/math/edd/uni-archiv/gumbel.htm. Reproduced with permission of the University of Heidelberg.

[3]Source: https://commons.wikimedia.org/wiki/File:Frechet.jpeg. Public Domain

[4]Source: The photo of Waloddi Weibull was taken by Sam C. Saunders. It is on the cover of The New Weibull Handbook, 5th Edition, ISBN 978-0-9653062-3-2, by Dr. Robert B. Abernethy, Author and Publisher. The 5th edition was originally published December 2006 with subsequent updates. http://www.weibullnews.com/ybullbio.html. Reproduced with permission of Paul Barringer and Robert B. Abernethy.

(ii) *Fréchet*—Φ_α: $E[X] = \Gamma(1 - 1/\alpha)$, *for* $\alpha > 1$; $Var[X] = \Gamma(1 - 2/\alpha) - \Gamma^2(1 - 1/\alpha)$, *for* $\alpha > 2$; Mode= $(1 + 1/\alpha)^{-1/\alpha}$;

(iii) *Weibull*—Ψ_α: $E[X] = -\Gamma(1 + 1/\alpha)$; $Var[X] = \Gamma(1 + 2/\alpha) - \Gamma^2(1 + 1/\alpha)$; *Mode* $= -(1 - 1/\alpha)^{-1/\alpha}$, *for* $\alpha > 1$, *and Mode* $= 0$, *for* $0 < \alpha \leq 1$.

(notation: Γ *is the gamma function* $\Gamma(s) := \int_0^\infty x^{s-1} e^{-x} dx, s > 0$)

DEFINITION 4.6 (Max-domain of attraction) *If there exist real sequences* $a_n > 0$ *and* b_n *such that*

$$\lim_{n \to \infty} P(M_n \leq a_n x + b_n) = \lim_{n \to \infty} F^n(a_n x + b_n) = G(x) \tag{4.3}$$

for every continuity point x of G, we say that the c.d.f. F belongs to the max-domain of attraction of G, and we write $F \in \mathcal{D}(G)$.

Richard von Mises (1883–1953) studied the EVT in 1936 (see von Mises, 1936), establishing the well-known von Mises sufficient conditions on the hazard rate (assuming the density exists), leading to one of the aforementioned three types of limit law, while providing one extreme domain of attraction $\mathcal{D}(G)$. Later on, and motivated by a storm surge in the North Sea (31 January–1 February 1953) which caused extensive flooding and many causalities, the Netherlands government gave top priority to understanding the causes of such tragedies with a view to risk mitigation. The study of the sea-level maxima projected EVT to a Netherlands scientific priority. A celebrated work in the field is the doctoral thesis of Laurens de Haan (1970). The fundamental extreme value theorem, worked out by Fisher–Tippett (1928) and Gnedenko (1943), ascertains the GEV distribution in the von Mises–Jenkinson parametrization (von Mises, 1936; Jenkinson, 1955) as a unified version of all possible nondegenerate weak limits of the partial maxima of a sequence $X_1, X_2, \ldots, X_n, \ldots$ of i.i.d. random variables.

THEOREM 4.7 (Asymptotic distribution of the sample maximum) *If* $F \in \mathcal{D}(G)$, *the limiting c.d.f. G of the sample maximum, suitably normalized, is then*

$$G(x) = G_\xi(x) := \begin{cases} \exp(-(1 + \xi x)^{-1/\xi}), & 1 + \xi x > 0, & \text{if } \xi \neq 0 \\ \exp(-\exp(-x)), & x \in \mathbb{R}, & \text{if } \xi = 0 \end{cases} \tag{4.4}$$

the GEV distribution, where the shape parameter ξ *is denominated extreme value index (EVI), which can be seen as a gauge of tail heaviness of the underlying c.d.f. F. Moreover, the Gumbel c.d.f.* $\Lambda(x)$ *reads in the limiting sense as* $\xi \to 0$.

Notice that for $\xi < 0$, $\xi = 0$ and $\xi > 0$, the c.d.f. G_ξ reduces to Weibull, Gumbel and Fréchet distributions, respectively. More precisely,

$$\Lambda(x) \equiv G_0(x), \quad \Phi_\alpha(x) \equiv G_{1/\alpha}(\alpha(x - 1)) \quad \text{and} \quad \Psi_\alpha(x) \equiv G_{-1/\alpha}(\alpha(1 + x)).$$

The EVI ξ is closely related to the tail heaviness of the distribution. In that sense, the value $\xi = 0$ concerns exponential tails, with finite or infinite right endpoint x^F and can be regarded as a change point: $\xi < 0$ refers to short tails with finite right endpoint x^F, whereas for $\xi > 0$ the c.d.f.'s have a polynomial decay, that is, are heavy tailed with infinite right endpoint x^F.

In many applied sciences where extremes come into play, it is assumed that the EVI ξ of the underlying c.d.f. F is equal to zero, and all subsequent statistical inference procedures concerning rare events on the tail of F, such as the estimation of high quantiles, small exceedance probabilities or return periods, bear on this assumption. Moreover, Gumbel and exponential models are also preferred because of the greater simplicity of inference associated with Gumbel or exponential populations. For other details on EV models see Chapter 22 of Johnson et al. (1995) and a brief entry of Fraga Alves and Neves in the International Encyclopedia of Statistical Science (Fraga Alves and Neves, 2011).

PROPOSITION 4.8 (Moments and mode of GEV) *The mean, variance and mode of the GEV as in Theorem 4.7 are, respectively:* $E[X] = -\frac{1}{\xi}[1 - \Gamma(1 - \xi)]$, *for $\xi < 1$;* $Var[X] = \frac{1}{\xi^2}[\Gamma(1 - 2\xi) - \Gamma^2(1 - \xi)]$,   *for $\xi < 1/2$;* $Mode = \frac{1}{\xi}$ $[(1 + \xi)^{-\xi} - 1]$, *for $\xi \neq 0$.*

PROPOSITION 4.9 (Skewness of GEV) *The skewness coefficient of GEV distribution, defined as*

$$skew_{G_\xi} := E[\{X - E[X]\}^3]/\{Var[X]\}^{3/2},$$

is equal to zero at $\xi_0 \simeq -0.28$. Moreover, $skew_{G_\xi} > 0$, for $\xi > \xi_0$, and $skew_{G_\xi} < 0$, for $\xi < \xi_0$. Furthermore, for the Gumbel distribution, $skew_{G_0} \simeq 1.14$.

DEFINITION 4.10 (Univariate max-stable distributions) *A random variable X with c.d.f. F is max-stable if there are normalizing real sequences $a_n > 0$ and $b_n \in \mathbb{R}$ such that, for all $n \in \mathbb{N}$, the r.v.'s $X_1, X_2, \ldots, X_n$ i.i.d. to X satisfy (notation: $\overset{d}{=}$ equality in distribution)*

$$\max(X_1, \ldots, X_n) \overset{d}{=} a_n X + b_n, \text{ or equivalently, } [F(x)]^n = F((x - b_n)/a_n).$$
$$(4.5)$$

The class GEV, up to location and scale parameters, that is,

$$\{G_\xi(x; \lambda, \delta) = G_\xi((x - \lambda)/\delta), \lambda \in \mathbb{R}, \delta > 0\}$$

represents the only possible max-stable distributions. The GEV model is used as an approximation to model the maxima of large (finite) random samples. In applications the GEV distribution is also known as the Fisher–Tippett distribution, named after Sir Ronald Aylmer Fisher (1890–1962) and Leonard Henry Caleb Tippett (1902–1985) who proved that these are the only three possible types of limiting functions as in Definition 4.3.

At this stage, a pertinent question is:

What is the limiting distribution (if there is one) that is obtained for the maximum from a given F?

One research topic in EVT comprehends the characterization of the max-domains of attraction; this means to characterize the class of c.d.f.'s F that belong to a certain max-domain $\mathcal{D}(G_\xi)$ and to find the suitable sequences b_n e a_n such that $F \in \mathcal{D}(G_\xi)$. We consider first the case of absolutely continuous c.d.f.'s F.

THEOREM 4.11 (von Mises's sufficient conditions) *Suppose that there exist the probability density function (p.d.f.) $f := F'(x)$ and $F''(x)$ for a c.d.f. F; define the* hazard function *and its algebraic inverse by $h(x) := \frac{f(x)}{1-F(x)}$ and $r(x) := \frac{1-F(x)}{f(x)}$.*
If

$$\lim_{x \to x^F} r'(x) = \xi \quad \text{then} \quad F \in \mathcal{D}(G_\xi)$$

with normalizing constants

$$b_n = F^\leftarrow(1 - 1/n) = U(n), \quad a_n = r(b_n) = \frac{1}{nf(b_n)} = nU'(n),$$

where

$$F^\leftarrow(u) = \inf\{x : F(x) \geq u\} \quad \text{and} \quad U(t) := F^\leftarrow(1 - 1/t), t \in]1, \infty]$$

the latter designated by tail quantile function.

Example 4.2 Maximum of exponential r.v.'s

$F(x) = 1 - \exp(-x)$, $f(x) = \exp(-x)$, $r(x) := \frac{1-F(x)}{f(x)} = 1$ for all $x > 0$.
Then $r'(x) = 0$ for all $x > 0$, and $F \in \mathcal{D}(G_0)$, that is, the exponential model belongs to Gumbel domain. The normalizing constants are

$$b_n = F^\leftarrow(1 - 1/n) \Leftrightarrow 1 - F(b_n) = 1/n$$

and one gets

$$\exp(-b_n) = 1/n \Longleftrightarrow b_n = \log\ n$$

and

$$a_n = r(b_n) = 1.$$

Consequently,

$$(M_n - b_n)/a_n = M_n - \log\ n$$

converges to a Gumbel distribution as it was obtained in Example 4.1.

THEOREM 4.12 (von Mises's sufficient conditions for $\xi > 0$) *Suppose that $x^F = \infty$ and $F' = f$ exists. If for some ξ positive*

$$\lim_{t \to \infty} \frac{tF'(t)}{1 - F(t)} = \lim_{t \to \infty} t\, h(t) = \frac{1}{\xi} \quad \text{then } F \in \mathcal{D}(G_\xi).$$

THEOREM 4.13 (von Mises's sufficient conditions for $\xi < 0$) *Suppose that* $x^F < \infty$ *and that* $F' = f$ *exists. If for any* ξ *negative*

$$\lim_{t \uparrow x^F} \frac{(x^F - t)F'(t)}{1 - F(t)} = \lim_{t \uparrow x^F}(x^F - t)h(t) = -\frac{1}{\xi} \quad then \quad F \in D(G_\xi).$$

The next theorem presents necessary and sufficient conditions for $F \in D(G_\xi), \xi \in \mathbb{R}$.

THEOREM 4.14 (Gnedenko (1943)) $F \in D(G_\xi), \xi \in \mathbb{R}$ *if and only if*

1. *For* $\xi > 0$: $x^F = \infty$ *and* $\lim_{t \to \infty} \frac{1 - F(tx)}{1 - F(t)} = x^{-1/\xi}$, *for all* $x > 0$;

   that is, $1 - F$ *is of regular variation[5] with index* $-1/\xi$ *(notation:* $F \in \mathcal{RV}_{-1/\xi}$)

2. *For* $\xi < 0$: $x^F < \infty$ *and* $\lim_{t \downarrow 0} \frac{1 - F(x^F - tx)}{1 - F(x^F - t)} = x^{-1/\xi}$, *for all* $x > 0$;

3. *For* $\xi = 0$: $x^F < \infty$ *or* $x^F = \infty$ *and* $\lim_{t \uparrow x^F} \frac{1 - F(t + xg(t))}{1 - F(t)} = e^{-x}$, *for all x, with* $\int_t^{x^F}(1 - F(s))ds < \infty$, *and g can be chosen as*

$$g(t) := \frac{\int_t^{x^F}(1 - F(s))ds}{1 - F(t)} = E[X - t | X > t], \quad for \ t < x^F.$$

The function $g(t)$ is denominated as *mean excess function*. The following result is also useful to obtain the normalizing constants for the EVDs: $F \in D(\Psi_\alpha)$, $D(\Lambda)$, $D(\Phi_\alpha)$.

THEOREM 4.15 (Normalizing constants) *Suppose* $F \in D(G_\xi)$; *then*

1. *For* $\xi > 0$:

$$\lim_{n \to \infty} F^n(a_n x) = \exp(-x^{-1/\xi}) = \Phi_{1/\xi}(x),$$

   for $x > 0$, *with* $a_n = U(n)$;

2. *For* $\xi < 0$:

$$\lim_{n \to \infty} F^n(a_n x + x^F) = \exp(-(-x)^{-1/\xi}) = \Psi_{-1/\xi}(x),$$

   for $x < 0$, *with* $a_n = x^F - U(n)$;

3. *For* $\xi = 0$:

$$\lim_{n \to \infty} F^n(a_n x + b_n) = \exp(-e^{-x}) = \Lambda(x),$$

   for all x, with $a_n = g(U(n))$ *and* $b_n = U(n)$ *and* $g(t) = E[X - t | X > t]$ *is the mean excess function.*

---

[5]If a positive function h is such that $\lim_{t \to \infty} \frac{h(tx)}{h(t)} = x^\beta$, for $x > 0$, we say that h is *regularly varying with index* β (at infinity) and denote by $h \in \mathcal{RV}_\beta$; if a satisfies $\lim_{t \to \infty} \frac{a(tx)}{a(t)} = 1$, for $x > 0$, then a is *slowly varying* (at infinity) and denote $a \in \mathcal{RV}_0$.

📖 **Example 4.3 (Uniform $\mathcal{U}_{(0,1)}$)**

$F(x) = x$, for $0 < x < 1$; since $x^F = 1 < \infty$, the Fréchet domain is discarded. We are going to check that the necessary and sufficient condition for Weibull domain holds. Indeed, we have that

$$\lim_{t \downarrow 0} \frac{1 - F(x^F - xt)}{1 - F(x^F - t)} = \lim_{t \downarrow 0} \frac{1 - (1 - xt)}{1 - (1 - t)} = \lim_{t \downarrow 0} \frac{xt}{t} = x,$$

meaning that

$$F \in \mathcal{D}(G_\xi), \quad \text{with } \xi = -1.$$

The suitable normalizing constants are
$b_n = x^F = 1$ and $a_n = x^F - U(n) = 1 - U(n) = 1 - (1 - 1/n) = 1/n$ and
$n(M_n - 1)$ converges to a r.v. with c.d.f. Weibull $\Psi_1(x)$. Notice that in
Figure 4.4 the $Beta(1,1)$ model equals the Uniform $\mathcal{U}_{(0,1)}$.

📖 **Example 4.4 (Pareto(α))**

$F(x) = 1 - x^{-\alpha}$, for $x > 1$ and $\alpha > 0$; since $x^F = \infty$, the Weibull domain is discarded. For this case, the necessary and sufficient condition for Fréchet domain holds. Indeed, we have that

$$\lim_{t \to \infty} \frac{1 - F(tx)}{1 - F(t)} = \lim_{t \to \infty} \frac{(tx)^{-\alpha}}{t^{-\alpha}} = x^{-\alpha} \iff \bar{F} \in \mathcal{RV}_{-\alpha},$$

and then

$$F \in \mathcal{D}(G_\xi), \quad \text{with } \xi = 1/\alpha.$$

The normalizing constants are
$b_n = 0$ and $a_n = U(n)$; since $U(t) = (1/t)^{-1/\alpha}$, then $a_n = n^{1/\alpha}$ and
$n^{-1/\alpha} M_n$ converges to a r.v. with c.d.f. Fréchet $\Phi_\alpha(x)$.

There are distributions that do not belong to any max-domain of attraction.

📖 **Example 4.5 (Log-Pareto)**

$F(x) = 1 - \frac{1}{\log x}$, for $x > e$. For this c.d.f. there is no possible linearization for the maximum in order to obtain a nondegenerate limiting distribution.

- Since $x^F = \infty$, the Weibull domain is discarded.

- Consider now the necessary and sufficient condition for the Fréchet domain:

$$\lim_{t \to \infty} \frac{1 - F(tx)}{1 - F(t)} = \lim_{t \to \infty} \frac{\log t}{\log (tx)} = 1;$$

so the condition $\bar{F} \in RV_{-1/\xi}$, for some value $\xi > 0$ fails.

- Finally we consider the Gumbel domain: we see that $\int_t^{x^F} (1 - F(s))ds = \int_t^{+\infty} \frac{1}{\log s}ds > \int_t^{+\infty} \frac{1}{s}ds = \infty$. Hence the necessary condition for F to belong to the Gumbel domain also fails.

Note: (Super-heavy tails) A c.d.f. such that its tail is of slow variation, that is, $1 - F \in RV_0$, is called superheavy tail, which does not belong to any max-domain of attraction. For more information about superheavy tails, see Fraga Alves et al. (2009).

It is possible also to characterize the max-domains of attraction in terms the tail quantile function U. The following result constitutes a necessary and sufficient condition for $F \in D(G_\xi)$, $\xi \in \mathbb{R}$.

THEOREM 4.16 (First-order condition: Extended regular variation)

$$F \in D(G_\xi), \xi \in \mathbb{R} \quad \text{if and only if} \quad \lim_{t \to \infty} \frac{U(tx) - U(t)}{a(t)} = \frac{x^\xi - 1}{\xi},$$

for some positive function $a(\cdot)$ and with $x > 0$. The 2nd member is interpreted as $\log x$, for $\xi = 0$.

The following result gives necessary conditions for $F \in D(G_\xi)$, in terms of U.

THEOREM 4.17 (Necessary conditions) *Suppose $F \in D(G_\xi)$, $\xi \in \mathbb{R}$. If*

1. $\xi > 0$, *then* $U(\infty) = \infty$ *and* $\lim_{t \to \infty} \frac{U(t)}{a(t)} = \frac{1}{\xi}$.
2. $\xi < 0$, *then* $U(\infty) < \infty$ *and* $\lim_{t \to \infty} \frac{U(\infty) - U(t)}{a(t)} = -\frac{1}{\xi}$.
3. $\xi = 0$, *then* $\lim_{t \to \infty} \frac{U(tx)}{U(t)} = 1$, *for all* $x > 0$ *and* $\lim_{t \to \infty} a(t)/U(t) = 0$. *Moreover, if* $U(\infty) < \infty$, *then* $\lim_{t \to \infty} \frac{U(\infty) - U(tx)}{U(\infty) - U(t)} = 1$, *for* $x > 0$ *and* $\lim_{t \to \infty} \frac{a(t)}{U(\infty) - U(t)} = 0$. *Adding to this, $a \in RV_0$, that is, $\lim_{t \to \infty} \frac{a(tx)}{a(t)} = 1$, for $x > 0$ (a slowly varying).*

The following result encloses necessary and sufficient conditions for $F \in D(G_\xi)$, $\xi \neq 0$, involving the tail quantile function U.

THEOREM 4.18 (Necessary and sufficient conditions) $F \in D(G_\xi), \xi \neq 0$ *if and only if*

1. *For $\xi > 0$:*

$$U \in \mathcal{R}\mathcal{V}_\xi, \text{ that is, } \lim_{t \to \infty} \frac{U(tx)}{U(t)} = x^\xi, \quad \text{for } x > 0.$$

2. *For $\xi < 0$: $x^F = U(\infty) < \infty$ and*

$$x^F - U \in \mathcal{R}\mathcal{V}_\xi, \text{ that is, } \lim_{t \to \infty} \frac{U(\infty) - U(tx)}{U(\infty) - U(t)} = \lim_{t \to \infty} \frac{x^F - U(tx)}{x^F - U(t)} = x^\xi,$$

$$\text{for } x > 0.$$

A brief catalog of some usual distributions concerning the respective max-domain of attraction is listed as follows.

Fréchet domain: The following models belong to $D(G_\xi)$ with $\xi > 0$:

- Pareto Pa(α): $F(x) = 1 - x^{-\alpha}, x > 1, \alpha > 0$; EVI: $\xi = \frac{1}{\alpha}$;
- Generalized Pareto GP(σ, ξ): $F(x) = 1 - \left(1 + \xi\frac{x}{\sigma}\right)^{-\frac{1}{\xi}}, x > 0$; $\sigma, \xi > 0$, EVI: ξ
- Burr(η, τ, λ): $F(x) = 1 - \left(\frac{\eta}{\eta + x^\tau}\right)^\lambda, x > 0$; $\eta, \tau, \lambda > 0$, EVI: $\xi = \frac{1}{\lambda\tau}$;
- Fréchet(α): $F(x) = \exp(-x^{-\alpha}), x > 0$; $\alpha > 0$, EVI: $\xi = \frac{1}{\alpha}$;
- t-student with v degrees of freedom: EVI: $\xi = \frac{1}{v}$;
- Cauchy: $F(x) = \frac{1}{2} + \frac{1}{\pi} \arctan x, x \in \mathbb{R}$, EVI: $\xi = 1$;
- Log-gamma(α, λ): $F(x) = \int_1^x \frac{\lambda^\alpha}{\Gamma(\alpha)}(\log t)^{\alpha-1}t^{-\lambda-1} \, dt$, EVI: $\xi = \frac{1}{\lambda}$.

Weibull domain: The following models belong to $D(G_\xi)$ with $\xi < 0$:

- Uniform $\mathcal{U}(0, 1)$: $F(x) = x, 0 < x < 1$; EVI: $\xi = -1$;
- Beta(a, b): $F(x) = \int_0^x \frac{\Gamma(a+b)}{\Gamma(a)\Gamma(b)}u^{a-1}(1 - u)^{b-1} \, du, x < 1, a, b > 0$; EVI: $\xi = \frac{-1}{q}$
- Reversed Burr(β, τ, λ): $F(x) = 1 - \left(\frac{\beta}{\beta + (-x)^{-\tau}}\right)^\lambda$, $x < 0$; $\beta, \tau, \lambda > 0$; EVI: $\xi = \frac{-1}{\lambda\tau}$;
- Weibull *for maxima*: $F(x) = 1 - \exp(-x^{-\alpha}), x > 0$; $\alpha > 0$; EVI: $\xi = \frac{-1}{\alpha}$.

Gumbel domain: These distributions are from $D(G_0)$:

- EXP(1): $F(x) = 1 - \exp(-x), x > 0$;

- Weibull for minima: $F(x) = 1 - \exp(-\lambda x^\tau), x > 0; \ \lambda, \tau > 0$;
- Logistic: $F(x) = 1 - \frac{1}{1 + \exp(x)}, x \in \mathbb{R}$;
- Gumbel: $\Lambda(x) = \exp(-\exp(-x)), x \in \mathbb{R}$;
- Normal: $\int_{-\infty}^{x} \frac{1}{\sqrt{2\pi}} \exp(-t^2/2) \mathrm{d}t, x \in \mathbb{R}$;
- Lognormal: The r.v. X has a lognormal distribution if $\log X$ is a normal random variable;
- Gamma(α, β): $F(x) = \int_0^x \frac{\alpha^\beta}{\Gamma(\alpha)} (\log \ t)^{\beta-1} t^{-\alpha-1} \ \mathrm{d}t$;
- Fréchet *for* *minima*: $\Phi_\alpha^*(x) = 1 - \Phi_\alpha(-x) = 1 - \exp(-(-x)^{-\alpha}), x < 0$; $\alpha > 0$.

4.2.3   Parametric and Semiparametric Inference Methodologies

When we are interested in modeling large observations, we are usually confronted with two extreme value models: the GEV c.d.f. introduced in (4.4) and the GP c.d.f. defined as

$$H_\xi(x) := \begin{cases} 1 - (1 + \xi x)^{-1/\xi}, & 1 + \xi x > 0 \ \ \text{and} \ \ x \in \mathbb{R}^+, & \text{if } \xi \neq 0, \\ 1 - \exp(-x), & x \in \mathbb{R}^+, & \text{if } \xi = 0. \end{cases} \quad (4.6)$$

The GP c.d.f. is defined more generally with the incorporation of location/scale parameters, $u \in \mathbb{R}$ and $\sigma > 0$, for values $x > u$, as

$$H_\xi(x; u, \sigma) := H_\xi((x - u)/\sigma).$$

4.2.3.1   Parametric methodologies

Statistical inference about rare events can clearly be deduced only from those observations which are extreme in some sense. There are different ways to define such observations and respective alternative approaches to statistical inference on extreme values: classical Gumbel method of *maxima per blocks of size n*, also designated AM (see Figure 4.8), a parametric approach that uses GEV c.d.f. to approximate the c.d.f. of the maximum, $F_{M_n}(x) \approx G_\xi(x; \lambda, \delta)$, and the (POT) parametric method, which picks up the *excesses* of the observations (*exceedances*), above a *high* threshold u (see Figure 4.9(a)), using GP class of c.d.f.'s to approximate $F_u(y) \approx H_\xi(y; \sigma_u)$, for $y \in [0, x^F - u]$, if $\xi \geq 0$, and for $y \in [0, -\sigma_u/\xi]$, if $\xi < 0$.

Pickands (1975) and Balkema and de Haan (1974) established the duality between the GEV(ξ) and GP(ξ), in a result summarized as follows. Given an r.v. X with c.d.f. F, it is important to characterize the distribution F_u of the excesses above a threshold u,

$$F_u(y) = P[X - u \leq y | X > u], 0 \leq y \leq x^F - u,$$

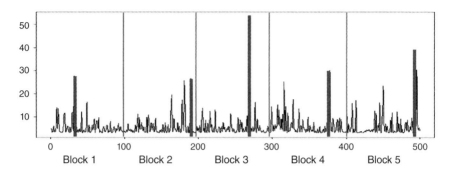

FIGURE 4.8 AM or Gumbel parametric method.

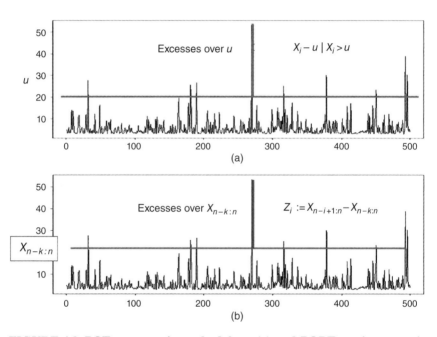

FIGURE 4.9 POT parametric methodology (a) and PORT semiparametric methodology (b).

that is,

$$F_u(y) = \frac{F(u+y) - F(u)}{1 - F(u)}. \tag{4.7}$$

THEOREM 4.19 (Pickands (1975) and Balkema–de Haan (1974))

$$F \in \mathcal{D}(G_\xi), \xi \in \mathbb{R} \iff \lim_{u \to x^F} \sup_{0 < y < x^F - u} |F_u(y) - H_\xi(y; \sigma_u)| = 0,$$

where $\sigma = \sigma_u$ is used to imply that the scale parameter depends on the threshold u.

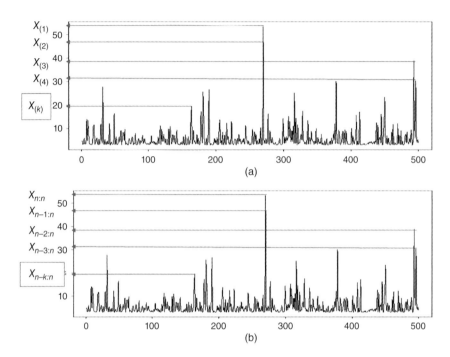

FIGURE 4.10 **LO parametric methodology (a) and largest intermediate order statistics semiparametric methodology (b).**

Another parametric approach for statistical inference is to fit a parametric model to the largest observations (LO), as sketched in Figure 4.10(a). Consider now that those k largest observations, after properly normalized with suitable location and scale real parameters λ and $\delta > 0$, $Z_{(i)} = (X_{(i)} - \lambda)/\delta$, $i = 1, \ldots, k$, are reasonably modeled by the joint p.d.f. given by

$$f_\xi(\mathbf{z}) := f_\xi(z_{(1)}, \ldots, z_{(k)}) = g_\xi(z_{(k)}) \prod_{i=1}^{k-1} \{g_\xi(z_{(i)})/G_\xi(z_{(i)})\}, z_{(1)} > \cdots > z_{(k)}, \quad (4.8)$$

where $g_\xi(z) = \partial G_\xi(z)/\partial z$ is the p.d.f. associated with GEV c.d.f. In general, $f_\xi(\mathbf{z})$ is the form of the p.d.f. of the nondegenerate limiting distributions of the top k o.s.'s from a set of n i.i.d. r.v.'s, as stated in the result.

THEOREM 4.20 (Asymptotic distribution of k top o.s.'s) $F \in D(G_\xi)$, *for normalizing sequences* $b_n, a_n > 0$ *and with* $G'_\xi = g_\xi$ *if and only if the k-vector* $\left(\frac{X_{n:n} - b_n}{a_n}, \ldots, \frac{X_{n-k+1:n} - b_n}{a_n}\right)$, *with k fixed, has the limiting joint p.d.f. in (4.8), as* $n \to \infty$.

Although in some practical cases only the annual maxima are available, and constituting AM approach a natural method, there are other situations for which the data are more complete, with the registration of the k largest values per year. For such cases, a possible parametric approach combines AM and LO methods, which considers a blocking split of the sample data and the largest k observations in each of the m blocks through what is called the *multidimensional GEV$_\xi$ model*, as follows: a set of i.i.d. k-dimensional random vectors $\{\mathbf{X}_i : i = 1, \dots, m\}$, normalized for λ and δ, where the common p.d.f. of the vectors $\mathbf{Z}_i = (\mathbf{X}_i - \lambda)/\delta$ is given by $f_\xi(\mathbf{z})$ defined in (4.8). Note that both AM and LO approaches can be particular cases of this multidimensional model, taking $k = 1$ and $m = 1$, respectively. Some references on these two last approaches are Gomes (1981), Smith (1986), Gomes and Alpuim (1986), Gomes (1989), Fraga Alves and Gomes (1996), and Fraga Alves (1999).

4.2.3.2 Semiparametric methodologies

In a semiparametric context, rather than fitting a model to the whole sample, built on whatever chosen extreme values as described before, the only assumption on F, the c.d.f. underlying the original random sample $\{X_i\}_{i=1}^n$, is that condition

$$F \in \mathcal{D}(G_\xi), \quad \text{for some} \quad \xi \in \mathbb{R} \tag{4.9}$$

is satisfied. In this setup, any inference concerning the tail of the underlying distribution F can be based on the k largest observations above a random threshold (see Figure 4.10b). Theoretically, the designated threshold corresponds to an intermediate o.s., $X_{n-k:n}$, letting k increase to infinity at a lower rate than the sample size n; formally, k is an *intermediate sequence* of positive integers such that

$$k = k_n \to \infty \quad \text{and} \quad k_n/n \to 0 \quad \text{as} \quad n \to \infty. \tag{4.10}$$

In the context of statistical choice of extreme models, Neves and Alves (2006) and Neves et al. (2006) proposed testing procedures which depend on the observations from the sample lying above a random threshold, with test statistics that are only based on the k excesses over $X_{n-k:n}$:

$$Z_i := X_{n-i+1:n} - X_{n-k:n}, \quad i = 1, \dots, k. \tag{4.11}$$

This setup represents an analogy to the POT approach, but here the random threshold $X_{n-k:n}$ plays the role of the deterministic threshold u. This motivates the peaks-over-random-threshold (PORT) methodology, as drafted in Figure 4.9(b). Another publication related with PORT methodology, in the context of high quantile estimation with relevance to VaR in finance, is Araújo e Santos et al. (2013).

4.2.3.3 The non-i.i.d. case: a brief note

For the previous presented results in EVT, with special relevance to the main EV Theorem 4.7, the main assumption is that the observed values can be fairly considered as outcomes of an i.i.d. sample $\{X_i\}_{i=1}^{n}$; however, in many real-world applications, dependence and/or nonstationarity is inherent to the actual processes generating the data. In particular, for statistical inference of rare events, it is of interest to account for dependence at high levels, seasonality, or trend. A simple approach for the latter is given by de Haan et al. (2015). Altogether, the EVT presented so far has to be adapted, and, for instance in AM and POT approaches, it is important to analyze how the respective GEV and GP distributions need to be modified in order to incorporate those features.

Week dependence. For the case of temporal dependence, a case of utmost importance in financial applications, the EV theorem can be extended by assuming the existence of a condition that controls the long-range dependence at extreme levels u_n of a target process. This is known in the literature as the $D(u_n)$ condition, rigorously defined by Leadbetter et al. (1983). For stationary sequences $\{X_i\}_{i \geq 1}$, for which the local weak dependence *mixing condition D* holds, it is still possible to obtain a limiting distribution of GEV type. More precisely, let $\{X_i^*\}_{i \geq 1}$ be the an i.i.d. associated sequence to $\{X_i\}_{i \geq 1}$, that is, with the same marginal F. The limiting distributions of partial maxima $M_n^* := X_{n:n}^*$ and $M_n := X_{n:n}$ for both sequences, respectively, $G_{\xi^*}(x; \lambda^*, \delta^*)$ and $G_{\xi}(x; \lambda, \delta)$, are related by the so-called *extremal index* parameter θ through the equality

$$G_{\xi}(x; \lambda, \delta) = \{G_{\xi^*}(x; \lambda^*, \delta^*)\}^{\theta}. \tag{4.12}$$

Consequently, a GEV c.d.f. is still present in this case, due to the max-stability property for GEV, defined in (4.5); the respective parameters in (4.12) satisfy

$$\xi = \xi^*, \lambda = \lambda^* - \delta^*(1 - \theta^{\xi})/\xi, \quad \text{and} \quad \delta = \delta^*\theta^{\xi}. \tag{4.13}$$

The extremal index θ, verifying $0 \leq \theta \leq 1$, is a measure of the tendency of the process to cluster at extreme levels, and its existence is guaranteed by a second condition D'' defined by Leadbetter and Nandagopalan (1989). For independent sequences, $\theta = 1$, but the converse is not necessarily true. Smaller values of θ imply stronger local dependence, and clusters of extreme values appear; moreover, the concept of the extremal index is identified as the reciprocal of the mean cluster size for high levels. Summing up, in the case of block of maxima, provided long-range independence conditions, inference is similar to that of the i.i.d. case, but in this case the AM approach is adapted to $F_{M_n}(x) \approx F^{n\theta}(x) \approx G_{\xi}(x; \lambda, \delta)$ for location/scale parameters as in (4.13). For details on the weak dependence approach, please see Leadbetter (2017).

Nonstationarity. The absence of stationarity is another situation common in most applications, with process of interest for which the marginal distribution does not remain the same as time changes (seasonality, trends, and volatility, for instance). For these cases, extreme value models are still useful, and parameters dependent of t can be the answer to some specific problems. In the adapted POT approach, for instance, the GP model incorporates then parameters with functional forms on time t, as dictated by the data, $H_{\xi_t}(x; \sigma_t)$. With the main goal of estimating one-day-ahead VaR forecast, and within this adapted POT framework, Araújo Santos and Fraga Alves (2013), Araújo Santos et al. 2013) proposed the presence of durations between excesses over high thresholds (DPOT) as covariates. For a general overview of EVT and its application to VaR, including the use of explanatory variables, see Tsay (2010), for instance. Recent works providing inference for non-stationary extremes are Gardes (2015), de Haan et al. (2015) and Einmahl et al. (2017).

4.2.3.4 Statistical inference: EVT "at work"

This section devoted to the illustration of how statistical inference for extreme values develops from EVT, using some of the approaches presented before. Two data sets, worked out by Beirlant et al. (2004), will be used with this purpose:

- `maasmax.txt` —Annual maximal river discharges (m³/2) of the Meuse river from year 1911 to 1995 at Borgharen in Holland.
  Available at http://lstat.kuleuven.be/Wiley/Data/maasmax.txt.
- `soa.txt` —SOA Group Medical Insurance Large Claims Database; claim amounts of at least 25,000 USD in the year 1991.
  Available at http://lstat.kuleuven.be/Wiley/Data/soa.txt.

Meuse river. This is a data set $\{Y_j\}_{j=1}^m$ of $m = 85$ annual maxima, considered here with the objective of illustrating the AM methodology. Figure 4.11(a) is the time series plot of the annual maxima. From figure 4.11(b) it seems clear that a positive asymmetrical distribution underlies the sample of maxima. With the main goal of making statistical inference on interesting rare events in the field of hydrology, EVT supports the GEV approximation of the c.d.f. of the annual maximum $Y :=$ $\max\{X_i\}_{i=1}^n$, with $n = 12$ for monthly maxima river discharges (or $n = 365$ daily records),

$$F_Y(y) \approx G_\xi(y; \lambda, \delta)$$

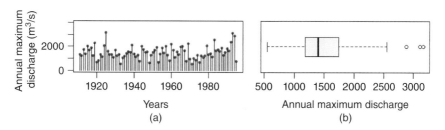

FIGURE 4.11 Annual maximal river discharges (m³/s) of the Meuse river from 1911 to 1995.

and the subsequent estimation of the EVI, ξ, jointly with location/scale parameters λ/δ. Then, for the annual maximum Y, the interesting parameters are

- *Exceedance probability* of a high level u:

$$P[Y > u] \approx 1 - G_\xi(u; \lambda, \delta) = \begin{cases} 1 - \exp\left\{ -\left[1 + \xi\left(\dfrac{u - \lambda}{\delta}\right)\right]^{-1/\xi} \right\}, & \xi \neq 0 \\ 1 - \exp\left\{ -\exp\left[-\dfrac{u - \lambda}{\delta}\right] \right\}, & \xi = 0 \end{cases};$$

- *Return period* for level u :

$$T_u := \frac{1}{P[Y > u]} \approx \frac{1}{1 - G_\xi(u; \lambda, \delta)};$$

- T-years *Return level*:

$$U(T) = G_\xi^\leftarrow\left(1 - \frac{1}{T}; \lambda, \delta\right)$$

$$= \begin{cases} \lambda + \dfrac{\delta}{\xi}\left[(-\log(1 - p))^{-\xi} - 1\right], & \xi \neq 0, \\ \lambda - \delta \log(-\log(1 - p)), & \xi = 0 \end{cases}, \quad p := \frac{1}{T};$$

- *Right endpoint*: If $\xi < 0$,

$$x^F = \lambda - \frac{\delta}{\xi}.$$

R package (R Development Core Team, 2011) incorporates several libraries aimed to work with statistics for extreme values, for instance, `ismev`, `evir`, `evd`, `fExtremes`. For Meuse data set, the ML parameter estimates obtained by `evir` for the EVI and location and scale parameters from GEV are $\hat{\xi} = -0.092$ (remember that $skew_{G_\xi} > 0$, for $\xi > -0.28$; Proposition 4.9),

$$\hat{\lambda} = 1267.227, \quad \hat{\delta} = 466.793$$

and the estimated 100-years return level is $\hat{U}(100) = 3016.410$ m^3/s. Notice that a nonparametric estimation for this high $(1 - p)$ quantile of the annual maxima, $p = 0.01$, is given by the empirical quantile of the sample of maxima, $x_{[n(1-p)]+1:n} = x_{85:85} = 3175$, and the answer remains the same for any $p < 0.01$. The `evir` still has the possibility of returning confidence intervals (CI) for the parameters involved. For the return level $U(100)$, for instance, the 95% CI based on *profile likelihood* is $CI = (2686.727, 3778.092)$. As the EVI is negative, the right endpoint for the annual maximum of the river discharges is estimated by $\hat{x}^F = 6317.558$ m^3/s, a value beyond the largest value in the sample of annual maxima. Since EVI is close to zero, it is also pertinent to fit the Gumbel model to the sample of 85 annual maxima; the estimated location and scale parameters are then

$$\hat{\lambda} = 1243.567, \quad \hat{\delta} = 456.454,$$

leading to an estimated 100-years return level of $\hat{U}(100) = 3343.324$ m^3/s. In this case study, it is observed that a small change in the value of the EVI has big repercussion on the estimated high quantile. So, it seems important to make beforehand a statistical choice between Gumbel model and the other GEV distributions, Weibull and Fréchet. This can be accomplished by a statistical test for the EVI on the hypothesis

$$H_0 : \xi = 0 \text{ versus } H_1 : \xi \neq 0.$$

Overviews on testing extreme value conditions can be found in Hüsler and Peng (2008) and Neves and Fraga Alves (2008). For other useful preliminary statistical analysis, like QQ-quantile plot or mean excess plot, see Coles (2001), Beirlant (2004), or Castillo et al. (2005), for instance.

SOA claims. This data set comprises $n = 75,789$ large claims[6] $\{X_i\}_{i=1}^{n}$ registered in 1991 from Group Medical Insurance Large Claims Database. The box plot in Figure 4.12(b) indicates a substantial right skewness.

POT approach. Keeping in mind the main goal of estimating a *high quantile* and a *probability of exceedance of a high level*, the POT approach will be considered, supported by the Pickands–Balkema–de Haan theorem 4.19. In Figure 4.12(a) a number of $n_u = 397$ exceedances is provided by a high threshold $u = 400,000$ and the respective observed excesses of $\{Y_j := X_i - u | X_i > u\}_{j=1}^{n_u}$, replicas of the excess $Y := X - u | X > u$, with c.d.f. in (4.7). Denoting by F the c.d.f. of the large claim X, the probability of exceedance of the high level $x = u + y$ is

$$1 - F(u + y) = \{1 - F(u)\}[1 - F_u(y)].$$

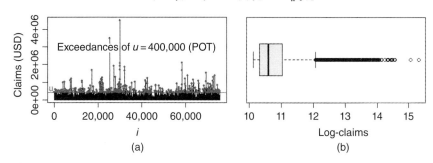

FIGURE 4.12 **Large claims (*USD*) of SOA Group Medical Insurance Large Claims Database, 1991.**

- Suppose that in order to set the reinsurance premium someone is interested in the probability of a large claim exceeding the maximum observed value, $x_{n:n} = 4,518,420$,

$$p_0 := P[X > x_{n:n}] = 1 - F(u + y_{n_u:n_u}) = \{1 - F(u)\}[1 - F_u(y_{n_u:n_u})],$$

---

[6]A *large claim X* is here considered as an amount of at least 25,000 USD.

for the maximum observed excess $y_{n_u:n_u} = x_{n:n} - u = 4{,}518{,}420 - 400{,}000 = 4{,}118{,}420$. From now on we simplify the notation, with $x_0 := x_{n:n}$ and $y_0 := y_{n_u:n_u} = x_0 - u$. Consider now the approximation of the distribution of the excesses to GP distribution $F_u(y_0) \approx H_\xi(y_0; \sigma_u)$; with ML estimates of EVI and scale returned by evir library, respectively, $\hat{\xi} = 0.3847$ and $\hat{\sigma}_u = 142{,}147$, it obtained

$$F_u(y_0) \approx H_{\hat{\xi}}(y_0; \hat{\sigma}_u) = 0.9985 \ ;$$

consequently, estimating the probability of a large claim exceeding the threshold u, by $1 - \widehat{F(u)} = \frac{n_u}{n} = \frac{397}{75{,}789} = 0.00524$, the target small **probability of exceedance of a high level** x_0 is estimated by

$$\hat{p}_0 = 1 - \widehat{F(x_0)} = \hat{P}[X > x_0] = \frac{n_u}{n} \, H_{\hat{\xi}}(x_0 - u; \hat{\sigma}_u);$$

consequently,

$$\hat{p}_0 = \begin{cases} \dfrac{n_u}{n} \left(1 + \dfrac{\hat{\xi}}{\hat{\sigma}_u}(x_0 - u)\right)^{-1/\hat{\xi}} , & \text{for } \xi \neq 0, \\[3mm] \dfrac{n_u}{n} \, \exp\left(-\dfrac{x_0 - u}{\hat{\sigma}_u}\right) , & \text{for } \xi = 0. \end{cases} \tag{4.14}$$

For SOA data is $\hat{p}_0 = 7.949e^{-06}$, if we assume $\xi \neq 0$ in (4.14).

- Consider a high quantile of F, the c.d.f. of a large claim X, that is, a value x_p, p small, such that $x_p = U\left(\frac{1}{p}\right) = F^{\leftarrow}(1 - p)$. The **estimator of the high quantile**, x_p, is obtained by similar arguments to the ones for the probability of exceedance, and it is given by

$$\hat{U}\left(\frac{1}{p}\right) = \begin{cases} u + \dfrac{\hat{\sigma}_u}{\hat{\xi}} \left(\left(\dfrac{np}{N_u}\right)^{-\hat{\xi}} - 1\right) , & \text{for } \xi \neq 0, \\[3mm] u - \hat{\sigma}_u \log\left(\dfrac{np}{N_u}\right) , & \text{for } \xi = 0, \end{cases} \tag{4.15}$$

which is accomplished by making $F(x_p) = 1 - p$ in expression (4.14) and inverting. For SOA data, with $u = 400{,}000$ as before, expression (4.15) provides the estimate for a high (1-p) quantile, $p = 1/100{,}000$, the value $\hat{U}\left(\frac{1}{p}\right) = \hat{U}(100{,}000) = 4{,}139{,}022$ USD. In Figure 4.13 it represented the sample path for the estimation, with POT approach, of the high quantile, $\hat{U}(100{,}000)$, for a decreasing value of the threshold.

For SOA data, the previous chosen threshold $u = 400{,}000$ is such that it is between the $k_1 = 397$ and $k_2 = 398$ largest data values, respectively, $x_{75{,}392:n} = 400{,}360$ and $x_{75{,}391:n} = 399{,}888$, that is, $x_{n-k_2+1:n} < u < x_{n-k_1+1:n}$.

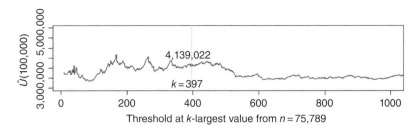

FIGURE 4.13 SOA insurance data: sample path for POT high quantile estimates, $\hat{U}(100,000)$, versus k-largest.

- For $\xi < 0$, an **estimator of the right endpoint** x^F is

$$\hat{x}^F = \hat{U}(\infty) = u - \frac{\hat{\sigma}_u}{\hat{\xi}} \,,$$

which can be easily checked by making $p = 0$ in expression (4.15). Indeed, for admissibility of any right endpoint estimator $\hat{x}^F$, one should take

$$\tilde{x}^F = \max(X_{n:n}, \hat{x}^F) \,.$$

Semiparametric approach. It is assumed that the random sample $X_1, X_2, \ldots, X_n$ is i.i.d. from c.d.f.

$$F \in \mathcal{D}(G_\xi), \quad \text{for some} \quad \xi \in \mathbb{R},$$

or, equivalently, by Theorem 4.16, the *first-order condition* for some positive function $a(\cdot)$:

$$\lim_{t \to \infty} \frac{U(tx) - U(t)}{a(t)} = \frac{x^\xi - 1}{\xi}.$$

Statistical inference is based on the top sample

$$X_{n:n} \geq X_{n-1:n} \geq \cdots \geq X_{n-k:n},$$

with $X_{n-k:n}$ an intermediate o.s., that is,

$$k \equiv k_n \to \infty, \text{ with } k/n \to 0, \text{ as } n \to \infty \,.$$

- **Estimation of EVI ξ and scale** $a\left(\frac{n}{k}\right)$: In a semiparametric setup, the EVI is the crucial parameter to be estimated.

  - $\xi > 0$: **Hill estimator**—In heavy tails, an usual case in financial applications, the most popular is the classical estimator introduced by Hill (1975), which has played as the starting point for some other more sophisticated estimators:

  $$\hat{\xi}_{k,n}^H = \frac{1}{k} \sum_{i=1}^{k} \log X_{n-i+1:n} - \log X_{n-k:n} \,. \tag{4.16}$$

– $\xi \in \mathbb{R}$: **Moments estimator**—The estimator in (4.16) has been extended to real EVI by Dekkers et al. (1989) using the log-Moments

$$M_{k,n}^{(r)} = \frac{1}{k} \sum_{i=1}^{k} (\log X_{n-i+1:n} - \log X_{n-k:n})^r, \quad r = 1, 2 \ ;$$

with $M_{k,n}^{(1)} \equiv \hat{\xi}_{k,n}^H$ and

$$\hat{\xi}_{k,n}^- = 1 - \frac{1}{2} \left\{ 1 - \frac{(M_{k,n}^{(1)})^2}{M_{k,n}^{(2)}} \right\}^{-1}, \tag{4.17}$$

the moments EVI estimator is defined by

$$\hat{\xi}_{k,n}^M = \hat{\xi}_{k,n}^H + \hat{\xi}_{k,n}^- . \tag{4.18}$$

– $\xi \in \mathbb{R}$: **Pickands estimator**—To simplify the presentation, denote the ith largest observation by

$$X_{(i)} = X_{n-i+1}, \quad i = 1, \ldots, n \ .$$

This EVI estimator only involves three observations from the top $k = 4m$

$$\cdots \geq X_{(m)} \geq \cdots \geq X_{(2m)} \geq \cdots \geq X_{(4m)}$$

and is defined by

$$\hat{\xi}_{m,n}^P = \frac{1}{\log 2} \log \left[\frac{X_{(m)} - X_{(2m)}}{X_{(2m)} - X_{(4m)}} \right], \quad m = 1, 2, \ldots, [n/4]. \tag{4.19}$$

Under extra conditions on the rate of $k_n \to \infty$ and on the tail of $1 - F$, a normal asymptotic distributional behavior is attained for Hill (H), moments (M), and Pickands (P) estimators:

$$\sqrt{k}(\hat{\xi}_{k,n}^E - \xi) \xrightarrow[n \to \infty]{d} \mathcal{N}(0, \sigma_\xi^2(E)), \quad E = H, M, P \ ,$$

with

$$\sigma_\xi^2(H) = \xi^2, \text{if } \xi > 0;$$

$$\sigma_\xi^2(M) = \begin{cases} \xi^2 + 1, & \text{if } \xi \geq 0; \\ \dfrac{(1 - \xi)^2(1 - 2\xi)(1 - \xi + 6\xi^2)}{(1 - 3\xi)(1 - 4\xi)}, & \text{if } \xi < 0 \ ; \end{cases}$$

$$\sigma_\xi^2(P) = \begin{cases} \dfrac{\xi^2(2^{2\xi+1}+1)}{(\log 2)^2(2^\xi-1)^2}, & \text{if } \xi \neq 0; \\[2ex] \dfrac{3}{(\log 2)^4}, & \text{if } \xi = 0 . \end{cases}$$

In Figure 4.14 the asymptotic variances are compared for Hill, Pickands, and moments estimators as functions of ξ, σ_ξ^2.

For n finite, these semiparametric estimators exhibit the following pattern: for small k less bias, and big variance, and the other way around for large k.

- **Scale estimator** of $a\left(\dfrac{n}{k}\right)$—With $M_{k,n}^{(1)}$ the Hill EVI estimator and $\hat\xi_{k,n}^-$ defined in (4.17), an estimator of the scale, in semiparametric setup, is given by

$$\hat a\left(\frac{n}{k}\right) = X_{n-k:n} M_{k,n}^{(1)}(1 - \hat\xi_{k,n}^-) .$$

- **Probability of exceedance of a high level** x_0: $p_0 = 1 - F(x_0)$.
  Theoretically, the results for estimating p_0 are established for high levels

$$x_0 = x_n, \quad \text{such that} \quad 1 - F(x_n) =: p_n \to 0, \quad \text{as} \quad n \to \infty.$$

A consistent estimator for p_n, in the sense that $\dfrac{\hat p_n}{p_n} \overset{P}{\to} 1$, is

$$\hat p_n = \begin{cases} \dfrac{k}{n}\left\{1 + \dfrac{\hat\xi}{\hat a\left(\frac{n}{k}\right)}(x_n - X_{n-k:n})\right\}^{-1/\hat\xi}, & \text{for } \xi \neq 0, \\[3ex] \dfrac{k}{n}\exp\left\{-\dfrac{x_n - X_{n-k:n}}{\hat a\left(\frac{n}{k}\right)}\right\}, & \text{for } \xi = 0 \end{cases} \qquad (4.20)$$

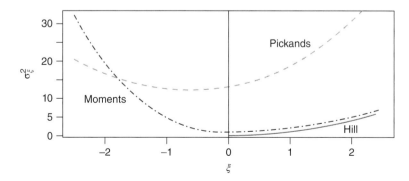

FIGURE 4.14 Asymptotic variances for EVI estimators $\sigma_\xi^2 = \sigma_\xi^2(E)$, $E = H, M,$ **and** P.

with $\hat{\xi}$ and $\hat{a}\left(\frac{n}{k}\right)$ consistent estimators of EVI ξ and scale $a\left(\frac{n}{k}\right)$. In particular,

$$\hat{a}\left(\frac{n}{k}\right) = X_{n-k:n}M_{k,n}^{(1)}(1 - \hat{\xi}_{k,n}^-) \text{ and } \hat{\xi} = \hat{\xi}_{k,n}^M . \tag{4.21}$$

For EVI ξ positive, the following simpler version of (4.20) is valid:

$$\hat{p}_n = \frac{k}{n}\left\{ \frac{x_n}{X_{n-k:n}} \right\}^{-1/M_{k,n}^{(1)}} .$$

Obs: Compare the semiparametric estimation (4.20) with expressions in (4.14) under parametric POT approach.

- **High quantile** x_p: with $p = p_n \rightarrow 0$, as $n \rightarrow \infty$.

$$\hat{U}\left(\frac{1}{p}\right) = \begin{cases} X_{n-k:n} + \dfrac{\hat{a}\left(\frac{n}{k}\right)}{\hat{\xi}}\left(\left(\frac{np}{k}\right)^{-\hat{\xi}} - 1\right) , & \text{for } \xi \neq 0 \\ X_{n-k:n} - \hat{a}\left(\frac{n}{k}\right)\log\left(\frac{np}{k}\right) , & \text{for } \xi = 0 \end{cases} , \tag{4.22}$$

with $\hat{\xi}$ and $\hat{a}\left(\frac{n}{k}\right)$ consistent estimators of EVI ξ and scale $a\left(\frac{n}{k}\right)$, in particular for estimators in (4.21).

Obs: Compare the semiparametric estimation (4.22) with expressions (4.15) under parametric POT approach.

For EVI ξ positive, the simpler version of (4.22) is valid:

$$\hat{U}\left(\frac{1}{p}\right) = X_{n-k:n}\left(\frac{k}{np}\right)^{\hat{\xi}} , \quad \hat{\xi} = \hat{\xi}_{k,n}^H \text{ or } \hat{\xi}_{k,n}^M, \tag{4.23}$$

introduced by Weissman (1978).

- For $\xi < 0$, an **estimator of the right endpoint** is

$$\hat{x}^F = X_{n-k:n} - \frac{\hat{a}\left(\frac{n}{k}\right)}{\hat{\xi}}, \quad \text{with } \hat{a}\left(\frac{n}{k}\right), \hat{\xi} \text{ as in (4.21)} .$$

All the classical presented semiparametric estimators are asymptotic normal, under convenient extra conditions on the rate of $k_n \rightarrow \infty$ and on the tail of $1 - F$, which enables the construction of CI for the target parameters. Details can be found, for instance, in de Haan and Ferreira (2006). Another area of current and future research, closely related with semiparametric methodology in EV, is the estimation of the right endpoint for distributions in the Gumbel domain of attraction, which has been innovated by Fraga Alves and Neves (2014). Therein, an application was pursued to statistical EVA of Anchorage International Airport Taxiway Centerline Deviations for Boeing 747 aircraft. For SOA data from 1991 of Group Medical Insurance Large Claims Database, the semiparametric estimation of the EVI ξ and of the high quantile $U(100,000)$ are represented in Figures 4.15 and 4.16, respectively, in comparison with POT estimation. Close to this subject on statistical analysis on extreme values, see also Beirlant et al. (2017) and Gomes et al. (2017).

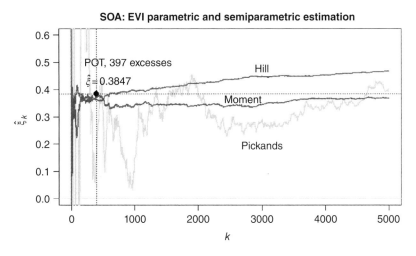

FIGURE 4.15 SOA insurance data: sample paths for semiparametric EVI estimates, $\hat{\xi}$, as in (4.16), (4.18), and (4.19), versus k-largest.

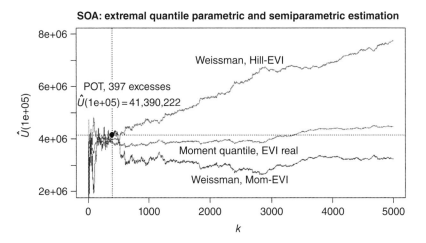

FIGURE 4.16 SOA insurance data: sample paths for semiparametric high quantiles estimates, $\hat{U}(100,000)$ as in (4.22) and (4.23), versus k-largest.

4.3   MULTIVARIATE CASE: SOME HIGHLIGHTS

There is no obvious ordering in multivariate observations, but there are too many possibilities. Hence, the interest is not in extraordinary high levels but rather in extreme probabilities or probability of an extreme or a failure set. A fruitful approach in multivariate extreme value (MEV) theory is the modeling of component-wise maxima. We define the vector of component-wise maxima (and minima) as follows. Let

$$\{\mathbf{X}_i\}_{i=1}^n = \{(X_{i,1}, X_{i,2}, \ldots, X_{i,d})\}_{i=1}^n$$

be a random sample of d-variate outcomes from

$$\mathbf{X} = (X_1, X_2, \ldots, X_d)$$

with the same joint distribution function F. The pertaining random vector of component-wise maxima is defined as

$$\mathbf{M}_n = (M_{n,1}, \ldots, M_{n,d}) := \left(\max_{i=1,\ldots,n} X_{i,1}, \ldots, \max_{i=1,\ldots,n} X_{i,d} \right).$$

Analogously for the vector of component-wise minima, we observe that

$$\mathbf{M}_n^* = (M_{n,1}^*, \ldots, M_{n,d}^*) := \left(\min_{i=1,\ldots,n} X_{i,1}, \ldots, \min_{i=1,\ldots,n} X_{i,d} \right)$$

$$= -\left(\max_{i=1,\ldots,n} (-X_{i,1}), \ldots, \max_{i=1,\ldots,n} (-X_{i,d}) \right).$$

It is worthy of note that the sample maximum may not be an observed sample value. Hence, there is not a direct transfer of the block maxima method from the univariate to the multivariate case. Nevertheless, a rich theory emanates from looking at maximal components individually. Let

$$P[\mathbf{M}_n \le \mathbf{x}] = P[M_{n,1} \le x_1, \ldots, M_{n,d} \le x_d] = F^n(x_1, \ldots, x_d) = F^n(\mathbf{x}), \mathbf{x} \in \mathbb{R}^d,$$

be the distribution function of the component-wise maximum $\mathbf{M}_n$. As in the univariate case, the usual approach is to find sequences of constants $\mathbf{a}_n = (a_{n,i})_{i=1}^d \in \mathbb{R}_+^d$ and $\mathbf{b}_n = (b_{n,i})_{i=1}^d \in \mathbb{R}^d$ such that we get a nontrivial limit for sufficiently large n, that is, such that

$$\lim_{n \to \infty} F^n(a_{n,1} x_1 + b_{n,1}, \ldots, a_{n,d} x_d + b_{n,d}) = G(\mathbf{x}), \tag{4.24}$$

for every continuity point $\mathbf{x}$ of G, with G a c.d.f. with nondegenerate margins $G_1, \ldots, G_d$. Any distribution function G arising in the limit is called a MEV distribution, and we then say that F belongs to the max-domain of attraction of G (notation: $F \in \mathcal{D}(G)$). It is important to note that (4.24) implies convergence of the pertaining marginal distributions,

$$\lim_{n\to\infty} F_j^n(a_{n,j}\, x_j + b_{n,j}) = G_j(x_j), \quad j = 1, \ldots, d,$$

which entails, in turn, a known parametric structure in the limit of the corresponding sequence of marginal distributions, that is, $G = G_j(x_j) = \exp\{-(1 + \xi_j\, x_j)^{-1/\xi_j}\}$, for all x_j such that $1 + \xi_j x_j > 0$. Similarly to the univariate case, the parameters $\xi_j \in \mathbb{R}$, $j = 1, \ldots, d$, are called (marginal) extreme value indices. Defining $U_j(t) = F_j^{\leftarrow}(1 - 1/t)$, $t > 1$, then the extended regular variation (see Theorem 4.16) of each marginal tail quantile function U_j holds with auxiliary functions $a_j > 0$, $j = 1, \ldots, d$, that is,

$$\lim_{t\to\infty} \frac{U_j(ty) - U_j(t)}{a_j(t)} = \frac{y^{\xi_j} - 1}{\xi_j}, \tag{4.25}$$

for all $y > 0$ (cf. de Haan and Ferreira, 2006, p. 209). Furthermore, since F is monotone and G itself is continuous, because its components are continuous, then the convergence in (4.24) holds locally uniformly. Considering for all $j = 1, \ldots, d$, the sequences

$$x_{j,n} := \frac{U_j(nx_j) - U_j(n)}{a_j(n)}, \quad \text{for which } \lim_{n\to\infty} x_{j,n} = \frac{x_j^{\xi_j} - 1}{\xi_j} \text{ holds}$$

by (4.25), then we may write

$$F^n(U_1(nx_1), \ldots, U_d(nx_d)) = F^n(a_1(n)x_{1,n} + U_1(n), \ldots, a_d(n)x_{d,n} + U_d(n)).$$

Therefore, for a suitable choice of constants $a_{n,j} = a_j(n)$ and $b_{n,j} = U_j(n)$ in Eq. (4.24), we write

$$\lim_{n\to\infty} F^n(U_1(nx_1), \ldots, U_d(nx_d)) = G\left(\frac{x_1^{\xi_1} - 1}{\xi_1}, \ldots, \frac{x_d^{\xi_d} - 1}{\xi_d}\right) =: G_0(x_1, \ldots, x_d), \tag{4.26}$$

for all $\mathbf{x} \in \mathbb{R}_+^d$. This leads to the statement in Theorem 6.1.1 of de Haan and Ferreira (2006). We now go back to the MEV condition (4.24): suppose that the random vector $\mathbf{X} = (X_1, X_2, \ldots, X_d)$ of dimension d belongs to the max-domain of attraction of the random vector $\mathbf{Z} = (Z_1, Z_2, \ldots, Z_d)$. That is, there exist constants $\mathbf{a}_n = (a_{n,i})_{i=1}^d \in \mathbb{R}_+^d$ and $\mathbf{b}_n = (b_{n,i})_{i=1}^d \in \mathbb{R}^d$ such that

$$\left(\frac{M_{n,1} - b_{n,1}}{a_{n,1}}, \ldots, \frac{M_{n,d} - b_{n,d}}{a_{n,d}}\right) \xrightarrow[n\to\infty]{d} \mathbf{Z}, \tag{4.27}$$

where $\mathbf{Z}$ is a nontrivial random vector and $\{\mathbf{X}_i\}_{i=1}^n$ are independent copies of $\mathbf{X}$. Unlike the univariate case (4.1), the MEV distribution of $\mathbf{Z}$ cannot be represented as a parametric family in the form of a finite-dimensional parametric vector. Instead, the family of MEV distributions is characterized by a class of finite measures. To this effect we reformulate the domain of attraction condition (4.27) as follows: suppose that the marginal distribution functions $F_j(x) = P\{X_j \leq x\}$, $j = 1, 2, \ldots, d$ are all continuous functions. Define the random vector

$$\widetilde{\mathbf{M}}_n = (\widetilde{M}_{n,1}, \ldots, \widetilde{M}_{n,d}) = \left(\max_{i=1,\ldots,n} \frac{1}{1 - F_1(X_{i,1})}, \ldots, \max_{i=1,\ldots,n} \frac{1}{1 - F_d(X_{i,d})} \right).$$

By virtue of (4.26), we have, as $n \to \infty$,

$$(n^{-1}\widetilde{M}_{n,1}, \ldots, n^{-1}\widetilde{M}_{n,d}) \xrightarrow[n \to \infty]{d} \mathbf{Z}_0,$$

where $\mathbf{Z}_0$ has joint distribution function G_0, meaning that the marginal distributions no longer intervene in the limiting sense. Hence it is possible to disentangle the marginal distributions from the inherent dependence structure. This process of transformation to standard marginals (Pareto in this case; another popular choice is the tail equivalent Fréchet marginals) does not pose theoretical difficulties (see, e.g., Resnick, 1987; Deheveuls, 1984). From a practical viewpoint, margins may be estimated via the e.d.f and then standardized into a unit Fréchet or standard Pareto distributions. This approach is also well established in the literature; see, for example, Genest et al. (1995). For a motivation and implications of choosing other standardized marginals, see Section 8.2.6 in Beirlant et al. (2004).

We proceed with the study of the dependence structure in the limit. Like in the univariate case, we may apply logarithm everywhere in order to find that (4.26) is equivalent to

$$\lim_{n \to \infty} n\{1 - F(U_1(nx_1), \ldots, U_d(nx_d))\} = -\log\ G_0(x_1, x_2, \ldots, x_d).$$

With some effort (see Corollary 6.1.4 of de Haan and Ferreira, 2006), we can replace n with t in the foregoing, ending up with a variable running through the real line, in a continuous path, that is, for any $\mathbf{x}$ such that $0 < G_0(\mathbf{x}) < 1$,

$$\lim_{t \to \infty} t\{1 - F(U_1(tx_1), \ldots, U_d(tx_d))\} = -\log\ G_0(x_1, x_2, \ldots, x_d) = \Psi(\mathbf{x}).$$

If we take $a > 0$ and multiply this scalar with the vector $\mathbf{x}$, we obtain

$$\lim_{t \to \infty} t\{1 - F(U_1(t\,ax_1), \ldots, U_d(t\,ax_d))\}$$
$$= -\log\ G_0(ax_1, ax_2, \ldots, ax_d) = \Psi(a\mathbf{x})$$

and

$$\frac{1}{a}\left[\lim_{t \to \infty} ta\{1 - F(U_1(ta\,x_1), \ldots, U_d(ta\,x_d))\} \right]$$
$$= -\log\ G_0(x_1, x_2, \ldots, x_d) = \Psi(\mathbf{x}).$$

Therefore, a measure characterizing the distribution of $\mathbf{Z}$ in (4.27) should satisfy the homogeneity relation

$$\Psi(a\mathbf{x}) = \Psi(ax_1, ax_2, \ldots, ax_d) = \frac{1}{a}\Psi(\mathbf{x}).$$

This is particularly true in the case of the exponent measure (see, e.g., Definition 6.1.7 of de Haan and Ferreira, 2006; p. 256 of Beirlant et al., 2004). The *exponent measure* v^* is concentrated on $[0, \infty]^d \setminus \{\mathbf{0}\}$ such that

$$G_0(\mathbf{x}) = \exp(-v^*([\mathbf{0}, \infty] \setminus [\mathbf{0}, \mathbf{x}])), \quad \mathbf{x} \in [0, \infty]^d,$$

with $av^*(aB) = v^*(B)$, for all $a > 0$ and B a Borel subset of $[0, \infty]^d \setminus \{\mathbf{0}\}$. This homogeneity property suggests transformation using pseudopolar coordinates, yielding the *spectral measure H* with respect to the sum-norm L_1:

$$G_0(\mathbf{x}) = \exp\left(-d \int_\Omega \bigvee_{j=1}^d \frac{\omega_j}{x_j} H(d\mathbf{w})\right),$$

$\Omega = \{\mathbf{w} = (\omega_1, \ldots, \omega_d) : \omega_1 + \cdots + \omega_d = 1, \omega_j \geq 0, j = 1, \ldots, d\}$ the unit simplex (notation: $\vee$ stands for max), with

$$\int_\Omega \omega_j H(d\mathbf{w}) = \frac{1}{d}, \quad j = 1, \ldots, d.$$

Section 6.1.4 of de Haan and Ferreira (2006) contains results that expound a direct link between convergence in distribution and convergence of exponent measures for sequences of max-stable distributions, in the sense of closure with respect to convergence in distribution. Section 8.2.3 in Beirlant et al. (2004) is fully dedicated to the spectral measure starting from arbitrary norms. Another way of characterizing max-stable distributions is by the *stable tail dependence function*

$$l(\mathbf{x}) = \Psi\left(\frac{1}{x_1}, \ldots, \frac{1}{x_d}\right) = -\log G\left(\frac{x_1^{-\xi_1} - 1}{\xi_1}, \ldots, \frac{x_d^{-\xi_d} - 1}{\xi_d}\right).$$

The exponent measure and the stable tail dependence function are related via $l(\mathbf{x}) = v^*([\mathbf{0}, \infty] \setminus [\mathbf{0}, (1/x_1, \ldots, 1/x_d)]), \mathbf{x} \in [0, \infty]$. Here the marginal distributions are featured through their extreme value indices ξ_j. Among the properties of the function l, listed in Proposition 6.1.21 of de Haan and Ferreira (2006), we mention that $l(\mathbf{x})$ is a convex function, satisfies the homogeneity property of order 1, and is such that $\max(x_1, \ldots, x_d) \leq l(x_1, \ldots, x_n) \leq x_1 + \cdots + x_d$, for all $\mathbf{x} \in [0, \infty)$. We also note that only the bivariate $d = 2$ is straightforward in this respect (cf. p. 257 of Beirlant et al., 2004). *Pickands dependence function* is also a common tool in the bivariate context (Pickands, 1981). On the unit simplex, it is defined as

$$A(t) = \Psi\left(\frac{1}{1-t}, \frac{1}{t}\right) = l(1-t, t), \quad t \in [0, 1],$$

where l denotes again the stable dependence function. By homogeneity of the function Ψ, Pickands dependence function A completely determines the limit G_0. Important properties of the function A are that (P1) A is convex, (P2) $A(0) = A(1) = 1$, and (P3) $((1 - t) \vee t) \leq A(t) \leq 1$. Moreover, A is related with the spectral measure H via

$$A(t) = 2 \int_0^1 (\omega(1 - t) \vee (1 - \omega)t) \, H(d\omega).$$

A similar relation with respect to an arbitrary choice of norms, possibly other than the sum-norm, is given in Eq. (8.49) of Beirlant et al. (2004). The d-variate extension of Pickands dependence function also relies on the homogeneity of the tail dependence function l, entailing the restriction to the unit simplex:

$$l(x_1, \dots, x_d) = (x_1 + \cdots + x_d) A \left(\frac{x_1}{x_1 + \cdots + x_d}, \dots, \frac{x_d}{x_1 + \cdots + x_d} \right),$$

$$\mathbf{x} \in [\mathbf{0}, \infty) \backslash \{\mathbf{0}\}.$$

We now turn to conditions fulfilled by a distribution function F in the domain of attraction of a max-stable distribution G (notation: $F \in D(G)$) in the d-variate setting. In the bivariate case, Lemmas 2.2 and 2.3 of Barão et al. (2007) can be used to generate distributions which are in the domain of attraction of a multivariate extreme distribution G. An extension of the latter to higher dimension is detailed in Section 3.1 of Segers (2012). As expected at this point, MEV conditions approach the marginal distributions and the dependence structure in a separate way. In order to be prepared for applying at least one of the previous measures, we consider the random vector $\tilde{\mathbf{X}}$ with standard Pareto margins, provided the transformation

$$\tilde{\mathbf{X}} = (\tilde{X}_j)_{j=1}^d = \left(\frac{1}{1 - F_j(X_j)} \right)_{j=1}^d.$$

Denote the joint distribution function of $\tilde{\mathbf{X}}$ with $\tilde{F}$, that is, $\tilde{F}(\mathbf{x}) = F(U_1(x_1), \dots, U_d(x_d))$. If $F \in D(G)$, then the following are equivalent:

1. $\displaystyle \lim_{t \to \infty} \frac{-\log \tilde{F}(t\mathbf{x})}{-\log \tilde{F}(t\mathbf{1})} = \lim_{t \to \infty} \frac{1 - \tilde{F}(t\mathbf{x})}{1 - \tilde{F}(t\mathbf{1})} = \frac{\Psi(\mathbf{x})}{\Psi(\mathbf{1})} = \frac{v^*([\mathbf{0}, \infty] \backslash [\mathbf{0}, \mathbf{x}])}{v^*([\mathbf{0}, \infty] \backslash [\mathbf{0}, \mathbf{1}])}.$

2. For all $r > 1$,

$$\lim_{t \to \infty} tP[t^{-1} \|\tilde{\mathbf{X}}\| > r, \quad \frac{\tilde{\mathbf{X}}}{\|\tilde{\mathbf{X}}\|} \in A] = r^{-1} H(A),$$

for all continuity set A for the spectral measure H.

3. The point processes associated with the normalized random sample $(n^{-1}\tilde{\mathbf{X}}_1, \dots, n^{-1}\tilde{\mathbf{X}}_n)$ converges weakly to a nonhomogeneous point processes on $[\mathbf{0}, \infty] \backslash \{\mathbf{0}\}$ (de Haan and Resnick, 1977).

Points 1 and 2 reveal nonparametric estimation procedures in the sense that probabilities involved can be translated and replaced by their empirical analogs. The latter also entails that empirical measures are in demand. An estimator for the spectral measure is introduced by Einmahl et al. (1997). We also refer the reader to Einmahl et al. (2001) in this respect. The problem of estimating the dependence structure is tackled in depth by de Haan and Ferreira (2006) (see their Chapter 7 and references therein). Parametric estimators evolve from point 3 by means of likelihood statistical inference. In this respect we refer to Coles and Tawn (1991, 1994). Other parametric threshold estimation methods, evolving from point 1, are presented by Ledford and Tawn (1996) and Smith et al. (1997). In these works, the sum-norm L_1 is in order. Others have used the L_2 (Einmahl et al., 1993) and L_∞ (Einmahl et al., 2001) norms in nonparametric estimation. Estimation of the probability of a failure set is expounded in Chapter 8 of de Haan and Ferreira (2006). A class of corrected bias estimators for the stable tail dependence function is proposed by Fougères et al. (2014). Finite sample comparison of several estimators by means of a simulation study is laid out in Barão et al. (2007) for the bivariate case. Altogether, the class of MEV distributions, being infinite dimensional, yields modeling and statistical inference a cumbersome task in practice. When we are dealing with realizations of stochastic processes, any difficulties in this task can be aggravated, although de Haan and Ferreira (2006, p. 293) point out that the theory of infinite-dimensional extremes is quite analogous to the MEV addressed in this chapter. For a review of the existing estimation techniques for max-stable processes, see, for example, Padoan et al. (2010), Reich and Shaby (2012), Einmahl et al. (2012), and Yuen and Stoev (2014a). Within the scope of finance and actuarial applications, Yuen and Stoev (2014b) advocate the use of a specific finite-dimensional max-stable model for extreme risks, which can be effectively estimated from the data, rather than to proceed in the infinite-dimensional setting.

At the two opposite ends of the dependence spectrum of max-stable or MEV distributions are the cases of asymptotic independence and complete dependence. Here, the stable tail dependence function proves to be useful. The main advantage of the stable function l arises from the possibility of setting levels in order to get a graphical depict of the dependence structure. Setting $l(x_1, \ldots, x_d) = x_1 + \cdots + x_n$ yields independent components of the limit vector $\mathbf{Z}_0$. On the opposite end, $l(x_1, \ldots, x_d) = \max(x_1, \ldots, x_d)$ means that the d-components are the same r.v.'s. There are several accounts on that the asymptotic independence assumption fails to provide a satisfactory way to estimate joint tails using MEV distributions (see, e.g., de Haan and Ferreira, 2006; Eastoe et al., 2014). A test for independence is constructed in Genest and Rémillard (2004). A comprehensive essay on the tail dependence function intertwined with the tail copula function is the work by Gudendorf and Segers (2010). The copula function represents the dependence structure of a multivariate random vector; hence the description of extreme or tail dependence does not escape its grasp. In fact, copula theory (cf. Nelsen, 1999; Joe, 1997) and copula estimation have been extensively used in financial applications. Concerning the estimation of general copula functions, several parametric, semiparametric, and nonparametric procedures have already been proposed in the literature (see, e.g., Stute, 1984; Genest and Rivest, 1993; Genest et al., 1995). Estimation of tail-related copula has been tackled, for instance, by Huang (1992), Peng (1998), and Durrleman et al. (2000).

Further reading

A recent up-to-date review of univariate EVT and respective statistical inference can be found in Gomes and Guillou (2014). Reference books in EVT and in the field of real-world applications of EVDs and extremal domains of attraction are Embrechts et al. (2001), Beirlant et al. 2004, Coles (2001), de Haan and Ferreira (2006), David and Nagaraja (2003), Gumbel (1958), Castillo et al. (2005), and Reiss and Thomas (2007). Seminal works on MEV theory are the papers by Tiago de Oliveira (1958), Sibuya (1960), de Haan and Resnick (1977), Deheuvels (1978), and Pickands (1981). For books predicated on this subject, we refer to Resnick (1987, 2007), Coles (2001), Beirlant et al. (2004), de Haan and Ferreira (2006), and Salvadori et al. (2007). Applications of MEV theory range from environmental risk assessment (Coles and Tawn, 1991; Joe, 1994; de Haan and de Ronde, 1998; Schlather and Tawn, 2003), financial risk management (Embrechts, 2000; Longin, 1996; Longin, 2000; Longin and Solnik, 2001; Stǎricǎ, 1999; Poon et al., 2003), and Internet traffic modeling (Maulik et al., 2002; Resnick, 2002) to sports (Barão and Tawn, 1999).

Acknowledgments

This work was funded by FCT – Fundação para a Ciência e a Tecnologia, Portugal, through the project UID/MAT/00006/2013.

References

Araújo Santos, P., Fraga Alves, M.I. Forecasting value-at-risk with a duration based POT method. Mathematics and Computers in Simulation 2013;**94**:295–309.

Araújo Santos, P., Fraga Alves, I., Hammoudeh, S. High quantiles estimation with quasi-PORT and DPOT: an application to value-at-risk for financial variables. The North American Journal of Economics and Finance 2013;**26**:487–496.

Balkema, A.A., de Haan, L. Residual life time at great age. Annals of Probability 1974;**2**(5):792–804.

Barão, M.I., de Haan, L., Li, D. Comparison of estimators in multivariate EVT. International Journal of Statistics and Systems (IJSS) 2007;**2**(1):75–91.

Barão, M.I., Tawn, J.A. Extremal analysis of short series with outliers: sea-levels and athletic records. Journal of the Royal Statistical Society: Series C – Applied Statistics, 1999;**48**(4):469–487.

Beirlant, J., Goegebeur, Y., Segers, J., Teugels, J. *Statistics of Extremes: Theory and Applications*. England: John Wiley & Sons, Ltd; 2004.

Beirlant, J., Herrmann, K., Teugels, J. Estimation of the extreme value index. In: Longin, F., editor. *Extreme Events in Finance*. Berlin Heidelberg: John Wiley & Sons; 2017.

Castillo, E., Hadi, A.S., Balakrishnan, N., Sarabia, J.M. *Extreme Value and Related Models with Applications in Engineering and Science*. Hoboken (NJ): John Wiley & Sons, Inc.; 2005.

Coles, S. *An Introduction to Statistical Modeling of Extreme Values*. London: Springer-Verlag; 2001.

Coles, S.G., Tawn, J.A. Modelling extreme multivariate events. Journal of the Royal Statistical Society: Series B 1991;**53**:377–392.

Coles, S.G., Tawn, J.A. Statistical methods for multivariate extremes: an application to structural design. Applied Statistics 1994;**43**:1–48.

David, H.A., Nagaraja, H.N. *Order Statistics*. 3rd ed. Hoboken (NJ): John Wiley & Sons, Inc.; 2003.

de Haan, L. On regular variation and its application to the weak convergence of sample extremes. *Mathematical Centre Tracts 32*. Amsterdam: Mathematisch Centrum; 1970.

de Haan, L., Ferreira, A. *Extreme Value Theory - An Introduction*, Springer Series in Operations Research and Financial Engineering. New York: Springer-Verlag; 2006.

de Haan, L., Resnick, S. Limit theory for multivariate sample extremes. Z Wahrsc Verw Geb 1977;**40**:317–337.

de Haan, L., Ronde, J. Multivariate extremes at work. Extremes 1998;**1**:7–45.

de Haan, L., Klein Tank, A., Neves, C. On tail trend detection: modeling relative risk. Extremes 2015;**18**(2):141–178.

Deheuvels, P. Caractérisation complète des lois extrêmes multivariées et de la convergence des types extrêmes. Publ Inst Stat Univ Paris 1978;**23**:1–36.

Deheuvels, P. Probabilistic aspects of multivariate extremes. In: Tiago de Oliveira, J, editor. *Statistical Extremes and Applications*. Dordrecht: D. Reidel; 1984. 117–130.

Dekkers, A., Einmahl, J.H.J., de Haan, L. A moment estimator for the index of an extreme-value distribution. Ann Stat 1989;**17**(4):1833–1855.

Durrleman, V., Nikeghbali, A., Roncalli, T. Which copula is the right one? Groupe de Recherche Opérationnelle, Crédit Lyonnais, working paper; 2000.

Eastoe, E.F., Heffernan, J.E., Tawn, A.J. Nonparametric estimation of the spectral measure, and associated dependence measures, for multivariate extreme values using a limiting conditional representation. Extremes 2014;**17**:25–43.

Einmahl, J.H.J., de Haan, L., Huang, X. Estimating a multidimensional extreme-value distribution. Journal of Multivariate Analysis 1993;**47**:35–47.

Einmahl, J.H.J., de Haan, L., Piterbarg, V. Multivariate extremes estimation. Annals of Statistics 2001;**19**:1401–1423.

Einmahl, J.H.J., de Haan, L., Sinha, A.K. Estimating the spectral measure of an extreme value distribution. Stochastic Processes and their Applications 1997;**70**: 143–171.

Einmahl, J.H.J., de Haan, L., Zhou, C. Statistics of heteroscedastic extremes. J. R. Statist. Soc. B, 2017;**78**(1):31–51.

Einmahl, J.H.J., Krajina, A., Segers, J. An *M*-estimator for tail dependence in arbitrary dimension. Annals of Statistics 2012;**40**:1764–1793.

Embrechts, P., de Haan, L., Huang, X. Modelling multivariate extremes. In: Embrechts, P., editor. *Extremes and Integrated Risk Management*. London: RISK Books; 2000. 59–67.

Embrechts, P., Klüppelberg, C., Mikosch, T. *Modelling Extremal Events for Insurance and Finance*. 3rd ed. Berlin, Heidelberg: Springer-Verlag; 2001.

Fisher, R.A., Tippett, L.H.C. Limiting forms of the frequency distribution of the largest and smallest member of a sample. Proc. Camb. Philol. Soc. 1928;**24**:180–190.

Fougères, A.-L., de Haan, L., Mercadier, C. Bias correction in multivariate extremes. Working paper; 2014.

Fraga Alves, M.I. Asymptotic distribution of Gumbel statistic in a semi-parametric approach. Portugaliæ Mathematica 1999;**56**(3):282–298.

Fraga Alves, M.I., de Haan, L., Neves, C. A test procedure for detecting super-heavy tails. Journal of Statistical Planning and Inference 2009;**139**:213–227.

Fraga Alves, M.I., Gomes, M.I. Statistical choice of extreme value domains of attraction—a comparative analysis. Communications in Statistics Theory Methods 1996;**25**(4):789–811.

Fraga Alves, M.I., Neves, C. Extreme value distributions. In: Lovric, M, editor. *International Encyclopedia of Statistical Science*. Berlin Heidelberg: Springer-Verlag; 2011. 493–496.

Fraga Alves, M.I., Neves, C. Estimation of the finite right endpoint in the Gumbel domain. Statistica Sinica 2014;**24**:1811–1835.

Fréchet, M. Sur la loi de probabilité de l'écart maximum. Annales de la Société Polonaise de Mathématique 1927;**6**(printed in 1928):92–116.

Gardes, L. A general estimator for the extreme value index: applications to conditional and heteroscedastic extremes. Extremes 2015;**18**(3):479–510.

Genest, C., Ghoudi, K., Rivest, L.-P. A semiparametric estimation procedure of dependence parameters in multivariate families of distributions. Biometrika 1995;**82**:543–552.

Genest, C., Rémillard, B. Test of independence and randomness based on the empirical copula process. Test 2004;**13**:335–369.

Genest, C., Rivest, L.-P. Statistical inference procedures for bivariate archimedean copulas. Journal of the American Statistical Association 1993;**88**:1034–1043.

Gnedenko, B.V. Sur la distribution limite du terme maximum d'une série aléatoire. Annals of Mathematics 1943;**44**:423–453.

Gomes, M.I. An *i*-dimensional limiting distribution function of largest values and its relevance to the statistical theory of extremes. In: Taillie, C., Patil, G.P., Baldessari, B.A., editors. *Statistical Distributions in Scientific Work*, Dordrecht: D. Reidel; 1981;**6**:389–410.

Gomes, M.I. Comparison of extremal models through statistical choice in multidimensional backgrounds. In: Hüsler, J., Reiss, R.-D., editors. *Extreme Value Theory, Oberwolfach 1987*. Lecture Notes in Statistics. Berlin, Heidelberg: Springer-Verlag; 1989. 191–203.

Gomes, M., Alpuim, M. Inference in a multivariate generalized extreme value model—asymptotic properties of two test statistics. Scandinavian Journal of Statistics 1986;**13**:291–300.

Gomes, M.I., Caeiro, F., Henriques-Rodrigues, L., Manjunath, B.G. Bootstrap methods in statistics of extremes. In: Longin, F., editor. *Extreme Events in Finance*. John Wiley & Sons; 2017.

Gomes, M.I., Guillou, A. Extreme value theory and statistics of univariate extremes: a review. International Statistical Review 2014;**83**(2):263–292.

Gudendorf, G., Segers, J. Extreme-value copulas. In: *Copula Theory and its Applications*. **198**, Lecture Notes in Statistics. Berlin, Heidelberg: Springer-Verlag; 2010. 127–145.

Gumbel, E.J. *Statistics of Extremes*. New York: Columbia University Press; 1958.

Hill, B. A simple general approach to inference about the tail of a distribution. Annals of Statistics 1975;**3**(5):1163–1174.

Huang, X. Statistics of Bivariate Extreme Values [PhD thesis]. Tinbergen Institute Research Series, Thesis Publishers and Tinbergen Institute; 1992.

Hüsler, J., Peng, L. Review of testing issues in extremes: in honor of Professor Laurens de Haan. Extremes 2008;**11**(1):99–111.

Jenkinson, A.F. The frequency distribution of the annual maximum (or minimum) values of meteorological elements. Quarterly Journal of the Royal Meteorological Society 1955;**81**:158–171.

Joe, H. Multivariate extreme-value distributions with applications to environmental data. The Canadian Journal of Statistics 1994;**22**:47–64.

Joe, H. *Multivariate Models and Dependence Concepts*. Monographs on Statistics and Applied Probability. London: Chapman and Hall;**73** 1997.

Johnson, N.L., Balakrishnan, N., Kotz, S. *Continuous Univariate Distributions*. 2nd ed. New York: John Wiley & Sons, Inc.; 1995.

Leadbetter, M.R. Extremes under dependance: historical development and parallels with central limit theory. In: Longin, F., editor. *Extreme Events in Finance*. John Wiley & Sons; 2017.

Leadbetter, M.R., Lindgren, G., Rootzén, H. *Extremes and Related Properties of Random Sequences and Processes*. New York, Berlin: Springer-Verlag; 1983.

Leadbetter, M.R., Nandagopalan, S. On exceedance point processes for stationary sequences under mild oscillation restrictions. In: Hüsler, J., Reiss, R.-D., editor. *Extreme Value Theory*. New York: Springer-Verlag; 1989. 69–80.

Ledford, A., Tawn, J. Statistics for near independence in multivariate extreme values. Biometrika 1996;**83**:169–187.

Longin, F. The asymptotic distribution of extreme stock market returns. Journal of Business 1996;**63**:383–408.

Longin, F. From value at risk to stress testing: the extreme value approach. Journal of Banking and Finance 2000;**24**:1097–1130.

Longin, F., Solnik, B. Extreme correlation of international equity markets. Journal of Finance 2001;**56**:651–678.

Maulik, K., Resnick, S.I., Rootzén, H. Asymptotic independence and a network traffic model. Journal of Applied Probability 2002;**39**:671–699.

Nelsen, R. *An Introduction to Copulas*. Volume **139**, Lecture Notes in Statistics. New York: Springer-Verlag; 1999.

Neves, C., Fraga Alves, M.I. Semi-parametric approach to Hasofer-Wang and Greenwood statistics in extremes. Test 2006;**16**:297–313.

Neves, C., Fraga Alves, M.I. Testing extreme value conditions - an overview and recent approaches. In: Beirlant, J., Fraga Alves, M.I., Leadbetter, R., editors. *Statistics of Extremes and Related Fields*. REVSTAT - Statistical Journal, Special issue Volume **6**(1); 2008. 83–100.

Neves, C., Picek, J., Fraga Alves, M.I. The contribution of the maximum to the sum of excesses for testing max-domains of attraction. Journal of Statistical Planning and Inference 2006;**136**(4):1281–1301.

Padoan, S., Ribatet, M., Sisson, S. Likelihood-based inference for max-stable processes. Journal of the American Statistical Association 2010;**105**(489):263–277.

Peng, L. Second order condition and extreme value theory [Volume 178 of PhD thesis]. Tinbergen Institute Research Series, Thesis Publishers and Tinbergen Institute; 1998.

Pickands, J. Statistical inference using extreme order statistics. Annals of Statistics 1975;**3**:119–131.

Pickands, J. Multivariate extreme value distributions. Proceedings of the 43rd Session of the International Statistics Institute; 1981. 859–878.

Poon, S.-H., Rockinger, M., Tawn, J.A. Modelling extreme-value dependence in international stock markets. Statistica Sinica 2003;**13**:929–953.

R Development Core Team. *R: A Language and Environment for Statistical Computing*. Vienna, Austria: The R Foundation for Statistical Computing; 2011. ISBN: 3-900051-07-0. Available online at http://www.R-project.org/.

Reich, B.J., Shaby, B. A finite-dimensional construction of a max-stable process for spatial extremes. Annals of Applied Statistics 2012;**6**(4):1430–1451.

Reiss, R.-D., Thomas, M. *Statistical Analysis of Extreme Values, with Application to Insurance, Finance, Hydrology and Other Fields*. 3rd ed. Basel, Switzerland: Birkhäuser Verlag; 2007.

Resnick, S.I. *Extreme Values, Regular Variation and Point Processes*. New York: Springer-Verlag; 1987.

Resnick, S.I. Hidden regular variation, second order regular variation and asymptotic independence. Extremes 2002;**5**:303–336.

Resnick, S.I. *Heavy-Tail Phenomena: Probabilistic and Statistical Modeling*. New York: Springer-Verlag; 2007.

Salvadori, G., De Michele, C., Kottegoda, T.N., Rosso, R. *Extremes in Nature: An approach using copulas*. Volume **56**, Water Science and Technology Library. Dordrecht: Springer-Verlag; 2007.

Schlather, M., Tawn, J.A. A dependence measure for multivariate and spatial extreme values: properties and inference. Biometrika 2003;**90**:139–156.

Segers, J. Max-stable models for multivariate extremes. REVSTAT –Statistical Journal 2012;**10**(1):61–82.

Sibuya, M. Bivariate extreme statistics. Annals of the Institute of Statistical Mathematics 1960;**11**:195–210.

Smith, R.L. Extreme value theory based on the r largest annual events. Journal of Hydrology 1986;**86**:27–43.

Smith, R.L., Tawn, J.A., Coles, S.G. Markov chain models for threshold exceedances. Biometrika 1997;**84**:249–268.

Stărică, C. Multivariate extremes for models with constant conditional correlations. Journal of Empirical Finance 1999;**6**(5):515–553.

Stute, W. The oscillation behavior of empirical processes: the multivariate case. Annals of Probability 1984;**12**:361–379.

Tiago de Oliveira, J. Extremal distributions. Revista Faculdade de Ciências de Lisboa, 2 Ser. A, Mat., 1958;**2**(7):219–227.

Tsay, R. *Analysis of Financial Time Series*, Wiley Series in Probability and Statistics. Hoboken, New Jersey, USA: John Wiley & Sons; 2010.

von Mises, R. *La distribution de la plus grande de* n *valeurs*. Reprinted in *Selected Papers Volumen II*. Providence (RI): American Mathematical Society, 1954; 1936. 271–294.

Weibull, W. *A statistical theory of the strength of materials*. Ingeniors Vetenskaps Akademien, Handlingar, 1939. Vol. **151-3**, 45–55.

Weissman, I. Estimation of parameters and large quantiles based on the k largest observations. Journal of the American Statistical Association 1978;**73**:812–815.

Yuen, R., Stoev, S. CRPS M-estimation for Max-stable models. Extremes 2014a; **17**:387–410.

Yuen, R., Stoev, S. Upper bounds on value-at-risk for the maximum portfolio loss. Extremes 2014b;**17**(4):585–614.

Chapter Five

Estimation of the Extreme Value Index

Beirlant J., Herrmann K., and Teugels J.L.
Department of Mathematics and LStat, KU Leuven, Belgium

5.1 INTRODUCTION

In Chapter 4, we learned that the stochastic behavior of extremes is well known and can be modeled by the extreme value distribution. The key parameter of this distribution is the extreme value index, or tail index. In this chapter, we deal with the statistical estimation techniques of this parameter. We assume that we have a sample $(X_1, \ldots, X_n)$ of n independent identically distributed (i.i.d.) or possibly stationary, weakly dependent random variables from an underlying cumulative distribution function F, and we use the notation $X_{1,n} \leq \cdots \leq X_{n,n}$ for the order statistics. Statistical methods of univariate extremes help us to learn from disastrous or almost disastrous events of high relevance in society and with high societal impact. The recent financial crisis has shown that the field of financial statistics certainly fits into this definition. Since the work of Gumbel, summarized in his book in 1958, methodology has been based on the extremal types theorem of Gnedenko (1943). Since then, the scientific output in this field has grown significantly. It is impossible within a brief review to provide an exhaustive list of references, even when focusing on the estimation of tail parameters. Recent books that have appeared on the subject of extreme value theory and extreme value analysis are, of course, important sources of information: for example, Embrechts et al. (1997), Coles (2001), Reiss and Thomas (2001, 2007), Castillo et al. (2005), Beirlant et al. (2004), de Haan and Ferreira (2006), Fraga Alves and Neves (2017) and Resnick (2007).

We will concentrate on the case of heavy-tailed distributions, as this is most prominent in financial applications and provide the most important ideas behind the different methods of tail estimation. We illustrate the methodology explained in this review using the weekly returns R_t from an important European bank from

Extreme Events in Finance: A Handbook of Extreme Value Theory and its Applications,
First Edition. Edited by François Longin.

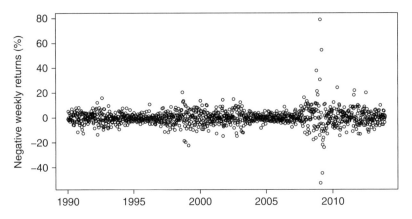

FIGURE 5.1 Negative weekly returns of a European bank from January 1990 till December 2013 (in %).

January 1990 till the end of 2013. Figure 5.1 shows the returns $-R_t$ as a function of time. We clearly see the effect of the financial crisis of 2008 with a maximum negative return of 80%.

5.2 THE MAIN LIMIT THEOREM BEHIND EXTREME VALUE THEORY

The main limiting results in extreme value theory date back to the papers by Fréchet (1927), Fisher and Tippett (1928), von Mises (1936), and Gnedenko (1943). Gnedenko's extremal types theorem provides the possible limiting behavior of the sequence of maximum or minimum values, linearly normalized. The characterization of the domains of attraction of the so-called max-stable or min-stable laws, however, was fully achieved by de Haan (1970). Here we deal only with the right tail, which means that in our case study of weekly financial returns, we are interested in the weeks with negative returns R_t, that is, with losses. We change signs and discuss the right tail of $-R_t$.

Max-stable laws are defined as laws S for which the functional equation $S^n(\alpha_n x + \beta_n) = S(x)$ $(n \geq 1)$ holds for some $\alpha_n > 0$ and real-valued β_n. More specifically, all possible nondegenerate weak limit distributions of the normalized partial maxima $X_{n,n}$ of i.i.d. random variables $X_1, \ldots, X_n$ are (generalized) *extreme value distributions*, that is, if there are normalizing constants $a_n > 0$ and b_n and some nondegenerate distribution function G such that, for all x,

$$\lim_{n \to \infty} P((X_{n,n} - b_n)/a_n \leq x) = G(x), \tag{5.1}$$

we can define the constants in such a way that

$$G(x) = G_\xi(x) := \exp\left\{-(1 + \xi x)^{-1/\xi}\right\} \quad \text{if } x > -1/\xi \tag{5.2}$$

for some real value ξ, termed *the extreme value index*, which is of prime interest in extreme value analysis. When $\xi = 0$, $G_0(x)$ is to be read as $\exp\{-\exp(-x)\}$. The form (5.2) is the so-called von Mises–Jenkinson form (von Mises (1936); Jenkinson (1955)). If (5.1) holds, we then say that F, which is underlying the data $X_1, X_2, \cdots$, is in *the max-domain of attraction* of G_ξ. The limiting distribution functions in (5.1) are then max-stable. Moreover, they are the only max-stable laws.

The extreme value index ξ governs the behavior of the right tail of F. The Fréchet domain of attraction ($\xi > 0$) contains heavy-tailed distributions like the Pareto and the Student t-distributions, that is, tails of a negative polynomial type and infinite right endpoint. Short-tailed distributions, with finite right endpoint like the beta distributions, belong to the Weibull max-domain of attraction with $\xi < 0$. Finally, the Gumbel max-domain of attraction corresponding to $\xi = 0$ contains a great variety of distributions with an exponentially decreasing tail, such as the exponential, the normal, and the gamma distributions, but not necessarily with an infinite right endpoint. An example of a distribution function in the Gumbel max-domain of attraction and with a finite right endpoint x_+ is given by $F(x) = K \exp\{-c/(x_+ - x)\}$ with $x < x_+$, $c > 0$, and $K > 0$.

Here we concentrate especially on the Fréchet domain of attraction, since in financial data positive values of the extreme value index are most prominent. However, we will also highlight the most important estimators of tail quantities that are consistent, whatever the sign of ξ may be.

5.3 CHARACTERIZATIONS OF THE MAX-DOMAINS OF ATTRACTION AND EXTREME VALUE INDEX ESTIMATORS

In order to characterize the max-domains of attraction in a mathematically correct way under the extremal types theorem, there are now two possibilities: model descriptions through the distribution function $F(x) = P(X \leq x)$ or the right tail function $\bar{F} = 1 - F$ (*probability view*), or through the quantile function Q, defined as the inverse of F (*quantile view*).

5.3.1 The Probability View: The Peaks-Over-Threshold Methodology

First, one can characterize a max-domain of attraction through the stochastic behavior of the so-called peaks over threshold (POTs) $X - t$, given that $X > t$. Pickands' (1975) theorem states that the extremal types theorem holds if and only if for some sequence $\sigma_t > 0$ the conditional distribution of the scaled excesses as $t \to x_+$ converges to *the generalized Pareto distribution* P_ξ

$$P((X - t)/\sigma_t \leq x \mid X > t) \to P_\xi(x) = 1 - (1 + \xi x)^{-1/\xi} \tag{5.3}$$

$(1 + \xi x > 0, x > 0)$. We remark here that, in case $\xi = 0$, the generalized Pareto distribution is nothing but the exponential distribution $1 - \exp(-x)$ $(x > 0)$.

From this, choosing an appropriate threshold t and hoping for a reasonable rate of convergence in (5.3), one estimates ξ and σ by fitting the generalized Pareto distribution with the survival function $\left(1 + \frac{\xi}{\sigma}x\right)^{-1/\xi}$ to the excesses $X_i - t$ for those data X_i for which $X_i > t$.

Estimation can now happen in several ways, such as maximum likelihood (Smith, 1987; Davison, 1984), method of (weighted) moments (Hosking, 1985; Hosking and Wallis, 1987), and Bayesian methods (Coles, 2001; Diebolt et al., 2005), among others.

In the specific case of the Fréchet max-domain of attraction with $\xi > 0$, the POT property can be specified using the relative POTs X/t given $X > t$. Indeed, the distributions in the max-domain of attraction with $\xi > 0$ are characterized by

$$P(X/t > x | X > t) = \frac{\bar{F}(xt)}{\bar{F}(t)} \to x^{-1/\xi} \tag{5.4}$$

with $x > 1$ as $t \to \infty$. The limit relation (5.4) is often rephrased as the regular variation property of $\bar{F}$ with index $-1/\xi$. Maximum likelihood estimation of ξ in this POT setting leads to the Hill (1975) estimator, which is a basic tool in the estimation of a positive ξ:

$$\hat{\xi}_t^H = \frac{\sum_{X_i > t} \log X_i}{\text{nr of } X_i > t} - \log t \tag{5.5}$$

or, when choosing the threshold t in a random way as one of the largest observations, say $X_{n-k,n}$,

$$\hat{\xi}_{k,n}^H = \frac{1}{k} \sum_{i=1}^{k} \log X_{n-i+1,n} - \log X_{n-k,n}. \tag{5.6}$$

The use of random thresholds $(X_{n-i+1,n} - X_{n-k,n}; i = 1, \ldots, k)$ has been generalized to real-valued ξ cases by Drees et al. (2004) for the maximum likelihood approach, by Diebolt et al. (2007), de Haan and Ferreira (2006), and Caeiro and Gomes (2011) for the probability weighted moments technique.

5.3.2   The Quantile View

Second, through the work of de Haan (1970, 1984), the max-domain of attraction characterization based on the regular varying behavior of the *tail function U* appeared. *U* is associated with the quantile function Q by $U(x) := Q(1 - \frac{1}{x})$. The max-domains of attraction can indeed be characterized by the *extended regular variation property*, specifying the difference between high quantiles corresponding to tail proportions that differ by $100x\%$:

$$F \text{ is in the max-domain of attraction } (\xi) \iff \lim_{u \to \infty} \frac{U(ux) - U(u)}{a(u)} = \frac{x^\xi - 1}{\xi}$$
$$(5.7)$$

for every real-valued x and some positive function a, and where the limit of expression on the right equals $\log x$ for $\xi = 0$.

As many estimators are written in terms of the logarithms of the data, one needs also a $\log U$ version of (5.7):

$$\lim_{u \to \infty} \frac{\log U(ux) - \log U(u)}{a(u)/U(u)} = \log x \quad \text{if } \xi \geq 0, \text{ and } (x^\xi - 1)/\xi \text{ if } \xi < 0. \quad (5.8)$$

5.3.2.1 Estimation of a positive extreme value index

In the specific case of the Fréchet max-domain of attraction with $\xi > 0$, the extended regular variation property corresponds to classical regular variation of U with index $\xi > 0$:

$$F \text{ is in max-domain of attraction with } \xi > 0 \iff \lim_{u \to \infty} \frac{U(ux)}{U(u)} = x^\xi. \quad (5.9)$$

The Hill estimator $\hat{\xi}_{k,n}^H$ can now also be written from a quantile point of view. Indeed, it can be written as the average of the scaled log-spacings $U_i = i$ $\log\left(\frac{X_{n-i+1,n}}{X_{n-i,n}}\right)$ or of log-excesses $V_{i,k} = \log\left(\frac{X_{n-i+1,n}}{X_{n-k,n}}\right)$, $1 \leq i \leq k < n$.
The Hill (1975) estimator can also be obtained from the Pareto QQ-plot

$$(\log((n+1)/i), \log X_{n-i+1,n}), \ i = 1, \dots, n \quad (5.10)$$

as the slope of the least squares regression line based on the highest k points in the QQ-plot and passing through the point $(\log((n+1)/(k+1)), \log X_{n-k,n})$ (Beirlant et al., 1996a). More flexible regression methods can be applied to this setting as proposed, for instance, in Beirlant et al. (1996a), Schultze and Steinebach (1996), Kratz and Resnick (1996), Csörgő and Viharos (1998), and Oliveira et al. (2006).

Based on the interpretation of $\xi > 0$ as the slope of the right end of a Pareto QQ-plot, it appears natural to plot those estimators as a function of $\log k$ rather than k. This idea was worked out in detail in Drees et al. (2000) for the case of the Hill estimator.

A more general class of estimators for a positive ξ was introduced in Csörgő et al. (1985), given by

$$\frac{\sum_{i=1}^n K(i/(n\lambda))U_i}{\sum_{i=1}^n K(i/(n\lambda))}$$

with some bandwidth parameter $\lambda > 0$ and K a nonnegative, non-increasing kernel defined on $(0, \infty)$ and with unit integral.

5.3.2.2 Estimation of a real-valued extreme value index

Based on (5.7), several classes of estimators were proposed for real-valued ξ:
Pickands-type estimators. Pickands (1975) proposed

$$\hat{\xi}^P_{k,n} = \log\{(X_{n-[k/4]+1,n} - X_{n-[k/2]+1,n})/(X_{n-[k/2]+1,n} - X_{n-k+1,n})\}/\log 2, \quad (5.11)$$

where $[x]$ denotes the integer part of x. The large variance of the Pickands (1975) estimator has motivated different generalizations of the type

$$-\log\{(X_{n-[\theta^2 k]+1,n} - X_{n-[\theta k]+1,n})/(X_{n-[\theta k]+1,n} - X_{n-k+1,n})\}/\log\theta,$$

(Fraga Alves, 1995; Yun, 2002). Drees (1995) considered linear combinations of Pickands-type estimators, while Segers (2005) considered a generalization that includes all previously known variants.

The moment estimator. Dekkers et al. (1989) considered the moments

$$M^{(j)}_{k,n} = \frac{1}{k}\sum_{i=1}^{k} V^j_{i,k}, \quad j \geq 1,$$

leading to the moment estimator

$$\hat{\xi}^M_{k,n} = M^{(1)}_{k,n} + 1 - \frac{1}{2}\left(1 - \frac{(M^{(1)}_{k,n})^2}{M^{(2)}_{k,n}}\right)^{-1}. \quad (5.12)$$

The mixed moment estimator. Fraga Alves et al. (2009) introduced an alternative, termed the mixed moment estimator, involving not only the log-excesses but also another type of moment statistics defined by

$$\hat{\phi}_{k,n} = \left(M^{(1)}_{k,n} - L^{(1)}_{k,n}\right)\Big/\left(L^{(1)}_{k,n}\right)^2$$

with $L^{(1)}_{k,n} = \frac{1}{k}\sum_{i=1}^{k}\left(1 - \frac{X_{n-k,n}}{X_{n-i+1,n}}\right)$:

$$\hat{\xi}^{MM}_{k,n} = \frac{\hat{\phi}_{k,n} - 1}{1 + 2\min\{\hat{\phi}_{k,n} - 1, 0\}}. \quad (5.13)$$

Estimators based on generalized quantiles. Beirlant et al. (1996b) proposed to replace $X_{n-i+1,n}$ by $X_{n-i+1,n}\hat{\xi}^H_{i-1,n}$ $(1 \leq i \leq k)$ in the basic components of the Hill estimator in order to arrive at graphs and estimators that are consistent in case of a real-valued ξ. A generalized Pareto QQ-plot is then defined as

$$(\log((n+1)/i), \log(X_{n-i+1,n}\hat{\xi}^H_{i-1,n})), \quad i = 1, \ldots, n, \quad (5.14)$$

from which slope estimators can be developed for a general ξ. In that sense, one can also consider generalized scaled log-spacings and log-excesses.

Other estimators.

- Falk (1995) proposed the location-invariant estimator

$$\frac{1}{k} \sum_{i=1}^{k-1} \log\{(X_{n,n} - X_{n-i,n})/(X_{n,n} - X_{n-k,n})\}$$

  as a complement of the POT maximum likelihood approach with random threshold $X_{n-k,n}$ for $\xi > -1/2$. Such an estimator has been improved on the basis of an iterative procedure in Hüsler and Müller (2005).

- Matthys and Beirlant (2003) proposed to generalize the scaled log-spacings U_i defined in the estimation of a positive ξ toward

$$i \log \frac{X_{n-i+1,n} - X_{n-k,n}}{X_{n-i,n} - X_{n-k,n}}, \quad 1 \le i \le k < n$$

  in order to obtain location-invariant estimators.

- The non-invariance for shifts of the Hill estimator led Fraga Alves (2001) to consider, with k_0 appropriately chosen, the location-invariant Hill-type estimator

$$\frac{1}{k_0} \sum_{i=1}^{k_0} \log \frac{X_{n-i+1,n} - X_{n-k,n}}{X_{n-k_0+1,n} - X_{n-k,n}}, \quad k > k_0.$$

- Drees (1998) considered a general class of estimators based on arbitrarily smooth functionals of the empirical tail quantile function $Q_n(t) = X_{n-[k_n t],n}$ ($t \in [0, 1]$), including Hill, Pickands, and regression estimators.

- Kernel estimators for a real-valued ξ are considered in Groeneboom et al. (2003).

5.4 CONSISTENCY AND ASYMPTOTIC NORMALITY OF THE ESTIMATORS

Weak consistency of any of the aforementioned estimators of ξ is achieved in the subdomain of the max-domain of attraction where they are valid, whenever (5.7) holds and k is intermediate, that is, $k = k_n \to \infty$ as $n \to \infty$ and $k/n \to 0$. In order to guarantee asymptotic normality, one needs a second-order condition refining (5.7), through which one can specify the rate of convergence in (5.7). Here, one leaves the universality that is present in the characterization of max-domains of attraction, and hence in practice such a second-order condition should not be taken for granted.

It is common, however, to assume the existence of a function A^*, not changing in sign and tending to 0 as $u \to \infty$, such that

$$\lim_{u \to \infty} \frac{\frac{U(ux)-U(u)}{a(u)} - \frac{x^\xi - 1}{\xi}}{A^*(u)} = \frac{1}{\rho^*} \left(\frac{x^{\xi+\rho^*} - 1}{\xi + \rho^*} - \frac{x^\xi - 1}{\xi} \right), \tag{5.15}$$

where $\rho^* < 0$ is a second-order parameter describing the speed of convergence of maximum values, linearly normalized, toward the limit law in (5.7). Then, $\lim_{u \to \infty} A^*(ux)/A^*(u) = x^{\rho^*}$ $(x > 0)$. Similar expressions exist in case $\rho^* = 0$. For more details, see de Haan and Ferreira (2006).

For heavy tails $\xi > 0$, the second-order condition is usually written as

$$\lim_{u \to \infty} \frac{\log U(ux) - \log U(u) - \xi \log x}{A(u)} = \frac{x^\rho - 1}{\rho}, \qquad (5.16)$$

where $\rho \leq 0$ and $A(u) \to 0$ as $u \to \infty$.

With T denoting any of the above estimators of ξ, under (5.15), or (5.16) in case $\xi > 0$, one can then state asymptotic normality of $\hat{\xi}_{k,n}^T$: with $B(u)$, a bias function converging to 0 as $u \to \infty$, which is closely related with the A^* function in (5.15), it is possible to guarantee the existence of constants b_T and $\sigma_T > 0$, such that

$$\hat{\xi}_{k,n}^T =_d \xi + \sigma_T P_k^T / \sqrt{k} + b_T B(n/k) + o_p(B(n/k)) \qquad (5.17)$$

with P_k^T an asymptotically standard normal random variable. Consequently, for values k such that $\sqrt{k}B(n/k) \to \lambda$, finite, as $n \to \infty$

$$\sqrt{k}\left(\hat{\xi}_{k,n}^T - \xi\right) \to_d \mathcal{N}(\lambda b_T, \sigma_T^2). \qquad (5.18)$$

The values b_T and σ_T^2 are usually called the asymptotic bias and asymptotic variance of $\hat{\xi}_{k,n}^T$, respectively. Details on the values of (b_T, σ_T^2) and the function B are given in the papers associated with the estimators.

5.5 SECOND-ORDER REDUCED-BIAS ESTIMATION

In general, the above-mentioned extreme value index estimators have a high asymptotic bias for a large range of k values, including the optimal k in the sense of minimal mean squared error. Accommodation of bias has been considered recently in a number of papers. This line of research was started by Peng (1998), Beirlant et al. (1999), and Feuerverger and Hall (1999) based on log-excesses and on scaled log-spacings in the case of a Pareto-type distribution. Gomes et al. (2000) considered the use of the generalized jackknife methodology from Gray and Schucany (1972). Such estimators, termed *second-order reduced-bias* estimators, have an asymptotic mean 0 instead of the value λb_T in (5.18), whatever the value of λ. However, the asymptotic variance increases typically compared to the corresponding asymptotic variance σ_T^2 of the original biased estimator.

A first set of second-order reduced-bias estimators was obtained by Beirlant et al. (1999) and Feuerverger and Hall (1999) with $\rho < 0$, and $A(u) = \xi\beta u^\rho$ (with β a real-valued constant) in (5.16) using the approximation

$$U_i \approx (\xi + A(n/k)(i/(k+1))^{-\rho})E_i, \quad 1 \leq i \leq k \qquad (5.19)$$

or

$$U_i \approx \xi \exp \left(\xi^{-1} A(n/k)(i/(k+1))^{-\rho} \right) E_i, \quad 1 \le i \le k, \tag{5.20}$$

where E_i denotes a sequence of independent, standard exponentially distributed random variables. For each k, models (5.19) and (5.20) can be considered as non-linear regression models in which one can estimate the intercept ξ, the slope β, and the power $-\rho$ with the covariate i/k. This can done jointly as in the original 1999 papers, or by using external parameters for ρ, or by using external estimation for ρ and β. Gomes et al. (2008) found that external estimation of β and ρ should be based on k_1 extreme order statistics, where $k = o(k_1)$ and $\hat{\rho} - \rho = o_p(1/\log n)$. Such an estimator for ρ was presented, for instance, in Fraga Alves et al. (2003). Given an estimator for ρ, an estimator for β follows by linear regression as in Beirlant et al. (2002) or as in Gomes and Martins (2002) by

$$\hat{\beta}_{k,n}^{\hat{\rho}} = \left(\frac{k}{n}\right)^{\hat{\rho}} \frac{\left(\frac{1}{k}\sum_{i=1}^k (i/k)^{-\hat{\rho}}\right)\hat{C}_0 - \hat{C}_1}{\left(1k\sum_{i=1}^k (i/k)^{-\hat{\rho}}\right)\hat{C}_1 - \hat{C}_2}, \quad \hat{C}_j = \frac{1}{k}\sum_{i=1}^k (i/k)^{-j\hat{\rho}} U_i.$$

When the three parameters are jointly estimated for each k, the asymptotic variance turns out to be $\xi^2((1-\rho)/\rho)^4$, which is to be compared with the asymptotic variance ξ^2 for the Hill estimator.

When a linear regression is performed on (5.19) importing an external estimator for ρ, the asymptotic variance drops down to $\xi^2((1-\rho)/\rho)^2$.

Finally, when both β and ρ are externally estimated, the following estimator can be easily deduced from (5.19):

$$\hat{\xi}_{k,n}^{\mathrm{MVRB}}(\hat{\beta}_{k_1},\hat{\rho}_{k_1}) := \hat{\xi}_{k,n}^H \left(1 - \hat{\beta}_{k_1}(n/k)^{\hat{\rho}_{k_1}}/(1-\hat{\rho}_{k_1})\right) \tag{5.21}$$

and for this estimator the bias is decreased without increasing the variance, which equals the variance ξ^2 of the Hill estimator $\hat{\xi}_{k,n}^H$. Such estimators are termed *minimum-variance reduced-bias* (MVRB) estimators. One should remark, however, that third-order regular variation conditions are needed to obtain such results, thereby reducing the original extremal types theorem's universality even further.

Other second-order reduced-bias estimators can be obtained using the generalized jackknife (GJ) from Gray and Schucany (1972) as demonstrated in Gomes et al. (2000, 2002). If the second-order condition (5.16) holds, we can easily find two statistics $\hat{\xi}_{k,n}^{(j)}$ for both of which (5.17) holds. The ratio between the dominant components of the bias of $\hat{\xi}_{k,n}^{(1)}$ and $\hat{\xi}_{k,n}^{(2)}$ is $q = b_1/b_2 = q(\rho)$, and we get the GJ estimator

$$\hat{\xi}_{k,n}^{\mathrm{GJ}} = (\hat{\xi}_{k,n}^{(1)} - q(\rho)\hat{\xi}_{k,n}^{(2)})/(1 - q(\rho)).$$

For a second-order reduced-bias estimator of a positive extreme value index based on the POT approach in the probability view, we refer to Beirlant et al. (2009). Here one uses the *extended Pareto distribution*

$$G_{\xi,\delta,\tau}(y) = 1 - \{y(1+\delta - \delta y^\tau)\}^{-1/\xi}.$$

Second-order reduced-bias estimation of a real-valued extreme value index has received much less attention. We can refer to Beirlant et al. (2005) based on generalized quantiles methodology, to Matthys and Beirlant (2003) for regression models based on location-invariant spacings, and to Cai et al. (2013) for ξ around 0 for the probability-weighted moments approach.

However, a serious warning is in order. A proper use of all of the above second-order reduced-bias and MVRB techniques is guaranteed only in case $\rho < 0$. The characteristics involved in these techniques typically deteriorate when ρ approaches 0. The example given in Figure 4.1.13 in Embrechts et al. (1997) illustrates this clearly.

5.6   CASE STUDY

The Pareto QQ-plot from (5.10) given in Figure 5.2 for the negative weekly returns clearly shows an upward linear trend due to the 2009 crisis, which starts at the 15th largest observation. This is confirmed by fitting a line with the slope equal to the corresponding Hill estimate $\hat{\xi}^H_{n-15,n} = 0.553$. The plot of the Hill estimates as a function of $\log k$ in Figure 5.3 indeed shows a rather stable behavior around 0.5 for $\log k \leq 5$, while for larger values of k a smaller extreme value index appears. The two regimes are confirmed in Figure 5.4, which shows the Hill estimates, the maximum likelihood POT estimates, and reduced-bias estimates by the joint estimation of (ξ, A, ρ) in (5.19). Based on the reduced-bias version, two ξ values, one near 0.4 and the other near 0.5, seem possible.

The impact on the data from September 2008 onward clearly shows in Figures 5.5 and 5.6, where a similar analysis is shown with the data stopped at

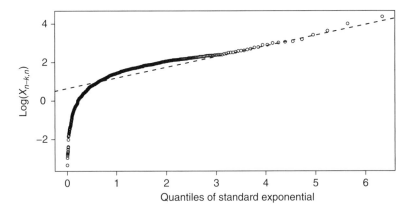

FIGURE 5.2 Pareto QQ-plot (5.10) of the negative weekly returns with regression line anchored in $\log(X_{n-15,n})$ with slope $\hat{\xi}^H_{n-15,n} = 0.553$.

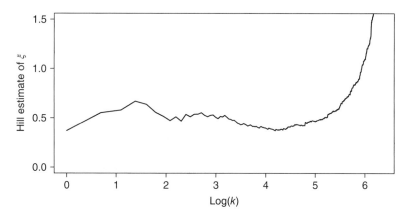

FIGURE 5.3 **Hill estimates for the negative weekly returns as a function of** **log** k.

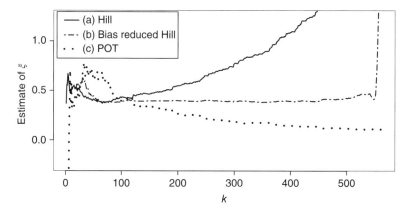

FIGURE 5.4 **Hill (full line), reduced-bias Hill (dash dotted line), and POT** **maximum likelihood (dotted line) estimates for the negative weekly returns** **as a function of** k.

the end of August 2008. In Figure 5.5, the Hill and the maximum likelihood POT estimates show much different pictures. The Hill estimates are constantly decreasing with decreasing value of k, indicating a nonlinear behavior of the Pareto QQ-plot and illustrating that Pareto-type modeling is inappropriate here. The POT values confirm this with even slightly negative values of ξ. A value of the extreme value index near 0 is also confirmed by the generalized Pareto QQ-plot (4.14) in Figure 5.6, which indicates an almost horizontal behavior for increasing values of $\log((n + 1)/i)$. We can conclude that the impact of the returns

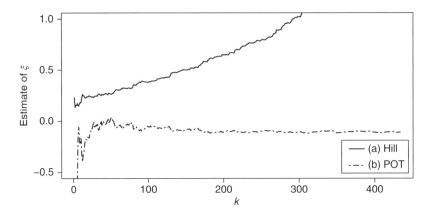

FIGURE 5.5 Hill (full line) and POT maximum likelihood (dash dotted line) estimates based on the negative weekly returns up to August 2008.

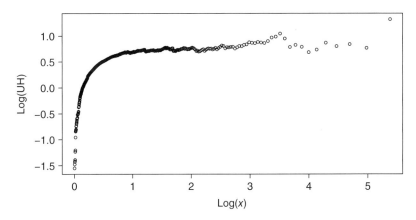

FIGURE 5.6 Generalized Pareto QQ-plot (5.14) based on the negative weekly returns up to August 2008.

during the crisis is quite large, and that during that period a different regime was attained.

5.7   OTHER TOPICS AND COMMENTS

5.7.1   Adaptive Selection of the Sample Fraction k or Threshold t

The choice of the threshold t in the POT approach or, equivalently, of the number k of top-order statistics to be used is an important topic in practice. It is of the same importance as the problem of adaptive choice of the bandwidth in nonparametric density estimation. Reduced-bias estimators help to stabilize the plots and weaken this problem. Choosing k or t can be viewed as a dual problem to bias reduction, and some methods have been based on the models forming the basis of bias reduction techniques. Almost all papers look for threshold values that minimize the asymptotic mean-squared error following from (5.17). We can refer here to Hall and Welsh (1985), Hall (1990), Jansen and de Vries (1991), Beirlant et al. (1996a, 1999, 2002), Drees and Kaufmann (1998), Danielsson et al. (2001), Gomes and Oliveira (2001), Csörgő and Viharos (1998), Guillou and Hall (2001), and Gomes et al. (2008). A numerical comparison between these techniques is provided in Matthys and Beirlant (2000).

5.7.2 Estimation of Other Tail Parameters

The estimation of the extreme value index is quite often only a step toward the estimation of the even more important tail characteristics, such as high quantile or value-at-risk estimation, and the estimation of other risk measures. From the quantile view, estimators of a quantile $Q(1 - p) = U(1/p) = VaR_p$ with p small can be easily derived from (5.7) through the approximation

$$U(ux) \approx U(u) + a(u)(x^\xi - 1)/\xi.$$

If one takes $u = n/k$, and since $X_{n-k+1} \sim U(n/k)$, one obtains estimators for extreme quantiles using estimators for ξ and $a(n/k)$. In the specific case of Pareto-type tails based on (5.9) taking $ux = 1/p$ and $u = n/k$, one obtains the estimator for $U(1 - p)$:

$$\hat{U}(1/p) = X_{n-k,n}(k/(np))^{\hat{\xi}}.$$

This type of estimator was proposed by Weissman (1978) using the Hill estimator for $\xi > 0$. More references can be found in the monographs mentioned in the introduction. For reduced-bias estimators in this context, see Matthys et al. (2004) and Gomes and Pestana (2007).

Inverting the preceding quantile estimators leads to estimators for probabilities of exceedances of a high level v. Such estimators can also be derived using the POT approach starting from (5.3)

$$P(X > t + x\sigma) \approx P(X > t)(1 + \xi x)^{-1/\xi}.$$

Setting $t + x\sigma = v$ and using appropriate POT estimates for ξ and σ leads to estimators of the type

$$\hat{p}_v = \frac{(\text{nr of data} > t)}{n}\left(1 + \hat{\xi}\left(\frac{v - t}{\hat{\sigma}}\right)\right)^{-1/\hat{\xi}}.$$

In the specific case of the Fréchet max-domain of attraction with $\xi > 0$ based on (5.4), we find then

$$\hat{p}_v = \frac{(\text{nr of data} > t)}{n}\left(\frac{v}{t}\right)^{-1/\hat{\xi}}.$$

5.7.3   Dependent Frameworks

Evidently, dependent frameworks with local dependence conditions for station-ary sequences are important for extreme value index estimation in a financial data setting, especially when treating high-frequency data. Here, the framework intro-duced in Leadbetter et al. (1983) is of major importance. Under appropriate local dependence conditions, the limiting distribution of the maximum $X_{n,n}$ of the sta-tionary sequence can be directly related to the maximum $Y_{n,n}$ of an i.i.d. associated sequence through the *extremal index* θ: for every $\tau > 0$, one may find a sequence of levels $u_n = u_n(\tau)$ such that

$$P(Y_{n,n} \leq u_n) \to_{n \to \infty} e^{-\tau} \text{ and } P(X_{n,n} \leq u_n) \to_{n \to \infty} e^{-\theta\tau}.$$

Concerning the value-at-risk estimation for dependent data, we can refer to Drees (2003). For more details, see Leadbetter (2017).

5.7.4   Robustness and Extremes

In the last few decades, some papers have appeared concerning robust estimation methods. Robust methods can improve the quality of extreme value data analysis by providing information on influential observations, deviating substructures, and possible misspecification of a model while guaranteeing good statistical properties over a whole set of underlying distributions around the assumed one. On the other hand, one performs an extreme value analysis just to consider and emphasize the role of extremes. Hence, in a risk management context it can hardly be the pur-pose to delete the most extreme observations when they were correctly reported. It is recommended to compare robust and non-robust estimators, which then yield different scenarios in risk assessment. An interesting discussion on this can be found in Dell'Aquila and Embrechts (2006), while more technicalities are found in Dupuis and Victoria-Feser (2006), Peng and Welsh (2001), Finkelstein et al. (2006), Brazauskas and Serfling (2000), Beran and Schell (2012), and Dierckx et al. (2013).

5.7.5   The Bayesian Approach

In Section 3.1, we mentioned Bayesian estimation methods as an alternative to obtaining estimates for the extreme value index. Markov-chain Monte Carlo meth-ods have been applied in an extreme value analysis context. However, it is also worthwhile importing a priori expert information in an extreme value analysis exercise. A nice review paper on this can be found in Coles and Powell (1996).

5.7.6   Bounded Versus Unbounded Distributions

For applications in risk management, there may be practical problems with the Pareto distribution because positive probabilities can still be assigned to loss amounts that are unreasonably large or even physically impossible. For instance, a gross loss return larger than 100% is impossible. Also, interest rates are bounded. In other situations, the true maximum possible loss may not be easily determined. In Aban et al. (2006), a generalization of the Hill estimator is proposed so as to include the possibility of using a truncated Pareto distribution. In Beirlant et al. (2016), appropriate statistical modeling and extreme quantile estimators are provided. Starting from a Pareto-distributed random variable W and considering the conditional distribution X of W given $W < \tau$ for some high truncation point τ, that is,

$$P(X > x) = \frac{P(W > x) - P(W > \tau)}{1 - P(W > \tau)}, \quad x < \tau,$$

the adaptation of the Hill estimator is defined as the solution of the following equation in ξ:

$$\hat{\xi}_{k,n}^{H} = \xi + \frac{R_{k,n}^{1/\xi} \log R_{k,n}}{1 - R_{k,n}^{1/\xi}},$$

where $R_{k,n} = X_{n-k,n}/X_{n,n}$.

References

Aban, I.B., Meerschaert, M.M., Panorska, A.K. Parameter estimation for the truncated Pareto distribution. J Am Stat Assoc 2006;**101**:270–277.

Beirlant, J., Alves, M.I., Gomes, M.I. Tail fitting for truncated and non-truncated Pareto-type distributions; Extremes 2017; doi:10.1007/s10687-016-0247-3.

Beirlant, J., Dierckx, G., Goegebeur, Y., Matthys, G. Tail index estimation and an exponential regression model. Extremes 1999;**2**:157–180.

Beirlant, J., Dierckx, G., Guillou, A. Estimation of the extreme-value index and generalized quantile plots. Bernoulli 2005;**11**:949–970.

Beirlant, J., Dierckx, G., Guillou, A., Starica, C. On exponential representations of log-spacings of extreme order statistics. Extremes 2002;**5**:257–180.

Beirlant, J., Goegebeur, Y., Teugels, J., Segers, J. *Statistics of Extremes: Theory and Applications*. UK: John Wiley & Sons, Ltd; 2004.

Beirlant, J., Joossens, E., Segers, J. Second-order refined peaks-over-threshold modelling for heavy-tailed distributions. J Stat Plann Inference 2009;**139**:2800–2815.

Beirlant, J., Vynckier, P., Teugels, J. Tail index estimation, Pareto quantile plots and regression diagnostics. J Am Stat Assoc 1996a;**91**:1659–1667.

Beirlant, J., Vynckier, P., Teugels, J.L. Excess functions and estimation of the extreme-value index. Bernoulli 1996b;**2**:293–318.

Beran, J., Schell, D. On robust tail index estimation. Comput Stat Data Anal 2012;**56**:3430–3443.

Brazauskas, V., Serfling, R. Robust and efficient estimation of the tail index of a single-parameter Pareto disribution. North Am Actuar J 2000;**4**:12–27.

Caeiro, F., Gomes, M.I. Semi-parametric tail inference through probability weighted moments. J Stat Plann Inference 2011;**141**:937–950.

Cai, J., de Haan, L., Zhou, C. Bias correction in extreme value statistics with index around zero. Extremes 2013;**16**:173–201.

Castillo, E., Hadi, A., Balakrishnan, N., Sarabia, J.M. *Extreme Value and Related Models with Applications in Engineering and Science*. Hoboken (NJ): John Wiley & Sons, Inc.; 2005.

Coles, S.G. *An Introduction to Statistical Modelling of Extreme Values*, Springer Series in Statistics. London: Springer-Verlag; 2001.

Coles, S.G., Powell, E.A. Bayesian methods in extreme value modelling: a review and new developments. Int Stat Rev 1996;**64**:119–136.

Csörgő, S., Deheuvels, P., Mason, D. Kernel estimates of the tail index of a distribution. Ann Stat 1985;**13**:1050–1077.

Csörgő, S., Viharos, L. Estimating the tail index. In: Szyszkowicz, B., editor. *Asymptotic Methods in Probability and Statistics*. Amsterdam: North-Holland; 1998. p 833–881.

Danielsson, J., de Haan, L., Peng, L., de Vries, C.G. Using a bootstrap method to choose the sample fraction in the tail index estimation. J Multivariate Anal 2001;**76**:226–248.

Davison, A. Modeling excesses over high threshold with an application. In: Tiago de Oliveira, J., editor. *Statistical Extremes and Applications*. Dordrecht, Holland: D. Reidel; 1984. p 461–482.

de Haan, L. *On Regular Variation and its Applications to the Weak Convergence of Sample Extremes*, Mathematical Centre Tract 32. Amsterdam: North-Holland; 1970.

de Haan, L. Slow variation and characterization of domains of attraction. In: de Oliveira, T, editor. *Statistical Extremes and Applications*. Dordrecht, Holland: D., Reidel; 1984. p 31–48.

de Haan, L., Ferreira, A. *Extreme Value Theory: an Introduction*. New York: Springer Science and Business Media, LLC; 2006.

Dekkers, A., Einmahl, J., de Haan, L. A moment estimator for the index of an extreme-value distribution. Ann Stat 1989;**17**:1795–1832.

Dell'Aquila, R., Embrechts, P. Extremes and robustness: a contradiction? Fin. Markets Portfolio Mgmt. 2006;**20**:103–118.

Diebolt, J., El-Aroui, M.A., Garrido, M., Girard, S. Quasi-conjugate Bayes estimates for generalized Pareto distribution parameters and application to heavy tail modeling. Extremes 2005;**8**:57–78.

Diebolt, J., Guillou, A., Rached, I. Approximation of the distribution of excesses through a generalized probability-weighted moments method. J Stat Plann Inference 2007;**137**:841–857.

Dierckx, G., Goegebeur, Y., Guillou, A. An asymptotically unbiased minimum density power divergence estimator for the Pareto-tail index. J Multivariate Anal 2013;**121**:70–86.

Drees, H. Refined Pickands estimator of the extreme value index. Ann Stat 1995;**23**:2059–2080.

Drees, H. A general class of estimators of the extreme value index. J Stat Plann Inference 1998;**66**:95–112.

Drees, H. Extreme quantile estimation for dependent data with applications to finance. Bernoulli 2003;**9**:617–657.

Drees, H., de Haan, L., Resnick, S. How to make a Hill plot. Ann Stat 2000;**28**: 254–274.

Drees, H., Ferreira, A., de Haan, L. On maximum likelihood estimation of the extreme value index. Ann Appl Probab 2004;**14**:1179–1201.

Drees, H., Kaufmann, E. Selecting the optimal sample fraction in univariate extreme value estimation. Stoch Proc Appl 1998;**75**:149–172.

Dupuis, D.J., Victoria-Feser, M.P. A robust prediction error criterion for Pareto modelling of upper tails. Can J Stat 2006;**34**:639–658.

Embrechts, P., Klüppelberg, C., Mikosch, T. *Modelling Extremal Events for Insurance and Finance*. Berlin, Heidelberg: Springer-Verlag; 1997.

Falk, M. Some best parameter estimates for distributions with finite endpoint. Statistics 1995;**27**:115–125.

Feuerverger, A., Hall, P. Estimating a tail exponent by modelling departure from a Pareto distribution. Ann Stat 1999;**27**:760–781.

Finkelstein, M., Tucker, H.G., Veeh, J.A. Pareto tail index estimation revisited. North Am Actuar J 2006;**10**:1–10.

Fisher, R.A., Tippett, L.H.C. Limiting forms of the frequency of the largest and smallest member of a sample. Math Proc Cambridge Philos Soc 1928;**24**:180–190.

Fraga Alves, M.I. Estimation of the tail parameter in the domain of attraction of an extremal distribution. J Stat Plann Inference 1995;**45**:143–173.

Fraga Alves, M.I. A location invariant Hill-type estimator. Extremes 2001;**4**:199–217.

Fraga Alves, M.I., Gomes, M.I., de Haan, L. A new class of semi-parametric estimators of the second order parameter. Port Math 2003;**60**:193–214.

Fraga Alves, M.I., Gomes, M.I., de Haan, L., Neves, C. The mixed moment estimator and location invariant alternatives. Extremes 2009;**12**:149–185.

Fraga Alves, M.I., Neves, C. Extreme value theory: an introductory overview. In: Longin, F., editor. *Extreme Events in Finance*. John Wiley & Sons; 2017.

Fréchet, M. Sur la loi de probabilité de l'écart maximum. Ann Soc Polon Math 1927;**6**:93–116.

Gnedenko, B.V. Sur la distribution limite du terme maximum d'une série aléatoire. Ann Math Stat 1943;**44**:423–453.

Gomes, M.I., de Haan, L., Henriques-Rodrigues, L. Tail index estimation for heavy-tailed models: accomodation of bias in weighted log-excesses. J R Stat Soc Ser B 2008;**70**:31–52.

Gomes, M.I., Martins, M.J. Asymptotically unbiased estimators of the tail index based on external estimation of the second order parameter. Extremes 2002;**5**:5–31.

Gomes, M.I., Martins, M.J., Neves, M. Alternatives to a semi-parametric estimator of parameters of rare events—the Jackknife methodology. Extremes 2000;**3**:207–229.

Gomes, M.I., Martins, M.J., Neves, M. Generalized Jackknife semi-parametric estimators of the tail index. Port Math 2002;**59**:393–408.

Gomes, M.I., Oliveira, O. The bootstrap methodology in Statistics of Extremes: choice of the optimal sample fraction. Extremes 2001;**4**:331–358.

Gomes, M.I., Pestana, D. A sturdy reduced-bias extreme quantile (VaR) estimator. J Am Stat Assoc 2007;**102**:280–292.

Gray, H.L., Schucany, W.R. *The Generalized Jackknife Statistic*. New York: Dekker; 1972.

Groeneboom, P., Lopuhaa, H., de Wolf, P. Kernel-type estimators for the extreme value index. Ann Stat 2003;**31**:1956–1995.

Guillou, A., Hall, P. A diagnostic for selecting the threshold in extreme-value analysis. J R Stat Soc Ser B 2001;**63**:293–305.

Hall, P. Using the bootstrap to estimate mean squared error and selecting smoothing parameter in nonparametric problems. J Multivariate Anal 1990;**32**:177–203.

Hall, P., Welsh, A.H. Adaptative estimates of parameters of regular variation. Ann Stat 1985;**13**:331–341.

Hill, B.M. A simple general approach about the tail of a distribution. Ann Stat 1975;**3**:1163–1174.

Hosking, J.R.M. Algorithm AS 215: maximum likelihood estimation of the parameters of the extreme value distribution. J R Stat Soc Ser C Appl Stat 1985;**34**:301–310.

Hosking, J.R.M, Wallis, J.R. Parameter and quantile estimation for the generalized Pareto distribution. Technometrics 1987;**27**:251–261.

Hüsler, J., Müller, S. Iterative estimation of the extreme value index. Math Comput Appl Probab 2005;**7**:139–148.

Jansen, D.W., de Vries, C.W. On the frequency of large stock returns: putting booms and busts into perspective. Rev Econ Stat 1991;**73**:18–24.

Jenkinson, A.F. The frequency distribution of the annual maximum (or minimum) values of meteorological elements. Q J R Meteorol Soc 1955;**81**:158–171.

Kratz, M., Resnick, S. The QQ-estimator of the index of regular variation. Stoch Models 1996;**12**:699–724.

Leadbetter, M.R. Extremes under dependence: historical development and parallels with central limit theory. In: Longin, F., editor. *Extreme Events in Finance: A Handbook of Extreme Value Theory and its Applications*. John Wiley & Sons, Inc.; 2017.

Leadbetter, M.R., Lindgren, G., Rootzén, H. *Extremes and Related Properties of Random Sequences and Processes*. New York: Springer-Verlag; 1983.

Matthys, G., Beirlant, J. Adaptive threshold selection in tail index estimation. In: Embrechts, P., editor. *Extremes and Integrated Risk Management*. London: UBS Warburg and Risk Books; 2000.

Matthys, G., Beirlant, J. Estimating the extreme value index and high quantiles with exponential regression models. Stat Sin 2003;**13**:853–880.

Matthys, G., Delafosse, M., Guillou, A., Beirlant, J. Estimating catastrophic quantile levels for heavy-tailed distributions. Insur Math Econ 2004;**34**:517–537.

Oliveira, O., Gomes, M.I., Fraga Alves, M.I. Improvements in the estimation of a heavy tail. Revstat 2006;**6**:83–100.

Peng, L. Asymptotically unbiased estimator for the extreme-value index. Stat Probab Lett 1998;**38**:107–115.

Peng, L., Welsh, A.W. Robust estimation of the generalized Pareto distribution. Extremes 2001;**4**:63–65.

Pickands, J III. Statistical inference using extreme order statistics. Ann Stat 1975;**3**:119–131.

Reiss, R.-D., Thomas, M. *Statistical Analysis of Extreme Values, with Applications to Insurance, Finance, Hydrology and Other Fields*. 1st ed. Basel: Birkhaüser Verlag, 2nd ed. 2001, 3rd ed., 2007.

Resnick, S.I. *Heavy-Tail Phenomena: Probabilistic and Statistical Modeling.* New York: Springer-Verlag; 2007.

Schultze, J., Steinebach, J. On least squares estimators of an exponential tail coefficient. Stat Decis 1996;**14**:353–372.

Segers, J. Generalized Pickands estimators for the extreme value index. J Stat Plann Inference 2005;**28**:381–396.

Smith, R.L. Estimating tails of probability distributions. Ann Stat 1987;**15**:1174–1207.

von Mises, R. La distribution de la plus grande de *n* valeurs. Rev Math Union Interbalcanique 1936;**1**:141–160. Reprinted in Selected Papers of Richard von Mises, Am Math Soc 1964;**2**:517–537.

Weissman, I. Estimation of parameters and large quantiles based on the *k* largest observations. J Am Stat Assoc 1978;**73**:812–815.

Yun, S. On a generalized Pickands estimator of the extreme value index. J Stat Plann Inference 2002;**102**:389–409.

Chapter Six

Bootstrap Methods in Statistics of Extremes

M. Ivette Gomes[1], Frederico Caeiro[2], Lígia Henriques-Rodrigues[3], and B.G. Manjunath[4]

[1] *Universidade de Lisboa, FCUL, DEIO and CEAUL, Portugal*
[2] *Universidade Nova de Lisboa, FCT and CMA, Portugal*
[3] *Universidade de São Paulo, IME and CEAUL, Brazil*
[4] *Universidade de Lisboa, CEAUL, Portugal*

AMS **2010** *subject classification. Primary 62G32, 62E20; Secondary 65C05.*
AMS 2000 *subject classification. Primary 62G32, 62E20; Secondary **62G09**,*
***62G30**.*

6.1 INTRODUCTION

Let $(X_1, \ldots, X_n)$ be a random sample from an underlying *cumulative distribution function* (CDF) F. If we assume that F is known, we can easily estimate the sampling distribution of any estimator $\hat{\theta} = \hat{\theta}(X_1, \ldots, X_n)$ of an unknown parameter θ through the use of a Monte Carlo simulation, described in the following algorithm:

S1. For $r = 1, \ldots, R$,

   S1.1 generate random samples $x_{1r}, \ldots, x_{nr} \frown F$,

   S1.2 and compute $\hat{\theta}_r = \hat{\theta}(x_{1r}, \ldots, x_{nr})$.

S2. On the basis of the output $(\hat{\theta}_1, \hat{\theta}_2, \ldots, \hat{\theta}_R)$, after the R iterations in Step S1, use such a sample to estimate the sampling distribution of $\hat{\theta}$, through either the associated empirical distribution function or any kernel estimate, among others.

If R goes to infinity, something not achievable in practice, we should then get a perfect match to the theoretical calculation, if available, that is, the Monte Carlo

---

Extreme Events in Finance: A Handbook of Extreme Value Theory and its Applications,
First Edition. Edited by François Longin.
© 2017 John Wiley & Sons, Inc. Published 2017 by John Wiley & Sons, Inc.

error should disappear. But F is usually unknown. How to proceed? The use of the bootstrap methodology is a possible way.

Bootstrapping (Efron, 1979) is essentially a computer-based and computer-intensive method for assigning measures of accuracy to sample estimates (see Efron and Tibshirani, 1994; Davison and Hinkley, 1997, among others). Concomitantly, this technique also allows estimation of the sampling distribution of almost any statistic using only very simple resampling methods, based on the observed value of the empirical distribution function, given by

$$F_n^*(x) := \frac{1}{n} \sum_{i=1}^{n} I_{\{X_i \leqslant x\}}. \tag{6.1}$$

We can replace in the previously sketched algorithm F by F_n^*, the empirical distribution function associated with the original observed data, $x_1, \ldots, x_n$, which puts mass $1/n$ on each of the $x_j, 1 \leqslant j \leqslant n$, generating with replacement $x_{1r}^*, \ldots, x_{nr}^* \frown F_n^*$, in Step S1.1 of the algorithm in the preceding text, computing $\hat{\theta}_r^* = \hat{\theta}(x_{1r}^*, \ldots, x_{nr}^*)$, $1 \leqslant r \leqslant R$, in Step S1.2, and using next such a sample in Step S2.

The main goal of this chapter is to enhance the role of the *bootstrap* methodology in the field of statistics of univariate extremes, where the bootstrap has been commonly used in the choice of the number k of top order statistics or of the optimal sample fraction, k/n, to be taken in the semiparametric estimation of a parameter of extreme events. For an asymptotically consistent choice of the *threshold* to use in the adaptive estimation of a positive *extreme value index* (EVI), ξ, the primary parameter in statistics of extremes, we suggest and discuss a double-bootstrap algorithm. In such algorithm, apart from the classical Hill (1975) and *peaks over random threshold* (PORT)-Hill EVI estimators (Araújo Santos et al., 2006), we consider a class of *minimum-variance reduced-bias* (MVRB), the simplest one in Caeiro et al. (2005), and associated PORT-MVRB (Gomes et al., 2011a, 2013) EVI estimators. Other bootstrap methods for the choice of k can be found in Hall (1990), Longin (1995), Caers et al. (1999), Draisma et al. (1999), Danielsson et al. (2001), and Gomes and Oliveira (2001), among others. For a recent comparison between the simple-bootstrap and the double-bootstrap methodology, see Caeiro and Gomes (2014b), where an improved version of Hall's bootstrap methodology was introduced.

After providing, in Section 6.2, a few technical details in the area of *extreme value theory* (EVT), related to the EVI estimators under consideration in this chapter, we shall briefly discuss, in Section 6.3, the main ideas behind the bootstrap methodology and optimal sample fraction estimation. In the lines of Gomes et al. (2011b, 2012, 2015a), we propose an algorithm for the adaptive consistent estimation of a positive EVI, through the use of resampling computer-intensive methods. The *Algorithm* is described for the Hill EVI estimator and associated PORT-Hill, MVRB, and PORT-MVRB EVI estimators, but it can work similarly for the estimation of other parameters of extreme events, like a high quantile, the probability of exceedance, or the return period of a high level. The associated code in R language for the adaptive EVI estimation is available upon request. Section 6.4 is entirely dedicated to the application of the **Algorithm** to three simulated samples. Finally, in Section 6.5, we draw some overall conclusions.

6.2 A FEW DETAILS ON EVT

The key results obtained by Fisher and Tippett (1928) on the possible limiting laws of the sample maxima, formalized by Gnedenko (1943), and used by Gumbel (1958) for applications of EVT in engineering subjects are some of the key tools that led to the way statistical EVT has been exploding in the last decades. In this chapter, we focus on the behavior of extreme values of a data set, dealing with maximum values and other top order statistics in a univariate framework, working thus in the field of statistics of extremes.

Let us assume that we have access to a random sample $(X_1, \ldots, X_n)$ of independent, identically distributed, or possibly stationary and weakly dependent random variables from an underlying model F, and let us denote by $(X_{1:n} \leqslant \cdots \leqslant X_{n:n})$ the sample of associated ascending order statistics. As usual, let us further assume that it is possible to linearly normalize the sequence of maximum values, $\{X_{n:n}\}_{n \geqslant 1}$, so that we get a nondegenerate limit. Then (Gnedenko, 1943), that limiting random variable has a CDF of the type of the extreme value distribution, given by

$$
G_\xi(x) = \begin{cases} \exp\left(-(1+\xi x)^{-1/\xi}\right), & 1+\xi x \geqslant 0, & \text{if} \quad \xi \neq 0, \\ \exp\left(-\exp\left(-x\right)\right), & x \in \mathbb{R}, & \text{if} \quad \xi = 0, \end{cases} \tag{6.2}
$$

and ξ is the so-called EVI, the primary parameter in statistics of extremes. We then say that F is in the max-domain of attraction of G_ξ, in (6.2), and use the notation $F \in \mathcal{D}_\mathcal{M}(G_\xi)$. The EVI measures essentially the weight of the right tail function, $\overline{F} := 1 - F$. If $\xi < 0$, the right tail is short and light, since F has compulsory a finite right end point, that is, $x^F := \sup\{x : F(x) < 1\}$ is finite. If $\xi > 0$, the right tail is heavy and of a negative polynomial type, and F has an infinite right end point. A positive EVI is also often called tail index. If $\xi = 0$, the right tail is of an exponential type, and the right end point can then be either finite or infinite.

Slightly more restrictively than the full max-domain of attraction of the extreme value distribution, we now consider a positive EVI, that is, we work with heavy-tailed models F in $\mathcal{D}_\mathcal{M}(G_\xi)_{\xi > 0} =: \mathcal{D}_\mathcal{M}^+$. Heavy-tailed models appear often in practice in fields like bibliometrics, biostatistics, finance, insurance, and telecommunications. Power laws, such as the Pareto distribution and Zipf's law, have been observed a few decades ago in some important phenomena in economics and biology and have seriously attracted scientists in recent years. As usual, we shall further use the notations $F^\leftarrow(y) := \inf\{x : F(x) \geqslant y\}$ for the *generalized inverse* function of F and $\mathcal{R}_a$ for the class of *regularly varying* functions at infinity with an index of regular variation a, that is, positive Borel measurable functions $g(\cdot)$ such that $g(tx)/g(t) \to x^a$, as $t \to \infty$, for all $x > 0$ (see Bingham et al., 1987, for details on regular variation). Let us further use the notation $U(t) := F^\leftarrow(1 - 1/t)$ for the tail quantile function. For heavy-tailed models we have the validity of the following *first-order conditions*:

$$
F \in \mathcal{D}_\mathcal{M}^+ \quad \Longleftrightarrow \quad \overline{F} \in \mathcal{R}_{-1/\xi} \quad \Longleftrightarrow \quad U \in \mathcal{R}_\xi. \tag{6.3}
$$

The first necessary and sufficient condition in the preceding text, related to the right tail function behavior, was proved by Gnedenko (1943), and the second one, related to the tail quantile function behavior, was proved by de Haan (1984).

For these heavy-tailed models, and given a sample $\underline{X}_n = (X_1, \ldots, X_n)$, the classical EVI estimators are Hill estimators (Hill, 1975), with the functional expression

$$H_{k,n} \equiv H(k; \underline{X}_n) := \frac{1}{k} \sum_{i=1}^{k} \ln \frac{X_{n-i+1:n}}{X_{n-k:n}}, \quad 1 \leqslant i \leqslant k < n. \tag{6.4}$$

They are thus the average of the k log-excesses, $V_{ik} := \ln X_{n-i+1:n} - \ln X_{n-k:n}$, $1 \leqslant i \leqslant k$, above the random level or threshold $X_{n-k:n}$. To have consistency of Hill EVI estimators, we need to have $k = k_n \to \infty$, and such a random threshold $X_{n-k:n}$ needs further to be an *intermediate* order statistic, that is, we need to have

$$k = k_n \to \infty \quad \text{and} \quad k/n \to 0, \text{ as } n \to \infty, \tag{6.5}$$

if we want to have consistent EVI estimation in the whole $\mathcal{D}_{\mathcal{M}}^+$. Indeed, under any of the first-order frameworks in (6.3), the *log-excesses*, $V_{ik}, 1 \leqslant i \leqslant k$, are approximately the k order statistics of an exponential sample of size k, with mean value ξ, hence the reason for the EVI estimators in (6.4).

Under adequate second-order conditions that rule the rate of convergence in any of the first-order conditions in (6.3), Hill estimators, $H_{k,n}$, have usually a high asymptotic bias, and recently, several authors have considered different ways of reducing bias (see the overviews in Gomes et al., 2007b, Chapter 6 of Reiss and Thomas, 2007; Gomes et al., 2008a; Beirlant et al., 2012; Gomes and Guillou, 2015). A simple class of MVRB EVI estimators is the class studied in Caeiro et al. (2005), to be introduced in Section 6.2.2. These MVRB EVI estimators depend on the adequate estimation of second-order parameters, and the kind of second-order parameter estimation that enables the building of MVRB EVI estimators, that is, EVI estimators that outperform the Hill estimator for all k, is sketched in Sections 6.2.1 and 6.2.2.

Both Hill and MVRB EVI estimators are invariant to changes in scale but not invariant to changes in location. And particularly the Hill EVI estimators can suffer drastic changes when we induce an arbitrary shift in the data, as can be seen in Figure 6.1.

Indeed, even if a Hill plot (a function of $H_{k,n}$ vs k) looks stable, as happens in Figure 6.1, with the $H|0$ sample path, where data, $(x_1, \ldots, x_n)$, $n = 1000$, come from a unit standard Pareto CDF, $F(x) = F_0(x) = 1 - x^{-\alpha}, x \geqslant 1$, for $\alpha = 1$ ($\xi = 1/\alpha = 1$), we easily come to the so-called Hill horror plots, a terminology used in Resnick (1997), when we induce a shift to the data. This can be seen also in Figure 6.1 (look now at $H|5$), where we present the Hill plot associated with the shifted sample $(x_1 + 5, \ldots, x_n + 5)$, from the CDF $F_s(x) = 1 - (x - s)^{-1}, x \geqslant 1 + s$, now for $s = 5$. This led Araújo Santos et al. (2006) to introduce the so-called PORT methodology, to be sketched in Section 6.2.3. The asymptotic behavior of the EVI estimators under consideration is discussed in Section 6.2.4.

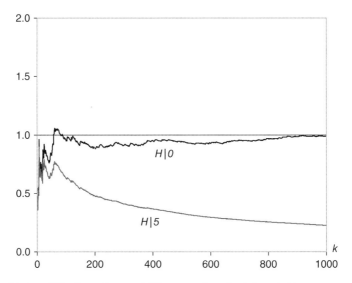

FIGURE 6.1 Hill plots, denoted $H|s$, associated with unit Pareto samples of size $n = 1000$, from the model $F_s(x) = 1 - (x - s)^{-1}, x \geqslant 1 + s$, for $s = 0$ and $s = 5$.

6.2.1 Second-Order Reduced-Bias EVI Estimation

For consistent semiparametric EVI estimation, in the whole $\mathcal{D}_{\mathcal{M}}^+$, we have already noticed that we merely need to work with adequate functionals, dependent on an intermediate tuning or control parameter k, the number of top order statistics involved in the estimation, that is, (6.5) should hold. To obtain full information on the nondegenerate asymptotic behavior of semiparametric EVI estimators, we often need to further assume a *second-order condition*, ruling the rate of convergence in any of the *first-order conditions*, in (6.3). It is often assumed that there exists a function $A(\cdot)$, such that

$$\lim_{t \to \infty} \frac{\ln U(tx) - \ln U(t) - \xi \ln x}{A(t)} = \psi_\rho(x) := \begin{cases} (x^\rho - 1)/\rho, & \text{if } \rho \neq 0, \\ \ln x, & \text{if } \rho = 0. \end{cases} \quad (6.6)$$

Then, we have $|A| \in \mathcal{R}_\rho$. Moreover, if the limit in the left-hand side of (6.6) exists, we can choose $A(\cdot)$ so that such a limit is compulsory equal to the previously defined $\psi_\rho(\cdot)$ function (Geluk and de Haan, 1987).

   Whenever dealing with reduced-bias estimators of parameters of extreme events, and essentially due to technical reasons, it is common to slightly restrict the domain of attraction, $\mathcal{D}_{\mathcal{M}}^+$, and to consider a Pareto-type class of models, assuming that, with $C, \xi > 0, \rho < 0, \beta \neq 0$, and as $t \to \infty$,

$$U(t) = Ct^\xi(1 + A(t)/\rho + o(t^\rho)), \quad A(t) := \xi\beta t^\rho. \quad (6.7)$$

The class in (6.7) is however a wide class of models that contains most of the heavy-tailed parents useful in applications, like the *Fréchet*, the *generalized*

Pareto, and the *Student-t_ν*, with ν degrees of freedom. For Fréchet parents, we get $\beta = 0.5$ and $\rho = -1$ in (6.7). For a generalized Pareto distribution, $H_\xi(x) = 1 + \ln G_\xi(x)$, with $G_\xi(\cdot)$ given in (6.2), we get $\beta = 1$ and $\rho = -\xi$. For Student-t_ν parents, we get $\xi = 1/\nu$ and $\rho = -2/\nu$. For further details and an explicit expression of β as a function of ν, see Caeiro and Gomes (2008), among others. Note that the validity of (6.6) with $\rho < 0$ is equivalent to (6.7). To obtain information on the bias of MVRB EVI estimators, it is even common to slightly restrict the class of models in (6.7), further assuming the following third-order condition:

$$U(t) = Ct^\xi(1 + A(t)/\rho + \beta' t^{2\rho} + o(t^{2\rho})), \tag{6.8}$$

as $t \to \infty$, with $\beta' \neq 0$. All the aforementioned models still belong to this class. Slightly more generally, we could have assumed a *general third-order condition*, ruling now the rate of convergence in the second-order condition in (6.6), which guarantees that, for all $x > 0$,

$$\lim_{t\to\infty} \frac{\frac{\ln U(tx) - \ln U(t) - \xi \ln x}{A(t)} - \psi_\rho(x)}{B(t)} = \psi_{\rho+\rho'}(x), \tag{6.9}$$

where $|B|$ must then be in $\mathcal{R}_{\rho'}$. Equation (6.8) is equivalent to equation (6.9) with $\rho = \rho' < 0$. Further details on the topic can be found in de Haan and Ferreira (2006).

Provided that (6.5) and (6.6) hold, Hill EVI estimators, $H_{k,n}$, have usually a high asymptotic bias. The adequate accommodation of this bias has recently been extensively addressed. Among the pioneering papers, we mention Peng (1998), Beirlant et al. (1999), Feuerverger and Hall (1999), and Gomes et al. (2000). In these papers, authors are led to reduced-bias EVI estimators, with asymptotic variances larger than or equal to $(\xi(1-\rho)/\rho)^2$, where $\rho(<0)$ is the aforementioned "shape" second-order parameter in (6.6). Recently, as sketched in Section 6.2.2, Caeiro et al. (2005) and Gomes et al. (2007a, 2008c) have been able to *reduce the bias without increasing the asymptotic variance*, kept at ξ^2, just as happens with the Hill EVI estimator.

6.2.2　MVRB EVI Estimation

To reduce bias, keeping the asymptotic variance at the same level, we merely need to use an adequate "external" and a bit more than consistent estimation of the pair of second-order parameters, $(\beta, \rho) \in (\mathbb{R}, \mathbb{R}^-)$, in (6.7). The MVRB EVI estimators outperform the classical Hill EVI estimators for all k, and among them, we now consider the simplest class by Caeiro et al. (2005), used for value-at-risk (VaR) estimation by Gomes and Pestana (2007b). Such a class, denoted by $\overline{H} \equiv \overline{H}_{k,n}$, has the functional form

$$\overline{H}_{k,n} \equiv \overline{H}_{\hat\beta,\hat\rho}(k; \underline{\mathbf{X}}_n) := H_{k,n}(1 - \hat\beta(n/k)^{\hat\rho}/(1-\hat\rho)), \tag{6.10}$$

where $(\hat\beta, \hat\rho)$ is an adequate consistent estimator of (β, ρ), with $\hat\beta$ and $\hat\rho$ based on a number of top order statistics k_1 usually of a higher order than the number of top order statistics k used in the EVI estimation, as explained in Sections 6.2.1 and 6.2.2. For different algorithms for the estimation of (β, ρ), see Gomes and Pestana (2007a,b).

6.2.2.1 Estimation of the "shape" Second-order Parameter

We consider the most commonly used ρ-estimators, the ones studied by Fraga Alves et al. (2003), briefly introduced in the sequel. Given the sample $\underline{\mathbf{X}}_n$, the ρ-estimators by Fraga Alves et al. (2003) are dependent on the statistics

$$V_\tau(k;\underline{\mathbf{X}}_n) := \begin{cases} \dfrac{\left(M_n^{(1)}(k;\underline{\mathbf{X}}_n)\right)^\tau - (M_n^{(2)}(k;\underline{\mathbf{X}}_n)/2)^{\tau/2}}{\left(M_n^{(2)}(k;\underline{\mathbf{X}}_n)/2\right)^{\tau/2} - \left(M_n^{(3)}(k;\underline{\mathbf{X}}_n)/6\right)^{\tau/3}}, & \text{if } \tau \neq 0, \\[2em] \dfrac{\ln M_n^{(1)}(k;\underline{\mathbf{X}}_n) - \ln(M_n^{(2)}(k;\underline{\mathbf{X}}_n)/2)/2}{\ln\left(M_n^{(2)}(k;\underline{\mathbf{X}}_n)/2\right)/2 - \ln\left(M_n^{(3)}(k;\underline{\mathbf{X}}_n)/6\right)/3}, & \text{if } \tau = 0, \end{cases} \tag{6.11}$$

defined for any *tuning parameter* $\tau \in \mathbb{R}$ and where

$$M_n^{(j)}(k;\underline{\mathbf{X}}_n) := \frac{1}{k}\sum_{i=1}^{k}\{\ln X_{n-i+1:n} - \ln X_{n-k:n}\}^j, \quad j = 1, 2, 3.$$

Under mild restrictions on k, that is, if (6.5) holds and $\sqrt{k}\,A(n/k) \to \infty$, with $A(\cdot)$ the function in (6.7), the statistics in (6.11) converge toward $3(1-\rho)/(3-\rho)$, independently of the *tuning* parameter τ, and we can consequently consider the class of admissible ρ-estimators:

$$\hat{\rho}_\tau(k) \equiv \hat{\rho}_\tau(k;\underline{\mathbf{X}}_n) := -\left|\frac{3(V_\tau(k;\underline{\mathbf{X}}_n) - 1)}{V_\tau(k;\underline{\mathbf{X}}_n) - 3}\right|. \tag{6.12}$$

Under adequate general conditions, and for an appropriate tuning parameter τ, the ρ-estimators in (6.12) show highly stable sample paths as functions of k, the number of top order statistics used, for a range of large k-values. Again, it is sensible to advise practitioners not to choose blindly the value of τ in (6.12). Sample paths of $\hat{\rho}_\tau(k)$, as functions of k, for a few values of τ, should be drawn, in order to elect the value of τ, which provides higher stability for large k, by means of any stability criterion. For the most common stability criterion, see Gomes and Pestana (2007b) and Remark 6.5. The value $\tau = 0$, considered in the description of the *Algorithm* in Section 6.3.2, has revealed to be the most adequate choice whenever we are in the region $|\rho| \leqslant 1$, a common region in applications, and the region where bias reduction is indeed needed. Distributional properties of the estimators in (6.12) can be found in Fraga Alves et al. (2003). Interesting alternative classes of ρ-estimators have recently been introduced by Goegebeur et al. (2008, 2010), Ciuperca and Mercadier (2010), and Caeiro and Gomes (2014a, 2015).

6.2.2.2   Estimation of the "scale" Second-order Parameter

For the estimation of the scale second-order parameter β, on the basis of

$$d_\alpha(k) := \frac{1}{k} \sum_{i=1}^{k} \left(\frac{i}{k}\right)^{-\alpha} \quad \text{and} \quad D_\alpha(k) := \frac{1}{k} \sum_{i=1}^{k} \left(\frac{i}{k}\right)^{-\alpha} i \ln \frac{X_{n-i+1:n}}{X_{n-i:n}}, \quad \alpha \in \mathbb{R},$$

we shall consider the estimator in Gomes and Martins (2002):

$$\hat{\beta}_{\hat{\rho}}(k) \equiv \hat{\beta}_{\hat{\rho}}(k; \underline{\mathbf{X}}_n) := \left(\frac{k}{n}\right)^{\hat{\rho}} \frac{d_{\hat{\rho}}(k)}{d_{\hat{\rho}}(k)} \frac{D_0(k) - D_{\hat{\rho}}(k)}{D_{\hat{\rho}}(k) - D_{2\hat{\rho}}(k)}, \tag{6.13}$$

dependent on an adequate ρ-estimator, $\hat{\rho}$. It has been advised the computation of these second-order parameter estimators at a k-value given by

$$k_1 = \lfloor n^{1-\epsilon} \rfloor, \quad \epsilon = 0.001. \tag{6.14}$$

The estimator $\hat{\rho}$, to be plugged in (6.13), is thus $\hat{\rho} := \hat{\rho}_\tau(k_1; \underline{\mathbf{X}}_n)$, with $\hat{\rho}_\tau(k; \underline{\mathbf{X}}_n)$ and k_1 given in (6.12) and (6.14), respectively.

REMARK 6.1   *Note that only the external estimation of both β and ρ at an adequately chosen level k_1 and the EVI-estimation at a level $k = o(k_1)$, or at a specific value $k = O(k_1)$, can lead to an MVRB EVI-estimator, with an asymptotic variance ξ^2. Such a choice of (k, k_1) is theoretically possible, as shown in Gomes et al. (2009) and Caeiro et al. (2009), but under conditions difficult to guarantee in practice. As a compromise between theoretical and practical results, we have so far advised any choice $k_1 = \lfloor n^{1-\epsilon} \rfloor$, with ϵ small (see Caeiro et al., 2005, 2009; Gomes et al., 2007a,b, 2008c, among others). With the choice of k_1 in (6.14), we have obviously the validity of condition (6.5), and whenever $\sqrt{k_1} A(n/k_1) \to \infty$, as $n \to \infty$ (an almost irrelevant restriction, from a practical point of view), we get $\hat{\rho} - \rho := \hat{\rho}_\tau(k_1) - \rho = o_p(1/\ln n)$, a condition needed, in order not to have any increase in the asymptotic variance of the bias-corrected Hill EVI-estimator in equation (6.10), comparatively with the one of the Hill EVI-estimator, in (6.4).*

REMARK 6.2   *Further note that the estimation of ξ, β, and ρ at the same value k would lead to a high increase in the asymptotic variance of the second-order reduced-bias EVI-estimators $\overline{H}_{k,n;\hat{\beta},\hat{\rho}}$ in (6.10), which would become $\xi^2((1-\rho)/\rho)^4$ (see Feuerverger and Hall, 1999; Beirlant et al., 1999; and Peng and Qi, 2004, among others). The external estimation of ρ at k_1 together with the estimation of ξ and β at the same $k = o(k_1)$ enables a slight decreasing of the asymptotic variance to $\xi^2((1-\rho)/\rho)^2$, still greater than ξ^2 (see Gomes and Martins, 2002, again among others).*

Details on the distributional behavior of the estimator in (6.13) can be found in Gomes and Martins (2002) and more recently in Gomes et al. (2008c) and Caeiro et al. (2009). Again, consistency is achieved for models in (6.7) and k-values such that (6.5) holds and $\sqrt{k}\,A(n/k) \to \infty$, as $n \to \infty$. Alternative estimators of β can be found in Caeiro and Gomes (2006) and Gomes et al. (2010). Due to the fact that $\hat{\beta} = \hat{\beta}_{\hat{\rho}}(k_1)$ and $\hat{\rho} = \hat{\rho}_\tau(k_1)$, with $\hat{\rho}_\tau(k)$, $\hat{\beta}_{\hat{\rho}}(k)$, and k_1 given in (6.12)–(6.14), respectively, depending on $\tau \in \mathbb{R}$, we often use the notation $\overline{H}_\tau$. But when we work with $\tau = 0$ only, as happens in Section 6.3.2, we shall not use the subscript $\tau = 0$. Note however that the *Algorithm* in Section 3.2 can also be used for another fixed choice of τ, as well as for a data-driven choice of τ provided by any of the algorithms in Gomes and Pestana (2007a,b), among others.

6.2.3 PORT EVI Estimation

The estimators in (6.4) and (6.10) are scale invariant but not location invariant. In order to achieve location invariance for a class of modified Hill EVI estimators and adequate properties for VaR estimators, Araújo Santos et al. (2006) introduced the so-called PORT methodology. The estimators are then functionals of a sample of excesses over a random level $X_{n_q:n}$, $n_q := \lfloor nq \rfloor + 1$, that is, functionals of the sample

$$\underline{\mathbf{X}}_n^{(q)} := (X_{n:n} - X_{n_q:n}, \dots, X_{n_q+1:n} - X_{n_q:n}). \tag{6.15}$$

Generally, we can have $0 < q < 1$, for any $F \in \mathcal{D}_{\mathcal{M}}^+$ (*the random level is an empirical quantile*). If the underlying model F has a finite *left end point*, $x_F := \inf\{x : F(x) \geqslant 0\}$, we can also use $q = 0$ (*the random level can then be the minimum*).

If we think, for instance, on Hill EVI estimators, in (6.4), the new classes of PORT-Hill EVI estimators, theoretically studied in Araújo Santos et al. (2006), and for finite samples in Gomes et al. (2008b), are given by

$$H_{k,n}^{(q)} := H(k; \underline{\mathbf{X}}_n^{(q)}) = \frac{1}{k} \sum_{i=1}^{k} \left\{ \ln \frac{X_{n-i+1:n} - X_{n_q:n}}{X_{n-k:n} - X_{n_q:n}} \right\}, \quad 0 \leqslant q < 1. \tag{6.16}$$

Similarly, if we think on the MVRB EVI estimators, in (6.10), the new classes of PORT-MVRB EVI estimators, studied for finite samples in Gomes et al. (2011a, 2013), are given by

$$\overline{H}_{k,n}^{(q)} := \overline{H}_{\hat{\beta}^{(q)}, \hat{\rho}^{(q)}}(k; \underline{\mathbf{X}}_n^{(q)}) = H_{k,n}^{(q)} \left(1 - \frac{\hat{\beta}^{(q)}(n^{(q)}/k)^{\hat{\rho}^{(q)}}}{1 - \hat{\rho}^{(q)}} \right), \quad 0 \leqslant q < 1, \tag{6.17}$$

with $H_{k,n}^{(q)}$ in (6.16), $n^{(q)} = n - n_q$ and $(\hat{\beta}^{(q)} := \hat{\beta}(k_1, \underline{\mathbf{X}}_n^{(q)}), \hat{\rho}^{(q)} := \hat{\rho}(k_1, \underline{\mathbf{X}}_n^{(q)}))$ any adequate estimator of (β_q, ρ_q), the vector of second-order parameters associated with the shifted model, based on the sample $\underline{\mathbf{X}}_n^{(q)}$, in (6.15).

These PORT EVI estimators are thus dependent on a *tuning parameter q*, $0 \leqslant q < 1$, that makes them highly flexible. Moreover, they are invariant to changes in both location and scale. Just as in Gomes et al. (2013, 2015a), we shall further include in the algorithm the value $q = 1$, so that with H, $\overline{H}$, $H^{(q)}$, and $\overline{H}^{(q)}$, given in (6.4), (6.10), (6.16), and (6.17), respectively, we can consider that $H = H^{(q)}$ and

$\overline{H} = \overline{H}^{(q)}$ for $q = 1$ (with the notations $n_1 = n + 1 \equiv 0$, $X_{n+1:n} = X_{0:n} \equiv 0$, so that $\underline{X}_n^{(1)} = \underline{X}_n$, $n^{(1)} = n - n_1 = n$, $\hat{\beta}^{(1)} = \hat{\beta}$, $\hat{\rho}^{(1)} = \hat{\rho}$).

REMARK 6.3 *The PORT VaR$_p$ estimators at a level p, $0 < p < 1$, introduced by Araújo Santos et al. (2006), are also semiparametric in nature and connected to the Weissman–Hill estimator:*

$$\hat{\chi}_p(k) \equiv \hat{\chi}_p(k; X_n) := X_{n-k:n}(k/(np))^{H_{k,n}}, \tag{6.18}$$

studied in Weissman (1978). However, they satisfy the empirical counterpart of the theoretical linear property of a quantile $\chi_p(X) := F^{\leftarrow}(1 - p)$, given by $\chi_p(\lambda + \delta X) = \lambda + \delta \chi_p(X)$ for any real λ and positive real δ. Up to an adequate translation, they have the same functional expression of the VaR$_p$ estimators in (6.18), but applied to the sample of excesses in (6.15). More precisely, they are given by

$$\hat{\chi}_p^{(q)}(k) := (X_{n-k:n} - X_{n_q:n})(k/(np))^{H_{k,n}^{(q)}} + X_{n_q:n}, \tag{6.19}$$

with $H_{k,n}^{(q)}$ the PORT-Hill EVI-estimator in (6.16). An expression similar to (6.19) can be written for a PORT-MVRB VaR$_p$ estimator, provided that we replace in (6.19), $H_{k,n}^{(q)}$ by $\overline{H}_{k,n}^{(q)}$, defined in (6.17).

Further applications of the PORT methodology can be found in Henriques-Rodrigues *et al.* (2014, 2015), Caeiro *et al.* (2016) and Gomes *et al.* (2016), among others.

6.2.4 Asymptotic Properties of the EVI Estimators

The Hill estimator reveals usually a high asymptotic bias. Indeed, from the results of de Haan and Peng (1998), and with $\mathcal{N}_{\mu,\sigma^2}$ denoting a normal random variable with mean value μ and variance σ^2, there exists b_H such that

$$\sqrt{k}(H_{k,n} - \xi) \stackrel{d}{=} \mathcal{N}_{0,\xi^2} + b_H \sqrt{k}A(n/k) + o_p\left(\sqrt{k}A(n/k)\right), \tag{6.20}$$

where the bias $b_H \sqrt{k}A(n/k) = \xi \beta \sqrt{k} (n/k)^\rho/(1 - \rho)$ under condition (6.8) can be very large, moderate, or small, going, respectively, to ∞, a nonnull constant, or 0, as $n \to \infty$. This nonnull asymptotic bias, together with a rate of convergence of the order of $1/\sqrt{k}$, leads to sample paths with a high variance for small k, a high bias for large k, and a very sharp mean square error (MSE) pattern, as a function of k. Under the same conditions as before, $\sqrt{k}(\overline{H}_{k,n} - \xi)$ is asymptotically normal with variance also equal to ξ^2 but with a null mean value. Indeed, under the validity of the aforementioned third-order condition in (6.8), related to Pareto-type class of models, we can adequately estimate the vector of second-order parameters (β, ρ) so that $\overline{H}_{k,n}$ outperforms $H_{k,n}$ for all k. Indeed, and for an adequate $b_{\overline{H}}$, computed by Caeiro et al. (2009), we can write

$$\sqrt{k}(\overline{H}_{k,n} - \xi) \stackrel{d}{=} \mathcal{N}_{0,\xi^2} + b_{\overline{H}} \sqrt{k}A^2(n/k) + o_p\left(\sqrt{k}A^2(n/k)\right). \tag{6.21}$$

We can further summarize the aforementioned results in the following theorem.

THEOREM 6.4 *(de Haan and Peng, 1998; Caeiro et al., 2009) Assume that condition (6.6) holds, and let $k \equiv k_n$ be an intermediate sequence, that is, (6.5) holds. Then $H_{k,n}$, in (6.4), is consistent for the estimation of ξ. Moreover, there exists a real number $b_H =: b_{H,1}$, such that the asymptotic distributional representation in (6.20) holds.*

If we further assume that (6.8) holds, there exists an extra real number $b_{H,2}$, such that we can write

$$\sqrt{k}(H_{k,n} - \xi) \overset{d}{=} \mathcal{N}_{0,\xi^2} + b_{H,1} \sqrt{k}A(n/k) + b_{H,2} \sqrt{k}A^2(n/k)(1 + o_p(1)).$$

If under the validity of the second-order condition in (6.6), we estimate β and ρ consistently through $\hat{\beta}$ and $\hat{\rho}$, in such a way that $\hat{\rho} - \rho = o_p(1/\ln n)$, the asymptotic distributional representation

$$\sqrt{k}(\overline{H}_{k,n} - \xi) \overset{d}{=} \mathcal{N}_{0,\xi^2} + o_p(\sqrt{k}A(n/k))$$

holds. Under the validity of equation (6.8), we can guarantee that there exists a pair of real numbers $(b_{\overline{H},1}, b_{\overline{H},2})$, with $b_{\overline{H},1} = 0$ and $b_{\overline{H},2} = b_{\overline{H}}$, given in (6.21), and

$$\sqrt{k}(\overline{H}_{k,n} - \xi) \overset{d}{=} \mathcal{N}_{0,\xi^2} + b_{\overline{H},1} \sqrt{k}A(n/k) + b_{\overline{H},2} \sqrt{k}A^2(n/k)(1 + o_p(1))$$

$$\overset{d}{=} \mathcal{N}_{0,\xi^2} + b_{\overline{H},2} \sqrt{k}A^2(n/k)(1 + o_p(1)),$$

for adequate k-values such that $\sqrt{k}A^2(n/k) \to \lambda_A$, finite.

For the asymptotic behavior of the PORT-Hill EVI estimators, we refer to Araújo Santos et al. (2006). The full asymptotic behavior of the PORT-MVRB EVI estimators is still under development. It is known that the rate of convergence and asymptotic variance do not change. There are however big changes in the bias but for adequate q-values the PORT-MVRB EVI estimators are indeed MVRB EVI estimators. Contrarily to what has been done by Gomes et al. (2015a), we shall thus consider for them the same double-bootstrap *Algorithm* we used for the MVRB EVI estimation.

6.3 THE BOOTSTRAP METHODOLOGY IN STATISTICS OF UNIVARIATE EXTREMES

The use of bootstrap resampling methodologies has revealed to be promising in the choice of the nuisance tuning or control parameter k or equivalently of the optimal sample fraction, k/n, in the semiparametric estimation of any parameter of extreme events. If we ask how to choose the tuning parameter k in the EVI estimation, either through $H_{k,n}$ or $\overline{H}_{k,n}$ or $H_{k,n}^{(q)}$ or $\overline{H}_{k,n}^{(q)}$, $0 \leqslant q < 1$, generally denoted $E_{k,n}$, we usually consider the estimation of

$$k_{0|E}(n) := \arg \min_k \mathrm{MSE}(E_{k,n}). \qquad (6.22)$$

To obtain estimates of $k_{0|E}(n)$, one can use the so-called *double-bootstrap* method based on two related bootstrap samples of size $m_1 = o(n)$ and $m_2 = m_1^2/n$. Such a method is applied to an adequate *auxiliary statistic* like

$$T_{k,n} \equiv T_{k,n|E} := E_{\lfloor k/2 \rfloor,n} - E_{k,n}, \quad k = 2, \dots, n-1, \qquad (6.23)$$

which tends to the well-known value *zero* and has an asymptotic behavior similar to the one of $E_{k,n}$ (see Gomes and Oliveira, 2001, among others, for the estimation through $H_{k,n}$ and Gomes et al., 2012, for the estimation through $\overline{H}_{k,n}$). See also Gomes et al. (2015a,b) and Section 6.3.2.

On the basis of (6.20) and (6.21), and with AMSE standing for "asymptotic MSE," the sum of the asymptotic variance and the squared dominant component of the bias, we get

$$k_{A|E}(n) := \arg \min_k \mathrm{AMSE}(E_{k,n})$$

$$= \arg \min_k \begin{cases} \xi^2/k + b_E^2 \ A^2(n/k), & \text{if} \quad E = H \\ \xi^2/k + b_E^2 \ A^4(n/k), & \text{if} \quad E = \overline{H} \end{cases}$$

$$= k_{0|E}(n)(1 + o(1)) \qquad (6.24)$$

with $k_{0|E}(n)$ defined in (6.22). See Theorem 1 of Draisma et al. (1999), for a proof of this result, in the case of H. The proof is similar for the cases of $\overline{H}$, as already mentioned by Gomes et al. (2012). Things work more intricately for the PORT-MVRB EVI estimators, and as mentioned in the preceding text, we shall consider an algorithm similar to the one devised for the MVRB EVI estimators in case we are working with $\overline{H}^{(q)}$, $0 \leqslant q < 1$, since we are interested in the possible specific value of q that makes these PORT estimators MVRB EVI estimators. The bootstrap methodology enables us to estimate $k_{0|E}(n)$, in (6.22), in a way similar to the one used for the classical EVI estimators, on the basis of a consistent estimator of $k_{A|E}(n)$, in (6.24), and now through the use of an auxiliary statistic like the one in (6.23), a method detailed in Gomes et al. (2011b, 2012) for the MVRB EVI estimation. For the sake of simplicity, we shall next describe the methodology for $(H, \overline{H})$, but similar formulas work for $(H^{(q)}, \overline{H}^{(q)})$ provided that we replace $(n, \underline{X}_n, \beta, \rho)$ by $(n^{(q)}, \underline{X}_n^{(q)}, \beta_q, \rho_q)$, $0 \leqslant q \leqslant 1$. Indeed, under the aforementioned third-order framework in (6.8),

$$T_{k,n|E} \overset{d}{=} \frac{\xi \ P_k^E}{\sqrt{k}} + \begin{cases} b_{E,1} \ (2^\rho - 1) \ A(n/k)(1 + o_p(1)), & \text{if} \quad E = H, \\ b_{E,2} \ (2^{2\rho} - 1) \ A^2(n/k)(1 + o_p(1)), & \text{if} \quad E = \overline{H}, \end{cases}$$

with P_k^E asymptotically standard normal.

Consequently, denoting $k_{0|T,E}(n) := \arg \min_k \text{MSE}(T_{k,n|E})$, we have

$$k_{0|E}(n) = k_{0|T,E}(n) \times \begin{cases} (1 - 2^\rho)^{\frac{2}{1-2\rho}} (1 + o(1)), & \text{if } E = H, \\ (1 - 2^{2\rho})^{\frac{2}{1-4\rho}} (1 + o(1)), & \text{if } E = \overline{H}. \end{cases} \tag{6.25}$$

6.3.1 The Resampling Methodology in Action

How does the resampling methodology then work? Given the sample $\underline{X}_n = (X_1, \ldots, X_n)$ from an unknown model F, and the functional in (6.23), $T_{k,n|E} =: \phi_k(\underline{X}_n)$, $1 < k < n$, consider for any $m_1 = O(n^{1-\epsilon})$, $0 < \epsilon < 1$, the bootstrap sample

$$\underline{X}^*_{m_1} = (X_1^*, \ldots, X_{m_1}^*),$$

from F_n^*, in (6.1), the empirical distribution function associated with the available random sample, $\underline{X}_n$.

Next, associate with the bootstrap sample the corresponding bootstrap auxiliary statistic, $T^*_{k_1,m_1|E} := \phi_{k_1}(\underline{X}^*_{m_1})$, $1 < k_1 < m_1$. Then, with $k^*_{0|T,E}(m_1) = \arg \min_{k_1} \text{MSE}(T^*_{k_1,m_1|E})$,

$$\frac{k^*_{0|T,E}(m_1)}{k_{0|T,E}(n)} = \left(\frac{m_1}{n}\right)^{-\frac{c\rho}{1-c\rho}} (1 + o(1)), \quad c = \begin{cases} 2 & \text{if } E = H, \\ 4 & \text{if } E = \overline{H}. \end{cases}$$

Consequently, for another sample size m_2, and for every $a > 1$,

$$\frac{(k^*_{0|T,E}(m_1))^a}{k^*_{0|T,E}(m_2)} = \left(\frac{m_1^a}{n^a} \frac{n}{m_2}\right)^{-\frac{c\rho}{1-c\rho}} (k_{0|T,E}(n))^{a-1} (1 + o(1)).$$

It is then enough to choose $m_2 = \lfloor n(m_1/n)^a \rfloor + 1$, in order to have independence of ρ. If we consider $a = 2$, that is, $m_2 = \lfloor m_1^2/n \rfloor + 1$, we have

$$(k^*_{0|T,E}(m_1))^2 / k^*_{0|T,E}(m_2) = k_{0|T,E}(n)(1 + o(1)), \quad \text{as } n \to \infty. \tag{6.26}$$

On the basis of (6.26), we are now able to consistently estimate $k_{0|T,E}$ and next $k_{0|E}$ through (6.25), on the basis of any estimate $\hat{\rho}$ of the second-order parameter ρ. With $\hat{k}^*_{0|T,E}$ denoting the sample counterpart of $k^*_{0|T,E}$ and $\hat{\rho}$, an adequate ρ-estimate, we thus have the k_0 estimate

$$\hat{k}^*_{0|E} \equiv \hat{k}_{0|E}(n; m_1) := \min \left(n - 1, \left\lfloor \frac{c_{\hat{\rho}} \, (\hat{k}^*_{0|T,E}(m_1))^2}{\hat{k}^*_{0|T,E}(\lfloor m_1^2/n \rfloor)} \right\rfloor + 1 \right), \tag{6.27}$$

with

$$c_\rho = \begin{cases} (1 - 2^\rho)^{\frac{2}{1-2\rho}} & \text{if } E = H, \\ (1 - 2^{2\rho})^{\frac{2}{1-4\rho}} & \text{if } E = \overline{H}. \end{cases}$$

The adaptive estimate of ξ is then given by

$$E^* \equiv E^*_{n,m_1|T} := E_{\hat{k}^*_{0|E},n}.$$

6.3.2   Adaptive EVI Estimation

In the following *Algorithm* we include the Hill, the MVRB, the PORT-Hill and the PORT-MVRB EVI estimators in the overall selection.

Algorithm: *Adaptive bootstrap estimation of ξ*

1. Consider a finite set Q with values in $[0, 1)$ and define $Q_1 := Q \cup \{1\}$. For example, if F has a finite left end point, we can select $Q = \{0(0.05)0.95\}$. On the other hand, if F has an infinite left end point, we should not select values close to zero.

2. Given an observed sample $\mathbf{x}_n = (x_1, \dots, x_n)$, execute the following steps, for each $q \in Q_1$:

   2.1 Obtain the sample $\mathbf{x}_n^{(q)}$, in (6.15). If $q = 1$, $\mathbf{x}_n^{(1)} \equiv \mathbf{x}_n$.

   2.2 Compute, for the tuning parameter $\tau = 0$, the observed values of $\hat{\rho}^{(q)}(k) := \hat{\rho}_\tau(k; \mathbf{X}_n^{(q)})$, with $\hat{\rho}_\tau(k)$ defined in (6.12).

   2.3 Work with $\hat{\rho}^{(q)} \equiv \hat{\rho}_0^{(q)}(k_1)$ and $\hat{\beta}^{(q)} = \hat{\beta}_{\hat{\rho}^{(q)}}^{(q)}(k_1)$, with $\hat{\beta}_{\hat{\rho}}(k)$ and k_1 given in (6.13) and (6.14), respectively.

   2.4 Compute $H_{k,n}^{(q)}$, in (6.16), and $\overline{H}_{k,n}^{(q)}$, in (6.17), for $k = 1, 2, \cdots$.

   2.5 Consider subsamples of size $m_1 = o(n)$ and $m_2 = \lfloor m_1^2/n \rfloor + 1$.

   2.6 For l from 1 to B, independently generate from the observed empirical distribution function, $F_n^*(x)$, associated with the observed sample $(x_1, \dots, x_n)$, B bootstrap samples

   $$(x_1^*, \dots, x_{m_2}^*) \quad \text{and} \quad (x_1^*, \dots, x_{m_2}^*, x_{m_2+1}^*, \dots, x_{m_1}^*),$$

   with sizes m_2 and m_1, respectively.

   2.7 Generally denoting by $E_{k,n}$ any of the estimators under study, let us denote by $T_{k,n}^* \equiv T_{k,n|E}^*$ the bootstrap counterpart of the auxiliary statistic in (6.23), obtain

   $$t_{k,m_1,l|E}^*, 1 < k < m_1, \quad t_{k,m_2,l|E}^*, 1 < k < m_2, 1 \leqslant l \leqslant B,$$

   the observed values of the statistics $T_{k,m_i}^*, i = 1, 2$, compute

   $$\mathrm{MSE}_E^*(m_i, k) = \frac{1}{B} \sum_{l=1}^{B} (t_{k,m_i,l|E}^*)^2, \quad k = 2, \dots, m_i - 1, \; i = 1, 2,$$

   and obtain $\hat{k}_{0|T,E}^*(m_i) := \arg \min_{1 < k \leqslant m_i-1} \mathrm{MSE}_E^*(m_i, k), i = 1, 2$.

   2.8 Compute $\hat{k}_{0|E}^*$ in (6.27).

2.9 Obtain $H^{*(q)} := H^{(q)}_{\hat{k}^*_{0|H^{(q)}},n}$ and $\overline{H}^{*(q)} := \overline{H}^{(q)}_{\hat{k}^*_{0|\overline{H}^{(q)}},n}.$

3. With $B_E^*(m_i,k) = \frac{1}{B}\sum_{l=1}^{B} t^*_{k,m_i,l|E}$, $k = 2,\ldots,m_i - 1$, $i = 1,2$, compute for $k = \hat{k}^*_{0|H^{(q)}}$ and all values $q \in \mathcal{Q}_1,$

$$\widehat{\mathrm{RMSE}}_H(k;q) := \sqrt{\frac{(H^{*(q)})^2}{k} + \left(\frac{\left(B^*_{H^{(q)}}(m_1,k)\right)^2}{(2\hat{\rho}^{(q)}-1)B^*_{H^{(q)}}(m_2,k)}\right)^2},$$

as well as

$$\widehat{\mathrm{RMSE}}_{\overline{H}}(k;q) := \sqrt{\frac{(\overline{H}^{*(q)})^2}{k} + \left(\frac{(B^*_{\overline{H}^{(q)}}(m_1,k)^2}{(2^{2\hat{\rho}^{(q)}}-1)B^*_{\overline{H}^{(q)}}(m_2,k)}\right)^2}.$$

4. Compute $\hat{q}_H := \arg\min_q \widehat{\mathrm{RMSE}}_H(\hat{k}^*_{0|H^{(q)}};q)$ and $\hat{q}_{\overline{H}} := \arg\min_q \widehat{\mathrm{RMSE}}_{\overline{H}}(\hat{k}^*_{0|\overline{H}^{(q)}};q).$

5. Obtain the adaptive EVI estimates:

$$H^{**} \equiv H^{**}|\hat{q}_H \equiv H^{*(\hat{q}_H)}_{n,m_1} := H^{(\hat{q}_H)}_{\hat{k}^{(\hat{q}_H)}_0,n} \quad \text{and}$$

$$\overline{H}^{**} \equiv \overline{H}^{**}|\hat{q}_{\overline{H}} \equiv \overline{H}^{*(\hat{q}_{\overline{H}})}_{n,m_1} := \overline{H}^{(\hat{q}_{\overline{H}})}_{\hat{k}^{(\hat{q}_{\overline{H}})}_0,n}.$$

REMARK 6.5 *Instead of **Steps 2.2** and **2.3**, we could have considered **Steps 2.2′** and **2.3′** in the succeeding text, reproduced from the algorithm provided by Gomes and Pestana (2007b) for the estimation of the second-order parameters β and ρ.*

2.2′ *Compute, for the tuning parameters $\tau = 0$ and $\tau = 1$, the observed values of $\hat{\rho}^{(q)}(k) := \hat{\rho}_\tau(k;\mathbf{X}_n^{(q)})$, with $\hat{\rho}_\tau(k)$ defined in (6.12). Consider $\{\hat{\rho}^{(q)}(k)\}_{k\in\mathcal{K}}$, with $\mathcal{K} = (\lfloor n_q^{0.995}\rfloor, \lfloor n_q^{0.999}\rfloor)$; compute their median, denoted χ_τ; and further compute $I_\tau := \sum_{k\in\mathcal{K}}(\hat{\rho}^{(q)}(k) - \chi_\tau)^2$, $\tau = 0,1$. Next choose the tuning parameter $\tau^* = 0$ if $I_0 \leqslant I_1$; otherwise, choose $\tau^* = 1$.*

2.3′ *Work with $\hat{\rho}^{(q)} \equiv \hat{\rho}^{(q)}_{\tau^*}(k_1)$ and $\hat{\beta}^{(q)} = \hat{\beta}^{(q)}_{\hat{\rho}^{(q)}}(k_1)$, with $\hat{\beta}_{\hat{\rho}}(k)$ and k_1 given in (6.13) and (6.14), respectively.*

REMARK 6.6 *If there are negative elements in any of the samples in the* algorithm, *the sample size must be replaced by the number of positive elements in the sample.*

REMARK 6.7 *An analogue procedure can be used for any other parameter of extreme events.*

REMARK 6.8 *A few practical questions may be raised under the setup developed: How does the asymptotic method work for moderate sample sizes? What is the type of the sample path of the new estimator for different values of m_1? What is the dependence of the method on the choice of m_1? What is the sensitivity of the method with respect to the choice of the ρ-estimator? Although aware of the theoretical need of $m_1 = o(n)$, what happens if we choose $m_1 = n$? Answers to these questions were given by Gomes and Oliveira (2001) for the estimation of ξ through the* Hill *estimator and can be addressed here. Quite often, the method is only moderately dependent on the choice of the nuisance parameter m_1, in* **Step 5** *of the algorithm, particularly for the* MVRB *EVI-estimators. This enhances the practical value of the method. Moreover, although aware of the need of $m_1 = o(n)$, it seems that we get good results up till n, again particularly for the* MVRB *EVI-estimator, $\overline{H}_{k,n}$, in (6.10). To detect the sensitivity of the algorithm to changes of m_1, we have run it for $q = 1$ and values of $m_1 = \lfloor n^b \rfloor$, $b = 0.950\ (0.005)\ 0.995$, different values of n, and different models. In Figure 6.2, as an illustration, we present for a Fréchet underlying parent, from a CDF $F(x) = \exp(-x^{-1/\xi})$, $x \geqslant 0$, with $\xi = 0.25$, the bootstrap ξ-estimates H^* and $\overline{H}^*$ as a function of b, for $n = 100$ and $n = 1000$.*

A few comments on the results:

- *As expected, and due to the fact that the method works asymptotically, there is a general improvement in the estimation as the sample size, n, increases.*

- *The sensitivity of the **Algorithm** in Section 6.3.2 to the nuisance parameter m_1 is quite weak for both H and $\overline{H}$, particularly if n is large.*

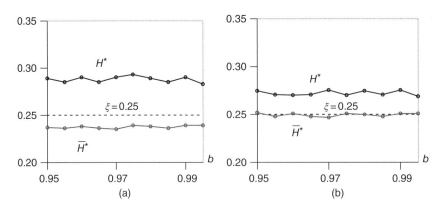

FIGURE 6.2 **Bootstrap adaptive EVI estimates, H^* and $\overline{H}^*$, as a function of b, in $m_1 = \lfloor n^b \rfloor$, for $n = 100$ (a) and $n = 1000$ (b).**

REMARK 6.9 *Note that bootstrap confidence intervals associated with the adaptive* EVI *estimates are easily computed on the basis of the replication of the Algorithm R times, for an adequate R. The value of B can also be adequately chosen.*

REMARK 6.10 *We would like to stress again that the use of the random sample of size m_2 $(x_1^*, \ldots, x_{m_2}^*)$ and the extended sample of size m_1 $(x_1^*, \ldots, x_{m_2}^*, x_{m_2+1}^*, \ldots, x_{m_1}^*)$ leads to a higher precision of the result with a smaller B. Indeed, if we had generated the sample of size m_1 independently of the sample of size m_2, just as done by Draisma et al. (1999), we would have got a wider confidence interval for the* EVI, *should we have kept the same value for B. This is quite similar to the use of the simulation technique of* "common random numbers" *in comparison algorithms, when we want to decrease the variance of a final answer to $z = y_1 - y_2$, inducing a positive dependence between y_1 and y_2.*

6.4   APPLICATIONS TO SIMULATED DATA

To enhance the importance of the PORT-Hill and PORT-MVRB EVI estimation in the field of finance, we refer to Gomes and Pestana (2007b) and Gomes et al. (2013), where, respectively, the MVRB and the PORT-MVRB EVI estimation have been applied to log returns associated with a few sets of financial data. Due to the specificity of such real data sets and to the fact that log returns have often been modeled by a Student-t or its skewed versions (see Jones and Faddy, 2003, among others), we have simulated a random sample of size $n = 1000$, from a Student's t_ν model with $\nu = 4$ degrees of freedom ($\xi = 1/\nu = 0.25$ and $\rho = -2/\nu = -0.5$). Due to the specificity of the data (infinite left end point), we have considered for both the PORT-Hill and the PORT-MVRB EVI estimation q-values from 0.15 to 1, with step 0.05. When $q = 1$, we elect the Hill or the MVRB EVI estimates. If $q < 1$, the PORT methodology is elected. We have further considered $m_1 = \lfloor n^b \rfloor$, with b from 0.950 to 0.995, with step 0.0025, and $B = 400$.

Figure 6.3 is related to the Student-t_4 generated sample, and we there present as an illustration of the obtained results the PORT-Hill/Hill and PORT-MVRB/MVRB EVI estimates (a), the q-estimates (b), and the RMSE estimates (c). The notation PORT ●/● means that we are playing with both the PORT-● ($q < 1$) and the ● ($q = 1$) EVI estimators. We have however been led to a PORT estimator, that is, to q-estimates smaller than 1.

6.5   CONCLUDING REMARKS

- For the previous simulated sample, we know the true value of ξ and the value 0.25, and we can easily assess the reliability of the estimates provided by the *Algorithm* in Section 6.3.2, immediately coming to the conclusion that, as

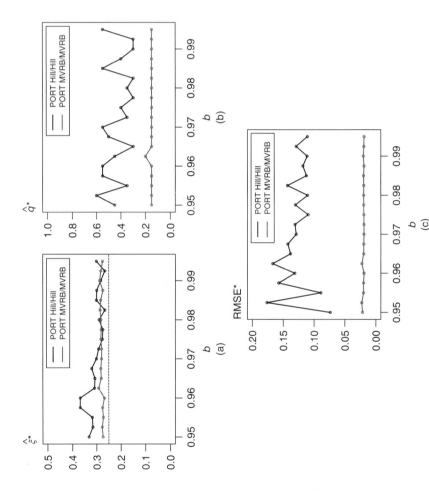

FIGURE 6.3 PORT-Hill/Hill and PORT-MVRB/MVRB adaptive EVI estimates (a), the *q*-estimates (b), and the RMSE estimates (c) for the generated Student-t_4 sample.

expected, the PORT-MVRB methodology provides the more reliable EVI estimation.

- It is clear that, similarly to what usually happens with the Hill EVI estimators, even the PORT-Hill EVI estimation leads to an overestimation of the EVI. The adaptive PORT-MVRB are generally closer to the target.

- Moreover, the RMSE estimates associated with the adaptive PORT-MVRB EVI estimates are always below the RMSE estimates associated with the adaptive PORT-Hill, another point in favor of the PORT-MVRB methodology.

- The performed case studies, including the one used here for illustration, claim obviously for a simulation study of the *Algorithm* and its application to real data sets. These are however topics out of the scope of this chapter.

- As a general conclusion, we advise the use of the PORT-MVRB methodology for the estimation of a heavy right tail function.

Acknowledgments

Research partially supported by national funds through **FCT**—Fundação para a Ciência e a Tecnologia, projects UID/MAT/UI0006/2013 (CEA/UL) and UID/MAT/0297/2013 (CMA/UNL) and postdoc grants SFRH/BPD/77319/2011 and SFRH/BPD/72184/2010.

References

Araújo Santos, P., Fraga Alves, M.I., Gomes, M.I. Peaks over random threshold methodology for tail index and quantile estimation. Revstat 2006;**4**(3):227–247.

Beirlant, J., Dierckx, G., Goegebeur, Y., Matthys, G. Tail index estimation and an exponential regression model. Extremes 1999;**2**:177–200.

Beirlant, J., Caeiro, F., Gomes, M.I. An overview and open research topics in the field of statistics of univariate extremes. Revstat 2012;**10**(1):1–31.

Bingham, N.H., Goldie, C.M., Teugels, J.L. *Regular Variation*. Cambridge: Cambridge University Press; 1987.

Caeiro, F., Gomes, M.I. A new class of estimators of a "scale" second order parameter. Extremes 2006;**9**:193–211, 2007.

Caeiro, F., Gomes, M.I. Minimum-variance reduced-bias tail index and high quantile estimation. Revstat 2008;**6**(1):1–20.

Caeiro, F., Gomes, M.I. A semi-parametric estimator of a shape second order parameter. In: Pacheco, A., Oliveira, M.R., Santos, R., Paulino, C.D., editors. *New Advances in Statistical Modeling and Application*, Studies in Theoretical and Applied Statistics, Selected Papers of the Statistical Societies. Berlin and Heidelberg: Springer-Verlag; 2014a. 137–144.

Caeiro, F., Gomes, M.I. On the bootstrap methodology for the estimation of the tail sample fraction. In: Gilli, M., Gonzalez-Rodriguez, G., Nieto-Reyes, A., editors. *Proceedings of COMPSTAT 2014*. Genéva, Switzerland; The International

Statistical Institute/International Association for Statistical Computing 2014b. 545–552.

Caeiro, F., Gomes, M.I. Bias reduction in the estimation of a shape second-order parameter of a heavy tailed model. J. Stat Comput Simul 2015;**85**(17):3405–3419.

Caeiro, F., Gomes, M.I., Henriques-Rodrigues, L. Reduced-bias tail index estimators under a third order framework. Commun Stat Theory Methods 2009;**38**(7):1019–1040.

Caeiro, F., Gomes, M.I., Pestana, D. Direct reduction of bias of the classical Hill estimator. Revstat 2005;**3**(2):111–136.

Caeiro, F., Gomes, M.I., Henriques-Rodrigues, L. A location invariant probability weighted moment EVI estimator. *International Journal of Computer Mathematics* 2016;**93**(4):676–695.

Caers, J., Beirlant, J., Maes, M.A. Statistics for modeling heavy tailed distributions in geology: Part I. Methodology. Math Geol 1999;**31**:391–410.

Ciuperca, G., Mercadier, C. Semi-parametric estimation for heavy tailed distributions. Extremes 2010;**13**(1):55–87.

Danielsson, J., de Haan, L., Peng, L., de Vries, C.G. Using a bootstrap method to choose the sample fraction in tail index estimation. Journal of Multivariate Analysis 2001;**76**:226–248.

Davison, A., Hinkley, D.V. *Bootstrap Methods and their Application*. Cambridge: Cambridge University Press; 1997.

de Haan, L. Slow variation and characterization of domains of attraction. In: de Oliveira, T., editor. *Statistical Extremes and Applications*. Dordrecht: D. Reidel; 1984. 31–48.

de Haan, L., Ferreira, A. *Extreme Value Theory: An Introduction*. New York: Springer Science+Business Media, LLC; 2006.

de Haan, L., Peng, L. Comparison of tail index estimators. Stat Neerl 1998;**52**:60–70.

Draisma, G., de Haan, L., Peng, L., Pereira, M.T. A bootstrap-based method to achieve optimality in estimating the extreme value index. Extremes 1999;**2**(4):367–404.

Efron, B. Bootstrap methods: another look at the jackknife. Ann Stat 1979;**7**(1):1–26.

Efron, B., Tibshirani, R.J. *An Introduction to the Bootstrap*. Boca Raton (FL): CRC Press; 1994.

Feuerverger, A., Hall, P. Estimating a tail exponent by modelling departure from a Pareto distribution. Ann Stat 1999;**27**:760–781.

Fisher, R.A., Tippett, L.H.C. Limiting forms of the frequency of the largest or smallest member of a sample. Proc Cambridge Philos Soc 1928;**24**:180–190.

Fraga Alves, M.I., Gomes, M.I., de Haan, L. A new class of semi-parametric estimators of the second order parameter. Portugaliae Mathematica 2003;**60**(2):194–213.

Geluk, J., de Haan, L. *Regular Variation, Extensions and Tauberian Theorems*. Amsterdam, Netherlands: CWI Tract 40, Center for Mathematics and Computer Science; 1987.

Gnedenko, B.V. Sur la distribution limite du terme maximum d'une série aléatoire. Ann Math 1943;**44**:423–453.

Goegebeur, Y., Beirlant, J., de Wet, T. Linking Pareto-tail kernel goodness-of-fit statistics with tail index at optimal threshold and second order estimation. Revstat 2008;**6**(1):51–69.

Goegebeur, Y., Beirlant, J., de Wet, T. Kernel estimators for the second order parameter in extreme value statistics. J Stat Plann Inference 2010;**140**(9):2632–2652.

Gomes, M.I., Guillou, A. Extreme value theory and statistics of univariate extremes: a review. Int Stat Rev 2015;**83**(2):263–292.

Gomes, M.I., Martins, M.J. "Asymptotically unbiased" estimators of the tail index based on external estimation of the second order parameter. Extremes 2002;**5**(1):5–31.

Gomes, M.I., Oliveira, O. The bootstrap methodology in Statistical Extremes—choice of the optimal sample fraction. Extremes 2001;**4**(4):331–358.

Gomes, M.I., Pestana, D. A simple second order reduced-bias' tail index estimator. J Stat Comput Simul 2007a;**77**(6):487–504.

Gomes, M.I., Pestana, D. A sturdy reduced-bias extreme quantile (VaR) estimator. J Am Stat Assoc 2007b;**102**(477):280–292.

Gomes, M.I., Martins, M.J., Neves, M.M. Alternatives to a semi-parametric estimator of parameters of rare events—the Jackknife methodology. Extremes 2000;**3**(3):207–229.

Gomes, M.I., Martins, M.J., Neves, M.M. Improving second order reduced-bias tail index estimation. Revstat 2007a;**5**(2):177–207.

Gomes, M.I., Reiss, R.-D., Thomas, M. Reduced-bias estimation. In: Reiss, R.-D., Thomas, M., editors. *Statistical Analysis of Extreme Values with Applications to Insurance, Finance, Hydrology and Other Fields*. 3rd ed., Chapter 6. Basel, Boston (MA), Berlin: Birkhäuser Verlag; 2007b. p 189–204.

Gomes, M.I., Canto e Castro, L., Fraga Alves, M.I., Pestana, D. Statistics of extremes for IID data and breakthroughs in the estimation of the extreme value index: Laurens de Haan leading contributions. Extremes 2008a;**11**(1):3–34.

Gomes, M.I., Fraga Alves, M.I., Araújo Santos, P. PORT hill and moment estimators for heavy-tailed models. Commun Stat Simul Comput 2008b;**37**:1281–1306.

Gomes, M.I., de Haan, L., Henriques-Rodrigues, L. Tail index estimation for heavy-tailed models: accommodation of bias in weighted log-excesses. J R Stat Soc B 2008c;**70**(1):31–52.

Gomes, M.I., Pestana, D., Caeiro, F. A note on the asymptotic variance at optimal levels of a bias-corrected Hill estimator. Stat Probab Lett 2009;**79**:295–303.

Gomes, M.I., Henriques-Rodrigues, L., Pereira, H., Pestana, D. Tail index and second order parameters' semi-parametric estimation based on the log-excesses. J Stat Comput Simul 2010;**80**(6):653–666.

Gomes, M.I., Henriques-Rodrigues, L., Miranda, C. Reduced-bias location-invariant extreme value index estimation: a simulation study. Commun Stat Simul Comput 2011a;**40**(3):424–447.

Gomes, M.I., Mendonça, S., Pestana, D. Adaptive reduced-bias tail index and VaR estimation via the bootstrap methodology. Commun Stat Theory Methods 2011b;**40**(16):2946–2968.

Gomes, M.I., Figueiredo, F., Neves, M.M. Adaptive estimation of heavy right tails: resampling-based methods in action. Extremes 2012;**15**:463–489.

Gomes, M.I., Henriques-Rodrigues, L., Fraga Alves, M.I., Manjunath, B.G. Adaptive PORT-MVRB estimation: an empirical comparison of two heuristic algorithms. J Stat Comput Simul 2013;**83**(6):1129–1144.

Gomes, M.I., Henriques-Rodrigues, L., Figueiredo, F. Resampling-based methodologies in statistics of extremes: environmental and financial applications. In: Bourguignon, J.-P., Jeltsch, R., Adrega Pinto, A., Viana, M., editors. *Mathematics of Planet Earth: Energy and Climate*, CIM Series in Mathematical Sciences, Chapter 8. Switzerland: Springer-Verlag; 2015a. p 197–215.

Gomes, M.I., Figueiredo, F., Martins, M.J., Neves, M.M. Resampling methodologies and reliable tail estimation. S Afr Stat J 2015b;**49**:1–20.

Gomes, M.I., Henriques-Rodrigues, L., Manjunath, B.L. Mean-of-order-p location-invariant extreme value index estimation. *Revstat* 2016;**14**(3):273–296.

Gumbel, E.J. *Statistics of Extremes*. New York: Columbia University Press; 1958.

Hall, P. Using the bootstrap to estimate mean squared error and select smoothing parameter in nonparametric problems. J Multivariate Anal 1990;**32**:177–203.

Hill, B.M. A simple general approach to inference about the tail of a distribution. Ann Stat 1975;**3**:1163–1174.

Henriques-Rodrigues, L., Gomes, M.I., Fraga Alves, M.I., Neves, C. PORT estimation of a shape second-order parameter. *Revstat* 2014;**12**(3):299–328.

Henriques-Rodrigues, L., Gomes, M.I., Manjunath, B.G. Estimation of a scale second-order parameter related to the PORT methodology. *Journal of Statistical Theory and Practice* 2015;**9**(3):571–599.

Jones, M.C., Faddy, M.J. A skew extension of the *t*-distribution, with applications. J R Stat Soc B 2003;**65**(1):159–174.

Longin, F. Le choix de la loi des rentabilités d'actifs financiers: les valeurs extrémes peuvent aider. Finance 1995;**16**:25–47.

Peng, L. Asymptotically unbiased estimator for the extreme-value index. Stat Probab Lett 1998;**38**(2):107–115.

Peng, L., Qi, Y. Estimating the first and second order parameters of a heavy tailed distribution. Aust N Z J Stat 2004;**46**:305–312.

Reiss, R.-D., Thomas, M. *Statistical Analysis of Extreme Values with Applications to Insurance, Finance, Hydrology and Other Fields*. 3rd ed. Basel, Boston (MA), Berlin: Birkhäuser Verlag; 2007.

Resnick, S. Heavy tail modelling and teletraffic data. Ann Stat 1997;**25**(5):1805–1869.

Weissman, I. Estimation of parameters and large quantiles based on the *k* largest observations. J Am Stat Assoc 1978;**73**:812–815.

Chapter Seven

Extreme Values Statistics for Markov Chains with Applications to Finance and Insurance

Patrice Bertail[1], Stéphan Clémençon[2], and Charles Tillier[1]

[1]*MODAL'X, Université Paris-Ouest, Nanterre, France*
[2]*TSI, TelecomParisTech, Paris, France*

AMS 2000 Mathematics Subject Classification: 60G70, 60J10, 60K20.

7.1 INTRODUCTION

Extremal events for (strongly or weakly) dependent data have received an increasing attention in the statistical literature in the last past years (see (Newell, 1964); (Loynes, 1965); (O'Brien, 1974), (O'Brien, 1987); (Hsing, 1988), (Hsing, 1991), (Hsing, 1993); (Resnick and Stărică, 1995); (Rootzén, 2009), for instance). A major issue for evaluating risks and understanding extremes and their possible replications is to take into account some dependencies. Indeed, whereas extreme values naturally occur in an isolated fashion in the identically independent distributed (i.i.d.) setup, since extreme values may be highly correlated, they generally tend to take place in small clusters for weakly dependent sequences. Most methods for statistical analysis of extremal events in weakly dependent setting rely on (fixed length) *blocking techniques*, which consist, roughly speaking, in dividing an observed data series into (overlapping or nonoverlapping) blocks of fixed length. Examining how extreme values occur over these data segments allows to capture the tail and the dependency structure of extreme values.

As originally pointed out in Rootzén (1988), the extremal behavior of instantaneous functionals $f(X) = \{f(X_n)\}_{n \in \mathbb{N}}$ of a Harris recurrent Markov chain X may be described through the regenerative properties of the underlying chain. This chapter emphasizes the importance of renewal theory and regeneration from the perspective of statistical inference for extremal events. Indeed, as observed by Rootzén (1988) (see also (Asmussen, 1998a); (Asmussen, 1998b); (Haiman et al., 1995); (Hansen and Jensen, 2005)), certain parameters of extremal behavior features of Harris Markov chains may be also expressed in terms of *regeneration cycles*, namely, data segments between consecutive regeneration times $\tau_1, \tau_2, \ldots$, that is, random times at which the chain completely forgets its past. Following in the footsteps of the seminal contribution of Rootzén (1988) (see also (Asmussen, 1998a)), Bertail et al. (2009) and Bertail et al. (2013) have recently investigated the performance of regeneration-based statistical procedures for estimating key parameters, related to the extremal behavior analysis in a Markovian setup. In the spirit of the works of Bertail and Clémençon (2006b) (refer also to (Bertail and Clémençon, 2004a); (Bertail and Clémençon, 2004b); (Bertail and Clémençon, 2006a)), they developed a statistical methodology, called the "pseudoregenerative method," based on approximating the pseudoregeneration properties of general Harris Markov chains, for tackling various estimation problems in a Markovian setup. Most of their works deal with regular differentiable functionals like the mean (see (Bertail and Clémençon, 2004a), (Bertail and Clémençon, 2007)), the variance, quantiles, L-statistics and their robustified versions (Bertail et al., 2015), as well as U-statistics (Bertail et al., 2011). Bootstrap versions of these estimates have also been proposed. For regular functionals, they possess the same nice second-order properties as the bootstrap in the i.i.d. case, that is, the rate of the convergence of the bootstrap distribution which is close to n^{-1}, for regular Markov chains, instead of $n^{-1/2}$ for the asymptotic (Gaussian) benchmark (see (Bertail and Clémençon, 2006b)).

The purpose of this chapter is to review and give some extensions of this approach in the framework of extreme values for general Markov chains. The proposed methodology consists in splitting up the observed sample path into regeneration data blocks (or into data blocks drawn from a distribution approximating the regeneration cycle's distribution, in the general case when regeneration times cannot be observed). We mention that the estimation principle exposed in this chapter is by no means restricted to the sole Markovian setup, but indeed applies to any process for which a regenerative extension can be constructed and simulated from available data (see Chapter 10 in Thorisson (2000)). Then, statistical tools are built over the sequence of maxima over the resulting data segments, as if these maxima were i.i.d. In order to illustrate the interest of this technique, we focus on the question of estimating the sample maximum's tail, the *extremal dependence index*, and the *tail index* by means of the (pseudo)regenerative method. To motivate this approach in financial and insurance applications (as well as queuing or inventory models), we illustrate how these tools may be used in order to estimate ruin probabilities or extremal index, in ruin models with a dividend barrier, exhibiting some regenerative properties. Such applications have also straightforward extensions (for continuous Markov chains) in the field of finance, for instance for put option pricing (for which the "strike" plays here the role of the ruin level).

7.2 ON THE (PSEUDO) REGENERATIVE APPROACH FOR MARKOVIAN DATA

Here and throughout, $X = (X_n)_{n \in \mathbb{N}}$ denotes a ψ-irreducible aperiodic time-homogeneous Markov chain, valued in a (countable generated) measurable space $(E, \mathcal{E})$ with transition probability $\Pi(x, dy)$ and initial distribution v. We recall that the Markov property means that, for any set B, such that $\psi(B) > 0$, for any sequence $(x_n, x_{n-1}, \ldots)$ in E,

$$P(X_{n+1} \in B | \{X_j = x_j, j \leq n\}) = P(X_{n+1} \in B | X_n = x_n)$$

$$= \Pi(x_n, B).$$

For homogeneous Markov chains, the transition probability does not depend on n. Refer to Revuz (1984) and Meyn and Tweedie (1996) for basic concepts of the Markov chain theory. For sake of completeness, we specify the two following notions:

- The chain is *irreducible* if there exists a σ-finite measure ψ such that for all set $B \in \mathcal{E}$, when $\psi(B) > 0$, the chain visits B with a strictly positive probability, no matter what the starting point.
- Assuming ψ-irreducibility, there are $d' \in \mathbb{N}^*$ and disjointed sets $D_1, \ldots, D_{d'}$ $(D_{d'+1} = D_1)$ weighted by ψ such that $\psi(E \setminus \cup_{1 \leq i \leq d'} D_i) = 0$ and $\forall x \in D_i$, $\Pi(x, D_{i+1}) = 1$. The *period* of the chain is the greatest common divisor d of such integers. It is *aperiodic* if $d = 1$.
- The chain is said to be recurrent if any set B with positive measure $\psi(B) > 0$, if and only if (i.f.f.) the set B is visited an infinite number of times.

The first notion formalizes the idea of a communicating structure between subsets, and the second notion considers the set of time points at which such communication may occur. Aperiodicity eliminates deterministic cycles. If the chain satisfies these three properties, it is said to be *Harris recurrent*.

In what follows, $\mathbb{P}_v$ (respectively, $\mathbb{P}_x$ for x in E) denotes the probability measure on the underlying space such that $X_0 \sim v$ (resp., conditioned upon $X_0 = x$), $\mathbb{E}_v[\cdot]$ the $\mathbb{P}_v$-expectation (resp. $\mathbb{E}_x[\cdot]$ the $\mathbb{P}_x(.)$-expectation), and $\mathcal{I}\{\mathcal{A}\}$ the indicator function of any event $\mathcal{A}$. We assume further that X is positive recurrent and denote by μ its (unique) invariant probability distribution.

7.2.1 Markov Chains with Regeneration Times: Definitions and Examples

A Markov chain X is said *regenerative* when it possesses an accessible atom, that is, a measurable set A such that $\psi(A) > 0$ and $\Pi(x, \cdot) = \Pi(y, \cdot)$ for all x, y in A. A recurrent Markov chain taking its value in a finite set is always atomic since each visited point is itself an atom. Queuing systems or ruin models visiting an infinite number of time the value 0 (the empty queue) or a given level (for instance, a barrier in the famous Cramér–Lundberg model; see Embrechts et al. (1997) and the following examples) are also naturally atomic. Refer also to Asmussen (2003) for regenerative models involved in queuing theory, and see also the examples and the following applications.

Denote then by $\tau_A = \tau_A(1) = \inf\{n \geq 1, X_n \in A\}$ the hitting time on A or first return time to A. Put also $\tau_A(j) = \inf\{n > \tau_A(j-1), X_n \in A\}, j \geq 2$ for the so-called *successive return times* to A, corresponding to the time of successive visits to the set A.

In the following $\mathbb{E}_A[\cdot]$ denotes the expectation conditioned on the event $\{X_0 \in A\}$. When the chain is Harris recurrent, for any starting distribution, the probability of returning infinitely often to the atom A is equal to one. Then, for any initial distribution v, by the *strong Markov property*, the sample paths of the chain may be divided into *i.i.d. blocks* of random length corresponding to consecutive visits to A, generally called *regeneration cycles*:

$$B_1 = (X_{\tau_A(1)+1}, \ldots, X_{\tau_A(2)}), \ldots, B_j = (X_{\tau_A(j)+1}, \ldots, X_{\tau_A(j+1)}), \ldots$$

taking their values in the torus $\mathbb{T} = \cup_{n=1}^{\infty} E^n$. The renewal sequence $\{\tau_A(j)\}_{j \geq 1}$ defines successive times at which the chain forgets its past, termed *regeneration times*.

Example 1: Queuing system or storage process with an empty queue. We consider here a storage model (or a queuing system), evolving through a sequence of *input times* $(T_n)_{n \in \mathbb{N}}$ (with $T_0 = 0$ by convention), at which the storage is refilled. Such models appear naturally in not only many domains like hydrology and operation research but also for modeling computer CPU occupancy.

Let X_n be the size of the input into the storage system at time T_n. Between each input time, it is assumed that withdrawals are done from the storage system at a constant rate r. Then, in a time period $[T, T + \Delta T]$, the amount of stored contents which disappears is equal to $r\Delta T$. If X_n denotes the amount of contents immediately before the input time T_n, we have, for all $n \in \mathbb{N}$,

$$X_{n+1} = (X_n + U_{n+1} - r\Delta T_{n+1})_+$$

with $(x)_+ = \sup(x, 0)$, $X_0 = 0$ by convention and $\Delta T_n = T_n - T_{n-1}$ for all $n \geq 1$ and $T_0 = 0$. ΔT_n is sometimes called the waiting time period.

This model can be seen as a reflected random walk on $\mathbb{R}^+$. Assume that, conditionally to $X_1, \ldots, X_n$, the amounts of input $U_1, \ldots, U_n$ are independent from each other and independent from the interarrival times $\Delta T_1, \ldots, \Delta T_n$ and that the distribution of U_i is given by $K(X_i, \cdot)$ for $0 \leq i \leq n$. Under the further assumption that $(\Delta T_n)_{n \geq 1}$ is an i.i.d. sequence, independent from $U = (U_n)_{n \in \mathbb{N}}$, the storage process X is a Markov chain. The case with exponential input–output has been extensively studied in Asmussen (1998a).

It is known that the chain Π is irreducible as soon as $K(x, \cdot)$ has an infinite tail for all $x \geq 0$ and if in addition $EU_n - rE\Delta T_{n+1} < 0$, $\{0\}$ is an accessible atom of

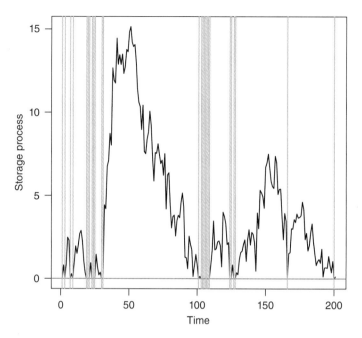

FIGURE 7.1 **Splitting a reflected random walk, with an atom at {0}; vertical lines corresponds to regeneration times, at which the chain forgets its past. A block is a set of observations between two lines (it may be reduced to {0} in some case).**

the chain X_n. Moreover, if $U_{n+1} - r\Delta T_{n+1}$ has exponential tails, then the chain is exponentially geometrically ergodic. The case with heavy tails has been studied in detail by Asmussen (1998b) and Asmussen et al. (2000). Under some technical assumptions, the chain is recurrent positive, and the times at which the storage process X reaches the value 0 are regeneration times. This property allows to define regeneration blocks dividing the sample path into independent blocks, as shown in the following. Figure 7.1 represents the storage process with ΔT_i and X_i with $\gamma(1)$ distribution and $r = 1.05$. The horizontal line corresponds to the atom $A = \{0\}$ and the vertical lines are the corresponding renewal times (visit to the atom).

Notice that the blocks are of random size. Some are rather long (corresponding to large excursion of the chain); others reduce to the point {0} if the chain stays at 0 for several periods. In this example, for the given values of the parameters, the mean length of a block is close to 50.5. It is thus clear that we need a lot of observations to get enough blocks. The behavior of the maximum of this process for subexponential arrivals has been studied at length in Asmussen (1998b).

Example 2: Cramér–Lundberg with a dividend barrier. Ruin models, used in insurance, are dynamic models in continuous time which describe the behavior of the reserve of a company as a function of:

(i) Its initial reserve u (which may be chosen by the insurer)

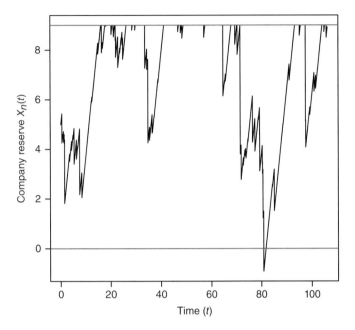

FIGURE 7.2 Cramér–Lundberg model with a dividend barrier at $b = 9$ (where the chain is reflected); ruin occurs at $t = 81$ when the chain goes below 0.

(ii) The claims which happen at some random times (described by a arrival claims process)

(iii) The premium rate which is the price paid by customers per unit of time

In the classical Cramér–Lundberg model (Figure 7.2), the claims arrival process $\{N(t), t \geqslant 0, N(0) = 0\}$ is supposed to be an homogeneous Poisson process with rate λ, modeling the number of claims in an interval $[0, t]$. The claims sizes $U_i, i = 1, \ldots, \infty$, which an insurance company has to face, are assumed to be strictly positive and independent, with cumulative distribution function (c.d.f.) F. The premium rate is supposed to be constant equal to c. Then, the total claims process, given by $S(t) = \sum_{i=1}^{N(t)} U_i$, is a compound Poisson process. Starting with an initial reserve $U(0) = u$, the reserve of the company evolves as

$$R(t) = u + ct - S(t)$$

$$= u + \sum_{n=1}^{N(t)} (c\Delta T_n - U_n).$$

One of the major problems in ruin models for insurance company is how to choose the initial amount to avoid the ruin or at least ensure that the probability of ruin over a finite horizon (or an infinite one) is small, equal to some given error of first kind, for instance, 10^{-3}. The probability of ruin for an initial reserve u over an horizon $[0, T]$ is given by

$$\psi(u, T) = P\left(\inf_{t \in [0,T]} (R(t)) < 0\right).$$

Notice that this model is very close to the queuing process considered in Example 1. The *input times* $(T_n)_{n \in \mathbb{N}}$ correspond here to the times of the claims. It is easy to see that under the given hypotheses, the interarrival times $(\Delta T_n)_{n \in \mathbb{N}}$ are i.i.d. with exponential distribution $\gamma(1, \lambda)$ (with $E\Delta T_n = 1/\lambda$). However, most of the time, for a given company, we only observe (at most) one ruin (since it is an absorbing state), and the reserve is not allowed to grow over a given barrier. Actually, if the process $R(t)$ crosses a given threshold b, the money is redistributed in some way to the shareholders of the company. This threshold is called a *dividend barrier*. In this case the process of interest is rather 1

$$X(t) = (u + ct - R(t)) \wedge b,$$

where $a \wedge b$ designs the infimum between a and b. Of course, the existence of a barrier reinforces the risk of ruin especially if the claims size may be large in particular if their distributions have a fat tail. The embedded chain is defined as the value of $X(t)$ at the claim times, say, $X_n = X(T_n)$ then it is easy to see that we have

$$X_{n+1} = \inf(X_n + c\Delta T_n - U_{n+1}, b) \text{ with } X_0 = u.$$

Otherwise, the probability of no ruin is clearly linked to the behavior of $Max_{1 \leq i \leq n}(-X_n)$.

In comparison to Example 1, this model is simply a mirror process, with this time an atom at $\{b\}$ instead of $\{0\}$ as shown in the following two graphics. In this example, the $(\Delta T_n)_{n \in \mathbb{N}}$ are exponential and the claims with exponential tails; the initial reserve is 5 and the barrier at 9. In this simulation the "ruin" is attained at time $t = 81$.

The embedded chain shows that the barrier is attained several times and allows to build regeneration times (vertical lines) and independent blocks just as in the first example. Because of the choice of the parameters (fat tail for the claims), the number of blocks is small on this short period, but in practical insurance applications, we may hope to have more regenerations (Figure 7.3).

7.2.2 Basic Regeneration Properties

When an accessible atom exists, the *stochastic stability* properties of the chain are reduced to properties concerning the speed of return time to the atom only. Theorem 10.2.2 in Meyn and Tweedie (1996) shows, for instance, that the chain X is positive recurrent i.f.f. $\mathbb{E}_A[\tau_A] < \infty$. The (unique) invariant probability distribution μ is then the Pitman occupation measure given by

$$\mu(B) = \frac{1}{\mathbb{E}_A[\tau_A]} \mathbb{E}_A\left[\sum_{i=1}^{\tau_A} \mathbb{I}\{X_i \in B\}\right], \text{ for all } B \in \mathcal{E}. \tag{7.1}$$

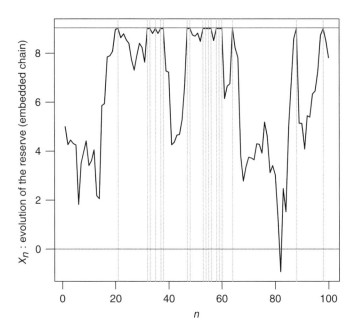

FIGURE 7.3 Splitting the embedded chain of a Cramér–Lundberg model with a dividend barrier. Vertical lines corresponds to regeneration times (when the chain attains the barrier $b = 9$). The blocks of observations between two vertical lines are independent.

In the case $\mathbb{E}_A[\tau_A] = \infty$, if there exists $0 < \beta < 1$ such that $E\tau_A^{\beta} < \infty$ and $E\tau_A^{\beta+\eta} = \infty$, for any $\eta > 0$, the chain is said $\beta - null\ recurrent$, and there exists an invariant measure (not a probability) for the chain. The splitting into independent blocks still holds (see, for instance, Tjöstheim, 1990; Karlsen and Tjöstheim, 2001). This includes the case of the random walk (with $\beta = 1/2$), and such procedure may be useful for studying the properties of the maximum for Markovian processes which have somehow the same kind of behavior as long-range memory processes. We will not consider this more technical case here. For atomic chains, limit theorems can be derived from the application of the corresponding results to the i.i.d. blocks $(\mathcal{B}_n)_{n \geq 1}$ (see (Smith, 1992) and the references therein). For instance, using this kind of techniques, Meyn and Tweedie (1996) have proved the law of large number (LLN), the central limit theorem (CLT), and laws of iterated logarithm (LIL) for Markov chains. Bolthausen (1980) obtained a Berry–Esseen-type theorem, and Malinovskĭ (1985), Malinovskĭ (1987, 1989); Bertail and Clémençon (2006b) have proved other refinements of the CLT, in particular Edgeworth expansions. The same technique can also be applied to establish moment and probability inequalities, which are not asymptotic results (see (Clémençon, 2001); (Bertail and Clémençon, 2010)).

Recall that a set $S \in \mathcal{E}$ is said to be *small* for X if there exist $m \in \mathbb{N}^*$, $\delta > 0$ and a probability measure Φ supported by S such that, for all $x \in S$, $B \in \mathcal{E}$,

$$\Pi^m(x, B) \geq \delta\ \Phi(B), \tag{7.2}$$

denoting by Π^m the mth iterate of the transition kernel Π. In the sequel, (7.2) is referred to as the *minorization condition* $\mathcal{M}(m, S, \delta, \Phi)$. Recall that accessible small sets always exist for ψ-irreducible chains: any set $B \in \mathcal{E}$ such that $\psi(B) > 0$ contains such a set (cf (Jain and Jamison, 1967)). In many models of interest $m = 1$ but even if it is not the case it is possible to vectorize the Markov chains to reduce the study of this condition to $m = 1$. Even if it entails replacing the initial chain X by the chain $\{(X_{nm}, \ldots, X_{n(m+1)-1})\}_{n \in \mathbb{N}}$, we now suppose $m = 1$. From a practical point of view, the minorizing probability measure may be chosen by the user. For instance, $\Phi(B)$ may be the uniform distribution over a given small set, typically a compact set which is often visited by the chain; then in this case δ may simply be seen as the minimum of the $\Pi(x, B)$ over S. Of course in practice Π is unknown but easily estimable so that plug-in estimators of these quantities may be easily constructed (see following text).

7.2.3 The Nummelin Splitting Trick and A Constructive Approximation

We now precise how to construct the atomic chain onto which the initial chain X is embedded. Suppose that X satisfies $\mathcal{M} = \mathcal{M}(m, S, \delta, \Phi)$ for $S \in \mathcal{E}$ such that $\psi(S) > 0$. The sample space is expanded so as to define a sequence $(Y_n)_{n \in \mathbb{N}}$ of independent Bernoulli random variables (r.v.'s) with parameter δ by defining the joint distribution $\mathbb{P}_{v, \mathcal{M}}$ whose construction relies on the following randomization of the transition probability Π each time the chain hits S. If $X_n \in S$ and

- if $Y_n = 1$ (with probability $\delta \in]0, 1[$), then $X_{n+1} \sim \Phi$.
- if $Y_n = 0$, then $X_{n+1} \sim (1 - \delta)^{-1}(\Pi(X_{n+1}, \cdot) - \delta\Phi(\cdot))$.

The key point of the construction relies on the fact that $A_S = S \times \{1\}$ is an atom for the bivariate Markov chain (X, Y), which inherits all its communication and stochastic stability properties from X (refer to Chapter 14 in Meyn and Tweedie (1996)).

Here we assume further that the conditional distributions $\{\Pi(x, dy)\}_{x \in E}$ and the initial distribution v are dominated by a σ-finite measure λ of reference, so that $v(dy) = f_v(y)\lambda(dy)$ and $\Pi(x, dy) = \pi(x, y)\lambda(dy)$ for all $x \in E$. For simplicity, we suppose that condition $\mathcal{M}$ is fulfilled with $m = 1$. Hence, Φ is absolutely continuous with respect to λ too, and, setting $\Phi(dy) = \phi(y) \cdot \lambda(dy)$,

$$\forall x \in S, \pi(x, y) \geq \delta\phi(y), \lambda(dy)\text{-almost surely.} \tag{7.3}$$

If we were able to generate binary random variables $Y_1, \ldots, Y_n$, so that $((X_1, Y_1), \ldots, (X_n, Y_n))$ be a realization of the split chain described previously, then we could divide the sample path $X^{(n)} = (X_1, \ldots, X_n)$ into regeneration blocks. Given the sample path $X^{(n+1)}$, it may be shown that the Y_i's are independent r.v.'s and the conditional distribution of Y_i is the Bernoulli distribution with parameter

$$\frac{\delta\phi(X_{i+1})}{\pi(X_i, X_{i+1})} \cdot \mathbb{I}\{X_i \in S\} + \delta \cdot \mathbb{I}\{X_i \notin S\}. \tag{7.4}$$

Therefore, knowledge of π over S^2 is required to draw $Y_1, \ldots, Y_n$ by this way.

A natural way of mimicking the Nummelin splitting construction consists in computing first an estimate $\hat{\pi}_n(x, y)$ of the transition density over S^2, based on the available sample path and such that $\hat{\pi}_n(x, y) \geq \delta\phi(y)$ a.s. for all $(x, y) \in S^2$, and then generating independent Bernoulli random variables $\hat{Y}_1, \ldots, \hat{Y}_n$ given $X^{(n+1)}$, the parameter of $\hat{Y}_i$ being obtained by plugging $\hat{\pi}_n(X_i, X_{i+1})$ into (7.4) in place of $\pi(X_i, X_{i+1})$. We point out that, from a practical point of view, it actually suffices to draw the $\hat{Y}_i$'s only at times i when the chain hits the small set S. $\hat{Y}_i$ indicates whether the trajectory should be cut at time point i or not. Proceeding this way, one gets the sequence of *approximate regeneration times*, namely, the successive time points at which $(X, \hat{Y})$ visits the set $A_S = S \times \{1\}$. Setting $\hat{l}_n = \sum_{1 \leqslant k \leqslant n} \mathbb{I}\{(X_k, \hat{Y}_k) \in S \times \{1\}\}$ for the number of splits (i.e., the number of visits of the approximated split chain to the artificial atom), one gets a sequence of *approximate renewal times*,

$$\hat{\tau}_{A_S}(j + 1) = \inf\{n \geq 1 + \hat{\tau}_{A_S}(j) / (X_n, \hat{Y}_n) \in S \times \{1\}\}, \text{ for } 1 \leq j \leq \hat{l}_n - 1 \quad (7.5)$$

with $\hat{\tau}_{A_S}(0) = 0$ by convention and forms the *approximate regeneration blocks* $\hat{B}_1, \ldots, \hat{B}_{\hat{l}_n - 1}$.

The knowledge of the parameters (S, δ, ϕ) of condition (7.3) is required for implementing this approximation method. A practical method for selecting those parameters in a fully data-driven manner is described at length in Bertail and Clémençon (2007). The idea is essentially to select a compact set around the mean of the time series and to increase its size. Indeed, if the small set is too small, then there will be no data in it and the Markov chain could not be split. On the contrary, if the small set is too large, the minimum δ over the small set will be very small, and there is little change that the we observe $Y_i = 1$. As the size increases, the number of regenerations increases up to an optimal value and then decreases; the choice of the small set and of the corresponding splitting is then entirely driven by the observations. To illustrate these ideas, we apply the method to a financial time series, assuming that it is Markovian (even if there are some structural changes, the Markovian nature still remains).

Example 3: Splitting a nonregenerative financial time series. Many financial time series exhibit some nonlinearities and structural changes both in level and variance. To illustrate how it is possible to divide such kind of data into "almost" independent blocks, we will study a particular model exhibiting such behavior.

Consider the following Smooth Exponential Threshold AutoRegressive Model with AutoRegressive Conditional Heteroskedasticity (SETAR(1)-ARCH(1)) model defined by

$$X_{t+1} = (\alpha_1 + \alpha_2 e^{-X_t^2})X_t + (1 + \beta X_t^2)^{1/2}\varepsilon_{t+1},$$

where the noise $(\varepsilon_t)_{t=1,\ldots,n}$ are i.i.d with variance σ^2. See Fan and Yao (2003) for a detailed description of these kinds of nonlinear models. It may be used to model log returns or log prices. Notice that this Markov chain (of order 1) may be seen as a continuous approximation of a threshold model. Assume that $|\alpha_1| < 1$, then for large values of $|X_t|$, it is easy to see that in mean X_{t+1} behaves like a simple $AR(1)$ model with coefficient α_1 (ensuring that the process will come back to its mean, equal to 0). Conversely, for small values of X_t (close to 0), the process behaves like an $AR(1)$ model with coefficient $\alpha_1 + \alpha_2$ (eventually explosive if $\alpha_1 + \alpha_2 > 1$). This process is thus able to engender bursting bubbles. The heteroscedastic part implies that the conditional variance $Var(X_{t+1}|X_t) = \sigma^2(1 + \beta X_t^2)^{1/2}$ may be strongly volatile when large values (the bubble) of the series occur. To ensure stationarity, we require $0 < \beta < 1$.

In the following simulation, we choose $n = 200$, $\alpha_1 = 0.60$, $\alpha_2 = 0.45$, $\beta = 0.35$, and $\sigma^2 = 1$. The following graph panel shows the Nadaraya estimator of the transition density and the number of blocks obtained as the size of the small set increases. For a small set of the form $[-0.8, 0.8]$, we obtain $\widehat{l}_n = 21$ pseudoblocks and the mean length of a block is close to 10. The estimated lower bound for the density over the small set $\widehat{\delta}_n$ is 0.15. The third graphic shows the level sets of the density and the corresponding optimal small set (containing the possible points at which the times series may be split). The last graph shows the original time series and the corresponding pseudoblocks obtained for an optimal data-driven small set.

Beyond the consistency property of the estimators that we will later study, this method has an important advantage that makes it attractive from a practical perspective: blocks are here entirely determined by the data (up to the approximation step), in contrast to standard blocking techniques based on fixed length blocks. Indeed, it is well known that the choice of the block length is crucial to obtain satisfactory results and is a difficult technical task.

7.2.4 Some Hypotheses

The validity of this approximation has been tackled in Bertail and Clémençon (2006a) using a *coupling approach*. Precisely, the authors established a sharp bound for the deviation between the distribution of $((X_i, Y_i))_{1 \leq i \leq n}$ and the one of $((X_i, \widehat{Y}_i))_{1 \leq i \leq n}$ in the sense of Wasserstein distance. The coupling "error" essentially depends on the rate of the *mean squared error* (MSE) of the estimator of the transition density

$$R_n(\widehat{\pi}_n, \pi) = \mathbb{E}[(\sup_{(x,y) \in S^2} |\widehat{\pi}_n(x, y) - \pi(x, y)|)^2] \tag{7.6}$$

with the sup norm over $S \times S$ as a loss function under the next conditions:

A1. The parameters S and ϕ in (7.3) are chosen so that $\inf_{x \in S}\phi(x) > 0$.

A2. $\sup_{(x,y) \in S^2} \pi(x, y) < \infty$ and $\mathbb{P}_v$-almost surely $\sup_{n \in \mathbb{N}}\sup_{(x,y) \in S^2} \widehat{\pi}_n(x, y) < \infty$.

Throughout the next sections, f denotes a fixed real-valued measurable function defined on the state space E. To study the properties of the block, we will also need the following usual moment conditions on the time return (Figure 7.4).

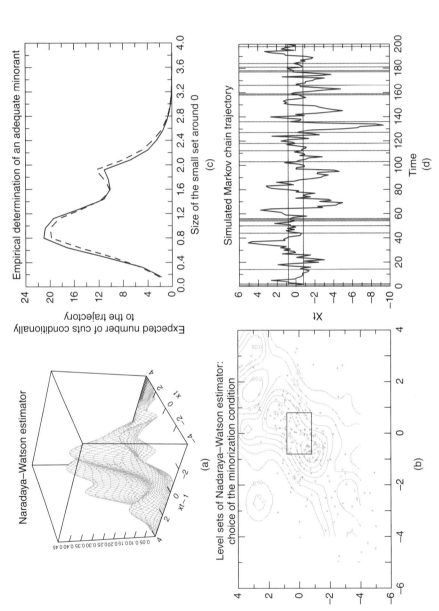

FIGURE 7.4 Splitting a Smooth Exponential Threshold Arch time series, with $n = 200$, $\alpha_1 = 0.60$, $\alpha_2 = 0.45$, $\beta = 0.35$ and $\sigma^2 = 1$. (a) Estimator of the transition density. (b) Visit of the chain to the small set $[-\varepsilon, \varepsilon]^2$ and the level sets of the transition density estimator: the optimal small set should contain a lot of points in a region with high density. (c) Number of regenerations according to the size ε of the small set, optimal for $\varepsilon_{opt} = 0.8$. (d) Splitting (vertical bars) of the original time series, with horizontal bars corresponding to the optimal small set.

A3 (Regenerative case)

$$\mathcal{H}(\kappa) \quad : \quad \mathbb{E}_A[\tau_A^\kappa] < \infty,$$

$$\mathcal{H}(v,\kappa) \quad : \quad \mathbb{E}_v[\tau_A^\kappa] < \infty,$$

and their analog versions in the nonregenerative case.

A4 (General Harris recurrent case)

$$\tilde{\mathcal{H}}(\kappa) \quad : \quad \sup_{x \in S} \mathbb{E}_x[\tau_S^\kappa] < \infty,$$

$$\tilde{\mathcal{H}}(v,\kappa) \quad : \quad \sup_{x \in S} \mathbb{E}_x[\tau_S^\kappa] < \infty.$$

7.3 PRELIMINARY RESULTS

Here we begin by briefly recalling the connection between the (pseudo) regeneration properties of a Harris chain X and the extremal behavior of sequences of type $f(X) = \{f(X_n)\}_{n \in \mathbb{N}}$, firstly pointed out in the seminal contribution of Rootzén (1988) (see also (Asmussen, 1998b); (Hansen and Jensen, 2005)).

7.3.1 Cycle Submaxima for Regenerative Markov Chains

We first consider the case when X possesses a known accessible atom A. In the following we denote $\alpha = \mathbb{E}_A[\tau_A]$. For $j \geq 1$, define the *submaximum* over the jth cycle of the sample path:

$$\zeta_j(f) = \max_{1+\tau_A(j) \leq i \leq \tau_A(j+1)} f(X_i). \tag{7.7}$$

In the following $l_n = \sum_{i=1}^{n} \mathbb{I}\{X_i \in A\}$ denotes the number of visits of X to the regeneration set A until time n . $\zeta_0(f) = \max_{1 \leq i \leq \tau_A} f(X_i)$ denotes the maximum over the first cycle (starting from an initial distribution v). Because of the "initialization" phase, its distribution is different from the others and essentially depends on v. $\zeta_{l_n}^{(n)}(f) = \max_{1+\tau_A(l_n) \leq i \leq n} f(X_i)$ denotes the maximum over the last nonregenerative data block (meaning by that it may be an incomplete block, since we may not observe the return to the atom A) with the usual convention that maximum over an empty set equals to $-\infty$.

With these definitions, it is easy to understand that the maximum value $M_n(f) = \max_{1 \leq i \leq n} f(X_i)$, taken by the sequence $f(X)$ over a trajectory of length n, may be naturally expressed in terms of *submaxima* over cycles

$$M_n(f) = \max\{\zeta_0(f), \max_{1 \leq j \leq l_n - 1} \zeta_j(f), \zeta_{l_n}^{(n)}(f)\}. \tag{7.8}$$

By the strong Markov property and independence of the blocks, the $\zeta_j(f)$'s are i.i.d. r.v.'s with common distribution function (d.f.) $G_f(x) = \mathbb{P}_A(\max_{1 \le i \le \tau_A} f(X_i) \le x)$. Moreover, by Harris recurrence, the number of blocks is of order $l_n \sim n/\alpha$ $\mathbb{P}_\nu$-almost surely as $n \to \infty$. Thus, $M_n(f)$ behaves like the maximum of n/α i.i.d. r.v.'s. The following result established in Rootzén (1988) shows that the limiting distribution of the sample maximum of X is entirely determined by the tail behavior of the d.f. G_f and relies on this crucial asymptotic independence of the blocks.

PROPOSITION 7.1 (Rootzén, 1988) *Let $\alpha = \mathbb{E}_A[\tau_A]$ be the mean return time to the atom A. Under the assumption that the first block does not affect the extremal behavior, that is to say that*

$$\mathbb{P}_\nu(\zeta_0(f) > \max_{1 \le k \le l} \zeta_k(f)) \to 0 \text{ as } l \to \infty, \tag{7.9}$$

we have then

$$\sup_{x \in \mathbb{R}} |\mathbb{P}_\nu(M_n(f) \le x) - G_f(x)^{n/\alpha}| \to 0 \text{ as } n \to \infty. \tag{7.10}$$

In the terminology of O'Brien (see (O'Brien, 1974, 1987), $G_f(x)^{1/\alpha}$ may be seen as a so-called phantom distribution, that is, an artificial distribution which gives the same distribution for the maximum as in the i.i.d. case. Indeed the preceding theorem shows that the distribution of the maximum behaves exactly as if the observations were independent with distribution $G_f(x)^{1/\alpha}$. As a consequence, the limiting behavior of the maximum in this dependent setting may be simply retrieved by using the famous Fischer–Tippett–Gnedenko theorem (obtained in the i.i.d. case), with the marginal distribution replaced by the phantom distribution $G_f(x)^{1/\alpha}$. Then, the asymptotic behavior of the sample maximum is entirely determined by the tail properties of the d.f. $G_f(dx)$. In particular, the limiting distribution of $M_n(f)$ (for a suitable normalization) is the generalized extreme value distribution function $H_\xi(dx)$ with parameter $\xi \in \mathbb{R}$, given by

$$H_\xi(x) = \begin{array}{ll} \exp(-x^{-1/\xi})\mathbb{I}\{x > 0\}, & \text{when } \xi > 0. \\ \exp(-\exp(-x)), & \text{when } \xi = 0. \\ \exp(-(-x)^{-1/\xi})\mathbb{I}\{x < 0\}, & \text{if } \xi < 0. \end{array}$$

In the following ξ will be referred as extreme value index. When $\xi > 0$, we will also call it the tail index, corresponding to a Pareto-like distribution. The smaller ξ, the heavier the tail is.

REMARK 7.2 *To explain the link between the transition and the behavior of the submaximum, consider the case where A is reduced to a point (which will be the case in our applications). Here to simplify $A = \{0\}$ and positive r.v.'s $X_k, k \in \mathbb{N}$, it is easy to see that*

$$G_f(x) = \mathbb{P}_A(\max_{1 \le i \le \tau_A} X_i \le x) = \sum_{k=1}^{\infty} a_k$$

$$a_k = \mathbb{P}_A(\max_{1 \le i \le \tau_A} X_i \le x, \tau_A = k)$$

but for $k \geqslant 2$

$$a_k = P_A(X_i \leq x, X_i > 0, i = 1, \ldots, k-1, X_k = 0)$$

$$= P_A(0 < X_1 \leq x | X_0 = 0) \prod_{i=2}^{k-1} P_A(0 < X_i \leq x | 0 < X_{i-1} < x)$$

$$\times P_A(X_k = 0 | 0 < X_{k-1} \leq x)$$

$$= \Pi(0,]0, x]) \Pi(]0, x],]0, x])^{k-2} \Pi(]0, x], 0)$$

so that

$$G_f(x) = \Pi(0, 0) + \frac{\Pi(0,]0, x]) \Pi(]0, x], 0)}{1 - \Pi(]0, x],]0, x])}.$$

Thus, it follows that the tail of G_f essentially depends on the behavior of $\Pi(,)$ for large values of x. The invariant measure depends itself on this quantity.

In the following, we assume that G_f belongs to the maximum domain of attraction $H_\xi(x)$ say, $MDA(H_\xi)$ (refer to (Resnick, 1987) for basics in extreme value theory). Then, there exist some sequences a_n and c_n such that $G_f(a_n x + c_n)^n \to H_\xi(x)$ as $n \to \infty$ and we have $\mathbb{P}_v(M_n(f) \leq a'_n x + c_n) \to H_\xi(x)$ as $n \to \infty$, with $a'_n = a_n / \alpha^\xi$.

7.3.1.1 Estimation of the cycle submaximum cumulative distribution function

In the atomic case, the c.d.f. G_f of the cycle submaxima, $\zeta_j(f)$ with $j \geqslant 1$, may be naturally estimated by the empirical counterpart d.f. from the observation of a random number $l_n - 1$ of complete regenerative cycles, namely,

$$G_{f,n}(x) = \frac{1}{l_n - 1} \sum_{j=1}^{l_n - 1} \mathbb{I}\{\zeta_j(f) \leqslant x\} \tag{7.11}$$

with $G_{f,n} \equiv 0$ by convention when $l_n \leq 1$. Notice that the first and the last (nonregenerative blocks) are dropped in this estimator. As a straightforward consequence of Glivenko-Cantelli's theorem for i.i.d. data, we have that

$$\Delta_n = \sup_{x \in \mathbb{R}} |G_{f,n}(x) - G_f(x)| \to 0, \mathbb{P}_v\text{-almost surely.} \tag{7.12}$$

Furthermore, by the LIL, we also have $\Delta_n = O(\sqrt{\log \log(n)/n})$ a.s.

7.3.1.2   Estimation of submaxima in the pseudoregenerative case

Cycle submaxima of the split chain are generally not observable in the general Harris case, since Nummelin extension depends on the true underlying transition probability. However, our regeneration-based statistical procedures may be directly applied to the submaxima over the approximate regeneration cycles. Define the pseudoregenerative block maxima by

$$\widehat{\zeta}_j(f) = \max_{1+\widehat{\tau}_{A_S}(j) \leq i \leq \widehat{\tau}_{A_S}(j+1)} f(X_i), \tag{7.13}$$

for $i = 1, \ldots, \widehat{l}_n - 1$. The empirical d.f. counterpart is now given by

$$\widehat{G}_{f,n}(x) = \frac{1}{\widehat{l}_n - 1} \sum_{j=1}^{\widehat{l}_n - 1} \mathbb{I}\{\widehat{\zeta}_j(f) \leq x\}, \tag{7.14}$$

with, by convention, $\widehat{G}_{f,n} \equiv 0$ if $\widehat{l}_n \leq 1$. As shown by the next theorem, using the approximate cycle submaxima instead of the "true" ones does not affect the convergence under assumption A1. Treading in the steps of Bertail and Clémençon (2004a), the proof essentially relies on a *coupling argument*.

THEOREM 7.3 *Let $f : (E, \mathcal{E}) \to \mathbb{R}$ be a measurable function. Suppose that conditions (7.3), A1, and A2 are fulfilled by the chain X. Assume further that $R_n(\widehat{\pi}_n, \pi) \to 0$ as $n \to \infty$. Then, $\widehat{G}_{f,n}(x)$ is a consistent estimator of $G_f(x) = \mathbb{P}_{A_S}(\max_{1 \leq i \leq \tau_{A_S}} f(X_i) \leq x)$, uniformly over $\mathbb{R}$, as $n \to \infty$,*

$$\widehat{\Delta}_n = \sup_{x \in \mathbb{R}} |\widehat{G}_{f,n}(x) - G_f(x)| = O_{\mathbb{P}_v}(R_n(\widehat{\pi}_n, \pi)^{1/2}). \tag{7.15}$$

For smooth Markov chains with smooth C^∞ transition kernel density, the rate of convergence of $\widehat{\Delta}_n$ will be close to $n^{-1/2}$. Under standard Hölder constraints of order s, the typical rate for the MSE (7.6) is of order $n^{-s/(s+1)}$ so that $\widehat{\Delta}_n = O_{\mathbb{P}_v}(n^{-s/(2(s+1))})$.

7.4 REGENERATION-BASED STATISTICAL METHODS FOR EXTREMAL EVENTS

The core of this paragraph is to show that, in the regenerative setup, consistent statistical procedures for extremal events may be derived from the application of standard inference methods introduced in the i.i.d. setting.

In the case when assumption (7.9) holds, one may straightforwardly derive from (7.10) estimates of $H^{(b_n)}(x) = \mathbb{P}_v(M_{b_n}(f) \leq x)$ as $n \to \infty$ and $b_n \to \infty$ based on the observation of (a random number of) submaxima $\zeta_j(f)$ over a sample path of length n, as proposed in Glynn and Zeevi (2000). Because of the estimation step, we will require that $\frac{b_n}{n} \to 0$. Indeed, if we want to obtain convergent estimators of the distribution of the maximum, we need to subsample the size of the maximum to ensure that the empirical estimation procedure does not alter the limiting distribution. For this, put

$$H_{n,l}(x) = (G_{f,n}(x))^l \tag{7.16}$$

with $l \geq 1$. The next limit result establishes the asymptotic validity of estimator (7.16) for an adequate choice of l depending both on the number of regenerations and of the size b_n, extending this way Proposition 3.6 of Glynn and Zeevi (2000). If computations are carried out with the pseudoregeneration cycles, under some additional technical assumptions taking into account the order of the approximation of the transition kernel, the procedure remains consistent. In this case, one would simply consider estimates of the form $\hat{H}_{n,l}(x) = (\hat{G}_{f,n}(x))^l$. The following theorem is a simple adaption of a theorem given in Bertail et al. (2009).

PROPOSITION 7.4

(i) *(Regenerative case) Suppose that assumption (7.9) holds. Assume that $b_n \to \infty$ is chosen in such a way that $b_n = o(\sqrt{n/\log\log n})$. Let $(u_n)_{n\in\mathbb{N}}$ be a (deterministic) sequence of real numbers such that $b_n(1 - G_f(u_n))/\alpha \to \eta < \infty$ as $n \to \infty$. Then, we have*

$$H^{(b_n)}(u_n) \to \exp(-\eta) \text{ as } n \to \infty. \tag{7.17}$$

In the regenerative setup, suppose furthermore that $\mathcal{H}(\nu, 1)$ is fulfilled. If we choose $l = l(b_n) \sim \frac{b_n}{\alpha}$ as $n \to \infty$. Then,

$$H_{n,l(b_n)}(u_n)/H^{(b_n)}(u_n) \to 1 \tag{7.18}$$

in $\mathbb{P}_\nu$- probability, as $n \to \infty$.

(ii) *(General Harris recurrent case) Suppose that **A1**, **A2**, and $\tilde{\mathcal{H}}(\nu, 1)$ hold and $R_N(\hat{\pi}_n, \pi) = O(n^{-1+\epsilon})$, as $n \to \infty$ for some $\epsilon \in]0, 1[$. If l is chosen so that, as $b_n \to \infty$, $l \sim \hat{l}_{b_n}$ and $b_n = o(n^{(1-\epsilon)/2})$, then*

$$\hat{H}_{n,l(n)}(u_n)/H^{(b_n)}(u_n) \to 1 \text{ in } \mathbb{P}_\nu \text{ - probability, as } n \to \infty. \tag{7.19}$$

(iii) *The same results hold if the deterministic threshold is replaced by an estimator based on the empirical distribution, for instance, $u_n = G_{f,n}^{-1}(1 - \eta\alpha/b_n)$.*

This result indicates that, in the most favorable case, we can recover the behavior of the maximum only over b_n observations with b_n much smaller than n. However, it is still possible to estimate the tail behavior of $M_n(f)$ by extrapolation techniques (as it is done, for instance, in Bertail et al. (2004)). If, in addition, one assumes that G_f belongs to some specific domain of attraction $MDA(H_\xi)$, for instance, to the Fréchet domain with $\xi > 0$, it is possible to use classical inference procedures (refer to Section 6.4 in (Embrechts et al., 1997), for instance) based on the submaxima $\zeta_1(f), \ldots, \zeta_{l_n - 1}(f)$ or the estimated submaxima over pseudocycles to estimate the shape parameter ξ, as well as the normalizing constants a_n and c_n.

7.5 THE EXTREMAL INDEX

The problem of estimating the extremal index of some functionals of this quantity has been the subject of many researches in the strong mixing framework (see, for instance, (Hsing, 1993); (Ferro and Segers, 2003); and more recently (Robert, 2009); (Robert et al., 2009)). However, we will show that in a Markov chain setting, the estimators are much more simpler to study. Recall that $\alpha = \mathbb{E}_A[\tau_A]$ is the mean return to the atom A. In the following, when the regenerative chain X is positive recurrent, we denote $F_\mu(x) = \alpha^{-1} \mathbb{E}_A[\sum_{i=1}^{\tau_A} \mathbb{I}\{f(X_i) \leqslant x\}]$, the empirical distribution function of the limiting stationary measure μ given by (7.1). It has been shown (see (Leadbetter and Rootzén, 1988), for instance) that there exists some index $\theta \in [0, 1]$, called the *extremal index* of the sequence $\{f(X_n)\}_{n \in \mathbb{N}}$, such that

$$\mathbb{P}_\mu(M_n(f) \leq u_n) \underset{n \to \infty}{\sim} F_\mu(u_n)^{n\theta}, \tag{7.20}$$

for any sequence $u_n = u_n(\eta)$ such that $n(1 - F_\mu(u_n)) \to \eta$. Once again, $F_\mu(\cdot)^\theta$ may be seen as an another phantom distribution. The inverse of the extremal index measures the clustering tendency of high threshold exceedances and how the extreme values cluster together. It is a very important parameter to estimate in risk theory, since it indicates somehow how many times (in mean) an extremal event will reproduce, due to the dependency structure of the data.

As notice in Rootzén (1988), because of the nonunicity of the phantom distribution, it is easy to see from Proposition 7.1 and (7.20) that

$$\theta = \lim_{n \to \infty} \frac{\log(G_f(u_n))/\alpha}{\log(F_\mu(u_n))} \tag{7.21}$$

$$= \lim_{n \to \infty} \frac{\log(1 - \bar{G}_f(u_n))/\alpha}{\log(1 - \bar{F}_\mu(u_n))} \tag{7.22}$$

$$= \lim_{n \to \infty} \frac{\bar{G}_f(u_n))}{\alpha \bar{F}_\mu(u_n)}. \tag{7.23}$$

The last equality is followed by a simple Taylor expansion. In the i.i.d. setup, by taking the whole state space as an atom ($A = \mathcal{X}$, so that $\tau_A = \alpha \equiv 1$, $G_f = F_\mu$), one immediately finds that $\theta = 1$. In the dependent case, the index θ may be interpreted as the proportionality constant between the probability of exceeding a sufficiently high threshold within a regenerative cycle and the mean time spent above the latter between consecutive regeneration times.

It is also important to notice that Proposition 7.1 combined with (7.20) also entail that, for all ξ in $\mathbb{R}$, G_f and F_μ belong to the same domain of attraction (when one of them is in a domain attraction of the maximum). Their tail behavior only differs from the slowly varying functions appearing in the tail behavior. We recall that a slowly varying function is a function L such that $L(tx)/L(x) \to 1$ as $x \to \infty$ for any $t > 0$. For instance, log, iterated logarithm, $1/\log$, $1 + 1/x^\beta$, $\beta > 0$ are slowly varying functions.

Suppose that G_f and F_μ belong to the Fréchet domain of attraction; then it is known (cf Theorem 8.13.2 in Bingham et al. (1987)) that there exist $\xi > 0$ and two slowly varying functions $L_1(x)$ and $L_2(x)$ such that $\bar{G}_f(x) = L_1(x) \cdot x^{-\frac{1}{\xi}}$ and $\bar{F}_\mu(x) = L_2(x) \cdot x^{-\frac{1}{\xi}}$. In this setup, the extremal index is thus simply given by the limiting behavior of

$$\theta(u) = \frac{L_1(u)}{\alpha L_2(u)}.$$

However, estimating slowly varying functions is a difficult task, which requires a lot of data (see (Bertail et al., 2004)). Some more intuitive empirical estimators of θ will be proposed in the following.

In the regenerative case, a simple estimator of θ is given by the empirical counterpart of expression (7.21). $F_n(x) = n^{-1} \sum_{1 \le i \le n} \mathbb{I}\{f(X_i) \le x\}$ is a natural a.s. convergent empirical estimate of $F_\mu(x)$. Recalling that $\frac{n}{l_n} \to \alpha$ a.s., define for a given threshold u,

$$\theta_n(u) = \frac{\sum_{j=1}^{l_n-1} \mathbb{I}\{\zeta_j(f) > u\}}{\sum_{i=1}^n \mathbb{I}\{f(X_i) > u\}}, \tag{7.24}$$

with the convention that $\theta_n(u) = 0$ if $M_n(f) < u$. For general Harris chains, the empirical counterpart of Eq. (7.21) computed from the approximate regeneration blocks is now given by

$$\hat{\theta}_n(u) = \frac{\sum_{j=1}^{\hat{l}_n-1} \mathbb{I}\{\hat{\zeta}_j(f) > u\}}{\sum_{i=1}^n \mathbb{I}\{f(X_i) > u\}}, \tag{7.25}$$

with $\hat{\theta}_n(u) = 0$ by convention when $M_n(f) < u$. The following result has been recently proved in Bertail et al. (2013). Other estimators based on fixed length blocks in the framework of strong mixing processes are given in Robert (2009) and Robert et al. (2009).

PROPOSITION 7.5 *Let $(r_n)_{n \in \mathbb{N}}$ be increasing to infinity in a way that $r_n = o(\sqrt{n/\log\log n})$ as $n \to \infty$. And consider $(v_n)_{n \in \mathbb{N}}$ such that $r_n(1 - G_f(v_n)) \to \eta < \infty$ as $n \to \infty$.*

(i) In the regenerative case, suppose that $\mathcal{H}(v, 1)$ and $\mathcal{H}(2)$ are fulfilled. Then,

$$\theta_n(v_n) \to \theta \ \mathbb{P}_v\text{-almost surely, as } n \to \infty. \tag{7.26}$$

Moreover we have

$$\sqrt{n/r_n}(\theta_n(v_n) - \theta(v_n)) \Rightarrow \mathcal{N}(0, \theta^2/\eta), \; as \; n \to \infty. \qquad (7.27)$$

(ii) In the general case, assume that A1 − A3, $\tilde{\mathcal{H}}(v, 1)$, and $\tilde{\mathcal{H}}(4)$ are satisfied. Then,

$$\widehat{\theta}_n(v_n) \to \theta \; in \; \mathbb{P}_v\text{-probability}, \, as \; n \to \infty. \qquad (7.28)$$

We also have the following CLT:

$$\sqrt{n/r_n}(\widehat{\theta}_n(v_n) - \theta(v_n)) \Rightarrow \mathcal{N}(0, \theta^2/\eta) \; as \; n \to \infty. \qquad (7.29)$$

REMARK 7.6 *In practice, the levels v_n are unknown since they are defined as upper quantiles of the true underlying submaximum distribution. However, if these thresholds are chosen empirically by taking r_n equal to $G_n^{-1}(1 - \eta/r_n)$ in the regenerative case or $\hat{G}_n^{-1}(1 - \eta/r_n)$ in the pseudoregenerative case, then the limiting results remain valid. Because of the condition $r_n = o(\sqrt{n/\log\log n})$, notice that the best attainable rate with our method is close to $n^{1/4}$ in the regenerative case.*

REMARK 7.7 *(The extremal index θ seen as a limiting conditional probability) (Rootzén, 1988) also showed that the extremal index may also be defined as*

$$\theta = \lim_{n \to \infty} \mathbb{P}_A \left(\max_{2 \leq i \leq \tau_A} f(X_i) \leq u_n \mid X_1 > u_n \right) \qquad (7.30)$$

for any sequence u_n defined as before. This may be seen as a regenerative version of the so-called runs *representation of the extremal index (see (Hsing, 1993), for instance). This also indicates that the extremal index measures the clustering tendency of high threshold exceedances within regeneration cycles only. An empirical estimator is then simply given by the empirical counterpart based on blocks (or pseudoblocks)*

$$\theta_n'(u) = \frac{\sum_{j=1}^{l_n - 1} \mathbb{I}\{f(X_{1+\tau_A(j)}) > u, \max_{2+\tau_A(j) \leq i \leq \tau_A(j+1)} f(X_i) \leq u\}}{\sum_{j=1}^{l_n - 1} \mathbb{I}\{f(X_{1+\tau_A(j)}) > u\}} \qquad (7.31)$$

for a properly chosen level $u > 0$. The same kind of results may be obtained for this estimator: however, a moderate sample simulation proposed in Bertail et al. (2013) shows that our first estimator outperforms this long-run version as far as coverage of confidence intervals are concerned. This is probably due to the second-order properties of these estimators which may be quite difficult to investigate.

REMARK 7.8 *Notice that the recentering value in the preceding theorem is $\theta(v_n)$, which converges asymptotically to θ. To control the induced bias (which is a common phenomenon in extreme value parameter estimation), some additional* *second-order conditions are needed. Typically, if one assumes some second-order Hall-type conditions, say,*

$$L_i(x) = \lim_{y \to \infty} L_i(y) + C_i \cdot x^{-\beta_i} + o(x^{-\beta_i})$$

as $x \to \infty$ where $C_i < \infty$ and $\beta_i > 0$, $i = 1, 2$, then it can be shown that $\theta(v_n)$ converges to θ at the rate $v_n^{-\beta}$ with $\beta = \beta_1 \wedge \beta_2$ and $v_n \sim r_n^{1/\beta_1}$. Hence, as soon as r_n is chosen such that $n/r_n^{1+2\beta/\beta_1} \to 0$, we have that $\sqrt{n/r_n}(\theta_n(v_n) - \theta) \Rightarrow \mathcal{N}(0, \theta^2/\eta)$ as $n \to \infty$. Similar result holds true in the pseudoregenerative case. From a practical point of view, to control for the bias, a graphical-based techniques is generally used for choosing the level by screening different values of u_n and detecting the region of stability of the estimator (see the following simulations).

7.6   THE REGENERATION-BASED HILL ESTIMATOR

As pointed out in Section 7.5, provided that the extremal index of $\{f(X_n)\}_{n \in \mathbb{N}}$ exists and is strictly positive, the equivalence $G_f \in MDA(H_\xi) \iff F_\mu \in MDA(H_\xi)$ holds true, in particular in the Fréchet case, for $\xi > 0$. Classically, the d.f. F belongs to $MDA(H_\xi)$ i.f.f. it fulfills the tail regularity condition

$$1 - F(x) = L(x)x^{-1/\xi}, \tag{7.32}$$

where $L(x)$ is a slowly varying function. Statistical estimation of the tail risk index $\xi > 0$ of a regularly varying d.f. based on i.i.d. data has been the subject of a good deal of attention since the seminal contribution of Hill (1975). Most methods that boil down to computing a certain functional of an increasing sequence of upper order statistics have been proposed for dealing with this estimation problem, just like the celebrated *Hill estimator*, which can be viewed as a conditional maximum likelihood approach. Given i.i.d. observations $Z_1, \dots, Z_n$ with common distribution $F(dx)$, the Hill estimator is

$$H_{k,n}^Z = k^{-1} \sum_{i=1}^{k} \log \frac{Z_{(i)}}{Z_{(k+1)}}, \text{ with } 1 \le k < n, \tag{7.33}$$

where $Z_{(i)}$ denotes the ith largest order statistic of the data sample $Z^{(n)} = (Z_1, \dots, Z_n)$. The asymptotic behavior of this estimator has been extensively investigated when stipulating that $k = k_n$ goes to ∞ at a suitable rate. Strong consistency is proved when $k_n = o(n)$ and $\log \log n = o(k_n)$ as $n \to \infty$ in Deheuvels et al. (1988). Its asymptotic normality is established in Goldie (1991): under further conditions on L (referred to as *second-order regular variation*) and k_n, we have the convergence in distribution $\sqrt{k_n}(H_{k_n,n}^Z - \xi) \Rightarrow \mathcal{N}(0, \xi^2)$.

The *regeneration-based Hill estimator* based on the observation of the $l_n - 1$ submaxima $\zeta_1(f), \ldots, \zeta_{l_n-1}(f)$, denoting by $\zeta_{(j)}(f)$ the jth largest submaximum, is naturally defined as

$$\xi_{n,k} = k^{-1} \sum_{i=1}^{k} \log \frac{\zeta_{(i)}(f)}{\zeta_{(k+1)}(f)}, \tag{7.34}$$

with $1 \leq k \leq l_n - 1$ when $l_n > 1$. Observing that, as $n \to \infty$, $l_n \to \infty$ with $\mathbb{P}_\nu$ probability one, limit results holding true for i.i.d. data can be immediately extended to the present setting (cf assertion (i) of Proposition 7.9). In the general Harris situation, an estimator of exactly the same form can be used, except that approximate submaxima are involved in the computation:

$$\widehat{\xi}_{n,k} = k^{-1} \sum_{i=1}^{k} \log \frac{\widehat{\zeta}_{(i)}(f)}{\widehat{\zeta}_{(k+1)}(f)}, \tag{7.35}$$

with $1 \leq k \leq \widehat{l}_n - 1$ when $\widehat{l}_n > 1$. As shown by the next result, the approximation stage does not affect the consistency of the estimator, on the condition that the estimator $\widehat{\pi}$ involved in the procedure is sufficiently accurate. For the purpose of building Gaussian asymptotic confidence intervals (CI) in the nonregenerative case, the estimator $\widehat{\xi}_{n,k}$ is also considered, still given by Eq. (7.35).

PROPOSITION 7.9 *Suppose that $F_\mu \in MDA(H_\xi)$ with $\xi > 0$. Let $\{k(n)\}$ be an increasing sequence of integers such that $k(n) < n$, $k(n) = o(n)$, and $\log \log n = o(k(n))$ as $n \to \infty$.*

(i) *Then the regeneration-based Hill estimator is strongly consistent*

$$\xi_{n,k(l_n)} \to \xi \; \mathbb{P}_\nu\text{- almost surely, as } n \to \infty. \tag{7.36}$$

Under the further assumption that F_μ satisfies the von Mises condition and that $k(n)$ is chosen accordingly (cf (Goldie, 1991)), it is moreover asymptotically normal in the sense that

$$\sqrt{k(l_n)}(\xi_{n,k(l_n)} - \xi) \Rightarrow \mathcal{N}(0, \xi^2) \; under \; \mathbb{P}_\nu, \text{as } n \to \infty. \tag{7.37}$$

(ii) *In the general Harris case, if A1 and A2 are furthermore fulfilled and $k = k(n)$ is chosen accordingly to the von Mises conditions such that $\mathcal{R}_n(\widehat{\pi}_n, \pi)^{1/2} n \log n = o(k(n))$, then*

$$\widehat{\xi}_{n,k(\widehat{l}_n)} \to \xi \text{ in } \mathbb{P}_\nu\text{- probability, as } n \to \infty. \tag{7.38}$$

(iii) *Under A1 and A2, if one chooses a sequence $(m_n)_{n \in \mathbb{N}}$ of integers increasing to infinity such that $m_n \mathcal{R}_n(\widehat{\pi}_n, \pi)^{1/2} / \sqrt{k(m_n)} \to 0$ as $n \to \infty$, then,*

$$\sqrt{k(\widehat{l}_{m_n})}(\widehat{\xi}_{m_n,k(\widehat{l}_{m_n})} - \xi) \Rightarrow \mathcal{N}(0, \xi^2) \; under \; \mathbb{P}_\nu, \text{as } n \to \infty. \tag{7.39}$$

Before showing how the extreme value regeneration-based statistics reviewed in the present article practically perform on several examples, a few comments are in order.

The tail index estimator (7.34) is proved strongly consistent under mild conditions in the regenerative setting, whereas only (weak) consistency has been established for the alternative method proposed in Resnick and Stărică (1995) under general strong mixing assumptions. The condition stipulated in assertion (ii) may not be satisfied for some $k(n)$. When the slowly varying function $L(u) = G_f(u)/u^{-1/\xi}$ equals, for instance, $\log(\cdot)$, it cannot be fulfilled. Indeed in this case, $k(n)$ should be chosen of order $o(\log(n))$ according to the von Mises conditions. In contrast, choosing a subsampling size m_n such that the conditions stipulated in assertion (iii) hold is always possible. The issue of picking m_n in an optimal fashion in this case remains open.

Given the number $l > 2$ (l_n or $\widehat{l}_n$) of (approximate) regeneration times observed within the available data series, the tuning parameter $k \in 1, \ldots, l - 1$ can be selected by means of standard methods in the i.i.d. context. A possible solution is to choose k so as to minimize the estimated MSE

$$\widehat{\gamma}_{n,k}^2/k + (a_{n,k} - \widehat{\gamma}_{n,k})^2,$$

where $\widehat{\gamma}_{n,k}$ is a bias-corrected version of the Hill estimator. Either the jackknife method or else an analytical method (see (Feuerverger and Hall, 1999) or (Beirlant et al., 1999)) can be used for this purpose. The randomness of the number of submaxima is the sole difference here.

7.7 APPLICATIONS TO RUIN THEORY AND FINANCIAL TIME SERIES

As an illustration, we now apply the inference methods described in the previous section to two models from the insurance and the financial fields.

7.7.1 Cramér–Lundberg model with a barrier: Example 2

Considering Example 2, we apply the preceding results to obtain an approximation of the distribution of the subminimum, the global minimum (i.e., the probability of ruin over a given period), and the extremal index. We will not consider here the subexponential case (heavy-tailed claims) for which it is known that the extremal index is equal to $\theta = 0$, corresponding to infinite clusters of extreme values (see (Asmussen, 1998b)). Recall that the continuous process of interest is given by

$$X(t) = (u + ct - R(t)) \wedge b$$

and that the embedded chain satisfies

$$X_{n+1} = \inf(X_n + c\Delta T_n - U_{n+1}, b) \text{ with } X_0 = u.$$

Notice that if the barrier b is too high in comparison to the initial reserve u, then the chain will regenerate very rarely (unless the price c is very high) and the method will not be useful. But if the barrier is attained at least one time, then the probability of ruin will only depend on b not on u. Assume that ΔT_n is $\gamma(\lambda)$ and the claims are distributed as $\gamma(1/\mu)$ with $EW_n = \mu$. The safety loading is then given by $\rho = \frac{c}{\lambda\mu} - 1$ and is assumed to be nonnegative to ensure that the probability of ruin is not equal to 1 a.s.

Using well-known results in the case of i.i.d. exponential inputs and outputs, the extremal index is given by $\theta = (1 - \frac{1}{1+\rho})^2 = (1 - \frac{\lambda\mu}{c})^2$. In our simulation we choose $\mu = 0.2$ and $c = 0.3\lambda$ with $\lambda = 10^{-2}$ so that the extremal index is given here by $\theta = 0.111$. We emphasize the fact that we need to observe the times series over a very long period (5000 days) so as to observe enough cycles. The barrier is here at $b = 44$ with a initial reserve $u = 43$.

For $n = 5000$ and if we choose b_n of order $\sqrt{n} \approx 70.7$, with proposition 3 by calculating the quantile of $G_{f,n}$ of order $1 + \log(\eta)\alpha/b_n$ for $\eta = 0.95$, we obtain that $Prob(\min_{1 \leqslant i \leqslant \sqrt{n}}(X_i) \leqslant 4.8) = 5\%$. This is an indicator that in the next 70 days there is a rather high probability of being ruined. Inversely, some straightforward inversions (here $G_{f,n}(b) = \Pr(\min_{1 \leq i \leq \tau_A}(X_i) \geq 0) = P(\min_{1 \leq i \leq \tau_A}(X_i - b) \geq -b) = P(\max_{1 \leq i \leq \tau_A}(b - X_i) \leq b))$ show that the probability of ruin

$$P(\min_{1 \leqslant i \leqslant \sqrt{n}}(X_i) \leqslant 0) = 1 - H_{n,l(b_n)}(b)$$

and that

$$\simeq 1 - (G_{f,n}(b))^{b_n/\alpha} = 1 - 0.9583 \simeq 4.2.$$

This strongly suggests that the dividend barrier and the initial reserve are too low.

As far as the extremal index is concerned, we obtain a rather good estimator of θ as shown in Figure 7.5 (see also the simulation results in Bertail et al. (2013) in a slightly different setting (M/M/1 queues)). It represents the value of $\theta(v_n)$ for a sequence of high value of the threshold. The stable part of $\theta(v_n)$ for a large range of value of levels corresponding to v_n is very close to the true value. It should be noticed that when v_n is too high, the quantiles of $G_{f,n}$ are badly estimated, resulting in a very bad estimation of θ. Although we did not present in this chapter the validity of the regenerative bootstrap (i.e., bootstrapping regenerative blocks) as shown in Bertail et al. (2013), we represent the corresponding bootstrap CI on the graphics. It is also interesting to notice that the change in width of the CI is a good indicator in order to choose the adequate level v_n.

7.7.2   Pseudoregenerative financial time series: extremal index and tail estimation

We will consider the model exhibited in Example 3 for a much more longer stretch of observations. Recall that the process is given by the nonlinear autoregressive form

$$X_{t+1} = (\alpha_1 + \alpha_2 e^{-X_t^2})X_t + (1 + \beta X_t^2)^{1/2}\varepsilon_{t+1}, \quad t = 0, \ldots, n-1.$$

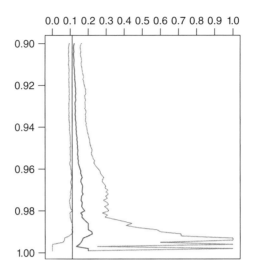

FIGURE 7.5 **Estimator (continuous line) and bootstrap confidence interval (dotted lines) of the extremal index** $\theta(v_n)$**, for a sequence of high values of the threshold** v_n **(seen as a quantile of the y-coordinate). True value of** $\theta = 0.111$**.**

Indeed the methods used here will only be of interest when $\sqrt{n/\alpha}$ and the number of pseudoregeneration is not too small. The rate of convergence of the Hill estimator is also strongly influenced by the presence of the slowly varying function (here in the distribution of the submaxima). Recall that if the slowly varying function belongs to the Hall's family, that is, is of the form, for some $D \in \mathbb{R}$ and $\beta > 0$,

$$L(x) = 1 + Dx^{-\beta}(1 + o(1)),$$

then the optimal rate of convergence of the Hill estimator is of order at most $n^{\beta/(2\beta+1/\xi)}$ (see (Goldie, 1991)). Thus, if β is small, the rate of convergence of the Hill estimator may be very slow. In practice, we rarely estimate the slowly varying function, but the index is determined graphically by looking at range k_n of extreme values, where the index is quite stable. We also use the bias correction methods (Feuerverger and Hall, (1999) or Beirlant et al., (1999)) mentioned before, which greatly improve the stability of the estimators.

We now present in Figure 7.6 a path of an SETAR-ARCH process, with a large value of $n = 5000$. We choose $\alpha_1 = 0.6$, $\alpha_2 = 0.45$, and $\beta = 0.35$, which ensure stationarity of the process. This process clearly exhibits the features of many log returns encountered in finance. The optimal small set (among those of the form $[-c, c]$) is given by $[-1.092, 1.092]$, which is quite large, because of the variability of the time series, with a corresponding value of $\delta = 0.145$.

The true value of θ (obtained by simulating several very long time series $N = 10^7$) is close to 0.50. This means that maxima clusterize by pair. Figure 7.7 presents the dependence index estimator for a range of values of the threshold (the level of the quantile is given on the axe). The estimator is rather unstable for

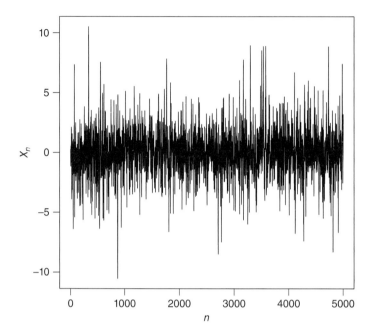

FIGURE 7.6 Simulation of the SETAR-ARCH process for $n = 5000$, $\alpha_1 = 0.6$, $\alpha_2 = 0.45$, and $\beta = 0.35$, exhibiting strong volatility and large excursions.

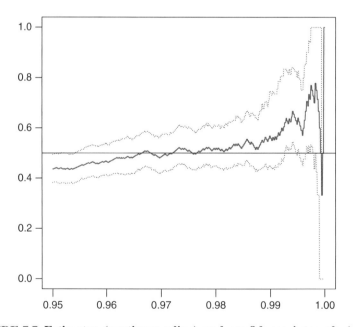

FIGURE 7.7 Estimator (continuous line) and confidence intervals (dotted lines) of the extremal index as a function of the quantile level $\theta(v_n)$, for a sequence of high values of the threshold v_n (seen as a quantile of the x-coordinate). True value of θ close to 0.5.

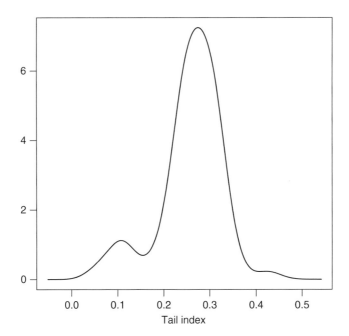

FIGURE 7.8 **Bootstrap distribution of the pseudoregenerative Hill estimator (smoothed with a Gaussian kernel), based on $B = 999$ bootstrap replications. Mode around 2.8.**

large quantiles, but we clearly identify a zone of stability near the true value of θ. Bootstrap CI lead to an estimator of θ, between 0.428 and 0.587 at the level 95% (which is in the range of the limit theorem given before). The problem of choosing the optimal value of k_n in this case is still an open problem.

Figure 7.8 presents the regenerative Bootstrap distribution (Bertail and Clémençon (2006b)) of the Hill estimator, with a choice of the optimal fraction $k(\widehat{l}_{m_n})$ obtained by minimizing the MSE. This leads to a CI for the tail (with a error rate of 5%) of the distribution given by $[0.090, 0.345]$. This suggests that for this process, the tail may be quite heavy, since even the moment of order 3 may not exist.

7.8 AN APPLICATION TO THE CAC40

We will apply our method to the daily log return of the CAC40, from 10/07/1987 to 06/16/2014, assuming that this time series follows a Markov chain. Such hypothesis has been tested by several authors (using discretization methods) on other periods, suggesting that the usual stochastic volatility models (Black and Scholes) may not be appropriate in this case (see, for instance, McQueen and Thorley (1991), Jondeaua and Rockinger (2003), Bhat and Kuma (2010), and Cont (2001)). The log returns are plotted in Figure 7.9. Notice that the time series exhibits the same features as the SETAR-ARCH model studied before. However,

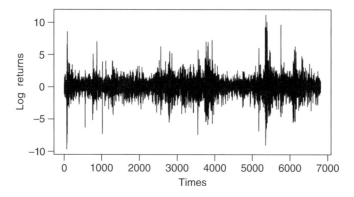

FIGURE 7.9 Log returns of the CAC40, from 10/07/1987 to 06/16/2014.

we do not assume here any specific model for the underlying Markov chain. We observe a lot of regeneration blocks (1567 over 6814 observations) in a small set of optimal size close to $\varepsilon = 0.985$ (a minorizing constant close to $\delta = 0.188$), yielding blocks of mean size 4.35 (Figure 7.9).

We have used two different specifications for the Markov chains, a Markov chain of order 1 and 2. The results are very similar, and we thus present only the results for a specification of a Markov chain of order 1. We distinguish between the behavior of the Markov chain for the minimum and the maximum, for which both the tail index and the extremal index may be different, leading to an asymmetric behavior between gains and losses. The following table summarizes the main results: we give the value of the estimators of the tail and extremal index as well as Bootstrap CI, respectively, for the minimum and the maximum of the time series.

Estimators/left and right tail	Min (left tail)	Max (right tail)
Hill tail index estimator	0.307	0.328
Lower CI tail index 2.5%	0.242	0.273
Upper CI tail index 97.5%	0.361	0.389
Extremal index estimator	0.440	0.562
Lower CI extremal index 2.5%	0.359	0.494
Upper CI extremal index 97.5%	0.520	0.614

Estimators and confidence intervals for tails and extremal indexes.

The extremal index estimators are very stable when the threshold u is changed, yielding very robust estimators. We emphasize that the tail of the process is very heavy since we are close to the nonexistence of the moment of order 4. A simple test based on the Bootstrap CI allows us to accept the hypothesis that $H_0 : \xi < 1/3$ against $\xi > 1/3$ but reject the existence of the moment of order four, $H_0 : \xi < 1/4$ against $\xi > 1/4$ for a type I error of 5%.

A striking feature of these results is seemingly some asymmetry in the times series between the minimum and the maximum log returns. In both case, the process has heavy tails with a much more heavy tail for positive log returns, but with a dynamic which creates smaller clusters of extremum values for maximum (of mean size 1.78) than for minimum (of mean size 2.27). This means that losses may be less strong than gains but may be more persistent. However, a simple test (consisting in comparing the confidence regions) yields that we do not reject the hypothesis of similar tail. This goes in the same direction as Jondeaua and Rockinger (2003) on a different period with different method, rather based on the notion of weak dependence.

7.9 CONCLUSION

Given the ubiquity of the Markov assumption in time series modeling and applied probability models, we review in this chapter several statistical methods, specifically tailored for the Markovian framework with a view toward the extremal behavior of such processes. Precisely, this chapter looks at statistical inference for extremal events from the renewal theory angle. We recalled that certain extremal behavior features of Harris Markov chains may be also expressed in terms of *regeneration cycles*, namely, data segments between consecutive regeneration times $\tau_1, \tau_2, \ldots$ (i.e., random times at which the chain forgets its past). Working on this approach, the methodology proposed in this chapter boils down to split up the observed sample path into regeneration data blocks (or into data blocks drawn from a distribution approximating the regeneration cycle's distribution, in the general case when regeneration times cannot be observed). Then the analysis boils down to examining the sequence of maxima over the resulting data segments, as if they were i.i.d., via standard statistical methods. In order to illustrate the interest of this technique, we have concentrated on several important inference problems concerning the question of estimating the sample maximum's tail, the *extremal dependence index*, and the *tail index*. However many other parameters of interest may be investigated in the same manner. The two examples given here—ruin models in insurance and times series exhibiting threshold and/or strong conditional heteroscedasticity—clearly show the potentiality of such methods in these fields. An illustration of the estimation methods to the CAC40 shows the potential of the method for real data applications.

References

Asmussen, S. Extreme value theory for queues via cycle maxima. Extremes 1998a;**1**(2):137–168.

Asmussen, S. Subexponential asymptotics for stochastic processes: extremal behavior, stationary distributions and first passage probabilities. Adv Appl Probab 1998b;**8**(2):354–374.

Asmussen, S. *Applied Probability and Queues*. New York: Springer-Verlag; 2003.

Asmussen, S., Binswanger, K., Höjgaard, B. Rare events simulation for heavy-tailed distributions. Bernoulli 2000;**6**:303–322.

Beirlant, J., Dierckx, G., Goegebeur, Y., Matthys, G. Tail index estimation and an exponential regression model. Extremes 1999;**2**(2):177–200.

Bertail, P., Clémençon, S. Edgeworth expansions for suitably normalized sample mean statistics of atomic Markov chains. Probab Theory Relat Fields 2004a;**130**(3):388–414.

Bertail, P., Clémençon, S. Note on the regeneration-base bootstrap for atomic Markov chains. Test 2004b;**16**:109–122.

Bertail, P., Clémençon, S. Regeneration-based statistics for Harris recurrent Markov chains. In: Bertail, P., Doukhan, P., Soulier, P., editors. *Probability and Statistics for Dependent Data*. Volume **187** of Lecture Notes in Statistics. Springer-Verlag; 2006a. pp 3–54.

Bertail, P., Clémençon, S. Regenerative-block bootstrap for Markov chains. Bernoulli 2006b;**12**(4):689–712.

Bertail, P., Clémençon, S. Approximate regenerative block-bootstrap for Markov chains. Computational Statistics and Data Analysis 2007;**52**(5):2739–2756.

Bertail, P., Clémençon, S. Sharp bounds for the tails of functionals of Markov chains; 2010. **54**(3):505–515.

Bertail, P., Clémençon, S., Tressou, J. Extreme value statistics for Markov chains via the (pseudo-)regenerative method. Extremes 2009;**12**:327–360.

Bertail, P., Clémençon, S., Tressou, J. A renewal approach to Markovian U-statistics. Mathematical Methods of Statistics 2011;**20**:79–105.

Bertail, P., Clémençon, S., Tressou, J. Regenerative block-bootstrap confidence intervals for the tail and extremal indexes. Electronic Journal of Statistics 2013;**7**:1224–1248.

Bertail, P., Clémençon, S., Tressou, J. Bootstrapping robust statistics for Markovian data applications to regenerative R- and L-statistics. J Times Ser Anal 2015;**36**(3):462–480.

Bertail, P., Haeffke, C., Politis, D., White, H. A subsampling approach to estimating the distribution of diverging statistics with applications to assessing financial market risks. Journal of Econometrics 2004;**120**:295–326.

Bhat, H., Kuma, N. Markov tree options pricing. Proceedings of the 4th SIAM Conference on Mathematics for Industry; 2010.

Bingham, N.H., Goldie, C.M., Teugels, J.L. Regular variation. *Encyclopedia of Mathematics and its Applications*. Cambridge: Cambridge University Press; 1987.

Bolthausen, E. The Berry-Esseen theorem for functionals of discrete Markov chains. Z Wahrsch Verw Geb 1980;**54**(1):59–73.

Clémençon, S. Moment and probability inequalities for sums of bounded additive functionals of a regular Markov chains via the Nummelin splitting technique. Statistics and Probability Letters 2001;**55**:227–238.

Cont, R. Empirical properties of asset returns: stylized facts and statistical issues. Quantitative Finance 2001;**1**:223–236.

Deheuvels, P., Häusler, E., Mason, D. Almost sure convergence of the Hill estimator. Math Proc Camb Philos Soc 1988;**104**:371–381.

Embrechts, P., Klüppelberg, C., Mikosch, T. *Modelling Extremal Events for Insurance and Finance. Applications of Mathematics*. Berlin: Springer-Verlag; 1997.

Fan, J., Yao, Q. *Nonlinear Time Series - Nonparametric and Parametric Methods*. New York: Springer-Verlag; 2003. 576pp.

Ferro, C., Segers, J. Inference for clusters of extreme values. J R Stat Soc Ser B Stat Methodol 2003;**65**(2):545–556.

Feuerverger, A., Hall, P. Estimating a tail exponent by modelling departure from a Pareto Distribution. Ann Stat 1999;**27**:760–781.

Glynn, P., Zeevi, A. Estimating tail probabilities in queues via extremal statistics. In: McDonald, D., Turner, S., editors. *Analysis of Communication Networks: Call Centres, Traffic, and Performance*. Providence (RI): AMS Press; 2000. p 135–158.

Goldie, C. Implicit renewal theory and tails of solutions of random equations. Ann Appl Probab 1991;**1**:126–166.

Haiman, G., Kiki, M., Puri, M. Extremes of Markov sequences. Journal of Statistical Planning Inference 1995;**45**:185–201.

Hansen, N., Jensen, A. The extremal behaviour over regenerative cycles for Markov additive processes with heavy tails. Stoch Proc Appl 2005;**115**:579–591.

Hill, B. A simple approach to inference about the tail of a distribution. Ann Stat 1975;**3**:1163–1174.

Hsing, T. On the extreme order statistics for a stationary sequence. Stoch Proc Appl 1988;**29**(1):155–169.

Hsing, T. On tail estimation using dependent data. Ann Stat 1991;**19**:1547–1569.

Hsing, T. Extremal index estimation for a weakly dependent stationary sequence. Ann Stat 1993;**21**(4):2043–2071.

Jain, J., Jamison, B. Contributions to Doeblin's theory of Markov processes. Z Wahrsch Verw Geb 1967;**8**:19–40.

Jondeaua, E., Rockinger, M. Testing for differences in the tails of stock-market returns. Journal of Empirical Finance 2003;**10**(5):559–581.

Karlsen, H.A., Tjöstheim, D. Nonparametric estimation in null recurrent time series. Ann Stat 2001;**29**:372–416.

Leadbetter, M., Rootzén, H. Extremal theory for stochastic processes. Ann Probab 1988;**16**:431–478.

Loynes, R. Extreme values in uniformly mixing stochastic processes. Ann Math Stat 1965;**36**:993–999.

McQueen, G., Thorley, S. Are stock returns predictable? A test using Markov chains. The Journal of Finance 1991;**46**:239–63.

Malinovskii, V. On some asymptotic relations and identities for Harris recurrent Markov chains. In: *Statistics and Control of Stochastic Processes (Steklov seminar, Moscow, 1984)*. New York: Optimization Software; 1985. p 317–336.

Malinovskii, V. Limit theorems for Harris Markov chains I. Theory Probab Appl 1987;**31**:269–285.

Malinovskii, V. Limit theorems for Harris Markov chains II. Theory Probab Appl 1989;**34**:252–265.

Meyn, S., Tweedie, R. *Markov Chains and Stochastic Stability*. London: Springer-Verlag; 1996.

Newell, G. Asymptotic extremes for m-dependent random variables. Ann Math Stat 1964;**35**:1322–1325.

O'Brien, G. The maximum term of uniformly mixing stationary processes. Z Wahrsch Verw Geb 1974;**30**:57–63.

O'Brien, G. Extreme values for stationary and Markov sequences. Ann Probab 1987;**15**:281–291.

Resnick, S. *Extreme Values, Point Processes and Regular Variation*. New York: Springer-Verlag; 1987.

Resnick, S., Stărică, C. Consistency of Hill's estimator for dependent data. J Appl Probab 1995;**32**:139–167.

Revuz, D. *Markov Chains*. 2nd ed. Amsterdam: North-Holland; 1984.

Robert, C,Y. Inference for the limiting cluster size distribution of extreme values. Ann Stat 2009;**37**(1):271–310.

Robert, C., Segers, J., Ferro, C. A sliding blocks estimator for the extremal index. Electron J Stat 2009;**3**:993–1020.

Rootzén, H. Maxima and exceedances of stationary Markov chains. Adv Appl Probab 1988;**20**:371–390.

Rootzén, H. Weak convergence of the tail empirical process for dependent sequences. Stoch Proc Appl 2009;**119**(2):468–490.

Smith, R. The extremal index for a Markov chain. J Appl Probab 1992;**29**(4):37–45.

Thorisson, H. *Coupling Stationarity and Regeneration*, Probability and its Applications. New York: Springer-Verlag; 2000.

Tjöstheim, D. Non-linear time series and Markov chains. Adv Appl Probab 1990;**22**:587–611.

Chapter Eight

Lévy Processes and Extreme Value Theory

Olivier Le Courtois[1] and Christian Walter[2]

[1] *EM Lyon Business School, Ecully Cedex, France*
[2] *Fondation Maison des Sciences de l'Homme, Paris, France*

8.1 INTRODUCTION

There are fundamentally two different ways of viewing the uncertainty of financial asset prices in continuous time. The first assumes the principle of continuity, the second does not. According to the first view, following Bachelier (1900) legacy, price movements are modeled by continuous diffusion processes, such as, for instance, Brownian motion. According to the other view, following Mandelbrot's (1963) legacy, price movements are modeled by discontinuous processes, such as, for instance, Lévy processes. In this chapter, we develop on the relationships connecting the Lévy processes and extreme value theory (EVT).

We begin by defining the modeling alternative and the challenges contemporary finance has to tackle. Next, we present the link with EVT. A convenient way of thinking the modeling alternative for today's financial stakes is to come back to the history of science to exhibit the roots of the puzzle. The story begins in the eighteenth century: Leibniz and Newton, the inventors of differential calculus, stated that "Natura non facit saltus" (nature does not make jumps). In other words, in physics, the so-called principle of continuity states that change is continuous rather than discrete. This same principle underpinned the thoughts of Linné on the classification of species and later Charles Darwin's theory of evolution (1859). If we move to economics, we find Alfred Marshall's Principles of Economics (1890) in which the principle of continuity is assumed, allowing the use of differential calculus in economics and the subsequent development of neoclassical economic theory. As modern financial theory grew out of neoclassical economics, the same principle of continuity is assumed in the conceptual framework

Extreme Events in Finance: A Handbook of Extreme Value Theory and its Applications,
First Edition. Edited by François Longin.

of financial modeling. As a surprising consequence of this assumption, one of the great success stories of modern financial theory was the valuation of derivatives. Celebrated examples include the formulas of Black et al. (1900) for valuing options, and the subsequent fundamental theorem of asset pricing that emerged from the work of Michael Harrison, Daniel Kreps, and Stanley Pliska between 1979 and 1981. These success stories rest on the principle of continuity.

In the twentieth century, both physics and genetics abrogated the principle of continuity. Quantum mechanics postulated discrete energy levels, while genetics took discontinuities into account. But economics—including modern financial theory—stood back from this intellectual revolution. An early attempt by Benoit Mandelbrot in 1962 to take explicit account of discontinuities on all scales in stock market prices led to huge controversies in the financial industry for almost 40 years; see (Walter 2009). But, by the 1980s, the academic consensus reaffirmed the principle of continuity—despite the repeated financial crises following the 1987 stock market crash. Many popular financial techniques, such as portfolio insurance or the calculation of capital requirements in the insurance industry, assume that (financial) nature does not make jumps and therefore promote continuity (see, however, Bertrand and Prigent (2017) for a recent account on the Constant proportion portfolio insurance (CPPI) method and the EVT approach). Most statistical descriptions of time series in finance assume continuity.

It follows that Brownian representation became the standard model, part and parcel of finance curricula across the globe. It was the dominant view in the financial industry itself; and it still underlies almost all prudential regulation frameworks: for instance, the so-called square-root-of-time-rule underlying the regulatory requirements (Basle III and Solvency II) for calculating minimum capital, which is a very narrow subset of time scaling rule of risk, comes directly from the hypothesis that returns are independent, stationary (identically distributed),and normal, that is, Brownian-based representation. Brownian motion has the very important property of independence and stationarity of increments. The processes with independent and stationary increments are called Lévy processes, which constitute the class of stochastic process having this property. Brownian motion is a specific Lévy process: it assumes continuity. Other Lévy processes do not.

Now let us turn our attention to the extreme values in the tails. The classic theory of extreme values distinguishes between small and large quantities. One of the difficulties often encountered in the practical application of this theory is the choice of a threshold beyond which a variation is considered large. One of the main goals of this chapter is to show how the Lévy process approach can be reconciled with that of extreme values. Another objective is to be able to bypass the dead-end of the mixture of diffusions and EVT approaches to tail modeling. An important and puzzling consequence of assuming continuous dynamics is the truncation of financial time series into the so-called "normal" periods and periods of "insanity" or "irrationality." Adopting continuity implies adding an extra component, precisely the EVT framework, to the continuous part of the model. But this *ad hoc* mechanism has a negative spillover: it implies considering crises as "irrational exceptions" and evacuating every possibility of detecting the frailty of the market by describing jumps at any scale. In other words, this dichotomy leaves the profession unable to explain the transition from one period to another. For example, Alan Greenspan, former chairman of the US central bank, commented on the financial crisis of 2007–2008 with these words: "We can never anticipate all discontinuities" (Financial Times, March 16, 2008). This demonstrates the limits of the diffusion + EVT approach.

This chapter contains five parts. We start by recalling the main definitions of the EVT framework. Then, we move to a presentation of Lévy processes. Section 4 is dedicated to the study of stable Lévy processes. In Section 5, we examine two subclasses of semi-heavy-tailed Lévy processes that are based on tempered stable and generalized hyperbolic distributions. Section 8.6 deals with the relationships between Lévy processes and extreme value distributions.

8.2   EXTREME VALUE THEORY

We start with a study of the Fisher–Tippett theorem, then we examine the Generalized Jenkinson–von Mises distribution, and finally we concentrate on the maximum domains of attraction.

8.2.1   The Fisher–Tippett theorem

Let $\{X_1, X_2, \cdots, X_n\}$ be n independent, identically distributed (i.i.d.) random variables equipped with the cumulative distribution function (c.d.f) $F_X(x) = \Pr(X \leq x)$. Consider a sample that consists of the n realizations $\{x_1, \cdots, x_n\}$. We rank them by decreasing order, and introduce the following convention:

$$x_{(1)} \geq x_{(2)} \geq \cdots \geq x_{(n)}.$$

The largest of these realizations, $x_{(1)}$, can be considered to represent the realization of a new random variable $X_{(1)}$. The same idea prevails for the other observations $x_{(k)}$. Thus, we introduce n new random variables with the convention

$$X_{(1)} = \max(X_1, \cdots, X_n),$$

which represents the random variable giving the largest value in a sample of size n. In the statistics literature, this quantity is also sometimes denoted by $X_{(1:n)}$. Similarly,

$$X_{(n)} = \min(X_1, \cdots, X_n)$$

represents the random variable giving the smallest value observed in a sample of size n. More generally, $X_{(k)}$—or $X_{(k:n)}$—is the random variable related to the k th value $x_{(k)}$ obtained among n realizations. These n new random variables can be ordered in the following way:

$$X_{(1)} \geq X_{(2)} \geq \cdots \geq X_{(n)}.$$

We want to show how it is traditionally possible to determine the values that can be taken by maxima over a given observation period, that is, we want to characterize the probability law of maxima. Because extreme values are by definition rare, one needs to be able to extrapolate from past observed values to future hypothetical large values. EVT proposes a framework adapted to this extrapolation: it describes the asymptotic behavior of $F_{1:n}$ when n tends to plus infinity. For technical reasons, this is not the maximum $X_{(1:n)}$, which is the object of study, but the centered and reduced maximum $(X_{(1:n)} - b_n)/a_n$.

The Fisher–Tippett theorem provides the shape of the possible asymptotic cdfs of the centered reduced maximum of a sample of size n. We remain in the context of a set of n random variables $\{X_1, \cdots, X_n\}$ that are i.i.d, and that have the cdf $F_X(x)$. We stress that this theory requires the validation of the i.i.d. hypothesis in order to be applied in an adequate way.

THEOREM 8.1 (Laws of maxima: Fisher–Tippett (1928)) *Let us assume a sequence of n i.i.d. random variables $\{X_1, \cdots, X_n\}$ with the cdf $F_X(x)$. If there are two sequences $\{a_n\}_{n \in \mathbb{N}}$ and $\{b_n\}_{n \in \mathbb{N}}$ with $\forall n$, $a_n \in \mathbb{R}^{+*}$ and $b_n \in \mathbb{R}$, and a nondegenerate limit cdf H such that*

$$\lim_{n \to \infty} \Pr\left(\frac{X_{(1:n)} - b_n}{a_n} \le x\right) = H(x), \tag{8.1}$$

then H belongs to one of the three classes:

- *Fréchet. $H(z) = \Phi_\alpha(z) = \exp(-z^{-\alpha})$ if $z > 0$, 0 if $z \le 0$,*
- *Weibull. $H(z) = \Psi_\alpha(z) = \exp(-(-z)^\alpha)$ if $z \le 0$, 1 if $z > 0$,*
- *Gumbel. $H(z) = \Lambda(z) = \exp(-e^{-z})$, $z \in \mathbb{R}$*

with $z = \frac{x-b}{a}$, where $a > 0$, $b \in \mathbb{R}$, and $\alpha > 0$.

The three classes of distributions denoted by Φ_α, Ψ_α, and Λ are called the laws of maxima. The Fréchet and Weibull laws are linked by the relation

$$\Phi_\alpha\left(-\frac{1}{z}\right) = \Psi_\alpha(z). \tag{8.2}$$

The parameters a and b are scale and localization parameters, whereas α is a shape parameter. These laws are stable with respect to maxima: for a sample of independent random variables $\{Z_1, \cdots, Z_n\}$ that satisfy one of these laws, and for $Z_{(1:n)}$, the maximum of these variables, we have

$$Z_{(1:n)} \overset{d}{=} a_n Z + b_n, \tag{8.3}$$

where Z is a random variable that has the same distribution as $\{Z_1, \cdots, Z_n\}$ and that is independent of these latter random variables.

In particular, we have

- Fréchet law: $Z_{(1:n)} \overset{d}{=} n^{1/\alpha}Z,$
- Weibull law: $Z_{(1:n)} \overset{d}{=} n^{-1/\alpha}Z,$
- Gumbel law: $Z_{(1:n)} \overset{d}{=} Z + \ln n.$

We illustrate the previous developments with a simple example. Suppose that $\mathbb{E}[Z] = 1$ and consider the Fréchet (with, e.g., $\alpha = \frac{1}{2}$) and Gumbel laws. We do not select the Weibull law because its support is bounded on the right (it is therefore of little use for financial problems). In the first case, we see that $\mathbb{E}[Z_{(1:n)}] = n^2$, while in the second case $\mathbb{E}[Z_{(1:n)}] \approx \ln n$. Written differently, with the Fréchet law the maximum increases much more quickly than with the Gumbel law, and consequently the same behavior is also observed for the contribution of the maximum within the sum.

There is a formal analogy between this theorem for the maximum (expressed through the formula (8.1)) and the central limit theorem for the mean, which we recall here:

$$\lim_{n \to \infty} \Pr\left(\frac{\bar{X}_n - \mathbb{E}[X]}{\sigma(X)/\sqrt{n}} \leq x \right) = \Phi(x), \tag{8.4}$$

where Φ is the cdf of the centered reduced Gaussian law.

This comparison between the two theorems, as well as the two formulas (8.1) and (8.4), allows us to interpret the parameters a_n and b_n. The parameter b_n corresponds to the mean $\mathbb{E}[X]$ in the central limit theorem and is therefore a localization parameter. The parameter a_n corresponds to $\sigma(X)/\sqrt{n}$ in the central limit theorem and is therefore a scale parameter. However, the parameter α has no equivalent in the central limit theorem. The elements of this analogy are displayed synthetically in Table 8.1, which displays a comparison between two laws of large numbers, respectively associated with the means and the extreme values. In the two cases, limit theorems and standard distributions exist. We note that, in the case of the α-stable distribution, $\mathbb{E}(X)$ and $\sigma(X)$ do not necessarily exist (case of Pareto-power laws). Indeed, when the first moments of distributions are not defined, we asymptotically obtain a stable distribution, where the coefficient α of the central limit theorem is identical to the inverse of the coefficient ξ of EVT. The two laws of large numbers focus on two distinct quantities: the fluctuation of means and the fluctuation of maxima. For more details, see (Leadbetter 2017).

8.2.2 Generalized Jenkinson–von Mises distribution

The expressions of the Fréchet, Weibull, and Gumbel distributions can be united in a general expression using the condensed representation of Jenkinson and von Mises (1954–1955), which defines a generalized distribution for the maxima H_ξ:

$$H_\xi(x) = \exp\left(-\left[1 + \xi\left(\frac{x - \mu}{\sigma} \right) \right]^{-\frac{1}{\xi}} \right), \tag{8.5}$$

TABLE 8.1   **Limit laws of means and maxima**

Laws of large numbers	
Central limit theorems	Extreme value theorems
Convergence of empirical means	Convergence of empirical maxima
$\bar{X}_n = \frac{1}{n}\sum_{i=1}^{n} X_i$	$X_{(n)} = \max(X_1, \cdots, X_n)$
$\Phi(x) = \lim_{n\to\infty} \Pr\left(\frac{\bar{X}_n - \mathbb{E}[X]}{\sigma(X)/\sqrt{n}} \leq x\right)$	$H(x) = \lim_{n\to\infty} \Pr\left(\frac{X_{(n)} - b_n}{a_n} \leq x\right)$
Centered reduced Gaussian distribution	Standardized distribution
if $\mathbb{E}[X]$ and $\sigma(X)$ exist	of extreme values
	Fréchet:
Gaussian density:	$H(x) = \exp(-x^{-\alpha})$
$\Phi(x) = \frac{1}{\sqrt{2\pi}} \int_{-\infty}^{x} e^{-t^2/2}\, dt$	Weibull:
Gaussian characteristic exponent:	$H(x) = \exp(-(-x)^\alpha)$
$\Psi_X(u) = -\frac{u^2}{2}$	Gumbel:
	$H(x) = \exp(-e^{-x})$
Moivre (1730)–Laplace (1812)	Fisher–Tippett (1928)
α-stable distributions	Generalized distribution
if $\mathbb{E}[X]$ and/or $\sigma(X)$ do not exist	of extreme values
$\Psi_X(u) = i\mu u - \gamma^\alpha \lvert u\rvert^\alpha \left(1 - i\beta \frac{u}{\lvert u\rvert} \mathrm{tg}\frac{\pi\alpha}{2}\right)$	$H_\xi(x) = \exp\left(-\left[1 + \xi\left(\frac{x-\mu}{\sigma}\right)\right]^{-\frac{1}{\xi}}\right)$
Lévy (1937)	Jenkinson–von Mises (1954–1955)
Fluctuations of means	Fluctuations of maxima

for all x such that $1 + \xi(x - \mu)/\sigma > 0$.

The density function of this generalized law of maxima is

$$h_\xi(x) = \frac{1}{\sigma}\left[1 + \xi\left(\frac{x-\mu}{\sigma}\right)\right]^{-\frac{1+\xi}{\xi}} \exp\left(-\left[1 + \xi\left(\frac{x-\mu}{\sigma}\right)\right]^{-\frac{1}{\xi}}\right). \qquad (8.6)$$

We can interpret the parameters μ and σ by comparing Eqs (8.1) and (8.5):

$$\lim_{n\to\infty} \Pr\left(\frac{X_{(n)} - b_n}{a_n} \leq x\right) = \exp\left(-\left[1 + \xi\left(\frac{x-\mu}{\sigma}\right)\right]^{-\frac{1}{\xi}}\right).$$

This equality shows that the parameters μ and σ are the limits of b_n and a_n when n is large. Therefore, $\mu \in \mathbb{R}$ is a localization parameter and $\sigma > 0$ is a scale parameter. Finally, the parameter $\xi \in \mathbb{R}$ models the shape of the distribution tail. It is therefore called the shape of the extreme value index. More precisely, three situations can be encountered:

1. $\xi > 0$, this is the Fréchet law. The distribution tail is thick and $\xi = \alpha^{-1} > 0$, where α is the tail index. The larger the ξ, the thicker the distribution tail.
2. $\xi < 0$, this is the Weibull law. The distribution tail is thin and $\xi = -\alpha^{-1} < 0$.

3. $\xi = 0$, this is the Gumbel law. The distribution tail decreases exponentially. This is a limit case between the two preceding situations, where $\xi \to 0$.

8.2.3 Maximum Domain of Attraction

Let us now reformulate the Fisher–Tippett theorem in order to introduce the concept of the maximum domain of attraction (MDA). Because

$$\Pr\left(\frac{X_{(1:n)} - b_n}{a_n} \leq x\right) = \Pr\left(X_{(1:n)} < a_n x + b_n\right),$$

we have, using the definition of $X_{(1:n)}$

$$\Pr\left(X_{(1:n)} < a_n x + b_n\right) = \left[F(a_n x + b_n)\right]^n.$$

Then, the Fisher–Tippett theorem states that

$$\lim_{n \to \infty} \left[F\left(a_n x + b_n\right)\right]^n = H(x). \tag{8.7}$$

We say that the Fisher–Tippett theorem defines a MDA for the cdf $F(\cdot)$, and we write $F \in \text{MDA}(H)$.

This result is equivalent for the largest values to what the central limit theorem is for the mean values. A probability distribution of the cdf F belongs to the MDA of H if the distribution of the renormalized maximum converges to H.

Which types of probability distribution belong to which maximum domains of attraction and what are the renormalization constants? The answer to this question depends on the variation of the cdf of the random variable. If a random variable varies regularly, then it belongs to the MDA of Fréchet; if this random variable varies rapidly, then it belongs to the MDA of Gumbel. We now examine these two cases.

In the first situation, $\bar{F}$ is a regular function of index $-\alpha$. Recall that f is a regular function of index α if, for all $x > 0$, we have

$$\lim_{t \to +\infty} \frac{f(tx)}{f(t)} = x^\alpha.$$

In this case, $F \in \text{MDA}(\Phi_\alpha)$: the MDA is that of the Fréchet law with $a_n = F^{-1}(1 - n^{-1})$ and $b_n = 0$. This result was obtained by Gnedenko in 1943. In order to verify that $F \in \text{MDA}(\Phi_\alpha)$, we check that

$$\lim_{t \to \infty} \frac{1 - F(tx)}{1 - F(t)} = x^{-\alpha}.$$

Assume, for instance, that F is the cdf of a Pareto distribution of type I, so that $F(x) = 1 - x^{-\alpha}$. Then

$$\lim_{t \to \infty} \frac{1 - F(tx)}{1 - F(t)} = \lim_{t \to \infty} \frac{(tx)^{-\alpha}}{t^{-\alpha}} = x^{-\alpha}.$$

Thus, a Pareto distribution of type I belongs to the MDA of the Fréchet law. We can also check the Fisher–Tippett theorem by calculating F^n. We have here $a_n = F^{-1}(1 - n^{-1}) = n^{1/\alpha}$. This yields

$$\lim_{n\to\infty} [F(a_n x + b_n)]^n = \lim_{n\to\infty} [F(n^{1/\alpha}x)]^n = \lim_{n\to\infty} (1 - \frac{x^{-\alpha}}{n})^n,$$

so that

$$\lim_{n\to\infty} [F(a_n x + b_n)]^n = \exp(-x^{-\alpha}),$$

and we have recovered the Fréchet law.

The second situation is that in which the distributions belong to the MDA of the Gumbel law and have an infinite right endpoint. These distributions are of rapid variation. Recall that a function f is of rapid variation if it satisfies

$$\begin{cases} \lim_{t\to+\infty} \frac{f(tx)}{f(t)} = 0, & x > 1, \\ \lim_{t\to+\infty} \frac{f(tx)}{f(t)} = +\infty, & 0 < x < 1. \end{cases}$$

These results conclude this first section on EVT. We will come back later on to these asymptotic results. Before that, let us conduct a study of infinitely divisible distributions and Lévy processes.

8.3 INFINITE DIVISIBILITY AND LÉVY PROCESSES

We start by recalling the definition of a characteristic exponent. Then we study infinitely divisible distributions, before examining Lévy processes, defined as the class of processes with independent and stationary increments, and Lévy measures.

8.3.1 Characteristic Exponent

Recall that the characteristic function of a random variable Y is the Fourier transform of its density function, that is,

$$\Phi_Y(u) = \mathbb{E}\left[e^{iuY}\right] = \underbrace{\sum_{k=0}^{\infty} e^{iuk} \Pr(Y = k)}_{\text{discrete } r.v.} = \underbrace{\int_{-\infty}^{+\infty} e^{iux} f_Y(x)dx}_{\text{continuous } r.v.},$$

where $f_Y(x)$ is the density function. The characteristic function can be expressed in the following way:

$$\Phi_Y(u) = \exp\left(\Psi_Y(u)\right), \tag{8.8}$$

where $\Psi_Y(u)$ is called the characteristic exponent of Y.

In the case of Lévy processes, the exponent Ψ is proportional to time. This follows from a very important property of these processes: their marginal distributions are infinitely divisible. We now examine this property in greater detail.

8.3.2 Infinitely Divisible Distributions

Roughly speaking, the property of infinite divisibility states that it is possible to write a random variable as a sum of n identical independent random variables, for any given n. More precisely, for any Lévy process X and any positive integer n, it is clear that

$$X_n = X_1 + (X_2 - X_1) + \cdots + (X_n - X_{n-1})$$

and

$$
\begin{aligned}
\Phi_{X_n}(u) &= \mathbb{E}\left[e^{iuX_n}\right] \\
&= \mathbb{E}\left[e^{iu(X_1 + (X_2 - X_1) + \cdots + (X_n - X_{n-1}))}\right] \\
&= \mathbb{E}\left[e^{iuX_1} \times e^{iu(X_2 - X_1)} \times \cdots \times e^{iu(X_n - X_{n-1})}\right].
\end{aligned}
$$

From the independence of the increments of X, it follows that

$$\Phi_{X_n}(u) = \mathbb{E}\left[e^{iuX_1}\right] \times \mathbb{E}\left[e^{iu(X_2 - X_1)}\right] \times \cdots \times \mathbb{E}\left[e^{iu(X_n - X_{n-1})}\right].$$

The stationarity of the increments of X then implies that

$$\Phi_{X_n}(u) = \underbrace{\mathbb{E}\left[e^{iuX_1}\right] \times \mathbb{E}\left[e^{iuX_1}\right] \times \cdots \times \mathbb{E}\left[e^{iuX_1}\right]}_{n \text{ times}} = \left(\mathbb{E}\left[e^{iuX_1}\right]\right)^n.$$

Finally, we obtain

$$\Phi_{X_n}(u) = \left(\Phi_{X_1}(u)\right)^n. \tag{8.9}$$

This result can be generalized in the case of continuous time t to

$$\Phi_{X_t}(u) = \left(\Phi_{X_1}(u)\right)^t. \tag{8.10}$$

If we now consider characteristic exponents, we readily have

$$\exp\left(\Psi_{X_t}(u)\right) = \left(\exp\left(\Psi_{X_1}(u)\right)\right)^t = \exp\left(t\Psi_{X_1}(u)\right).$$

From this equation, we deduce the relation between the distributions of the process X at time 1 and at time t:

$$\Psi_{X_t}(u) = t\,\Psi_{X_1}(u). \tag{8.11}$$

Thus, the characteristic exponent of a Lévy process is equal to t times that of its underlying infinitely divisible distribution, which is the distribution of X_1.

8.3.3 Characteristic Exponent of Lévy Processes

Lévy processes are described by their characteristic exponent, which can, in general, be decomposed as follows:

$$\Psi_{X_t}(u) = \underbrace{t\left(i\mu u - \frac{1}{2}\sigma^2 u^2\right)}_{\substack{\text{Gaussian law} \\ \text{Diffusion}}} +$$

$$\underbrace{\underbrace{t\int_{|x|<1}\left(e^{iux} - 1 - iux\right)v(dx)}_{\text{small jumps}} + \underbrace{t\int_{|x|\geq 1}\left(e^{iux} - 1\right)v(dx)}_{\text{large jumps}}}_{\text{Jump Component}}. \qquad (8.12)$$

The three terms of this formula represent the characteristic exponents of the normal distribution (diffusive component), of a generalized (in the sense that the arrival rate of jumps may be infinite) compensated compound Poisson process, and of a compound Poisson process, respectively. The second term corresponds to modeling small jumps, that is (by arbitrary construction), those jumps of size less than 1 in absolute value, and the third one to large jumps.

The last two terms can be written together in the same integral using an indicator function:

$$\Psi_{X_t}(u) = t\left(i\mu u - \frac{1}{2}\sigma^2 u^2\right) + t\int_{\mathbb{R}^*}\left(e^{iux} - 1 - iux\,\mathbf{1}_{|x|<1}(x)\right)v(dx). \qquad (8.13)$$

This is the Lévy–Khintchine formula. The characteristic exponent is indeed proportional to time:

$$\begin{cases} \Psi_{X_1}(u) = i\mu u - \frac{1}{2}\sigma^2 u^2 + \int_{\mathbb{R}^*}\left(e^{iux} - 1 - iux\,\mathbf{1}_{|x|<1}(x)\right)v(dx), \\ \Psi_{X_t}(u) = t\,\Psi_{X_1}(u). \end{cases} \qquad (8.14)$$

A Lévy process is therefore completely determined by the following three quantities:

1. The expectation μ of the diffusion component. This is the drift of the process.

2. The diffusion coefficient σ. This coefficient functions as a scale of the diffusive fluctuations.

3. The measure $v(dx)$, called the Lévy measure, determines the fluctuations of the jumps, as well as the skewness and the kurtosis of the process. Note that for the integral in Eq. (8.13) to be defined, we impose the following restriction:

$$\int_{\mathbb{R}}(x^2 \wedge 1)v(dx) < +\infty$$

TABLE 8.2   **Comparison of characteristic exponents**

Process/characteristic exponent	$\int_{-\infty}^{+\infty} \nu(dx)$
Compound Poisson: $t \int_{-\infty}^{+\infty}(e^{iux} - 1)\nu(dx)$	Finite
Compensated compound Poisson: $t \int_{-\infty}^{+\infty}(e^{iux} - 1 - iux)\nu(dx)$	Finite
Lévy pure jump: $t\int_{|x|\geq1}(e^{iux} - 1)\nu(dx) + t\int_{|x|<1}(e^{iux} - 1 - iux)\nu(dx)$ $t\int_{\mathbb{R}^*}\left(e^{iux} - 1 - iux\, \mathbf{1}_{|x|<1}(x)\right)\nu(dx)$	Infinite
Lévy: $t\left(i\mu u - \frac{1}{2}\sigma^2 u^2\right) + t\int_{\mathbb{R}^*}\left(e^{iux} - 1 - iux\,\mathbf{1}_{|x|<1}(x)\right)\nu(dx)$	Infinite

Table 8.2 gives an overview of the jump component in the Lévy–Khintchine formula of the Poisson processes we have seen so far, which are written in terms of their Lévy measure.

8.3.4 Lévy Measure

The important term of the characteristic exponent is the Lévy measure. To explain its meaning intuitively, we choose the example, given in the preceding paragraph, of a compound Poisson process with intensity λ(the Poisson parameter). We assume that this process has the density function $f_Y(x)$ for the jump size given by Y. The Lévy measure can then be written as

$$\nu(x) = \lambda\, f_Y(x). \tag{8.15}$$

Intuitively, the Lévy measure gives the average number of jumps per unit of time in terms of their size. We can therefore view the Lévy measure as the mathematical object that quantifies the arrival of jumps and their size. It can be used to create discontinuities in the paths of the stochastic processes that represent fluctuations on the stock market.

For the Poisson processes introduced previously, the average number λ of jumps per unit of time is finite. However, in a very general way, we can arbitrarily adjust both the frequency with which jumps occur and their size by using the Lévy measure. We call the average number of jumps per unit of time the intensity of the process (also called activity of the process in analogy to turbulence). Then, if we also know the density function that determines the size of the jumps, we can join them together:

$$\text{intensity} \times \text{density},$$

which is exactly the Lévy measure in the case when it is finite. Let us now come to the study of two important classes of Lévy processes. We start with the heavy-tailed ones.

8.4 HEAVY-TAILED LÉVY PROCESSES

This section is dedicated to the study of stable Lévy processes. We first examine stable distributions, and then stable processes, and finally stable characteristic exponents and measures.

8.4.1 Stable Distributions

Let X, Y, and Z be three i.i.d. random variables, and A, B, C, and D four real numbers (the first three being strictly positive). Then, if the relation

$$AX + BY \stackrel{d}{=} CZ + D$$

holds, the random variable X(and its independent copies) is said to be stable.

This relation can be generalized for all $n \geq 2$ as follows:

$$X_1 + X_2 + \cdots + X_n \stackrel{d}{=} C_n X + D_n,$$

where X_1, X_2, ..., X_n, and X are i.i.d. random variables, and C_n and D_n are real numbers (the first of which is strictly positive). If this last relation holds, X(and its independent copies) is said to be stable.

Stable distributions are described by four parameters $(\alpha, \beta, \gamma, \mu)$, which correspond to the fatness of the tails, the asymmetry, the width, and the mean of these distributions, respectively (when this last quantity does not exist, μ is interpreted as a shift parameter). We will denote stable distributions by $S(\alpha, \beta, \gamma, \mu)$ in the following.

8.4.2 Stable Processes

A stable process is a process whose underlying distributions, marginal or joint, are stable. We call a stable process whose marginal distributions are symmetric and normalized, an alpha-stable process such as

$$X_t - X_s \sim S(\alpha, 0, |t - s|^{\frac{1}{\alpha}}, 0).$$

These symmetric and normalized alpha-stable distributions are often denoted by $S\alpha S$.

If X is an alpha-stable process, then it has the following property:

$$X(at) - X(as) \stackrel{d}{=} a^{1/\alpha}(X(t) - X(s)), \tag{8.16}$$

for all $\alpha \in \,]0, 2]$, where we use $\stackrel{d}{=}$ to denote equality in distribution. In this case, the stochastic process X is said to be self-similar with exponent $1/\alpha$, or $1/\alpha$-self-similar with stationary increments ($1/\alpha$-sssi), or also fractal. This means that the distribution of the return at date at (hence $X(at)$), where a determines some multiple or fraction of t(e.g., a year-fraction, or a noninteger multiple of a year, if a year is the unit of time), is related to the distribution at date t by simple invariance of scale. Graphically, the dilation of the time axis is equivalent to a dilation of the axis of cumulative returns, up to normalization (and stressing the fact that this is a dilation of the distributions, and not of the paths).

8.4.3 Characteristic Function and Lévy Measure

To obtain the characteristic function of the marginal distribution of a stable process at a given time t, we take the t th power of the characteristic function of a reference stable distribution taken at time $t = 1$(see Eq. (8.10)). In the general case, the density function is not known in closed form and the characteristic function is used. For a stable random variable X, we have by definition

$$\Psi_X(u) = i\mu u + \int_{-\infty}^{0} \psi(u, x) \frac{C_-}{|x|^{1+\alpha}} dx + \int_{0}^{+\infty} \psi(u, x) \frac{C_+}{x^{1+\alpha}} dx \qquad (8.17)$$

with

$$\psi(u, x) = e^{iux} - 1 - iux \, \mathbf{1}_{|x|<1}. \qquad (8.18)$$

The parameter μ gives the drift, while the term α describes the form of the distribution and the force of the jumps affecting the paths. The tails of the distribution become fatter and fatter as α decreases. C_- and C_+ are two constants, called the tail amplitudes, which represent scale parameters for the distribution tails. In practice, C_- and C_+ give the order of magnitude of large fluctuations (negative or positive). Comparing Eq. (8.17) to the Lévy–Khintchine formula (8.13), we see that the Lévy measure of a stable distribution is

$$v(dx) = \frac{C_-}{|x|^{1+\alpha}} \mathbf{1}_{(-\infty,0)}(x)dx + \frac{C_+}{x^{1+\alpha}} \mathbf{1}_{(0,+\infty)}(x)dx \qquad (8.19)$$

or, more intuitively,

$$v(x) = \begin{cases} \frac{C_-}{|x|^{1+\alpha}}, & \text{if} \quad x < 0, \\ \\ \frac{C_+}{x^{1+\alpha}}, & \text{if} \quad x > 0, \end{cases} \qquad (8.20)$$

which is the equation also found in (Samorodnitsky and Taqqu 1994).

An important feature evident in this form is a decrease given by a power law, which is slow for large values of x compared to the fast decrease observed for exponential laws. This slow decrease of the distribution tails is a key characteristic of Pareto distributions. Here, the Lévy measure is defined by a Pareto type I distribution, or simply Pareto distribution.

8.5   SEMI-HEAVY-TAILED LÉVY PROCESSES

In these section, we examine two subclasses of semi-heavy-tailed Lévy processes that are based on tempered stable and generalized hyperbolic distributions.

8.5.1   Tempered Stable Distributions

To remedy the inconvenience of not having any moments for those Lévy processes whose measure is given by a power function built on the model

$$
v(x) = \begin{cases} \dfrac{C_-}{|x|^{1+\alpha}}, & \text{if } \quad x < 0, \\[3mm] \dfrac{C_+}{x^{1+\alpha}}, & \text{if } \quad x > 0, \end{cases}
$$

it has been suggested to weight this measure by an exponential quantity in order to reduce large fluctuations, and therefore recover the moments. This idea corresponds to a set of Lévy processes whose marginal distributions are stable distributions truncated, or "tempered," by exponential functions, hence their name *tempered stable processes*. The distribution tails of these stable models, tempered by the truncation, are semi-light.

The first model to be built on this principle was that of (Koponen 1995), later taken up by (Bouchaud and Potters 2003) and again by (Boyarchenko and Levendorskii 2002), in which the Lévy measure is given by

$$
v(x) = \begin{cases} \dfrac{C_-}{|x|^{1+\alpha}}\, e^{-a_-\,|x|}, & \text{if } \quad x < 0, \\[3mm] \dfrac{C_+}{x^{1+\alpha}}\, e^{-a_+\,x}, & \text{if } \quad x > 0. \end{cases} \tag{8.21}
$$

Observe that the parameterization is asymmetric in the decay rate of large jumps, but symmetric in the parameter α, which is the same for up and down jumps. The Variance Gamma and CGMY (Carr, Geman, Madan, and Yor) models are well-known special cases of this model. In the CGMY model, the coefficients C_- and C_+ have been symmetrized.

This model has the following Lévy measure:

$$
v(x) = \begin{cases} \dfrac{C}{|x|^{1+\alpha}}\, e^{-a_-\,|x|}, & \text{if } \quad x < 0, \\[3mm] \dfrac{C}{x^{1+\alpha}}\, e^{-a_+\,x}, & \text{if } \quad x > 0. \end{cases} \tag{8.22}
$$

As before, interpreting the parameters exposes two types of risk: size and shape. The parameter C is a measure of size (affecting all moments), whereas α, a_-, and a_+ determine the shape (force of the jumps for α and asymmetry for a_- and a_+). When $a_- > a_+$, the distribution is curtailed on the left and stretched to the right (the left part is squashed by the exponential factor), and vice versa.

Finally, for asymmetrical distributions, a change in α will result in a change in the asymmetry. In other words, α has an indirect leverage effect on the asymmetry.

8.5.2 Generalized hyperbolic distributions

We first concentrate on the simple hyperbolic distribution by developing an intuitive understanding of what motivates the name "hyperbolic." If we draw the graph of a Gaussian density in a semilogarithmic chart (i.e., one in which the ordinate is given on a logarithmic scale), then the density function (with e^{-x^2}) will have the shape of a parabola (since we have $-x^2$ now). This parabola is characterized visually by the rapid fall (rapid decline) of the distribution's tails. If we try to obtain more drawn-out distribution tails, we can slow down the fall by replacing the parabola by a hyperbola. In this case, the distribution's density function will be of hyperbolic form in a semilogarithmic chart. This is the reason why distributions constructed in this manner are called hyperbolic. Their usefulness for the modeling of price movements on the stock markets stems from the slower decrease of their tails.

This intuition allows us to reach in a simple way the general complicated form of these distributions. In fact, the equation defining a hyperbola (with vertex on top in order to obtain a density) is easily obtained as

$$y(x) = -\alpha\sqrt{1+x^2} + \beta x, \tag{8.23}$$

where α and β are two constants that determine the shape of the hyperbola. As x goes to $\pm\infty$, the asymptotes are the two lines with slope $-\alpha + \beta$ (for $x \to +\infty$) and $\alpha + \beta$ (for $x \to -\infty$). It follows directly from Eq. (8.23) that the general form of the density function of a hyperbolic distribution is given by

$$f(x) = a \, \exp\left(-\alpha\sqrt{1+x^2} + \beta x\right), \tag{8.24}$$

where a is a normalization constant for the integral of the density function.

By considering the slopes of the two asymptotes, we obtain a direct interpretation of the parameters: $\alpha > 0$ and $0 < |\beta| < \alpha$ determine the shape of the distribution, affecting the fatness of the tails (for α) and the asymmetry (for β). Introducing a localization parameter denoted by μ and a dispersion (or scale) parameter denoted by γ, we obtain a more general version of the preceding equation:

$$f(x) = a' \, \exp\left(-\alpha\sqrt{\gamma^2 + (x-\mu)^2} + \beta(x-\mu)\right). \tag{8.25}$$

We must now define the normalization constant. Since the density must integrate to 1, we compute its integral and deduce the value of the normalization constant from it. In this way, we obtain the result that the density function of a hyperbolic distribution (H) is given by

$$f_H(x) = \frac{\sqrt{\alpha^2 - \beta^2}}{2\alpha\gamma K_1\left(\gamma\sqrt{\alpha^2 - \beta^2}\right)} \, \exp\left(-\alpha\sqrt{\gamma^2 + (x-\mu)^2} + \beta(x-\mu)\right), \tag{8.26}$$

where $K_1(\cdot)$ is a modified Bessel function of the third kind of order 1.

We see that, like alpha-stable distributions, hyperbolic distributions are defined by four parameters: the kurtosis, the asymmetry, the dispersion, and the localization of the distribution. In other words, here too we have completed the size of the random movements (their dispersion, or scale: γ) with their form (fatness of tails and asymmetry: α and β). The localization parameter keeps the same meaning in all cases. Although different in their asymptotic behavior, all hyperbolic distributions retain a twofold notion of risk in their description of price movements on an exchange (size–form, or amplitude–structure).

The construction of the density function of a hyperbolic distribution can therefore be carried out in two steps.

1. By defining the hyperbolic part of the exponential function in its general form with four parameters $(\alpha, \beta, \gamma, \mu)$:

$$-\alpha \sqrt{\gamma^2 + (x - \mu)^2} + \beta(x - \mu);$$

2. By adjusting the exponential of the hyperbola by a normalization constant that depends on the parameters: $a(\alpha, \beta, \gamma)$. This constant involves modified Bessel functions denoted by $K_\lambda(\cdot)$.

We recall that Bessel functions are solutions to the second-order differential equation

$$x^2 y'' + xy' + (x^2 - \lambda^2)y = 0.$$

The solutions to this equation are denoted by $J_\lambda(x)$ and $Y_\lambda(x)$, depending on whether they are defined at $x = 0$, and are called Bessel function of the first kind of order λ and Bessel function of the second kind of order λ, respectively.

If at present we consider the following modified differential equation

$$x^2 y'' + xy' - (x^2 + \lambda^2)y = 0$$

then its solutions are called modified Bessel functions of the first and second kinds, denoted by $I_\lambda(x)$ and $K_\lambda(x)$.

We can generalize the density (8.26) by choosing an order λ different from 1 for the modified Bessel function to obtain a generalized version of the hyperbolic distribution. The Bessel function of the second kind of order λ is defined for all $x > 0$ by

$$K_\lambda(x) = \int_0^\infty y^{\lambda-1} e^{-\frac{1}{2}x(y+y^{-1})} \, dy.$$

- For $\lambda = 1$, we have the case K_1 of the simple hyperbolic distribution described above.

- For $\lambda = -1/2$, we obtain the density of the normal inverse Gaussian (NIG) distribution

$$f_{\text{NIG}}(x) = \frac{\alpha\gamma}{\pi} \frac{K_1(\alpha\sqrt{\gamma^2 + (x-\mu)^2})}{\sqrt{\gamma^2 + (x-\mu)^2}} \exp\left(\gamma\sqrt{\alpha^2 - \beta^2} + \beta(x-\mu)\right).$$

(8.27)

The dispersion parameter γ takes values between 0 and infinity. Starting from the simple hyperbolic distribution with density (8.26), it can be shown that

- when $\gamma \to +\infty$ and $\beta \to 0$, then $\gamma/\sqrt{\alpha^2 - \beta^2} \to \sigma^2$, and the simple hyperbolic density converges toward a Gaussian one with mean μ and standard deviation σ;

- when $\gamma \to 0$, the simple hyperbolic density converges toward an asymmetric Laplace density

$$f(x) = C \begin{cases} e^{-(\alpha-\beta)(|x|-\mu)}, & \text{if} \quad x \geq \mu, \\ e^{-(\alpha+\beta)(|x|-\mu)}, & \text{if} \quad x < \mu. \end{cases}$$

(8.28)

- For $\lambda \neq 1$, we have the case of the generalized hyperbolic distribution(GH), whose density function is given by

$$f_{\text{GH}}(x) = a(\gamma^2 + (x-\mu)^2)^{\left(\lambda-\frac{1}{2}\right)/2} K_{\lambda-\frac{1}{2}}\left(\alpha\sqrt{\gamma^2 + (x-\mu)^2}\right) e^{\beta(x-\mu)} \quad (8.29)$$

with normalizing constant

$$a = \frac{(\alpha^2 - \beta^2)^{\lambda/2}}{\sqrt{2\pi}\alpha^{\lambda-\frac{1}{2}}\gamma^\lambda K_\lambda\left(\gamma\sqrt{\alpha^2 - \beta^2}\right)}.$$

8.6 LÉVY PROCESSES AND EXTREME VALUES

The infinitely divisible distributions whose underlying Lévy measure density is the product of an exponential function by a power function belong to the MDA of the Gumbel law. The asymptotic behavior of these distributions is studied in detail in (Albin and Sundén 2009). Consider, for instance, the infinitely divisible distributions having the Lévy measure density

$$\nu(x) = Cx^\rho e^{-\alpha x}.$$

(8.30)

It appears that both the distribution densities and the cdfs of these laws have, up to a constant, a mixed exponential-power form. It can also be noted that the distributions constructed from such Lévy measure densities (in particular the Variance Gamma, CGMY, or generalized hyperbolic distributions) possess cdfs that can be written as

$$F(x) = 1 - e^{-\int_{-\infty}^{x} c(t)\, dt},$$

where $\lim_{t \to +\infty} c(t) = \alpha$. This representation is that of a von Mises function. It readily implies that these distributions belong to the MDA of the Gumbel law.

Let us conclude on the behavior of distribution tails:

1. The MDA of the Fréchet law contains all distributions having stretched or heavy tails, such as power functions.

2. The MDA of the Gumbel law contains all thin and medium-tailed distributions. Examples of such distributions are the exponential distributions with semi-heavy tails thicker than the Gaussian, such as the distributions resulting from mixing a power function with an exponential function. The previous section gave a representative sample of such distributions.

3. The MDA of the Weibull law contains all distributions with a support bounded to the right. These distributions are said to be short-tailed.

These results are summarized in Table 8.3. It appears that most distributions of interest to the field of finance belong to the MDA of Gumbel, whereas distributions of interest to the field of insurance rather belong to the MDA of Fréchet.

To describe the behavior of the largest values of Lévy processes, it is sufficient to consider the Lévy measure. Indeed, this measure directly yields the asymptotic pattern of the density and cdf of any marginal X_t. Because Lévy processes have independent and stationary increments, considering a marginal distribution at time t, as we do in the next subsections, exhausts the discussion for the whole process.

8.6.1 CGMY and VG Distributions

We first consider the asymptotic behavior of the CGMY (see Carr, Geman, Madan, and Yor (2002) and Variance Gamma (see, e.g., Madan and Seneta (1990) or Madan and Milne (1991)) processes satisfying the relationship (8.30) with,

TABLE 8.3 Laws of maxima and maximum domain of attraction

Laws of maxima	Shape parameter	Basic distributions
Weibull	$\xi < 0$	Uniform
		Beta
Gumbel	$\xi = 0$	Gaussian
		Exponential
		Lognormal
		Gamma
		CGMY
Fréchet	$\xi > 0$	Cauchy
		Pareto
		α-Stable
		Student
		Loggamma

respectively, $\rho < -1$ and $\rho = -1$. For a process X of the CGMY type that has the Lévy measure density

$$v(x) = C \frac{e^{Gx}}{(-x)^{1+Y}} \mathbf{1}_{x<0} + C \frac{e^{-Mx}}{x^{1+Y}} \mathbf{1}_{x>0},$$

where $Y > 0$, (Albin and Sundén 2009) showed that, when u is large,

$$\Pr(X_t > u) \overset{+\infty}{\sim} \frac{Ct}{M} \, \mathbb{E}\left[e^{MX(t)}\right] \frac{e^{-Mu}}{u^{1+Y}}.$$

From the computation of the moment generating function $\mathbb{E}(e^{MX(t)})$, we deduce that

$$\Pr(X_t > u) \overset{+\infty}{\sim} \frac{Ct}{M} \, e^{Ct\Gamma(-Y)} \left[(G+M)^Y - M^Y - G^Y\right] \frac{e^{-Mu}}{u^{1+Y}},$$

so that

$$\Pr(X_t > u) \overset{+\infty}{\sim} \tilde{C}(t) \, \frac{e^{-Mu}}{u^{1+Y}},$$

where

$$\tilde{C}(t) = \frac{Ct}{M} \, e^{Ct\Gamma(-Y)\left[(G+M)^Y - M^Y - G^Y\right]}.$$

This confirms that the CGMY distribution tail is a mix of power and exponential functions, similar to the CGMY Lévy measure density.

In the case of a Variance Gamma process $Z = Z_1 + Z_2$ with the Lévy density

$$v(x) = C \frac{e^{Gx}}{(-x)} \mathbf{1}_{x<0} + C \frac{e^{-Mx}}{x} \mathbf{1}_{x>0},$$

where Z_1 is a gamma process describing the positive jumps and Z_2 is a gamma process describing the negative jumps, (Albin and Sundén 2009) showed that, when u is large

$$\Pr(X_t > u) \overset{+\infty}{\sim} \frac{M^{Ct-1}}{\Gamma(Ct)} \, \mathbb{E}\left[e^{MZ_2(t)}\right] \frac{e^{-Mu}}{u^{1-Ct}}.$$

From the computation of the moment-generating function $\mathbb{E}\left[e^{MZ_2(t)}\right]$ of the gamma process associated with negative jumps, we deduce that

$$\Pr(X_t > u) \overset{+\infty}{\sim} \frac{M^{Ct-1}}{\Gamma(Ct)} \left(\frac{G}{G+M}\right)^{Ct} \frac{e^{-Mu}}{u^{1-Ct}},$$

so that

$$\Pr(X_t > u) \overset{+\infty}{\sim} \tilde{C}(t) \, \frac{e^{-Mu}}{u^{1-Ct}},$$

where

$$\tilde{C}(t) = \frac{M^{Ct-1}}{\Gamma(Ct)} \left(\frac{G}{G+M}\right)^{Ct}.$$

Recall that

$$C = \frac{1}{v}, \quad G = \left(\sqrt{\frac{\theta^2 v^2}{4} + \frac{\sigma^2 v}{2}} - \frac{\theta v}{2} \right)^{-1}, \quad M = \left(\sqrt{\frac{\theta^2 v^2}{4} + \frac{\sigma^2 v}{2}} + \frac{\theta v}{2} \right)^{-1}.$$

Again, the distribution tail is a mix of power and exponential functions.

8.6.2 Alpha-Stable Distributions

In the case of an alpha-stable motion, described by the Lévy measure (8.19), we have, by extending Proposition 1.2.15 in (Samorodnitsky and Taqqu 1994) to an unconstrained time,

$$\Pr(X_t > u) \overset{+\infty}{\sim} \tilde{C}(t) \frac{1+\beta}{u^\alpha}, \tag{8.31}$$

and

$$\Pr(X_t < u) \overset{-\infty}{\sim} \tilde{C}(t) \frac{1-\beta}{(-u)^\alpha}, \tag{8.32}$$

where $\tilde{C}(t) = \frac{(1-\alpha)\sigma^\alpha t}{2\, \Gamma(2-\alpha)\, \cos\left(\frac{\pi\alpha}{2}\right)}$ in both situations, provided $\alpha \neq 1$.

8.6.3 Generalized Hyperbolic Distributions

Recall that generalized hyperbolic distributions (see, e.g., (Prause 1999)) have the density

$$f_{\mathrm{HG}}(x) = a \frac{K_{\lambda-\frac{1}{2}}\left(\alpha \sqrt{\gamma^2 + (x-\mu)^2} \right) e^{\beta(x-\mu)}}{\left(\gamma^2 + (x-\mu)^2 \right)^{\left(\frac{1}{2} - \lambda \right)/2}},$$

where a is defined by

$$a = \frac{(\alpha^2 - \beta^2)^{\lambda/2}}{\sqrt{2\pi} \alpha^{\lambda-\frac{1}{2}} \gamma^\lambda\, K_\lambda\left(\gamma \sqrt{\alpha^2 - \beta^2} \right)}.$$

From (Abramowitz and Stegun 1965), we have

$$K_v(z) \overset{\pm\infty}{\sim} \sqrt{\frac{\pi}{2z}}\, e^{-z},$$

so that

$$f_{\mathrm{HG}}(x) \overset{\pm\infty}{\sim} a \frac{\sqrt{\frac{\pi}{2\alpha\sqrt{\gamma^2+(x-\mu)^2}}}\, e^{-\alpha\sqrt{\gamma^2+(x-\mu)^2}}\, e^{\beta(x-\mu)}}{\left(\gamma^2 + (x-\mu)^2 \right)^{\left(\frac{1}{2} - \lambda \right)2}}.$$

Because

$$\sqrt{\gamma^2 + (x-\mu)^2} \overset{\pm\infty}{\sim} |x|,$$

we can write

$$f_{HG}(x) \overset{\pm\infty}{\sim} a \frac{\sqrt{\frac{\pi}{2\alpha|x|}}\ e^{-\alpha|x|}\ e^{\beta(x-\mu)}}{|x|^{\frac{1}{2}-\lambda}},$$

so that, finally,

$$f_{HG}(x) \overset{\pm\infty}{\sim} \tilde{C}\ \frac{e^{-\alpha|x|+\beta x}}{|x|^{1-\lambda}} \tag{8.33}$$

with

$$\tilde{C} = \frac{(\alpha^2 - \beta^2)^{\lambda/2}\ e^{-\beta\mu}}{2\ \alpha^\lambda\ \gamma^\lambda\ K_\lambda\left(\gamma\sqrt{\alpha^2-\beta^2}\right)}.$$

This asymptotic expression corresponds to a mix of exponential and power functions. Consider the shape of the asymptotic density in the two particular cases below:

1. $\lambda = 1$: hyperbolic distribution. The asymptotic behavior of the density is

$$f_H(x) \overset{\pm\infty}{\sim} \tilde{C}\ e^{-\alpha|x|+\beta x}$$

with

$$\tilde{C} = \frac{\sqrt{\alpha^2-\beta^2}\ e^{-\beta\mu}}{2\ \alpha\ \gamma\ K_1\left(\gamma\sqrt{\alpha^2-\beta^2}\right)}.$$

2. $\lambda = -1/2$: NIG distribution. The asymptotic behavior of the density is

$$f_{NGI}(x) \overset{\pm\infty}{\sim} \tilde{C}\ \frac{e^{-\alpha|x|+\beta x}}{|x|^{\frac{3}{2}}}$$

with

$$\tilde{C} = \frac{\sqrt{\alpha\gamma}e^{-\beta\mu}}{2\left(\alpha^2-\beta^2\right)^{\frac{1}{4}}K_{-\frac{1}{2}}\left(\gamma\sqrt{\alpha^2-\beta^2}\right)}.$$

Compared to the alpha-stable distribution, whose tail is a power function, we observe here a faster asymptotic decrease due to the presence of an exponential function in the tail. The distribution tail remains, however, thicker than in the Gaussian case. Generalized hyperbolic distributions, similar to CGMY and VG distributions, show a medium asymptotic decrease and therefore represent a compromise between the Gaussian and alpha-stable distributions.

Table 8.4 concludes this chapter by presenting the main asymptotic behaviors of Lévy process marginals.

TABLE 8.4 **Infinitely divisible distributions and asymptotic behavior**

Basic distributions	Density function	Tail function	Laws of maxima
Gaussian	Exp. of parabola	Exp. of power	Gumbel
Hyperbolic	Exp. of hyperbola	Exp.-power mix	Gumbel
Trunc. α-stable		Exp.-power mix	Gumbel
α-stable		Power	Fréchet

8.7 CONCLUSION

This chapter started by recalling the important features of EVT. Then, it presented a synthetic account of infinite divisibility and Lévy processes. Further, it explained distinct studies of heavy-tailed and semi-heavy-tailed processes. Finally, it provided a recombination of all these elements and allowed us to understand the tail behaviors associated with the marginals of the most standard classes of Lévy processes.

References

Abramowitz, M., Stegun, I.A. *Handbook of Mathematical Functions: with Formulas, Graphs, and Mathematical Tables*. New York: Dover Publications; 1965.

Albin, J.M.P., Sundén, M. On the asymptotic behaviour of Lévy processes, Part I: Subexponential and exponential processes. Stochastic Processes and their Applications 2009;**119**(1):281–304.

Bachelier, L. *Théorie de la Spéculation*. Paris: Gauthier-Villars; 1900.

Barndorff-Nielsen, O.E. Normal inverse Gaussian distributions and stochastic volatility modeling. Scandinavian Journal of Statistics 1997;**24**(1):1–13.

Bertrand, P., Prigent, J.-L. Portfolio insurance: the extreme value approach applied to the CPPI method. In: Longin, F., editor. *Extreme Events in Finance*. New York: John Wiley & Sons, Inc.; 2017.

Black, Fischer, Scholes, Myron. The Pricing of Options and Corporate Liabilities. Journal of Political Economy **81**(3):637-654.

Bouchaud, J.-P., Potters, M. *Theory of Financial Risk and Derivative Pricing*. 2nd ed. Cambridge: Cambridge University Press; 2003.

Boyarchenko, S.I., Levendorskii, S. *Non-Gaussian Merton–Black–Scholes Theory*. Singapore: World Scientific Publishing; 2002.

Carr, P., Geman, H., Madan, D.B., Yor, M. The fine structure of asset returns: an empirical investigation. Journal of Business 2002;**75**(2):305–332.

Carr, P., Wu, L. The finite moment log-stable process and option pricing. Journal of Finance 2003;**58**(2):753–777.

Eberlein, E., Keller, U. Hyperbolic distributions in finance. Bernoulli 1995;**1**(3):281–299.

Eberlein, E., Keller, U., Prause, K. New insights into smile, mispricing and Value at Risk: the hyperbolic model. Journal of Business 1998;**71**(3):371–405.

Koponen, I. Analytic approach to the problem of convergence of truncated Lévy flights towards the Gaussian stochastic process. Physical Review E 1995;**52**(1):1197–1199.

Leadbetter, M.R. Extremes under dependence: historical development and parallels with central limit theory. In: Longin, F., editor. *Extreme Events in Finance*. New York: John Wiley & Sons, Inc.; 2017.

Madan, D.B., Carr, P., Chang, E.C. The Variance Gamma process and option pricing. European Finance Review 1998;**2**(1):79–105.

Madan, D.B., Milne, F. Option pricing with V.G. martingale components. Mathematical Finance 1991;**1**(4):39–55.

Madan, D.B., Seneta, E. The variance gamma (V.G.) model for share market returns. Journal of Business 1990;**63**(4):511–524.

Mandelbrot, B. The variation of certain speculative prices. Journal of Business 1963;**36**(4):394–419.

Merton, Robert. Theory of Rational Option Pricing. The Bell Journal of Economics and Management Science **4** (1): 141–183.

Prause, K. The generalized hyperbolic model: estimation, financial derivatives, and risk measures [PhD thesis]. University of Freiburg; 1999.

Samorodnitsky, G., Taqqu, M.S. *Stable Non-Gaussian Random Processes*. New York: Chapman and Hall; 1994.

Walter, C. Research of scaling laws on stock market variations. In: Abry, P., Gonçalvés, P., Lévy Véhel, J., editors. *Scaling, Fractals and Wavelets*. London: John Wiley & Sons, Ltd; 2009. p 437–464.

Chapter Nine

Statistics of Extremes: Challenges and Opportunities

M. de Carvalho[*]
Faculty of Mathematics, Pontificia Universidad Católica de Chile, Santiago, Chile

9.1 INTRODUCTION

My experience on discussing concepts of risk and statistics of extremes with practitioners started in 2009 while I was a visiting researcher at the Portuguese Central Bank (*Banco de Portugal*). At the beginning, colleague practitioners were intrigued about the methods I was applying; the questions were recurrent: "What is the difference between statistics of extremes and survival analysis (or duration analysis)?[1] And why don't you apply empirical estimators?" The short answer is that when modeling rare catastrophic events, we need to extrapolate beyond observed data—into the tails of a distribution—and standard inference methods often fail to deal with this properly. To see this, suppose that we observe a random sample of losses $L_1, \dots, L_N \overset{\text{i.i.d.}}{\sim} S_L$ and that we estimate the survivor function $S_L(x) := P(L > x)$, using the empirical survivor function, $\widehat{S}_L(x) := N^{-1} \sum_{i=1}^{N} I(L_i > x)$, for $x > 0$. Now, suppose that we want to assess

---

[*]I would like to thank, without implicating, Holger Rootzén and Ross Leadbetter for helpful comments on the penultimate version of this document and to François Longin for encouraging discussion group participants of the ESSEC Conference on Extreme Events in Finance to write down their viewpoints. I would like to thank other conference participants including Isabel Fraga Alves, Jan Beirlant, Frederico Caeiro, Ivette Gomes, Serguei Novak, Michał Warchoł, and Chen Zhou, among others, for stimulating discussions and for pointing out many fascinating directions for the future of statistics of extremes. The research was partially funded by the Chilean NSF through the Fondecyt project 11121186 "Constrained Inference Problems in Extreme Value Modeling."

[1]In econometrics, survival analysis is also known as duration analysis; see Wooldridge (2015), Chapter 22.

Extreme Events in Finance: A Handbook of Extreme Value Theory and its Applications,
First Edition. Edited by François Longin.
© 2017 John Wiley & Sons, Inc. Published 2017 by John Wiley & Sons, Inc.

what is the probability of observing a loss just ϵ larger than the maximum observed loss, $M_N := \max\{L_1, \ldots, L_N\}$. Obviously, the probability of that event turns out to be zero $[\widehat{S}_L(M_N + \epsilon) = 0$, for all $\epsilon > 0]$, thus illustrating that the empirical survivor function fails to be able to extrapolate into the right tail of the loss distribution. As put simply by Taleb (2012, p. 46), "the fool believes that the tallest mountain in the world will be equal to the tallest one he has observed."

In this chapter, I resume some viewpoints that I shared with the discussion group "Future of Statistics of Extremes" at the ESSEC *Conference on Extreme Events in Finance*, which took place in Royaumont Abbey, France, on 15–17 December 2014

`extreme-events-in-finance.essec.edu`

and which originated the invitation by the editor for writing this chapter. My goal is on providing a personal view on some recent concepts and methods of statistics of extremes and to discuss challenges and opportunities that could lead to potential future developments. The scope is far from encyclopedic, and many other interesting perspectives are found all over this monograph.

In Section 9.2, I note that a bivariate extreme value distribution is an example of what I call here a measure-dependent measure, I briefly review kernel density estimators for the spectral density, and I discuss families of spectral measures. In Section 9.3, I argue that the spectral density ratio model (de Carvalho and Davison, 2014), the proportional tails model (Einmahl et al., 2015), and the exponential families for heavy-tailed data (Fithian and Wager, 2015) share similar construction principles; in addition, I discuss en passant a new nonparametric estimator for the so-called scedasis function, which is one of the main estimation targets on the proportional tails model. Comments on potential future developments are scattered across the chapter and a miscellanea of topics are included in Section 9.4.

Throughout this chapter I use the acronym EVD to denote extreme value distribution.

9.2 STATISTICS OF BIVARIATE EXTREMES

9.2.1 The Bivariate EVD is a Measure-dependent Measure

Let G be a probability measure on $(\Omega, \mathcal{A})$, and let Θ be a parameter space. The family $\{G_\theta : \theta \in \Theta\}$ is a statistical model. Obviously not every statistical model is appropriate for modeling risk. As mentioned in Section 9.1, candidate statistical models should possess the ability to extrapolate into the tails of a distribution, beyond existing data.

THEOREM 9.1 *If there exist sequences $\{a_n > 0\}$ and $\{b_n\}$ such that $P\{(M_n - b_n)/a_n \leq y\} \to G_\theta(y)$, as $n \to \infty$, for some nondegenerate distribution G_θ, then*

$$G_\theta(y) = \exp\left[-\left\{1 + \xi\left(\frac{y - \mu}{\sigma}\right)\right\}^{-1/\xi}\right], \quad \theta = (\mu, \sigma, \xi), \quad (9.1)$$

defined on $\{y : 1 + \xi(y - \mu)/\sigma > 0\}$ where $\mu \in \mathbb{R}$, $\sigma \in \mathbb{R}_+$, and $\xi \in \mathbb{R}$.[2]

See Coles (2001, Theorem 3.1.1). Here, μ and σ are location and scale parameters, while ξ is a shape parameter that determines the rate decay of the tail: $\xi \to 0$, light tail (Gumbel); $\xi > 0$, heavy tail (Fréchet); $\xi < 0$, short tail (Weibull). The generalized EVD (G_θ in (9.1)) is a three-parameter family that plays an important role in statistics of univariate extremes.

In some cases we want to assess the risk of observing simultaneously large values of two random variables (say, two simultaneous large losses in a portfolio), and the mathematical basis for such modeling is that of statistics of bivariate extremes. In this context, "extremal dependence" is often interpreted as a synonym of risk. Moving from one dimension to two dimensions increases sharply the complexity of models for the extremes. The first challenge one faces when modeling bivariate extremes is that the estimation object of interest is infinite dimensional, whereas in the univariate case only three parameters (μ, σ, ξ) are needed. The intuition is the following. When modeling bivariate extremes, apart from the marginal distributions, we are also interested in the extremal dependence structure of the data, and—as we shall see in Theorem 9.4—only an infinite-dimensional object is flexible enough to capture the "spectrum" of all possible types of dependence.

Let $(Y_{1,1}, Y_{1,2}), \ldots, (Y_{N,1}, Y_{N,2}) \overset{\text{i.i.d.}}{\sim} F_{Y_1,Y_2}$, where I assume that Y_1 and Y_2 are unit Fréchet $[G_{(1,1,1)}]$ marginally distributed, that is, $P(Y_1 \leq y) = P(Y_2 \leq y) = \exp(-1/y)$, for $y > 0$. Similarly to the univariate case, the classical theory for characterizing the extremal behavior of bivariate extremes is based on block maxima, here given by the componentwise maxima $M_N = (\max\{Y_{i,1}\}_{i=1}^N, \max\{Y_{i,2}\}_{i=1}^N) = (M_{N,1}, M_{N,2})$; note that the componentwise maxima M_N needs not to be a sample point. Similarly to the univariate case, we focus on the standardized maxima, which for Fréchet marginals is given by the standardized componentwise maxima, that is, $M_N^\star = N^{-1}(\max\{Y_{i,1}\}_{i=1}^N, \max\{Y_{i,2}\}_{i=1}^N) = (M_{N,1}^\star, M_{N,2}^\star)$. Next, I define a special type of statistical model that plays a key role on bivariate extreme value modeling.

DEFINITION 9.2 *Let $\mathcal{F}$ be the space of all probability measures that can be defined over $(\Omega_0, \mathcal{A}_0)$. If G_H is a probability measure on $(\Omega_1, \mathcal{A}_1)$, for all $H \in \mathcal{H} \subseteq \mathcal{F}$, then we say that G_H is a measure-dependent measure. The family $\{G_H : H \in \mathcal{H}\}$ is said to be a set of measure-dependent measures, if G_H is a measure-dependent measure.*

---

[2]Following the standard convention that for $\xi = 0$, Eq. (9.1) is to be understood with $\xi \to 0$.

REMARK 9.3 *Throughout the definitions and theorems presented in the succeeding text,* $\mathcal{H}$ *denotes the space of all probability measures H that can be defined over* $([0, 1], \mathbb{B}_{[0,1]})$, *where* $\mathbb{B}_{[0,1]}$ *is the Borel sigma-algebra on* $[0, 1]$, *and which obey the mean constraint*

$$\int_{[0,1]} wH(dw) = \frac{1}{2}. \tag{9.2}$$

What are the relevant statistical models for statistics of bivariate extremes? Is there an extension of the generalized EVD for the bivariate setting? The following is a bivariate analogue to Theorem 9.1.

THEOREM 9.4 *If* $P(M_{N,2}^{\star} \leq y_1, M_{N,1}^{\star} \leq y_2) \to G_H(y_1, y_2)$, *as* $n \to \infty$, *with* G *being a nondegenerate distribution function, then*

$$G_H\{(0, y_1) \times (0, y_2)\} := G_H(y_1, y_2)$$
$$= \exp\left\{-2 \int_{[0,1]} \max\left(\frac{w}{y_1}, \frac{1-w}{y_2}\right) H(dw)\right\}, \quad y_1, y_2 > 0, \tag{9.3}$$

for some $H \in \mathcal{H}$.

See Coles (2001, Theorem 8.1). Throughout I refer to G_H as a bivariate EVD. Note the similarities between (9.1) and (9.3): both start with an "exp," but for bivariate EVD $\Theta = \mathcal{H}$, whereas for univariate EVD $\Theta \subseteq \mathbb{R} \times \mathbb{R}_+ \times \mathbb{R}$. To understand why H needs to be an element of $\mathcal{H}$, let $y_1 \to \infty$ or $y_2 \to \infty$ in (9.3). Some further comments are in order. First, since (9.2) is the only constraint on H, neither H nor G_H can have a finite parameterization. Second, a bivariate extreme value distribution G_H is an example of a *measure-dependent measure*, as introduced in Definition 9.2.

A pseudo-polar transformation is useful for understanding the role of H, which is the so-called spectral measure. Define $(R, W) = (Y_1 + Y_2, Y_1/(Y_1 + Y_2))$, and denote R and W as the radius and pseudo-angle, respectively. If Y_1 is relatively large, then $W \approx 1$; if Y_2 is relatively large, then $W \approx 0$. de Haan and Resnick (1977) have shown that $P(W \in \cdot \mid R > u) \to H(\cdot)$, as $u \to \infty$. Thus, when the radius R_i is large, the pseudo-angles W_i are approximately distributed according to H. Perfect (extremal) dependence corresponds to H being degenerate at $1/2$, whereas independence corresponds to H being a binomial distribution function, with half of the mass in 0 and the other half in 1. The spectral probability measure H determines the interactions between joint extremes and is thus an estimating target of interest; other functionals of the spectral measure are also often used, such as the spectral density $h = dH/dw$ or Pickands (1981) dependence function $A(w) = 1 - w + 2 \int_0^w H(v) \, dv$, for $w \in [0, 1]$. The cases of extremal independence and extremal dependence, respectively, correspond to the bivariate EVDs, $G_H(y_1, y_2) = \exp\{-1/y_1 - 1/y_2\}$ and $G_H(y_1, y_2) = \exp\{-\max(1/y_1, 1/y_2)\}$, for $y_1, y_2 > 0$.

9.2.2 Nonparametric Spectral Density Estimation

In practice, we have to deal with a statistical problem—lack of knowledge on H—and an inference challenge—that is, obtaining estimates that obey the marginal moment constraints and define a density on the unit interval. Indeed, as posed by Coles (2001, p. 146) "it is not straightforward to constrain non-parametric estimators to satisfy functional constraints of the type" of Eq. (9.2). Inference should be conducted by using $n = \sum_{i=1}^{N} I(Y_{i,1} + Y_{i,2} > u)$ pseudo-angles $W_1, \dots, W_n$, which are constructed from a sample of size N, thresholding the pseudo-radius at a sufficiently high threshold u. Kernel smoothing estimators for h have been recently proposed by 2013 and are based on

$$\widehat{h}(w) = \sum_{i=1}^{n} p_i \, \beta(w; W_i v, (1 - W_i)v). \tag{9.4}$$

Here $\beta(w; a, b)$ denotes the beta density with shape parameters $a, b > 0$, and $v > 0$ is a parameter responsible for the level of smoothing, which can be obtained through cross validation. Each beta density is centered around a pseudo-angle in the sense that $E(W_i^*) = W_i$, for $W_i^* \sim \text{Beta}(W_i v; (1 - W_i)v)$. And how can we obtain the probability masses, p_i? There are at least two options. A simple one is to consider Euclidean likelihood methods (Owen, 2001, pp. 63–66), in which case the vector of probability masses $\boldsymbol{p} = (p_1, \dots, p_n)$ solves

$$\max_{\boldsymbol{p} \in \mathbb{R}^n} \quad -\tfrac{1}{2} \sum_{i=1}^{n} (np_i - 1)^2$$

$$\text{s.t.} \qquad \sum_{i=1}^{n} p_i = 1 \tag{9.5}$$

$$\sum_{i=1}^{n} W_i p_i = 1/2.$$

By the method of Lagrange multipliers, we obtain $p_i = n^{-1}\{1 - (\overline{W} - 1/2)S^{-2}(W_i - \overline{W})\}$, where $\overline{W} = n^{-1} \sum_{i=1}^{n} W_i$, and $S^2 = n^{-1} \sum_{i=1}^{n} (W_i - \overline{W})^2$. This yields the following estimator, known as the smooth Euclidean likelihood spectral density:

$$\widehat{h}_{\text{Euc}}(w) = \frac{1}{n} \sum_{i=1}^{n} \{1 - (\overline{W} - 1/2)S^{-2}(W_i - \overline{W})\} \, \beta(w; W_i v, (1 - W_i)v). \tag{9.6}$$

Another option proposed by de Carvalho et al. (2013) is to consider a similar approach to that of Einmahl and Segers (2009), in which case the vector of probability masses $\boldsymbol{p} = (p_1, \dots, p_n)$ solves the following empirical likelihood (Owen, 2001) problem:

$$\max_{\boldsymbol{p} \in \mathbb{R}^n_+} \quad \sum_{i=1}^{n} \log p_i$$

$$\text{s.t.} \quad \sum_{i=1}^{n} p_i = 1 \tag{9.7}$$

$$\sum_{i=1}^{n} W_i p_i = 1/2.$$

Again by the method of Lagrange multipliers, the solution is $p_i = [n\{1 + \lambda(W_i - 1/2)\}]^{-1}$, for $i = 1, \ldots, n$, where λ is the Lagrange multiplier associated with the second equality constraint in (9.7), defined implicitly as the solution to the equation

$$\frac{1}{n} \sum_{i=1}^{n} \frac{W_i - 1/2}{1 + \lambda(W_i - 1/2)} = 0.$$

This yields the following estimator, known as the smooth empirical likelihood spectral density:

$$\hat{h}_{\text{Emp}}(w) = \frac{1}{n} \sum_{i=1}^{n} \frac{\beta(w; W_i \nu, (1 - W_i)\nu)}{1 + \lambda(W_i - 1/2)}. \tag{9.8}$$

One can readily construct smooth estimators for the corresponding spectral measures; the smooth Euclidean spectral measure and smooth empirical likelihood spectral measure are, respectively, given by

$$\hat{H}_{\text{Euc}}(w) = \frac{1}{n} \sum_{i=1}^{n} \{1 - (\overline{W} - 1/2)S^{-2}(W_i - \overline{W})\} \, B(w; W_i \nu, (1 - W_i)\nu),$$

$$\hat{H}_{\text{Emp}}(w) = \frac{1}{n} \sum_{i=1}^{n} \frac{B(w; W_i \nu, (1 - W_i)\nu)}{1 + \lambda(W_i - 1/2)},$$

where $B(w; a, b)$ is the regularized incomplete beta function, with $a, b > 0$. By construction both estimators, (9.6) and (9.8), obey the moment constraint, so that, for example,

$$\int_0^1 w \, \hat{h}_{\text{Euc}}(w) \, dw = \sum_{i=1}^{n} p_i \left\{ \frac{\nu W_i}{\nu W_i + \nu(1 - W_i)} \right\} = \sum_{i=1}^{n} p_i W_i = 1/2. \tag{9.9}$$

Put differently, realizations of the random probability measures $\hat{H}_{\text{Euc}}$ and $\hat{H}_{\text{Emp}}$ are elements of $\mathcal{H}$. Examples of applications of these estimators in finance can be found in Kiriliouk et al. (2015, Figure 4). At the moment, the large sample properties of these estimators remain unknown.

Other estimators for the spectral measure (obeying (9.2)) can be found in Boldi and Davison (2007), Guillotte et al. (2011), and Sabourin and Naveau (2014).

9.2.3   Predictor-Dependent Spectral Measures

Formally, $\{F_x : x \in \mathcal{X}\}$ is a set of predictor-dependent (henceforth pd) probability measures if the F_x are probability measures on $(\Omega, \mathbb{B}_\Omega)$, indexed by a covariate $x \in \mathcal{X} \subseteq \mathbb{R}^p$; here $\mathbb{B}_\Omega$ is the Borel sigma-algebra on Ω. Analogously, I define the following:

DEFINITION 9.5 *The family $\{H_x : x \in \mathcal{X}\}$ is a set of pd spectral measures if $H_x \in \mathcal{H}$, for all $x \in \mathcal{X}$.*

And why do we care about pd spectral measures? Pd spectral measures allow us to assess how extremal dependence evolves over a certain covariate x, that is, they allow us to model nonstationary extremal dependence structures. Pd spectral measures are a natural probabilistic concept for modeling extremal dependence structures that may change according to a covariate. Indeed, in many settings of applied interest, it seems natural to regard risk from a covariate-adjusted viewpoint, and this leads us to ideas of "conditional risk." However, if we want to develop ideas of "conditional risk" for bivariate extremes, that is, if we want to assess systematic variation of risk according to a covariate, we need to allow for nonstationary extremal dependence structures.

To describe how extremal dependence may change over a predictor, I now introduce the concept of spectral surface.

DEFINITION 9.6 *Suppose $H_x \in \mathcal{H}$ is absolutely continuous for all $x \in \mathcal{X}$. The pd spectral density is defined as $h_x = dH_x/dw$, and we refer to the set $\{h_x(w) : w \in [0, 1], x \in \mathcal{X}\}$ as the spectral surface.*

A simple spectral surface can be constructed with the pd spectral density $h_x(w) = \beta(w; a_x, a_x)$, where $a : \mathcal{X} \mapsto (0, \infty)$. In Figure 9.1, I represent a spectral surface based on this model, with $a_x = x$, for $x \in \mathcal{X} = [0.5, 50]$. (Larger values of the predictor x lead to larger levels of extremal dependence.) Other spectral surfaces can be readily constructed from parametric models for the spectral density; see, for instance, Coles (2001, Section 8.2.1).

Let's now regard the subject of pd bivariate extremes from another viewpoint. Modeling nonstationarity in marginal distributions has been the focus of

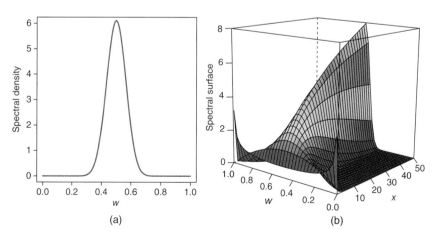

(a) (b)

FIGURE 9.1 **(a) Example of a spectral density. (b) Spectral surface from a predictor-dependent beta family, with $a_x = x$, for $x \in \mathcal{X} = [0.5, 50]$.**

much recent literature in applied extreme value modeling; see for instance Coles (2001, Chapter 6). The simplest approach in this setting was popularized long ago by Davison and Smith (1990), and it is based on indexing the location and scale parameters of the generalized EVD by a predictor, say, by taking

$$G_{(\mu_x, \sigma_x, \xi)}(y) = \exp\left[-\left\{1 + \xi\left(\frac{y - \mu_x}{\sigma_x}\right)\right\}^{-1/\xi}\right], \quad x \in \mathcal{X}. \tag{9.10}$$

And how to model "nonstationary bivariate extremes" if one must? Surprisingly, by comparison to the marginal case, approaches to modeling nonstationarity in the extremal dependence structure have received relatively little attention. These should be important to assess the dynamics governing extremal dependence of variables of interest. For example, has extremal dependence between returns of CAC 40 and DAX 30 been constant over time, or has this level been changing over the years?

By using pd spectral measures, we are essentially indexing the parameter of the bivariate extreme value distribution (H) with a covariate, and thus the approach can be regarded as an analogue of the Davison–Smith paradigm in (9.10), but for the bivariate setting. In the same way that (9.10) is a covariate-adjusted version of the generalized EVD (9.1), the following concept can be regarded as a pd version of the bivariate EVD in (9.3).

DEFINITION 9.7 *The family* $\{G_{H_x} : H_x \in \mathcal{H}\}$ *is a set of (measure-dependent) pd bivariate extreme value distributions if for* $y_1, y_2 > 0$:

$$G_{H_x}\{(0, y_1) \times (0, y_2)\} := G_{H_x}(y_1, y_2)$$

$$= \exp\left\{-2 \int_{[0,1]} \max\left(\frac{w}{y_1}, \frac{1 - w}{y_2}\right) H_x(dw)\right\}, \quad x \in \mathcal{X}.$$

Similarly to Section 2.2, in practice we need to obtain estimates that obey the marginal moment constraint and define a density on the unit interval, for all $x \in \mathcal{X}$. It is not straightforward to construct nonparametric estimators able to yield valid pd spectral measures. Indeed, any such estimator, $\hat{h}_x$, needs to obey the moment constraint, that is, $\int_0^1 w\, \hat{h}_x(w)\, dw = 1/2$, for all $x \in \mathcal{X}$. Castro and de Carvalho (2016) and Castro et al. (2015) are currently developing models for these contexts, but there are still plenty of opportunities here.[3]

Needless to say that other pd objects of interest can be readily constructed. For example, a pd version of Pickands (1981) dependence function can be defined as $A_x(w) = 1 - w + 2 \int_0^w H_x(v)\, dv$, and a pd $\chi = \lim_{u \to \infty} P(Y_1 > u \mid Y_2 > u)$ can also be constructed. Using the fact that $\chi = 2 - 2A(1/2)$ (de Carvalho and Ramos, 2012, p. 91), the pd χ can be defined as $\chi_x = 2 - 2A_x(1/2)$, for $x \in \mathcal{X}$.

---

[3]A natural option could be on using dependent Bernstein polynomials (Barrientos et al., 2016)— although it may be challenging to impose the moment constraint. It seems conceivable that similar ideas to those in Guillotte et al. (2011) could be used to construct a prior over a family $\{H_x : x \in \mathcal{X}\}$.

9.2.4 Other Families of Spectral Measures

Beyond pd spectral measures other families of spectral measures are of interest. In a recent paper, de Carvalho and Davison (2014) proposed a model for a family of spectral measures $\{H_1, \ldots, H_K\}$. The applied motivation for the concept was to track the effect of explanatory variables on joint extremes. Put differently, their main concern was on the joint modeling of extremal events when data are gathered from several populations, to each of which corresponds a vector of covariates. Thus, conceptually, there are already in de Carvalho and Davison (2014) some of the ingredients of pd spectral measures and related modeling objectives. Each element in the family should be regarded as a "distorted version," of a baseline spectral measure H_0, in a sense that I will precise in the succeeding text. Formally, spectral density ratio families are defined as follows.

DEFINITION 9.8 *Let $H_k \in \mathcal{H}$ be absolutely continuous, for $k = 1, \ldots, K$. The family $\{H_1, \ldots, H_K\}$ is a spectral density ratio family, if there exists an absolutely continuous $H_0 \in \mathcal{H}$, tilting parameters $(\alpha_k, \beta_k) \in \mathbb{R}^2$, and $c : [0, 1] \mapsto \mathbb{R}$ such that*

$$\frac{dH_k}{dH_0}(w) = \exp\{\alpha_k + \beta_k c(w)\}, \quad k = 1, \ldots, K. \tag{9.11}$$

🖥 **Example 9.1**

> Consider a family of symmetric beta distributions, $dH_k = \beta(w; \phi_k, \phi_k)\, dw$, for $k = 0, \ldots, K$. If $c(w) = \log\{w(1-w)\}$ we can write that $dH_k = \exp\{a_k + b_k c(w)\}\, dw$, where $(a_k, b_k) = (-\log B(\phi_k), \phi_k - 1)$, with $B(\phi) = \int_0^1 \{u(1-u)\}^{\phi-1}\, du$. Hence, $dH_k/dH_0 = \exp\{\alpha_k + \beta_k c(w)\}$, where the tilting parameters are $(\alpha_k, \beta_k) = (\log\{B(\phi_0)/B(\phi_k)\}, \phi_k - \phi_0)$. Note that $(\alpha_0, \beta_0) = (0, 0)$, and thus this parametrization is identifiable. This version of the model is closed, since tilting always produces a symmetric beta distribution.

From (9.11), we can write all the normalization and moment constraints for this family as a function of the baseline spectral measure and the tilting parameters, that is,

$$\begin{cases} \int_0^1 dH_0(w) = 1, & \int_0^1 w\, dH_0(w) = 1/2, \\[2mm] \int_0^1 \exp\{\alpha_1 + \beta_1 c(w)\}\, dH_0(w) = 1, & \int_0^1 w \exp\{\alpha_1 + \beta_1 c(w)\}\, dH_0(w) = 1/2, \\[2mm] \vdots & \vdots \\[2mm] \int_0^1 \exp\{\alpha_K + \beta_K c(w)\}\, dH_0(w) = 1, & \int_0^1 w \exp\{\alpha_K + \beta_K c(w)\}\, dH_0(w) = 1/2. \end{cases} \tag{9.12}$$

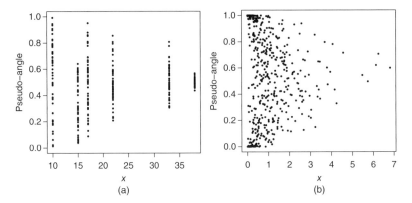

FIGURE 9.2 **Scatter plots presenting two configurations of data (predictor, pseudo-angles): one (a) where there are sample pseudo-angles per each observed covariate and another (b) where to each observed covariate may correspond a single pseudo-angle.**

Inference is based on the combined sample $\{W_{1,0}, \ldots, W_{n_0,0}, \ldots, W_{1,K}, \ldots, W_{n_K,K}\}$ from the spectral distributions $H_0, \ldots, H_k$. Details on estimation and inference through empirical likelihood methods can be found in de Carvalho and Davison (2011), de Carvalho and Davison (2014). An extremely appealing feature of their model is that it allows for borrowing strength across samples, in the sense that the estimate of H_k is based on $n = n_0 + \cdots + n_K$ pseudo-angles, instead of simply n_k. Although flexible, their approach requires however a substantial computational investment; in particular, inference entails intensive constrained optimization problems—even for a moderate K—so that estimates of H_k obey empirical versions of the normalization and moment constraints in (9.12). Their approach allows for modeling extremal dependence in settings such as Figure 9.2a, but it excludes data configurations such as Figure 9.2b. The pd-based approach of Castro et al. (2015) allows for inference to be conducted in both settings in Figure 9.2.

9.3   MODELS BASED ON FAMILIES OF TILTED MEASURES

The main goal of this section is on describing the link between the specifications underlying the spectral density ratio model, discussed in Section 2.4, the proportional tails model (Einmahl et al., 2015), and the exponential families for heavy-tailed data (Fithian and Wager, 2015).

9.3.1 Proportional Tails Model

The proportional tails model is essentially an approach for modeling non-stationary extremes. Suppose that at time points $t = 1, \ldots, N$ we gather independent observations $Y_1^{(N)}, \ldots, Y_N^{(N)}$, respectively, sampled from the continuous distribution functions $F_{N,1}, \ldots, F_{N,N}$, all with a common right end point $y^* = \sup\{y : F_{N,t}(y) < 1\}$. Suppose further that there exists a (time-invariant) baseline distribution function F_0, also with right end point y^*, and a continuous function $s : [0, 1] \mapsto [0, \infty)$, such that

$$s\left(\frac{t}{N}\right) := \lim_{y \to y^*} \frac{1 - F_{N,t}(y)}{1 - F_0(y)}, \quad t = 1, \ldots, N. \tag{9.13}$$

Here s is the so-called scedasis density, and following Einmahl et al. (2015) I assume the following normalization constraint $\int_0^1 s(u)\, du = 1$. Equation (9.13) is the key specification of the proportional tails model. Roughly speaking, the scedasis density tells us how much more/less mass there is on the tail $1 - F_{N,t}$, relatively to the baseline tail, $1 - F_0$, for a large y; uniform scedasis corresponds to a constant frequency of extremes over time.

The question arises naturally: "If the scedasis density provides an indication of the 'relative frequency' of extremes over time, would it seem natural that such function could be somehow connected to the intensity measure of the point process characterization of univariate extremes (Coles 2001, Section 7.3)?" To have an idea on how the concepts relate, I sketch here a heuristic argument. I insist, the argument is heuristic, and my aim here does not go beyond shedding some light on how these ideas connect. Consider the following artificial setting. Suppose that we could gather a large sample from F_0, say, $\{Y_{1,0}, \ldots, Y_{m,0}\}$, and that at each time point we could also collect a large sample from $F_{N,t}$, say, $\{Y_{1,t}, \ldots, Y_{m,t}\}$, for $t = 1, \ldots, N$. For concreteness let's focus on $t = 1$. Then, the definition of scedasis in (9.13) and similar arguments as in Coles (2001, Section 4.2.2) suggest that for a sufficiently large y,

$$s\left(\frac{1}{N}\right) \approx \frac{1 - F_{N,1}(y)}{1 - F_0(y)} \approx \frac{\{1 + \xi(y - \mu_1)/\sigma_1\}^{-1/\xi}}{\{1 + \xi(y - \mu_0)/\sigma_0\}^{-1/\xi}} = \frac{\Lambda_1\{(0, 1) \times (y, \infty)\}}{\Lambda_0\{(0, 1) \times (y, \infty)\}}, \tag{9.14}$$

where $\Lambda_i\{[t_1, t_2] \times (z, \infty)\} := (t_2 - t_1)\{1 + \xi(z - \mu_i)/\sigma_i\}^{-1/\xi}$, for $i = 0, 1$, is the intensity measure of the limiting Poisson process for univariate extremes (cf Coles 2001, Theorem 7.1.1). Thus, it can be seen from (9.14) that in this artificial setting the scedasis density can be literally interpreted as a measure of the relative intensity of the extremes at period $t = 1$, with respect to a (time-invariant) baseline.

Another important question is: "How can we estimate the scedasis density?" Einmahl et al. (2015) propose a kernel-based estimator

$$\hat{s}(w) = \frac{1}{n} \sum_{t=1}^{N} I(Y_t^{(N)} > Y_{N,N-n}) K_b(w - t/N), \quad w \in (0, 1), \tag{9.15}$$

where $K_b(\cdot) = (1/b)K(\cdot/b)$, with $b > 0$ being a bandwidth and K being a kernel; in addition, $Y_{N,1} \leq \cdots \leq Y_{N,N}$ are the order statistics of $Y_1^{(N)}, \ldots, Y_N^{(N)}$. Specifically, Einmahl et al. (2015) recommend K to be a symmetric kernel on $[-1, 1]$. A conceptual problem with using a kernel on $[-1, 1]$ is that it allows for the scedasis density to put mass outside $[0, 1]$.[4] Using similar ideas to the ones involved in the construction of the smooth spectral density estimators in Section 2.2, I propose here the following estimator:

$$\tilde{s}(w) = \frac{1}{n} \sum_{t=1}^{N} I(Y_t^{(N)} > Y_{N,N-n})\beta(w; vt/(N+1), v\{1 - t/(N+1)\}), \quad w \in (0, 1).$$

(9.16)

Indeed, each beta density is centered close to t/N in the sense that $E(Z_t) = t/(N+1)$, for $Z_t \sim \text{Beta}(vt/(N+1); v\{1 - t/(N+1)\})$, where v is the parameter controlling the level of smoothing. My goal here will not be on trying to recommend an estimator over the other, but rather on providing a brief description of strengths and limitations with both approaches. In Figure 9.3, I illustrate how the two estimators, (9.15) and (9.16), perform on the same data used by Einmahl et al. (2015) and on simulated data (single-run experiment).[5] The data consist of daily negative returns of the Standard and Poor's index from 1988 to 2007 ($N = 5043$), and I use the same value for n (130) and the same bandwidth ($h = 0.1$) and (biweight) kernel $[K(y) = 15(1 - y^2)^2/16$, for $y \in [-1, 1]]$ as authors; I also follow the author's settings for the simulated data. Finally, I consider $v = 100$ for illustration.

In the Standard and Poor's example in Figure 9.3a, it can be seen that both estimators capture similar dynamics; the gray rectangles represent contraction periods of the US economy as dated by the National Bureau of Economic Research (NBER). It is interesting to observe that the local maxima of the scedasis density are relatively close to economic contraction periods. Indeed, "turning points" (local maxima and minima) of the scedasis density seem like an interesting estimation target for many settings of applied interest.

The estimator in (9.16) has the appealing feature of putting all mass of the scedasis density inside the $(0, 1)$ interval, and some further numerical experiments suggest that it tends to have a similar behavior to that in (9.15) except at the boundary. However, a shortcoming with the method in (9.16) is that it may not be defined at the vertex 0 or 1, and hence it could be inappropriate for forecasting purposes.

The proportional tails model is extremely appealing and simple to fit. A possible shortcoming is that it does not allow for $\xi > 0$ to change over time. For applications in which we suspect that ξ may change over time, the generalized additive approach by Chavez-Demoulin and Davison (2005) is a sensible alternative, and although the model is more challenging to implement, it can be readily fitted with the R package QRM by typing in the command game.

---

[4]For a discussion on the challenges surrounding kernel density estimation on the unit interval, see, for instance, Chen (1999), Jones and Henderson (2007), de Carvalho et al. (2013), Geenens (2014), and references therein.

[5]The dashed line in Figure 9.3a differs slightly (close to 0 and 1) from Einmahl et al. (2015, Figure 1), because here I do not use boundary correction.

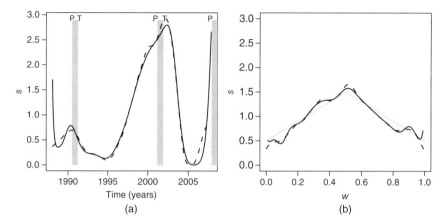

FIGURE 9.3 Scedasis density estimates. The solid line represents the beta kernel estimate from (9.16), whereas the dashed line represents the estimate from (9.15). (a) Daily Standard and Poor's index from 1988 to 2007; the gray rectangles correspond to contraction periods in the US economy. (b) Simulated data illustration from $F_{N,t}(y) = \exp\{-s(t/N)/y\}$, **for** $y > 0$, **with** $N = 5000$ **and** $n = 400$; **the grey line represents the true scedasis** $s(w) = 2w + 0.5$, **for** $w \in [0, 0.5)$, **and** $s(w) = -2w + 2.5$, **for** $w \in [0.5, 1]$.

A problem that seems relevant for practice is that of cluster analysis for the proportional tails model. To see this, suppose that one estimates the scedasis density and tail index for several stocks. It seems natural to wonder: "How can we cluster stocks whose scedasis looks more alike, or—perhaps more interestingly—how can we cluster stocks with a similar scedasis and tail index?"

Lastly, I would like to comment that it seems conceivable that Bernstein polynomials could be used for scedasis density estimation. In particular, a natural question is "Would it be possible to construct a prior over the space of all integrated scedasis functions?" Random Bernstein polynomials could seem like the way to go; see Petrone (1999) and references therein.

9.3.2 Exponential Families for Heavy-Tailed Data

In this section I sketch some basic ideas on exponential families for heavy-tailed data; I will be more brief here than in Section 3.1. My goal is mainly on introducing the model specification and to move on; further details can be found in Fithian and Wager (2015).

The starting point for the Fithian–Wager approach is on modeling the conditional right tail law from a population, $G_1^*(y) = P(Y_1 - u \le y \mid Y_1 > u)$, as an exponential family with carrier measure $G_0^* = P(Y_0 - u \le y \mid Y_0 > u)$, for a sufficiently large threshold u. Two random samples are assumed to be available, $Y_{1,0}, \ldots, Y_{N_0,0} \overset{\text{i.i.d.}}{\sim} F_0$ and $Y_{1,1}, \ldots, Y_{N_1,1} \overset{\text{i.i.d.}}{\sim} F_1$, with $N_0 \gg N_1$; hence, the applied setting of interest is one where the size of the sample from F_0 is much larger than the one from F_1. The model specification is

$$\frac{dG_1^*}{dG_0^*}(y) = \exp\{\eta T(y) - \psi(\eta)\}, \quad y \in [0, \infty), \tag{9.17}$$

where the sufficient statistic $T(y)$ is of the form $y/(y + \kappa)$ for a certain κ; the functional form of $T(y)$ is motivated from the case where G_0^* and G_1^* are generalized Pareto distributions (cf. Fithian and Wager, 2015, p. 487).

In common with the spectral density ratio model, the Fithian–Wager model is motivated by the gains from borrowing strength across samples. Fithian and Wager are not however concerned about spectral measures, but rather on estimating a (small-sample) mean of a heavy-tailed distribution, by borrowing information from a much larger sample from a related population with the same $0 < \xi < 1$. More concretely, the authors propose a semiparametric method for estimating the mean of Y_1, by using the decomposition $\mu = p \, \mu_L + (1 - p) \, \mu_R$, where $\mu = E(Y_1)$, $p = P(Y_1 \leq u)$, $\mu_L = E(Y_1 \mid Y_1 \leq u)$, and $\mu_R = E(Y_1 \mid Y_1 > u)$. The Fithian–Wager estimator for the (small-sample) mean can be written as

$$\hat{\mu} = \hat{p} \, \hat{\mu}_L + (1 - \hat{p}) \, \hat{\mu}_R$$

$$= \frac{n_L}{N_1} \frac{1}{n_L} \sum_{\{i : Y_{i,1} \leq u\}} Y_{i,1} + \frac{n_R}{N_1} \frac{1}{\sum_{\{i : Y_{i,0} > u\}} \exp\{\hat{\eta} \, T(Y_{i,0} - u)\}}$$

$$\sum_{\{i : Y_{i,0} > u\}} Y_{i,0} \exp\{\hat{\eta} \, T(Y_{i,0} - u)\}, \tag{9.18}$$

where $n_L = |\{i : Y_{i,1} \leq u\}|$ and $n_R = |\{i : Y_{i,1} > u\}|$, for a large threshold u. Here $\hat{\eta}$ can be computed through a logistic regression with an intercept and predictor $T(y - u)$, as a consequence of results on imbalanced logistic regression (Owen, 2007). As it can be observed from (9.18), the main trick on the estimation of μ is on the exponential tilt-based estimator for the mean residual lifetime μ_R.

9.3.3   Families of Tilted Measures

From previous sections it may have became obvious that the common link underlying the specification of the spectral density ratio model, the proportional tails model, and the exponential families for heavy-tailed data was the assumption that all members in a family of interest were obtained through a suitable "distortion" of a certain baseline measure. In this section I make this link more precise.

DEFINITION 9.9 *Let $\mathcal{F}$ be the space of all probability measures that can be defined on $(\Omega, \mathcal{A})$. Let $g_{i,I} : \Omega \mapsto \mathbb{R}$, for $i = 1, \dots, I$. A family of probability measures in $\mathcal{F}$, $\{F_1, \dots, F_I\}$, is a g-tilted family if there exists $F_0 \in \mathcal{F}$ and a functional θ such that*

$$\Phi_\theta(y) := \left(\frac{\theta(F_i)}{\theta(F_0)} \right)(y) = g_{i,I}(y), \quad y \in \Omega.$$

Some examples are presented in the succeeding text.

▣ Example 9.2 **Spectral Density Ratio Model**

For the spectral density ratio model, the family of interest is $\{H_1, \ldots, H_K\}$ and thus $I = K$. Tilting is conducted through $g_k(w) = \exp\{\alpha_k + \beta_k c(w)\}$, for $w \in (0,1)$; let $\theta(H) = dH$, for absolutely continuous $H \in \mathcal{H}$. Thus, Eq. (9.11) can be written as

$$\Phi_\theta(w) := \frac{dH_k}{dH_0}(w) = \exp\{\alpha_k + \beta_k c(w)\} =: g_k(w), \quad w \in (0,1).$$

▣ Example 9.3 **Proportional Tails Model**

For the proportional tails model, for a fixed N, the family of interest is $\{F_{N,1}, \ldots, F_{N,N}\}$ and hence $I = N$. Tilting is conducted through $g_{t,N}(y) = s(t/N)$, for $y \in \mathbb{R}$; let $\theta(F) = \lim_{y \to y^*} 1 - F(y)$, with F denoting a continuous distribution function. Thus, Eq. (9.13) can be rewritten as

$$\Phi_{\theta_{\mathrm{pt}}}(y) := \lim_{y \to y^*} \frac{1 - F_{N,t}(y)}{1 - F_0(y)} = s\left(\frac{t}{N}\right) =: g_{t,N}(y), \quad y \in \mathbb{R}.$$

▣ Example 9.4 **Exponential Families for Heavy-Tailed Data**

In Section 3.2 the "family" of interest is $\{G_1^*\}$ and thus $I = 1$. Tilting is conducted through $g(y) = \exp\{\eta T(y) + \psi(\eta)\}$, for $y \in [0, \infty)$; let θ to be defined as in Example 9.2. Thus, Eq. (9.17) can be rewritten as

$$\Phi_\theta^*(y) := \frac{dG_1^*}{dG_0^*}(y) = \exp\{\eta T(y) - \psi(\eta)\} =: g(y), \quad y \in [0, \infty).$$

9.4 MISCELLANEA

9.4.1 Asymptotic (in)dependence

Here, I comment on the need for further developing models compatible with both asymptotic dependence and asymptotic independence. In two influential papers, Poon et al. (2003, 2004) put forward that asymptotic independence was observed on many pairs of stock market returns. This had important consequences in finance, mostly because inferences in a seminal paper (Longin and Solnik, 2001) had been based on the assumption of asymptotic dependence, and hence perhaps risk had been overestimated earlier. However, an important questions is: "What if pairs of financial losses can move over time from asymptotic independence to asymptotic dependence and the other way around?" Some markets are believed to be more integrated these days than in the past, so for such markets it is relevant to ask whether they could have entered an "asymptotic dependence regime." An accurate answer to this question would require however models able to allow for smooth transitions from asymptotic independence to asymptotic dependence, and vice versa, but as already mentioned in Section 2.3 at the moment, there is a shortage of models for nonstationary extremal dependence structures. Wadsworth et al. (2016) presents an interesting approach for modeling asymptotic (in)dependence.

9.4.2   Spatial Multivariate Extremes

An important reference here is Genton et al. (2015), but there is a wealth of problems to work in this direction, so I stop my comment here.

9.4.3   Dimension Reduction for Multivariate Extremes

Is there a way to reduce dimension in such a way that the interesting features of the data—in terms of tails of multivariate distributions—are preserved?[6] I think it is fair to say that, apart from some remarkable exceptions, most models for multivariate extremes have been applied only to low-dimensional settings. I remember that at a seminal workshop on high-dimensional extremes, organized by Anthony Davison, at the Ecole Polytechnique Fédérale de Lausanne (September 14–18, 2009), for most talks high dimensional actually meant "two dimensional," and all speakers were top scientists in the field.

Principal component analysis (PCA) itself would seem inappropriate, since principal axes are constructed in a way to find the directions that account for most variation, and for our axes of interest (whatever they are …), variation does not seem to be the most reasonable objective. A naive approach could be to use PCA for compositional data (Jolliffe, 2002, Section 13.3) and apply it to the pseudo-angles themselves. Such approach could perhaps provide a simple way to disentangle dependence into components that could be of practical interest.

9.4.4   Should the Journal *Extremes* Include an *Applications and Case Studies* Section?

Theory and methods are the backbone of our field, without regular variation we wouldn't have gone far anyway. But, beyond theory, should our community be investing even more than it already is, in modeling and applications? As put simply by Box (1979), "all models are wrong, but some are useful." However, while most of us agree that models only provide an approximation to reality, we seem to

---

[6]An interesting paper on dimension reduction for multivariate extremes appeared in the meantime at the *Electronic Journal of Statistics* (Chautru, 2015), after the discussion took place. Anne Sabourin and colleagues are also currently working on the topic.

be very demanding about the way that we develop theory about such—wrong yet useful—models. Some models entail ingenious approximations to reality and yet are very successful in practice. Should we venture more on this direction in the future? Applied work can also motivate new, and useful, theories. Should we venture more on collaborating with researchers from other fields or on creating more conferences such as the ESSEC Conference on Extreme Events in Finance, where one has the opportunity to regard risk and extremes from a broader perspective, so to think out of the box? Should the journal *Extremes* include an *Applications and Case Studies* section?

9.4.5 Communicating Risk and Extremes

What has our community been supplying in terms of communication of risk and extremes? Silence, for the most part. Definitely there have been some noteworthy initiatives, but perhaps mostly from people outside of our field such as those of David Spiegelhalter and David Hand. My own view is that it would be excellent if, in a recent future, leading scientists in our field could be more involved in communicating risk and extremes to the general public, either by writing newspaper and magazine articles or by promoting science vulgarization. Our community is becoming more and more aware of this need, I think. I was happy to see Paul Embrechts showing recently his concern about this matter at EVA 2015 in Ann Arbor.

9.4.6 Prior Elicitation in Contexts Where a Conflict of Interest Exists

How can we accurately elicit prior information when modeling extreme events in finance, in cases where a conflict of interest may exist? Suppose that a regulator requires a bank to report an estimate. If prior information is gathered from a bank expert—and if the bank is better off by misreporting—then how can we trust in the accuracy of the inferences? In such cases, I think the only Bayesian analysis a regulator should be willing to accept would be an objective Bayes-based analysis; see Berger (2006) for a review on objective Bayes.

References

Barrientos, A.F., Jara, A., Quintana, F.A. Fully nonparametric regression for bounded data using dependent Bernstein polynomials. J Am Stat Assoc 2016. In press.

Berger, J. The case for objective bayesian analysis. Bayesian Anal 2006;**1**:385–402.

Boldi, M.-O., Davison, A.C. A mixture model for multivariate extremes. Journal of the Royal Statistical Society, Series B 2007;**69**:217–229.

Box, G.E.P. Some problems of statistics and everyday life. Journal of the American Statistical Association 1979;**74**:1–4.

Castro, D., de Carvalho, M. Spectral density regression for bivariate extremes. Stochastic Environmental Research and Risk Assessment 2016. In press. DOI: 0.1007/s00477-016-1257-z.

Castro, D., de Carvalho, M., Wadsworth, J. Time-varying extremal dependence with application to leading european stock markets. 2015. Submitted.

Chautru, E. Dimension reduction in multivariate extreme value analysis. Electronic Journal of Statistics 2015;**9**:383–418.

Chavez-Demoulin, V., Davison, A.C. Generalized additive modelling of sample extremes. Journal of the Royal Statistical Society, Ser. C, 2005;**54**:207–222.

Chen, S.X. Beta Kernel estimators for density functions. Comput Stat Data Anal 1999;**31**:131–145.

Coles, S. *An Introduction to Statistical Modeling of Extreme Values*. New York: Springer-Verlag; 2001.

Davison, A.C., Smith, R.L. Models for exceedances over high thresholds (with Discussion). Journal of the Royal Statistical Society, Ser. B 1990;**52**:393–442.

de Carvalho, M., Davison, A.C. Semiparametric estimation for K-sample multivariate extremes. Proceedings 58th World Statistical Congress; 2011. 2961–2969.

de Carvalho, M., Davison, A.C. Spectral density ratio models for multivariate extremes. J Am Stat Assoc 2014;**109**:764–776.

de Carvalho, M., Oumow, B., Segers, J., Warchoł, M. A Euclidean likelihood estimator for bivariate tail dependence. Communications in Statistics—Theory and Methods 2013;**42**:1176–1192.

de Carvalho, M., Ramos, A. Bivariate extreme statistics, II. RevStat—Statistical Journal 2012;**10**:81–104.

de Haan, L., Resnick, S.I. Limit theory for multivariate sample extremes. Zeitschrift für Wahrscheinlichkeitstheorie und verwandte Gebiete 1977;**40**:317–377.

Einmahl, J.H.J., de Haan, L., Zhou, C. Statistics of heteroscedastic extremes. Journal of the Royal Statistical Society, Ser. B 2015;**78**(1):31–51. DOI: 10.1111/rssb.12099.

Einmahl, J.H.J., Segers, J. Maximum empirical likelihood estimation of the spectral measure of an extreme-value distribution. The Annals of Statistics 2009;**37**: 2953–2989.

Fithian, W., Wager, S. Semiparametric exponential families for heavy-tailed data. Biometrika 2015;**102**:486–493.

Geenens, G. Probit transformation for kernel density estimation on the unit interval. Journal of the American Statistical Association, 2014;**109**:346–359.

Genton, M.G., Padoan, S.A., Sang, H. Multivariate max-stable spatial processes. Biometrika 2015;**102**:215–230.

Guillotte, S., Perron, F., Segers, J. Non-parametric bayesian inference on bivariate extremes. Journal of the Royal Statistical Society, Ser. B, 2011;**73**:377–406.

Jolliffe, I.T. *Principal Component Analysis*. New York: Springer-Verlag; 2002.

Jones, M.C., Henderson, D.A. Kernel-type density estimation on the unit interval. Biometrika 2007;**94**:977–984.

Kiriliouk, A., Segers, J., Warchoł, M. Nonparametric estimation of extremal dependence. In: Dey, D.K., Yan, J., editors. *Extreme Value Modelling and Risk Analysis: Methods and Applications*. Boca Raton (FL): Chapman and Hall/CRC; 2015.

Longin, F., Solnik, B. Extreme correlation of international equity markets. The Journal of Finance 2001;**56**:649–676.

Owen, A.B. *Empirical Likelihood*. Boca Raton (FL): Chapman and Hall/CRC; 2001.

Owen, A.B. Infinitely imbalanced logistic regression. Journal of Machine Learning Research 2007;**8**:761–773.

Petrone, S. Random Bernstein polynomials. Scand inavian Journal of Statistics 1999;**26**:373–393.

Pickands, J. Multivariate extreme value distributions. Proceedings 43rd World Statistical Congress; 1981. p 859–878.

Poon, S.-H., Rockinger, M., Tawn, J. Modelling extreme-value dependence in international stock markets. Statistica Sinica 2003;**13**:929–953.

Poon, S.-H., Rockinger, M., Tawn, J. Extreme value dependence in financial markets: diagnostics, models, and financial implications. Review of Financial Studies 2004;**17**:581–610.

Sabourin, A., Naveau, P. Bayesian dirichlet mixture model for multivariate extremes: a re-parametrization. Comput Stat Data Anal 2014;**71**:542–567.

Taleb, N. *Antifragile: Things that Gain from Disorder*. New York: Random House; 2012.

Wadsworth, J.L., Tawn, J.A., Davison, A.C., Elton, D.M. Modelling across extremal dependence classes. J R Stat Soc, Ser B 2016. In press.

Wooldridge, J.M. *Econometric Analysis of Cross Section and Panel Data*. 2nd ed. Cambridge (MA): MIT Press; 2015.

Chapter Ten

Measures of Financial Risk

S.Y. Novak

School of Science and Technology, Middlesex University, London, UK

*AMS 2000 Subject Classification: primary 60G70; secondary 60G55, 60E15.
JEL Classification: C53, G17.*

10.1 INTRODUCTION

Accurate evaluation of risk is fundamental to the financial well-being of financial institutions as well as individual investors. However, the issue is demanding. It involves sophisticated statistical analysis of market data.

The traditional approach to risk measurement is capable of forecasting the magnitude of a possible sharp market movement (see, e.g., Novak and Beirlant, 2006). However, the estimates appear static: they barely change with the inflow of new information, and may be unsuitable for active portfolio management. The "Technical Analysis" (TA) approach offers a truly dynamic risk measure m_{TA} (cf. Novak, 2011, Chapter 10). However, the lack of statistical scrutiny affects its credibility. The main obstacle that prevents building a body of empirical evidence either in favor or against the use of m_{TA} is the computational difficulty caused by the fact that price charts appear objects of fractal geometry.

Section 10.2 briefly overviews the popular measures of risk, including value at risk (VaR) and a related measure called conditional VaR (CVaR) or Expected Shortfall. Section 10.3 discusses the strengths and weaknesses of the traditional approach to risk measurement. In Section 10.4, we briefly overview the basic tools of the Technical Analysis approach. Section 10.5 presents properties of a dynamic risk measure. Section 10.6 concentrates on a number of open questions concerning computational and statistical issues related to dynamic risk measurement.

Extreme Events in Finance: A Handbook of Extreme Value Theory and its Applications,
First Edition. Edited by François Longin.

10.2 TRADITIONAL MEASURES OF RISK

Let X denote the underlying financial/insurance data (e.g., the rate of return of a particular financial asset, the daily log-return of a share price, claim sizes, etc.), and let

$$F(x) = \mathbb{P}(X \leq x)$$

be the distribution function (d.f.) of $\mathcal{L}(X)$. Traditional measures of risk are the standard deviation

$$\sigma_X$$

and the beta

$$\beta_X = \text{cov}(X; M)/\sigma_M^2,$$

where X is the rate of return of a particular financial asset, M is the rate of return of the market portfolio (often approximated by the S&P 500 index), and σ_M^2 is the variance of M. In the case of autoregressive conditional heteroscedasticity (ARCH)/generalized ARCH (GARCH) models, one often deals with the conditional standard deviation σ_{X_n} of X_n given $(X_{n-1}, X_{n-2}, \cdots)$.

Among traditional measure of risk is Value-at-Risk (VaR). Up to a sign, VaR is an extreme quantile:

$$m\%\text{-VaR} = -F^{-1}(m/100).$$

Equivalently,

$$q\text{-VaR} = -F^{-1}(q) \qquad (0 < q < 1).$$

Recall that

$$F^{-1}(q) = \inf\{x : F(x) \geq q\}.$$

If F is continuous, then q-VaR is such that

$$\mathbb{P}(X \leq -q\text{-VaR}) = q.$$

$m\%$-VaR indicates how far the quantity of interest (say, daily log-return X) can fall in approximately $m\%$ "worst" cases. For instance, if 1%-VaR equals 0.04, then in approximately 1% cases the quantity of interest, X, can be below -4%.

One often deals with log-returns $X_k = \ln(P_k/P_{k-1})$ instead of prices $\{P_k\}$, as log-returns are more likely to form a stationary sequence. If 1%-VaR for daily log-returns equals y, then roughly once in 100 days the value of a portfolio may be below e^{-y} times the previous day's value.

VaR is probably the most popular measure of risk. Many banks routinely calculate VaR in order to monitor the current exposure of their portfolios to market risk. Knowing VaR allows a bank to decide how much money it needs to put aside to offset the risk of an undesirable market movement. For instance, Goldman Sachs deals with 5%-VaR; Citigroup, Credit Suisse First Boston, Deutsche Bank,

JP Morgan Chase, and Morgan Stanley use 1%-VaR (see, e.g., Wells et al., 2004; Gurrola-Perez and Murphy, 2015).

Closely related is another measure of risk known as CVaR, the Expected Shortfall or BVaR (Artzner et al., 1999; Longin, 2001; Pflug, 2000; Rockafellar and Uryasev, 1999). It represents the average loss, given there is a fall beyond VaR: assuming $\mathbb{E}|X| < \infty$,

$$\text{CVaR} = -\mathbb{E}\{X|X \leq -\text{VaR}\}.$$

One often prefers to deal with positive numbers (e.g., we speak about "20.5% fall" of the S&P 500 index on the "Black Monday" instead of "−20.5% rate of return"). If we switch from X to $-X$, then VaR is the upper quantile (the inverse of $F_c = 1 - F$):

$$q\text{-VaR} = F_c^{-1}(q), \tag{10.1}$$

and

$$\text{CVaR} = \mathbb{E}\{X|X \geq \text{VaR}\} = \text{VaR} + \mathbb{E}\{X - \text{VaR}|X \geq \text{VaR}\} \tag{10.2}$$

(we sometimes omit prefix q-). Recall that

$$\mathbb{E}\{X - x|X \geq x\}$$

is the *mean excess function*, also known as the mean residual life function.

Properties of VaR and CVaR can be found, for example, in Alexander (2008), Nadarajah and Chan (2017), Novak (2011), and Pflug (2000).

📖 **Example 10.1**

Let $\{X_n, n \geq 1\}$ be the ARCH(1) process with parameters $b > 0$ and $c \geq 0$:

$$X_n = \xi_n \sqrt{b + cX_{n-1}^2} \qquad (n \geq 2), \tag{10.3}$$

where $\{\xi_i\}$ is a sequence of independent normal $\mathcal{N}(0; 1)$ random variables. The conditional standard deviation of X_n given $(X_{n-1}, X_{n-2}, \cdots)$ is

$$\sigma_{X_n} = \sqrt{b + cX_{n-1}^2},$$

$$q\text{-VaR}_{X_n} \simeq -t_q \sqrt{b + cX_{n-1}^2},$$

$$q\text{-CVaR}_{X_n} \simeq \exp(-t_q^2/2)\sigma_{X_n}/q\sqrt{2\pi}, \tag{10.4}$$

where $t_q = \Phi^{-1}(q)$ and Φ is the standard normal distribution function. The estimate of c is typically close to 0, making the random variables σ_{X_n}, $q\text{-VaR}_{X_n}$ and $q\text{-CVaR}_{X_n}$ rather static.

Note that σ, β, VaR and CVaR (as well as m_{TA} below) measure the risk on the basis of the past ("historical") data. A different approach based on "future values only" was suggested by Artzner et al. (1999): "The basic objects of our study shall be possible future values of positions or portfolios." Artzner et al. (1999) define a measure of risk related to the "acceptance set" A as

$$\rho_A(X) = \inf\{m : mr_o + X \in A\},$$

where X is "the final net worth of a position" and r_o is the rate of return of the risk-free asset.

10.3 RISK ESTIMATION

This section is devoted to the problem of estimating risk measures assuming a particular model. The topic of testing the goodness of fit of particular models is beyond the scope of this article.

One has to distinguish a quantity one wants to estimate (e.g., 1%-VaR) from a model (i.e., the assumptions on the class of distributions the unknown distribution $\mathcal{L}(X)$ belongs to).

If data is light-tailed (this, of course, needs to be checked), it hardly can exhibit extreme movements, and the assumption that $\mathcal{L}(X)$ has normal $\mathcal{N}(\mu; \sigma^2)$ distribution is not unreasonable. In the case of frequent data μ is typically negligible, and hence

$$q\text{-VaR}_{\mathcal{N}} \simeq -\sigma t_q, \quad q\text{-CVaR}_{\mathcal{N}} \simeq \exp\left(-t_q^2/2\right)\sigma/q\sqrt{2\pi} \simeq q\text{-VaR}_{\mathcal{N}}. \tag{10.5}$$

According to (10.5), one only needs to estimate the standard deviation $\sigma \equiv \sigma_X$ (cf. Alexander, 2001, Section 9.3).

Financial/insurance data often exhibits heavy tails (see Embrechts et al., 1997; Fama and Roll, 1968; Longin, 1996; Mandelbrot, 1963). This is particularly common to "frequent" data (e.g., daily log-returns of stock prices and stock indexes), while log-returns of less frequent data can exhibit light tails–well in line with the central limit theorem. Note that the stationary distribution of the ARCH(1) process (10.3) is heavy-tailed (see Goldie, 1991; Embrechts et al., 1997, pp. 465–466).

The feature of heavy-tailed distributions is that a single observation can be of the same order of magnitude as the whole sum of sample elements: a single claim to an insurance company or a 1-week market movement can cause a loss comparable to a 1-year profit.

A number of procedures to check whether the distribution is heavy-tailed are mentioned in Markovich (2007) and Novak (2011).

The problem of evaluating risk from dependent heavy-tailed data is attracting increasing attention of researchers (see Nadarajah and Chan, 2017; Novak, 2011, and references therein).

The distribution of a random variable X has a *heavy right tail* if

$$\mathbb{P}(X \geq x) = L(x)x^{-\alpha} \qquad (\alpha > 0), \tag{10.6}$$

where the (unknown) function L is slowly varying at ∞:

$$\lim_{x \to \infty} L(xt)/L(x) = 1 \qquad (\forall t > 0).$$

Number α in (10.6) is called the *tail index*. It is the main characteristic describing the tail of a heavy-tailed distribution.

If the distribution of a random variable X has a heavy right tail with tail index $\alpha > 1$, then

$$\mathbb{E}\{X|X \geq x\} \simeq \frac{\alpha}{\alpha - 1}\, x$$

for large x (see, e.g., Embrechts et al., 1997, p. 162). For small q

$$q\text{-VaR} = \ell(q)q^{-1/\alpha},$$

where ℓ is a slowly varying function (see Seneta, 1976; Bingham et al., 1987), and hence

$$q\text{-CVaR} \simeq \frac{\alpha}{\alpha - 1}\, q\text{-VaR}$$

(cf. Longin (2001), Equation (4); Novak (2011), p. 168).

Heavy-tailed distributions form a domain of attraction to one of the possible limit laws for the sample maximum (see Gnedenko, 1943). Interest in heavy-tailed distributions is inspired also by their rich applications in hydrology, meteorology, etc. (see, e.g., Fraga Alves and Neves, 2017).

The problem of reliable estimation of the tail index α,

$$y_q := q\text{-VaR} \quad \text{and} \quad z_q := q\text{-CVaR}$$

from heavy-tailed data is demanding (cf. Embrechts et al., 1997; Novak, 2011). The following estimators of VaR and CVaR are asymptotically normally distributed (see Novak, 2002, 2011) and appear reasonably accurate in examples of simulated data:

$$y_{n,q} \equiv y_{n,q}(x) = x(N_n(x)/qn)^{\hat{a}_n^{\text{RE}}}, \tag{10.7}$$

$$z_{n,q} \equiv z_{n,q}(x) = y_{n,q}/(1 - \hat{a}_n^{\text{RE}}). \tag{10.8}$$

Here, the threshold x is a tuning parameter (it needs to be chosen), q is the given level, and $\hat{a}_n^{\text{RE}}$ is the Ratio Estimator (RE) of index $a = 1/\alpha$:

$$\hat{a}_n^{\text{RE}} \equiv \hat{a}_n^{\text{RE}}(x) = \sum_{i=1}^{n} \ln\,(X_i/x)\mathbb{I}\{X_i > x\} \Big/ \sum_{i=1}^{n} \mathbb{I}\{X_i > x\} \tag{10.9}$$

(equivalently, $1/\hat{a}_n^{\text{RE}}$ is the Ratio Estimator of the tail index).

This approach is nonparametric. The comparison of finite-sample properties and asymptotic mean-squared errors of a number of tail index estimators in Novak (2011), p. 150, is in favor of the RE.

There are doubts that parametric models accurately describe real financial data: one usually cannot be sure whether the unknown distribution comes from a chosen parametric family. The advantage of the nonparametric approach is that such a problem is void: the nonparametric class is so rich that one typically has no doubt that the unknown distribution belongs to it. The disadvantage of the non-parametric inference is the presence of a tuning ("nuisance") parameter.

A procedure of choosing the tuning parameter for estimators (10.7–10.9) has been suggested in Novak (2002), see also Novak (2011). It is data-driven, model-free, and suggests to

(i) plot an estimator $\hat{a}_n$ (e.g., $\hat{a}_n^{RE}$) as a function of the tuning parameter,

(ii) choose an interval $[x_-; x_+]$ formed by a significant number of sample elements, in which the plot demonstrates stability (the theoretical results in Novak (2002) state there should be such an interval of stability),

(iii) take the average value $\hat{a}$ of the estimator $\hat{a}_n$ in the interval $[x_-; x_+]$ as the estimate of a (i.e., we choose the threshold $\hat{x}_n \in [x_-; x_+]$ such that $\hat{a}_n(\hat{x}_n) = \hat{a}$).

Since we take the average over an interval formed by a significant number of sample points, the procedure yields almost one and the same estimate despite the individual choice of the interval of stability: the variability with the choice of end-points is almost eliminated.

Example 10.2

The "Black Monday" crash. Forecasting the scale of possible extreme movements of financial markets is one of the main tasks of a risk manager. A particular question of this kind was raised in McNeil (1998): having the data over the period January 1, 1960 to 16, October 1987, was is possible to predict the magnitude of the next crash?

If data is heavy-tailed, then the standard deviation does not appear to be a proper tool to describe the risk associated with extreme movements of the portfolio returns even if a portfolio is optimal in the sense of the mean-variance portfolio theory.

Figure 10.1 presents the standard deviations of daily log-returns of the S&P 500 index over the period 01.01.1960 to 16.10.1987 (the standard deviations were calculated using a 1-year of preceding data). The value of the standard deviation on 16.10.1987 is close to that on 16.10.1982, 16.10.1970, and 16.10.1962, and hardly can serve an indicator of a possible crash. Yet, on Monday 19.10.1987 the S&P 500 index fell by 20.5% – the worst daily fall of the index (see Figure 10.2).

Recall that if data is heavy-tailed, then a single sample element, for example, the loss over one particular day, can make a major contribution to the total loss over a considerable period. In particular, the "Black Monday" crash erased all the index had gained since March 1986.

Sometimes, the data exhibits such heavy tails that the variance is likely to be infinite. In all such situations, VaR and CVaR appear more suitable measures of risk.

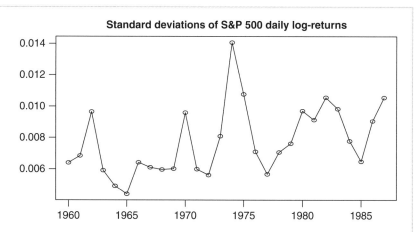

FIGURE 10.1 Standard deviations of daily log-returns of the S&P 500 index during the period from January 1960 – October 1987. The value of the standard deviation on 16.10.1987 is close to those on 16.10.1982, 16.10.1970, and 16.10.1962, and hardly can serve an indicator of a possible crash.

We have applied estimators (10.7), (10.8), and the procedure of choosing the tuning parameter to daily log-returns of the S&P 500 index over the period from 01.01.1960 to 16.10.1987 (formed by approximately 10,000 trading days). The Dickey–Fuller test does not reject the hypothesis of stationarity. We use the Ratio estimator in order to estimate the tail index (a comparison of a number of tail index estimators can be found in Markovich (2007) and Novak (2011)).

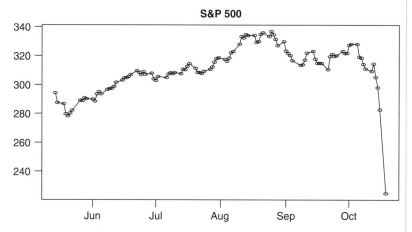

FIGURE 10.2 The S&P 500 index during the period from May 1987 to October 1987. On Monday, October 19, 1987, the index fell by 20.5%.

The plot of the Ratio estimator $\hat{a}_n^{RE}(\cdot)$ is stable in the interval $[1.4; 5.4]$. The curve over that interval is formed by 285 points. There were 3319 falls during that period, while only 512 of them exceeded the 1% level. We conclude that interval $[1.4; 5.4]$ is formed by a significant number of sample elements. The average value of $\hat{a}_n^{RE}(x)$ as $x \in [1.4; 5.4]$ is

$$\hat{a} = 0.2515,$$

and threshold $\hat{x}_n$ is chosen so that $\hat{a}_n^{RE}(\hat{x}_n) = \hat{a}$. Thus, the tail index has been estimated at

$$1/\hat{a} = 3.97.$$

VaR and CVaR estimators (10.7), (10.8) with $q = 0.01\%$ and the threshold already chosen yield 18.1% for 0.01%-VaR and 24.2% for the corresponding CVaR. Hence the worst possible fall of the daily log-return of the S&P 500 index in 40 years, according to the data available on the eve of the "Black Monday," was likely to be around 24.2%.

This is remarkably close to the value of the actual fall on 19.10.1987. The closing price of S&P 500 on 16.10.87 was 282.94 (already 5% down on the previous day); the closing price of S&P 500 on 19.10.1987 was 225.06, and the log-return was equal to -0.229.

10.4 "TECHNICAL ANALYSIS" OF FINANCIAL DATA

In this section we overview the approach to the analysis of financial data known as "Technical Analysis" (TA).

Measures of risk we discussed so far were static: they barely change with the inflow of new information and hence are suitable only for long-term investment decisions; one hardly would use them for short-term investment decisions.

Measures like the standard deviation or VaR are static by the definition (it is not the standard deviation or VaR that changes but the values of our estimates of σ and VaR). Moreover, a long-term trend can be replaced with the trend in the opposite direction within few days, leaving static measures no time to react to the change (cf. the recent volatility of the crude oil prices). Therefore, a short-term investor would prefer a dynamic risk measure.

It is widely believed that there are moments of time when investing in a particular financial instrument is less risky, and moments of time when the level of risk is high. One would prefer to invest when the risk is low, and reduce or close a position when risk is high (cf. e.g., Choffray and de Mortanges, 2017). Determining such moments can be a key to successful investing, yet it is a difficult task. One way to locate such moments is by using a dynamic measure of risk.

We call a measure of risk dynamic if it changes considerably with the change of market data.

The first step toward developing a dynamic measure of risk was made with the introduction of the ARCH model (10.3). If the sequence $\{X_i, i \geq 1\}$ of random variables (say, daily log-returns) obeys (10.3), then the conditional variance

$$\sigma_n^2 \equiv \mathbb{E}\{(X_n - \mathbb{E}X_n)^2 | X_1, \ldots, X_{n-1}\} = b + cX_{n-1}^2$$

is a function of the previous observation.

A more general (not necessarily more accurate) model is ARCH(k):

$$X_n = \xi_n \sqrt{b + c_1 X_{n-1}^2 + \cdots + c_k X_{n-k}^2} \qquad (n \geq k+1, k \geq 1),$$

where $\{\xi_n, n \geq 1\}$ are independent normal $\mathcal{N}(0; 1)$ random variables. Estimates of parameters $c, c_1, \ldots, c_k$ are usually small, meaning that the influence of the past on the conditional variance is not dramatic.

A very different approach to risk measurement is based on Technical Analysis tools.

Just like the traditional approach, which is sometimes called "Fundamental Analysis" (FA), Technical Analysis deals with a set of past (historical) data (e.g., daily closing share prices $\{P_n\}$ of a particular stock over the past 2 years).

Following the traditional approach, one starts by computing a handful of numbers (e.g., the rate of return

$$r_n = P_n / P_{n-1} - 1,$$

the standard deviation of $\{r_n\}$, the beta, the price to earnings ratio, etc.), displays them, and makes an executive decision (see, e.g., Elton and Gruber, 1995; Luenberger, 1997). A practical advice on the use of the FA approach can be found, for example, in Choffray and de Mortanges (2017).

Following TA, one also starts by computing a set of numbers (e.g., daily Open-High-Low-Close prices, moving averages, etc.). The main difference is that the results of calculation are displayed not in a numerical form but in a graphical form (TA is sometimes called "charting").

Both approaches aim at spotting trends and points of entrance and exit. The idea behind TA is that a human eye can spot trends and regions of entrance and exit well before numerical measures like price-to-earnings ratio, VaR, etc., change considerably.

10.4.1 Background to the Technical Analysis

TA presumes that price movements form patterns, those price patterns can be studied, classified, etc., and an observer is capable of recognizing a price pattern before the formation of the pattern is complete.

These assumptions mean that the price movements are not considered completely random. Indeed, it is widely observed that prices often appear to exhibit trends, levels of support and resistance, etc. Not always is an observer capable of recognizing a pattern the price is currently forming. However, an observer is free to invest only when he or she recognizes a particular pattern. Moreover, the mere fact that many investors/speculators are aware of certain price patterns makes their reaction to corresponding price formations predictable, causing a plausible pattern even more likely to become a reality.

Note that TA assumptions contradict to those of ARCH and the Geometric Brownian Motion models, and suggest searching for models that allow for patterns of cyclical behavior. TA assumptions contradict also the efficient market hypothesis (EMH). The arguments in favor of and against EMH and TA can be found, for example, in Akram et al. (2006), Brock et al. (1992), Clarke et al. (2001), Elder (2002), Fama (1970), French (1980), Higson (2001), Irwin & Park (2007), Lo et al. (2000), Osler and Chang (1995), Poser (2003), Prechter and Parker (2007), Williams (1994).

The present chapter looks at TA tools from a different angle. The main point for us is that TA ideas lead to a dynamic measure of risk m_{TA}, which does change considerably as price changes.

We overview a few popular price patterns before discussing TA tools for dynamic risk measurement.

10.4.2   Basic Elliott Waves

The price chart appears an object of fractal geometry. A common way to simplify the chaotic structure of the chart is by using price bars (Figure 10.3).

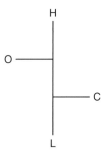

FIGURE 10.3   Open-High-Low-Close price bar. Figure 10.5 is an example of a price chart with Open-High-Low-Close price bars. Many web-cites offer displaying price charts as a sequence of price bars.

Price charts often appear to exhibit patterns like those in Figure 10.4: the general trend is up, but it is interrupted by "corrections". Such patterns are called Elliott waves.

The basic Elliott wave is a 5-leg zigzag (see Figure 10.4 for an up-trend); it is typically followed by a 3-leg wave in the opposite direction. The use of straight lines in Figure 10.4 is, of course, a simplification: each wave has "inside" a set of smaller scale waves, each "sub-wave" has again a set of even smaller waves inside, etc. (cf. monthly, weekly, daily, hourly, 10-min, and 1-min price charts of the same stock or index).

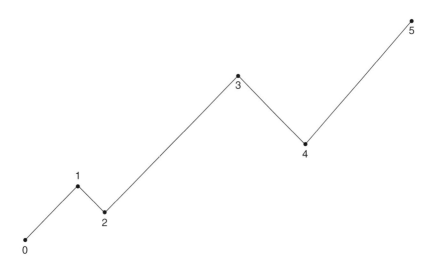

FIGURE 10.4 Basic Elliott wave for an up-trend (see also see Figure 10.5).
The use of straight lines is, of course, a simplification (we consider an
up-trend): each wave has "inside" a set of smaller scale waves, each
"sub-wave" has again a set of even smaller waves inside, etc.

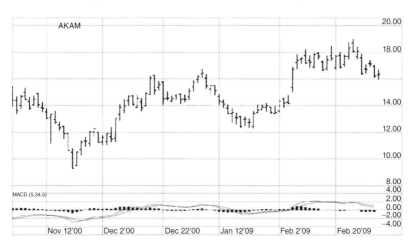

FIGURE 10.5 Prices of the Akamai stock in November 2008 – March 2009.
In early December an investor might have concluded that the price was in
wave 2. With vertex 0 identified when the price was near \$9.50, the risk of
holding a "long" position was around \$2 per share. The potential profit (if
the position held till the end of wave 3) was around \$5. *Source:* Novak (2011).
Reproduced with permission of Taylor and Francis.

Recognizing an Elliott wave is not easy, and different observers can mark
vertexes differently (cf. Fig. 10.5). A few empirically observed facts can be helpful
in determining vertexes (we consider an up-trend):
{**1**} The level of vertex 2 can be within 38% of the range of wave 1.

{**2**} The range of wave 3 (sections 2–3) can be up to 262% of the range of wave 1. Moving average convergence–divergence (MACD) histogram is positive during the third wave.

{**3**} Vertex 4 almost nether goes beyond the level of vertex 1. The range of wave 4 (sections 3–4) is 38–50% of the range of wave 3. MACD histogram during the fourth wave is negative.

{**4**} The range of the fifth wave (sections 4–5) is often within 62–100% of the third one.

These are empirically observed facts (cf. Williams, 1994), and there seems to be no statistical study behind these observations so far.

One can only be sure about locating a vertex after the price has passed it. Making an investment decision on the basis of an assumption that the price is, say, in vicinity of vertex 2, one understands that an element of uncertainty is inevitable. However, dealing with imprecise objects is not uncommon in Statistics. Recall that, if θ_n is an estimator of a certain quantity, θ, then $(1 + 1/n)\theta_n$ is often an "equally good" estimator (e.g., the sample variance estimator

$$\hat{\sigma}_n^2 = n^{-1} \sum_{i=1}^{n} X_i^2 - \bar{X}^2,$$

where $\bar{X} = \sum_{i=1}^{n} X_i/n$ is a natural estimator constructed by the method of moments, while

$$\tilde{\sigma}_n^2 = \sum_{i=1}^{n} (X_i - \bar{X})^2/(n - 1)$$

is an unbiased estimator).

Among TA signals/indicators, one can mention

Moving average (MA) – a basic indicator of a trend (MA(k) is the average of k past prices);

MACD, one of the most popular TA indicators;

Relative strength index (RSI);

Breakout signal.

Formal definitions can be found, for example, in Pring (2002), Williams (1994), Novak (2011), Chapter 10. These indicators are functions of certain "tuning" parameters (e.g., the time scale).

10.5 DYNAMIC RISK MEASUREMENT

Measures of risk discussed in Sections 10.1–10.3 (the standard deviation, VaR, CVaR) were static. In addition to static measures of risk suitable for long-term investment decisions, a short-term investor would like to consider a dynamic measure of risk.

In this section we discuss a particular approach to dynamic risk measurement based on an idea of "stop-loss" from the Technical Analysis of financial data.

Namely, we deal in this section with measure m_{TA} that measures a level of risk by the distance from the current price to the stop-loss level identified by the nearest local price minimum or maximum (see Novak, 2011, Chapter 10).

Definition of m_{TA}: for a holder of a "long" position, it is the distance between the current price, P_n, and the last local price minimum below P_n:

$$m_{TA} = P_n - P_{n_*}, \tag{10.10}$$

where n_* is the time of the last local price minimum below P_n. For a holder of a "short" position, n_* is the time of the last local price maximum above P_n and $m_{TA} = |P_n - P_{n_*}|$.

We denote by $m_{TA} \equiv m_{TA}(cP_n)$ the measure of risk when investing in c units of instrument P at time n (we sometimes omit P_n and c).

The following example illustrates the definition.

📖 **Example 10.3**

In the case of a basic Elliott wave, the local extrema are the vertexes of the wave.

If the price is considered to be in wave 2, then for a holder of a "long" position m_{TA} is the distance between the current price and the level of vertex 0, which is the nearest local price minimum (Figure 10.4); for a holder of a "short" position m_{TA} is the distance between the current price and the level of vertex 1.

Suppose a long position is opened when price is in wave 2. As the price moves down toward vertex 2, the paper loss increases while m_{TA} decreases. If the price falls below the level of vertex 0, the assumption that the price was in wave 2 is proved to be wrong; m_{TA} resets using the level of the last local minimum below the level of vertex 0, one would have also a breakout signal that the price was in the bear trend.

If the price is in wave 3 below the level of vertex 1, then for a holder of a "long" position m_{TA} is the distance between P_n and the level of vertex 2 (until the next local minimum is formed); for a holder of a "short" position m_{TA} is the distance between P_n and the level of vertex 1. After passing the level of vertex 1, m_{TA} is the distance between P_n and the level of the last local price minimum (typically, wave 3 is again a pattern with a number of local extrema, and m_{TA} is reset when a new local price minimum is formed and recognized); for a holder of a "short" position the level of risk jumps: m_{TA} is now the distance between P_n and the last local price maximum above the level of vertex 1.

If the price is in wave 4, then for a holder of a "long" position m_{TA} is the distance between P_n and the last local price minimum below P_n; for a holder of a "short" position m_{TA} is the distance between P_n and the level of vertex 3.

In wave 5 for a holder of a "long" position m_{TA} is the distance between P_n and the last local price minimum; for a holder of a "short" position, the risk may be unlimited.

Note that a price chart is virtually an object of fractal geometry; a local extremum of a fractal cannot be identified. To be precise, a price chart is not exactly a fractal, and local extrema can be formally identified. However, by the local extremum a practitioner would mean a "recognizable" local minimum or maximum, cf. Figures 10.4 and 10.5. Thus, m_{TA} is not uniquely defined (similarly, the definitions of patterns in TA are not mathematically strict). Just like TA patterns and signals, local extrema may be identified differently by different investors.

One approach to deal with this problem is to use data-smoothing; the degree of smoothing is the "tuning" parameter. However, the choice of a tuning parameter becomes an issue.

■ Example 10.4

Consider, for instance, Figure 10.5. In early December, when the price of Akamai stock was around $11.50, an investor might have concluded the price was in wave 2. With vertex 0 identified when the price was near $9.50, risk of holding a "long" position was around $2 per share, that is, about 15%–20% of the value of the investment. The potential profit if the position held till the end of wave 3, according to property {2}, was around $5.

Note that wave 4 can be identified, as the MACD histogram is negative in the first half of January 2009. As the price almost never falls below the level of vertex 1, an investor could have added a long position mid-January when the price was around $13 with $m_{TA} < \$1$. We know the range of wave 5 is usually at least 62% of the range of Section 0–3, that is, one would expect the price to move up by $4.2–$7; the ratio of the potential gain to the potential loss is greater than 4. The price did move up by about $5; the S&P 500 index was still declining during that period.

One could have used other TA indicators as well. For instance, Figure 10.5 shows the MACD divergence signal: the price makes higher highs while the MACD histogram makes lower highs around December 10, mid-December, and early January. Expecting a short-term bear trend, an investor could have decided to open a short position in early January when the MACD histogram made a local maximum. The measure of risk (the distance between the price $\approx \$15.50$ and the last local maximum under $17) is $m_{TA} \approx \$1.5$. The chart shows that the potential profit would be around $3 per share.

Properties of m_{TA}

Property 10.1. m_{TA} *is not symmetric.*

The level of risk for a holder of a long position is not equal, in general, to the level of risk for a holder of a short position. Note also that m_{TA} may grow as price moves in investor's favor.

Property 10.2. $m_{TA} \geq 0$ and $m_{TA}(\lambda c P_n) = \lambda m_{TA}(c P_n)$.

Note that for a holder of a long position $m_{TA}(c P_n) \leq c P_n$.

For a holder of a short position $m_{TA} \leq \infty$ – not always the last local maximum can be identified (e.g., the price makes the new global maximum), meaning that the amount of a possible loss for a holder of a short position is potentially unlimited.

Property 10.3. m_{TA} *is typically sub-additive.*

Indeed, let X and Y be two instruments, and suppose that the last local minima of instruments X, Y and $X + Y$ have been identified within the period $[n_*, \ldots, n]$. Then for a holder of a long position

$$m_{TA}(X_n + Y_n) = X_n + Y_n - \min_{n_* \leq i \leq n} (X_i + Y_i)$$

$$\leq \left(X_n - \min_{n_* \leq i \leq n} X_i \right) + \left(Y_n - \min_{n_* \leq i \leq n} Y_i \right) = m_{TA}(X_n) + m_{TA}(Y_n).$$

If the last local maxima of instruments X, Y and $X + Y$ have been identified within the period $[n_*, \ldots, n]$, then for a holder of a short position

$$m_{TA}(X_n + Y_n) = \max_{n_* \leq i \leq n} (X_i + Y_i) - X_n - Y_n$$

$$\leq \left(\max_{n_* \leq i \leq n} X_i - X_n \right) + \left(\max_{n_* \leq i \leq n} Y_i - Y_n \right)$$

$$= m_{TA}(X_n) + m_{TA}(Y_n).$$

Property 10.4. m_{TA} *does not change if an investor adds cash to the portfolio.*

This property looks rather natural, as only investing in the risky assets contributes to risk.

Note that Artzner et al. (1999) have on the list of "desirable properties for measures of risk" the property of a measure to shrink by the amount of cash added. This is because Artzner et al. do not distinguish a measure of risk from a capital reserve/margin requirement: "the measures to the risk will be interpreted as the minimum extra cash the agent has to add to the risky position." The traditional approach (e.g., using σ, β, VaR, CVaR) does distinguish a measure of risk from a capital reserve/margin requirement. In other words, measuring risk is a separate act with respect to calculating a capital reserve/margin requirement.

Property 10.5. Let X and Y be two instruments with prices $\{X_i\}$ and $\{Y_i\}$, respectively, and assume that

$$X_n = Y_n$$

(one can always consider rescaling $\{Y_i\}$, i.e., one compares investing in $\{X_i\}$ vs investing in $\{zY_i\}$, where $z = X_n/Y_n$). If the last local minima of instruments X and Y have been identified within the period $[n_*, \ldots, n]$ and

$$X_i \leq Y_i \quad (n_* \leq i < n),$$

then for a holder of a long position

$$m_{TA}(X_n) \geq m_{TA}(Y_n). \qquad (10.11)$$

If the last local maxima of instruments X and Y have been identified within the period $[n_*, \ldots, n]$ and $X_i \geq Y_i$ as $n_* \leq i < n$, then (10.11) holds for a holder of a short position. In other words, in both cases Y is less volatile than X.

Property 10.6. m_{TA} *is not continuous.*

When a new local extremum is formed and recognized, it replaces the previous one in the calculation of m_{TA}(cf. Table 10.1).

TABLE 10.1   The S&P 500 index, its standard deviations, and m_{TA} on the eve of the Black Monday. While the standard deviation decreases, suggesting a reduction of the level of risk, m_{TA} exhibits spikes, indicating high level of risk

Date	S&P 500	σ	m_{TA}
8.10.1987	314.16	28.55	3.62
9.10.1987	311.07	28.42	0.53
12.10.1987	309.39	28.27	6.45
13.10.1987	314.52	28.14	3.98
14.10.1987	305.23	27.99	2.29
15.10.1987	298.08	27.84	9.62
16.10.1987	282.7	27.67	4.49

Note that definition (10.10) of m_{TA} ignores the rate r_o of return of the risk-free asset (the same can be said about the definitions of a number of risk measures, e.g., the standard deviation, VaR, and CVaR). One can adjust the definition of m_{TA} to take r_o into account: denote

$$m^*_{TA} = |P_n/(1 + r_o)^{n-n_*} - P_{n_*}|,$$

where for a holder of a long position n_* is the time of the last local price minimum below P_n (for a holder of a short position n_* is the time of the last local price maximum above P_n). In particular, $m^*_{TA}(P^o_n) = 0$ if P^o_n is the risk-free asset.

The advantage of m_{TA} is that it changes considerably as the price changes. Traditional risk measures (estimated, say, from a 1-year-long sample of preceding data) are rather static (see Example 10.5). Actually, they have to be static by the definition (it is not the standard deviation or VaR that changes but the values of our estimates of σ and VaR). By contrast, m_{TA} by definition has to change as the price changes.

The disadvantage of m_{TA} is that it is not defined uniquely (like other tools of the TA). That is because the nearest local minima/maxima of a fractal curve cannot be uniquely identified. One way to address the problem is to deal with price bars on a certain time scale (e.g., daily or weekly price bars). Note that some local extrema identified on a chart of daily price bars will not be present on weekly price charts. Moreover, some local extrema may be "too close" one to another. A practitioner may skip one of those "close" local extrema, effectively looking for minima/maxima of a group of "close" local extrema (i.e., zooming out on a particular chart area). For instance, in Example 10.5 we only considered local minima separated by two consecutive price bars. Thus, the time scale is the "tuning" parameter of m_{TA}. The presence of a tuning parameter is common in nonparametric estimation problems.

Example 10.2 (continued) We have calculated m_{TA} on the eve of the "Black Monday" (Table 10.1).

From mid-August 1987, the S&P 500 index was mainly declining (see Figure 10.2). Table 10.1 and Figure 10.6 show steady decrease of the standard deviation of the S&P 500 index since early September 1987 till 16.10.1987, suggesting a lower level of risk (the conditional standard deviation was more dynamic, see Figure 1 in McNeil and Frey (2000)).

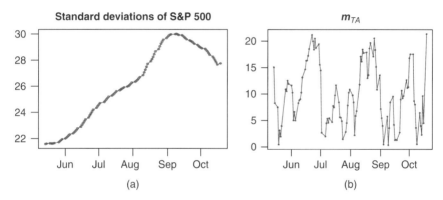

FIGURE 10.6 Standard deviations of the S&P 500 index (a) and m_{TA} (b) in 14.05.1987–19.10.1987. The standard deviation decreases, suggesting lower risk; m_{TA} exhibits spikes, indicating high level of risk.

The behavior of m_{TA} is very different: Figure 10.6 shows spikes of m_{TA} on the eve of the Black Monday. On 12.10.1987, the index closed at 309.39, that is, below the "last" local minimum identified on 21.09.1987 at 310.54 ("breakout" signal in TA terminology). This means that m_{TA} has to be reset from $P_n - 310.54$ to $P_n - x_*$, where x_* is the last local minimum below P_n (x_* has been identified on 01.07.1987 at 302.94). Hence on 12.10.1987 $m_{TA} = 6.45$.

On the previous trading day, that is, 9.10.1987, the risk was $m_{TA} = 0.53$. The market has shown a 12-fold increase of the level of risk. The data was ringing a bell, but would anyone hear it using the standard deviation?

While traditional measures of risk are too static, measure m_{TA} may appear too volatile. One may ask if there is anything in between?

As a possible candidate, we suggest the following measure:

$$m^+ \equiv m_c^+ = m_s + cm_{TA}. \tag{10.12}$$

Here m_s is a traditional (static) measure of risk (e.g., the standard deviation, VaR, or CVaR), and $c \geq 0$ is a "tuning" parameter.

This approach suggests setting aside a somewhat larger amount of capital reserve, meaning smaller profits during quiet periods in return for higher financial stability during turbulent periods.

Example 10.5

In 2007, the S&P 500 index had a level of resistance at 1406 (see Figure 10.7). The presence of a level of resistance does not mean, of course, an increase of the level of risk – markets often bounce up from the levels of resistance (breaking through a level of resistance does, however, indicate a short-term downtrend and hence an increase of the level of risk).

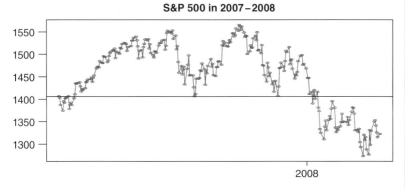

FIGURE 10.7 The S&P 500 index in March 2007 – March 2008 had a level of resistance at 1406. After breaking through the level of resistance in January 2008, the index lost half of its value (see Figure 10.8).

In 2007, the market did bounce up after touching the level of resistance. Eventually, after breaking through the level of resistance in January 2008, the index lost half of its value (see Figure 10.8).

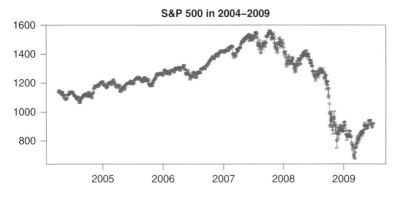

FIGURE 10.8 S&P 500 index in April 2004–June 2009. After reaching 1565 in October 2007, the index fell to 678 in March 2009.

One would like to get a warning earlier, and the measure m_s may come handy. It appears more suitable for the risk managers' purposes, providing both a warning signal as well as a numerical measure of the increased level of risk.

We have calculated m_{TA} for the daily closing prices of the S&P 500 index for the period from 27.11.2007 till 28.03.2008 (see Figure 10.9). A local minimum is recognized if the daily closing price is smaller than the daily closing prices of two preceding and two consequent days.

Figure 10.9 shows spikes of m_{TA} in January 2007; the highest value $m_{TA} = 135.07$ was achieved on 11.01.2008, indicating increased risk as well as providing a numerical measure of the level of risk. The S&P 500

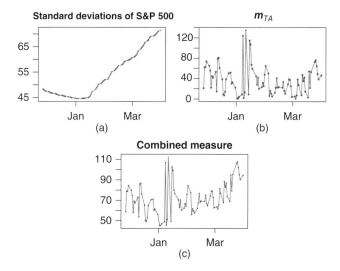

FIGURE 10.9 Standard deviation (a), measure m_{TA}(b), and the combined measure m^+(c) of the S&P 500 index for the period November 2007–March 2008.

index was still at 1416.25 on 14.01.2008, providing time to act. After that it went on downtrend, briefly bounced back in May 2008, and then took a nose dive to reach 682.55 in March 2009 (see Figure 10.8).

Figure 10.9 presents also the combined measure (10.12) with the standard deviation as m_s and $c = 0.5$ for the period from 27.11.2007 till 31.03.2008. It is easy to see that the chart of measure m^+ is more dynamic than the chart of the standard deviation, yet less volatile than the chart of measure m_{TA}.

The peak values of m_{TA} and m^+ were achieved on 11.01.2008. The index closed at 1401.02 that day, breaking through the level of resistance. The preceding peak value was achieved on 08.01.2008, again with a break of the level of resistance. On both occasions, the peak values of m^+ were more than twice the values of the recent local minima of m^+. The jumps of m_{TA} through to the peak in January 2008 were more than

100-fold. Thus, measures m_{TA} and m^+ signaled increased risk and provided a numerical measure of the level of risk.

What happened next suggests that one would be right to act in January 2008 on the basis of the indicator of increased risk provided by measures m_{TA} and m^+.

10.6 OPEN PROBLEMS AND FURTHER RESEARCH

TA approach is based on a large body of empirical observations (see, e.g., Elder, 2002; Pring, 2002; Williams, 1994), yet we are not aware of any comprehensive statistical study that would provide rigorous statistical background to the approach. Many questions appear to be left unanswered so far. We formulate below a few natural questions:

(•) What can be said about the empirical distribution of the process $\{m_{TA}$ $(P_n)\}$ for major stock indexes, commodity prices, and major currency exchange rates?

The answer may be different for a holder of a long position and for a holder of a short position. It may be worth considering separately the periods of bull and bear trends.

(•) What is the distribution of the gain-to-risk ratio tested on major stock indexes, commodity prices, and major currency exchange rates?

The answer may depend on the trigger signal, the stop/exit strategy, and the chosen time scale (say, weekly or daily data).

(•) How often is a particular TA indicator profitable?

What is the empirical distribution of the rate of return when using a particular indicator?

Does the mean rate of return when using a particular indicator change considerably over time?

These questions are not easy to answer, as the answers depend on the choice of the stop/exit strategy. For instance, an institutional investor often buys a stake and holds it, say, for two years. The natural question is

(•) if an indicator is triggered, how often will the position be "in black" in 2 years' time?

For a short-term investor, the question can be formulated as follows:

(•) if a particular indicator has triggered opening a long position, the stop is at the level of the recent local minimum and the exit strategy is based on a specified signal, how often will the position be "in black"?

A considerable amount of empirical research is required to answer these questions, as one would like to analyze a variety of markets as well as a variety of trigger signal/stop/exit strategy combinations.

The computational difficulty is due to the fact that identifying local extrema of a near fractal is not straightforward: every price bar with a bar minimum lower than those of neighboring bars is formally a local minimum. In fact, a local minimum of a fractal cannot be identified, and one needs a reasonable substitute to the local minimum. One approach to overcome the problem is to use data-smoothing (e.g., moving average); variation with the degree of smoothing (the tuning parameter) may affect the results. Another approach is to use the minimum over an interval of size s, where s is a tuning parameter. The open problem is to suggest a procedure of choosing the tuning parameters. Besides, one would like to consider more than one time frame (e.g., daily and weekly price charts).

10.7 CONCLUSION

This chapter provided an overview of modern approaches to financial risk measurement, aiming to encourage interdisciplinary research on the topic of dynamic measures of risk.

We find that the traditional approach appears static from a short-term investor point of view.

The approach involving m_{TA} appears more suitable for dynamic risk measurement. Risk measure m_{TA} is truly dynamic (e.g., while the standard deviation was declining on the eve of the Black Monday, m_{TA} was indicating increased volatility). However, the definition of the dynamic risk measure involves local extrema of the price series. The computational difficulty of identifying local extrema is linked to the fact that price charts appear objects of fractal geometry. As a result, the approach involving m_{TA} lacks proper statistical scrutiny and requires considerable amount of empirical research.

Acknowledgment

The author is grateful to the editor for helpful comments.

References

Akram Q.F., Rime D., Sarno L. Arbitrage in the foreign exchange market: turning on the microscope. Research Report No 42. Stockholm, Sweden: Swedish Institute for Financial Research; 2006.

Alexander C. *Market Models*. New York: John Wiley & Sons, Inc.; 2001.

Alexander C. *Value-at-Risk Models*. New York: John Wiley & Sons, Inc.; 2008.

Artzner P., Delbaen F., Eber J.-M., Heath D. Coherent measures of risk. Math. Finance 1999; **9**: 203–228.

Bingham N.H., Goldie C.M., Teugels J.L. *Regular Variation*. Cambridge: Cambridge University Press; 1987.

Brock W., Lakonishok J., LeBaron B. Simple technical trading rules and the stochastic properties of stock returns. J. Finance 1992; **47**(5): 1731–1764.

Choffray J.-M., de Mortanges C.P. Protecting assets under non-parametric market conditions. In: Longin F., editor. *Extreme Events in Finance*. John Wiley & Sons; 2017.

Clarke J., Jandik T., Mandelker G. The efficient markets hypothesis. In: Arffa R., editor. *Expert Financial Planning: Advice from Industry Leaders*. New York: John Wiley & Sons, Inc.; 2001. p 126–141.

Elder A. *Come Into My Trading Room*. New York: John Wiley & Sons, Inc.; 2002.

Elton E.J., Gruber M.J. *Modern Portfolio Theory and Investment Analysis*. New York: John Wiley & Sons, Inc.; 1995.

Embrechts P., Klüppelberg C., Mikosch T. *Modelling Extremal Events for Insurance and Finance*. Berlin: Springer-Verlag; 1997.

Fama E.F. Efficient capital markets: a review of theory and empirical work. J. Finance 1970; **25**: 383–417.

Fama E.F., Roll R. Some properties of symmetric stable distributions. J. Am. Stat. Assoc., 1968; **63**: 817–836.

Fraga Alves M.I., Neves C. Extreme value theory: an introductory overview. In: Longin F, editor. *Extreme Events in Finance: A Handbook of Extreme Value Theory and its Applications*. John Wiley & Sons; 2017.

French K.R. Stock returns and the weekend effect. J. Financ. Econ. 1980;**8**:55–69.

Gnedenko B.V. Sur la distribution limite du terme maximum d'une serie aleatoire. Ann. Math 1943; **44**: 423–453.

Goldie C.M. Implicit renewal theory and tails of solutions of random equations. Ann. Appl. Probab., 1991; **1**: 126–166.

Gurrola-Perez P., Murphy D. Filtered historical simulation Value-at-Risk models and their competitors. Working Paper No 525, Bank of England; 2015.

Higson C. Did Enron's investors fool themselves? Business Strategy Rev 2001; **12**(4): 1–6.

Irwin S.H., Park C.-H. What do we know about the profitability of Technical Analysis? J. Economic Surveys 2007; **21**(4): 786–826.

Lo A.W., Mamaysky H., Wang J. Foundations of Technical Analysis: computational algorithms, statistical inference and empirical implementation. J. Finance 2000; **55**(4): 1705–1765.

Longin F. The asymptotic distribution of extreme stock market returns. J. Business, 1996; **69**(3): 383–408.

Longin F. Beyond the VaR. J Derivatives 2001; **8**: 36–48.

Luenberger D.G. *Investment Science*. Oxford: Oxford University Press; 1997. ISBN: 10: 0195108094.

Mandelbrot B.B. New methods in statistical economics. J Polit Econ 1963; **71**: 421–440.

Markovich N. *Nonparametric Analysis of Univariate Heavy-Tailed Data*. Chichester: John Wiley & Sons; 2007.

McNeil A.J. On extremes and crashes. Risk 1998; **11**: 99–104.

McNeil A.J., Frey R. Estimation of tail-related risk measures for heteroscedastic financial time series: an extreme value approach. J. Empir. Finance, 2000; **7**: 271–300.

Nadarajah S., Chan S. Estimation methods for Value-at-Risk. In: Longin F., editor. *Extreme Events in Finance: A Handbook of Extreme Value Theory and its Applications*. John Wiley & Sons; 2017.

Novak S.Y. Inference on heavy tails from dependent data. Siberian Adv. Math., 2002; **12**(2): 73–96.

Novak S.Y. *Extreme Value Methods with Applications to Finance*. London: CRC; 2011. ISBN: 978-1-43983-574-6.

Novak S.Y., Beirlant J. The magnitude of a market crash can be predicted. J. Banking & Finance, 2006; **30**: 453–462.

Osler C., Chang K. Head and shoulders: not just a flaky pattern. Staff Report No 4. New York: Federal Reserve Bank of New York; 1995.

Pflug G.C. Some remarks on the Value–at–Risk and the conditional Value-at-Risk. In: Uryasev S.P., editor. *Probabilistic Constrained Optimization*. Netherlands: Kluwer; 2000. p 272–281.

Poser S.W. *Applying Elliott Wave Theory Profitably*. New York: John Wiley & Sons, Inc.; 2003.

Prechter R.R., Parker W.D. The financial/economic dichotomy in social behavioral dynamics: the socionomic perspective. J. Behavioral Finance, 2007; **8**(2): 84–108.

Pring M.J. *Technical Analysis Explained*. New York: McGraw-Hill; 2002. ISBN: 0-07-138193-7.

Rockafellar R.T., Uryasev S. Optimization of conditional Value-at-Risk; 1999. Available at http://www.ise.ufl.edu/uryasev.

Seneta E. *Regularly Varying Functions*. Volume **508**, Lecture Notes Mathematics. Berlin: Springer-Verlag; 1976.

Wells D., Pretzlik C., Wighton D. The balancing act that is Value-at-Risk. Financial Times; 25. 03. 2004.

Williams B.M. *Trading Chaos: Applying Expert Techniques to Maximise Your Profits*. New York: John Wiley & Sons, Inc.; 1994.

Chapter Eleven

On the Estimation of the Distribution of Aggregated Heavy-Tailed Risks: Application to Risk Measures

Marie Kratz
ESSEC Business School, CREAR, Paris, France

AMS 2000 subject classification. 60F05; 62G32; 62G30; 62P05; 62G20; 91B30; 91G70.

11.1 INTRODUCTION

A universally accepted lesson of the last financial crisis has been the urgent need to improve risk analysis within financial institutions. Taking into account extreme risks is recognized nowadays as a necessary condition for good risk management in any financial institution and not restricted anymore to reinsurance companies. Minimizing the impact of extreme risks, or even ignoring them because of a small probability of occurrence, has been considered by many professionals and supervisory authorities as a factor of aggravation of the last financial crisis. The American Senate and the Basel Committee on Banking Supervision confirm this statement in their report. Therefore it became crucial to include and evaluate correctly extreme risks. It is our goal here, when considering a portfolio of heavy-tailed risks, notably when the tail risk is larger than 2, that is, when there is a finite variance. It is the case when studying not only financial assets but also insurance liabilities. It concerns life insurance as well, because of investment risks and interest rates; to have omitted them was at the origin of the bankruptcy of several insurance life

Extreme Events in Finance: A Handbook of Extreme Value Theory and its Applications,
First Edition. Edited by François Longin.

companies as, for instance, Executive Life in the United States, Mannheimer in Germany, or Scottish Widows in the United Kingdom.

11.1.1   Motivation and Objective

When considering financial assets, because of a finite variance, a normal approximation is often chosen in practice for the unknown distribution of the yearly log returns, justified by the use of the central limit theorem (CLT), when assuming independent and identically distributed (i.i.d.) observations. Such a choice of modeling, in particular using light-tailed distributions, has shown itself grossly inadequate during the last financial crisis when dealing with risk measures because it leads to underestimating the risk.

Recently, a study was done by Furrer (2012) on simulated i.i.d. Pareto random variables (r.v.'s) to measure the impact of the choice and the use of the limiting distribution of aggregated risks, in particular for the computation of standard risk measures (value-at-risk or expected shortfall). In this study, the standard general central limit theorem (GCLT) (see, e.g., (Samorodnitsky and Taqqu, 1994)) is recalled, providing a limiting stable distribution or a normal one, depending on the value of the shape parameter of the Pareto r.v.'s. Then, considering Pareto samples of various sizes and for different values of the shape parameter, Furrer compared the distance between the empirical distribution and the theoretical limiting distribution; then computed the empirical value-at-risk (denoted VaR) and expected shortfall, called also tail value-at-risk (denoted ES or TVaR); and compared them with the ones computed from the limiting distribution. It appeared clearly that not only the choice of the limiting distribution but also the rate of convergence matters, hence the way of aggregating the variables. From this study, we also notice that the normal approximation appears really inadequate when considering aggregated risks coming from a moderately heavy-tailed distribution, that is, a Pareto with a shape parameter or tail index larger than 2, but below 4.

A few comments can be added to this study. First, the numerical results obtained in Furrer (2012) confirm what is already known in the literature. In particular, there are two main drawbacks when using the CLT for moderate heavy-tailed distributions (e.g., Pareto with a shape parameter larger than 2). On one hand, if the CLT may apply to the sample mean because of a finite variance, we also know that it provides a normal approximation with a very slow rate of convergence, which may be improved when removing extremes from the sample (see, e.g., (Hall, 1984)). Hence, even if we are interested only in the sample mean, samples of small or moderate sizes will lead to a bad approximation. To improve the rate of convergence, existence of moments of order larger than 2 is necessary (see, e.g., Section 3.2 in Embrechts et al. (1997) or, for more details, Petrov (1995)). On the other hand, we know that it has also been proved theoretically (see, e.g., (Pictet et al., 1998)) as well as empirically (see, e.g., (Dacorogna et al., 2001), Section 5.4.3) that the CLT approach applied to a heavy-tailed distributed sample does not bring any information on the tail and therefore should not be used to evaluate risk measures. Indeed, a heavy tail may appear clearly on high-frequency data (e.g., daily ones) but become not visible anymore when

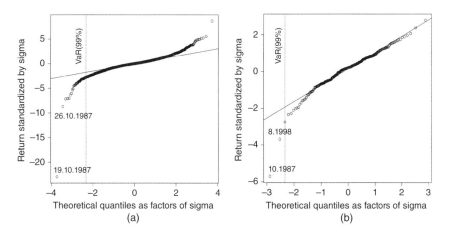

FIGURE 11.1 (a) *QQ* plot of the S&P 500 daily returns from 1987 to 2007, plotted against the Gaussian one (same scaling) that appears as a straight line. (b) *QQ* plot of the S&P 500 monthly returns from 1987 to 2007, plotted against the Gaussian one (same scaling) that appears as a straight line.

aggregating them in, for example, yearly data (i.e., short samples), although it is known, by Fisher theorem, that the tail index of the underlying distribution remains constant under aggregation. It is a phenomenon on which many authors insisted, as, for example, in Dacorogna et al. (2001). Figure 11.1 on the S&P 500 returns illustrate very clearly this last issue.

Based on these figures above, the *QQ* plot of the S&P 500 daily returns from 1987 to 2007 helps to detect a heavy tail. When aggregating the daily returns into monthly returns, the *QQ* plot looks more as a normal one, and the very few observations appearing above the threshold of VaR$_{99\%}$, such as the financial crises of 1998 and 1987, could almost be considered as outliers, as it is well known that financial returns are symmetrically distributed.

Now, look at Figure 11.2. When adding data from 2008 to 2013, the *QQ* plot looks pretty the same, that is, normal, except that another "outlier" appears ... with the date of October 2008! Instead of looking again on daily data for the same years, let us consider a larger sample of monthly data from 1791 to 2013.[1] With a larger sample size, the heavy tail becomes again visible. And now we see that the financial crisis of 2008 does belong to the heavy tail of the distribution and cannot be considered anymore as an outlier. So we clearly see the importance of the sample size when dealing with moderately heavy tails to estimate the risk. Thus we need a method that does not depend on the sample size, but looks at the shape of the tail.

The main objective is to obtain the most accurate evaluation of the distribution of aggregated risks and of risk measures when working on financial data under the presence of fat tail. We explore various approaches to handle this problem,

---

[1] As compiled by Global Financial Data (https://www.globalfinancialdata.com/index.html).

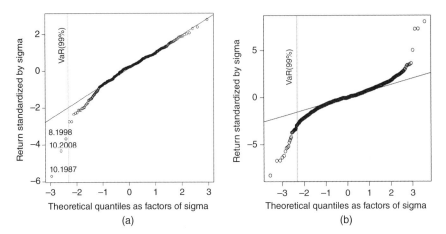

FIGURE 11.2 **(a)** *QQ* **plot of the S&P 500 monthly returns from 1987 to 2013, plotted against the Gaussian one (same scaling) that appears as a straight line. (b)** *QQ* **plot of the S&P 500 monthly returns from 1791 to 2013, plotted against the Gaussian one (same scaling) that appears as a straight line.**

theoretically, empirically, and numerically. The application on log returns, which motivated the construction of this method, illustrates the case of time aggregation, but the method is general and concerns any type of aggregation, for example, of assets.

After reviewing briefly the existing methods, from the GCLT to extreme value theory (EVT), we will propose and develop two new methods, both inspired by the work of Zaliapin et al. (2005) in which the sum of n i.i.d. r.v.'s is rewritten as the sum of the associated order statistics.

The first method, named *Normex*, answers the question of how many largest order statistics would explain the divergence between the underlying moderately heavy-tailed distribution and the normal approximation, whenever the CLT applies, and combines a normal approximation with the exact distribution of this number (independent of the size of the sample) of largest order statistics. It provides in general the sharpest results among the different methods, whatever the sample size is and for any heaviness of the tail.

The second method is empirical and consists of a weighted normal approximation. Of course, we cannot expect such a sharp result as the one obtained with Normex. However it provides a simple tool allowing to remain in the Gaussian realm. We introduce a shift in the mean and a weight in the variance as correcting terms for the Gaussian parameters.

Then we will proceed to an analytical comparison between the exact distribution of the Pareto sum and its approximation given by Normex before turning to the application of evaluating risk measures.

Finally a numerical study will follow, applying the various methods on simulated samples to compare the accuracy of the estimation of extreme quantiles, used as risk measures in solvency calculation.

In the rest of the chapter, with financial/actuarial applications in mind, and without loss of generality, we will use power law models for the marginal distributions of the risks such as the Pareto distribution.

11.1.2 Preliminaries

11.1.2.1 Main notation

$[x]$ will denote the integer part of any nonnegative real x such that $[x] \leq x < [x] + 1$.

Let $(\Omega, \mathcal{A}, \mathbb{P})$ be the probability space on which we will be working.

Let Φ and φ denote, respectively, the cumulative distribution function (cdf) and the probability density function (pdf) of the standard normal distribution $\mathcal{N}(0, 1)$ and Φ_{μ,σ^2} and φ_{μ,σ^2} the cdf and pdf of the normal distribution $\mathcal{N}(\mu, \sigma^2)$ with mean μ and variance σ^2.

Let X be a random variable (r.v.) Pareto (type I) distributed with shape parameter 0, pdf denoted by f and cdf F defined by

$$\overline{F}(x) := 1 - F(x) = x^{-\alpha}, \quad x \geq 1, \tag{11.1}$$

and probability density function (pdf) denoted by f.

Note that the inverse function $F^{\leftarrow}$ of F is given by

$$F^{\leftarrow}(z) = (1 - z)^{-1/\alpha}, \quad \text{for } 0 < z < 1. \tag{11.2}$$

Recall that for $\alpha > 1$, $\mathbb{E}(X) = \frac{\alpha}{\alpha-1}$ and for $\alpha > 2$, $\text{var}(X) = \frac{\alpha}{(\alpha-1)^2(\alpha-2)}$.

We will consider i.i.d. Pareto r.v.'s in this study and denote by S_n the Pareto sum $S_n := \sum_{i=1}^{n} X_i$ ($X_i, i = 1, \ldots, n$) being an n-sample with parent r.v. X and associated order statistics $X_{(1)} \leq \cdots \leq X_{(n)}$.

When dealing with financial assets (market risk data), we define the returns as

$$X_i^{(n)} := \ln P_i - \ln P_{i-n}, \quad n \geq 1,$$

P_i being the daily price and n representing the aggregation factor.

Note that we can also write

$$X_i^{(n)} = \sum_{i=1}^{n} X_i^{(1)}.$$

In what follows, we will denote $X_i^{(1)}$ by X_i.

Further comments or questions

– Is it still worth considering i.i.d. r.v.'s, whereas most recent research focus on dependent ones?

Concerning the i.i.d. condition, note that this study fills up a gap in the literature on the sum of i.i.d. moderate heavy r.v.'s (see, e.g., (Feller, 1966); (Hahn et al., 1991), and (Petrov, 1995)). Moreover, in our practical example of log returns (the motivation of this work), the independence condition is satisfied (see, e.g., (Taylor, 1986); (Dacorogna et al., 2001)) and hence is not a restriction in this case of time aggregation.

Another theoretical reason comes from the EVT; indeed we know that the tail index of the aggregated distribution corresponds to the one of the marginal with the heaviest tail and hence does not depend on considering the issue of dependence.

Finally, there was still mathematically a missing "brick" when studying the behavior of the sum of i.i.d. r.v.'s with a moderately heavy tail, for which the CLT applies (for the center of distribution!) but with a slow convergence for the mean behavior and certainly does not provide satisfactory approximation for the tail. With this work, we aim at filling up the gap by looking at an appropriate limit distribution.

– Why considering Pareto distribution?
  It is justified by the EVT (see, e.g., (Leadbetter et al., 1983); (Resnick, 1987), and (Embrechts et al., 1997)). Indeed recall the Pickands theorem (see (Pickands, 1975) for the seminal work) proving that for sufficiently high threshold u, the generalized Pareto distribution (GPD) $G_{\xi,\sigma(u)}$ (with tail index ξ and scale parameter $\sigma(u)$) is a very good approximation to the excess cdf of a r.v. X defined by $F_u(x) = \mathbb{P}[X - u \leq x | X > u]$:

$$F_u(y) \underset{u \to \infty}{\approx} G_{\xi,\sigma(u)}(y)$$

if and only if the distribution of X is in the domain of attraction of one of the three limit laws. When considering risks under the presence of heavy tail, it implies that the extreme risks follow a GPD with a positive tail index (called also extreme value index) $\xi > 0$, which corresponds to say that the risks belong to the Fréchet maximum domain of attraction (see, e.g., (Galambos, 1978); (Leadbetter et al., 1983); (Resnick, 1987), or (Embrechts et al., 1997)). In particular, for $\xi > 0$,

$$\overline{G}_{\xi,\sigma(u)}(y) \underset{y \to \infty}{\sim} cy^{-1/\xi} \tag{11.3}$$

for some constant $c > 0$. It is then natural and quite general to consider a Pareto distribution (with shape parameter $1/\xi$) for heavy-tailed risks.
  A natural extension would then be considering r.v.'s with other distributions belonging to the Fréchet maximum domain of attraction.

– A last remark concerns the parameter α that we consider as given in our study. A prerequisite, when working on real data, would be to estimate α. Recall that there are various ways to test the presence of a heavy tail and to estimate the tail index, for example, the Hill estimator (see (Hill, 1975)) or the QQ-estimator (see (Kratz and Resnick, 1996)) (see also (Huston McCulloch, 1997); (Beirlant et al., 2004); (Resnick, 2006), and references therein). We will not provide an inventory of the methods, except a brief recall in the next section of an important empirical EVT method used for estimating the heaviness of the tail. Let us also mention a test, easy to use in practice, for the existence of fat tails, namely, the scaling law (see (Dacorogna et al., 2001), Section 5.5). It consists of comparing the two plots, for $p = 1$ and 2, respectively, of $\left(\ln(n), \ln\left(\|\sum_{i=1}^{n} X_i\|_p\right)\right)$, $n \geq 1$; if the scaling exponent for $p = 1$ is larger than for $p = 2$, then it is a sign of the existence of a fat tail. For financial data, there are numerous empirical studies that show the existence of fat tail and that the shape parameter is between 2 and 4 for developed markets (see, e.g., (Jansen and De Vries, 1991); (Longin, 1996); (Müller et al., 1998); (Dacorogna2 et al., 2001); (Dacorogna et al., 2001), and references therein).

11.2 A BRIEF REVIEW OF EXISTING METHODS

Limit theorems for the sum of i.i.d. r.v.'s are well known. Nevertheless, they can be misused in practice for various reasons such as a too small sample size, as we have seen. As a consequence, it leads to wrong estimations of the risk measures for aggregated data. To help practitioners to be sensitive to this issue, we consider the simple example of aggregated heavy-tailed risks, where the risks are represented by i.i.d. Pareto r.v.'s. We start by reviewing the existing methods, from the GCLT to EVT, before applying them on simulated Pareto samples to show the pros and cons of those methods.

11.2.1 A GCLT Approach

- For sake of completeness, let us recall the GCLT (see, e.g., (Samorodnitsky and Taqqu, 1994); (Nolan, 2012)), which states that the properly normalized sum of a large number of i.i.d. r.v.'s belonging to the domain of attraction of an α-stable law may be approximated by a stable distribution with index α ($0 < \alpha \leq 2$).

THEOREM 11.1 (GCLT) *Let $(X_i, i \geq 1)$ be i.i.d. r.v.'s, with parent r.v. X and parent distribution F attracted by an α-stable law F_α, with $\alpha > 0$ (recall that Z is said to be (sum or Lévy) stable if and only if $\forall n > 1$, $\sum_{i=1}^{n} Z_i \stackrel{d}{=} n^{1/\alpha} Z + d_n$, $d_n \in \mathbb{R}$ where $(Z_i)_i$ are i.i.d. copies of Z).*
(i) If $\alpha > 2$, that is, if $\mathbb{E}(X^2) < \infty$, then

$$\frac{S_n - n\mu}{\sigma\sqrt{n}} \stackrel{d}{\to} \Phi$$

with $\mu = \mathbb{E}(X)$ and $\sigma^2 = var(X)$.
(ii) If $\alpha \leq 2$, that is, if $\mathbb{E}(X^2) = \infty$ or $\alpha = 2$, then

$$\frac{S_n - \mu_n}{n^{1/\alpha} L(n)} \stackrel{d}{\to} G_\alpha \text{ normalized } \alpha\text{-stable distribution}$$

with $\mu_n := n\int_{|x|\le a_n} x\, dF(x)$, $a_n = \inf\{x : \mathbb{P}(|X| > x) < 1/n\}$, *and L an appropriate slowly varying function, that is, satisfying* $\lim\limits_{x\to\infty} \frac{L(tx)}{L(t)} = 1$, $\forall t > 0$.

- It applies in our specific case where we consider i.i.d. Pareto r.v.'s with shape parameter α and we can identify the normalizing constants. We have

$$\text{if } 0 < \alpha < 2, \quad \frac{S_n - b_n}{n^{1/\alpha} C_\alpha} \overset{d}{\to} G_\alpha \text{ normalized } \alpha\text{-stable distribution,} \quad (11.4)$$

$$\text{if } \alpha \ge 2, \quad \frac{1}{d_n}\left(S_n - \frac{n\alpha}{\alpha - 1}\right) \overset{d}{\to} \Phi, \quad (11.5)$$

with

$$b_n = \begin{cases} 0, & \text{if } 0 < \alpha < 1, \\ \dfrac{\pi n^2}{2}\displaystyle\int_1^\infty \sin\left(\dfrac{\pi x}{2n}\right) dF(x) \\ \quad \simeq n(\log n + 1 - \gamma - \log(2/\pi)), & \text{if } \alpha = 1, \\ n\,\mathbb{E}(X) = n\alpha/(\alpha - 1) & \text{if, } 1 < \alpha < 2, \end{cases}$$

$$(\gamma = \text{Euler constant } 0.5772);$$

$$C_\alpha = \begin{cases} (\Gamma(1 - \alpha)\cos(\pi\alpha/2))^{1/\alpha} & \text{if } \alpha \ne 1, \\ \pi/2 & \text{if } \alpha = 1, \end{cases} ;$$

$$d_n = \begin{cases} \sqrt{n\,\text{var}(X)} = \sqrt{\dfrac{n\alpha}{(\alpha - 1)^2(\alpha - 2)}} & \text{if } \alpha > 2, \\ \inf\left\{x : \dfrac{2n\log x}{x^2} \le 1\right\} & \text{if } \alpha = 2. \end{cases}$$

Note that the tail distribution of G_α satisfies (see (Samorodnitsky and Taqqu, 1994)):

$$1 - G_\alpha(x) \sim (C_\alpha x)^{-\alpha} \text{ as } x \to \infty. \quad (11.6)$$

11.2.2   An EVT Approach

When focusing on the tail of the distribution, in particular for the estimation of the risk measures, the information on the entire distribution is not necessary, hence the alternative of the EVT approach.

Recall the Fisher–Tippett theorem (see (Fisher and Tippett, 1928)) which states that the limiting distribution for the rescaled sample maximum can only be of three types: Fréchet, Weibull, and Gumbel. The three types of extreme value distribution have been combined into a single three-parameter family ((Jenkinson, 1955); (von Mises, 1936); 1985) known as the generalized extreme value (GEV) distribution given by

$$H_\xi(x) = H_{\mu,\sigma,\xi}(x) = \exp\left[-\left(1 + \xi\frac{x - \mu}{\sigma}\right)^{-\frac{1}{\xi}}\right], \quad \text{for } 1 + \xi\frac{x - \mu}{\sigma} > 0,$$

with $\sigma > 0$ (scale parameter), $\mu \in \mathbb{R}$ (location parameter), and $\xi \in \mathbb{R}$ (tail index or extreme value index). The tail index ξ determines the nature of the tail distribution:
$\xi > 0$: Fréchet, $\xi = 0$: Gumbel, $\xi < 0$: Weibull.

Under the assumption of regular variation of the tail distribution, the tail of the cdf of the sum of i.i.d. r.v.'s is mainly determined by the tail of the cdf of the maximum of these r.v.'s. Indeed, we have the following lemma.

LEMMA 11.1 (See, e.g., (Feller, 1966); (Embrechts et al., 1997)) *Assuming that $X_i, i = 1, \ldots, n$ are i.i.d. r.v.'s with cdf F_X having a regularly varying tail with tail index $\beta \geq 0$, then for all $n \geq 1$,*

$$\overline{F^{n*}}(x) \sim n\overline{F}(x) \quad \text{as } x \to \infty, \tag{11.7}$$

which means that

$$\mathbb{P}[S_n > x] \sim \mathbb{P}[\max_{1 \leq i \leq n} X_i > x] \quad \text{as } x \to \infty. \tag{11.8}$$

It applies of course to Pareto r.v.'s.

Combining (11.8) with the GEV limiting distribution in the case of α-Pareto r.v.'s provides that the tail distribution of the rescaled sum S_n of Pareto r.v.'s is asymptotically Fréchet:

$$\mathbb{P}\left[n^{-1/\alpha}\left(S_n - b_n\right) > x\right] \underset{n \to \infty}{\to} 1 - e^{-x^{-\alpha}}, \quad \text{for large } x, \tag{11.9}$$

where b_n is defined as in (2.1).

11.3 NEW APPROACHES: MIXED LIMIT THEOREMS

An alternative approach to the GCLT one has been proposed by Zaliapin et al. (see (Zaliapin et al., 2005)) when the Pareto shape parameter satisfies $1/2 < \alpha < 2$, a case where the variance of the Pareto r.v.'s X_i does not exist. The neat idea of the method is to rewrite the sum of the X_i's as the sum of the order statistics $X_{(1)} \leq \cdots \leq X_{(n)}$ and to separate it into two terms, one with the first $n - 2$ order statistics having finite variance and the other as the complement

$$S_n = \sum_{i=1}^{n} X_i = \sum_{i=1}^{n-2} X_{(i)} + (X_{(n-1)} + X_{(n)}), \text{ with } \text{var}(X_{(i)}) < \infty, \ \forall i = 1, \ldots, n-2.$$

They can then treat these two subsums separately. Even if not always rigorously developed in this paper, or, say, quite approximative, as we will see later, their method provides better numerical results than the GCLT does for any number of summands and any quantile. Nevertheless, there are some mathematical issues in this paper. One of them is that the authors consider these two subsums as independent. Another one is that they approximate the quantile of the total (Pareto) sum with the direct summation of the quantiles of each subsum, although the quantiles are not additive. For the case $1/2 < \alpha < 2/3$, they reduce the behavior of the sum arbitrarily to the last two upper order statistics.

Another drawback of this method would be, when considering the case $\alpha > 2$, to remain with one sum of all terms with a finite variance, hence in general with a poor or slow normal approximation.

We are mainly interested in the case of a shape parameter larger than 2, since it is the missing part in the literature and of practical relevance when studying market risk data, for instance. For such a case, the CLT applies because of the finiteness of the second moment, but using it to obtain information on something else than the average is simply wrong in presence of fat tails, even if in some situations (e.g., when working on aggregated data or on short samples), the plot of the empirical distribution fits a normal one. The CLT only concentrates on the mean behavior; it is equivalent to the CLT on the trimmed sum (i.e., S_n minus a given number of the largest order statistics (or tail)) (see (Mori, 1984)), for which the rate of convergence improves (see, e.g., (Hahn et al., 1991); (Hall, 1984)).

Inspired by Zaliapin et al.'s paper, we go further in the direction of separating mean and extreme behaviors in order to improve approximations, for any α, and we build two alternative methods, called *Normex* and the *weighted normal limit*, respectively. It means to answer rigorously the question of how many largest order statistics $X_{(n-j)}$, $j > k$ would explain the divergence between the underlying distribution and the normal approximation when considering a Pareto sum with $\alpha \geq 2$ or the stable approximation when considering a Pareto sum with $\alpha < 2$.

Both methods rely initially on Zaliapin et al.'s approach of splitting the Pareto sum into a trimmed sum to which the CLT applies and another sum with the remaining largest order statistics. The main idea of the two methods is to determine in an "optimal way" (in order to improve at most the distribution approximation), which we are going to explain, the number k that corresponds to a threshold when splitting the sum of order statistics into two subsums, with the second one constituted by the k largest order statistics. We will develop these methods under realistic assumptions, dropping in particular Zaliapin's et al.'s assumption of independence between the two subsums. Our two methods differ from each other in two points:

- The way of selecting this number k.
- The way of evaluating the sum determined by the k largest order statistics, which is of course related to the choice of k

Our study is developed on the Pareto example, but its goal is to propose a method that may be applied to any heavy-tailed distribution (with positive tail index) and to real data, hence this choice of looking for limit theorems in order to approximate the true (and most of the time unknown) distribution.

11.3.1 A Common First Step

11.3.1.1 How to fit for the best mean behavior of aggregated heavy-tailed distributed risks?

Let us start by studying the behavior of the trimmed sum T_k when writing down the sum S_n of the i.i.d. α-Pareto r.v.'s (with $\alpha > 0$), $S_n := \sum_{i=1}^{n} X_i$, as

$$S_n = T_k + U_{n-k} \quad \text{with} \quad T_k := \sum_{j=1}^{n-k} X_{(j)} \quad \text{and} \quad U_{n-k} := \sum_{j=0}^{k-1} X_{(n-j)}. \quad (11.10)$$

Much literature, since the 1980s, has been concerned with the behavior of trimmed sums by removing extremes from the sample; see, for example, Hall (1984), Mori (1984), and Hahn et al. (1991).

The main issue is the choice of the threshold k, in order to use the CLT but also to improve its fit since we want to approximate the behavior of T_k by a normal one.

We know that a necessary and sufficient condition for the CLT to apply on T_k is to require the summands $X_{(j)}, j = 1, \ldots, n - k$, to be L^2-r.v.'s. But we also know that requiring only the finitude of the second moment may lead to a poor normal approximation, if higher moments do not exist, as occurs, for instance, with financial market data. In particular, including the finitude of the third moment provides a better rate of convergence to the normal distribution in the CLT (Berry–Esséen inequality). Another information that might be quite useful to improve the approximation of the distribution of S_n with its limit distribution is the Fisher index, defined by the ratio $\gamma = \frac{\mathbb{E}[(X-\mathbb{E}(X))^4]}{(\text{var}(X))^2}$, which is a kurtosis index. The skewness $\mathbb{E}[(X - \mathbb{E}(X))^3]/(\text{var}(X))^{3/2}$ of X and $(\gamma - 3)$ measures the closeness of the cdf F to Φ. Hence we will choose k based on the condition of existence of the fourth moment of the summands of T_k (i.e., the first $n - k$ order statistics).

The following Edgeworth expansion involving the Hermite polynomials $(H_n, n \geq 0)$ points out that requiring the finitude of the fourth moments appears as what we call the "optimal" solution (of course, the higher order moments exist, the finer the normal approximation becomes, but it would imply too strong conditions and difficult to handle). If F_n denotes the cdf of the standardized S_n defined by $\frac{S_n - n\mathbb{E}(X)}{\sqrt{n \; \text{var}(X)}}$, then

$$F_n(x) - \Phi(x) = \frac{1}{\sqrt{n}} Q_1(x) + \frac{1}{n} Q_2(x) + o(1/n) \quad (11.11)$$

uniformly in x, with

$$Q_1(x) = -\varphi(x) \frac{H_2(x)}{6} \frac{\mathbb{E}[(X - \mathbb{E}(X))^3]}{(\text{var}(X))^{3/2}},$$

$$Q_2(x) = -\varphi(x) \left\{ \frac{H_5(x)}{72} \frac{(\mathbb{E}[(X - \mathbb{E}(X))^3])^2}{(\text{var}(X))^3} + \frac{H_3(x)}{24} (\gamma - 3) \right\},$$

TABLE 11.1   Necessary and sufficient condition on α for having $\mathbb{E}[|X_{(n-k)}|^p] < \infty, p = 2, 3, 4$

k	0	1	2	3	4	5	6	7
$\mathbb{E}(X^2_{(n-k)}) < \infty$	$\alpha > 2$	$\alpha > 1$	$\alpha > 2/3$	$\alpha > 1/2$	$\alpha > 2/5$	$\alpha > 1/3$	$\alpha > 2/7$	$\alpha > 1/4$
$\mathbb{E}(X^3_{(n-k)}) < \infty$	$\alpha > 3$	$\alpha > 3/2$	$\alpha > 1$	$\alpha > 3/4$	$\alpha > 3/5$	$\alpha > 1/2$	$\alpha > 3/7$	$\alpha > 3/8$
$\mathbb{E}(X^4_{(n-k)}) < \infty$	$\alpha > 4$	$\alpha > 2$	$\alpha > 4/3$	$\alpha > 1$	$\alpha > 4/5$	$\alpha > 2/3$	$\alpha > 4/7$	$\alpha > 1/2$

and

$$H_2(x) = x^2 - 1, \quad H_3(x) = x^3 - 3x, \quad H_5(x) = x^5 - 10x^3 + 15x.$$

The rate of convergence appears clearly as $n^{-\delta/2}$ whenever $\mathbb{E}[X^{2+\delta}] < \infty, \delta > 0$.

Note that in our Pareto case, the skewness and the excess kurtosis are, respectively,

$$\gamma = \frac{2(1+\alpha)}{\alpha - 3} \sqrt{\frac{\alpha - 2}{\alpha}} \text{ if } \alpha > 3 \text{ and } \gamma - 3 = \frac{6(\alpha^3 + \alpha^2 - 6\alpha - 2)}{\alpha(\alpha - 3)(\alpha - 4)} \text{ if } \alpha > 4.$$

Therefore we set $p = 4$ (but prefer to keep the notation p so that it remains general) to obtain what we call an "optimal" approximation. Then we select the threshold $k = k(\alpha)$ such that

$$\mathbb{E}\left[X^p_{(j)}\right] \begin{cases} < \infty & \forall j \leq n - k, \\ = \infty & \forall j > n - k, \end{cases}$$

which when applied to our case of α-Pareto i.i.d. r.v.'s (using (11.17)) gives

$$k > \frac{p}{\alpha} - 1. \tag{11.12}$$

This condition allows then to determine a fixed number $k = k(\alpha)$ as a function of the shape parameter α of the underlying heavy-tailed distribution of the X_i's but not of the size n of the sample. We can take it as small as possible in order to fit for the best both the mean and tail behaviors of S_n. Note that we look for the smallest possible k to be able to compute explicitly the distribution of the last upper order statistics appearing as the summands of the second sum U_{n-k}. For this reason, based on condition (11.12), we choose

$$k = [p/\alpha - 1] + 1. \tag{11.13}$$

Let us summarize in Table 11.1 the necessary and sufficient condition on α(for $\alpha > 1/4$) to have the existence of the pth moments for the upper order statistics for $p = 2, 3, 4$, respectively, using (11.12) written as $\alpha > \frac{p}{k+1}$.

We deduce the value of the threshold $k = k(\alpha)$ satisfying (11.13) for which the fourth moment is finite according to the set of definition of α: We notice from Table 11.2 that we would use Zaliapin et al.'s decomposition only when $\alpha \in]\frac{4}{3}; 2]$.

TABLE 11.2 Value of $k(\alpha)$ for having up to $\mathbb{E}(|X_{(n-k(\alpha))}|^4) < \infty$

$\alpha \in I(k)$ with $I(k) =$	$]\frac{1}{2};\frac{4}{7}]$	$]\frac{4}{7};\frac{2}{3}]$	$]\frac{2}{3};\frac{4}{5}]$	$]\frac{4}{5};1]$	$]1;\frac{4}{3}]$	$]\frac{4}{3};2]$	$]2,4]$
$k = k(\alpha) =$	7	6	5	4	3	2	1

When considering, as they do, $2 > \alpha > 2/3$, we would rather introduce the decomposition $S_n = \sum_{j=1}^{n-k} X_{(j)} + \sum_{j=0}^{k-1} X_{(n-j)}$, with k varying from 2 to 5 depending on the value of α, to improve the approximation of the distribution of S_n, if we omit the discussion on their conditions.

11.3.1.2 Some properties of order statistics for Pareto random variables

First we apply known results on distribution of order statistics (see, e.g., (David and Nadaraja, 2003)) when considering Pareto distributions. Next we compute conditional distributions of order statistics, as well as conditional moments, to apply them to the Pareto case.

- **Distribution of Pareto order statistics**

  For α-Pareto r.v.'s, the pdf $f_{(i)}$ of $X_{(i)}$ ($1 \le i \le n$) and the pdf $f_{(n_1)\ldots(n_k)}$ of the order statistics $X_{(n_j)}, j = 1,\ldots,k$ ($1 \le k \le n$), with $1 \le n_1 < \cdots < n_k \le n$, are expressed, respectively, as

  $$f_{(i)}(x) = \frac{n!}{(i-1)!(n-i)!} \, \alpha(1 - x^{-\alpha})^{i-1} x^{-\alpha(n-i+1)-1}, \quad \text{for } x > 1, \quad (11.14)$$

  and, for $1 < x_1 \le \cdots \le x_k$,

  $$f_{(n_1)\ldots(n_k)}(x_1,\ldots,x_k) = n! \; \alpha^k \frac{(1 - x_1^{-\alpha})^{n_1-1}}{(n_1-1)!} \frac{x_k^{-\alpha(n-n_k+1)-1}}{(n-n_k)!}$$
  $$\prod_{j=1}^{k-1} \frac{x_j^{-\alpha-1}(x_j^{-\alpha} - x_{j+1}^{-\alpha})^{n_{j+1}-n_j-1}}{(n_{j+1}-n_j-1)!}. \quad (11.15)$$

  When considering successive order statistics, for $1 < x_1 \le \cdots \le x_j$, for $i \ge 1$, $j \ge 2$, with $i + j \le n$, we obtain

  $$f_{(i+1)\ldots(i+j)}(x_1,\ldots,x_j) = \frac{n! \; \alpha^j}{i! \; (n-i-j)!} (1 - x_1^{-\alpha})^i \, x_j^{-\alpha(n-i-j)} \prod_{l=1}^{j} \frac{1}{x_l^{\alpha+1}}. \quad (11.16)$$

  Moments of α-Pareto order statistics satisfy (see also, e.g., (Zaliapin et al., 2005); Theorem 1)

  $$\mathbb{E}[X_{(j)}^p] < \infty \text{ iff } \quad p < \alpha(n-j+1),$$
  $$\text{and } \mathbb{E}[X_{(j)}^p] = \frac{n! \; \Gamma(n-j+1-p/\alpha)}{(n-j)! \; \Gamma(n+1-p/\alpha)}, \quad (11.17)$$

and, for $1 \le i < j \le n$,

$$\mathbb{E}[X_{(i)}X_{(j)}] < \infty \text{ iff } \min(n - j + 1, (n - i + 1)/2) > 1/\alpha,$$

$$\text{and } \mathbb{E}[X_{(i)}X_{(j)}] = \frac{n! \; \Gamma(n - j + 1 - 1/\alpha)\Gamma(n - i + 1 - 2/\alpha)}{(n - j)! \; \Gamma(n - i + 1 - 1/\alpha)\Gamma(n + 1 - 2/\alpha)}.$$

- **Conditional distribution of order statistics. Application to Pareto r.v.'s**
  Now straightforward computations lead to new properties that will be needed
  to build Normex. We express them in the general case (and labeled), with the
  notation f and F, and then for Pareto r.v.'s.
  We deduce from (11.14) and (11.15) that the pdf of $X_{(i)}$ given $X_{(j)}$, for
  $1 \le i < j \le n$, is, for $x \le y$,

$$f_{X_{(i)}/(X_{(j)}=y)}(x) = \frac{(j - 1)!}{(i - 1)!(j - i - 1)!} \; f(x)(F(y) - F(x))^{j-i-1} \; \frac{F^{i-1}(x)}{F^{j-1}(y)}$$

$$= \frac{\alpha \; (j - 1)!}{(i - 1)!(j - i - 1)!} \; x^{-\alpha-1}(x^{-\alpha} - y^{-\alpha})^{j-i-1} \; \frac{(1 - x^{-\alpha})^{i-1}}{(1 - y^{-\alpha})^{j-1}},$$

$$(11.18)$$

and that the joint pdf of $(X_{(i)}, X_{(j)})$ given $X_{(k)}$, for $1 \le i < j < k \le n$, is, for
$x \le y \le z$,

$$f_{X_{(i)},X_{(j)}/(X_{(k)}=z)}(x, y) = \frac{(k - 1)!}{(i - 1)!(j - i - 1)!(k - j - 1)!} \; f(x)f(y)$$

$$\times \frac{F^{i-1}(x)(F(y) - F(x))^{j-i-1}(F(z) - F(y))^{k-j-1}}{F^{k-1}(z)}$$

$$= \frac{\alpha^2 \; (k - 1)! \; x^{-\alpha-1}y^{-\alpha-1} \; (1 - x^{-\alpha})^{i-1}(x^{-\alpha} - y^{-\alpha})^{j-i-1}(y^{-\alpha} - z^{-\alpha})^{k-j-1}}{(i - 1)!(j - i - 1)!(k - j - 1)! \; (1 - z^{-\alpha})^{k-1}}.$$

$$(11.19)$$

Using (11.14) and (11.16) provides, for $y \le x_1 \le \cdots \le x_{j-1}$,

$$f_{X_{(i+2)}\cdots X_{(i+j)}/X_{(i+1)}=y}(x_1, \ldots, x_{j-1})$$

$$= \frac{(n - i - 1)!}{(n - i - j)! \; (1 - F(y))^{n-i-1}} \; (1 - F(x_{j-1}))^{n-i-j} \prod_{l=1}^{j-1} f(x_l)$$

$$= \frac{(n - i - 1)! \; \alpha^{j-1}}{(n - i - j)! \; y^{-\alpha(n-i-1)}} \; \frac{1}{x_{j-1}^{\alpha(n-i-j+1)+1}} \prod_{l=1}^{j-2} \frac{1}{x_l^{\alpha+1}}. \qquad (11.20)$$

Then we can compute the first conditional moments. We obtain, using
(11.18) and the change of variables $u = F(x)/F(y)$,

$$\mathbb{E}[X_{(i)}/X_{(j)} = y] = \frac{(j - 1)!}{(i - 1)!(j - i - 1)!} \int_0^1 F^{\leftarrow}(uF(y)) \; u^{i-1}(1 - u)^{j-i-1} \; du$$

$$= \frac{(j-1)!}{(i-1)!(j-i-1)!} \int_0^1 (1-u(1-y^{-\alpha}))^{-\frac{1}{\alpha}} u^{i-1}(1-u)^{j-i-1} \, du$$

$$\simeq \frac{1}{B(i,j-i)} \left\{ B(i,j-i) + \sum_{l \geq 1} B(i+l,j-i) \frac{(1-y^{-\alpha})^l}{l!} \prod_{m=0}^{l-1}(m+1/\alpha) \right\}$$

$$= 1 + \frac{\Gamma(j)}{\Gamma(i)} \sum_{l \geq 1} \frac{\Gamma(i+l)}{l\,\Gamma(j+l)\Gamma(l)}(1-y^{-\alpha})^l \prod_{m=0}^{l-1}(m+1/\alpha), \qquad (11.21)$$

and $\mathbb{E}[X_{(i)}^2/X_{(j)} = y]$

$$= \frac{(j-1)!}{(i-1)!(j-i-1)!} \int_0^1 [F^{\leftarrow}(uF(y))]^2 \, u^{i-1}(1-u)^{j-i-1} \, du$$

$$= \frac{(j-1)!}{(i-1)!(j-i-1)!} \int_0^1 (1-u(1-y^{-\alpha}))^{-\frac{2}{\alpha}} u^{i-1}(1-u)^{j-i-1} \, du$$

$$\simeq 1 + \frac{\Gamma(j)}{\Gamma(i)} \sum_{l \geq 1} \frac{\Gamma(i+l)}{l\,\Gamma(j+l)\Gamma(l)}(1-y^{-\alpha})^l \prod_{m=0}^{l-1}(m+2/\alpha). \qquad (11.22)$$

For $1 \leq i < j < k \leq n$, via (11.19) and the change of variables $u = F(x_i)/F(y)$ and $v = F(x_j)/F(y)$, it comes

$$\mathbb{E}[X_{(i)}X_{(j)}/X_{(k)} = y]$$

$$= \frac{(k-1)!}{(i-1)!(j-i-1)!(k-j-1)!} \int_0^1 F^{\leftarrow}(uF(y)) \, u^{i-1}$$

$$\left(\int_u^1 F^{\leftarrow}(vF(y)) \, (v-u)^{j-i-1}(1-v)^{k-j-1} dv \right) du$$

$$= \frac{(k-1)!}{(i-1)!(j-i-1)!(k-j-1)!} \int_0^1 (1-u(1-y^{-\alpha}))^{-\frac{1}{\alpha}} u^{i-1}$$

$$\left(\int_u^1 (1-v(1-y^{-\alpha}))^{-\frac{1}{\alpha}} (v-u)^{j-i-1}(1-v)^{k-j-1} dv \right) du. \qquad (11.23)$$

Moreover, the joint conditional distribution of $(X_{(i+1)}, \ldots, X_{(p-1)})$ given $(X_{(k)} = x_k, p \leq k \leq i)$, for $1 \leq i < p \leq n$, denoted by $f_{X_{(i+1)}, \ldots, X_{(p-1)}/(X_{(k)} = x_k, p \leq k \leq i)}$, or $f_{(i+1),\ldots,(p-1)}\,/(X_{(k)}=x_k,p\le k\le i)$ when no ambiguity exists, is, for $x_1 < \cdots < x_n$,

$$f_{(i+1),\ldots,(p-1)\,/\,(X_{(k)}=x_k,k\le i,k\ge p)}(x_{i+1},\ldots,x_{p-1}) = \frac{(p-i-1)!}{(F(x_p)-F(x_i))^{p-i-1}} \prod_{l=i+1}^{p-1} f(x_l)$$

$$= \frac{(p-i-1)!\ \alpha^{p-i-1}}{(x_i^{-\alpha}-x_p^{-\alpha})^{p-i-1}} \prod_{l=i+1}^{p-1} \frac{1}{x_l^{\alpha+1}},$$

$$(11.24)$$

from which we get back the well-known result that $X_{(i+1)},\ldots,X_{(p-1)}$ are independent of $X_{(1)},\ldots,X_{(i-1)}$ and $X_{(p+1)},\ldots,X_{(n)}$ when $X_{(i)}$ and $X_{(p)}$ are given and that the order statistics form a Markov chain.

11.3.2   Method 1: Normex—A Mixed Normal Extreme Limit

(see (Kratz, 2014))

11.3.2.1   A conditional decomposition

Whatever the size of the sample is, because of the small magnitude of k, we are able to compute explicitly the distribution of the last upper order statistics appearing as the summands of the second sum U_{n-k} defined in (11.10). The choice of k allows also to obtain a good normal approximation for the distribution of the trimmed sum T_k. Nevertheless, since T_k and U_{n-k} are not independent, we decompose the Pareto sum S_n in a slightly different way than in (11.10) (but keeping the same notation), namely,

$$S_n = T_k + X_{(n-k+1)} + U_{n-k+1}, \qquad (11.25)$$

and use the property of conditional independence (recalled in Section 11.1.2) between the two subsums T_k and U_{n-k+1} conditional on $X_{(n-k+1)}$(for $k \ge 1$).

Then we obtain the following approximation of the distribution of S_n, for $k \ge 1$(i.e., when the pth moment of the k largest order statistics does not exist).

THEOREM 11.2   *The cdf of S_n expressed in (11.25) with $k = k(\alpha) \ge 1$ defined in (11.13) can be approximated by $G_{n,\alpha,k}$ defined for any $x \ge 1$ by*

$$G_{n,\alpha,k}(x) = \begin{cases} n\alpha \displaystyle\int_1^x \frac{1}{\sigma(y)} \frac{(1-y^{-\alpha})^{n-1}}{y^{1+\alpha}} \int_0^{x-y} \varphi\left(\frac{v-m_1(y)}{\sigma(y)}\right) dv\, dy, & \text{if } k=1, \\[4mm] \displaystyle\int_1^x f_{(n-k+1)}(y) \int_0^{x-y} \varphi_{m_1(y),\sigma^2(y)} * h_y^{(k-1)*}(v) dv\, dy, & \text{if } k \ge 2, \end{cases}$$

where $f_{(n-k+1)}(y) = \dfrac{\alpha\ n!}{(n-k)!(k-1)!}(1-y^{-\alpha})^{n-k}y^{-\alpha k-1}\ \mathbb{1}_{(y>1)}$; h_y *denotes the probability density function of a Pareto r.v. with parameters α and y, defined by*

$h_y(x) = \frac{\alpha}{x^{\alpha+1}} \mathbb{I}_{(x \geq y)}$, *and the mean* $m_1(y)$ *and the variance* $\sigma^2(y)$ *are defined, respectively, by*

$$m_1(y) = m_1(\alpha, n, k, y) = \frac{n - k(\alpha)}{1 - y^{-\alpha}} \times \begin{cases} \dfrac{1 - y^{1-\alpha}}{1 - 1/\alpha}, & \text{if } \alpha \neq 1, \\ \\ \ln(y), & \text{if } \alpha = 1, \end{cases} \tag{11.26}$$

and

$$\sigma^2(y) = \sigma^2(\alpha, n, k, y) := m_2(\alpha, n, k, y) - m_1^2(\alpha, n, k, y)$$

$$= (n - k(1)) \, y \left(1 - \frac{y \ln^2(y)}{(y - 1)^2} \right) \mathbb{I}_{(\alpha=1)} + 2(n - k(2)) \frac{y^2}{y^2 - 1} \left(\ln(y) - 2 \frac{y - 1}{y + 1} \right) \mathbb{I}_{(\alpha=2)}$$

$$+ \frac{n - k(\alpha)}{1 - y^{-\alpha}} \left(\frac{1 - y^{2-\alpha}}{1 - 2/\alpha} - \frac{1}{(1 - 1/\alpha)^2} \times \frac{(1 - y^{1-\alpha})^2}{1 - y^{-\alpha}} \right) \mathbb{I}_{(\alpha \neq 1,2)}. \tag{11.27}$$

Comments

1. The distribution $G_{n,\alpha,k}$ can also be expressed as

$$G_{n,\alpha,1}(x) = \alpha \, n \int\limits_1^x \frac{(1 - y^{-\alpha})^{n-1}}{y^{1+\alpha}} \left(\Phi\left(\frac{m_1(y)}{\sigma(y)} \right) - \Phi\left(\frac{m_1(y) - (x - y)}{\sigma(y)} \right) \right) dy$$

and, for $k \geq 2$,

$$G_{n,\alpha,k}(x) = \int\limits_1^x \frac{f_{(n-k+1)}(y)}{\sigma(y)} \int\limits_0^{x-y} \left(\int\limits_0^v \varphi\left(\frac{v - u - m_1(y)}{\sigma(y)} \right) h_y^{(k-1)*}(u) du \right) dv \, dy,$$

where the convolution product $h_y^{(k-1)*}$ can be numerically evaluated using either the recursive convolution equation $h_y^{j*}(x) = h_y^{*(j-1)} * h_y(x)$, for $j \geq 2$, (it will be fast, k being small) and $h_y^{1*} = h_y$ or, if $\alpha \in \mathbb{N}^*$, the explicit expression (12) (replacing β by y) given in Ramsay (2006).

2. Note that we considered i.i.d. Pareto r.v.'s only as an example to illustrate our method intended to be extended to unknown distributions using the CLT for the mean behavior and heavy-tailed distributions of the Pareto type for the tail. Since the exact distribution of the Pareto sum S_n of i.i.d. Pareto r.v.'s is known, we will be able to judge about the quality of the approximation proposed in Theorem 11.2 when comparing $G_{n,\alpha,k}$ with the exact distribution of S_n. We will then compare the respective associated risk measures.

3. Finally recall the following result by Feller (see 1966) on the convolution closure of distributions with regularly varying tails, which applies in our Pareto example but may also be useful when extending the method to distributions belonging to the Fréchet maximum domain of attraction.

LEMMA 11.2 (Feller). *If F_1 and F_2 are two cdfs with regularly varying tails with tail index $\beta \geq 0$, then the convolution $F_1 * F_2$ is also regularly varying with the same tail index β.*

Note that this lemma implies the result given in (11.7), and as a consequence in the Pareto case, we have

$$\int_x^\infty h_y^{(k-1)*}(u)du \underset{x\to\infty}{\sim} (k-1)\int_x^\infty h_y(u)du.$$

Proof of Theorem 11.2

▷ Let us express the cdf of S_n. Note that $\mathbb{P}(S_n \le x) = \mathbb{P}(1 \le S_n \le x)$. For any $x \ge 1$, we can write

$$\mathbb{P}(S_n \le x) = \int_1^x \mathbb{P}(T_k + U_{n-k+1} \le x - y \ / \ X_{(n-k+1)} = y) f_{(n-k+1)}(y)dy.$$

Hence, if $k = 1$,

$$\mathbb{P}(S_n \le x) = \int_1^x f_{(n)}(y) \int_0^{x-y} f_{T_1/X_{(n)}=y}(v)dv \ dy, \qquad (11.28)$$

and, for $k \ge 2$, using the conditional independence of T_k and U_{n-k+1} conditional on $X_{(n-k+1)}$:

$$\mathbb{P}(S_n \le x)$$

$$= \int_1^x f_{(n-k+1)}(y) \int_0^{x-y} f_{T_k/X_{(n-k+1)}=y} * f_{U_{n-k+1}/X_{(n-k+1)}=y}(v)dv \ dy. \qquad (11.29)$$

The next two steps consist in evaluating the limit distribution of $T_k \ / \ (X_{(n-k+1)} = y)$ and the exact distribution of $U_{n-k+1} \ / \ (X_{(n-k+1)} = y)$.

▷ *A limiting normal distribution for* $T_k/(X_{(n-k+1)} = y)$

PROPOSITION 11.1   *The conditional distribution of the trimmed sum* T_k *defined in (11.10) given the kth largest r.v.* $X_{(n-k+1)}$ *can be approximated, for large n, by the normal distribution* $\mathcal{N}(m_1(\alpha, n, k, y), \sigma^2(\alpha, n, k, y))$:

$$\mathcal{L}\left(T_k/(X_{(n-k+1)} = y)\right) \underset{n\to\infty}{\overset{d}{\sim}} \mathcal{N}\left(m_1(\alpha, n, k, y), \sigma^2(\alpha, n, k, y)\right)$$

with $y > 1$ *and where the mean* $m_1(\alpha, n, k, y)$ *and the variance* $\sigma^2(\alpha, n, k, y)$ *are defined in (11.26) and (11.27), respectively.*

Proof of Proposition 11.1 Since, conditionally on $X_{(n-k+1)}$, T_k has the same distribution as $\sum_{j=1}^{n-k} Y_j$ with (Y_j) an $(n-k)$ sample with parent cdf defined by $F_Y(\cdot) = \mathbb{P}(X_i \le \cdot \ / \ X_i < X_{(n-k+1)})$, we may apply the CLT whenever the second moment of Y_j is finite. Note that for the reasons explained previously, we will choose $p \ge 4$ for a better fit (after noticing that if $X_{(i)}$ has a finite pth moment, for $i \le n - k$, so does $X/X < X_{(n-k+1)}$).

We need to compute the first two moments of $T_k/(X_{(n-k+1)} = y)$, $m_1(\alpha, n, k, y)$, and $m_2(\alpha, n, k, y)$, respectively. We do it when considering the sum itself, since it involves less computations than the direct computation. Indeed, using (11.21)–(11.23), respectively, and applying the multinomial theorem lead to, for $k > p/\alpha - 1$,

$$m_1(y) := m_1(\alpha, n, k, y) := \sum_{j=1}^{n-k} \mathbb{E}(X_{(j)}/X_{(n-k+1)} = y)$$

$$= (n-k) \int_0^1 F^\leftarrow(uF(y)) \sum_{j=0}^{n-k-1} \binom{n-k-1}{j} u^j(1-u)^{n-k-1-j} du,$$

where $\binom{n-k-1}{j}$ denotes the binomial coefficient

$$= (n-k) \int_0^1 F^\leftarrow(uF(y)) du \quad \text{(using the binomial theorem)},$$

that is, when considering the α-Pareto distribution, using (11.2),

$$m_1(y) = (n - k(\alpha)) \int_0^1 (1 - uF(y))^{-1/\alpha} du = \frac{n - k(\alpha)}{F(y)} \times \begin{cases} \dfrac{1 - \left(\overline{F}(y)\right)^{1-1/\alpha}}{1 - 1/\alpha}, & \text{if } \alpha \neq 1, \\[2mm] |\ln \overline{F}(y)|, & \text{if } \alpha = 1, \end{cases}$$

hence (11.26).

Let us compute the second moment $m_2(y) := m_2(\alpha, n, k, y)$, introducing the notation $a = F(y)$:

$$m_2(y) = \sum_{j=1}^{n-k} \mathbb{E}(X_{(j)}^2/X_{(n-k+1)} = y) + 2 \sum_{j=2}^{n-k} \sum_{i=1}^{j-1} \mathbb{E}(X_{(i)}X_{(j)}/X_{(n-k+1)} = y)$$

$$= (n-k) \int_0^1 (F^\leftarrow(au))^2 du + 2(n-k)(n-k-1) \int_0^1 F^\leftarrow(au) \int_u^1 F^\leftarrow(av)$$

$$\times \sum_{j=0}^{n-k-2} \sum_{i=0}^{j} \binom{n-k-2}{i, j-i, n-k-2-j} u^i(v-u)^{j-i}(1-v)^{n-k-2-j} dv \, du,$$

where $\binom{n-k-2}{i, j-i, n-k-2-j}$ denotes the multinomial coefficient

$$= (n-k) \left\{ \int_0^1 (F^\leftarrow(au))^2 du + 2(n-k-1) \int_0^1 F^\leftarrow(au) \int_u^1 F^\leftarrow(av) dv \, du \right\}$$

(using the multinomial theorem).

Hence, for Pareto, via (11.2), it comes

$$
m_2(y) = (n-k)\left\{ \int_0^1 (1-au)^{-2/\alpha}\,du + 2(n-k-1)\int_0^1 (1-au)^{-1/\alpha}\int_u^1 (1-av)^{-1/\alpha}\,dv\,du \right\}
$$

$$
= (n-k)\int_0^1 (1-au)^{-2/\alpha}\,du + (n-k)(n-k-1)
$$

$$
\times\begin{cases} \dfrac{2}{a(1-1/\alpha)}\left(\displaystyle\int_0^1 (1-au)^{1-2/\alpha}\,du - (1-a)^{1-1/\alpha}\int_0^1 (1-au)^{-1/\alpha}\,du \right), & \text{if } \alpha \neq 1, \\[4mm] \dfrac{\ln^2(1-a)}{a^2}, & \text{if } \alpha = 1, \end{cases}
$$

that is, $m_2(y) = \dfrac{n-k(\alpha)}{\overline{F}(y)} \times \begin{cases} \dfrac{1-\left(\overline{F}(y)\right)^{1-2/\alpha}}{1-2/\alpha}, & \text{if } \alpha \neq 2 \\[4mm] |\ln \overline{F}(y)|, & \text{if } \alpha = 2 \end{cases}$

$$
+ \frac{(n-k(\alpha))(n-k(\alpha)-1)}{\overline{F}^2(y)} \times \begin{cases} \dfrac{\left(1-(\overline{F}(y))^{1-1/\alpha}\right)^2}{(1-1/\alpha)^2}, & \text{if } \alpha \neq 1, \\[4mm] \ln^2(\overline{F}(y)), & \text{if } \alpha = 1, \end{cases}
$$

hence (11.27) and the result given in Proposition 11.1.

▷ *A Pareto distribution for the conditional sum of the largest order statistics*
  Now, let us look at $U_{n-k+1}/(X_{(n-k+1)} = y)$ assuming $k \geq 2$. Its distribution may be computed explicitly via (11.20) that becomes, when taking $i = n - k$ and $j = k$, and for $y \leq x_1 \leq \cdots \leq x_{k-1}$ (h_y being the pdf of a Pareto r.v. with parameters α and y),

$$
f_{X_{(n-k+2)},\ldots,X_{(n)}/X_{(n-k+1)}=y}(x_1,\ldots,x_{k-1})
$$

$$
= \frac{(k-1)!}{(1-F(y))^{k-1}}\prod_{l=1}^{k-1}f(x_l) = \frac{(k-1)!\,\alpha^{k-1}}{y^{-\alpha(k-1)}}\prod_{l=1}^{k-1}x_l^{-\alpha-1},
$$

that is, $f_{X_{(n-k+2)},\ldots,X_{(n)}/X_{(n-k+1)}=y}(x_1,\ldots,x_{k-1}) = (k-1)!\prod_{l=1}^{k-1}h_y(x_l)\,\mathbb{1}_{(x_1\leq\cdots\leq x_{k-1})}.$

We deduce, taking into account the number of possible permutations, that the conditional density of the sum U_{n-k+1} given $(X_{(n-k+1)} = y)$ is defined, $\forall s \geq (k-1)y$, by

$$
f_{U_{n-k+1}/(X_{(n-k+1)}=y)}(s) = h_y^{(k-1)*}(s). \tag{11.30}
$$

Note that we could have retrieved this conditional density, noticing, as previously for T_k, that $U_{n-k+1}/X_{(n-k+1)}$ can be written as $U_{n-k+1}/X_{(n-k+1)} \overset{d}{=} \sum_{j=1}^{k-1} Z_j$ where the Z_j are i.i.d. r.v.'s with parent r.v. Z and parent cdf defined by $F_Z(\cdot) = \mathbb{P}[X \leq \cdot \ / \ X > X_{(n-k+1)}]$.

▷ Combining Proposition 11.1 and (11.30), (11.28), and (11.29) allows to conclude to Theorem 11.2.

11.3.2.2 On the quality of the approximation of the distribution of the Pareto sum S_n

To estimate the quality of the approximation of the distribution of the Pareto sum S_n, we compare analytically the exact distribution of S_n with the distribution $G_{n,\alpha;k}$ defined in Theorem 11.2. It could also be done numerically, as, for instance, in Furrer (2012) with the distance between two distributions F and G defined by $d_i(F, G) = \int_1^\infty |F(x) - G(x)|^i dx$, with $i = 1, 2$. We will proceed numerically only when considering the tail of the distributions and estimating the distance in the tails through the VaR measure (see Section 11.4.3). When looking at the entire distributions, we will focus on the analytical comparison mainly for the case $\alpha > 2$ (with some hints for the case $\alpha \leq 2$). Note that it is not possible to compare directly the expressions of the VaR corresponding to, respectively, the exact and approximative distributions, since they can only be expressed as the inverse function of a cdf. Nevertheless, we can compare the tails of these two distributions to calibrate the accuracy of the approximative VaR since

$$|\mathbb{P}(S_n > x) - \overline{G}_{n,\alpha;k}(x)| = |\mathbb{P}(S_n \leq x) - G_{n,\alpha;k}(x)|.$$

Moreover, we will compare analytically our result with a normal approximation made on the entire sum (and not the trimmed one) since, for $\alpha > 2$, the CLT applies and, as already noticed, is often used in practice.

Since Normex uses the exact distribution of the last upper order statistics, comparing the true distribution of S_n with its approximation $G_{n,\alpha;k}$ simply comes back to the comparison of the true distribution of $n - k$ i.i.d. r.v.'s with the normal distribution (when applying the CLT). Note that, when extending Normex to any distribution, an error term should be added to this latter evaluation; it comes from the approximation of the extreme distribution by a Pareto one.

Suppose $\alpha > 2$. Applying the CLT gives the normal approximation $\mathcal{N}(\mu_n, s_n^2)$, with $\mu_n := \mathbb{E}(S_n)$ and $s_n^2 := var(S_n)$, where in the case of a Pareto sum, $\mu_n = \frac{n\alpha}{\alpha-1}$, and $s_n^2 = \frac{n\alpha}{(\alpha-1)^2(\alpha-2)}$. We know that applying the CLT directly to S_n leads to nonsatisfactory results even for the mean behavior, since, for any x, the quantity $Q_1(x)$, involving the third moment of X and appearing in the error (11.11) made when approximating the exact distribution of S_n by a normal one, is infinite for any $2 < \alpha \leq 3$. The rate of convergence in n is reduced to $O(1)$. When $\alpha > 3$, even if the rate of convergence improves because $Q_1(x) < \infty$, we still have $Q_2(x) = \infty$ (because the fourth moment of X does not exist), which means that we cannot get a rate of order $1/n$.

Now let us look at the rate of convergence when approximating S_n with $G_{n,\alpha;k}$.

Considering the exact distribution of the Pareto sum S_n means taking, at given $y > 1$ and for any $k \geq 1$, $T_k \leq x - y \;/\; (X_{(n-k+1)} = y) \overset{d}{=} \sum_{j=1}^{n-k} Y_j$ with Y_j i.i.d. r.v.'s with parent r.v. Y with finite pth moment and pdf g defined, for $z \leq (n-k)y$, by

$$f_{T_k / X_{(n-k+1)} = y}(z) = g^{(n-k)*}(z) \text{ with } g(u) = \frac{\alpha}{F(y)} \, u^{-\alpha-1} \, \mathbb{1}_{(1 \leq u \leq y)}.$$

Let us look at the three first moments of Y. The direct dependence is on α (and y) and indirectly on k since $k = k(\alpha)$. We have

$$\mu_y := \mathbb{E}(Y) = \frac{m_1(\alpha, n, k; y)}{n-k} = \frac{1}{1 - 1/\alpha} \times \frac{1 - y^{1-\alpha}}{1 - y^{-\alpha}} \mathbb{1}_{(\alpha \neq 1)} + \frac{\ln(y)}{1 - y^{-1}} \mathbb{1}_{(\alpha=1)}$$

(11.31)

(note that $\mu_y > 1$, for any α that we consider, and any $y > 1$) and

$$\gamma_y^2 := var(Y) = \frac{\sigma^2(\alpha, n, k; y)}{n-k} = \frac{1}{1 - y^{-\alpha}} \left(\frac{1 - y^{2-\alpha}}{1 - 2/\alpha} - \frac{1}{(1 - 1/\alpha)^2} \times \frac{(1 - y^{1-\alpha})^2}{1 - y^{-\alpha}} \right) \mathbb{1}_{(\alpha \neq 1,2)}$$

$$+ y \left(1 - \frac{y \ln^2(y)}{(y-1)^2} \right) \mathbb{1}_{(\alpha=1)} + 2 \frac{y^2}{y^2 - 1} \left(\ln(y) - 2 \frac{y-1}{y+1} \right) \mathbb{1}_{(\alpha=2)},$$

(11.32)

using the expressions of $m_1(\alpha, n, k; y)$ and $\sigma^2(\alpha, n, k; y)$ given in Theorem 11.2. A straightforward computation of the third centered moment of Y provides

$$\mathbb{E}(|Y - \mu_y|^3) = \frac{\alpha}{1 - y^{-\alpha}} [2h(\mu) - h(1) - h(y)],$$

(11.33)

where h denotes the antiderivative of the function $H(z) = (\mu^3 - 3\mu^2 z + 3\mu z^2 - z^3) z^{-\alpha-1}$, that is, if $\alpha \neq 1, 2$,

$$\mathbb{E}(|Y - \mu_y|^3) = \frac{\alpha}{1 - y^{-\alpha}} \left[\frac{\mathbb{1}_{(\alpha \neq 3)}}{3 - \alpha} y^{3-\alpha} + \mathbb{1}_{(\alpha=3)} \ln(y) + \frac{3\mu_y}{\alpha - 2} y^{2-\alpha} - \frac{3\mu_y^2}{\alpha - 1} y^{1-\alpha} \right.$$

$$+ \frac{\mu_y^3}{\alpha} y^{-\alpha} + \frac{12 \, \mu_y^{3-\alpha} \, \mathbb{1}_{(\alpha \neq 3)}}{\alpha(\alpha-1)(\alpha-2)(\alpha-3)} - \left(2 \ln \mu_y + \frac{11}{3} \right) \mathbb{1}_{(\alpha=3)}$$

$$\left. + \frac{\mu_y^3}{\alpha} - \frac{3\mu_y^2}{\alpha-1} + \frac{3\mu_y}{\alpha-2} - \frac{\mathbb{1}_{(\alpha \neq 3)}}{\alpha-3} \right],$$

whereas, if $\alpha = 1$,

$$\mathbb{E}(|Y - \mu_y|^3) = \frac{1}{(1 - y^{-1})^2} \left[\frac{y^2}{2} - y \left(\frac{1}{2} + 3 \ln(y) \right) + \frac{\ln^3(y)}{1 - y^{-1}} \left(3 + \frac{1}{y-1} + \frac{1}{1-y^{-1}} \right) \right.$$

$$\left. + \frac{3\ln^2(y)}{1 - y^{-1}} \left[1 - 2\ln_2(y) + 2 \ln(1 - y^{-1}) \right] - 3 \ln(y) + \frac{1 - y^{-1}}{2} \right],$$

and, if $\alpha = 2$,

$$\mathbb{E}(|Y - \mu_y|^3) = \frac{4}{1 - y^{-1}} \left[\frac{2y}{1 + y^{-1}} - 3\ln(y) - \frac{6}{1 + y} + \frac{2}{(1 + y)^2} + \frac{1 + y^{-1}}{2} \right.$$
$$\left. + 3\left(1 + 2\ln 2 - 2\ln(1 + y^{-1})\right) - \frac{6}{1 + y^{-1}} + \frac{2}{(1 + y^{-1})^2} \right].$$

For simplicity, let us look at the case $2 < \alpha \leq 3$ and consider the Berry–Esséen inequality. For $\alpha > 3$, we would use the Edgeworth expansion, with similar arguments as developed later. Various authors have worked on this type of Berry–Esséen inequality, in particular to sharpen the accuracy of the constant appearing in it. In the case of Berry–Esséen bounds, the value of the constant factor c has decreased from 7.59 by Esséen (1942) to 0.4785 by Tyurin (2010), to 0.4690 by Shevtsova (2013) in the i.i.d. case, and to 0.5600 in the general case. Note also that these past decades, much literature ((Stein, 1972, 1986); (Chen and Shao, 2004); (Cai, 2012); (Pinelis, 2013), etc.) has been dedicated to the generalization of this type of inequality, such as the remarkable contribution by Stein.

We can propose the following bound.

PROPOSITION 11.2 *Suppose $2 < \alpha \leq 3$. Then the error between the true distribution of S_n and its approximation $G_{n,\alpha;1}$ is bounded by*

$$\left|\mathbb{P}(S_n \leq x) - G_{n,\alpha;1}(x)\right| \leq K(x) = \frac{c}{\sqrt{n-1}} \int_1^x \frac{C(y)}{\left(1 + \left|\frac{x - y - (n-1)\mu_y}{\sqrt{n-1}\ \gamma_y}\right|\right)^3} f_{(n)}(y)dy,$$

where $c = 0.4690$, μ_y, and γ_y are given in (11.31) and (11.32), respectively, $f_{(n)}(x) = n\alpha(1 - x^{-\alpha})^{n-1}x^{-\alpha-1} \mathbb{I}_{(x>1)}$, and

$$C(y) := \frac{\mathbb{E}(|Y - \mu_y|^3)}{\gamma_y^3}, \text{with } \mathbb{E}(|Y - \mu_y|^3) \text{ given in (11.33).} \tag{11.34}$$

Moreover, for any $n \geq 52$ and $\alpha \in (2;3]$, $0 \leq \max\limits_{x>1} K(x) < 5\%$ and K decreases very fast to 0 after having reached its maximum; the larger n, the faster to 0.

Proof of Proposition 11.2 Since $\alpha > 2$, we only have to consider the case $k = 1$(see Table 11.2). We can write

$$\left|\mathbb{P}(S_n \leq x) - G_{n,\alpha;1}(x)\right|$$

$$\leq \int_1^x \left|\mathbb{P}\left(T_1 \leq x - y \ / \ X_{(n)} = y\right) - \Phi_{(n-1)\mu_y,(n-1)\gamma_y^2}(x - y)\right| f_{(n)}(y)dy.$$

Since the conditions on moments of Y are satisfied, we can use the Berry–Esséen inequality to provide a nonuniform bound of the error made when approximating the exact distribution by $G_{n,\alpha;1}$. Indeed, we have

$$|\mathbb{P}(T_1 \leq x - y \; / \; X_{(n)} = y) - \Phi_{(n-1)\mu_y,(n-1)\gamma_y^2}(x - y)|$$

$$= \left| \mathbb{P}\left(\frac{\sum\limits_{i=1}^{n-1} Y_i - (n-1)\mu_y}{\sqrt{n-1} \; \gamma_y} \leq \frac{x - y - (n-1)\mu_y}{\sqrt{n-1} \; \gamma_y} \right) - \Phi\left(\frac{x - y - (n-1)\mu_y}{\sqrt{n-1} \; \gamma_y} \right) \right|$$

$$\leq \frac{c \; C(y)}{\sqrt{n-1}} \times \frac{1}{\left(1 + \left| \frac{x-y-(n-1)\mu_y}{\sqrt{n-1} \; \gamma_y} \right| \right)^3},$$

where μ_y, γ_y, and $C(y)$ are defined in (11.31), (11.32), and (11.34), respectively. We can deduce that, for any $x \geq 1$,

$$|\mathbb{P}(S_n \leq x) - G_{n,\alpha;1}(x)| \leq K(x) := \frac{c}{\sqrt{n-1}} \int_1^x \frac{C(y)}{\left(1 + \left| \frac{x-y-(n-1)\mu_y}{\sqrt{n-1} \; \gamma_y} \right| \right)^3} f_{(n)}(y) \; dy,$$

(11.35)

where $f_{(n)}$ is defined in (11.14). We can compute numerically the function $K(\cdot)$ given in (11.35), as there is no known analytical solution for the antiderivative. We use the software R for that.

Note that $K(\cdot)$ depends on the two parameters n and α. We represent this function on a same plot for a given value of α but for various values of n, namely, $n = 52, 100, 250, 500,$ and 1000, respectively, to compare its behavior according to the parameter n. Then we repeat the operation for different $\alpha \in (2; 3]$, namely, for $a = 2.01, 2.5, 3$, respectively (Figure 11.3).

We observe that the bound K is an increasing then decreasing function of x, with a maximum less than 5%, which is decreasing with n and α. The x-coordinate of the maximum is proportional to n, with the proportion decreasing with α. The interval on the x-axis for which the error is larger than 1% has a small amplitude, which is decreasing with α.

We show in Table 11.3 the values of the coordinates $(x_{\max}, y_{\max})$ of the maximum of K computed on R for $\alpha = 2.01, 2.5, 3$ and $n = 52$ (corresponding to aggregating weekly returns to obtain yearly returns), 100, 250 (corresponding to aggregating daily returns to obtain yearly returns), 500, 1000, respectively.

Hence the result of Proposition 11.2.

REMARK 11.1 *Let us briefly look at the case $(1/2 <)\alpha \leq 2$, which implies $k \geq 2$ (see Table 11.2). We obtain in this case the following result:*

$$|\mathbb{P}(S_n \leq x) - G_{n,\alpha;k}| \leq \frac{\tilde{c}}{(n-k)} \int_1^x \frac{C(y)}{\gamma_y} f_{(n-k+1)}(y) \int_0^{x-y} \int f_{U_{n-k+1}/X_{(n-k+1)}=y}(t) \, dt \, dv \, dy,$$

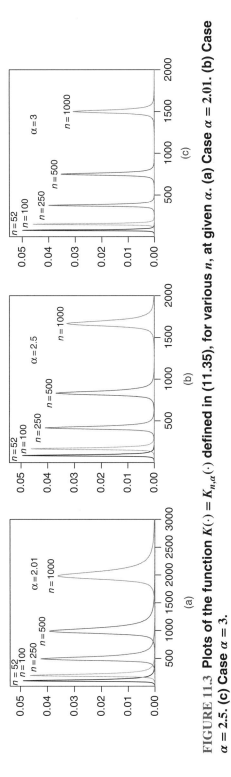

FIGURE 11.3 Plots of the function $K(\cdot) = K_{n,\alpha}(\cdot)$ defined in (11.35), for various n, at given α. **(a)** Case $\alpha = 2.01$. **(b)** Case $\alpha = 2.5$. **(c)** Case $\alpha = 3$.

TABLE 11.3   Coordinates $(x_{\max}, y_{\max})$ of the maximum of K(defined in (11.35)), as a function of n and α

n	$\alpha = 2.01$		$\alpha = 2.5$		$\alpha = 3.0$	
	$x_{\max}$	$y_{\max}(\%)$	$x_{\max}$	$y_{\max}(\%)$	$x_{\max}$	$y_{\max}(\%)$
52	101	4.9	86	4.9	78	4.9
100	196	4.6	166	4.6	150	4.6
250	494	4.2	417	4.1	376	4.0
500	990	3.9	834	3.7	751	3.5
1000	1984	3.6	1667	3.3	1501	3.0

where $\tilde{c} = 0.4014$ (see (Shevtsova, 2007)), $C(y)$ is defined in (11.34), and $f_{(n-k+1)}$ and $f_{U_{n-k+1}/X_{(n-k+1)}=y} = h_y^{(k-1)*}$ are defined in Theorem 11.2.

Indeed, we have

$$|\mathbb{P}(S_n \leq x) - G_{n,\alpha;k}(x)| \leq \int_1^x f_{(n-k+1)}(y) \int_0^{x-y} f_{U_{n-k+1}/X_{(n-k+1)}=y} *$$

$$\left| g^{(n-k)*} - \varphi_{(n-k)\mu_y,(n-k)\gamma_y^2} \right| (v) dv \, dy.$$

Note that the Berry–Esséen inequality has been proved by Petrov to hold also for probability density functions (see (Petrov, 1956) or (Petrov, 1995)). It has been refined by Shevtsova (2007), and we will use her result to evaluate $|g^{(n-k)*} - \varphi_{(n-k)\mu_y,(n-k)\gamma_y^2}|$. We need to go back to the pdf of the standardized sum $\sum_{i=1}^{n-k} \frac{Y_i - \mu_y}{\sqrt{n-k} \, \gamma_y}$ of i.i.d. r.v.'s with pdf $\tilde{g}$, which can be expressed as

$$\tilde{g}^{(n-k)*} \quad \text{where} \quad g(\cdot) = \frac{1}{\sqrt{n-k} \, \gamma_y} \tilde{g}\left(\frac{\cdot - \mu_y}{\sqrt{n-k} \, \gamma_y}\right).$$

It is straightforward to show by induction that

$$g^{(n-k)*}(v) = \frac{1}{\sqrt{n-k} \, \gamma_y} \tilde{g}^{(n-k)*}\left(\frac{v - (n-k)\mu_y}{\sqrt{n-k} \, \gamma_y}\right).$$

Then, since $\varphi_{a,b^2}(x) = \frac{1}{b}\varphi\left(\frac{x-a}{b}\right)$, we can write

$$g^{(n-k)*}(v) - \varphi_{(n-k)\mu_y,(n-k)\gamma_y^2}(v) = \frac{1}{\sqrt{n-k} \, \gamma_y}(\tilde{g}^{(n-k)*} - \varphi)\left(\frac{v - (n-k)\mu_y}{\sqrt{n-k} \, \gamma_y}\right).$$

$$(11.36)$$

Since we consider a sum of $(n-k)$ i.i.d. r.v.'s $Y_i (i = 1, \ldots, n-k)$ with parent r.v. Y having a finite pth moment, we obtain via (Petrov, 1956) and (Shevtsova, 2007) that there exists a constant $\tilde{c} = 0.4014$ such that

$$
\sup_v \left| \left(\tilde{g}^{(n-k)*} - \varphi \right) \left(\frac{v - (n-k)\mu_y}{\sqrt{n-k}\, \gamma_y} \right) \right| = \sup_v |\tilde{g}^{(n-k)*}(v) - \varphi(v)| \leq \frac{\tilde{c}\, C(y)}{\sqrt{n-k}},
$$

$$(11.37)$$

where $C(y)$ is defined in (11.34).

Hence, combining (11.36) and (11.37) gives

$$
\sup_v \left| g^{(n-k)*}(v) - \varphi_{(n-k)\mu_y, (n-k)\gamma_y^2}(v) \right| \leq \frac{\tilde{c}\, C(y)}{(n-k)\gamma_y} = \frac{\tilde{c}}{n-k} \times \frac{\mathbb{E}(|Y - \mu_y|^3)}{\mathrm{var}^2(Y)},
$$

from which we deduce that

$$
|\mathbb{P}(S_n \leq x) - G_{n,\alpha;k}| \leq \frac{\tilde{c}}{(n-k)} \int_1^x \frac{C(y)}{\gamma_y} f_{(n-k+1)}(y) \int_0^{x-y} \int f_{U_{n-k+1}/X_{(n-k+1)}=y}(t) dt \, dv \, dy.
$$

As in the case $k = 1$ (Proposition 11.2), this bound could be computed numerically.

11.3.3 Method 2: A Weighted Normal Limit

In this method, we go back to the first decomposition (11.10) of S_n and use limit theorems for both terms T_k and U_{n-k} instead of proceeding via conditional independence and considering a small given $k = k(\alpha)$. It means that we need to choose k as a function of n such that $k = k(n) \to \infty$ as $n \to \infty$ for the approximation of the distribution of U_{n-k} via its limit to be relevant.

First we consider a normal approximation for the trimmed sum T_k, which implies some conditions on the threshold k (see (Csörgö et al., 1986)). We need to select a threshold k such that

$$
\begin{cases}
k \text{ satisfies} (3.3) \\
k \to \infty \text{ as } n \to \infty \\
k/n \to 0 \text{ as } n \to \infty \text{ or } k = [n\rho] \text{ with } 0 < \rho < 1/2.
\end{cases}
$$

$$(11.38)$$

Note that the condition (11.12) will be implied by the condition $k \underset{n\to\infty}{\to} \infty$. Hence, for this method, k does not depend directly on the value of α.

We can then enunciate the following.

PROPOSITION 11.3 *Take $\alpha > 1/4$. Let $p \geq 2$ and $k = k(n,\alpha)$ satisfy (11.38). The distribution of the trimmed sum T_k defined in (11.10) can be approximated, for large n, by the normal distribution $\mathcal{N}(m_1(\alpha,n,k), \sigma^2(\alpha,n,k))$:*

$$
\mathcal{L}(T_k) \underset{n\to\infty}{\overset{d}{\sim}} \mathcal{N}(m_1(\alpha,n,k), \sigma^2(\alpha,n,k)),
$$

$$(11.39)$$

where the mean $m_1(\alpha, n, k)$ and the variance $\sigma^2(\alpha, n, k)$ are defined, respectively, by

$$m_1(\alpha, n, k) := \sum_{i=1}^{n-k} \mathbb{E}(X_{(i)}) = \sum_{i=1}^{n-k} \frac{n!\Gamma(n-i+1-1/\alpha)}{(n-i)!\Gamma(n+1-1/\alpha)}, \tag{11.40}$$

$$= \sum_{i=1}^{n-k} \prod_{j=0}^{i-1} \frac{n-j}{n-j-1/\alpha}, \tag{11.41}$$

$$\sigma^2(\alpha, n, k) := m_2(\alpha, n, k) - m_1^2(\alpha, n, k), \tag{11.42}$$

with

$$m_2(\alpha, n, k) := \sum_{i=1}^{n-k} \mathbb{E}(X_{(i)}^2) + 2\sum_{j=2}^{n-k}\sum_{i=1}^{j-1} \mathbb{E}(X_{(i)}X_{(j)})$$

$$= \frac{n!}{\Gamma(n+1-2/\alpha)} \left(\sum_{i=1}^{n-k} \frac{\Gamma(n-i+1-2/\alpha)}{(n-i)!} + \right. \tag{11.43}$$

$$\left. 2\sum_{j=2}^{n-k}\sum_{i=1}^{j-1} \frac{\Gamma(n-j+1-1/\alpha)\Gamma(n-i+1-2/\alpha)}{(n-j)!\Gamma(n-i+1-1/\alpha)} \right)$$

$$= \sum_{j=1}^{n-k} \left(\prod_{l=0}^{j-1} \frac{n-l}{n-l-2/\alpha} + 2\sum_{i=1}^{j-1}\prod_{l=0}^{i-1} \frac{n-l}{n-l-2/\alpha} \prod_{l=i}^{j-1} \frac{n-l}{n-l-1/\alpha} \right). \tag{11.44}$$

Note that $k = k(\alpha)$ is chosen in such a way that $\sigma^2(\alpha, n, k)$ is finite. The case $k = 2$ corresponds to the one developed in Zaliapin et al. (but with a different set of definition for α).

Proof of Proposition 11.3 It is sufficient to notice that T_k can be considered as the sum $T_k = \sum_{j=1}^{n-k} X_{(j)} = \sum_{j=1}^{n-k} Y_j$ with (Y_j) an $(n-k)$ sample with parent cdf defined by $F_Y(\cdot) = \mathbb{P}(X_i \leq \cdot \mid X_i < X_{(n-k+1)})$. Hence the CLT applies to T_k when requiring $p \geq 2$. The result follows directly using (11.17) and (11.18) to obtain the first equalities (11.40) and (11.43). The simplified expressions (11.41) and (11.44) come from straightforward computations using the recursive definition of the gamma function for nonnegative real numbers z, namely, $\Gamma(z+1) = z\Gamma(z)$. Indeed we can show by induction that, for $1 \leq i \leq n-k$, and assuming $\alpha \geq \max(1/(k+1), 1/4)$,

$$\Gamma(n+1-1/\alpha) = \prod_{j=0}^{i-1} (n-j-1/\alpha)\Gamma(n-i+1-1/\alpha)$$

from which we deduce that, for $1 \leq i \leq n - k$ with $k \geq 1$, for $\alpha \geq \max(1/(k+1), 1/4)$,

$$\mathbb{E}(X_{(i)}) = h(n, i, 1/\alpha) := \frac{n!}{(n-i)!} \times \frac{\Gamma(n - i + 1 - 1/\alpha)}{\Gamma(n + 1 - 1/\alpha)}$$

$$= \prod_{j=0}^{i-1} \frac{(n-j)}{(n-j-1/\alpha)} \tag{11.45}$$

and so (11.41). Let us proceed in the same way to simplify (11.43). Note that $m_2(\alpha, n, k)$ can be expressed, in terms of the function h introduced previously, as

$$m_2(\alpha, n, k) = h(n, 1, 2/\alpha) + \sum_{j=2}^{n-k} \left(h(n, j, 2/\alpha) + 2 \sum_{i=1}^{j-1} h(n, i, 2/\alpha) \; h(n - i, j - i, 1/\alpha) \right)$$

Therefore, using (11.45), it comes, for $\alpha \geq \max(2/k, 1/4)$,

$$m_2(\alpha, n, k) = \sum_{j=1}^{n-k} \left(\prod_{l=0}^{j-1} \frac{(n-l)}{(n-l-2/\alpha)} + 2 \sum_{i=1}^{j-1} \prod_{l=0}^{i-1} \frac{(n-l)}{(n-l-2/\alpha)} \; \prod_{l=0}^{j-i-1} \frac{(n-i-l)}{(n-i-l-1/\alpha)} \right)$$

$$= \sum_{j=1}^{n-k} \left(\prod_{l=0}^{j-1} \frac{(n-l)}{(n-l-2/\alpha)} + 2 \sum_{i=1}^{j-1} \prod_{l=0}^{i-1} \frac{(n-l)}{(n-l-2/\alpha)} \; \prod_{l=i}^{j-1} \frac{(n-l)}{(n-l-1/\alpha)} \right).$$

Let us turn now to the limit behavior of the partial sum U_{n-k}. The main idea of this method relies on using an estimation (involving the last order statistics) of the expected shortfall $ES(X)$ of X defined for an α-Pareto r.v. by $ES_q(X) = \frac{\alpha}{(\alpha-1)} (1-q)^{-1/\alpha}$, $q \in (0, 1)$ being the confidence level (see Section 11.4.1), in order to propose an approximation for the second term U_{n-k}. So it implies to assume $X \in L^1$, that is, $\alpha > 1$.

Let us recall the following result (see (Acerbi and Tasche, 2002) for the proof or (Embrechts et al., 1997)) that we are going to use.

LEMMA 11.3 *For a sequence $(L_i)_{i \in \mathbb{N}}$ of L^1-i.i.d. r.v.'s with cdf F_L, we have*

$$\lim_{n \to \infty} \frac{\sum_{i=0}^{[n(1-\gamma)]-1} L_{n-i,n}}{[n(1-\gamma)]} = ES_\gamma(L) \quad a.s.$$

where $L_{1,n} \leq \cdots \leq L_{n,n}$ are the order statistics of $L_1, \ldots, L_n$ and where $[n(1-\gamma)]$ denotes the largest integer not exceeding $n(1-\gamma)$, $0 < \gamma < 1$.

In other words, expected shortfall at confidence level γ can be thought of as the limiting average of the $[n(1-\gamma)]$ upper order statistics from a sample of size n from the loss distribution.

Now we can enunciate the main empirical result.

PROPOSITION 11.4   *Let X be a α-Pareto r.v. with cdf (11.1), with α > 2, and $(X_i, i = 1, \ldots, n)$ an n sample with parent r.v. X.*

Let us choose $k = k(n, \gamma)$ with $\gamma = 0.9$, such that

$$k = k(n, \gamma) = [n(1 - \gamma)] = [n/10]. \tag{11.46}$$

The distribution of S_n expressed in (11.10) can be approximated, for any n and any α > 2, by a normal approximation with mean $(m_1(\alpha, n, k) + kES_\gamma)$ and variance $\gamma^2 \sigma^2(\alpha, n, k) \, ES_\gamma^2$:

$$\mathcal{N}(m_1(\alpha, n, k) + k \, ES_\gamma(X), \quad \gamma^2 \sigma^2(\alpha, n, k) \, ES_\gamma^2), \tag{11.47}$$

where $m_1(\alpha, n, k)$, $\sigma^2(\alpha, n, k)$ are defined in (11.40) and (11.41), respectively, and $ES_\gamma(X) = \frac{\alpha}{(\alpha-1)} (1 - \gamma)^{-1/\alpha}$.

Proof of Proposition 11.4   Note that the choice (11.46) of k implies that it satisfies (11.38) with $\rho = 1 - \gamma$ and has been made according to Lemma 11.3 and Csörgö et al. (1986).

We deduce from Lemma 11.3 that U_{n-k} defined in (11.10) satisfies, with k chosen as in (11.46),

$$\frac{U_{n-k}}{k} = \frac{1}{k} \sum_{j=0}^{k-1} X_{(n-j)} \overset{a.s.}{\to} ES_\gamma(X) \quad \text{as } n \to \infty.$$

Recall that if, as $n \to \infty$, $Z_n \overset{d}{\to} Z$, and $W_n \overset{d}{\to} a$, then $Z_n + W_n \overset{d}{\to} Z + a$, for any r.v.'s (Z_n), Z, (W_n) and any constant a. On one hand, by Proposition 11.3, we have $T_k \underset{n\to\infty}{\sim} \mathcal{N}(m_1(\alpha, n, k), \sigma^2(\alpha, n, k))$. On the other hand, we have $U_{n-k} \underset{n\to\infty}{\sim} k \, ES_\gamma(X)$. Therefore, for large n,

$$\mathcal{L}(T_k + U_{n-k}) \overset{d}{\sim} \mathcal{N}(m_1(\alpha, n, k), \sigma^2(\alpha, n, k)) + k \, ES_\gamma(X)$$

$$\overset{d}{=} \mathcal{N}(m_1(\alpha, n, k) + k \, ES_\gamma(X), \sigma^2(\alpha, n, k)).$$

Note that $m_1(\alpha, n, k) + k \, ES_\gamma(X)$ is close to $\mathbb{E}(S_n) = n \, var(X) = m_1(\alpha, n, 0)$ (a bit larger), which makes sense when looking at the tool we used. But the variance $\sigma^2(\alpha, n, k)$ of T_k is too small compared with $var(S_n) = \sigma^2(\alpha, n, 0)$; hence a correction has to be made, of at least the order $var(S_n)/\sigma^2(\alpha, n, k)$, taking into account the number k of extremes we considered, α and ES_γ (as for the mean).

It has been checked numerically that considering a variance as $\gamma^2 \sigma^2(\alpha, n, k) \, ES_\gamma^2$, with $\gamma = 0.9$, allows to get a good approximation of the tail of the distribution of S_n, for any n and any $\alpha > 2$, as seen in the results tables.

Comments

1. This result is interesting since it shows that, even if we want to consider a normal approximation, there must be a correction based on ES_γ and the

number of extremes that we considered, such that both the mean and the variance become larger than the ones of S_n.

2. With the final approximation being normal, its tail distribution is light; hence we do not expect *a priori* an evaluation of the VaR as accurate as the one provided by Normex, but better than the normal one applied directly on S_n. The light tail should still lead to an underestimation of the VaR, but certainly not as gross as the one when applying directly the CLT, because of the correcting term expressed in terms of the ES.

3. We will compare numerically not only the tail approximation with the exact one but also the modified normal approximation with the normal one made directly on S_n.

4. To obtain a good fit requires a calibration of γ. Numerically, it appeared that the value $\gamma = 0.9$ provides a reasonable fit, for any n and any $\alpha > 2$. It is an advantage that γ does not have to be chosen differently, depending on these parameters n and α, in order to keep the generality of the method. The next research step will consist in the analytical evaluation of this method and to generalize it, if possible, to any $\alpha > 0$.

11.4 APPLICATION TO RISK MEASURES AND COMPARISON

11.4.1 Standard Risk Measures Based on Loss Distribution

Variance and standard deviation were historically the dominating risk measures in finance. However, they require the underlying distribution to have a finite second moment and are appropriate for symmetric distributions. Because of this restricted frame, they have often been replaced in practical applications by VaR, which was, until recently, the most popular downside risk measure in finance. VaR started to be criticized for a number of different reasons. Most important are its lack of the subadditivity property and the fact that it completely ignores the severity of losses in the far tail of the loss distribution. The coherent risk measure expected shortfall was introduced to solve these issues. Two years ago, ES has been shown not to be elicitable (Gneiting, 2012). Hence the search, meantime, of coherent and elicitable alternatives, as, for instance, expectiles (Bellini et al., 2013); (Ziegel, 2014). Properties of these popular risk measures, like coherence, comonotonic additivity, robustness, and elicitability, as well as their impact on important issues in risk management like diversification benefit and capital allocation, have been discussed in a recent paper (Emmer et al., 2015).

Here we are going to consider only the risk measures used in solvency calculations (the other risk measures would be treated in the same way), namely, the value-at-risk, denoted VaR, and the expected shorfall (named also tail value-at-risk) ES (or TVaR), of an r.v. X with continuous cdf F_X (and inverse function denoted by $F_X^{\leftarrow}$):

- The value-at-risk of order q of X is simply the quantile of F_X of order q, $q \in (0, 1)$:

$$\text{VaR}_q(X) = \inf\{y \in \mathbb{R} : P[X > y] \le 1 - q\} = F_X^{\leftarrow}(q).$$

- If $\mathbb{E}|X| < \infty$, the expected shortfall (ES) at confidence level $q \in (0, 1)$ is defined as

$$\text{ES}_q(X) = \frac{1}{1 - q} \int_q^1 \text{VaR}_\beta(X) \, d\beta \quad \text{or} \quad \text{ES}_q(X) = \mathbb{E}[X \mid X \ge \text{VaR}_q].$$

We will simplify the notation of those risk measures writing VaR_q or ES_q when no confusion is possible.

Note that, in the case of an α-Pareto distribution, analytical expressions of those two risk measures can be deduced from (11.2), namely,

$$\text{VaR}_q(X) = F^{\leftarrow}(q) = (1 - q)^{-\frac{1}{\alpha}}, \text{ and, if } \alpha > 1, \text{ES}_q(X) \;=\; \frac{\alpha}{(\alpha - 1)}(1 - q)^{-1/\alpha}.$$

Recall also that the shape parameter α totally determines the ratio ES_q/VaR_q when we go far enough out into the tail:

$$\lim_{q \to 1} \frac{\text{ES}_q}{\text{VaR}_q} = (1 - 1/\alpha)^{-1}, \quad \text{if } \alpha > 0 \text{ and } 1 \text{ otherwise.}$$

Note that this result holds also for the GPD with shape parameter $\xi = 1/\alpha$.

When looking at aggregated risks $\sum_{i=1}^n X_i$, it is well known that the risk measure ES is coherent (see (Artzner et al., 1999)). In particular it is subadditive, that is,

$$\text{ES}_q\left(\sum_{i=1}^n X_i\right) \le \sum_{i=1}^n \text{ES}_q(X_i)$$

whereas VaR is not a coherent measure, because it is not subadditive. Indeed many examples can be given where VaR is superadditive, that is,

$$\text{VaR}_q\left(\sum_{i=1}^n X_i\right) \ge \sum_{i=1}^n \text{VaR}_q(X_i)$$

see, e.g., Embrechts et al., (2009), Daníelsson et al., (2005).

PROPOSITION 11.5 (Embrechts et al., 2009) *Consider i.i.d. r.v.'s X_i, $i = 1, \dots, n$ with parent r.v. X and cdf F_X. Assume they are regularly varying with tail index $\beta > 0$, which means that the right tail $1 - F_X$ of its distribution satisfies*

$$\lim_{x \to \infty} \frac{1 - F_X(ax)}{1 - F_X(x)} = a^{-\beta}, \quad \forall a > 0.$$

Then the risk measure VaR is asymptotically subadditive for $X_1, \ldots, X_n$ if and only if $\beta \geq 1$:

$$\lim_{q \nearrow 1} \frac{\mathrm{VaR}_q \left(\sum_{i=1}^{n} X_i \right)}{\sum_{i=1}^{n} \mathrm{VaR}_q(X_i)} \leq 1 \iff \beta \geq 1.$$

In the case of α-Pareto i.i.d. r.v.'s, the risk measure VaR is asymptotically superadditive (subadditive, respectively) if $\alpha \in (0, 1)(\alpha \geq 1$, respectively).

Recently, numerical and analytical techniques have been developed in order to evaluate the risk measures VaR and ES under different dependence assumptions regarding the loss r.v.'s. It certainly helps for a better understanding of the aggregation and diversification properties of risk measures, in particular of non-coherent ones such as VaR. We will not review these techniques and results in this report, but refer to Embrechts et al. (2013) for an overview and references therein. Let us add to those references some recent work by Mikosch and Wintenberger (2013) on large deviations under dependence which allows an evaluation of VaR. Nevertheless, it is worth mentioning a new numerical algorithm that has been introduced by Embrechts et al., (2013), which allows for the computation of reliable lower and upper bounds for the VaR of high-dimensional (inhomogeneous) portfolios, whatever the dependence structure is.

11.4.2 Possible Approximations of VaR

As an example, we treat the case of one of the two main risk measures and choose the VaR, since it is the main one used for solvency requirement. We would proceed in the same way for the expected shortfall.

It is straightforward to deduce, from the various limit theorems, the approximations $z_q^{(i)}$ of the VaR of order q of the aggregated risks, $\mathrm{VaR}_q(S_n)$, that is, the quantile of order q of the sum S_n defined by $\mathbb{P}[S_n \leq \mathrm{VaR}_q(S_n)] = q$. The index (i) indicates the chosen method, namely, (i) for the GCLT approach, (ii) for the CLT one, (iii) for the max one, (iv) for the Zaliapin et al.'s method, (v) for Normex, and (vi) for the weighted normal limit. We obtain the following:

▷ Via the GCLT, for $0 < \alpha \leq 2$:

  −For $\alpha < 2$, via (2.1) :

  $z_q^{(1)} = n^{1/\alpha} C_\alpha \, G_\alpha^{\leftarrow}(q) + b_n$ (G_α being the limiting normalized α−stable,

  distribution in (2.1)) which, for large quantiles ($q > 0.95$),

  may be approximated, using (2.3), by $z_q^{(1bis)} = n^{1/\alpha}(1 - q)^{-1/\alpha} + b_n$;

  (see Zaliapin et al. (2005)).

  −For $\alpha = 2$, via (2.2) :

  $z_q^{(1)} = d_n \, \Phi^{\leftarrow}(q) + 2n.$

▷ Via the CLT, for $\alpha > 2$ (see (11.5)):

$$z_q^{(2)} = \frac{\sqrt{n\alpha}}{(\alpha-1)\sqrt{\alpha-2}} \ \Phi^{\leftarrow}(q) + \frac{n\alpha}{\alpha-1}.$$

▷ Via the Max (EVT) approach, using (11.9), for high-order q, for any positive α,

$$z_q^{(3)} = n^{1/\alpha}(\log(1/q))^{-1/\alpha} + b_n.$$

▷ Via the Zaliapin et al.'s method (Zaliapin et al., 2005), for $2/3 < \alpha < 2$:

$$z_q^{(4)} = (\sigma(\alpha, n, 2) \ \Phi^{\leftarrow}(q) + m_1(\alpha, n, 2)) \ + \ T_{\alpha,n}^{\leftarrow}(q)$$

$$\text{with } T_{\alpha,n} \text{ the cdf of } (X_{(n-1)} + X_{(n)}).$$

▷ Via Normex, for any positive α, and k satisfying (11.13):

$$z_q^{(5)} = G_{n,\alpha,k}^{\leftarrow}(q) \text{ with } G_{n,\alpha,k} \text{defined in Theorem 11.2, namely,}$$

$$G_{n,\alpha,k}(x) = \int_1^x \frac{f_{(n-k+1)}(y)}{\sigma(y)} \int_0^{x-y} \left(\int_0^v \varphi\left(\frac{v-u-m_1(y)}{\sigma(y)}\right) h_y^{\star(k-1)}(u)du \right) dv \ dy.$$

▷ Via the weighted normal limit, for $\alpha > 2$ (see (11.47)):

$$z_q^{(6)} = \gamma \ ES_\gamma \ \sigma(\alpha, n, k) \ \Phi^{\leftarrow}(q) \ + m_1(\alpha, n, k) + k \ ES_\gamma$$

$$\text{with } k = [n(1-\gamma)], \gamma = 0.9, ES_\gamma = \frac{\alpha}{(\alpha-1)} \ (1-\gamma)^{-1/\alpha},$$

$$m_1(\alpha, n, k) \text{ and } \sigma^2(\alpha, n, k) \text{ defined in (3.32) and (3.33), respectively.}$$

11.4.3 Numerical Study: Comparison of the Methods

Since there is no explicit analytical formula for the true quantiles of S_n, we will complete the analytical comparison of the distributions of S_n and $G_{n,\alpha,k}$ given in Section 11.3.2.2, providing here a numerical comparison between the quantile of S_n and the quantiles obtained by the various methods seen so far.

Nevertheless, in the case $\alpha > 2$, we can compare analytically the VaR obtained when doing a rough normal approximation directly on S_n, namely, $z_q^{(2)}$, with the one obtained via the shifted normal method, namely, $z_q^{(6)}$. So, we obtain the correcting term to the CLT as

$$z_q^{(6)} - z_q^{(2)} = \left(\frac{\gamma}{(1-\gamma)^{1/\alpha}} \frac{\alpha}{\alpha-1} \sigma(\alpha, n, k) - \frac{\sqrt{n\alpha}}{(\alpha-1)\sqrt{\alpha-2}} \right) \Phi^{\leftarrow}(q)$$

$$+ m_1(\alpha, n, k) + \frac{n\alpha}{\alpha-1} \left(\frac{[n(1-\gamma)]}{n} (1-\gamma)^{-1/\alpha} - 1 \right).$$

11.4.3.1 Presentation of the study

We simulate $(X_i, i = 1, \ldots, n)$ with parent r.v. X α-Pareto distributed, with different sample sizes, varying from $n = 52$ (corresponding to aggregating weekly returns to obtain yearly returns) through $n = 250$ (corresponding to aggregating daily returns to obtain yearly returns) to $n = 500$ representing a large size portfolio.

We consider different shape parameters, namely, $\alpha = 3/2; 2; 5/2; 3; 4$, respectively. Recall that simulated Pareto r.v.'s X_i's $(i \geq 1)$ can be obtained simulating a uniform r.v. U on $(0, 1]$ and then applying the transformation $X_i = U^{-1/\alpha}$.

For each n and each α, we aggregate the realizations x_i's $(i = 1, \ldots, n)$. We repeat the operation $N = 10^7$ times, thus obtaining 10^7 realizations of the Pareto sum S_n, from which we can estimate its quantiles.

Let z_q denote the empirical quantile of order q of the Pareto sum S_n (associated with the empirical cdf F_{S_n} and pdf f_{S_n}) defined by

$$z_q := \inf\{t \mid F_{S_n}(t) \geq q\}, \quad \text{with } 0 < q < 1.$$

Recall, for completeness, that the empirical quantile of S_n converges to the true quantile as $N \to \infty$ and has an asymptotic normal behavior, from which we deduce the following confidence interval at probability a for the true quantile: $z_q \pm \Phi^{\leftarrow}(a/2) \times \frac{\sqrt{q(1-q)}}{f_{S_n}(q)\sqrt{N}}$, where f_{S_n} can be empirically estimated for such a large N. We do not compute them numerically: N being very large, bounds are close.

We compute the values of the quantiles of order q, $z_q^{(i)}$ ((i) indicating the chosen method), obtained by the main methods, the GCLT method, the Max one, Normex, and the weighted normal method, respectively. We do it for various values of α and n. We compare them with the (empirical) quantile z_q obtained via Pareto simulations (estimating the true quantile). For that, we introduce the approximative relative error:

$$\delta^{(i)} = \delta^{(i)}(q) = \frac{z_q^{(i)}}{z_q} - 1.$$

We consider three possible order q: 95%, 99% (threshold for Basel II) and 99.5% (threshold for Solvency 2).

We use the software R to perform this numerical study, with different available packages. Let us particularly mention the use of the procedure *Vegas* in the package *R2Cuba* for the computation of the double integrals. This procedure turns out not to be always very stable for the most extreme quantiles, mainly for low values of α. In practice, for the computation of integrals, we would advise to test various procedures in R2Cuba (Suave, Divonne, and Cuhre, besides Vegas) or to look for other packages. Another possibility would be implementing the algorithm using altogether a different software, as, for example, Python.

11.4.3.2 Estimation of the VaR with the various methods

All codes and results are obtained for various n and α are given in Kratz (2013) (available upon request) and will draw conclusions based on all the results.

We start with a first example when $\alpha > 2$ to illustrate our main focus, when looking at data under the presence of moderate heavy tail. We present here the case $\alpha = 5/2$ in Table 11.4.

Let us also illustrate in table 11.5 the heavy tail case, choosing, for instance, $\alpha = 3/2$, which means that $k = 2$. Take, for example, $n = 52,100$ respectively, to illustrate the fit of Normex even for small samples. Note that the weighted normal does not apply here since $\alpha < 2$.

11.4.3.3 Discussion of the results

- Those numerical results are subject to numerical errors due to the finite sample of simulation of the theoretical value, as well as the choice of random generators, but the most important reason for numerical error of our methods resides in the convergence of the integration methods. Thus, one should read the results, even if reported with many significant digits, to a confidence we estimate to be around 0.1% (also for the empirical quantiles).

- The Max method overestimates for $\alpha < 2$ and underestimates for $\alpha \geq 2$; it improves a bit for higher quantiles and $\alpha \leq 2$. It is a method that practitioners should think about when wanting to have a first idea on the range of the VaR, because it is very simple to use and costless in terms of computations. Then they should turn to Normex for an accurate estimation.

- The GCLT method ($\alpha < 2$) overestimates the quantiles but improves with higher quantiles and when n increases.

- Concerning the CLT method ($\alpha \geq 2$), we find out that:
  - The higher the quantile, the higher the underestimation; it improves slightly when n increases, as expected.
  - The smaller α, the larger the underestimation.
  - The estimation improves for smaller-order q of the quantile and large $n(\geq 500)$, as expected, since, with smaller order, we are less in the upper tail.
  - The VaR estimated with the normal approximation is almost always lower than the VaR estimated via Normex or the weighted normal method. The lower n and α, the higher the difference with Normex.
  - The difference between the VaR estimated by the CLT and the one estimated with Normex appears large for relatively small n, with a relative error going up to 13%, and decreases when n becomes larger.

- With the Weighted Normal method ($\alpha > 2$), it appears that:

TABLE 11.4 **Approximations of extreme quantiles (95%; 99%; 99.5%) by various methods (CLT, Max, Normex, weighted normal) and associated approximative relative error to the empirical quantile** z_q**, for** $n = 52, 100, 250, 500$ **respectively, and** $\alpha = 2.5$

$n = 52$	Simul	CLT	Max	Normex	Weighted normal
q	z_q	$z_q^{(2)}$ $\delta^{(1)}(\%)$	$z_q^{(3)}$ $\delta^{(3)}(\%)$	$z_q^{(5)}$ $\delta^{(5)}(\%)$	$z_q^{(6)}$ $\delta^{(6)}(\%)$
95%	103.23	104.35	102.60	103.17	109.25
		1.08	−0.61	**−0.06**	5.83
99%	119.08	111.67	117.25	119.11	118.57
		−6.22	−1.54	**0.03**	−0.43
99.5%	128.66	114.35	127.07	131.5	121.98
		−11.12	**−1.24**	2.21	−5.19
$n = 100$	Simul	CLT	Max	Normex	Weighted normal
q	z_q	$z_q^{(2)}$ $\delta^{(1)}(\%)$	$z_q^{(3)}$ $\delta^{(3)}(\%)$	$z_q^{(5)}$ $\delta^{(5)}(\%)$	$z_q^{(6)}$ $\delta^{(6)}(\%)$
95%	189.98	191.19	187.37	189.84	197.25
		0.63	−1.38	**−0.07**	3.83
99%	210.54	201.35	206.40	209.98	209.74
		−4.36	−1.96	**−0.27**	−0.38
99.5%	222.73	205.06	219.14	223.77	214.31
		−7.93	−1.61	**0.47**	−3.78
$n = 250$	Simul	CLT	Max	Normex	Weighted normal
q	z_q	$z_q^{(2)}$ $\delta^{(1)}(\%)$	$z_q^{(3)}$ $\delta^{(3)}(\%)$	$z_q^{(5)}$ $\delta^{(5)}(\%)$	$z_q^{(6)}$ $\delta^{(6)}(\%)$
95%	454.76	455.44	446.53	453.92	464.28
		0.17	−1.81	**−0.18**	2.09
99%	484.48	471.5	473.99	483.27	483.83
		−2.68	−2.17	−0.25	**−0.13**
99.5%	501.02	477.38	492.38	501.31	490.98
		−4.72	−1.73	**0.06**	−2.00
$n = 500$	Simul	CLT	Max	Normex	Weighted normal
q	z_q	$z_q^{(2)}$ $\delta^{(1)}(\%)$	$z_q^{(3)}$ $\delta^{(3)}(\%)$	$z_q^{(5)}$ $\delta^{(5)}(\%)$	$z_q^{(6)}$ $\delta^{(6)}(\%)$
95%	888.00	888.16	872.74	886.07	900.26
		0.02	−1.72	−0.22	1.38
99%	928.80	910.88	908.97	925.19	927.80
		−1.93	−2.14	−0.39	**−0.11**
99.5%	950.90	919.19	933.23	948.31	937.89
		−3.33	−1.86	**−0.27**	−1.37

TABLE 11.5   **Approximations of extreme quantiles (95%; 99%; 99.5%) by various methods (GCLT, Max, Normex) and associated approximative relative error to the empirical quantile** z_q**, for** $n = 52, 100$**, respectively, and for** $\alpha = 3/2$

$n = 52$	Simul	GCLT	Max	Normex
q	z_q	$z_q^{(1)}$ $\delta^{(1)}(\%)$	$z_q^{(3)}$ $\delta^{(3)}(\%)$	$z_q^{(5)}$ $\delta^{(5)}(\%)$
95%	246.21	280.02	256.92	245.86
		13.73	4.35	**−0.14**
99%	450.74	481.30	455.15	453.92
		6.78	0.97	**0.71**
99.5%	629.67	657.91	631.66	645.60
		4.48	**0.31**	2.53

$n = 100$	Simul	GCLT	Max	Normex
q	z_q	$z_q^{(1)}$ $\delta^{(1)}(\%)$	$z_q^{(3)}$ $\delta^{(3)}(\%)$	$z_q^{(5)}$ $\delta^{(5)}(\%)$
95%	442.41	491.79	456.06	443.08
		11.16	3.09	**0.15**
99%	757.82	803.05	762.61	761.66
		5.97	0.63	**0.51**
99.5%	1031.56	1076.18	1035.58	1032.15
		4.33	0.39	**0.06**

- The method overestimates the 95% quantile but is quite good for the 99% one. In general, the estimation of the two upper quantiles improve considerably when compared with the ones obtained via a straightforward application of the CLT.

- The estimation of the quantiles improve with increasing n and increasing α.

- The results are generally not as sharp as the ones obtained via Normex, but better than the ones obtained with the max method, whenever $\alpha \geq 3$.

• Concerning Normex, we find out that:
  - The accuracy of the results appears more or less independent of the sample size n, which is the major advantage of our method when dealing with the issue of aggregation.

  - For $\alpha > 2$, it always gives sharp results (error less than 0.5% and often extremely close); for most of them, the estimation is indiscernible from the empirical quantile, obviously better than the ones obtained with the other methods.

  - For $\alpha \leq 2$, the results for the most extreme quantile are slightly less satisfactory than expected. We attribute this to a numerical instability in the integration procedure used in R. Indeed, for very large quantiles ($\geq 99.5\%$), the convergence of the integral seems a bit more unstable (due to the use of the package Vegas in R), which may explain why the accuracy decreases a bit and may sometimes be less than with the

Max method. This issue should be settled using other R-package or software.

- We have concentrated our study on the VaR risk measure because it is the one used in solvency regulations both for banks and insurances. However, the expected shortfall, which is the only coherent measure in presence of fat tails, would be more appropriate for measuring the risk of the companies. The difference between the risk measure estimated by the CLT and the one estimated with Normex would certainly be much larger than what we obtain with the VaR when the risk is measured with the expected shortfall, pleading for using this measure in presence of fat tails.

11.4.3.4 Normex in practice

From the results we obtained, Normex appears as the best method among the ones we studied, applicable for any n and $\alpha > 0$. This comparison was done on simulated data. A next step will be to apply it on real data.

Let us sketch up a step-by-step procedure on how Normex might be used and interpreted in practice on real data when considering aggregated heavy-tailed risks.

We dispose of a sample $(X_1, \ldots, X_n)$, with unknown heavy-tailed cdf having positive tail index α. We order the sample as $X_{(1)} \leq X_{(2)} \leq \cdots \leq X_{(n)}$ and consider the aggregated risks $S_n := \sum_{i=1}^{n} X_i$ that can be rewritten as $S_n = \sum_{i=1}^{n} X_{(i)}$.

1. Preliminary step: Estimation of α, with standard EVT methods (e.g., Hill estimator (Hill, 1975)), QQ-estimator (Kratz and Resnick, 1996); (Beirlant et al., 1996)), etc.); let $\hat{\alpha}$ be denoted as an estimate of α.

2. Define $k = [p/\hat{\alpha} - 1] + 1$ with $p = 4$(see (11.13)); the k largest order statistics share the property of having a pth infinite moment, contrary to the $n - k$ first ones. Note that k is independent of the aggregation size.

3. The $n - k$ first order statistics and the $k - 1$ last ones being, conditionally on $X_{(n-k+1)}$, independent, we apply the CLT to the sum of the $n - k$ first order statistics conditionally on $X_{(n-k+1)}$ and compute the distribution of the sum of the last $k - 1$ ones conditionally on $X_{(n-k+1)}$ assuming a Pareto distribution for the r.v.'s because of (11.3).

4. We can then approximate the cdf of S_n by $G_{n,\alpha,k}$ defined in Theorem 11.2, which provides a sharp approximation, easily computable whatever the size of the sample is.

5. We deduce any quantile z_q of order q of S_n as $z_q = G_{n,\alpha,k}^{\leftarrow}(q)$, which allows an accurate evaluation of risk measures of aggregated heavy-tailed risks.

11.5 CONCLUSION

The main motivation of this study was to propose a sharp approximation of the entire distribution of aggregate risks when working on financial or insurance data under the presence of fat tails. It corresponds to one of the daily duties of actuaries when modeling investment or insurance portfolios. In particular the aim is to obtain the most accurate evaluations of risk measures. After reviewing the existing methods, we built two new methods, *Normex* and the weighted normal method. *Normex* is a method mixing a CLT and the exact distribution for a small number (defined according to the range of α and the choice of the number of existing moments of order p) of the largest order statistics. The second approach is based on a *weighted normal* limit, with a shifted mean and a weighted variance, both expressed in terms of the tail distribution.

In this study, Normex has been proved, theoretically as well as numerically, to deliver a sharp approximation of the true distribution, for any sample size n and for any positive tail index α, and is generally better than existing methods. The weighted normal method consists of trimming the total sum by taking away a large number of extremes and approximating the trimmed sum with a normal distribution and then shifting it by the (almost sure) limit of the average of the extremes and correcting the variance with a weight depending on the shape of the tail. It is a simple and reasonable tool, which allows to express explicitly the tail contribution to be added to the VaR when applying the CLT to the entire sample. It has been developed empirically in this work and still requires further analytical study. It constitutes a simple and exploratory tool to remediate the underestimation of extreme quantiles over 99% .

An advantage of both methods, Normex and the weighted normal, is their generality. Indeed, trimming the total sum by taking away extremes having infinite moments (of order $p \geq 3$) is always possible and allows to better approximate the distribution of the trimmed sum with a normal one (via the CLT). Moreover, fitting a normal distribution for the mean behavior can apply, not only for the Pareto distribution but for any underlying distribution, without having to know about it, whereas for the extreme behavior, we pointed out that a Pareto type is standard in this context.

Normex could also be used from another point of view. We could apply it for a type of inverse problem to find out a range for the tail index α when fitting this explicit mixed distribution to the empirical one. Note that this topic of tail index estimation has been studied extensively in the literature on the statistics of extremes (see, e.g., (Beirlant et al., 2004); (Reiss and Thomas, 2007), and references therein). Approaches to this estimation may be classified into two classes, supervised procedures in which the threshold to estimate the tail is chosen according to the problem (as, e.g., for seminal references, the weighted moments (Hosking and Wallis, 1987)), the MEP (Davison and Smith, 1990); (Hill, 1975), QQ (Kratz and Resnick, 1996); (Beirlant et al., 1996)) methods, and unsupervised ones, where the threshold is algorithmically determined (as, e.g., in (Bengio and Carreau, 2009) and references therein, (Debbabi and Kratz, 2014)). Normex would then be classified as a new unsupervised approach, since the k is chosen algorithmically for a range of α.

Other perspectives concern the application of this study to real data, its extension to the dependent case, using CLT under weak dependence and some recent results on stable limits for sums of dependent infinite variance r.v. from

Bartkiewicz et al. (2012) and large deviation principles from (Mikosch and Wintenberger, 2013).

Finally this study may constitute a first step in understanding the behavior of VaR under aggregation and be helpful in analyzing the scaling behavior of VaR under aggregation, next important problem that we want to tackle.

References

Acerbi, C., Tasche, D. On the coherence of expected shortfall. Journal of Banking & Finance 2002;**26**:1487–1503.

Artzner, P., Delbaen, F., Eber, J.-M., Heath, D. Coherent measures of risks. Mathematical Finance 1999;**9**:203–228.

Bartkiewicz, K., Jakubowski, A., Mikosch, T., Wintenberger, O. Stable limits for sums of dependent infinite variance random variables. Probab Theory Relat Fields 2012;**150**:337–372.

Basel Committee on Banking Supervision. Developments in modelling risk aggregation. *Basel: Bank for International Settlements*; 2010.

Beirlant, J., Goegebeur, Y., Segers, J., Teugels, J. *Statistics of Extremes: Theory and Applications*. New York: John Wiley & Sons, Inc.; 2004.

Beirlant, J., Vynckier, P., Teugels, J. Tail index estimation, Pareto quantile plots, and regression diagnostics. J Am Stat Assoc 1996;**91**:1659–1667.

Bellini, F., Klar, B., Müller, A., Rosazza Gianin, E. Generalized quantiles as risk measures; 2013. Preprint http://ssrn.com/abstract=2225751. Accessed 2016 May 2.

Bengio, Y., Carreau, J. A hybrid Pareto model for asymmetric fat-tailed data: the univariate case. Extremes 2009;**1**:53–76.

Cai, G.-H. The Berry-Esséen bound for identically distributed random variables by Stein method. Appl Math J Chin Univ 2012;**27**:455–461.

Chen, L.H., Shao, Q.-M. Normal approximation under local dependence. Ann Probab 2004;**32**(3):1985–2028.

Csörgő, S., Horváth, L., Mason, D. What portion of the sample makes a partial sum asymptotically stable or normal? Probab Theory Relat Fields 1986;**72**:1–16.

Dacorogna, M.M., Gençay, R., Müller, U., Olsen, R., Pictet, O. *An Introduction to High-Frequency Finance*. New York: Academic Press; 2001.

Dacorogna, M.M., Müller, U.A., Pictet, O.V., de Vries, C.G. The distribution of extremal foreign exchange rate returns in extremely large data sets. Extremes 2001;**4**(2):105–127.

Daníelsson, J., Jorgensen, B., Samorodnitsky, G., Sarma, M., de Vries, C. Subadditivity re-examined: the case for Value-at-Risk. FMG Discussion Papers, London School of Economics; 2005.

David, H.A., Nadaraja, H.N. *Order Statistics*. 3rd ed. New York: John Wiley & Sons, Inc.; 2003.

Davison, A., Smith, R. Models for exceedances over high thresholds. J R Stat Soc Ser B 1990;**52**(3):393–442.

Debbabi, N., Kratz, M. A new unsupervised threshold determination for hybrid models. IEEE-ICASSP; 2014.

Embrechts, P., Klüppelberg, C., Mikosch, T. *Modelling Extremal Events for Insurance and Finance*. Berlin: Springer-Verlag; 1997.

Embrechts, P., Lambrigger, D., Wüthrich, M. Multivariate extremes and the aggregation of dependent risks: examples and counter-examples. Extremes 2009;**12**:107–127.

Embrechts, P., Puccetti, G., Rüschendorf, L. Model uncertainty and VaR aggregation. Journal of Banking & Finance 2013;**37**(8):2750–2764.

Emmer, S., Kratz, M., Tasche, D. What is the best risk measure in practice? A comparison of standard risk measures. J Risk 2015;**18**:31-60.

Esseen, C.-G. On the Liapunoff limit of error in the theory of probability. Ark Mat Astron Fysik 1942;**A28**:1–19. ISSN: 0365-4133.

Feller, W. *An Introduction to Probability Theory and its Applications*. Volume **II**. New York: Wiley; 1966.

Fisher, R.A., Tippett, L.H.C. Limiting forms of the frequency distribution of the largest or smallest member of a sample. Proc Camb Philos Soc 1928;**24**:180–190.

Furrer, H. Uber die Konvergenz zentrierter und normierter Summen von Zufallsvariablen und ihre Auswirkungen auf die Risikomessung; 2012. ETH preprint.

Galambos, J. *The Asymptotic Theory of Extreme Order Statistics*. New York: John Wiley & Sons, Inc.; 1978.

Gneiting, T. Making and evaluating point forecasts. J Am Stat Assoc 2012;**106**(494): 746–762.

Hahn, M.G., Mason, D.M., Weiner, D.C. *Sums, Trimmed Sums and Extremes. Progress in Probability*. Volume **23**. Cambridge (MA): Birkhäuser Boston; 1991.

Hall, P. On the influence of extremes on the rate of convergence in the central limit theorem. Ann Probab 1984;**12**:154–172.

Hill, B.M. A simple approach to inference about the tail of a distribution. Ann Stat 1975;**3**:1163–1174.

Hosking, J., Wallis, J. Parameter and quantile estimation for the Generalized Pareto distribution. Technometrics 1987;**29**(3):339–349.

Hosking, J.R.M., Wallis, J.R., Wood, E.F. Estimation of the generalized extreme-value distribution by the method of probability-weighted moments. Technometrics 1985;**27**:251–261. [321–323].

Huston, J., McCulloch, M. Measuring tail thickness to estimate the stable index α: a critique. J. of Business & Economic Statistics 1997;**15**:74–81.

Jansen, D.W., De Vries, C.G. On the frequency of large stock returns: putting booms and busts into perspectives. Review of Economics and Statistics 1991;**73**:18–24.

Jenkinson, A.F. The frequency distribution of the annual maximum (or minimum) values of meteorological elements. Q J R Meteorol Soc 1955;**81**:58–171.

Korolev, V.Y., Shevtsova, I.G. On the upper bound for the absolute constant in the Berry-Esseen inequality. J Theory Probab Appl 2010;**54**(4):638–658.

Kratz, M. There is a VaR beyond usual approximations. Towards a toolkit to compute risk measures of aggregated heavy tailed risks. FINMA report; 2013.

Kratz, M. Normex, a new method for evaluating the distribution of aggregated heavy tailed risks. Application to risk measures. Extremes 2014;**17**(4) (Special issue: Extremes and Finance. Guest Ed. P. Embrechts). 661–691.

Kratz, M., Resnick, S. The QQ-estimator and heavy tails. Stoch Models 1996;**12**: 699–724.

Leadbetter, R., Lindgren, G., Rootzén, H. *Extremes and Related Properties of Random Sequences and Processes*. New York: Springer-Verlag; 1983.

Longin, F. The asymptotic distribution of extreme stock market returns. J Bus 1996;**63**:383–408.

Mikosch, T., Wintenberger, O. Precise large deviations for dependent regularly varying sequences. Probab Theory Relat Fields 2013;**156**:851–887.

Mori, T. On the limit distribution of lightly trimmed sums. Math Proc Camb Philos Soc 1984;**96**:507–516.

Müller, U.A., Dacorogna, M.M., Pictet, O.V. Heavy tails in high-frequency financial data. In: Taqqu, M., editor. Published in the book *A Practical Guide to Heavy Tails: Statistical Techniques for Analysing Heavy Tailed Distributions*. Boston (MA): Birkhauser; 1998.

Nolan, J. 2012. Available at http://academic2.american.edu/jpnolan/stable/stable.html. Accessed 2016 May 2.

Petrov, V.V. A local theorem for densities of sums of independent random variables. J Theory Probab Appl 1956;**1**(3):316–322.

Petrov, V.V. *Limit Theorem of Probability Theory: Sequences of Independent Random Variables*. Oxford: Oxford Sciences Publications; 1995.

Pickands, J. Statistical inference using extreme order statistics. Ann Stat 1975;**3**:119–131.

Pictet, O., Dacorogna, M., Müller, U.A. Hill, Bootstrap and Jackknife Estimators for heavy tails, In: Taqqu, M., editor. *Practical Guide for Heavy Tails Distributions*. Boston (MA): Birkhäuser; 1998.

Pinelis, I. On the nonuniform Berry-Esséen bound; 2013. arxiv.org/pdf/1301.2828.

Ramsay, C.M. The distribution of sums of certain i.i.d. Pareto variates. Commun Stat Theory Methods 2006;**35**(3):395–405.

Reiss, R.-D., Thomas, M. *Statistical Analysis of Extreme Values: With Applications to Insurance, Finance, Hydrology and Other Fields*. 3rd ed. Birkhäuser Basel; 2007.

Resnick, S. *Extreme Values, Regular Variation, and Point Processes*. 1st ed. New York: Springer-Verlag; 1987, 2008.

Resnick, S. *Heavy-Tail Phenomena: Probabilistic and Statistical Modeling*. New York: Springer-Verlag; 2006.

Samorodnitsky, G., Taqqu, M.S. *Stable non-Gaussian Random Processes: Stochastic Models with Infinite Variance*. New York: Chapman & Hall; 1994.

Shevtsova, I.G. About the rate of convergence in the local limit theorem for densities under various moment conditions. Statistical Methods of Estimation and Hypotheses Testing Volume 20, Perm, Russia; 2007. p 1-26(in Russian).

Shevtsova, I.G. On the absolute constants in the Berry-Esséen inequality and its structural and nonuniform improvements. Informatics and its Applications 2013;**7**(1):124–125 (in Russian).

Stein, C. A bound for the error in the normal approximation to the distribution of a sum of dependent random variables. Proceedings of the 6th Berkeley Symposium on Mathematical Statistics and Probability, Volume 2; 1972. p 583–602.

Stein, C. *Approximate Computations of Expectations*. Volume **7**, Lecture Notes—Monograph Series. Hayward (CA): IMS; 1986.

Taylor, S.J. *Modelling Financial Time Series*. Chichester: John Wiley & Sons; 1986.

Tyurin, I.S. An improvement of upper estimates of the constants in the Lyapunov theorem. Russian Mathematical Surveys 2010;**65**(3):201–202.

von Mises, R. La distribution de la plus grande de n valeurs. Revue Mathématique de l'Union Interbalkanique 1936;**1**:141–160.

Zaliapin, I.V., Kagan, Y.Y., Schoenberg, F.P. Approximating the distribution of Pareto sums. Pure Appl Geophys 2005;**162**:1187–1228.

Ziegel, J.F. Coherence and elicitability. Mathematical Finance 2014 (online 2014).

Chapter Twelve

Estimation Methods for Value at Risk

Saralees Nadarajah and Stephen Chan
School of Mathematics, University of Manchester, Manchester, M13 9PL, UK

12.1 INTRODUCTION

12.1.1 History of VaR

In the last few decades, risk managers have truly experienced a revolution. The rapid increase in the usage of risk management techniques has spread well beyond derivatives and is totally changing the way institutions approach their financial risk. In response to the financial disasters of the early 1990s, a new method called Value at Risk (VaR) was developed as a simple method to quantify market risk (in recent years, VaR has been used in many other areas of risk including credit risk and operational risk). Some of the financial disasters of the early 1990s are the following:

- Figure 12.1 shows the effect of Black Monday, which occurred on October 19, 1987. In a single day, the Dow Jones stock index (DJIA) crashed down by 22.6% (by 508 points), causing a negative knock-on effect on other stock markets worldwide. Overall the stock market lost $0.5 trillion.

- The Japanese stock price bubble, creating a $2.7 trillion loss in capital; see Figure 12.2. According to this website, "the Nikkei Index after the Japanese bubble burst in the final days of 1989. Again, the market showed a substantial recovery for several months in mid-1990 before sliding to new lows."

- Figure 12.3 describes the dot-com bubble. During 1999 and 2000, the NASDAQ rose at a dramatic rate with all technology stocks booming.

Extreme Events in Finance: A Handbook of Extreme Value Theory and its Applications,
First Edition. Edited by François Longin.

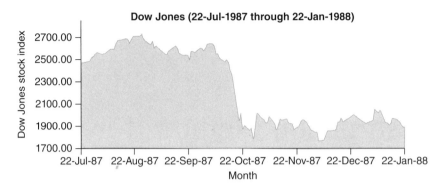

FIGURE 12.1 Black Monday crash on October 19, 1987. The Dow Jones stock index crashed down by 22.6% (by 508 points). Overall the stock market lost $0.5 trillion.

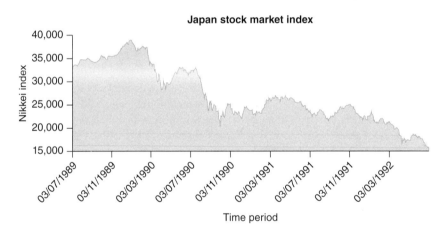

FIGURE 12.2 Japan stock price bubble near the end of 1989. A loss of $2.7 trillion in capital. A recovery happened after mid-1990.

However, on March 10, 2000, the bubble finally burst, because of sudden simultaneous sell orders in big technology companies (Dell, IBM, and Cisco) on the NASDAQ. After a peak at $5048.62 on that day, the NASDAQ fell back down and has never since been recovered.

- Figure 12.4 describes the 1997 Asian financial crisis. It first occurred at the beginning of July 1997. During that period a lot of Asia got affected by this financial crisis, leading to a pandemic spread of fear to a worldwide economic meltdown. The crisis was first triggered when the Thai baht (Thailand currency) was cut from being pegged to the US dollars and the government floated the baht. In addition, at the time Thailand was effectively bankrupt from the burden of foreign debt it acquired. A later period saw a contagious

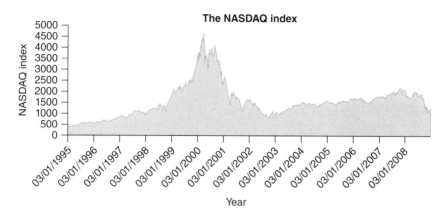

FIGURE 12.3 Dot-com bubble (the NASDAQ index) during 1999 and 2000. The bubble burst on March 10, 2000. The peak on that day was $5048.62. There is a recovery after 2002. Never recovered to attain the peak.

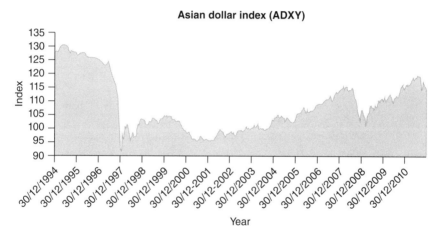

FIGURE 12.4 Asian financial crisis (Asian dollar index) in July 1997. Not fully recovered even in 2011.

spread of the crisis to Japan and to South Asia, causing a slump in asset prices, stock market, and currencies.

- The Black Wednesday, resulting in £800 million losses; see Figure 12.5; According to http://en.wikipedia.org/wiki/Black_Wednesday, Black Wednesday "refers to the events of September 16, 1992 when the British Conservative government was forced to withdraw the pound sterling from the European exchange rate mechanism (ERM) after they were unable to keep it above its agreed lower limit."

- The infamous financial disasters of Orange County, Barings, Metallgesellschaft, Daiwa, and so many more.

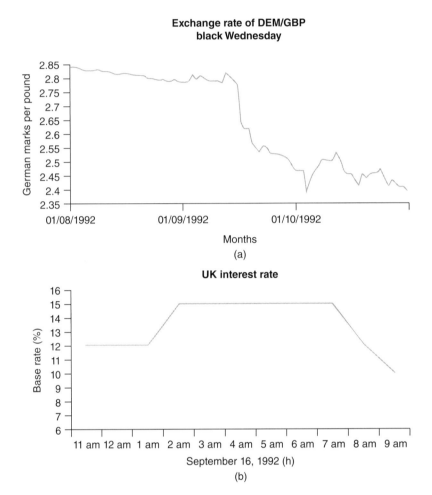

**FIGURE 12.5 Black Wednesday crash of September 16, 1992. (a) shows the
exchange rate of Deutsche mark to British pounds. (b) shows the UK interest
rate on the day.**

12.1.2   Definition of VaR

Till Guldimann is widely credited as the creator of value at risk (VaR) in the late
1980s. He was then the head of global research at J.P. Morgan. VaR is a method
that uses standard statistical techniques to assess risk. The VaR "measures the
worst average loss over a given horizon under normal market conditions at a
given confidence level" (Jorion, 2001, p. xxii). The value of VaR can provide
users with information in two ways: as a summary measure of market risk or
an aggregate view of a portfolio's risk. Overall VaR is a forward-looking risk
measure and used by financial institutions, regulators, nonfinancial corporations, and asset management exposed to financial risk. The most important

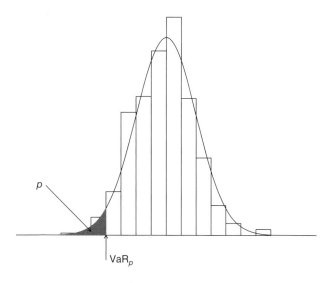

FIGURE 12.6 Value at risk illustrated.

use of VaR has been for capital adequacy regulation under Basel II and later
revisions.

Let $\{X_t, t = 1, 2, \ldots, n\}$ denote a stationary financial series with marginal
cumulative distribution function (cdf) F and marginal probability density function
(pdf) f. The VaR for a given probability p is defined mathematically as

$$\text{VaR}_p = \inf\{u : F(u) \geq p\}. \tag{12.1}$$

That is, VaR is the quantile of F exceeded with probability $1 - p$. Figure 12.6
illustrates the definition given by (12.1).

Sometimes, VaR is defined for log returns of the original time series. That is,
if $R_t = \ln (X_{t+h}/X_t)$, $t = 1, 2, \ldots, n$ are the log returns for some h with marginal
cdf F and then VaR is defined by (12.1). If α_h and σ_h denote the mean and standard
deviation of the log returns, then one can write

$$\text{VaR}_p = \alpha_h + \sigma_h \psi^{-1}(p), \tag{12.2}$$

where $\psi(\cdot)$ denotes the quantile function of the standardized log returns $Z_t = (R_t - \alpha_h)/\sigma_h$.

12.1.3 Applications of VaR

Applications of VaR can be classified as:

- Information reporting—it measures aggregate risk and corporation risk in a
  nontechnical way for easy understanding.

- Controlling risk—setting position limits for traders and business units, so they can compare diverse market risky activities.
- Managing risk—reallocating of capital across traders, products, business units, and whole institutions.

Applications of VaR have been extensive. Some recent applications and application areas have included estimation of highly parallel architectures (Dixon et al., 2012), estimation for crude oil markets (He et al., 2012a), multiresolution analysis-based methodology in metal markets (He et al., 2012b), estimation of optimal hedging strategy under bivariate regime switching ARCH framework (Chang, 2011b), energy markets (Cheong, 2011), Malaysian sectoral markets (Cheong and Isa, 2011), downside residential market risk (Jin and Ziobrowski, 2011), hazardous material transportation (Kwon, 2011), operational risk in Chinese commercial banks (Lu, 2011), longevity and mortality (Plat, 2011), analysis of credit default swaps (Raunig et al., 2011), exploring oil-exporting country portfolio (Sun et al., 2011), Asia-focused hedge funds (Weng and Trueck, 2011), measure for waiting time in simulations of hospital units (Dehlendorff et al., 2010), financial risk in pension funds (Fedor, 2010), catastrophic event modeling in the Gulf of Mexico (Kaiser et al., 2010), estimating the South African equity market (Milwidsky and Mare, 2010), estimating natural disaster risks (Mondlane, 2010), wholesale price for supply chain coordination (Wang, 2010), US movie box office earnings (Bi and Giles, 2009), stock market index portfolio in South Africa (Bonga-Bonga and Mutema, 2009), multiperiod supply inventory coordination (Cai et al., 2009), Toronto stock exchange (Dionne et al., 2009), modeling volatility clustering in electricity price return series (Karandikar et al., 2009), calculation for heterogeneous loan portfolios (Puzanova et al., 2009), measurement of HIS stock index futures market risk (Yan and Gong, 2009), stock index futures market risk (Gong and Li, 2008), estimation of real estate values (He et al., 2008), foreign exchange rates (Ku and Wang, 2008), artificial neural network (Lin and Chen, 2008), criterion for management of stormwater (Piantadosi et al., 2008), inventory control in supply chains (Yiu et al., 2008), layers of protection analysis (Fang et al., 2007), project finance transactions (Gatti et al., 2007), storms in the Gulf of Mexico (Kaiser et al., 2007), midterm generation operation planning in electricity market environment (Lu et al., 2007), Hong Kong's fiscal policy (Porter, 2007), bakery procurement (Wilson et al., 2007), newsvendor models (Xu and Chen, 2007), optimal allocation of uncertain water supplies (Yamout et al., 2007), futures floor trading (Lee and Locke, 2006), estimating a listed firm in China (Liu et al., 2006), Asian Pacific stock market (Su and Knowles, 2006), Polish power exchange (Trzpiot and Ganczarek, 2006), single loss approximation to VaR (Böcker and Klüppelberg, 2005), real options in complex engineered systems (Hassan et al., 2005), effects of bank technical sophistication and learning over time (Liu et al., 2004), risk analysis of the aerospace sector (Mattedi et al., 2004), Chinese securities market (Li et al., 2002), risk management of investment-linked household property insurance (Zhu and Gao, 2002), project risk measurement (Feng and Chen, 2001), long-term capital management for property/casualty insurers (Panning, 1999), structure-dependent securities and FX derivatives (Singh, 1997), and mortgage-backed securities (Jakobsen, 1996).

12.1.4 Aims

The aim of this chapter is to review known methods for estimating VaR given by (12.1). The review of methods is divided as follows: general properties (Section 12.2), parametric methods (Section 12.3), nonparametric methods (Section 12.4), semiparametric methods (Section 12.5), and computer software (Section 12.6). For each estimation method, we give the main formulas for computing VaR. We have avoided giving full details for each estimation method (e.g., interpretation, asymptotic properties, finite sample properties, finite sample bias, sensitivity to outliers, quality of approximations, comparison with competing estimators, advantages, disadvantages, and application areas) because of space concerns. These details can be read from the cited references.

12.1.5 Further Material

The review of value of risk presented here is not complete, but we believe we have covered most of the developments in recent years. For a fuller account of the theory and applications of value risk, we refer the readers to the following books: Bouchaud and Potters (2000, Chapter 3), Delbaen (2000, Chapter 3), Moix (2001, Chapter 6), Voit (2001, Chapter 7), Dupacova et al. (2002, Part 2), Dash (2004, Part IV), Franke et al. (2004), Tapiero (2004, Chapter 10), Meucci (2005), Pflug and Romisch (2007, Chapter 12), Resnick (2007), Ardia (2008, Chapter 6), Franke et al. (2008), Klugman et al. (2008), Lai and Xing (2008, Chapter 12), Taniguchi et al. (2008), Janssen et al. (2009, Chapter 18), Sriboonchitta et al. (2010, Chapter 4), Tsay (2010), Capinski and Zastawniak (2011), Jorion (2001), and Ruppert (2011, Chapter 19).

12.2 GENERAL PROPERTIES

This section describes general properties of VaR. The properties discussed are ordering properties (Section 12.2.1), upper comonotonicity (Section 12.2.2), multivariate extension (Section 12.2.3), risk concentration (Section 12.2.4), Hürlimann's inequalities (Section 12.2.5), Ibragimov and Walden's inequalities (Section 12.2.6), Denis et al.'s inequalities (Section 12.2.7), Jaworski's inequalities (Section 12.2.8), Mesfioui and Quessy's inequalities (Section 12.2.9), and Slim et al.'s inequalities (Section 12.2.10).

12.2.1 Ordering Properties

Pflug (2000) and Jadhav and Ramanathan (2009) establish several ordering properties of VaR_p. Given random variables X, Y, Y_1, Y_2 and a constant c, some of the properties given by Pflug (2000) and Jadhav and Ramanathan (2009) are the following:

(i) VaR_p is translation equivariant, that is, $\text{VaR}_p(Y + c) = \text{VaR}_p(Y) + c$.

(ii) VaR_p is positively homogeneous, that is, $\text{VaR}_p(cY) = c\text{VaR}_p(Y)$ for $c > 0$.

(iii) $\text{VaR}_p(Y) = -\text{VaR}_{1-p}(-Y)$.

(iv) VaR_p is monotonic with respect to stochastic dominance of order 1 (a random variable Y_1 is less than a random variable Y_2 with respect to stochastic dominance of order 1 if $E[\psi(Y_1)] \leq E[\psi(Y_2)]$ for all monotonic integrable functions ψ); that is, Y_1 is less than a random variable Y_2 with respect to stochastic dominance of order 1 and then $\text{VaR}_p(Y_1) \leq \text{VaR}_p(Y_2)$.

(v) VaR_p is comonotone additive, that is, if Y_1 and Y_2 are comonotone, then $\text{VaR}_p(Y_1 + Y_2) = \text{VaR}_p(Y_1) + \text{VaR}_p(Y_2)$. Two random variables Y_1 and Y_2 defined on the same probability space $(\Omega, \mathcal{A}, P)$ are said to be comonotone if for all $w, w' \in \Omega$, $[Y_1(w) - Y_2(w)][Y_1(w') - Y_2(w')] \geq 0$ almost surely.

(vi) if $X \geq 0$ then $\text{VaR}_p(X) \geq 0$.

(vii) VaR_p is monotonic, that is, if $X \geq Y$, then $\text{VaR}_p(X) \geq \text{VaR}_p(Y)$.

Let F denote the joint cdf of (X_1, X_2) with marginal cdfs F_1 and F_2. Write $F \equiv (F_1, F_2, C)$ to mean $F(X_1, X_2) \equiv C(F_1(X_1), F_2(X_2))$, where C is known as the copula (Nelsen, 1999), a joint cdf of uniform marginals. Let (X_1, X_2) have the joint cdf $F \equiv (F_1, F_2, C)$ and (X_1', X_2') have the joint cdf $F' \equiv (F_1, F_2, C')$, $X = wX_1 + (1 - w)X_2$, and $X' = wX_1' + (1 - w)X_2'$. Then, Tsafack (2009) shows that if C' is stochastically less than C, then $\text{VaR}_p(X') \geq \text{VaR}_p(X)$ for $p \in (0, 1)$.

12.2.2   Upper Comonotonicity

If two or more assets are comonotonic, then their values (whether they be small, medium, large, etc.) move in the same direction simultaneously. In the real world, this may be too strong of a relation. A more realistic relation is to say that the assets move in the same direction if their values are extremely large. This weaker relation is known as *upper comonotonicity* (Cheung, 2009).

Let X_i denote the loss of the ith asset. Let $\mathbf{X} = (X_1, \ldots, X_n)$ with joint cdf $F(x_1, \ldots, x_n)$. Let $T = X_1 + \cdots + X_n$. Suppose all random variables are defined on the probability space $(\Omega, \mathcal{F}, \text{Pr})$. Then, a simple formula for the VaR of T in terms of values at risk of X_i can be established if $\mathbf{X}$ is upper comonotonic.

We now define what is meant by upper comonotonicity. A subset $C \subset \mathbb{R}^n$ is said to be comonotonic if $(t_i - s_i)(t_j - s_j) \geq 0$ for all i and j whenever $(t_1, \ldots, t_n)$ and $(s_1, \ldots, s_n)$ belong to C. The random vector is said to be comonotonic if it has a comonotonic support.

Let $\mathcal{N}$ denote the collection of all zero probability sets in the probability space. Let $\overline{\mathbb{R}^n} = \mathbb{R}^n \cup (-\infty, \ldots, -\infty)$. For a given $(a_1, \ldots, a_n) \in \mathbb{R}^n$, let $U(\mathbf{a})$ denote the upper quadrant of $(a_1, \infty) \times \cdots \times (a_n, \infty)$ and let $L(\mathbf{a})$ denote the lower quadrant of $(-\infty, a_1] \times \cdots \times (-\infty, a_n]$. Let $R(\mathbf{a}) = \mathbb{R}^n \setminus (U(\mathbf{a}) \cup L(\mathbf{a}))$.

Then, the random vector $\mathbf{X}$ is said to be upper comonotonic if there exist $\mathbf{a} \in \overline{\mathbb{R}^n}$ and a zero probability set $N(\mathbf{a}) \in \mathcal{N}$ such that

(a) $\{\mathbf{X}(w) \mid w \in \Omega \backslash N(\mathbf{a})\} \cap U(\mathbf{a})$ is a comonotonic subset of $\mathbb{R}^n$,

(b) $\Pr(\mathbf{X} \in U(\mathbf{a})) > 0$,

(c) $\{\mathbf{X}(w) \mid w \in \Omega \backslash N(\mathbf{a})\} \cap R(\mathbf{a})$ is an empty set.

If these three conditions are satisfied, then the VaR of T can be expressed as

$$\text{VaR}_p(T) = \sum_{i=1}^{n} \text{VaR}_p (X_i) \qquad (12.3)$$

for $p \in (F(a_1^*, \ldots, a_n^*), 1)$ and $\mathbf{a}^* = (a_1^*, \ldots, a_n^*)$, a comonotonic threshold as constructed in Lemma 2 of Cheung (2009).

12.2.3 Multivariate Extension

In this chapter, we shall focus mainly on univariate VaR estimation. Multivariate VaR is a much more recent topic.

Let $\mathbf{X}$ be a random vector in $\mathbb{R}^r$ with joint cdf F. Prékopa (2012) gives the following definition of multivariate VaR:

$$\text{MVaR}_p = \{\mathbf{u} \in \mathbb{R}^r \mid F(\mathbf{u}) = p\}. \qquad (12.4)$$

Note that MVaR may not be a single vector. It will often take the form of a set of vectors.

Prékopa (2012) gives the following motivation for multivariate VaR: "A finance company generally faces the problem of constructing different portfolios that they can sell to customers. Each portfolio produces a random total return and it is the objective of the company to have them above given levels, simultaneously, with large probability. Equivalently, the losses should be below given levels, with large probability. In order to ensure it we look at the total losses as components of a random vector and find a multivariate p-quantile or MVaR to know what are those points in the r-dimensional space (r being the number of portfolios), that should surpass the vector of total losses, to guarantee the given reliability."

Cousin and Bernardinoy (2011) provide another definition of multivariate VaR:

$$\text{MVaR}_p = E[\mathbf{X} \mid \mathbf{X} \in \partial L(p)] = \begin{pmatrix} E\left[X_1 \mid \mathbf{X} \in \partial L(p)\right] \\ E[X_2 \mid \mathbf{X} \in \partial L(p)] \\ \vdots \\ E[X_r \mid \mathbf{X} \in \partial L(p)] \end{pmatrix}$$

or equivalently

$$\text{MVaR}_p = E[\mathbf{X} \mid F(\mathbf{X}) = p] = \begin{pmatrix} E\left[X_1 \mid F(\mathbf{X}) = p\right] \\ E[X_2 \mid F(\mathbf{X}) = p] \\ \vdots \\ E[X_r \mid F(\mathbf{X}) = p] \end{pmatrix},$$

where $\partial L(p)$ is the boundary of the set $\{\mathbf{x} \in \mathbb{R}_+^r : F(\mathbf{x}) \geq p\}$.

Cousin and Bernardinoy (2011) establish various properties of MVaR similar to those in the univariate case. For instance,

(i) the translation equivariant property holds, that is,

$$\text{MVaR}_p (\mathbf{c} + \mathbf{X}) = \mathbf{c} + \text{MVaR}_p(\mathbf{X}) = \begin{pmatrix} c_1 + E\left[X_1 \mid F(\mathbf{X}) = p\right] \\ c_2 + E[X_2 \mid F(\mathbf{X}) = p] \\ \vdots \\ c_r + E[X_r \mid F(\mathbf{X}) = p] \end{pmatrix};$$

(ii) the positively homogeneous property holds, that is,

$$\text{MVaR}_p(\mathbf{cX}) = \mathbf{c}\text{MVaR}_p(\mathbf{X}) = \begin{pmatrix} c_1 E\left[X_1 \mid F(\mathbf{X}) = p\right] \\ c_2 E[X_2 \mid F(\mathbf{X}) = p] \\ \vdots \\ c_r E[X_r \mid F(\mathbf{X}) = p] \end{pmatrix};$$

(iii) if F is quasi-concave (Nelsen, 1999) then

$$\text{MVaR}_p^i(\mathbf{X}) \geq \text{VaR}_p (X_i)$$

for $i = 1, 2, \ldots, r$, where $\text{MVaR}_p^i(\mathbf{X})$ denotes the ith component of $\text{MVaR}_p(\mathbf{X})$;

(iv) if $\mathbf{X}$ is a comonotone nonnegative random vector and if F is quasi-concave (Nelsen, 1999), then

$$\text{MVaR}_p^i(\mathbf{X}) = \text{VaR}_p (X_i)$$

for $i = 1, 2, \ldots, r$;

(v) if $X_i = Y_i$ in distribution for every $i = 1, 2, \ldots, s$, then

$$\text{MVaR}_p(\mathbf{X}) = \text{MVaR}_p(\mathbf{Y})$$

for all $p \in (0, 1)$;

(vi) if X_i is stochastically less than Y_i for every $i = 1, 2, \ldots, s$, then

$$\text{MVaR}_p(\mathbf{X}) \leq \text{MVaR}_p(\mathbf{Y})$$

for all $p \in (0, 1)$.

Bivariate VaR in the context of a bivariate normal distribution has been considered much earlier by Arbia (2002).

A matrix variate extension of VaR and its application for power supply networks are discussed in Chang (2011a).

12.2.4 Risk Concentration

Let $X_1, X_2, \ldots, X_n$ denote future losses, assumed to be nonnegative independent random variables with common cdf F and survival function $\overline{F}$. Degen et al. (2010) define *risk concentration* as

$$C(\alpha) = \frac{\text{VaR}_\alpha \left[\sum_{i=1}^{n} X_i \right]}{\sum_{i=1}^{n} \text{VaR}_\alpha(X_i)}.$$

If $\overline{F}$ is regularly varying with index $-1/\xi$, $\xi > 0$ (Bingham et al., 1989), meaning that $\overline{F}(tx)/\overline{F}(t) \to x^{-1/\xi}$ as $t \to \infty$, then it is shown that

$$C(\alpha) \to n^{\xi-1} \tag{12.5}$$

as $\alpha \to 1$. Degen et al. (2010) also study the rate of convergence in (12.5).

Suppose X_i, $i = 1, 2, \ldots, n$ are regularly varying with index $-\beta$, $\beta > 0$. According to Jang and Jho (2007), for $\beta > 1$,

$$C(\alpha) < 1$$

for all $\alpha \in [\alpha_0, 1]$ for some $\alpha_0 \in (0, 1)$. This property is referred to as subadditivity. If $C(\alpha) < 1$ holds as $\alpha \to 1$, then the property is referred to as asymptotic subadditivity. For $\beta = 1$,

$$C(\alpha) \to 1$$

as $\alpha \to 1$. This property is referred to as asymptotic comonotonicity. For $0 < \beta < 1$,

$$C(\alpha) > 1$$

for all $\alpha \in [\alpha_0, 1]$ for some $\alpha_0 \in (0, 1)$. If $C(\alpha) > 1$ holds as $\alpha \to 1$ then the property is referred to as asymptotic superadditivity.

Let $N(t)$ denote a counting process independent of $\{X_i\}$ with $E[N(t)] < \infty$ for $t > 0$. According to Jang and Jho (2007), in the case of subadditivity,

$$\text{VaR}_\alpha \left[\sum_{i=1}^{N(t)} X_i \right] \leq E[N(t)] \sum_{i=1}^{N(t)} \text{VaR}_\alpha (X_i)$$

for all $\alpha \in [\alpha_0, 1]$ for some $\alpha_0 \in (0, 1)$. In the case of asymptotic comonotonicity,

$$\text{VaR}_\alpha \left[\sum_{i=1}^{N(t)} X_i \right] \sim E[N(t)] \sum_{i=1}^{N(t)} \text{VaR}_\alpha (X_i)$$

as $\alpha \to 1$. In the case of superadditivity,

$$\text{VaR}_\alpha \left[\sum_{i=1}^{N(t)} X_i \right] \geq E[N(t)] \sum_{i=1}^{N(t)} \text{VaR}_\alpha (X_i)$$

for all $\alpha \in [\alpha_0, 1]$ for some $\alpha_0 \in (0, 1)$.

Suppose $\mathbf{X} = (X_1, X_2, \ldots, X_n)^T$ is multivariate regularly varying with index β according to Definition 2.2 in Embrechts et al. (2009a). If $\boldsymbol{\Phi} : \mathbb{R}^n \to \mathbb{R}$ is a measurable function such that

$$\lim_{x \to \infty} \frac{\Pr(\Psi(\mathbf{X}) > x)}{\Pr(X_1 > x)} \to q \in (0, \infty),$$

then it is shown that

$$\lim_{\alpha \to 1} \frac{\text{VaR}_\alpha(\Psi(\mathbf{X}))}{\text{VaR}_\alpha(X_1)} \to q^{1/\beta};$$

see Lemma 2.3 in Embrechts et al. (2009b).

12.2.5 Hürlimann's Inequalities

Let X denote a random variable defined over $[A, B]$, $-\infty \leq A < B \leq \infty$ with mean μ and variance σ. Hürlimann (2002) provides various upper bounds for $\text{VaR}_p(X)$: for $p \leq \sigma^2/\{\sigma^2 + (B - \mu)^2\}$,

$$\text{VaR}_p(X) \leq B;$$

for $\sigma^2/\{\sigma^2 + (B - \mu)^2\} \leq p \leq (\mu - A)^2/\{\sigma^2 + (\mu - A)^2\}$,

$$\text{VaR}_p(X) \leq \mu + \sqrt{\frac{1-p}{p}}\sigma;$$

for $p \geq (\mu - A)^2/\{\sigma^2 + (\mu - A)^2\}$,

$$\text{VaR}_p(X) \leq \mu + \frac{(\mu - A)(B - A)(1 - p) - \sigma^2}{(B - A)p - (\mu - A)}. \tag{12.6}$$

The equality in (12.6) holds if and only if $B \to \infty$.

Now suppose X is a random variable defined over $[A, B]$, $-\infty \leq A < B \leq \infty$ with mean μ, variance σ, skewness γ, and kurtosis γ_2. In this case, Hürlimann (2002) provides the following upper bound for $\text{VaR}_p(X)$:

$$\text{VaR}_p(X) \leq \mu + x_p\sigma,$$

where x_p is the $100(1 - p)$ percentile of the standardized Chebyshev–Markov maximal distribution. The latter is defined as the root of

$$p(x_p) = p$$

if $p \le (1/2)\{1 - \gamma/\sqrt{4 + \gamma^2}\}$ and as the root of

$$p(\psi(x_p)) = 1 - p$$

if $p > (1/2)\{1 - \gamma/\sqrt{4 + \gamma^2}\}$, where

$$p(u) = \frac{\Delta}{q^2(u) + \Delta(1 + u^2)},$$

$$\psi(u) = \frac{1}{2}\left[\frac{A(u) - \sqrt{A^2(u) + 4q(u)B(u)}}{q(u)}\right],$$

where $\Delta = \gamma_2 - \gamma^2 + 2$, $A(u) = \gamma q(u) + \Delta u$, $B(u) = q(u) + \Delta$, and $q(u) = 1 + \gamma u - u^2$.

12.2.6 Ibragimov and Walden's Inequalities

Let $R(\mathbf{w}) = \sum_{i=1}^{N} w_i R_i$ denote a portfolio return made up of N asset returns, R_i, and the nonnegative weights w_i. Ibragimov (2009) provides various inequalities for the VaR of $R(\mathbf{w})$. They suppose that R_i are independent and identically distributed and belong to either $\underline{CS}$, the class of distributions that are convolutions of symmetric stable distributions $S_\alpha(\sigma, 0, 0)$ with $\alpha \in [0, 1]$ and $\sigma > 0$, or $\overline{CSLC}$, convolutions of distributions from the class of symmetric log-concave distributions and the class of distributions that are convolutions of symmetric stable distributions $S_\alpha(\sigma, 0, 0)$ with $\alpha \in [1, 2]$ and $\sigma > 0$.

Here, $S_\alpha(\beta, \gamma, \mu)$ denotes a stable distribution specified by its characteristic function

$$\phi(t) = \begin{cases} \exp\left\{i\mu t - \gamma^\alpha |t|^\alpha \left[1 - i\beta \tan\left(\pi\frac{\alpha}{2}\right) \text{sign}(t)\right]\right\}, & \alpha \neq 1, \\[2ex] \exp\left\{i\mu t - \gamma|t| \left(1 + i\beta\text{sign}(t)\frac{2}{\pi} \ln t\right)\right\}, & \alpha = 1, \end{cases}$$

where $i = \sqrt{-1}$, $\alpha \in (0, 2]$, $|\beta| \le 1$, $\gamma > 0$, and $\mu \in \mathbb{R}$. The stable distribution contains as particular cases the Gaussian distribution for $\alpha = 2$, the Cauchy distribution for $\alpha = 1$ and $\beta = 0$, the Lévy distribution for $\alpha = 1/2$ and $\beta = 1$, the Landau distribution for $\alpha = 1$ and $\beta = 1$, and the dirac delta distribution for $\alpha \downarrow 0$ and $\gamma \downarrow 0$.

Furthermore, let $\mathcal{I}_N = \{(w_1, \ldots, w_N) \in \mathbb{R}_+^N : w_1 + \cdots + w_N = 1\}$. Write $\mathbf{a} \prec \mathbf{b}$ to mean that $\sum_{i=1}^{k} a_{[i]} \le \sum_{i=1}^{k} b_{[i]}$ for $k = 1, \ldots, N - 1$ and $\sum_{i=1}^{N} a_{[i]} = \sum_{i=1}^{N} b_{[i]}$, where $a_{[1]} \ge \cdots \ge a_{[N]}$ and $b_{[1]} \ge \cdots \ge b_{[N]}$ denote the components of $\mathbf{a}$ and $\mathbf{b}$ in descending order. Let $\underline{\mathbf{w}}_N = (1/N, 1/N, \ldots, 1/N)$ and $\overline{\mathbf{w}}_N = (1, 0, \ldots, 0)$.

With these notations, Ibragimov (2009) provides the following inequalities for $\text{VaR}_q(R(\mathbf{w}))$. Suppose first that $q \in (0, 1/2)$ and R_i belong to $\overline{CSLC}$. Then,

(i) $\text{VaR}_{1-q}[R(\mathbf{v})] \leq \text{VaR}_{1-q}[R(\mathbf{w})]$ if $\mathbf{v} \prec \mathbf{w}$;

(i) $\text{VaR}_{1-q}[R(\underline{\mathbf{w}}_N)] \leq \text{VaR}_{1-q}[R(\mathbf{w})] \leq \text{VaR}_{1-q}[R(\overline{\mathbf{w}}_N)]$ for all $\mathbf{w} \in \mathcal{I}_N$.

Suppose now that $q \in (0, 1/2)$ and R_i belong to $\underline{CS}$. Then,

(i) $\text{VaR}_{1-q}[R(\mathbf{v})] \geq \text{VaR}_{1-q}[R(\mathbf{w})]$ if $\mathbf{v} \prec \mathbf{w}$;

(i) $\text{VaR}_{1-q}[R(\overline{\mathbf{w}}_N)] \leq \text{VaR}_{1-q}[R(\mathbf{w})] \leq \text{VaR}_{1-q}[R(\underline{\mathbf{w}}_N)]$ for all $\mathbf{w} \in \mathcal{I}_N$.

Further inequalities for VaR are provided in Ibragimov and Walden (2011) when a portfolio return, say, R, is made up of a two-dimensional array of asset returns, say, R_{ij}. That is,

$$R(\mathbf{w}) = \sum_{i=1}^{r} \sum_{j=1}^{c} w_{ij} R_{ij}$$

$$= \sum_{i=1}^{r} w_{i0} R_i + \sum_{i=1}^{r} w_{0j} C_j + \sum_{i=1}^{r} \sum_{j=1}^{c} w_{ij} U_{ij}$$

$$= \mathcal{R}(\mathbf{w}_0^{(\text{row})}) + C(\mathbf{w}_0^{(\text{col})}) + U(\mathbf{w}),$$

where $\mathcal{R}_i, i = 1, \dots, r$ are referred to as "row effects," $C_j, j = 1, \dots, c$ are referred to as "column effects," and $U_{ij}, i = 1, \dots, r, j = 1, \dots, c$ are referred to as "idiosyncratic components."

Let $\underline{\mathbf{w}}_{rc} = (1/(rc), 1/(rc), \dots, 1/(rc))$, $\overline{\mathbf{w}}_{rc} = (1, 0, \dots, 0)$, $\underline{\mathbf{w}}_0^{(\text{row})} = (1/r, 1/r, \dots, 1/r)$, $\overline{\mathbf{w}}_0^{(\text{row})} = (1, 0, \dots, 0)$, $\underline{\mathbf{w}}_0^{(\text{col})} = (1/c, 1/c, \dots, 1/c)$, and $\overline{\mathbf{w}}_0^{(\text{col})} = (1, 0, \dots, 0)$.

With these notations, Ibragimov and Walden (2011) provide the following inequalities for $q \in (0, 1/2)$:

(i) if R_i, C_j, U_{ij} belong to $\overline{CSLC}$, then $\text{VaR}_{1-q}[R(\underline{\mathbf{w}}_{rc})] \leq \text{VaR}_{1-q}[R(\mathbf{w})] \leq \text{VaR}_{1-q}[R(\overline{\mathbf{w}}_{rc})]$ for all $\mathbf{w} \in \mathcal{I}_{rc}$.

(ii) if R_i, C_j, U_{ij} belong to $\overline{CS}$, then $\text{VaR}_{1-q}[R(\underline{\mathbf{w}}_{rc})] \geq \text{VaR}_{1-q}[R(\mathbf{w})] \geq \text{VaR}_{1-q}[R(\overline{\mathbf{w}}_{rc})]$ for all $\mathbf{w} \in \mathcal{I}_{rc}$.

(iii) if U_{ij} belong to $\overline{CSLC}$, then $\text{VaR}_{1-q}[U(\underline{\mathbf{w}}_{rc})] \leq \text{VaR}_{1-q}[U(\mathbf{w})] \leq \text{VaR}_{1-q}[U(\overline{\mathbf{w}}_{rc})]$ for all $\mathbf{w} \in \mathcal{I}_{rc}$.

(iv) if U_{ij} belong to $\overline{CS}$, then $\text{VaR}_{1-q}[U(\underline{\mathbf{w}}_{rc})] \geq \text{VaR}_{1-q}[U(\mathbf{w})] \geq \text{VaR}_{1-q}[U(\overline{\mathbf{w}}_{rc})]$ for all $\mathbf{w} \in \mathcal{I}_{rc}$.

(v) if R_i belong to $\overline{CSLC}$, then $\text{VaR}_{1-q}[R(\underline{\mathbf{w}}_r)] \leq \text{VaR}_{1-q}\left[R\left(\mathbf{w}_0^{(\text{row})}\right)\right] \leq \text{VaR}_{1-q}[R(\overline{\mathbf{w}}_r)]$ for all $\mathbf{w} \in \mathcal{I}_{rc}$.

(vi) if $\mathcal{R}_i$ belong to $\overline{CS}$, then $\text{VaR}_{1-q}[\mathcal{R}(\underline{\mathbf{w}}_r)] \geq \text{VaR}_{1-q}\left[\mathcal{R}\left(\mathbf{w}_0^{(\text{row})}\right)\right] \geq$ $\text{VaR}_{1-q}[\mathcal{R}(\overline{\mathbf{w}}_r)]$ for all $\mathbf{w} \in \mathcal{I}_{rc}$.

(vii) if C_j belong to $\overline{CSLC}$, then $\text{VaR}_{1-q}[C(\underline{\mathbf{w}}_c)] \leq \text{VaR}_{1-q}\left[C\left(\mathbf{w}_0^{(\text{col})}\right)\right] \leq$ $\text{VaR}_{1-q}[C(\overline{\mathbf{w}}_c)]$ for all $\mathbf{w} \in \mathcal{I}_{rc}$.

(viii) if C_j belong to $\overline{CS}$, then $\text{VaR}_{1-q}[C(\underline{\mathbf{w}}_c)] \geq \text{VaR}_{1-q}\left[C\left(\mathbf{w}_0^{(\text{col})}\right)\right] \geq$ $\text{VaR}_{1-q}[C(\overline{\mathbf{w}}_c)]$ for all $\mathbf{w} \in \mathcal{I}_{rc}$.

Ibragimov and Walden (2011, Section 12.4) discuss an application of these inequalities to portfolio component VaR analysis.

12.2.7 Denis et al.'s Inequalities

Let $\{P_t\}$ denote prices of financial assets. The process could be modeled by

$$P_t = m + \int_0^t \sigma_s \, dB_s + \int_0^t b_s \, ds + \sum_{i=1}^{N_t} \gamma_{T_i^-} Y_i,$$

where B is a Brownian motion; $\tilde{N}$ is a compound Poisson process independent of B; $T_1, T_2, \ldots$ are jump times for $\tilde{N}$; b is an adapted integrable process; and σ, γ are certain random variables.

Denis et al. (2009) derive various bounds for the VaR of the process

$$P_t^* = \sup_{0 \leq u \leq t} P_u.$$

The following assumptions are made:

(i) For all $t > 0$, $E\left(\int_0^t \sigma_s^2 \, ds\right) < \infty$.

(ii) Jumps of the compound Poisson process are nonnegative and Y_1 is not identically equal to zero.

(iii) The process $\sum_{i=1}^{N_t} \gamma_{T_i^-} Y_i$ for $t > 0$ is well defined and integrable.

(iv) The jumps have a Laplace transform, $L(x) = E[\exp(xY_1)]$, $x < c$ where c is a positive constant.

(v) There exists $\gamma^* > 0$ such that $\gamma_s \leq \gamma^*$ almost surely for all $s \in [0, t]$.

(vi) There exists $b^*(t) \geq 0$ and $a^*(t) \geq 0$ such that

$$\int_0^t \sigma_u^2 \, du \leq a^*(t), \quad \int_0^s b_u \, du \leq b^*(t)$$

almost everywhere for all $s \in [0, t]$. In this case, let

$$K_t(\delta) = \delta b^*(t) + \delta^2 \frac{a^*(t)}{2} + \lambda t[L(\delta \gamma^*) - 1]$$

for $0 < \delta < c/\gamma^*$.

With these assumptions, Denis et al. (2009) show that

$$\text{VaR}_{1-\alpha}(P_t^*) \le \inf_{\delta < c/\gamma^*} \left\{ m + \frac{K_t(\delta) - \ln \alpha}{\delta} \right\},$$

$$\text{VaR}_{1-\alpha}(P_t^*) \le \inf_{0 < \delta < c/\gamma^*} \left\{ m + b^*(t) + \frac{a^*(t)\delta}{2} + \lambda t \frac{L(\delta\gamma^*) - 1}{\delta} - \frac{\ln \alpha}{\delta} \right\}.$$

For $\gamma \le 0$, Denis et al. (2009) show that

$$\text{VaR}_{1-\alpha}(P_t^*) \le m + b^*(t) + \sqrt{-2a^*(t)\ln \alpha}.$$

If the jumps follow a simple Poisson process, Denis et al. (2009) show that

$$\text{VaR}_{1-\alpha}(P_t^*) \le \inf_{0 < \delta < \infty} \left\{ m + b^*(t) + \frac{a^*(t)\delta}{2} + \lambda t \frac{\exp(\delta\gamma^*) - 1}{\delta} - \frac{\ln \alpha}{\delta} \right\}.$$

If the jumps follow an exponential distribution with parameter $v > 0$, Denis et al. (2009) show that

$$\text{VaR}_{1-\alpha}(P_t^*) \le \inf_{0 < \delta < v/\gamma^*} \left\{ m + b^*(t) + \frac{a^*(t)\delta}{2} + \frac{\lambda t}{v/\gamma^* - \delta} - \frac{\ln \alpha}{\delta} \right\}.$$

About the issue of continuity/discontinuity of the market with jumps, see Walter (2015).

12.2.8   Jaworski's Inequalities

Jaworski (2007, 2008) considers the following situation: suppose s_i, $i = 1, \cdots, n$ are the quotients of the currency rates at the end and at the beginning of an investment; suppose that the joint cdf of $(s_1, \ldots, s_n)$ is $C(F_1(s_1), \ldots, F_n(s_n))$, where C is a copula (Nelsen, 1999) and F_i is the marginal cdf of s_i; suppose w_i is the part of the capital invested in the ith currency, where w_i are nonnegative and sum to one. Then, the final investment value is

$$W_1(\mathbf{w}) = (w_1 s_1 + \cdots + w_n s_n)W_0,$$

where $\mathbf{w} = (w_1, \ldots, w_n)$. Jaworski (2007, 2008) defines the value of risk for a given $\mathbf{w}$ and a probability α as

$$\text{VaR}_\alpha(\mathbf{w}) = \sup\{V : \Pr(W_0 - W_1(\mathbf{w}) \le V) \le \alpha\}.$$

Jaworski (2007) shows this VaR can be bounded as

$$\sum_{i=1}^{n} \text{VaR}_{\alpha'}(\mathbf{e}_i) \le \text{VaR}_\alpha \le \sum_{i=1}^{n} \text{VaR}_\alpha(\mathbf{e}_i)$$

for portfolios consisting of only one currency, where $\mathbf{e}_i = (0, \ldots, 0, 1, 0, \ldots, 0)^T$ and $\alpha' = \alpha^2/C(\alpha, \ldots, \alpha)$.

12.2.9 Mesfioui and Quessy's Inequalities

Suppose a portfolio is made up of n assets and let $X_1, X_2, \ldots, X_n$ denote the losses for the n assets. Suppose also that the joint cdf of $(X_1, \ldots, X_n)$ is $C(F_1(x_1), \ldots, F_n(x_n))$, where C is a copula (Nelsen, 1999) and F_i is the marginal cdf of X_i. Furthermore, define the dual of a given copula C (Definition 2.4, Mesfioui and Quessy, 2005) as

$$C^d(u_1, \ldots, u_n) = \Pr(U(0,1) \leq u_1 \text{ or } \cdots \text{ or } U(0,1) \leq u_n).$$

With these notations, Mesfioui and Quessy (2005) derive various inequalities for the VaR of $S = X_1 + \cdots + X_n$. If C is such that $C \geq qC_L$ and $C \leq C_U^d$ for some copulas C_L and C_U, then

$$\underline{\text{VaR}}_\alpha \leq \text{VaR}_\alpha(S) \leq \overline{\text{VaR}}_\alpha,$$

where

$$\underline{\text{VaR}}_\alpha = \sup_{C_U^d(u_1, \ldots, u_n) = \alpha} \sum_{i=1}^{n} F_i^{-1}(u_i)$$

and

$$\overline{\text{VaR}}_\alpha = \inf_{C_L(u_1, \ldots, u_n) = \alpha} \sum_{i=1}^{n} F_i^{-1}(u_i).$$

If $X_1, X_2, \ldots, X_n$ are identical random variables with common cdf F and if $x^* \in \mathbb{R}$ is such that $f(x) = dF(x)/dx$ is nonincreasing for $x \geq x^*$, then it is shown under certain conditions that

$$\text{VaR}_\alpha(S) \leq nF^{-1}(\delta_{C_L}^{-1}(\alpha)),$$

where $\delta_{C_L}(t) = C_L(t, \ldots, t)$ is the diagonal section of C_L.

Mesfioui and Quessy (2005) also show that if X is a random variable with mean μ and variance σ^2, then

$$g_{\mu,\sigma}(\alpha) \leq \text{VaR}_\alpha(X) \leq h_{\mu,\sigma}(\alpha),$$

where

$$g_{a,b}(u) = \{a - bq(1-u)\}I\left(u \geq \frac{b^2}{a^2 + b^2}\right)$$

and

$$gh_{a,b}(u) = a + aq^2(u)I\left(u \leq \frac{b^2}{a^2 + b^2}\right) + bq(u)I\left(u > \frac{b^2}{a^2 + b^2}\right),$$

where $q(u) = \sqrt{u/(1-u)}$. If X_i, $i = 1, \ldots, n$ have means μ_i, $i = 1, \ldots, n$ and variances σ_i^2, $i = 1, \ldots, n$, then it is shown that

$$g_{\mu,\sigma}(\alpha) \le \text{VaR}_\alpha(S) \le h_{\mu,\sigma}(\alpha),$$

where $\mu = \mu_1 + \cdots + \mu_n$ and $\sigma = \sigma_1 + \cdots + \sigma_n$.

12.2.10   Slim et al.'s Inequalities

Suppose a portfolio is made up of d assets. Let $X_1, X_2, \ldots, X_n$ denote the losses for the n assets. Let F_i and f_i denote the cdf and the pdf of X_i. Let x_i^* denote the value for which $f_i(x)$ is nonincreasing for all $x \le x_i^*$. Given this notation, the total portfolio loss can be expressed as $S = w_1 X_1 + w_2 X_2 + \cdots + w_n X_n$ for some nonnegative weights w_i summing to one. Slim et al. (2012) show that the VaR of S can be bounded as follows:

$$\underline{\text{VaR}}_p \le \text{VaR}_p(S) \le \overline{\text{VaR}}_p,$$

where

$$\overline{\text{VaR}}_p = \inf_{u_1 + \cdots + u_n = \alpha + n - 1} \sum_{i=1}^n F_i^{-1}(u_i)$$

and

$$\underline{\text{VaR}}_p = \max_{1 \le i \le n} \left\{ F_i^{-1}(\alpha) + \sum_{1 \le j \ne i \le n} F_j^{-1}(n) \right\}$$

for $\alpha \le \min\{F_1(x_1^*), \ldots, F_n(x_n^*)\}$. The use of the earlier results allows easy computation for explicit VaR bounds for possibly dependent risks.

12.3   PARAMETRIC METHODS

This section concentrates on estimation of VaR when data comes from a parametric distribution, and we want to make use of the parameters. The parametric methods summarized are based on Gaussian distribution (Section 12.3.1), Student's t distribution (Section 12.3.2), Pareto-positive stable distribution (Section 12.3.3), log-folded t distribution (Section 12.3.4), variance–covariance method (Section 12.3.5), Gaussian mixture distribution (Section 12.3.6), generalized hyperbolic distribution (Section 12.3.7), Fourier transformation method (Section 12.3.8), principal components method (Section 12.3.9), quadratic forms (Section 12.3.10), elliptical distribution (Section 12.3.11), copula method (Section 12.3.12), Gram–Charlier approximation (Section 12.3.13), delta–gamma approximation (Section 12.3.14), Cornish–Fisher approximation (Section

12.3.15), Johnson family method (Section 12.3.16), Tukey method (Section 12.3.17), asymmetric Laplace distribution (Section 12.3.18), asymmetric power distribution (Section 12.3.19), Weibull distribution (Section 12.3.20), ARCH models (Section 12.3.21), GARCH models (Section 12.3.22), GARCH model with heavy tails (Section 12.3.23), ARMA–GARCH model (Section 12.3.24), Markov switching ARCH model (Section 12.3.25), fractionally integrated GARCH model (Section 12.3.26), RiskMetrics model (Section 12.3.27), capital asset pricing model (Section 12.3.28), Dagum distribution (Section 12.3.29), location-scale distributions (Section 12.3.30), discrete distributions (Section 12.3.31), quantile regression method (Section 12.3.32), Brownian motion method (Section 12.3.33), Bayesian method (Section 12.3.34), and Rachev et al.'s method (Section 12.3.35).

12.3.1 Gaussian Distribution

If $X_1, X_2, \ldots, X_n$ are observations from a Gaussian distribution with mean μ and variance σ^2, then VaR can be estimated by

$$\widehat{\text{VaR}}_\alpha = \overline{X} + \Phi^{-1}(\alpha)s, \tag{12.7}$$

where $\overline{X}$ is the sample mean and s^2 is the sample variance

$$s^2 = \frac{1}{n} \sum_{i=1}^{n} (X_i - \overline{X})^2. \tag{12.8}$$

The estimator in (12.7) is biased and consistent. If the n in (12.8) is replaced by $n - 1$, then (12.7) becomes unbiased and consistent.

12.3.2 Student's t Distribution

If $X_1, X_2, \ldots, X_n$ are observations from a Student's t distribution with v degrees of freedom, then VaR can be estimated by (Arneric et al., 2008)

$$\widehat{\text{VaR}}_\alpha = \overline{X} + t_{v,\alpha} s \sqrt{\frac{3 + \kappa}{3 + 2\kappa}},$$

where κ is the excess sample kurtosis and $t_{v,\alpha}$ is the 100α percentile of a Student's t random variable with v degrees of freedom.

12.3.3 Pareto-Positive Stable Distribution

Sarabia and Prieto (2009) and Guillen et al. (2011) introduce the Pareto-positive stable distribution specified by the cdf

$$F(x) = 1 - \exp\{-\lambda[\ln (x/\sigma)]^v\} \tag{12.9}$$

for $x \geq \sigma$, $\lambda > 0$, and $v > 0$. Here, λ and v are shape parameters and σ is a scale parameter. The Pareto distribution is the particular case of (12.9) for $v = 1$.

The Pareto-positive stable distribution has been applied to risk management; see, for example, Guillen et al. (2011). If X is a random variable having the cdf (12.9), then it is easy to see that

$$\text{VaR}_\alpha = \sigma \exp \left\{ \left[-\frac{1}{\lambda} \ln (1 - \alpha) \right]^{1/v} \right\}$$

for $0 < \alpha < 1$. So, if $(\hat{\sigma}, \hat{\lambda}, \hat{v})$ are maximum likelihood estimators of (σ, λ, v), then

$$\widehat{\text{VaR}}_\alpha = \hat{\sigma} \exp \left\{ \left[-\frac{1}{\hat{\lambda}} \ln (1 - \alpha) \right]^{1/\hat{v}} \right\}$$

for $0 < \alpha < 1$.

12.3.4 Log-Folded t Distribution

Brazauskas and Kleefeld (2011) introduce the log-folded t distribution specified by the quantile function

$$F^{-1}(u) = \exp\{\sigma Q_{T(v)}((u + 1)/2)\}$$

for $0 < u < 1$, where $\sigma > 0$ is a scale parameter, $v > 0$ is a shape parameter, and $Q_{T(v)}(\cdot)$ denotes the quantile function of a Student's t random variable with v degrees of freedom. Brazauskas and Kleefeld (2011) also provide an application of this distribution to risk management.

Suppose $X_1, X_2, \ldots, X_n$ is a random sample from the log-folded t distribution with order statistics $X_{1:n} < X_{2:n} < \cdots < X_{n:n}$. Brazauskas and Kleefeld (2011) show that the VaR can be estimated by

$$\widehat{\text{VaR}}_{1-\alpha} = \exp\{\hat{\sigma} Q_{T(v)}(1 - \alpha/2)\},$$

where

$$\hat{\sigma} = \left[\frac{1}{n} \sum_{i=1}^{n} \ln^2 X_i \right]^{1/2}$$

or

$$\hat{\sigma} = \frac{1}{c(a,b)(n - m_n - m_n^*)} \sum_{i=m_n+1}^{n-m_n^*} \ln X_{i:n},$$

where

$$c(a,b) = \frac{1}{1 - a - b} \int_a^{1-b} Q_{T(\infty)}((u + 1)/2) du,$$

where m_n and m_n^* are integers $0 \le m_n < n - m_n^* \le n$ such that $m_n/n \to a$ and $m_n^*/n \to b$ as $n \to \infty$, where a and b are trimming proportions with $0 \le a + b < 1$.

12.3.5 Variance–Covariance Method

Suppose the portfolio return, say, R, is made up of N asset returns, R_i, $i = 1, 2, \ldots, N$, as

$$R = \sum_{i=1}^{N} w_i R_i,$$

where w_i are nonnegative weights summing to one. Suppose also $E(R_i) = \mu_i$, $Var(R_i) = \sigma_i^2$, and $Cov(R_i, R_j) = \sigma_i \sigma_j \rho_{ij}$. The variance–covariance method suggests that the VaR of R can be approximated by

$$VaR_\alpha(R) = \sum_{i=1}^{N} w_i \mu_i + \Phi^{-1}(\alpha) \sqrt{\sum_{i=1}^{N} w_i \sigma_i^2 + \sum_{i,j=1, i \ne j}^{N} w_i w_j \sigma_i \sigma_j \rho_{ij}}.$$

An estimator can be obtained by replacing the parameters μ_i, σ_i, and ρ_{ij} by their maximum likelihood estimators.

12.3.6 Gaussian Mixture Distribution

Let $\{P_t\}$ denote the financial asset prices and let $R_t = \ln P_t - \ln P_{t-1}$ denote the log return corresponding to the original financial series. Zhang and Cheng (2005) consider the model that R_t have a Gaussian mixture distribution specified by the pdf

$$f(r) = \sum_{k=1}^{K} p_k \frac{1}{\sqrt{2\pi}\sigma_k} \exp\left\{ -\frac{(r - \mu_k)^2}{2\sigma_k^2} \right\}$$

for $K \ge 1$, where the mixing coefficients p_k sum to one. Let VaR_α^k denote the VaR corresponding to the kth component, that is,

$$\int_{-\infty}^{VaR_\alpha^k} \frac{1}{\sqrt{2\pi}\sigma_k} \exp\left\{ -\frac{(r - \mu_k)^2}{2\sigma_k^2} \right\} dr = \alpha.$$

Let VaR_α denote the VaR corresponding to the mixture model, that is,

$$\int_{-\infty}^{VaR_\alpha} \sum_{k=1}^{K} p_k \frac{1}{\sqrt{2\pi}\sigma_k} \exp\left\{ -\frac{(r - \mu_k)^2}{2\sigma_k^2} \right\} dr = \alpha.$$

Then, Theorem 1 in Zhang and Cheng (2005) shows that

$$\min_{1 \le k \le K} \text{VaR}_\alpha^k \le \text{VaR}_\alpha \le \max_{1 \le k \le K} \text{VaR}_\alpha^k$$

always holds.

Furthermore, let α^k denote the significance level of VaR corresponding to the kth component, that is,

$$\alpha^{(k)} = \int_{-\infty}^{\text{VaR}} \frac{1}{\sqrt{2\pi}\sigma_k} \exp\left\{ -\frac{(r - \mu_k)^2}{2\sigma_k^2} \right\} dr.$$

Let α denote the significance level of VaR corresponding to the mixture model, that is,

$$\alpha = \int_{-\infty}^{\text{VaR}} \sum_{k=1}^{K} p_k \frac{1}{\sqrt{2\pi}\sigma_k} \exp\left\{ -\frac{(r - \mu_k)^2}{2\sigma_k^2} \right\} dr = \alpha.$$

Then, Theorem 2 in Zhang and Cheng (2005) shows that

$$\min_{1 \le k \le K} \alpha^{(k)} \le \alpha = \sum_{k=1}^{K} p_k \alpha^{(k)} \le \max_{1 \le k \le K} \alpha^{(k)}$$

always holds.

12.3.7   Generalized Hyperbolic Distribution

Suppose the log returns, $R_t = \ln X_t - \ln X_{t-1}$, follow the model

$$R_t = \sigma_t \epsilon_t,$$

where σ_t is the volatility process and ϵ_t are independent and identical random variables with zero mean and unit variance. Let $\text{VaR}_{\alpha,t}$ denote the corresponding VaR. Suppose ϵ_t are independent and identical and have the generalized hyperbolic distribution specified by the pdf

$$f(x) = \frac{(\eta/\delta)^\lambda}{\sqrt{2\pi}K_\lambda(\delta\eta)} \frac{K_{\lambda-1/2}(\alpha\sqrt{\delta^2 + (x - \mu)^2})}{\{\sqrt{\delta^2 + (x - \mu)^2}/\alpha\}^{1/2-\lambda}} \exp[\beta(x - \mu)],$$

where $\mu \in \mathbb{R}$ is a location parameter, $\alpha \in \mathbb{R}$ is a shape parameter, $\beta \in \mathbb{R}$ is an asymmetry parameter, $\delta \in \mathbb{R}$ is a scale parameter, $\lambda \in \mathbb{R}$, $\eta = \sqrt{\alpha^2 - \beta^2}$, and $K_\nu(\cdot)$ denotes the modified Bessel function of order ν.

Tian and Chan (2010) propose a method based on saddlepoint approximation for computing $\text{VaR}_{\alpha,t}$. It can be described as follows:

1. Estimate σ_t^2 by

$$\hat{\sigma}_t^2 = \left(\sum_{j=1}^{m} \omega_j R_{t-j} \right)^2$$

for $m > 1$, where ω_j are some nonnegative weights summing to one.

2. Compute $\hat{t}$ as the root of $\kappa'(t) = t$, where $\kappa'(\cdot)$ is defined in Step 3.

3. Compute $\hat{q}_p$ as the root of

$$
p = \begin{cases}
\exp\left\{ \kappa(\hat{t}) - \hat{t}t + \dfrac{1}{2}\hat{t}^2\kappa''(\hat{t}) \right\} \Phi(-\sqrt{\hat{t}^2\kappa''(\hat{t})}), & \text{if } t > E, \\[2ex]
\dfrac{1}{2}, & \text{if } t = E, \\[2ex]
1 - \exp\left\{ \kappa(\hat{t}) - \hat{t}t + \dfrac{1}{2}\hat{t}^2\kappa''(\hat{t}) \right\} \Phi(-\sqrt{\hat{t}^2\kappa''(\hat{t})}), & \text{if } t < E,
\end{cases}
$$

where

$$E = \mu + \frac{\delta\beta K_{\lambda+1}(\delta\eta)}{\eta K_{\lambda}(\delta\eta)},$$

$$\kappa(z) = \mu z + \ln \eta^{\lambda} - \lambda \ln \eta + \ln K_{\lambda}(\delta\eta) - \ln K_{\lambda}(\delta\eta),$$

$$\kappa'(z) = \mu + \frac{\delta(\beta + z)K_{\lambda+1}(\delta\eta)}{\eta K_{\lambda}(\delta\eta)},$$

$$\kappa''(z) = \frac{\delta K_{\lambda+1}(\delta\eta)}{\eta K_{\lambda}(\delta\eta)} + \frac{\delta^2(\beta + z)^2 K_{\lambda+2}(\delta\eta)}{\eta^2 K_{\lambda}(\delta\eta)} - \frac{\delta^2(\beta + z)^2 K_{\lambda+1}^2(\delta\eta)}{\eta^2 K_{\lambda}^2(\delta\eta)}.$$

4. Estimate $\text{VaR}_{\alpha,t}$ by $\widehat{\text{VaR}}_{\alpha,t} = \hat{\sigma}_t \hat{q}_p$.

12.3.8 Fourier Transformation Method

Siven et al. (2009) suggest a method for computing VaR by approximating the cdf F by a Fourier series. The approximation is given by the following result due to Hughett (1998): suppose

(a) that there exist constants A and $\alpha > 1$ such that $F(-y) \leq A|y|^{-\alpha}$ and $1 - F(y) \leq A|y|^{-\alpha}$ for all $y > 0$,

(b) that there exist constants B and $\beta > 0$ such that $|\phi(u)| \leq B|u/(2\pi)|^{-\beta}$ for all $u \in \mathbb{R}$, where $\phi(\cdot)$ denotes the characteristic function corresponding to $F(\cdot)$.

Then, for constants $0 < l < 2/3$, $T > 0$ and $N > 0$, the cdf F can be approximated as

$$F(x) \approx \frac{1}{2} + 2 \sum_{k=1}^{N/2-1} \text{Re}(G[k]\exp(2\pi ikx/T)),$$

where $i = \sqrt{-1}$, $\text{Re}(\cdot)$ denotes the real part, and

$$G(k) = \frac{1 - \cos(2\pi lk)}{2\pi ik}\phi(-2\pi k/T).$$

An estimator for VaR_p is obtained by solving the equation

$$\frac{1}{2} + 2 \sum_{k=1}^{N/2-1} \text{Re}(G[k]\exp(2\pi ikx/T)) = p$$

for x.

12.3.9   Principal Components Method

Brummelhuis et al. (2002) use an approximation based on the principal component method to compute VaR. If $\mathbf{S}(t) = (S_1(t), \ldots, S_n(t))$ is a vector of risk factors over time t and if $\Pi(t, \mathbf{S}(t))$ is a random variable, they define VaR to be

$$\Pr[\Pi(0, \mathbf{S}(0)) - \Pi(t, \mathbf{S}(t)) > \text{VaR}] = \alpha. \tag{12.10}$$

This equation is too general to be solved. So, Brummelhuis et al. (2002) consider the quadratic approximation

$$\Pi(t, \mathbf{S}(t)) - \Pi(0, \mathbf{S}(0)) \approx \Theta t + \Delta\xi + \frac{1}{2}\xi\Gamma\xi^T$$

and assume that ξ is normally distributed with mean $\mathbf{m}$ and covariance matrix $\mathbf{V}$. Under this approximation, we can rewrite (12.10) as

$$\Pr\left[\Theta + \Delta\xi + \frac{1}{2}\xi\Lambda\xi^T \leq -\text{VaR}\right] = \alpha.$$

Let $\mathbf{V} = \mathbf{H}^T\mathbf{H}$ denote the Cholesky decomposition and let

$$\widetilde{\Theta} = \Theta + \mathbf{m}\Delta + \frac{1}{2}\mathbf{m}\Gamma\mathbf{m}^T,$$

$$\widetilde{\Delta} = (\Delta + \mathbf{m}\Gamma)\mathbf{H}^T,$$

$$\widetilde{\Gamma} = \mathbf{H}\Gamma\mathbf{H}^T.$$

Also let $\widetilde{\mathbf{\Gamma}} = \mathbf{P}\widetilde{\mathbf{D}}\mathbf{P}^T$ denote the principal components decomposition of $\widetilde{\mathbf{\Gamma}}$, $\mathbf{v} = \widetilde{\mathbf{\Delta}}\mathbf{P}\widetilde{\mathbf{D}}^{-1}$, and $T = \Theta - \frac{1}{2}\mathbf{v}\mathbf{D}\mathbf{v}^T$. With these notations, Brummelhuis et al. (2002) show that VaR can be approximated by

$$\text{VaR} = K - T,$$

where K is the root of

$$\frac{1}{(2\pi)^{n/2}} \int_{\frac{1}{2}\mathbf{z}\widetilde{\mathbf{D}}\mathbf{z}^T \leq -\text{VaR}-T} \exp\left\{-\frac{1}{2}|z - v|^2\right\} dz = \alpha.$$

12.3.10 Quadratic Forms

Suppose the financial series are realizations of a quadratic form

$$V = \theta + \boldsymbol{\delta}^T\mathbf{Y} + \frac{1}{2}\mathbf{Y}^T\mathbf{\Lambda}\mathbf{Y} = \theta + \sum_{j=1}^{m}\left(\delta_j Y_j + \frac{1}{2}\lambda_j Y_j^2\right),$$

where $\mathbf{Y} = (Y_1, Y_2, \ldots, Y_m)^T$ is a standard normal vector, $\delta = (\delta_1, \delta_2, \ldots, \delta_m)^T$, and $\mathbf{\Lambda} = \text{diag}(\lambda_1, \lambda_2, \ldots, \lambda_m)$. Examples include nonlinear positions like options in finance or the modeling of bond prices in terms of interest rates (duration and convexity). Here, λs are the eigenvalues sorted in ascending order. Suppose there are $n \leq m$ distinct eigenvalues. Let i_j denote the highest index of the jth distinct eigenvalue with multiplicity μ_j. For $j = 1, 2, \ldots, n$, let

$$V_j = \begin{cases} \dfrac{1}{2}\lambda_{i_j} \displaystyle\sum_{\ell=i_{j-1}+1}^{i_j}\left(\dfrac{\delta_\ell}{\lambda_{i_j}} + Y_\ell\right)^2, & \text{if } \lambda_{i_j} \neq 0, \\[3ex] \lambda_{i_j} \displaystyle\sum_{\ell=i_{j-1}+1}^{i_j}\delta_\ell Y_\ell, & \text{if } \lambda_{i_j} = 0, \end{cases}$$

$$\bar{\delta}_j^2 = \sum_{\ell=i_{j-1}+1}^{i_j}\delta_\ell^2,$$

$$a_j^2 = \bar{\delta}_j^2 / \lambda_{i_j}^2.$$

Let b_j denote the moment-generating function of $V - V_j$ evaluated at $1/\lambda_{i_j}$. With this notation, Jaschke et al. (2004) derive various approximations for VaR. The first of these applicable for $\lambda_{i_1} < 0$ is

$$\text{VaR}_\alpha \approx \lambda_{i_1} \ln b_1 + \frac{\lambda_{i_1}}{2}\chi^2_{\mu_1, 1-\alpha}(a_1^2),$$

where $\chi^2_{\mu,\alpha}(\delta)$ denotes the 100α percentile of a noncentral chi-square random variable with degrees of freedom μ and noncentrality parameter δ. The second of the approximations applicable for $\lambda_{i_1} = 0$ and $\lambda_{i_n} = 0$ is

$$\text{VaR}_\alpha \approx \theta - \sum_{j=2}^{n} \frac{\overline{\delta}_j^2}{2\lambda_{i_j}} + (\widetilde{F}_1^t)^{-1}(\alpha),$$

where

$$\widetilde{F}_1^t(x) = \left[\frac{|\overline{\delta}_1|}{\sqrt{2\pi}} \exp\left(-\sum_{j=2}^{n} a_j^2/2 \right) \prod_{j=2}^{n} \left| \overline{\delta}_1^2/\lambda_{i_j} \right|^{\mu_j/2} \right] \frac{\exp[-x^2/(2\overline{\delta}_1^2)]}{(-x)^{1+\sum_{j=2}^{n} \mu_j/2}}.$$

The third of the approximations applicable for $\lambda_{i_1} > 0$ and $\lambda_{i_n} < 0$ is

$$\text{VaR}_\alpha \approx \theta - \sum_{j=1}^{n} \frac{\overline{\delta}_j^2}{2\lambda_{i_j}} + \left(\frac{m\alpha}{2d} \right)^{2/m},$$

where

$$d = \frac{1}{\Gamma(m/2)} \prod_{j=1}^{n} |\lambda_{i_j}|^{-\mu_j/2} \exp\left(-\sum_{j=1}^{n} a_j^2/2 \right).$$

12.3.11   Elliptical Distribution

Suppose a portfolio return, say, R, is made up of n asset returns, say, R_i, $i = 1, 2, \ldots, n$, as $R = \delta_1 R_1 + \cdots + \delta_n R_n = \boldsymbol{\delta}^T \mathbf{R}$, where δ_i are nonnegative weights summing to one, $\boldsymbol{\delta} = (\delta_1, \ldots, \delta_n)^T$ and $\mathbf{R} = (R_1, \ldots, R_n)^T$. Kamdem (2005) derives various expressions for the VaR of R by supposing that $\mathbf{R}$ has an elliptically symmetric distribution.

If $\mathbf{R}$ has the joint pdf $f_{\mathbf{R}}(\mathbf{r}) = |\boldsymbol{\Sigma}|^{-1/2} g((\mathbf{r} - \boldsymbol{\mu})^T \boldsymbol{\Sigma}^{-1}(\mathbf{r} - \boldsymbol{\mu}))$, where $\boldsymbol{\mu}$ is the mean vector, $\boldsymbol{\Sigma}$ is the variance–covariance matrix, and $g(\cdot)$ is a continuous and integrable function over $\mathbb{R}$, then it is shown that

$$\text{VaR}_\alpha(R) = \boldsymbol{\delta}^T \boldsymbol{\mu} + q\sqrt{\boldsymbol{\delta}^T \boldsymbol{\Sigma} \boldsymbol{\delta}},$$

where q is the root of

$$G(s) = \alpha,$$

where

$$G(s) = \frac{\pi^{(n-1)/2}}{\Gamma((n-1)/2)} \int_s^{-\infty} \int_{z_1^2}^{\infty} (u - z_1^2)^{(n-3)/2} g(u) \, du \, dz_1. \qquad (12.11)$$

If **R** follows a mixture of elliptical pdfs given by

$$f_{\mathbf{R}}(\mathbf{r}) = \sum_{i=1}^{m} \beta_j |\mathbf{\Sigma}_j|^{-1/2} g_j((\mathbf{r} - \mathbf{\mu}_j)^T \mathbf{\Sigma}_j^{-1} (\mathbf{r} - \mathbf{\mu}_j)),$$

where $\mathbf{\mu}_j$ is the mean vector for the jth elliptical pdf, $\mathbf{\Sigma}_j$ is the variance–covariance matrix for the jth elliptical pdf, and β_j are nonnegative weights summing to one, then it is shown that the VaR of **R** is the root of

$$\sum_{j=1}^{m} \beta_j G_j \left(\frac{\mathbf{\delta}^T \mathbf{\mu}_j + \mathrm{VaR}_\alpha}{\sqrt{\mathbf{\delta}^T \mathbf{\Sigma}_j \mathbf{\delta}}} \right) = \alpha,$$

where $G_j(\cdot)$ is defined as in (12.11).

12.3.12 Copula Method

Suppose a portfolio return, say, R, is made up of two asset returns, R_1 and R_2, as $R = wR_1 + (1 - w)R_2$, where w is the portfolio weight for asset 1 and $1 - w$ is the portfolio weight for asset 2. Huang et al. (2009) consider computation of VaR for this situation by supposing that the joint cdf of (R_1, R_2) is $C(F_1(R_1), F_2(R_2))$, where C is a copula (Nelsen, 1999), F_i is the marginal cdf of R_i, and f_i is the marginal pdf of R_i. Then, the cdf of R is

$$\Pr(R \leq r) = \Pr(wR_1 + (1 - w)R_2 \leq r)$$

$$= \Pr \left(R_1 \leq \frac{r}{w} - \frac{(1 - w)R_2}{w} \right)$$

$$= \int_{-\infty}^{\infty} \int_{-\infty}^{r/w - (1-w)R_2/w} c(F_1(r_1), F_2(r_2)) f_1(r_1) f_2(r_2) dr_1 \, dr_2,$$

where c is the copula pdf. So, $\mathrm{VaR}_p(R)$ can be computed by solving the equation

$$\int_{-\infty}^{\infty} \int_{-\infty}^{\mathrm{VaR}_p(R)/w - (1-w)R_2/w} C(F_1(r_1), F_2(r_2)) dr_1 \, dr_2 = p.$$

In general, this equation will have to be solved numerically or by simulation.

Franke et al. (2011) consider the more general case that the portfolio return R is made up of n asset returns, R_i, $i = 1, 2, \ldots, n$; that is,

$$R = \sum_{i=1}^{n} w_i R_i$$

for some nonnegative weights summing to one. Suppose as in the preceding text that the joint cdf of $(R_1, \ldots, R_n)$ is $C(F_1(R_1), \ldots, F_n(R_n))$, where F_i is the marginal cdf of R_i and f_i is the marginal pdf of R_i. Then, the cdf of R is

$$\Pr(R \leq r) = \int_{\mathcal{U}} c(u_1, \ldots, u_n)du_1 \cdots du_n,$$

where

$$u = \{[0, 1]^{n-1} \times [0, u_n(r)]\}$$

and

$$u_n(r) = F_n\left(r/w_n - \sum_{i=1}^{n-1} w_i F_i^{-1}(u_i)/w_n\right).$$

So, $\mathrm{VaR}_p(R)$ can be computed by solving the equation

$$\int_{u} c(u_1, \ldots, u_n)du_1 \cdots du_n = p.$$

Again, this equation will have to be computed by numerical integration or simulation.

12.3.13   Gram–Charlier Approximation

Simonato (2011) suggests a number of approximations for computing (12.2). The first of these is based on Gram–Charlier expansion.

Let $\kappa_3 = E[Z_t^3]$ denote the skewness coefficient and $\kappa_4 = E[Z_t^4]$ the kurtosis coefficient of the standardized log returns. Simonato (2011) suggests the approximation

$$\mathrm{VaR}_\alpha = \alpha_h + \sigma_h \psi_{\mathrm{GC}}^{-1}(p),$$

where $\psi_{\mathrm{GC}}^{-1}(\cdot)$ is the inverse function of

$$\psi_{\mathrm{GC}}(k) = \Phi(k) - \frac{\kappa_3}{6}(k^2 - 1)\phi(k) - \frac{\kappa_4 - 3}{24}k(k^2 - 3)\phi(k),$$

where $\Phi(\cdot)$ denotes the standard normal cdf and $\phi(\cdot)$ denotes the standard normal pdf.

12.3.14   Delta–Gamma Approximation

Let $\mathbf{R} = (R_1, \ldots, R_n)^T$ denote a vector of returns normally distributed with zero means and covariate matrix $\boldsymbol{\Sigma}$. Suppose the return of an associated portfolio takes the general form $Y = g(\mathbf{R})$. It will be difficult to find the value of risk of Y for general $g(\cdot)$. Some approximations are desirable. The delta–gamma approximation is a commonly used approximation (Feuerverger and Wong, 2000).

Suppose we can approximate $\mathbf{Y} = \mathbf{a}_1^T\mathbf{R} + \mathbf{R}^T\mathbf{B}_1\mathbf{R}$ for $\mathbf{a}_1$ a $n \times 1$ vector and $\mathbf{B}_1$ a $n \times n$ matrix. Let $\Sigma = \mathbf{HH}^T$ denote the Cholesky decomposition. Let $\lambda_1, \ldots, \lambda_n$ and $\mathbf{P}_1, \ldots, \mathbf{P}_n$ denote the eigenvalues and eigenvectors of $\mathbf{H}^T\mathbf{B}_1\mathbf{H}$. Let $\mathbf{a}_j$ denote the entries of $\mathbf{P}^T\mathbf{H}^T\mathbf{a}_1$, where $\mathbf{P} = (\mathbf{P}_1, \ldots, \mathbf{P}_n)$. Then, the delta–gamma approximation is that

$$Y \stackrel{d}{=} \sum_{j=1}^{n}(a_jZ_j + \lambda_jZ_j^2), \tag{12.12}$$

where $Z_1, \ldots, Z_n$ are independent standard normal random variables. The value of risk can be obtained by inverting the distribution of the right-hand side of (12.12).

12.3.15   Cornish–Fisher Approximation

Another approximation suggested by Simonato (2011) is based on Cornish–Fisher expansion. With the notation as in Section 12.3.13, the approximation is

$$\text{VaR}_\alpha = \alpha_h + \sigma_h\psi_{\text{CF}}^{-1}(p),$$

where $\psi_{\text{CF}}^{-1}(\cdot)$ is the inverse function of

$$\psi_{\text{CF}}^{-1}(p) = \Phi^{-1}(p) + \frac{\kappa_3}{6}\left[\left(\Phi^{-1}(p)\right)^2 - 1\right] + \frac{\kappa_4 - 3}{24}\left[\left(\Phi^{-1}(p)\right)^3 - 3\Phi^{-1}(p)\right]$$
$$- \frac{\kappa_3^2}{36}\left[2\left(\Phi^{-1}(p)\right)^3 - 5\Phi^{-1}(p)\right],$$

where $\Phi^{-1}(\cdot)$ denotes the standard normal quantile function.

12.3.16   Johnson Family Method

A third approximation suggested by Simonato (2011) is based on the Johnson family of distributions due to Johnson (1949).

Let Y denote a standard normal random variable. A Johnson random variable can be expressed as

$$Z = c + dg^{-1}\left(\frac{Y - a}{b}\right),$$

where

$$g^{-1}(u) = \begin{cases} \exp(u), & \text{for the lognormal family,} \\ \left[\exp(u) - \exp(-u)\right]/2, & \text{for the unbounded family,} \\ 1/[1 + \exp(-u)], & \text{for the bounded family,} \\ u, & \text{for the normal family.} \end{cases}$$

Here, a, b, c, and d are unknown parameters determined, for example, by the method of moments; see Hill et al. (1976).

With the notation as in the preceding text, the approximation is

$$\text{VaR}_\alpha = \alpha_h + \sigma_h \psi_J^{-1}(p; a, b, c, d),$$

where

$$\psi_J^{-1}(p; a, b, c, d) = c + dg^{-1}\left(\frac{\Phi^{-1}(p) - a}{b}\right),$$

where $\Phi^{-1}(\cdot)$ denotes the standard normal quantile function.

12.3.17   Tukey Method

Jiménez and Arunachalam (2011) present a method for approximating VaR based on Tukey's g and h family of distributions.

Let Y denote a standard normal random variable. A Tukey g and h random variable can be expressed as

$$Z = g^{-1}[\exp(gY) - 1]\exp(hY^2/2)$$

for $g \neq 0$ and $h \in \mathbb{R}$. The family of lognormal distributions is contained as the particular case for $h = 0$. The family of Tukey's h distribution is contained as the limiting case for $g \to 0$.

With the notation as in Section 12.3.13, the approximation suggested by Jiménez and Arunachalam (2011) is

$$\text{VaR}_p = A + BT_{g,h}(\Phi^{-1}(p)),$$

where A and B are location and scale parameters. For $g = 0$ and $h = 1$, Z is a normal random variable with mean μ and standard deviation σ, so $A = \mu$ and $B = \sigma$. For $g = 0.773$ and $h = -0.09445$, Z is an exponential random variable with parameter λ, so $A = (1/\lambda)\ln 2$ and $B = g/\lambda$. For $g = 0$ and $h = 0.057624$, Z is a Student's t random variable with ten degrees of freedom, so $A = 0$ and $B = 1$.

12.3.18   Asymmetric Laplace Distribution

Trindade and Zhu (2007) consider the case that the log returns of $X_1, X_2, \ldots, X_n$ are a random sample from the asymmetric Laplace distribution given by the pdf

$$f(x) = \frac{\kappa\sqrt{2}}{\tau(1 + \kappa^2)}\begin{cases}\exp\left(-\dfrac{\kappa\sqrt{2}}{\tau}|x - \theta|\right), & \text{if } x \geq \theta, \\[2ex] \exp\left(-\dfrac{\sqrt{2}}{\kappa\tau}|x - \theta|\right), & \text{if } x < \theta\end{cases}$$

for $x \in \mathbb{R}$, $\tau > 0$, and $\kappa > 0$. The maximum likelihood estimator of VaR_α is derived as

$$\widehat{\text{VaR}}_\alpha = -\frac{\hat{\tau}\ln\,[(1+\hat{\kappa}^2)(1-\alpha)]}{\hat{\kappa}\sqrt{2}},$$

where $(\hat{\tau}, \hat{\kappa})$ are the maximum likelihood estimators of (τ, κ). Trindade and Zhu (2007) show further that

$$\sqrt{n}(\widehat{\text{VaR}}_\alpha - \text{VaR}_\alpha) \to N(0, \sigma^2)$$

in distribution as $n \to \infty$, where $\sigma^2 = \tau^2[(\omega-1)^2\kappa^2 + 2\omega^2]/(4\kappa^2)$ and $\omega = \ln\,[(1+\kappa^2)(1-\alpha)]$.

12.3.19 Asymmetric Power Distribution

Komunjer (2007) introduces the asymmetric power distribution as a model for risk management. A random variable, say, X, is said to have this distribution if its pdf is

$$f(x) = \begin{cases} \dfrac{\delta^{1/\lambda}}{\Gamma(1+1/\lambda)}\exp\left[-\dfrac{\delta}{\alpha^\lambda}|x|^\lambda\right], & \text{if } x \le 0, \\[3mm] \dfrac{\delta^{1/\lambda}}{\Gamma(1+1/\lambda)}\exp\left[-\dfrac{\delta}{(1-\alpha)^\lambda}|x|^\lambda\right], & \text{if } x > 0 \end{cases} \tag{12.13}$$

for $x \in \mathbb{R}$, where $0 < \alpha < 1$, $\lambda > 0$ and $\delta = 2\alpha^\lambda(1-\alpha)^\lambda/\{\alpha^\lambda + (1-\alpha)^\lambda\}$. Note that λ is a shape parameter and α is a scale parameter. The cdf corresponding to (12.13) is shown to be (Lemma 1, Komunjer, 2007)

$$F(x) = \begin{cases} \alpha\left[1 - \mathcal{I}\left(\dfrac{\delta}{\alpha^\lambda}\sqrt{\lambda}|x|^\lambda, 1/\lambda\right)\right], & \text{if } x \le 0, \\[3mm] 1 - (1-\alpha)\left[1 - \mathcal{I}\left(\dfrac{\delta}{(1-\alpha)^\lambda}\sqrt{\lambda}|x|^\lambda, 1/\lambda\right)\right], & \text{if } x > 0, \end{cases} \tag{12.14}$$

where $\mathcal{I}(x, \gamma) = \int_0^{x\sqrt{\gamma}} t^{\gamma-1}\exp(-t)dt/\Gamma(\gamma)$. Inverting (12.14) as in Lemma 2 of Komunjer (2007), we can express $\text{VaR}_p(X)$ as

$$\text{VaR}_p(X) = \begin{cases} -\left[\dfrac{\alpha^\lambda}{\delta\sqrt{\lambda}}\right]^{1/\lambda}\left[\mathcal{I}^{-1}\left(1-\dfrac{p}{\alpha}, \dfrac{1}{\lambda}\right)\right]^{1/\lambda}, & \text{if } p \le \alpha, \\[3mm] -\left[\dfrac{(1-\alpha)^\lambda}{\delta\sqrt{\lambda}}\right]^{1/\lambda}\left[\mathcal{I}^{-1}\left(1-\dfrac{1-p}{1-\alpha}, \dfrac{1}{\lambda}\right)\right]^{1/\lambda}, & \text{if } p > \alpha, \end{cases} \tag{12.15}$$

where $\mathcal{I}^{-1}(\cdot, \cdot)$ denotes the inverse function of $\mathcal{I}(\cdot, \cdot)$. An estimator of $\mathrm{VaR}_p(X)$ can be obtained by replacing the parameters in (12.15) by their maximum likelihood estimators; see Proposition 2 in Komunjer (2007).

12.3.20   Weibull Distribution

Gebizlioglu et al. (2011) consider estimation of VaR based on the Weibull distribution. Suppose $X_1, X_2, \ldots, X_n$ is a random sample from a Weibull distribution with the cdf specified by $F(x) = 1 - \exp\{-(x/\theta)^\beta\}$ for $x > 0$, $\theta > 0$ and $\beta > 0$. Then, the estimator for VaR is

$$\widehat{\mathrm{VaR}}_\alpha = \{-\ln(1-\alpha)\}^{1/\hat{\beta}} \hat{\theta}.$$

Gebizlioglu et al. (2011) consider various methods for obtaining the estimators $\hat{\theta}$ and $\hat{\beta}$. By the method of maximum likelihood, $\hat{\theta}$ and $\hat{\beta}$ are the simultaneous solutions of

$$\frac{\bar{x}^2}{s^2} = \frac{\{\Gamma(1 + 1/\beta)\}^2}{\Gamma(1 + 2/\beta) - \Gamma^2(1 + 1/\beta)}$$

and

$$\hat{\theta} = \frac{\bar{x}}{\Gamma(1 + 1/\hat{\beta})},$$

where $\bar{X}$ is the sample mean and s^2 is the sample variance. By Cohen and Whitten (1982)'s modified method of maximum likelihood, $\hat{\theta}$ and $\hat{\alpha}$ are the simultaneous solutions of

$$-\frac{nX_{(1)}^\beta}{\ln\ [n/(n+1)]} = \sum_{i=1}^n X_i^\beta$$

and

$$\hat{\theta} = \left(\frac{1}{n} \sum_{i=1}^n X_i^{\hat{\beta}}\right)^{1/\hat{\beta}},$$

where $X_{(1)} \leq X_{(2)} \leq \cdots \leq X_{(n)}$ are the order statistics in ascending order. By Tiku (1967 and 1968) and Tiku and Akkaya (2004)'s modified method of maximum likelihood,

$$\hat{\theta} = \exp(\hat{\delta}), \hat{\beta} = 1/\hat{\eta},$$

where

$$\hat{\delta} = K + D\hat{\eta}, \quad \hat{\eta} = \{B + \sqrt{B^2 + 4nC}\}/(2n),$$

$$K = \sum_{i=1}^{n} \beta_i X_{(i)}/m, \quad D = \sum_{i=1}^{n} (\alpha_i - 1)/m,$$

$$B = \sum_{i=1}^{n} (\alpha_i - 1)(X_{(i)} - K), \quad C = \sum_{i=1}^{n} \beta_i (X_{(i)} - K)^2,$$

$$m = \sum_{i=1}^{n} \beta_i, \quad \alpha_i = [1 - t_{(i)}] \exp(t_{(i)}),$$

$$\beta_i = \exp(t_{(i)}), \quad t_{(i)} = \ln \left(-\ln \left(1 - i/(n+1) \right) \right).$$

By the least squares method, $\hat{\theta}$ and $\hat{\alpha}$ are those minimizing

$$\sum_{i=1}^{n} \left(1 - \exp \left\{ -\left[X_{(i)}/\theta \right]^{\beta} \right\} - \frac{i}{n+1} \right)^2$$

with respect to θ and α. By the weighted least squares method, $\hat{\theta}$ and $\hat{\alpha}$ are those minimizing

$$\sum_{i=1}^{n} \frac{(n+1)^2(n+2)}{i(n-i+1)} \left(1 - \exp \left\{ -\left[X_{(i)}/\theta \right]^{\beta} \right\} - \frac{i}{n+1} \right)^2$$

with respect to θ and α. By the percentile method, $\hat{\theta}$ and $\hat{\alpha}$ are those minimizing

$$\sum_{i=1}^{n} \left\{ X_{(i)} - \theta \left[-\ln \left(1 - \frac{i}{n+1} \right) \right]^{1/\beta} \right\}^2$$

with respect to θ and α.

12.3.21 ARCH Models

ARCH models are popular in finance. Suppose the log returns, say, R_t, of $\{X_1, X_2, \ldots, X_n\}$ follow the ARCH model specified by

$$R_t = \sigma_t \epsilon_t, \quad \sigma_t^2 = \beta_0 + \sum_{j=1}^{k} \beta_j R_{t-j}^2,$$

where ϵ_i are independent and identical random variables with zero mean, unit variance, pdf $f(\cdot)$, and cdf $F(\cdot)$, and $\beta = (\beta_0, \beta_1, \ldots, \beta_k)^T$ is an unknown parameter vector satisfying $\beta_0 > 0$ and $\beta_j \geq 0, j = 1, 2, \ldots, k$. If $\hat{\beta} = (\hat{\beta}_0, \hat{\beta}_1, \ldots, \hat{\beta}_k)^T$ are the maximum likelihood estimators, then the residuals are

$$\hat{\epsilon}_t = R_t/\hat{\sigma}_t,$$

where

$$\hat{\sigma}_t^2 = \hat{\beta}_0 + \sum_{j=1}^{k} \hat{\beta}_j R_{t-j}^2.$$

Taniai and Taniguchi (2008) show that VaR for this ARCH model can be approximated by

$$\widehat{\text{VaR}}_p \approx \hat{\sigma}_{n+1}[F^{-1}(p) + \hat{\sigma}\Phi^{-1}(\alpha)/\sqrt{n}],$$

where

$$\sigma^2 = \frac{1}{f^2(F^{-1}(p))} \left[p(1-p) \right.$$

$$+ F^{-1}(p)f(F^{-1}(p)) \left\{ \int_{-\infty}^{F^{-1}(p)} u^2 f(u) du - p \right\} \tau^T U^{-1} V$$

$$\left. + \frac{1}{4}(F^{-1}(p))^2 f^2(F^{-1}(p)) \tau^T U^{-1} S U^{-1} \tau \right],$$

where $V = E[\sigma_t^2 W_{t-1}]$, $S = 2E[\sigma_t^4 W_{t-1} W_{t-1}^T]$, $W = (1, R_t^2, \ldots, R_{t-k+1}^2)^T$, $U = E[W_{t-1} W_{t-1}^T]$, $\tau = (\tau_0, \tau_1, \ldots, \tau_k)^T$, $\tau_0 = E[1/\sigma_t^2]$, and $\tau_j = E[R_{t-j}^2/\sigma_t^2]$, $j = 1, 2, \ldots, k$.

12.3.22 GARCH Models

Suppose the financial returns, say, R_t, satisfy the model

$$[1 - \phi(L)]R_t = [1 - \theta(L)] \; \epsilon_t, \epsilon_t = \eta_t \sqrt{h_t}, \tag{12.16}$$

where η_t are independent and identical standard normal random variables, R_t is the return at time t, L denotes the lag operator satisfying $LR_t = R_{t-1}$, $\phi(L)$ is the polynomial $\phi(L) = 1 - \sum_{i=1}^{r} \phi_i L^i$, $\theta(L)$ is the polynomial $\theta(L) = 1 + \sum_{i=1}^{s} \theta_i L^i$, h_t is the conditional variance, and η_t are independent and identical residuals with zero means and unit variances. One popular specification for h_t is

$$h_t = \omega + \sum_{i=1}^{p} \alpha_i \epsilon_{t-i}^2 + \sum_{i=1}^{q} \beta_i h_{t-i}. \tag{12.17}$$

This corresponds to the GARCH (p, q) model.

For the model given by (12.16) and (12.17), Chan (2009b) proposes the following algorithm for computing VaR:

1. Estimate the maximum likelihood estimates of the parameters in (12.16) and (12.17).

2. Using the parameter estimates, compute the standardized residuals $\widehat{\eta}_t = (R_t - \widehat{r}_t)/\widehat{h}_t$.

3. Compute the first k sample moments for $\widehat{\eta}_t$.

4. Compute

$$\widehat{p}(\eta_t) = \exp\left(\sum_{i=1}^{k} \lambda_i \eta_t^i\right) \bigg/ \int \exp\left(\sum_{i=1}^{k} \lambda_i \eta_t^i\right) d\eta_t.$$

The parameters $\lambda_1, \lambda_2, \ldots, \lambda_k$ are determined from the sample moments of Step 3 in a way explained in Chan (2009a) and Rockinger and Jondeau (2002).

5. Compute $\widehat{\text{VaR}}_p$ as the root of the equation

$$\int_{-\infty}^{K} \widehat{p}(\eta_t) d\eta_t = p.$$

12.3.23 GARCH Model with Heavy Tails

Chan et al. (2007) consider the case that financial returns, say, R_t, come from a GARCH (p, q) specified by

$$R_t = \sigma_t \epsilon_t, \quad \sigma_t^2 = c + \sum_{i=1}^{p} b_i R_{t-i}^2 + \sum_{j=1}^{q} a_j \sigma_{t-j}^2,$$

where R_t is strictly stationary with $ER_t^2 < \infty$, and ϵ_t are zero mean, unit variance, independent, and identical random variables independent of $\{R_{t-k}, k \geq 1\}$. Further, Chan et al. (2007) assume that ϵ_t have heavy tails, that is, their cdf, say, G, satisfies

$$\lim_{x\to\infty} \frac{1 - G(xy)}{1 - G(x)} = y^{-\gamma}, \quad \lim_{x\to\infty} \frac{G(-x)}{1 - G(x)} = d$$

for all $y > 0$, where $\gamma > 0$ and $d \geq 0$. Chan et al. (2007) show that the VaR for this model given by

$$\text{VaR}_\alpha = \inf\{x\colon \Pr(R_{n+1} \leq x | R_{n+1-k}, k \geq 1) \geq \alpha\}$$

can be estimated by

$$\widehat{\text{VaR}}_\alpha = \widetilde{\sigma}_{n+1}(\widehat{a}, \widehat{b}, \widehat{c})(1 - \alpha)^{-1/\widehat{\gamma}} \left(\frac{k}{m}\right)^{1/\widehat{\gamma}} \widehat{\epsilon}_{m,m-k},$$

where

$$\widetilde{\sigma}_t^2(a, b, c) = \frac{c}{1 - \sum\limits_{j=1}^{q} a_j} + \sum_{i=1}^{p} b_i R_{t-i}^2$$

$$+ \sum_{i=1}^{p} b_i \sum_{k=1}^{\infty} \sum_{j_1=1}^{q} \cdots \sum_{j_k=1}^{q} a_{j_1} \cdots a_{j_k} R^2_{t-i-j_1-\cdots-j_k}$$

$$I\{t - i - j_1 - \cdots - j_k \geq 1\},$$

$$L_v(a, b, c) = \sum_{t=v}^{n} \{R^2_t / \tilde{\sigma}^2_t(a, b, c) + \ln \tilde{\sigma}^2_t(a, b, c)\},$$

$$(\hat{a}, \hat{b}, \hat{c}) = \underset{(a,b,c)}{\arg\min} L_v(a, b, c),$$

$$\hat{\epsilon}_t = R_t / \tilde{\sigma}^2_t(\hat{a}, \hat{b}, \hat{c}),$$

$$\hat{\gamma} = \left\{ \frac{1}{k} \sum_{i=1}^{k} \ln \frac{\hat{\epsilon}_{m,m-i+1}}{\hat{\epsilon}_{m,m-k}} \right\}^{-1},$$

where $v = v(n) \to \infty$ and $v/n \to 0$ as $n \to \infty$, $m = n - v + 1$, $\hat{\epsilon}_{m,1} \leq \hat{\epsilon}_{m,2} \leq \cdots \leq \hat{\epsilon}_{m,m}$ are the order statistics of $\hat{\epsilon}_v, \hat{\epsilon}_{v+1}, \ldots, \hat{\epsilon}_n$, and $k = k(m) \to \infty$ and $k/m \to 0$ as $n \to \infty$. Chan et al. (2007) also establish asymptotic normality of $\widehat{\text{VaR}}_\alpha$.

12.3.24   ARMA–GARCH Model

Suppose the financial returns, say, R_t, $t = 1, 2, \ldots, T$, satisfy the ARMA (p, q)–GARCH(r, s) model specified by

$$R_t = a_0 + \sum_{i=1}^{p} a_i R_{t-i} + \epsilon_t + \sum_{j=1}^{q} b_j \epsilon_{t-j},$$

$$\sigma^2_t = c_0 + \sum_{i=1}^{r} c_i \epsilon^2_{t-i} + \sum_{j=1}^{s} d_j \sigma^2_{t-j},$$

$$\epsilon_t = z_t \sigma_t,$$

where z_t are independent standard normal random variables. For this model, Hartz et al. (2006) show that the h-step ahead forecast of VaR can be estimated by

$$\hat{\mu}_{T+h} + \hat{\sigma}_{T+h} \Phi^{-1}(\alpha),$$

where

$$\hat{\epsilon}_t = R_t - \hat{a}_0 - \sum_{i=1}^{p} \hat{a}_i R_{t-i} - \sum_{j=1}^{q} \hat{b}_j \hat{\epsilon}_{t-j},$$

$$\hat{\sigma}^2_t = \hat{c}_0 + \sum_{i=1}^{r} \hat{c}_i \hat{\epsilon}^2_{t-i} + \sum_{j=1}^{s} \hat{d}_j \hat{\sigma}^2_{t-j},$$

$$\widehat{\mu}_{T+h} = \widehat{a}_0 + \sum_{i=1}^{p} \widehat{a}_i R_{T+h-i} + \sum_{j=1}^{q} \widehat{b}_j \widehat{\epsilon}_{T+h-j},$$

$$\widehat{\sigma}_{T+h}^2 = \widehat{c}_0 + \sum_{i=1}^{r} \widehat{c}_i \widehat{\epsilon}_{T+h-i}^2 + \sum_{j=1}^{s} \widehat{d}_j \widehat{\sigma}_{T+h-j}^2.$$

The parameter estimators required can be obtained, for example, by the method of maximum likelihood.

12.3.25 Markov Switching ARCH Model

Suppose the financial returns, say, R_t, $t = 1, 2, \ldots, T$, satisfy the Markov switching ARCH model specified by

$$R_t = u_{s_t} + \epsilon_t,$$

$$\epsilon_t = (g_{s_t} w_t)^{1/2},$$

$$w_t = (h_t e_t)^{1/2},$$

$$h_t = a_0 + a_1 w_{t-1}^2 + \cdots + a_q w_{t-q}^2,$$

where e_t are standard normal random variables, s_t is an unobservable random variable assumed to follow a first-order Markov process, and w_t is a typical ARCH(q) process. This model is due to Bollerslev (1986). An estimator of the VaR at time t can be obtained by inverting the cdf of R_t with its parameters replaced by their maximum likelihood estimators.

12.3.26 Fractionally Integrated GARCH Model

Suppose the financial returns, say, R_t, $t = 1, 2, \ldots, T$, satisfy the fractionally integrated GARCH model specified by

$$R_t = \sigma_t \epsilon_t,$$

$$\sigma_t^2 = w + \sum_{i=1}^{p} \beta_i (\sigma_{t-i}^2 - R_{t-i}^2) - \sum_{i=1}^{\infty} \lambda_i R_{t-i}^2,$$

where ϵ_t are random variables with zero means and unit variances. This model is due to Baillie et al. (1996). An estimator of the VaR at time t can be obtained by inverting the cdf of R_t with its parameters replaced by their maximum likelihood estimators. This of course depends on the distribution of ϵ_t. If, for example, ϵ_t are normally distributed, then $\widehat{\text{VaR}}_{t,\alpha} = \widehat{\sigma}_{t+1} \Phi^{-1}(\alpha)$, where $\widehat{\sigma}_{t+1}$ may be the maximum likelihood estimator of σ_{t+1}.

12.3.27   RiskMetrics Model

Suppose $\{R_t\}$ are the log returns of $\{X_1, X_2, \ldots, X_n\}$ and let Ω_t denote the information up to time t. The RiskMetrics model (RiskMetrics Group, 1996) is specified by

$$R_t = \epsilon_t,$$

$$\epsilon_t | \Omega_{t-1} \sim N(0, \sigma_t^2),$$

$$\sigma_t^2 = \lambda \sigma_{t-1}^2 + (1 - \lambda)\epsilon_{t-1}^2, 0 < \lambda < 1.$$

The VaR for this model can be computed by inverting

$$\Pr(R_t < \text{VaR}_{t,\alpha}) = \alpha$$

with the parameters, σ_t^2 and λ, replaced by their maximum likelihood estimators.

12.3.28   Capital Asset Pricing Model

Let R_i denote the return on asset i, let R_f denote the "risk-free rate," and let R_m denote the "return on the market portfolio." With this notation, Fernandez (2006) considers the capital asset pricing model given by

$$R_i - R_f = \alpha_i + \beta_i(R_m - R_f)\epsilon_i$$

for $i = 1, 2, \ldots, k$, where ϵ_i are independent random variables with $\text{Var}(\epsilon_i) = \sigma_{\epsilon_i}^2$ and $\text{Var}(R_m) = \sigma_m^2$. It is easy to see that

$$\text{Var}(R_i) = \beta_i^2 \sigma_m^2 + \sigma_e^2,$$

$$\text{Cov}(R_i, R_j) = \beta_i \beta_j \sigma_m^2.$$

Fernandez (2006) shows that the VaR of the portfolio of k assets can be expressed as

$$\text{VaR}_\alpha = V_0 \Phi^{-1}(\alpha)\sqrt{\mathbf{w}^T(\boldsymbol{\beta}\boldsymbol{\beta}^T \sigma_m^2 + \mathbf{E})\mathbf{w}}, \qquad (12.18)$$

where $\mathbf{w}$ is a $k \times 1$ vector of portfolio weights, V_0 is the initial value of the portfolio, $\boldsymbol{\beta} = (\beta_1, \ldots, \beta_k)^T$, and $\mathbf{E} = \text{diag}(\sigma_{\epsilon_1}^2, \ldots, \sigma_{\epsilon_k}^2)^T$. An estimator of (12.18) can be obtained by replacing the parameters by their maximum likelihood estimators.

12.3.29   Dagum Distribution

The Dagum distribution is due to Dagum (1977 and 1980). It has the pdf and cdf specified by

$$f(x) = \beta \lambda \delta \exp(-\delta x)[1 + \lambda \exp(-\delta x)]^{-\beta - 1}$$

and

$$F(x) = [1 + \lambda \exp(-\delta x)]^{-\beta},$$

respectively, for $x > 0$, $\lambda > 0$, $\beta > 0$, and $\delta > 0$. Domma and Perri (2009) discuss an application of this distribution for VaR estimation. They show that

$$\widehat{\text{VaR}}_p = \frac{1}{\hat{\delta}} \ln \left(\frac{\hat{\lambda}}{p^{-1/\hat{\beta}} - 1} \right),$$

where $(\hat{\lambda}, \hat{\beta}, \hat{\delta})$ are maximum likelihood estimators of (λ, β, δ) based on $\{X_1, X_2, \ldots, X_n\}$ being a random sample coming from the Dagum distribution. Domma and Perri (2009) show further that

$$\sqrt{n}(\widehat{\text{VaR}}_p - \text{VaR}_p) \rightarrow N(0, \sigma^2)$$

in distribution as $n \rightarrow \infty$, where $\sigma = \mathbf{g}\mathbf{I}^{-1}\mathbf{g}^T$ and

$$\mathbf{g} = \left[-\frac{p^{-1/\beta} \ln p}{\delta \beta^2 \left(p^{-1/\beta} - 1 \right)}, \frac{1}{\lambda \delta}, -\frac{1}{\delta^2} \ln \left(\frac{\lambda}{p^{-1/\beta} - 1} \right) \right].$$

Here, $\mathbf{I}$ is the expected information matrix of $(\hat{\lambda}, \hat{\beta}, \hat{\delta})$. An explicit expression for the matrix is given in the appendix of Domma and Perri (2009).

12.3.30 Location-Scale Distributions

Suppose $X_1, X_2, \ldots, X_n$ is a random sample from a location-scale family with cdf $F_{\mu,\sigma}(x) = F_0((x - \mu)/\sigma)$ and pdf $f_{\mu,\sigma}(x)$. Then,

$$\text{VaR}_p = \mu + z_p \sigma, \tag{12.19}$$

where $z_p = F_0^{-1}(p)$. The point estimator for VaR is

$$\widehat{\text{VaR}}_p = \hat{\mu}_n + z_p c_n \hat{\sigma}_n,$$

where

$$\hat{\mu}_n = \frac{1}{n} \sum_{i=1}^{n} X_i,$$

$$\hat{\sigma}_n^2 = \frac{1}{n-1} \sum_{i=1}^{n} (X_i - \hat{\mu}_n)^2,$$

and

$$c_n = (E[\hat{\sigma}_n/\sigma])^{-1}.$$

Bae and Iscoe (2012) propose various confidence intervals for VaR. Based on $c_n = 1 + O(n^{-1})$ and asymptotic normality, Bae and Iscoe (2012) propose the interval

$$\hat{\mu}_n + z_p \hat{\sigma}_n \pm \frac{\hat{\sigma}_n}{\sqrt{n}} z_{(1+\alpha)/2} \sqrt{1 + \frac{z_p^2}{4}(\kappa - 1) + z_p \omega}, \qquad (12.20)$$

where α is the confidence level, κ is the kurtosis of $F_0(x)$, and ω is the skewness of $F_0(x)$. Based on Bahadur (1966)'s almost sure representation of the sample quantile of a sequence of independent random variables, Bae and Iscoe (2012) propose the interval

$$\hat{\xi}_p \pm \frac{1}{\sqrt{n}} z_{(1+\alpha)/2} \frac{\sqrt{p(1-p)}}{f_{\mu,\sigma}(\hat{\xi}_p)},$$

where ξ_p is the pth quantile and $\hat{\xi}_p$ is its sample counterpart.

Sometimes the financial series of interest is strictly positive. In this case, if $X_1, X_2, \ldots, X_n$ is a random sample from a log location-scale family with cdf $G_{\mu,\sigma}(x) = \ln F_0((x - \mu)/\sigma)$, then (12.19) and (12.20) generalize to

$$\mathrm{VaR}_p = \exp(\mu + z_p \sigma)$$

and

$$\exp\left(\hat{\mu}_n + z_p \hat{\sigma}_n \pm \frac{\hat{\sigma}_n}{n} z_{(1+\alpha)/2} \sqrt{1 + \frac{z_p^2}{4}(\kappa - 1) + z_p \omega}\right),$$

respectively, as noted by Bae and Iscoe (2012).

12.3.31 Discrete Distributions

Göb (2011) considers VaR estimation for the three most common discrete distributions: Poisson, binomial, and negative binomial. Let

$$L_c(\lambda) = \sum_{y=0}^{c} \frac{\lambda^y \exp(-\lambda)}{y!}.$$

Then, the VaR for the Poisson distribution is

$$\mathrm{VaR}_p(\lambda) = \inf\{c = 0, 1, \ldots \mid L_c(\lambda) \geq p\}.$$

Letting

$$L_{n,c}(r) = \sum_{y=0}^{c} \binom{n}{y} r^y (1-r)^{n-y},$$

the VaR for the binomial distribution is

$$\mathrm{VaR}_p(r) = \inf\{c = 0, 1, \ldots \mid L_{n,c}(r) \geq p\}.$$

Letting

$$H_{n,c}(r) = \sum_{y=0}^{c} \binom{n+y-1}{y} (1-r)^y r^n,$$

the VaR for the negative binomial distribution is

$$\mathrm{VaR}_p(r) = \inf\{c = 0, 1, \ldots \mid H_{n,c}(r) \geq p\}.$$

Göb (2011) derives various properties of these VaR measures in terms of their parameters. For the Poisson distribution, the following properties were derived:

(a) For fixed $p \in (0, 1)$, $\mathrm{VaR}_p(\lambda)$ is increasing in $\lambda \in [0, \infty)$ with $\lim_{\lambda \to \infty} \mathrm{VaR}_p(\lambda) = \infty$. There are values $0 = \lambda_{-1} < \lambda_0 < \lambda_1 < \lambda_2 < \cdots$, $\lim_{c \to \infty} \lambda_c = \infty$, such that, for $c \in \mathbb{N}_0$, $\mathrm{VaR}_p(\lambda) = c$ on the interval $(\lambda_{c-1}, \lambda_c]$ and $L_c(\lambda) > L_c(\lambda_c) = p$ for $\lambda \in (\lambda_{c-1}, \lambda_c)$. In particular, $\lambda_0 = -\ln(p)$.

(b) For fixed $\lambda > 0$, $c = -1, 0, 1, \ldots$, let $p_c = L_c(\lambda)$. Then, for $c = 0, 1, 2, \ldots$, $\mathrm{VaR}_p(\lambda) = c$ for $p \in (p_{c-1}, p_c]$.

For the binomial distribution, the following properties were derived:

(a) For fixed $p \in (0, 1)$, $\mathrm{VaR}_p(r)$ is increasing in $r \in [0, 1]$. There are values $0 = r_{-1} < r_0 < r_1 < r_2 < \cdots < r_n = 1$ such that, for $c \in \{0, \ldots, n\}$, $\mathrm{VaR}_p(r) = c$ on the interval $(r_{c-1}, r_c]$ and $L_{n,c}(r) > L_{n,c}(r_c) = p$ for $r \in (r_{c-1}, r_c)$. In particular, $r_0 = 1 - p^{1/n}$ and $r_{n-1} = (1-p)^{1/n}$.

(b) For fixed $0 < r < 1$, $c = -1, 0, 1, \ldots$, let $p_c = L_{n,c}(r)$. Then, for $c = 0, 1, 2, \ldots, n$, $\mathrm{VaR}_p(r) = c$ for $p \in (p_{c-1}, p_c]$.

For the negative binomial distribution, the following properties were derived:

(a) For fixed $p \in (0, 1)$, $\mathrm{VaR}_p(r)$ is decreasing in $r \in [0, 1]$. There are values $1 = r_{-1} > r_0 > r_1 > r_2 > \cdots$, $\lim_{c \to \infty} r_c = 0$, such that, for $c \in \mathbb{N}_0$, $\mathrm{VaR}_p(r) = c$ on the interval $[r_c, r_{c-1})$ and $H_{n,c}(r) > H_{n,c}(r_c) = p$ for $r \in (r_c, r_{c-1})$. In particular, $r_0 = p^{1/n}$.

(b) For fixed $0 < r < 1$, $c = -1, 0, 1, \ldots$, let $p_c = H_{n,c}(r)$. Then, for $c = 0, 1, 2, \ldots, n$, $\mathrm{VaR}_p(r) = c$ for $p \in (p_{c-1}, p_c]$.

Empirical estimation of the three VaR measures can be based on asymptotic normality.

12.3.32 Quantile Regression Method

Quantile regressions have been used to estimate VaR; see Koenker and Bassett (1978), Koenker and Portnoy (1997), Chernozhukov and Umantsev (2001), and Engle and Manganelli (2004). The idea is to regress the VaR on some known covariates. Let X_t at time t denote the financial variable, let $\mathbf{z}_t$ denote a $k \times 1$ vector of covariates at time t, let $\boldsymbol{\beta}_\alpha$ denote a $k \times 1$ vector of regression coefficients, and let $\text{VaR}_{t,\alpha}$ denote the corresponding VaR. Then, the quantile regression model can be rewritten as

$$\text{VaR}_{t,\alpha} = g(\mathbf{z}_t; \boldsymbol{\beta}_\alpha). \tag{12.21}$$

In the linear case, (12.21) could take the form

$$\text{VaR}_{t,\alpha} = \mathbf{z}_t^T \boldsymbol{\beta}_\alpha.$$

The parameters in (12.21) can be estimated by least squares as in standard regression.

12.3.33 Brownian Motion Method

Cakir and Raei (2007) describe simulation schemes for computing VaR for single-asset and multiple-asset portfolios. Let P_t denote the price at time t, let T denote a holding period divided into small intervals of equal length Δt, let ΔP_t denote the change in P_t over Δt, let Z_t denote a standard normal shock, let μ denote the mean of returns over the holding period T, and let σ denote the standard deviation of returns over the holding period T. With these notations, Cakir and Raei (2007) suggest the model

$$\frac{\Delta P_t}{P_t} = \mu \Delta t + \sigma \sqrt{\Delta t} Z_t. \tag{12.22}$$

Under this model, the VaR for single-asset portfolios can be computed as follows:

(i) Starting with P_t, simulate $P_t, P_{t+1}, \dots, P_T$ using (12.22).
(ii) Repeat Step (i) 10, 000 times.
(iii) Compute the empirical cdf over the holding period.
(iv) Compute $\widehat{\text{VaR}}_\alpha$ as 100α percentile of the empirical cdf.

The VaR for multiple-asset portfolios can be computed as follows:

(i) Suppose the price at time t for the ith asset follows

$$\frac{\Delta P_t^i}{P_t^i} = \mu^i \Delta t + \sigma^i \sqrt{\Delta t} Z_t^i \tag{12.23}$$

for $i = 1, 2, \ldots, N$, where N is the number of assets and the notation is the same as that for single-asset portfolios. The standard normal shocks, $Z_t^i, i = 1, 2, \ldots, N$, need not be correlated.

(ii) Starting with P_t^i, $i = 1, 2, \ldots, N$, simulate $P_t^i, P_{t+1}^i, \ldots, P_T^i$, $i = 1, 2, \ldots, N$ using (12.23).

(iii) Compute the portfolio price for the holding period as the weighted sum of the individual asset prices.

(iv) Repeat Steps (ii) and (iii) 10,000 times.

(v) Compute the empirical cdf of the portfolio price over the holding period.

(vi) Compute $\widehat{\text{VaR}}_\alpha$ as 100α percentile of the empirical cdf.

12.3.34 Bayesian Method

Pollard (2007) defines a Bayesian VaR. Let X_t denote the financial variable of interest at time t. Let $p(X_t \mid \Theta, Z_t)$ denote the posterior pdf of X_t given some parameters Θ and "state" variables Z_t. Pollard (2007) defines the Bayesian VaR at time t as

$$\text{VaR}_\alpha = \left\{ x : \int_{-\infty}^{x} p\left(y \mid \Theta, Z_{t+1}\right) dy = \alpha \right\}. \tag{12.24}$$

The "state" variables Z_t are assumed to follow a transition pdf $f(Z_t, Z_{t+1})$.

Pollard (2007) also proposes several methods for estimating (12.24). One of them is the following:

(i) Use Markov chain Monte Carlo to simulate N samples $\{(Z_t^{(n)}, \Theta^{(n)}), n = 1, 2, \ldots, N\}$, from the joint conditional posterior pdf of (Z_t, Θ) given $Y_t = \{X_\tau, \tau = 1, 2, \ldots, t\}$.

(ii) For n from 1 to N, simulate $Z_{t+1}^{(n)}$ from the conditional posterior pdf of Z_{t+1} given $\Theta^{(n)}$ and $Z_t^{(n)}$.

(iii) For n from 1 to N, simulate $X_{t+1}^{(n)}$ from the conditional posterior pdf of X_{t+1} given $\Theta^{(n)}$ and $Z_{t+1}^{(n)}$.

(iv) Compute the empirical cdf

$$\widehat{G}(x) = \frac{1}{N} \sum_{n=1}^{N} I\{X_{t+1}^{(n)} \leq x\}. \tag{12.25}$$

(v) Estimate VaR as $\widehat{G}^{-1}(\alpha)$.

12.3.35 Rachev et al.'s Method

Let $R = \sum_{i=1}^{n} w_i R_i$ denote a portfolio return made up of n asset returns, R_i, and the nonnegative weights w_i summing to one. Suppose R_i are independent

$S_\alpha(\alpha_i, \beta_i, 0)$ random variables. Then, it can be shown that (Rachev et al., 2003) $R \sim S_\alpha(\alpha_p, \beta_p, 0)$, where

$$\alpha_p = \left[\sum_{i=1}^{n} \left(|w_i| \sigma_i \right)^\alpha \right]^{1/\alpha}$$

and

$$\beta_p = \frac{\sum_{i=1}^{n} \text{sign}(w_i) \beta_i (|w_i| \sigma_i)^\alpha}{\sum_{i=1}^{n} (|w_i| \sigma_i)^\alpha}.$$

Hence, the value of risk of R can be estimated by the following algorithm due to Rachev et al. (2003):

- Estimate α_i and β_i (to obtain, say, $\widehat{\alpha}_i$ and $\widehat{\beta}_i$) using possible data on the ith asset return.
- Estimate α_p and β_p by

$$\widehat{\alpha}_p = \left[\sum_{i=1}^{n} \left(|w_i| \widehat{\sigma}_i \right)^\alpha \right]^{1/\alpha}$$

    and

$$\widehat{\beta}_p = \frac{\sum_{i=1}^{n} \text{sign}(w_i) \widehat{\beta}_i (|w_i| \widehat{\sigma}_i)^\alpha}{\sum_{i=1}^{n} (|w_i| \widehat{\sigma}_i)^\alpha},$$

    respectively.
- Estimate $\text{VaR}_p(R)$ as the pth quantile of $S_\alpha(\widehat{\alpha}_p, \widehat{\beta}_p, 0)$.

12.4   NONPARAMETRIC METHODS

This section concentrates on estimation methods for VaR when the data are assumed to come from no particular distribution. The nonparametric methods summarized are based on historical method (Section 12.4.1), filtered historical method (Section 12.4.2), importance sampling method (Section 12.4.3), bootstrap method (Section 12.4.4), kernel method (Section 12.4.5), Chang et al.'s estimators (Section 12.4.6), Jadhav and Ramanathan's method (Section 12.4.7), and Jeong and Kang's method (Section 12.4.8).

12.4.1   Historical Method

Let $X_{(1)} \leq X_{(2)} \leq \cdots \leq X_{(n)}$ denote the order statistics in ascending order corresponding to the original financial series $X_1, X_2, \ldots, X_n$. The historical method suggests to estimate VaR by

$$\widehat{\text{VaR}}_\alpha(X) = X_{(i)}$$

for $\alpha \in ((i-1)/n, i/n]$.

12.4.2 Filtered Historical Method

Suppose the log returns, $R_t = \ln X_t - \ln X_{t-1}$, follow the model, $R_t = \sigma_t \epsilon_t$, discussed before, where σ_t is the volatility process and ϵ_t are independent and identical random variables with zero means. Let $\epsilon_{(1)} \le \epsilon_{(2)} \le \cdots \le \epsilon_{(n)}$ denote the order statistics of $\{\epsilon_t\}$. The filtered historical method suggests to estimate VaR by

$$\widehat{\text{VaR}}_\alpha = \epsilon_{(i)} \widehat{\sigma}_t$$

for $\alpha \in ((i-1)/n, i/n]$, where $\widehat{\sigma}_t$ denotes an estimator of σ_t at time t. This method is due to Hull and White (1998) and Barone-Adesi et al. (1999).

12.4.3 Importance Sampling Method

Suppose $\widehat{F}(\cdot)$ is the empirical cdf of $X_1, X_2, \ldots, X_n$. As seen in Section 12.4.1, an estimator for VaR is $\widehat{F}^{-1}(\alpha)$. This estimator is asymptotically normal with variance equal to

$$\frac{\alpha(1-\alpha)}{nf^2(\text{VaR}_\alpha)}.$$

This can be large if α is closer to zero or one. There are several methods for variance reduction. One popular method is importance sampling. Suppose $G(\cdot)$ is another cdf and let $S(x) = \widehat{F}(dx)/G(dx)$ and

$$\widehat{S}(x) = \frac{1}{n} \sum_{i=1}^{n} I\{X_i \le x\} S(X_i).$$

Hong (2011) shows that $\widehat{S}^{-1}(p)$ under certain conditions can provide estimators for VaR with smaller variance.

12.4.4 Bootstrap Method

Suppose $\widehat{F}(\cdot)$ is the empirical cdf of $X_1, X_2, \ldots, X_n$. The bootstrap method can be described as follows:

1. Simulate B independent sample from $\widehat{F}(\cdot)$.
2. For each sample estimate VaR_α, say, $\widehat{\text{VaR}}_\alpha^{(i)}$ for $i = 1, 2, \ldots, B$, using the historical method.

3. Take the estimate of VaR as the mean or the median of $\widehat{\text{VaR}}_\alpha^{(i)}$ for $i = 1, 2, \ldots, B$.

One can also construct confidence intervals for VaR based on the bootstrapped estimates $\widehat{\text{VaR}}_\alpha^{(i)}$, $i = 1, 2, \ldots, B$.

12.4.5   Kernel Method

Kernels are commonly used to estimate pdfs. Let $K(\cdot)$ denote a symmetric kernel, that is, a symmetric pdf. The kernel estimator of F can be given by

$$\widehat{F}(x) = \frac{1}{n} \sum_{i=1}^{n} G\left(\frac{x - X_i}{h}\right), \tag{12.26}$$

where h is a smoothing bandwidth and

$$G(x) = \int_{-\infty}^{x} K(u)du.$$

A variable width version of (12.26) is

$$\widehat{F}(x) = \frac{1}{n} \sum_{i=1}^{n} \frac{1}{hT_i} G\left(\frac{x - X_i}{hT_i}\right), \tag{12.27}$$

where $T_i = d_k(x_i)$ is the distance of X_i from its kth nearest neighbor among the remaining $(n-1)$ data points and $k = n^{-1/2}$. The kernel estimator of VaR, say, $\widehat{\text{VaR}}_p$, is then the root of the equation

$$\widehat{F}(x) = p \tag{12.28}$$

for x, where $\widehat{F}(\cdot)$ is given by (12.26) or (12.27). According to Sheather and Marron (1990), $\widehat{\text{VaR}}_p$ could also be estimated by

$$\widehat{\text{VaR}}_p = \frac{\sum_{i=1}^{n} \widehat{F}((i - 1/2)/n - p)X_{(i)}}{\sum_{i=1}^{n} \widehat{F}((i - 1/2)/n - p)},$$

where $\widehat{F}(\cdot)$ is given by (12.26) or (12.27) and $\{X_{(i)}\}$ are the ascending order statistics of X_i.

The estimator in (12.28) is due to Gourieroux et al. (2000). Its properties have been studied by many authors. For instance, Chen and Tang (2005) show under certain regularity conditions that

$$\sqrt{n}(\widehat{\text{VaR}}_p - \text{VaR}_p) \to N(0, \sigma^2(p)f^{-2}(\text{VaR}_p))$$

in distribution as $n \to \infty$, where

$$\sigma^2(p) = \lim_{n \to \infty} \sigma^2(p; n),$$

$$\sigma^2(p; n) = \left\{ p(1-p) + 2 \sum_{k=1}^{n-1} \left(1 - \frac{k}{n} \right) \gamma(k) \right\},$$

$$\gamma(k) = \text{Cov}\{I(X_1 < \text{VaR}_p), I(X_{k+1} < \text{VaR}_p)\}.$$

Here, $I\{\cdot\}$ denotes the indicator function.

12.4.6 Chang et al.'s Estimators

Chang et al. (2003) propose several nonparametric estimators for the VaR of log returns, say, R_t with pdf $f(\cdot)$. The first of these is $\widehat{\text{VaR}}_\alpha = (1-w)R_{(m)} + wR_{(m+1)}$, where $m = [n\alpha + 0.5]$ and $w = n\alpha - m + 0.5$, where $[x]$ denotes the greatest integer less than or equal to x. This estimator is shown to have the asymptotic distribution

$$\sqrt{n}(\widehat{\text{VaR}}_\alpha - \text{VaR}_\alpha) \to N(0, \alpha(1-\alpha)(p)f^{-2}(\text{VaR}_\alpha))$$

in distribution as $n \to \infty$. It is sometimes referred to as the historical simulation estimator. The second of the proposed estimators is

$$\widehat{\text{VaR}}_\alpha = \sum_{i=1}^{n} R_{(i)}[B_{i/n}((n+1)\alpha, (n+1)(1-\alpha))$$
$$- B_{(i-1)/n}((n+1)\alpha, (n+1)(1-\alpha))].$$

This estimator is shown to have the asymptotic distribution

$$\sqrt{n}(\widehat{\text{VaR}}_\alpha - \text{VaR}_\alpha) \to N(0, \alpha(1-\alpha)(p)f^{-2}(\text{VaR}_\alpha))$$

in distribution as $n \to \infty$. The third of the proposed estimators is

$$\widehat{\text{VaR}}_\alpha = \sum_{i=1}^{n} k_{i,n} R_{(i)},$$

where
$$k_{i,n} = B_{q_{i,n}}((n+1)\alpha, (n+1)(1-\alpha)) - B_{q_{i-1,n}}((n+1)\alpha, (n+1)(1-\alpha)),$$

$$q_{0,n} = 0, q_{i,n} = \sum_{j=1}^{i} w_{j,n}, j = 1, 2, \ldots, n,$$

$$w_{i,n} = \begin{cases} \dfrac{1}{2}\left[1 - \dfrac{n-2}{\sqrt{n(n-1)}} \right], & \text{if } i = 1, n, \\[3ex] \dfrac{1}{\sqrt{n(n-1)}}, & \text{if } i = 2, 3, \ldots, n-1. \end{cases}$$

This estimator is shown to have the asymptotic distribution

$$\sqrt{n}(\widehat{\text{VaR}}_\alpha - \text{VaR}_\alpha) \to N(0, \alpha(1 - \alpha)(p)f^{-2}(\text{VaR}_\alpha))$$

in distribution as $n \to \infty$.

12.4.7   Jadhav and Ramanathan's Method

Jadhav and Ramanathan (2009) provide a collection of nonparametric estimators for VaR$_\alpha$. Let $X_{(1)} \le X_{(2)} \le \cdots \le X_{(n)}$ denote the order statistics in ascending order corresponding to $X_1, X_2, \dots, X_n$. For given α, define $i = [n\alpha + 0.5]$, $j = [n\alpha]$, $k = [(n + 1)\alpha]$, $g = n\alpha - j$, $h = (n + 1)\alpha - k$, and $r = [(p + 1)\alpha]$. The collection provided is

$$\widehat{\text{VaR}}_\alpha = (1 - g)X_{(j)} + gX_{(j+1)},$$

$$\widehat{\text{VaR}}_\alpha = \begin{cases} X_{(j)}, & \text{if } g < 0.5, \\ X_{(j+1)}, & \text{if } g \ge 0.5, \end{cases}$$

$$\widehat{\text{VaR}}_\alpha = \begin{cases} X_{(j)}, & \text{if } g = 0, \\ X_{(j+1)}, & \text{if } g > 0, \end{cases}$$

$$\widehat{\text{VaR}}_\alpha = (1 - h)X_{(k)} + hX_{(k+1)},$$

$$\widehat{\text{VaR}}_\alpha = \begin{cases} \dfrac{X_{(j)} + X_{(j+1)}}{2}, & \text{if } g = 0, \\ X_{(j+1)}, & \text{if } g > 0, \end{cases}$$

$$\widehat{\text{VaR}}_\alpha = X_{(j+1)},$$

$$\widehat{\text{VaR}}_\alpha = (0.5 + i - np)X_{(i)} + (0.5 - i + np)X_{(i+1)}, \quad 0.5 \le n\alpha \le n - 0.5,$$

$$\widehat{\text{VaR}}_\alpha = \sum_{m=1}^{n} W_{n,m}X_{(m)},$$

$$\widehat{\text{VaR}}_\alpha = \sum_{m=r}^{r+n-p} \frac{\dbinom{m-1}{r-1}\dbinom{n-m}{p-r}}{\dbinom{n}{p}} X_{(m)},$$

where

$$W_{n,m} = I_{m/n}(\alpha(n + 1), (1 - \alpha)(n + 1)) - I_{(m-1)/n}(\alpha(n + 1), (1 - \alpha)(n + 1)),$$

where $I_x(a, b)$ denote the incomplete beta function ratio defined by

$$I_x(a, b) = \frac{\int_0^x t^{a-1}(1-t)^{b-1}dt}{B(a, b)} = \frac{\int_0^x t^{a-1}(1-t)^{b-1}dt}{\int_0^1 t^{a-1}(1-t)^{b-1}dt}.$$

The last of the estimators in the collection is due to Kaigh and Lachenbruch (1982). The second last is due to Harrell and Davis (1982).

12.4.8   Jeong and Kang's Method

Suppose the log returns, $R_t = \ln X_t - \ln X_{t-1}$, follow the model, $R_t = \sigma_t \epsilon_t$, discussed before. Let $\text{VaR}_{\alpha,t}$ denote the corresponding VaR. Jeong and Kang (2009) propose a fully nonparametric estimator for the $\text{VaR}_{\alpha,t}$ defined by

$$\Pr(R_t < \text{VaR}_{\alpha,t} | \mathcal{F}_{t-1}) = \alpha,$$

where $\mathcal{F}_t$ is the σ-field generated by $(\sigma_s)_{s \le t}$. Let

$$Q_n(\alpha) = \begin{cases} X_{(s)}, & \text{if } (s-1)/n < \alpha \le s/n, \\ X_{(1)}, & \text{if } \alpha = 0, \end{cases}$$

$$a_i = \int_0^1 (\alpha - s)^i K\left(\frac{\alpha - s}{h}\right) ds,$$

and

$$A_i(\alpha) = \int_0^1 (\alpha - s)^i K\left(\frac{\alpha - s}{h}\right) Q_n(s) ds$$

for some kernel function $K(\cdot)$ with bandwidth h. With this notation, Jeong and Kang (2009) propose the estimator

$$\widehat{\text{VaR}}_{\alpha,t} = \hat{\sigma}_t \hat{q}_2,$$

where

$$\hat{\sigma}_t^2 = \frac{1}{\hat{m}} \sum_{p=t-\hat{m}}^{t-1} R_p^2$$

and

$$\hat{q}_2 = \frac{A_0(\alpha)(a_2 a_4 - a_3^2) - A_1(\alpha)(a_1 a_4 - a_2 a_3) + A_2(\alpha)(a_1 a_3 - a_2^2)}{a_0(a_2 a_4 - a_3^2) - a_1(a_1 a_4 - a_2 a_3) + a_2(a_1 a_3 - a_2^2)}.$$

Here, $\hat{m}$ can be determined using a recursive algorithm presented in Section 12.2.1 of Jeong and Kang (2009).

12.5   SEMIPARAMETRIC METHODS

This section concentrates on estimation methods for VaR that have both para-metric and nonparametric elements. The semiparametric methods summarized are based on extreme value theory method (Section 12.5.1), generalized Pareto distribution (Section 12.5.2), Matthys et al.'s method (Section 12.5.3), Araújo Santos et al.'s method (Section 12.5.4), Gomes and Pestana's method (Section 12.5.5), Beirlant et al.'s method (Section 12.5.6), Caeiro and Gomes' method (Section 12.5.7), Figueiredo et al.'s method (Section 12.5.8), Li et al.'s method (Section 12.5.9), Gomes et al.'s method (Section 12.5.10), Wang's method (Section 12.5.11), M-estimation method (Section 12.5.12), and the generalized Champernowne distribution (Section 12.5.13).

12.5.1   Extreme Value Theory Method

Let $M_n = \max\{R_1, R_2, \ldots, R_n\}$ denote the maximum of financial returns. Extreme value theory says that under suitable conditions there exist norming constants $a_n > 0$ and b_n such that

$$\Pr\{a_n(M_n - b_n) \leq x\} \to \exp\{-(1 + \xi x)^{-1/\xi}\}$$

in distribution as $n \to \infty$. The parameter ξ is known as the extreme value index. It controls the tail behavior of the extremes.

There are several estimators proposed for ξ. One of the earliest estimators due to Hill (1975) is

$$\hat{\xi} = \frac{1}{k} \sum_{i=1}^{k} \ln \frac{R_{(i)}}{R_{(k+1)}}, \tag{12.29}$$

where $R_{(1)} > R_{(2)} > \cdots R_{(k)} > \cdots > R_{(n)}$ are the order statistics in descending order. Another earliest estimator due to Pickands (1975) is

$$\hat{\xi} = \frac{1}{\ln 2} \ln \frac{R_{(k+1)} - R_{(2k+1)}}{R_{(2k+1)} - R_{(4k+1)}}. \tag{12.30}$$

The tails of F for most situations in finance take the Pareto form, that is,

$$1 - F(x) = Cx^{-1/\xi} \tag{12.31}$$

for some constant C. Embrechts et al. (1997, p. 334) propose estimating C by $\hat{C} = (k/n)R_{k+1}^{1/\hat{\xi}}$.

Combining (12.29) and (12.31), Odening and Hinrichs (2003) propose esti-mating VaR by

$$\widehat{\text{VaR}}_{1-p} = R_{(k+1)} \left(\frac{k}{np}\right)^{\hat{\xi}}. \tag{12.32}$$

This estimator is actually due to Weissman (1978).

An alternative approach is to suppose that the maximum of financial returns follows the generalized extreme value cdf (Fisher and Tippett, 1928) given by

$$G(x) = \exp\left\{ -\left(1 + \xi \frac{x - \mu}{\sigma}\right)^{-1/\xi} \right\} \tag{12.33}$$

for $1 + \xi(x - \mu)/\sigma > 0$, $\mu \in \mathbb{R}$, $\sigma > 0$, and $\xi \in \mathbb{R}$. In this case, the VaR can be estimated by

$$\widehat{\text{VaR}}_p = \hat{\mu} - \frac{\hat{\sigma}}{\hat{\xi}}\left[1 - \{-\ln\ p\}^{-\hat{\xi}}\right],$$

where $(\hat{\mu}, \hat{\sigma}, \hat{\xi})$ are the maximum likelihood estimators of (μ, σ, ξ). Prescott and Walden (1990) provide details of maximum likelihood estimation for the generalized extreme value distribution.

The Gumbel distribution is the particular case of (12.33) for $\xi = 0$. It has the cdf specified by

$$G(x) = \exp\left\{ -\exp\left(-\frac{x - \mu}{\sigma}\right) \right\}$$

for $\mu \in \mathbb{R}$ and $\sigma > 0$. If the maximum of financial returns follows this cdf, then the VaR can be estimated by

$$\widehat{\text{VaR}}_p = \hat{\mu} - \hat{\sigma} \ln\{-\ln\ p\},$$

where $(\hat{\mu}, \hat{\sigma})$ are the maximum likelihood estimators of (μ, σ).

For more on extreme value theory, estimation of the tail index, and applications, we refer the readers to Longin (1996, 2000), Beirlant et al. (2017), Fraga Alves and Neves (2017), and Gomes et al. (2015).

12.5.2 Generalized Pareto Distribution

The Pareto distribution is a popular model in finance. Suppose the log return, say, R_t, of $X_1, X_2, \ldots, X_n$ comes from the generalized Pareto distribution with cdf specified by

$$F(y) = \frac{N_u}{n}\left(1 + \gamma \frac{y - u}{\sigma}\right)^{-1/\gamma}$$

for $u < y < \infty$, $\sigma > 0$, and $\gamma \in \mathbb{R}$, where u is some threshold and N_u is the number of observed exceedances above u.

For this model, several estimators are available for the VaR. Let $R_{(1)} \le R_{(2)} \le \cdots \le R_{(n)}$ denote the order statistics in ascending order. The first estimator due to Pickands (1975) is

$$\widehat{\text{VaR}}_{1-p} = R_{(n-k+1)} + \frac{1}{1 - 2^{-\hat{\gamma}}}\left[\left(\frac{k}{(n+1)p}\right)^{\hat{\gamma}} - 1\right](R_{(n-k+1)} - R_{(n-2k+1)}),$$

where

$$\hat{\gamma} = \frac{1}{\ln 2} \ln \frac{R_{(n-k+1)} - R_{(n-2k+1)}}{R_{(n-2k+1)} - R_{(n-4k+1)}}$$

for $k \neq n/4$. The second estimator due to Dekkers et al. (1989) is

$$\widehat{\text{VaR}}_{1-p} = R_{(n-k)} + \frac{\hat{a}}{\hat{\gamma}} \left[\left(\frac{k}{np} \right)^{\hat{\gamma}} - 1 \right],$$

where

$$\hat{\gamma} = M_{k+1}^{(1)} + 1 - \frac{1}{2} \left[1 - \frac{\left(M_{k+1}^{(1)} \right)^2}{M_{k+1}^{(2)}} \right]^{-1},$$

$$M_{(k+1)}^{\ell} = \frac{1}{k} \sum_{i=1}^{k} [\ln R_{(n-i+1)} - \ln R_{(n-k)}]^{\ell}, \ell = 1, 2,$$

$$\hat{a} = \frac{R_{(n-k)} M_{(k+1)}^{(1)}}{\rho_1},$$

$$\rho_1 = \begin{cases} 1, & \text{if } \gamma \geq 0, \\ \dfrac{1}{1-\gamma}, & \text{if } \gamma < 0. \end{cases}$$

Suppose now that the returns are from the alternative generalized Pareto distribution with cdf specified by

$$F(x) = 1 - \left(1 + \xi \frac{x - u}{\sigma} \right)^{-1/\xi}$$

for $1 + \xi(x - u)/\sigma > 0$. Then, the VaR is

$$\text{VaR}_p = u + \frac{\sigma}{\xi}[(1 - p)^{-\xi} - 1]. \tag{12.34}$$

If $\hat{\sigma}$ and $\hat{\xi}$ are the maximum likelihood estimators of σ and ξ, respectively, then the maximum likelihood estimator of VaR is

$$\widehat{\text{VaR}}_p = \hat{u} + \frac{\hat{\sigma}}{\hat{\xi}}[(1 - p)^{-\hat{\xi}} - 1].$$

There are several methods for constructing confidence intervals for (12.34). One popular method is the bias-corrected method due to Efron and

Tibshirani (1993). This method based on bootstrapping can be described as follows:

1. Given a random sample $\mathbf{r} = (r_1, r_2, \ldots, r_n)$, calculate the maximum likelihood estimate $\hat{\boldsymbol{\theta}} = (\hat{\sigma}, \hat{\xi})$ and $\hat{\boldsymbol{\theta}}_{(i)}$, the maximum likelihood estimate with the ith data point, r_i, removed.

2. Simulate $\mathbf{r}^{*i} = \{r_1^*, r_2^*, \ldots, r_n^*\}$ from the generalized Pareto distribution with parameters $\hat{\boldsymbol{\theta}}$.

3. Compute the maximum likelihood estimate, say, $\hat{\boldsymbol{\theta}}^{*i}$, for the sample simulated in Step 2.

4. Repeat Steps 2 and 3, B times.

5. Compute

$$\alpha_1 = \Phi\left(\hat{z}_0 + \frac{\hat{z}_0 + \Phi^{-1}(\alpha)}{1 - \hat{a}\left(\hat{z}_0 + \Phi^{-1}(\alpha)\right)}\right)$$

and

$$\alpha_2 = \Phi\left(\hat{z}_0 + \frac{\hat{z}_0 + \Phi^{-1}(1 - \alpha)}{1 - \hat{a}\left(\hat{z}_0 + \Phi^{-1}(1 - \alpha)\right)}\right),$$

where

$$\hat{z}_0 = \Phi^{-1}\left(\frac{\sum_{i=1}^{B} I\left\{\widehat{\text{VaR}}^{*i} < \widehat{\text{VaR}}\right\}}{B}\right)$$

and

$$\hat{a} = \frac{\sum_{i=1}^{n} I(\overline{\widehat{\text{VaR}}} - \widehat{\text{VaR}}_{(i)})^3}{6\left\{\sum_{i=1}^{n} I\left(\overline{\widehat{\text{VaR}}} - \widehat{\text{VaR}}_{(i)}\right)^2\right\}^{3/2}},$$

where $\overline{\widehat{\text{VaR}}}$ is the mean of $\widehat{\text{VaR}}^{*i}$.

6. Compute the bias-corrected confidence interval for VaR as

$$\left(\widehat{\text{VaR}}^{*(\alpha_1)}, \widehat{\text{VaR}}^{*(\alpha_2)}\right),$$

where $\widehat{\text{VaR}}^{*(\alpha)}$ is the 100α percentile of $\widehat{\text{VaR}}^{*i}$.

Note that $\hat{\boldsymbol{\theta}}^{*i}$ and $\widehat{\text{VaR}}^{*i}$ are the bootstrap replicates of $\boldsymbol{\theta}$ and VaR, respectively.

12.5.3   Matthys et al.'s Method

Several improvements have been proposed on (12.32). The one due to Matthys et al. (2004) takes account of censoring. Suppose only N of the n are actually observed; the remaining are considered to be censored or missing. In this case, Matthys et al. (2004) show that VaR can be estimated by

$$\widehat{\text{VaR}}_{1-p} = R_{(n-k)} \left[\frac{k+1}{(n+1)p} \right]^{\widehat{\gamma}} \exp \left\{ -\frac{\widehat{b}}{\widehat{\rho}} \left[1 - \left(\frac{(n+1)p}{k+1} \right)^{-\widehat{\rho}} \right] \right\},$$

where

$$H_{k,n}^{(c)} = \frac{1}{k-n+N} \left[\sum_{j=n-N+1}^{k} \ln \frac{R_{(n-j+1)}}{R_{(n-k)}} + (n-N) \ln \frac{R_{(N)}}{R_{(n-k)}} \right],$$

$$C = (n-N)/k, \; Z_{j,k} = j \ln \frac{R_{(n-j+1)}}{R_{(n-j)}},$$

$$\widehat{\rho} = -\frac{1}{\ln \lambda} \ln \frac{H_{[\lambda^2 k],n}^{(c)} - H_{[\lambda k],n}^{(c)}}{H_{[\lambda k],n}^{(c)} - H_{k,n}^{(c)}},$$

$$\widehat{\gamma} = \frac{1}{k-n+N} \sum_{j=n-N+1}^{k} Z_j - \widehat{b} \frac{1 - C^{1-\widehat{\rho}}}{(1-C)(1-\widehat{\rho})},$$

$$\widehat{b} = \frac{\frac{1}{k-n+N} \sum_{j=n-N+1}^{k} \left[\left(\frac{j}{k+1} \right)^{-\widehat{\rho}} - \frac{1-C^{1-\widehat{\rho}}}{(1-C)(1-\widehat{\rho})} \right] Z_j}{\left[\frac{1-C^{1-2\widehat{\rho}}}{(1-C)(1-2\widehat{\rho})} - \frac{1-C^{1-\widehat{\rho}}}{(1-C)(1-\widehat{\rho})} \right]^2}.$$

Here, λ is a tuning parameter and takes values in the unit interval. Among other properties, Matthys et al. (2004) establish asymptotic normality of VaR_{1-p}.

12.5.4   Araújo Santos et al.'s Method

The improvement of (12.32) due to Araújo Santos et al. (2006) takes the expression

$$\widehat{\text{VaR}}_{1-p} = R_{(n_q)} + (R_{(n-k)} - R_{(n_q)}) \left(\frac{k}{np} \right)^{H_n},$$

where $n_q = [nq] + 1$ and

$$H_n = \frac{1}{k} \sum_{i=1}^{k} \ln \frac{R_{(n-i+1)} - R_{(n_q)}}{R_{(n-k)} - R_{(n_q)}}.$$

12.5.5 Gomes and Pestana's Method

The improvement of (12.32) due to Gomes and Pestana (2007) takes the expression

$$\widehat{\text{VaR}}_{1-p} = R_{(n-k+1)} \exp\left[\overline{H}(k)\ln\left(\frac{k}{np}\right)\right],$$

where

$$\overline{H}(k) = H(k)\left[1 - \frac{\hat{\beta}}{1-\hat{\rho}}\left(\frac{n}{k}\right)^{\hat{\rho}}\right],$$

$$H(k) = \frac{1}{k}\sum_{i=1}^{k} U_i, \quad U_i = i\ln\left(\frac{R_{(n-i+1)}}{R_{(n-i)}}\right),$$

$$\hat{\rho} = \min\left[0, \frac{3\left(T_n^{(\tau)}(k) - 1\right)}{T_n^{(\tau)}(k) - 3}\right],$$

$$T_n^{(\tau)}(k) = \begin{cases} \dfrac{\left(M_n^{(1)}(k)\right)^{\tau} - (M_n^{(2)}(k)/2)^{\tau/2}}{(M_n^{(2)}(k)/2)^{\tau/2} - (M_n^{(3)}(k)/6)^{\tau/3}}, & \text{if } \tau \neq 0, \\[2em] \dfrac{\ln\left(M_n^{(1)}(k)\right) - \frac{1}{2}\ln(M_n^{(2)}(k)/2)}{\frac{1}{2}\ln\left(M_n^{(2)}(k)/2\right) - \frac{1}{3}\ln\left(M_n^{(3)}(k)/6\right)}, & \text{if } \tau = 0, \end{cases}$$

$$M_n^{(j)}(k) = \frac{1}{k}\sum_{i=1}^{k}[\ln R_{(n-i+1)} - \ln R_{(n-k)}]^j,$$

$$\hat{\beta} = \left(\frac{k}{n}\right)^{\hat{\rho}} \frac{d_{\hat{\rho}}(k)D_0(k) - D_{\hat{\rho}}(k)}{d_{\hat{\rho}}(k)D_{\hat{\rho}}(k) - D_{2\hat{\rho}}(k)},$$

$$d_\alpha(k) = \frac{1}{k}\sum_{i=1}^{k}\left(\frac{i}{k}\right)^{-\alpha}, \quad D_\alpha(k) = \frac{1}{k}\sum_{i=1}^{k}\left(\frac{i}{k}\right)^{-\alpha}U_i.$$

Here, τ is a tuning parameter. Under suitable conditions, Gomes and Pestana (2007) show further that

$$\frac{\sqrt{k}}{\ln k - \ln(np)}(\widehat{\text{VaR}}_{1-p} - \text{VaR}_{1-p}) \to N(0, \xi^2)$$

in distribution as $n \to \infty$.

12.5.6   Beirlant et al.'s Method

The improvement of (12.32) due to Beirlant et al. (2008) takes the expression

$$
\widehat{\mathrm{VaR}}_{1-p} = R_{(n-k)} \left[\frac{k+1}{(n+1)p} \right]^{\hat{\gamma}} \exp \left\{ -\frac{\hat{\gamma}\hat{\beta}}{\hat{\rho}} \left(\frac{n+1}{k+1} \right)^{\hat{\rho}} \left[1 - \left(\frac{(n+1)p}{k+1} \right)^{-\hat{\rho}} \right] \right\},
$$

where $\hat{\rho}$ is as given by Section 12.5.5, and

$$
\hat{\gamma} = \frac{1}{k} \sum_{i=1}^{k} i \ln \frac{R_{(n-i+1)}}{R_{(n-i)}},
$$

$$
\hat{\beta} = \left(\frac{k}{n} \right)^{\hat{\rho}} \frac{d_{\hat{\rho}}(k)D_0(k) - D_{\hat{\rho}}(k)}{d_{\hat{\rho}}(k)D_{\hat{\rho}}(k) - D_{2\hat{\rho}}(k)},
$$

$$
d_{\alpha}(k) = \frac{1}{k} \sum_{i=1}^{k} \left(\frac{i}{k} \right)^{-\alpha}, \quad D_{\alpha}(k) = \frac{1}{k} \sum_{i=1}^{k} \left(\frac{i}{k} \right)^{-\alpha} U_i.
$$

This estimator is shown to be consistent.

12.5.7   Caeiro and Gomes's Method

Caeiro and Gomes (2008 and 2009) propose several improvements on (12.32). The first of these takes the expression

$$
\widehat{\mathrm{VaR}}_{1-p} = R_{(n-k)} \left(\frac{k}{np} \right)^{\hat{\gamma}} \left\{ 1 - \frac{\hat{\gamma}\hat{\beta}}{\hat{\rho}} \left(\frac{n}{k} \right)^{\hat{\gamma}} \left[1 - \left(\frac{(n+1)p}{k+1} \right)^{-\hat{\rho}} \right] \right\},
$$

where $\hat{\rho}$ and $\hat{\beta}$ are as given by Section 12.5.5, and $\hat{\gamma}$ is as given by Section 12.5.6. The second of these takes the expression

$$
\widehat{\mathrm{VaR}}_{1-p} = R_{(n-k)} \left(\frac{k}{np} \right)^{\hat{\gamma}} \exp \left\{ -\frac{\hat{\gamma}\hat{\beta}}{\hat{\rho}} \left(\frac{n}{k} \right)^{\hat{\gamma}} \left[1 - \left(\frac{(n+1)p}{k+1} \right)^{-\hat{\rho}} \right] \right\},
$$

where $\hat{\rho}$ and $\hat{\beta}$ are as given by Section 12.5.5, and $\hat{\gamma}$ is as given by Section 12.5.6. The third of these takes the expression

$$
\widehat{\mathrm{VaR}}_{1-p} = \frac{R_{(n-[k/2])} - R_{(n-k)}}{2^{\hat{\gamma}} - 1} \left(\frac{k}{np} \right)^{\hat{\gamma}} [1 - B_{1/2}(\hat{\gamma}; \hat{\rho}, \hat{\beta})],
$$

where $\hat{\rho}$ and $\hat{\beta}$ are as given by Section 12.5.5, $\hat{\gamma}$ is as given by Section 12.5.6, and $B_x(a, b)$ denotes the incomplete beta function defined by

$$
B_x(a, b) = \int_0^x t^{a-1}(1-t)^{b-1} dt.
$$

The fourth of these takes the expression

$$\widehat{\text{VaR}}_{1-p} = \frac{R_{(n-[k/2])} - R_{(n-k)}}{2^{\overline{H}(k)} - 1} \left(\frac{k}{np}\right)^{\overline{H}(k)} [1 - B_{1/2}(\overline{H}(k); \widehat{\rho}, \widehat{\beta})],$$

where $\widehat{\rho}$, $\widehat{\beta}$, and $\overline{H}(k)$ are as given in Section 12.5.5. All of these estimators are shown to be consistent and asymptotically normal.

12.5.8 Figueiredo et al.'s Method

The latest improvement of (12.32) is due to Figueiredo et al. (2012). It takes the expression

$$\widehat{\text{VaR}}_{1-p} = R_{(n_q)} + (R_{(n-k)} - R_{(n_q)}) \left(\frac{k}{np}\right)^{\overline{H}_n},$$

where $n_q = [nq] + 1$ and

$$\overline{H}_n = H_n \left[1 - \frac{\widehat{\beta}(n/k)^{\widehat{\rho}}}{1 - \widehat{\rho}}\right]$$

with $(\widehat{\beta}, \widehat{\rho})$ as defined in Section 12.5.5 and H_n as defined in Section 12.5.4.

12.5.9 Li et al.'s Method

Let p_n be such that $p_n \to 0$ and $np_n \to q > 0$ as $n \to \infty$. Li et al. (2010) derive estimators for VaR_{1-p_n} for large n. They give the estimator

$$\widehat{\text{VaR}}_{1-p_n} = \widehat{c}^{1/\widehat{\alpha}} p_n^{-1/\widehat{\alpha}} \left[1 + \widehat{\alpha}^{-1}\widehat{c}^{-\widehat{\beta}/\widehat{\alpha}}\widehat{d}p_n^{\widehat{\beta}/\widehat{\alpha}-1}\right],$$

where

$$\widehat{c} = \frac{\widehat{\alpha}\widehat{\beta}}{\widehat{\alpha} - \widehat{\beta}}R_{(n-k)}^{\widehat{\alpha}} \left[\frac{1}{\widehat{\beta}} - \frac{1}{k}\sum_{i=1}^{k} \ln \frac{R_{(n-i+1)}}{R_{(n-k)}}\right]$$

and

$$\widehat{d} = \frac{\widehat{\alpha}\widehat{\beta}}{\widehat{\beta} - \widehat{\alpha}}R_{(n-k)}^{\widehat{\beta}} \left[\frac{1}{\widehat{\alpha}} - \frac{1}{k}\sum_{i=1}^{k} \ln \frac{R_{(n-i+1)}}{R_{(n-k)}}\right],$$

where $\widehat{\alpha}$ and $\widehat{\beta}$ are the simultaneous solutions of the equations

$$\frac{1}{k}\sum_{i=1}^{k} Q_i^{-1}(\alpha, \beta) = 1$$

and

$$\frac{1}{k} \sum_{i=1}^{k} Q_i^{-1}(\alpha, \beta) \ln \frac{R_{(n-i+1)}}{R_{(n-k)}} = \frac{1}{\beta},$$

where

$$Q_i(\alpha, \beta) = \frac{\alpha}{\beta} \left[1 + \frac{\alpha\beta}{\alpha - \beta} H(\alpha) \right] \left(\frac{R_{(n-i+1)}}{R_{(n-k)}} \right)^{\beta - \alpha} - \frac{\alpha\beta}{\alpha - \beta} H(\alpha)$$

and

$$H(\alpha) = \frac{1}{\alpha} - \frac{1}{k} \sum_{i=1}^{k} \ln \frac{R_{(n-i+1)}}{R_{(n-k)}}.$$

Li et al. (2010) show under suitable conditions that

$$\frac{\sqrt{k}}{\ln k - \ln(np_n)} \left[\frac{\widehat{\text{VaR}}_{1-p_n}}{F^{-1}(1 - p_n)} - 1 \right] \to N \left(0, \frac{\beta^4}{\alpha^2(\beta - \alpha)^4} \right)$$

in distribution as $n \to \infty$.

12.5.10   Gomes et al.'s Method

Gomes et al. (2011) propose a bootstrap-based method for computing VaR. The method can be described as follows:

1. For an observed sample, $r_1, r_2, \ldots, r_n$, compute $\widehat{\rho}$ as in Section 12.5.5 for $\tau = 0$ and $\tau = 1$.

2. Compute the median of $\widehat{\rho} = \widehat{\rho}(k)$, say, M, for $k \in ([n^{0.995}], [n^{0.999}])$. Also compute

$$I_\tau = \sum_{k \in ([n^{0.995}], [n^{0.999}])} (\widehat{\rho}(k) - M)^2$$

for $\tau = 0, 1$. Choose the tuning parameter, τ, as zero if $I_0 \leq I_1$ and as one otherwise.

3. Compute $\widehat{\rho} = \widehat{\rho}([n^{0.999}])$ and $\widehat{\beta} = \widehat{\beta}([n^{0.999}])$ using the formulas in Section 12.5.5 and the chosen tuning parameter.

4. Compute $\overline{H}(k)$, $k = 1, 2, \ldots, n - 1$ in Section 12.5.5 with the estimates $\widehat{\rho}$ and $\widehat{\beta}$ in Step 3.

5. Set $n_1 = [n^{0.95}]$ and $n_2 = [n_1^2/n] + 1$.

6. Generate B bootstrap samples $(r_1^*, r_2^*, \ldots, r_{n_2}^*)$ and $(r_1^*, r_2^*, \ldots, r_{n_2}^*, r_{n_2+1}^*, \ldots, r_{n_1}^*)$ from the empirical cdf of $r_1, r_2, \ldots, r_n$.

7. Compute $\overline{H}([k/2]) - \overline{H}(k)$ for the bootstrap samples in Step 6. Let $t_{1,\ell}(k)$, $\ell = 1, 2, \dots, B$ denote the estimates for the bootstrap samples of size n_1. Let $t_{2,\ell}(k)$, $\ell = 1, 2, \dots, B$ denote the estimates for the bootstrap samples of size n_2.

8. Compute

$$\mathrm{MSE}_1(j, k) = \frac{1}{B} \sum_{i=1}^{B} t_{j,\ell}^2(k)$$

and

$$\mathrm{MSE}_2(j, k) = \ln^2 \left(\frac{k}{np} \right) \mathrm{MSE}_1$$

for $j = 1, 2$ and $k = 1, 2, \dots, n_j - 1$.

9. Compute

$$\widehat{P}(j) = \arg \min_{1 \leq k \leq n_j - 1} \mathrm{MSE}_1(j, k), \ \widehat{Q}(j) = \arg \min_{1 \leq k \leq n_j - 1} \mathrm{MSE}_2(j, k)$$

for $j = 1, 2$.

10. Compute

$$\widehat{k}_0 = \min \left\{ n - 1, \left[\frac{\left(1 - 4\widehat{\rho}\right)^{2/(1-\widehat{\rho})} \widehat{P}^2(1)}{\widehat{P}([n_1^2/n] + 1)} \right] + 1 \right\}.$$

11. Compute $\overline{H}(\widehat{k}_0)$ with the estimates $\widehat{\rho}$ and $\widehat{\beta}$ in Step 3.

12. Compute

$$\widehat{\ell}_0 = \min \left\{ n - 1, \left[\frac{\left(1 - 4\widehat{\rho}\right)^{2/(1-\widehat{\rho})} \widehat{Q}^2(1)}{\widehat{Q}([n_1^2/n] + 1)} \right] + 1 \right\}.$$

13. Finally, estimate VaR_{1-p} as

$$\widehat{\mathrm{VaR}}_{1-p} = r_{(n-\widehat{\ell}_0+1)} \left(\frac{\widehat{\ell}_0}{np} \right)^{\overline{H}(\widehat{\ell}_0)}.$$

12.5.11 Wang's Method

Wang (2010) combined the historical method in Section 12.4.1 with the generalized Pareto model in Section 12.5.2 to suggest the following estimator for VaR:

$$\widehat{\text{VaR}}_p = \begin{cases} R_{(i)}, p \in ((i-1)/n, i/n] \,, & \text{if } p < p_0, \\ u + \dfrac{\widehat{\sigma}}{\widehat{\xi}}[(1-p)^{-\widehat{\xi}} - 1], & \text{if } p \geq p_0, \end{cases}$$

where $\widehat{\sigma}$ and $\widehat{\xi}$ are the maximum likelihood estimators of σ and ξ, respectively, and p_0 is an appropriately chosen threshold.

12.5.12 *M*-Estimation Method

Iqbal and Mukherjee (2012) provide an *M*-estimator for VaR. They consider a GARCH $(1, 1)$ model for returns $R_1, \dots, R_n$ specified by

$$R_t = \sigma_t \epsilon_t,$$

where

$$\sigma_t^2 = \omega_0 + \alpha_0 R_{t-1}^2 + \beta_0 \sigma_{t-1}^2 + \gamma_0 I(R_{t-1} < 0) R_{t-1}^2$$

and ϵ_t are independent and identical random variables symmetric about zero. The unknown parameters are $\boldsymbol{\theta}_0 = (\omega_0, \alpha_0, \gamma_0, \beta_0)^T$, and they belong to the parameter space, the set of all $\boldsymbol{\theta} = (\omega, \alpha, \gamma, \beta)^T$ with $\omega, \alpha, \beta > 0$, $\alpha + \gamma \geq 0$ and $\alpha + \beta + \gamma/2 < 1$. The *M*-estimator, say, $\widehat{\boldsymbol{\theta}}_T$, is obtained by solving the equation

$$\sum_{t=1}^{n} \widehat{m}_t(\boldsymbol{\theta}) = 0,$$

where

$$\widehat{m}_t(\boldsymbol{\theta}) = (1/2)\{1 - H(R_t/\widehat{v}_t^{1/2}(\boldsymbol{\theta}))\}[\dot{\widehat{v}}_t(\boldsymbol{\theta})/\widehat{v}_t(\boldsymbol{\theta})]$$

and

$$\widehat{v}_t(\boldsymbol{\theta}) = \frac{\omega}{1-\beta} + I(t \geq 2)\left\{ \alpha \sum_{j=1}^{t-1} \beta^{j-1} R_{t-j}^2 + \gamma \sum_{j=1}^{t-1} I\left(R_{t-j} < 0\right) \beta^{j-1} R_{t-j}^2 \right\},$$

where $H(x) = x\psi(x)$ for some skew-symmetric function $\psi : \mathbb{R} \to \mathbb{R}$ and $\dot{\widehat{v}}_t(\boldsymbol{\theta})$ denotes the derivative of $\widehat{v}_t(\boldsymbol{\theta})$. Iqbal and Mukherjee (2012) propose that VaR_p can be estimated by $\widehat{v}_t^{1/2}(\widehat{\boldsymbol{\theta}}_T)$ multiplied by the $([np] + 1)$th order statistic of $\{R_t/\{\widehat{v}_t(\widehat{\boldsymbol{\theta}}_T)\}^{1/2}, t = 2, 3, \dots, n\}$.

12.5.13 Generalized Champernowne Distribution

Generalized Champernowne distribution was introduced by Buch-Larsen et al. (2005) as a model for insurance claims. A random variable, say, X, is said to have this distribution if its cdf is

$$F(x) = \frac{(x+c)^a - c^a}{(x+c)^a + (M+c)^a - 2c^a} \tag{12.35}$$

for $x > 0$, where $\alpha > 0$, $c > 0$, and $M > 0$ is the median. Charpentier and Oulidi (2010) provide estimators of $\text{VaR}_p(X)$ based on beta kernel quantile estimators. They suggest the following algorithm for estimating $\text{VaR}_p(X)$:

- Suppose $X_1, X_2, \ldots, X_n$ is a random sample from (12.35).
- Let $(\hat{M}, \hat{\alpha}, \hat{c})$ denote the estimators of the parameters (M, α, c); if the method of maximum likelihood is used, then the estimators can be obtained by maximizing the log likelihood given by

$$\ln \ L(\alpha, M, c) = n\{\ln a + \ln[(M+c)^a - c^a]\} + (a-1) \sum_{i=1}^{n} \ln \ (X_i + c)$$

$$-2 \sum_{i=1}^{n} \ln[(X_i + c)^a + (M+c)^a - 2c^a].$$

- Transform $Y_i = F(X_i)$, where $F(\cdot)$ is given by (12.35) with (M, α, c) replaced by $(\hat{M}, \hat{\alpha}, \hat{c})$.
- Estimate the cdf of $Y_1, Y_2, \ldots, Y_n$ as

$$\hat{F}_{n,Y}(y) = \frac{\sum_{i=1}^{n} \int_0^y K_\beta(Y_i; b, t)dt}{\sum_{i=1}^{n} \int_0^1 K_\beta(Y_i; b, t)dt},$$

where $K_\beta(\cdot; b, t)$ is given by either

$$K_\beta(u; b, t) = k_{t/b+1,(1-t)/b+1}(u) = \frac{u^{t/b}(1-u)^{(1-t)/b}}{B(t/b + 1, (1-t)/b + 1)}$$

or

$$K_\beta(u; b, t) = \begin{cases} k_{t/b,(1-t)/b}(u), & \text{if } t \in [2b, 1-2b], \\ k_{\rho_b(t),(1-t)/b}(u), & \text{if } t \in [0, 2b), \\ k_{t/b,\rho_b(1-t)}(u), & \text{if } t \in (1-2b, 1], \end{cases}$$

where $\rho_b(t) = 2b^2 + 2.5 - \sqrt{4b^4 + 6b^2 + 2.25 - t^2 - t/b}$.
- Solve $\hat{F}_{n,Y}(q) = p$ for q by using some Newton algorithm.
- Estimate $\text{VaR}_p(X)$ by $\widehat{\text{VaR}}_p(X) = F_{\hat{M},\hat{\alpha},\hat{c}}^{-1}(q)$.

12.6 COMPUTER SOFTWARE

Software for computing VaR and related quantities are widely available. Some software available from the R package (R Development Core Team, 2015) are the following:

- The package actuar due to Vincent Goulet, Sébastien Auclair, Christophe Dutang, Xavier Milhaud, Tommy Ouellet, Louis-Philippe Pouliot, and Mathieu Pigeon. According to the authors, this package provides "additional actuarial science functionality, mostly in the fields of loss distributions, risk theory (including ruin theory), simulation of compound hierarchical models and credibility theory. The package also features 17 new probability laws commonly used in insurance, most notably heavy tailed distributions."

- The package ghyp due to David Luethi and Wolfgang Breymann. According to the authors, this package "provides detailed functionality for working with the univariate and multivariate Generalized Hyperbolic distribution and its special cases (Hyperbolic (hyp), Normal Inverse Gaussian (NIG), Variance Gamma (VG), skewed Student-t and Gaussian distribution). Especially, it contains fitting procedures, an AIC-based model selection routine, and functions for the computation of density, quantile, probability, random variates, expected shortfall and some portfolio optimization and plotting routines as well as the likelihood ratio test. In addition, it contains the Generalized Inverse Gaussian distribution."

- The package PerformanceAnalytics due to Peter Carl, Brian G. Peterson, Kris Boudt, and Eric Zivot. According to the authors, this package "aims to aid practitioners and researchers in utilizing the latest research in analysis of non-normal return streams. In general, it is most tested on return (rather than price) data on a regular scale, but most functions will work with irregular return data as well, and increasing numbers of functions will work with P & L or price data where possible."

- The package crp.CSFP due to Matthias Fischer, Kevin Jakob, and Stefan Kolb. According to the authors, this package models "credit risks based on the concept of 'CreditRisk+', First Boston Financial Products, 1997 and 'CreditRisk+ in the Banking Industry', Gundlach & Lehrbass, Springer, 2003. "

- The package fAssets due to Diethelm Wuertz and many others.

- The package fPortfolio due to the Rmetrics Core Team and Diethelm Wuertz.

- The package CreditMetrics due to Andreas Wittmann.

- The package fExtremes due to Diethelm Wuertz and many others.

- The package rugarch due to Alexios Ghalanos.

Some other software available for computing VaR and related quantities are the following:

- The package EC-VaR due to Rho-Works Advanced Analytical Systems, http://www.rhoworks.com/ecvar.php. According to the authors, this package implements "Conditional Value-at-Risk, BetaVaR, Component VaR, traditional VaR and backtesting measures for portfolios composed of stocks, currencies and indexes. An integrated optimizer can solve for the minimum CVaR portfolio based on market data, while a module capable of doing Stochastic Simulation allows to graph all feasible portfolios on the CVaR-Return space. EC-VaR employs a full-valuation historical-simulation approach to estimate Value-at-Risk and other risk indicators."

- The package VaR calculator and simulator due to Lapides Software Development Inc., http://members.shaw.ca/lapides/var.html. According to the authors, this package implements "simple, robust, down to earth implementation of JP Morgan's RiskMetrics. Build to answer day to day needs of medium size organisations. Ideal for managers with focus on performance, end result and value. Allows one to calculate the VaR of any portfolio. Calculates correlations, volatilities, valuates complex financial instruments and employs two methods: Analytical VaR calculation and Monte Carlo simulation."

- The package NtInsight for asset liability management due to Numerical Technologies, http://www.numtech.com/financial-risk-management-software/. According to the producers, this package is used by "banks and insurance companies that handles massive and complicated financial simulation without oversimplified approximations. It provides asset/liability management professionals an integrated balance sheet management environment to monitor, analyze, and manage liquidity risks, interest-rate risks, and earnings-at-risk."

- The package Protecht.ALM due to David Tattam and David Bergmark from the company Protecht, http://www.protecht.com.au/risk-management-software/asset-liability-risk. According to the authors, this package provides "a full analysis and measurement of interest rate risk using variety of complimentary best practice measures such as VaR, PVBP and gap reporting. Also offers web based scenario and risk reporting for in-house reporting of exposures";

- The package ProFintm Risk due to the company Entrion, http://www.entrion.com/software/. According to the authors, this package provides "a multi commodity Energy risk application that calculates VaR. The result is a system that minimizes the resource needed for daily risk calculator; which in turn, changes the focus from calculating risk to managing risk. VaR is calculated using the Delta-Normal method and this method calculates VaR using commodity prices and positions, volatilities, correlations and risk statistics. This application calculates volatilities and correlations using exponentially weighted historical prices."

- The package ALM Optimizer for asset allocation software due to Bob Korkie from the company RMKorkie & Associates, http://assetallocation software.org/. According to the author, this package provides "risk and expected return of Markowitz efficient portfolios but extended to include recent technical advances on the definition of risk, adjustments for input bias, non normal distributions, and enhancements that allow for overlays, risk budgets, and investment horizon adjustments." Also the package "is a true Portfolio Optimizer with lognormal asset returns and user specified return or surplus optimization; optimization, risk, and rebalancing horizons; volatility, expected shortfall, and two VaR risk variables tailored to the risk horizon; and user specified portfolio constraints including risk budget constraints."

- The package QuantLib due to StatPro, http://www.statpro.com/portfolio-analytics-products/risk-management-software/. According to the authors, this package provides "access to a complete universe of pricing functions for risk assessment covering every asset class from equity, interest rate-linked products to mortgage-backed securities." The package has key features including "Multiple ex-ante risk measures including Value-at-Risk and CVaR (expected shortfall) at a variety of confidence levels, potential gain, volatility, tracking error and diversification grade. These measures are available in both absolute and relative basis."

- The package FinAnalytica's Cognity risk management due to FinAnalytica, http://www.finanalytica.com/daily-risk-statistics/. According to the authors, this package provides "more accurate fat-tailed VaR estimates that do not suffer from the over-optimism of normal distributions. But Cognity goes beyond VaR and also provides the downside Expected Tail Loss (ETL) measure—the average or expected loss beyond VaR. As compared with volatility and VaR, ETL, also known as Conditional Value at Risk (CVaR) and Expected Shortfall (ES), is a highly informative and intuitive measure of extreme downside losses. By combining ETL with fat-tailed distributions, risk managers have access to the most accurate estimate of downside risk available today."

- The package CVaR Expert due to CVaR Expert Rho-Works Advanced Analytical Systems, http://www.rhoworks.com/software/detail/cvarxpert.htm. According to the authors, this package implements "total solution for measuring, analyzing and managing portfolio risk using historical VaR and CVaR methodologies. Traditional Value-at-Risk, Beta VaR, Component VaR, Conditional VaR and backtesting modules are incorporated on the current version, which lets you work with individual assets, portfolios, asset groups and multi currency investments (Enterprise Edition). An integrated optimizer can solve for the minimum CVaR portfolio based on market data and investor preferences, offering the best risk benchmark that can be produced. A module capable of doing Stochastic Simulation allows you to graph the CVaR-Return space for all feasible portfolios."

- The Kamakura Risk Manager software (KRM) due to ZSL Inc., http://www.zsl.com/solutions/banking-finance/enterprise-risk-management-krm. According to the authors, KRM "completely integrates credit portfolio management, market risk management, asset and liability management, Basel II and other capital allocation technologies, transfer pricing, and performance measurement. KRM is also directly applicable to operational risk, total risk, and accounting and regulatory requirements using the same analytical engine, GUI and reporting, and its vision is that completely integrated risk solution based on common assumptions and methodologies. KRM offers, dynamic VaR and expected shortfall, historical VaR measurement, Monte Carlo VaR measurement, etc."

- The package G@RCH 6, OxMetrics, due to Timberlake Consultants Limited, http://www.timberlake.co.uk/?id=64#garch. According to the authors, the package is "dedicated to the estimation and forecasting of univariate ARCH-type models. G@RCH provides a user-friendly interface (with rolling menus) as well as some graphical features (through the OxMetrics graphical interface). G@RCH helps the financial analysis: value-at-risk, expected shortfall, backtesting (Kupiec LRT, dynamic quantile test), forecasting, and realized volatility."

12.7 CONCLUSIONS

We have reviewed the current state of the most popular risk measure, VaR, with emphasis on recent developments. We have reviewed 10 of its general properties, including upper comonotonicity and multivariate extensions; 35 of its parametric estimation methods, including time series, quantile regression, and Bayesian methods; 8 of its nonparametric estimation methods, including historical methods and bootstrapping; 13 of its semiparametric estimation methods, including extreme value theory and M-estimation methods; and 20 known computer software, including those based on the R platform.

This review could encourage further research with respect to measures of financial risk. Some open problems to address are further multivariate extensions of risk measures and corresponding estimation methods; development of a comprehensive R package implementing a wide range of parametric, nonparametric, and semiparametric estimation methods (no such packages are available to date); estimation based on nonparametric Bayesian methods; estimation methods suitable for big data; and so on.

Acknowledgment

The authors would like to thank Professor Longin for careful reading and comments that greatly improved the chapter.

References

Araújo Santos, A., Fraga Alves, M.I., Gomes, M.I. Peaks over random threshold methodology for tail index and quantile estimation. Revstat 2006;**4**:227–247.

Arbia, G. Bivariate value-at-risk. Statistica 2002;**62**:231–247.

Ardia, D. *Financial Risk Management with Bayesian Estimation of GARCH Models: Theory and Applications*. Berlin: Springer-Verlag; 2008.

Arneric, J., Jurun, E., Pivac, S. Parametric forecasting of value at risk using heavy tailed distribution. Proceedings of the 11th International Conference on Operational Research; 2008. p 65–75.

Bae, T., Iscoe, I. Large-sample confidence intervals for risk measures of location-scale families. Journal of Statistical Planning and Inference 2012;**142**:2032–2046.

Bahadur, R. A note on quantiles in large samples. Annals of Mathematical Statistics 1966;**37**:577–580.

Baillie, R.T., Bollerslev, T., Mikkelsen, H.O. Fractionally integrated generalized autoregressive conditional heteroskedasticity. Journal of Econometrics 1996;**74**:3–30.

Barone-Adesi, G., Giannopoulos, K., Vosper, L. VaR without correlations for nonlinear portfolios. Journal of Futures Markets 1999;**19**:583–602.

Beirlant, J., Figueiredo, F., Gomes, M.I., Vandewalle, B. Improved reduced-bias tail index and quantile estimators. Journal of Statistical Planning and Inference 2008;**138**:1851–1870.

Beirlant, J., Herrmann, K., Teugels, J.L. Estimation of the extreme value index. In: Longin, F., editor. *Extreme Events in Finance*. Chichester: John Wiley & Sons; 2017.

Bi, G., Giles, D.E. Modelling the financial risk associated with U.S. movie box office earnings. Mathematics and Computers in Simulation 2009;**79**:2759–2766.

Bingham, N.H., Goldie, C.M., Teugels, J.L. *Regular Variation*. Cambridge: Cambridge University Press; 1989.

Böcker, K., Klüppelberg, C. Operational VaR: a closed-form approximation. Risk 2005;**18**:90–93.

Bollerslev, T. Generalized autoregressive conditional heteroskedasticity. Journal of Econometrics 1986;**28**:307–327.

Bonga-Bonga, L., Mutema, G. Volatility forecasting and value-at-risk estimation in emerging markets: the case of the stock market index portfolio in South Africa. South African Journal of Economic and Management Sciences 2009;**12**:401–411.

Bouchaud, J.-P., Potters, M. *Theory of Financial Risks: From Statistical Physics to Risk Management*. Cambridge: Cambridge University Press; 2000.

Brazauskas, V., Kleefeld, A. Folded and log-folded-*t* distributions as models for insurance loss data. Scandinavian Actuarial Journal 2011;**2011**(1):59–74.

Brummelhuis, R., Cordoba, A., Quintanilla, M., Seco, L. Principal component value at risk. Mathematical Finance 2002;**12**:23–43.

Buch-Larsen, T., Nielsen, J.P., Guillen, M., Bolance, C. Kernel density estimation for heavy-tailed distribution using the Champernowne transformation. Statistics 2005;**6**:503–518.

Caeiro, F., Gomes, M.I. Minimum-variance reduced-bias tail index and high quantile estimation. Revstat 2008;**6**:1–20.

Caeiro, F., Gomes, M.I. Semi-parametric second-order reduced-bias high quantile estimation. Test 2009;**18**:392–413.

Cai, Z.-Y., Xin, R., Xiao, R. Value at risk management in multi-period supply inventory coordination. Proceedings of the 2009 IEEE International Conference on e-Business Engineering; 2009. p. 335–339.

Cakir, S., Raei, F. Sukuk versus Eurobonds: is there a difference in value-at-risk? IMF Working Paper WP/07/237; 2007.

Capinski, M., Zastawniak, T. *Mathematics for Finance*. London: Springer-Verlag; 2011.

Chan, F. Modelling time-varying higher moments with maximum entropy density. Mathematics and Computers in Simulation 2009a;**79**:2767–2778.

Chan, F. Forecasting value-at-risk using maximum entropy density. Proceedings of the 18th World IMACS / MODSIM Congress; 2009b. p 1377–1383.

Chan, N.H., Deng, S.-J., Peng, L., Xia, Z. Interval estimation of value-at-risk based on GARCH models with heavy tailed innovations. Journal of Econometrics 2007;**137**:556–576.

Chang, C.-S. A matrix-based VaR model for risk identification in power supply networks. Applied Mathematical Modelling 2011a;**35**:4567–4574.

Chang, K.L. The optimal value at risk hedging strategy under bivariate regime switching ARCH framework. Applied Economics 2011b;**43**:2627–2640.

Chang, Y.P., Hung, M.C., Wu, Y.F. Nonparametric estimation for risk in value-at-risk estimator. Communications in Statistics—Simulation and Computation 2003;**32**:1041–1064.

Charpentier, A., Oulidi, A. Beta kernel quantile estimators of heavy-tailed loss distributions. Statistics and Computing 2010;**20**:35–55.

Chen, S.X., Tang, C.Y. Nonparametric inference of value-at-risk for dependent financial returns. Journal of Financial Econometrics 2005;**3**:227–255.

Cheong, C.W. Univariate and multivariate value-at-risk: application and implication in energy markets. Communications in Statistics—Simulation and Computation 2011;**40**:957–977.

Cheong, C.W., Isa, Z. Bivariate value-at-risk in the emerging Malaysian sectoral markets. Journal of Interdisciplinary Mathematics 2011;**14**:67–94.

Chernozhukov, V., Umantsev, L. Conditional value-at-risk: aspects of modeling and estimation. Empirical Economics 2001;**26**:271–292.

Cheung, K.C. Upper comonotonicity. Insurance: Mathematics and Economics 2009;**45**:35–40.

Cohen, A.C., Whitten, B. Modified maximum likelihood and modified moment estimators fort the three-parameter Weibull distribution. Communications in Statistics—Theory and Methods 1982;**11**:2631–2656.

Cousin, A., Bernardinoy, E.D. A multivariate extension of value-at-risk and conditional-tail-expectation; 2011. ArXiv: 1111.1349v1.

Dagum, C. A new model for personal income distribution: specification and estimation. Economie Appliquée, 1977;**30**:413–437.

Dagum, C. The generation and distribution of income, the Lorenz curve and the Gini ratio. Economie Appliquée, 1980;**33**:327–367.

Dash, J.W. *Quantitative Finance and Risk Management: A Physicist's Approach*. River Edge (NJ): World Scientific Publishing Company; 2004.

Degen, M., Lambrigger, D.D., Segers, J. Risk concentration and diversification: second-order properties. Insurance: Mathematics and Economics 2010;**46**:541–546.

Dehlendorff, C., Kulahci, M., Merser, S., Andersen, K.K. Conditional value at risk as a measure for waiting time in simulations of hospital units. Quality Technology and Quantitative Management 2010;**7**:321–336.

Dekkers, A.L.M., Einmahl, J.H.J., de Haan, L. A moment estimator for the index of an extreme-value distribution. Annals of Statistics 1989;**17**:1833–1855.

Delbaen, F. Coherent Risk Measures (Scuola Normale Superiore, Classe di Scienze, Pisa, Italy); 2000.

Denis, L., Fernandez, B., Meda, A. Estimation of value at risk and ruin probability for diffusion processes with jumps. Mathematical Finance 2009;**19**:281–302.

Dionne, G., Duchesne, P., Pacurar, M. Intraday value at risk (IVaR) using tick-by-tick data with application to the Toronto stock exchange. Journal of Empirical Finance 2009;**16**:777–792.

Dixon, M.F., Chong, J., Keutzer, K. Accelerating value-at-risk estimation on highly parallel architectures. Concurrency and Computation—Practice and Experience 2012;**24**:895–907.

Domma, F., Perri, P.F. Some developments on the log-Dagum distribution. Statistical Methods and Applications 2009;**18**:205–220.

Dupacova, J., Hurt, J., Stepan, J. *Stochastic Modeling in Economics and Finance*. Dordrecht: Kluwer Academic Publishers; 2002.

Efron, B., Tibshirani, R.J. *An Introduction to the Bootstrap*. New York: Chapman and Hall; 1993.

Embrechts, P., Klüppelberg, C., Mikosch, T. *Modeling Extremal Events for Insurance and Finance*. Berlin: Springer-Verlag; 1997.

Embrechts, P., Lambrigger, D.D., Wuthrich, M.V. Multivariate extremes and the aggregation of dependent risks: examples and counter-examples. Extremes 2009a;**12**:107–127.

Embrechts, P., Neslehova, J., Wuthrich, M.V. Additivity properties for value-at-risk under Archimedean dependence and heavy-tailedness. Insurance: Mathematics and Economics 2009b;**44**:164–169.

Engle, R.F., Manganelli, S. CAViaR: conditional autoregressive value at risk by regression quantiles. Journal of Business and Economic Statistics 2004;**22**:367–381.

Fang, J., Mannan, M., Ford, D., Logan, J., Summers, A. Value at risk perspective on layers of protection analysis. Process Safety and Environmental Protection 2007;**85**:81–87.

Fedor, M. Financial risk in pension funds: application of value at risk methodology. In: Micocci, G.N., Gregoriou, G., Batista, M., editors. *Pension Fund Risk Management: Financial and Actuarial Modelling*, Chapter 9. New York: CRC Press; 2010. p 185–209.

Feng, Y.J., Chen, A.D. The application of value-at-risk in project risk measurement. Proceedings of the 2001 International Conference on Management Science and Engineering; 2001. p 1747–1750.

Fernandez, V. The CAPM and value at risk at different time scales. Int Rev Financ Anal 2006;**15**:203–219.

Feuerverger, A., Wong, A.C.M. Computation of value at risk for non-linear portfolios. J Risk 2000;**3**:37–55.

Figueiredo, F., Gomes, M.I., Henriques-Rodrigues, L., Miranda, M.C. A computational study of a quasi-PORT methodology for VaR based on second-order reduced-bias estimation. Journal of Statistical Computation and Simulation 2012;**82**:587–602.

Fisher, R.A., Tippett, L.H.C. Limiting forms of the frequency distribution of the largest or smallest member of a sample. Proceedings of the Cambridge Philosophical Society 1928;**24**:180–290.

Fraga Alves, I., Neves, C. Extreme value theory: an introductory overview. In: Longin, F., editor. *Extreme Events in Finance*. Chichester: John Wiley & Sons; 2017.

Franke, J., Hardle, W.K., Hafner, C.M. *Statistics of Financial Markets: An Introduction*. Berlin: Springer-Verlag; 2004.

Franke, J., Hardle, W.K., Hafner, C.M. *Statistics of Financial Markets*. Berlin: Springer-Verlag; 2008.

Franke, J., Hardle, W.K., Hafner, C.M. Copulae and value at risk. In: *Statistics of Financial Markets*. Berlin: Springer-Verlag; 2011. p 405–446.

Gatti, S., Rigamonti, A., Saita, F. Measuring value at risk in project finance transactions. European Financial Management 2007;**13**:135–158.

Gebizlioglu, O.L., Senoglu, B., Kantar, Y.M. Comparison of certain value-at-risk estimation methods for the two-parameter Weibull loss distribution. Journal of Computational and Applied Mathematics 2011;**235**:3304–3314.

Göb, R. Estimating value at risk and conditional value at risk for count variables. Quality and Reliability Engineering International 2011;**27**:659–672.

Gomes, M.I., Caeiro, F., Henriques-Rodrigues, L., Manjunath, B.G. Bootstrap methods in statistics of extremes. In: Longin, F., editor. *Extreme Events in Finance*. Chichester: John Wiley & Sons; 2015.

Gomes, M.I., Mendonca, S., Pestana, D. Adaptive reduced-bias tail index and VaR estimation via the bootstrap methodology. Communications in Statistics—Theory and Methods 2011;**40**:2946–2968.

Gomes, M.I., Pestana, D. A sturdy reduced-bias extreme quantile (VaR) estimator. Journal of the American Statistical Association 2007;**102**:280–292.

Gong, Z., Li, D. Measurement of HIS stock index futures market risk based on value-at-risk. Proceedings of the 15th International Conference on Industrial Engineering and Engineering Management; 2008. p 1906–1911.

Gouriéroux, C., Laurent, J.-P., Scaillet, O. Sensitivity analysis of values at risk. Journal of Empirical Finance 2000;**7**:225–245.

Guillen, M., Prieto, F., Sarabia, J.M. Modelling losses and locating the tail with the Pareto positive stable distribution. Insurance: Mathematics and Economics 2011;**49**:454–461.

Harrell, F.E., Davis, C.E. A new distribution free quantile estimator. Biometrika 1982;**69**:635–640.

Hartz, C., Mittnik, S., Paolella, M. Accurate value-at-risk forecasting based on the (good old) normal-GARCH model. Center for Financial Studies (CFS), Working Paper Number 2006/23; 2006.

Hassan, R., de Neufville, R., McKinnon, D. Value-at-risk analysis for real options in complex engineered systems. Proceedings of the International Conference on Systems, Man and Cybernetics; 2005. p 3697–3704.

He, K., Lai, K.K., Xiang, G. Portfolio value at risk estimate for crude oil markets: a multivariate wavelet denoising approach. Energies 2012a;**5**:1018–1043.

He, K., Lai, K.K., Yen, J. Ensemble forecasting of value at risk via multi resolution analysis based methodology in metals markets. Expert Systems with Applications 2012b;**39**:4258–4267.

He, K., Xie, C., Lai, K.K. Estimating real estate value at risk using wavelet denoising and time series model. Proceedings of the 8th International Conference on Computational Science, Part II; 2008. p 494–503.

Hill, B.M. A simple general approach to inference about the tail of a distribution. Annals of Statistics 1975;**13**:331–341.

Hill, I., Hill, R., Holder, R. Fitting Johnson curves by moments. Applied Statistics 1976;**25**:180–192.

Hong, L.J. Monte Carlo estimation of value-at-risk, conditional value-at-risk and their sensitivities. Proceedings of the 2011 Winter Simulation Conference; 2011. p 95–107.

Huang, J.J., Lee, K.J., Liang, H.M., Lin, W.F. Estimating value at risk of portfolio by conditional copula-GARCH method. Insurance: Mathematics and Economics 2009;**45**:315–324.

Hughett, P. Error bounds for numerical inversion of a probability characteristic function. SIAM Journal on Numerical Analysis 1998;**35**:1368–1392.

Hull, J., White, A. Incorporating volatility updating into the historical simulation method for VaR. Journal of Risk 1998;**1**:5–19.

Hürlimann, W. Analytical bounds for two value-at-risk functionals. Astin Bull 2002;**32**:235–265.

Ibragimov, R. Portfolio diversification and value at risk under thick-tailedness. Quantitative Finance 2009;**9**:565–580.

Ibragimov, R., Walden, J. Value at risk and efficiency under dependence and heavy-tailedness: models with common shocks. Annals of Finance 2011;**7**:285–318.

Iqbal, F., Mukherjee, K. A study of value-at-risk based on M-estimators of the conditional heteroscedastic models. Journal of Forecasting 2012;**31**:377–390.

Jadhav, D., Ramanathan, T.V. Parametric and non-parametric estimation of value-at-risk. Journal of Risk Model Validation 2009;**3**:51–71.

Jakobsen, S. Measuring value-at-risk for mortgage backed securities. In: Bruni, F., Fair, D.E., O'Brien, R., editors. *Risk Management in Volatile Financial Markets*. Volume **32**. Dordrecht: Kluwer; 1996. p 184–206.

Jang, J., Jho, J.H. *Asymptotic super(sub)additivity of value-at-risk of regularly varying dependent variables*. Sydney: Preprint, MacQuarie University; 2007.

Janssen, J., Manca, R., Volpe di Prignano, E. *Mathematical Finance*. Hoboken (NJ): John Wiley & Sons, Inc.; 2009.

Jaschke, S., Klüppelberg, C., Lindner, A. Asymptotic behavior of tails and quantiles of quadratic forms of Gaussian vectors. Journal of Multivariate Analysis 2004;**88**:252–273.

Jaworski, P. Bounds for value at risk for asymptotically dependent assets—the copula approach. Proceedings of the 5th EUSFLAT Conference. Ostrava: Czech Republic; 2007.

Jaworski, P. Bounds for value at risk for multiasset portfolios. Acta Phys Pol A 2008;**114**:619–627.

Jeong, S.-O., Kang, K-H. Nonparametric estimation of value-at-risk. J Appl Stat 2009;**36**:1225–1238.

Jiménez, J.A., Arunachalam, V. Using Tukey's g and h family of distributions to calculate value-at-risk and conditional value-at-risk. J Risk 2011;**13**:95–116.

Jin, C., Ziobrowski, A.J. Using value-at-risk to estimate downside residential market risk. J Real Estate Res 2011;**33**:389–413.

Johnson, N.L. System of frequency curves generated by methods of translation. Biometrika 1949;**36**:149–176.

Jorion, P. *Value at Risk: The New Benchmark for Managing Financial Risk*. 2nd ed. New York: McGraw-Hill; 2001.

Kaigh, W.D., Lachenbruch, P.A. A generalized quantile estimator. Commun Stat Theory Methods 1982;**11**:2217–2238.

Kaiser, M.J., Pulsipher, A.G., Darr, J., Singhal, A., Foster, T., Vojjala, R. Catastrophic event modeling in the Gulf of Mexico II: industry exposure and value at risk. Energy Sources Part B—Economics Planning and Policy 2010;**5**:147–154.

Kaiser, M.J., Pulsipher, A.G., Singhal, A., Foster, T., Vojjala, R. Industry exposure and value at risk storms in the Gulf of Mexico. Oil and Gas Journal 2007;**105**:36–42.

Kamdem, J.S. Value-at-risk and expected shortfall for linear portfolios with elliptically distributed risk factors. International Journal of Theoretical and Applied Finance 2005;**8**. DOI: 10.1142/S0219024905003104.

Karandikar, R.G., Deshpande, N.R., Khaparde, S.A. Modelling volatility clustering in electricity price return series for forecasting value at risk. European Transactions on Electrical Power 2009;**19**:15–38.

Klugman, S.A., Panjer, H.H., Willmot, G.E. *Loss Models*. Hoboken (NJ): John Wiley & Sons, Inc.; 2008.

Koenker, R., Bassett, G. Regression quantiles. Econometrica 1978;**46**:33–50.

Koenker, R., Portnoy, S. Quantile regression. Working Paper 97-0100, University of Illinois at Urbana-Champaign; 1997.

Komunjer, I. Asymmetric power distribution: theory and applications to risk measurement. Journal of Applied Econometrics 2007;**22**:891–921.

Ku, Y.-H.H., Wang, J.J. Estimating portfolio value-at-risk via dynamic conditional correlation MGARCH model—an empirical study on foreign exchange rates. Applied Economics Letters 2008;**15**:533–538.

Kwon, C. Conditional value-at-risk model for hazardous materials transportation. Proceedings of the 2011 Winter Simulation Conference; 2011. p 1703–1709.

Lai, T.L., Xing, H. *Statistical Models and Methods for Financial Markets*, New York: Springer Verlag; 2008.

Lee, J., Locke, P. Dynamic trading value at risk: futures floor trading. Journal of Futures Markets 2006;**26**:1217–1234.

Li, D.Y., Peng, L., Yang, J.P. Bias reduction for high quantiles. Journal of Statistical Planning and Inference 2010;**140**:2433–2441.

Li, K., Yu, X.Y., Gao, F. The validity analysis of value-at-risk technique in Chinese securities market. Proceedings of the 2002 International Conference on Management Science and Engineering; 2002. p 1518–1521.

Lin, H.-Y., Chen, A.-P. Application of dynamic financial time-series prediction on the interval artificial neural network approach with value-at-risk model. Proceedings of the 2008 IEEE International Joint Conference on Neural Networks; 2008. p 3918–3925.

Liu, C.C., Ryan, S.G., Tan, H. How banks' value-at-risk disclosures predict their total and priced risk: effects of bank technical sophistication and learning over time. Review of Accounting Studies 2004;**9**:265–294.

Liu, R., Zhan, Y.R., Lui, J.P. Estimating value at risk of a listed firm in China. Proceedings of the 2006 International Conference on Machine Learning and Cybernetics; 2006. p 2137–2141.

Longin, F. The asymptotic distribution of extreme stock market returns. Journal of Business 1996;**69**:383–408.

Longin, F. From value at risk to stress testing: the extreme value approach. Journal of Business and Finance 2000;**24**:1097–1130.

Lu, Z. Modeling the yearly Value-at-Risk for operational risk in Chinese commercial banks. Math Comput Simul 2011;**82**:604–616.

Lu, G., Wen, F., Chung, C.Y., Wong, K.P. Conditional value-at-risk based mid-term generation operation planning in electricity market environment. Proceedings of the 2007 IEEE Congress on Evolutionary Computation; 2007. p 2745–2750.

Mattedi, A.P., Ramos, F.M., Rosa, R.R., Mantegna, R.N. Value-at-risk and Tsallis statistics: risk analysis of the aerospace sector. Physica A 2004;**344**:554–561.

Matthys, G., Delafosse, E., Guillou, A., Beirlant, J. Estimating catastrophic quantile levels for heavy-tailed distributions. Insurance: Mathematics and Economics 2004;**34**:517–537.

Mesfioui, M., Quessy, J.F. Bounds on the value-at-risk for the sum of possibly dependent risks. Insurance: Mathematics and Economics 2005;**37**:135–151.

Meucci, A. *Risk and Asset Allocation*. Berlin: Springer-Verlag; 2005.

Milwidsky, C., Mare, E. Value at risk in the South African equity market: a view from the tails. South African Journal of Economic and Management Sciences 2010;**13**:345–361.

Moix, P.-Y. *The Measurement of Market Risk: Modelling of Risk Factors, Asset Pricing, and Approximation of Portfolio Distributions*. Berlin: Springer-Verlag; 2001.

Mondlane, A.I. Value at risk in a volatile context of natural disaster risk. Proceedings of the 10th International Multidisciplinary Scientific Geo-Conference; 2010. p 277–284.

Nelsen, R.B. *An Introduction to Copulas*. New York: Springer-Verlag; 1999.

Odening, M., Hinrichs, J. Using extreme value theory to estimate value-at-risk. Agric Finance Rev 2003;**63**:55–73.

Panning, W.H. The strategic uses of value at risk: long-term capital management for property/casualty insurers. North American Actuarial Journal 1999;**3**:84–105.

Pflug, G.Ch. Some remarks on the value-at-risk and the conditional value-at-risk. In: Uryasev, S., editor. *Probabilistic Constrained Optimization: Methodology and Applications*. New York: Kluwer Academic Publishers; 2000. p 272–281.

Pflug, G.Ch., Romisch, W. *Modeling, Measuring and Managing Risk*. Hackensack (NJ): World Scientific Publishing Company; 2007.

Piantadosi, J., Metcalfe, A.V., Howlett, P.G. Stochastic dynamic programming (SDP) with a conditional value-at-risk (CVaR) criterion for management of storm-water. Journal of Hydrology 2008;**348**:320–329.

Pickands, J. III. Statistical inference using extreme order statistics. Annals of Statistics 1975;**3**:119–131.

Plat, R. One-year value-at-risk for longevity and mortality. Insurance: Mathematics and Economics 2011;**49**:462–470.

Pollard, M. Bayesian value-at-risk and the capital charge puzzle; 2007. Available at http://www.apra.gov.au/AboutAPRA/WorkingAtAPRA/Documents/Pollard-M_Paper-for-APRA.pdf. Accessed 2016 April 30.

Porter, N. Revenue volatility and fiscal risks—an application of value-at-risk techniques to Hong Kong's fiscal policy. Emerg Mark Finance Trade 2007;**43**:6–24.

Prékopa, A. Multivariate value at risk and related topics. Annals of Operations Research 2012;**193**:49–69.

Prescott, P., Walden, A.T. Maximum likelihood estimation of the parameters of the generalized extreme-value distribution. Biometrika 1990;**67**:723–724.

Puzanova, N., Siddiqui, S., Trede, M. Approximate value at risk calculation for heterogeneous loan portfolios: possible enhancements of the Basel II methodology. Journal of Financial Stability 2009;**5**:374–392.

Rachev, S.T., Schwartz, E., Khindanova, I. Stable modeling of market and credit value at risk. In: Rachev, S.T., editor. *Handbook of Heavy Tailed Distributions in Finance*. Chapter 7. New York: Elsevier; 2003. p 249–328.

Raunig, B., Scheicher, M. A value-at-risk analysis of credit default swaps. Journal of Risk 2011;**13**:3–29.

R Development Core Team. *R: A Language and Environment for Statistical Computing*. Vienna, Austria: R Foundation for Statistical Computing; 2015.

Resnick, S.I. *Heavy-Tail Phenomena*. New York: Springer-Verlag; 2007.

RiskMetrics Group. *RiskMetrics-Technical Document*. New York: J.P. Morgan; 1996.

Rockinger, M., Jondeau, E. Entropy densities with an application to autoregressive conditional skewness and kurtosis. Journal of Econometrics 2002;**106**:119–142.

Ruppert, D. *Statistics and Data Analysis for Financial Engineering*. New York: Springer-Verlag; 2011.

Sarabia, J.M., Prieto, F. The Pareto-positive stable distribution: a new descriptive method for city size data. Physica A—Statistical Mechanics and Its Applications 2009;**388**:4179–4191.

Sheather, S.J., Marron, J.S. Kernel quantile estimators. J Am Stat Assoc 1990;**85**:410–416.

Simonato, J.-G. The performance of Johnson distributions for computing value at risk and expected shortfall. Journal of Derivatives 2011;**19**:7–24.

Singh, M.K. Value at risk using principal components analysis. Journal of Portfolio Management 1997;**24**:101–112.

Siven, J.V., Lins, J.T., Szymkowiak-Have, A. Value-at-risk computation by Fourier inversion with explicit error bounds. Finance Research Letters 2009;**6**:95–105.

Slim, S., Gammoudi, I., Belkacem, L. Portfolio value at risk bounds using extreme value theory. International Journal of Economics and Finance 2012;**4**:204–215.

Sriboonchitta, S., Wong, W.-K., Dhompongsa, S., Nguyen, H.T. *Stochastic Dominance and Applications to Finance, Risk and Economics*. Boca Raton (FL): CRC Press; 2010.

Su, E., Knowles, T.W. Asian Pacific stock market volatility modelling and value at risk analysis. Emerging Markets Finance and Trade 2006;**42**:18–62.

Sun, X., Tang, L., He, W. Exploring the value at risk of oil exporting country portfolio: an empirical analysis from the FSU region. Procedia Computer Science 2011;**4**:1675–1680.

Taniai, H., Taniguchi, M. Statistical estimation errors of VaR under ARCH returns. Journal of Statistical Planning and Inference 2008;**138**:3568–3577.

Taniguchi, M., Hirukawa, J., Tamaki, K. *Optimal Statistical Inference in Financial Engineering*. Boca Raton (FL): Chapman and Hall/CRC; 2008.

Tapiero, C. *Risk and Financial Management*. Hoboken (NJ): John Wiley & Sons, Inc.; 2004.

Tian, M.Z., Chan, N.H. Saddle point approximation and volatility estimation of value-at-risk. Statistica Sinica, 2010;**20**:1239–1256.

Tiku, M.L. Estimating the mean and standard deviation from censored normal samples. Biometrika 1967;**54**:155–165.

Tiku, M.L. Estimating the parameters of lognormal distribution from censored samples. Journal of the American Statistical Association 1968;**63**:134–140.

Tiku, M.L., Akkaya, A.D. *Robust Estimation and Hypothesis Testing*. New Delhi: New Age International; 2004.

Trindade, A.A., Zhu, Y. Approximating the distributions of estimators of financial risk under an asymmetric Laplace law. Computational Statistics and Data Analysis 2007;**51**:3433–3447.

Trzpiot, G., Ganczarek, A. Value at risk using the principal components analysis on the Polish power exchange. From Data and Information Analysis to Knowledge Engineering; 2006. p 550–557.

Tsafack, G. Asymmetric dependence implications for extreme risk management. J Derivatives 2009;**17**:7–20.

Tsay, R.S. *Analysis of Financial Time Series*. 3rd ed. Hoboken (NJ): John Wiley & Sons, Inc.; 2010.

Voit, J. *The Statistical Mechanics of Financial Markets*. Berlin: Springer-Verlag; 2001.

Walter, Ch. Jumps in financial modelling: pitting the Black-Scholes model refinement programme against the Mandelbrot programme. In: Longin, F., editor. *Extreme Events in Finance*. Chichester: John Wiley & Sons; 2015.

Wang, C. Wholesale price for supply chain coordination via conditional value-at-risk minimization. Applied Mechanics and Materials 2010;**20-23**:88–93.

Weissman, I. Estimation of parameters and large quantiles based on the k largest observations. J Am Stat Assoc 1978;**73**:812–815.

Weng, H., Trueck, S. Style analysis and value-at-risk of Asia-focused hedge funds. Pacific Basin Finance Journal 2011;**19**:491–510.

Wilson, W.W., Nganje, W.E., Hawes, C.R. Value-at-risk in bakery procurement. Review of Agricultural Economics 2007;**29**:581–595.

Xu, M., Chen, F.Y. Tradeoff between expected reward and conditional value-at-risk criterion in newsvendor models. Proceedings of the 2007 IEEE International Conference on Industrial Engineering and Engineering Management; 2007. p 1553–1557.

Yamout, G.M., Hatfield, K., Romeijn, H.E. Comparison of new conditional value-at-risk-based management models for optimal allocation of uncertain water supplies. Water Resource Research 2007;**43**:W07430.

Yan, D., Gong, Z. Measurement of HIS stock index futures market risk based on value at risk. Proceedings of the 2009 International Conference on Information Management, Innovation Management and Industrial Engineering, Volume 3; 2009. p 78–81.

Yiu, K.F.C., Wang, S.Y., Mak, K.L. Optimal portfolios under a value-at-risk constraint with applications to inventory control in supply chains. Journal of Industrial and Management Optimization 2008;**4**:81–94.

Zhang, M.H., Cheng, Q.S. An approach to VaR for capital markets with Gaussian mixture. Applied Mathematics and Computation 2005;**168**:1079–1085.

Zhu, B., Gao, Y. Value at risk and its use in the risk management of investment-linked household property insurance. Proceedings of the 2002 International Conference on Management Science and Engineering; 2002. p 1680–1683.

Chapter Thirteen

Comparing Tail Risk and Systemic Risk Profiles for Different Types of U.S. Financial Institutions

Stefan Straetmans and Thanh Thi Huyen Dinh

School of Business and Economics, Maastricht University, Maastricht, The Netherlands

JEL codes: G21, G28, G29, G12, C49.

13.1   INTRODUCTION

The Basel II framework identifies credit risk, market risk, and operational risk as the key risk factors for financial institutions. Prior to the Crisis, the dominant opinion used to be that by appropriately managing these risks, financial institutions can maximize the probability of their continued survival while delivering appropriate profit to the capital providers. However, this financial regulatory framework is essentially micro-prudential in nature in the sense that it is designed to limit each institution's risk individually. However, Basel II typically did not take into account that distressed systemically important companies can destabilize the whole financial system as well as causing negative effects on real economic activity. The recent financial crisis created a conscience that there is an urgent need to complement Basel II with regulations that also take into account these macro-prudential concerns, that is, the need to monitor the so-called systemic risk. Thus, in order to preserve monetary and financial stability, central banks, as well as regulatory and supervisory authorities (often one and the same entity), ideally should have a regulatory and supervisory framework that both exhibits a micro-prudential layer as well as a set of tools to monitor the systemic importance

Extreme Events in Finance: A Handbook of Extreme Value Theory and its Applications,
First Edition. Edited by François Longin.

of individual financial institutions in order to get a feel of the potential for the overall financial sector instability. This is a particularly challenging task in large and complex economies with highly developed financial systems. In the United States, for example, tremendous consolidation as well as the removal of regulatory barriers to universal banking has made the financial system's interconnectedness extremely complex, giving rise to the popular reference to the so-called large and complex banking organizations (or LCBOs) as institutions that are "too complex to fail."

A significant body of theoretical and empirical literature on bank contagion and systemic risk developed throughout the years, but the amount of scientific contributions in this area has nearly exploded since the occurrence of the most recent systemic banking crisis. A majority of the empirical banking stability literature has proposed "market-based" indicators of systemic risk. That is because factors that are supposed to drive systemic instability, such as, for example, the financial system's interbank interconnectedness, the location of banks within the system's "network," or the correlations between loan or trading (investment) portfolios are often difficult to quantify. Banks' interconnectedness may be "direct," that is, related to money markets, the payment system, or derivatives markets and the resulting counterparty risk, see, for example, Allen and Gale (2000). However, it may also be of an "indirect" nature and induced by the overlap in banks' asset portfolios (Iori et al., 2006; De Vries, 2005; Zhou, 2010). Event studies are one of the oldest tools employed to measuring bank linkages by investigating the impacts of specific bank distress or bank failures on other banks' stock prices, see, for example, Swary (1986), Wall and Peterson (1990), or Slovin et al. (1999). Other studies ran regressions of abnormal bank stock returns on proxies for asset-side risk, for example, Smirlock and Kaufold (1987) or Kho et al. (2000). De Nicolo and Kwast (2002) explain increases in bank equity correlations over time by means of proxies for bank consolidation. Gropp and Moerman (2004) and Gropp and Vesala (2004) use (market-based) equity-derived distances to default to measure bank equity spillovers. More recent market-based measures of systemic risk include the Shapley value (Tarashev et al., 2010), conditional value at risk (VaR) (Adrian and Brunnermeier, 2011), marginal expected shortfall (MES) (Acharya et al., 2011), or SRISK (Brownlees and Engle, 2015).

All the studies mentioned above assumed that domino-type bank equity spillovers (often dubbed "bank contagion") are at the heart of systemic risk. An alternative strand in the literature assumes that banking crises are triggered by aggregate (nondiversifiable) shocks that affect all banks simultaneously. The systemic risk indicator we are going to work with fits into this latter tradition. Gorton (1988) argued that business cycles have often been leading indicators of bank panics. The studies by Gonzalez-Hermosillo et al. (1997) (for Mexico), Demirgüç-Kunt and Detragiache (1998) (multi-country-evidence), and Hellwig (1994) fit in the same tradition. The latter author argued that the fragility of financial institutions to large macro shocks may partly be due to the noncontingent character of deposit contracts to the state of the macro economy.

The use of market-based indicators for systemic risk is not without controversy and potential problems. First, it allows systemic risk assessment only for listed banks. This may lead to a biased view on the true level of financial fragility. Second, bank stocks can be truly informative about current or future systemic risk (i.e., market-based indicators as "early warning indicator") only if bank stocks reflect all relevant and available information about the risks that characterize a given financial institution, that is, if bank stocks are efficiently priced. In efficient stock markets, large drops in the market value of bank equity should occur only (i) when there is institution-specific news about that bank; (ii) when there is institution-specific news about related banks; (iii) in the presence of adverse aggregate shocks that impact all banks simultaneously. The evolution of bank stocks prior to 2007 rather suggests that the markets did not foresee the banking crisis. We nevertheless believe that the extreme spikes in bank stocks and their co-movements exhibit at least some informational content about systemic risk and stability.

This chapter builds on the statistical extreme value theory (EVT) approach followed by, for example, Hartmann et al. (2006) and Straetmans and Chaudhry (2015). More specifically, we use extreme downside risk measures that assume Pareto-type tail decline. To identify bank systemic risk, we employ the so-called tail-β indicator of "extreme systematic" risk as a tail equivalent of the traditional regression-based CAPM-β, introduced in Straetmans et al. (2008). Tail-β is defined as the probability of a collapse in the market value of a bank's equity capital conditional on a large adverse aggregate shock (typically an extreme negative return on a market portfolio like a banking index, overall stock market index, credit spread, etc.). Tail-β is obviously market-based because it uses stock prices of individual bank equity as well as market-based information about aggregate shocks (i.e., market indices for the banking sector).

Notice that the concept of MES and the conditional value at risk (CoVaR) resemble tail-β because these indicators are also probabilistic in nature: MES is the expected loss on individual bank equity capital conditional on large market portfolio losses; CoVaR is the VaR of the financial system conditional on institutions being under distress and is implicitly defined using a conditional co-crash probability. Also, and in contrast to previous correlation-based approaches toward modeling market linkages and spillovers, MES, CoVaR, and tail-β identify non-linear dependencies (if present) in the data. The crucial difference between our approach and competing approaches such as MES or CoVaR lies in the way the indicators are estimated: whereas we explicitly focus on the extreme tails of bank equity capital and the tail dependence structure between bank stock returns, parallel studies identifying MES or CoVaR typically use estimation techniques like quantile regressions that do not go as far in the tail. They typically assume that non-extreme outcomes are representative for what happens in the tail area but we believe this may be an overly restrictive assumption. Statistical EVT deals with events that are severe enough for regulators and supervisors caring about financial stability, which cannot be claimed about events that happen 5% of 1% of the time.

By applying techniques of univariate and multivariate EVT to the tails of bank equity returns, we make four contributions to the existing literature. First, we perform a "cross-industry" comparison of tail risk and systemic importance, that is, do traditional banks exhibit more or less tail risk and systemic risk as compared to, for example, investment banks or insurance companies? Indeed, besides deposit banks, insurance companies (including large reinsurers) and B&Ds (investment banks) played a crucial role in the narrative of the 2007–2009 banking and financial crisis. It is to be expected that these different segments of the financial industry also exhibit different risk profiles and risk-taking behavior. Previous empirical systemic risk studies were often limited to measuring tail risk and systemic risk of banks in the narrow sense of the word. Second, we assess the forward-looking characteristics of these risk measures by looking at the stability of tail risk and systemic risk rankings over time. We therefore calculate rank correlations between pre-crisis and crisis ranks. Third, we reinvestigate the corroboration that a financial institution's size is a prime factor fueling systemic risk. We also look into the relation between tail risk and institutional size. Finally, we want to assess whether the tail risk and systemic risk of the same institutions are positively or negatively related to each other. Suppose that both micro-prudential (tail) risk and macro-prudential (systemic) risk exhibit common drivers; the relation between the common factors and the two risk types and their common drivers will also determine whether tail risk and systemic risk are positively or negatively related. For example, if size is the single most important variable and bigger banks exhibit less tail risk (diversification effect) but more systemic risk (too big to fail effect), then it follows that tail risk and systemic risk should be negatively related to each other across financial institutions. Whether tail risk and systemic risk are positively or negatively correlated is assessed by means of cross-sectional rank correlations between tail risk and systemic risk for the pre-crisis and the crisis subsample separately.

Turning to the data, our panel contains roughly the same banks as in Acharya et al. (2011) and Brownlees and Engle (2015), that is, the top 102 U.S. financial firms with a market capitalization greater than 7 billion USD as of the end of June 2007 (just before the start of the subprime mortgage crisis). SIC codes are used to divide financial institutions into four buckets: deposit banks (e.g., JP Morgan, Bank of America, Citigroup), insurance companies (e.g., AIG, Berkshire Hathaway, Countrywide), B&Ds (e.g., Goldman Sachs, Morgan Stanley), and a residual category ("others") consisting of nondepository institutions or real estate agencies. Our dataset includes only 92 firms instead of the 102 as in the original panel due to mergers or bankruptcies. Stock prices and relevant balance sheet data to proxy institutional size are downloaded over the sample period January 1, 1990 to September 1, 2011.

Anticipating our results, we find that different groups of financial institutions exhibit different levels of tail risk and systemic risk. The heterogeneity in tail risks and systemic contributions across different types of financial institutions suggests that a tailor-made regulatory and supervisory approach may be advisable. The most salient outcome of our cross-industry risk comparison, however, seems to be that the insurance industry exhibits the highest tail risk but that deposit banks are characterized by the highest degree of extreme systematic risk. The latter outcome is surprising given the role investment banks (and more specifically the trading divisions) seem to have played in the narrative of the financial crisis. What is less surprising is that both tail risk and systemic risk dramatically increased during the financial crisis. However, this does not mean that EVT-based indicators of tail risk and systemic risk are of no value when making any judgment about the propensity toward future systemic crises: we actually observe that the ranking of institutions did not change dramatically when considering pre-crisis and crisis tail-βs: the riskiest institutions in terms of tail risk and systemic risk before the crisis stay the riskiest ones over the crisis sample. The ranking stability is nevertheless quite fluctuating across different types of financial institutions. Last but not least, financial institutions' size does not have much to say about financial institutions' tail risk; but size does seem to matter for their systemic risk. However, the size–systemic risk relationship is not very robust and varies with the considered size proxies, subsamples, and types of financial institutions.

The remainder of this chapter is organized as follows. Section 13.2 introduces indicators of downside risk and systemic risk based on statistical extreme value analysis. Section 13.3 provides estimation procedures for both measures. Section 13.4 summarizes the empirical results. Section 13.5 concludes.

13.2 TAIL RISK AND SYSTEMIC RISK INDICATORS

We first introduce alternative downside risk measures for financial institutions (Section 13.2.1). Next, we discuss a systemic risk indicator that reflects individual banks' sensitivity to systemwide, nondiversifiable shocks (tail-β) (Section 13.2.2).

13.2.1 Univariate Tail Risk Indicators

We define extreme downside risk (tail risk) measures for financial institutions by exploiting the empirical stylized fact that equity returns of financial institutions exhibit "heavy" tails. Mandelbrot (1963) was arguably the first to observe that sharp short-term fluctuations in financial markets (typically daily returns) are nonnormally distributed – and bank stocks do not constitute an exception. Let S_t stand for the dividend-corrected stock price of a financial institution. Define $X = -\ln(S_t/S_{t-1})$ as the loss variable we are interested in. For the sake of notational convenience, the left tail of equity returns (market losses on equity capital) is mapped into positive losses, which implies that all downside risk measures are expressed for the upper tail of a loss distribution. Loosely speaking, Mandelbrot's observation of the heavy-tail feature implies that the marginal tail probability for X as a function of the corresponding quantile can be approximately described by a power law

$$P\{X > x\} \sim ax^{-\alpha}, \tag{13.1}$$

for large x.

This contrasts with the (much faster) exponential tail decay of thin-tailed processes like the normal distribution. The so-called tail index α can be interpreted as the rate at which the tail decay takes place when making the quantile or crisis barrier x more extreme: a lower α implies a slower decay to zero and a higher probability mass for given values of x. The tail index also has an interesting statistical interpretation in terms of the higher moments of an empirical process: all distributional moment higher than α are unbounded and thus do not exist. In contrast, for the normal distribution, all statistical moments exist. Mandelbrot's empirical observation of heavy tails implies that the normal distribution is not a good choice if one wants to make probability assessment of extreme returns such as financial crises, bank failures, and so on. Why is the normality assumption still so common when applying statistical tools to social sciences? This can be partly explained by (i) its analytical tractability, and, more importantly, (ii) by the predominant focus on sample averages in social science, which implies that versions of the central limit theorem apply. However, if one is interested in assessing the likelihood of extreme events (financial crises, bank distress, etc.) away from the mean and the distributional center, other limit laws apply, such as the extremal types theorem, see Embrechts et al. (1997). The heavy-tailed model (13.1) is one possible outcome of this extremal types theorem.

Popular distributional models often used in the finance literature, such as the Student-t, the class of symmetric stable distributions, or the generalized autoregressive conditional heteroscedasticity (GARCH) model, all exhibit fat tails: they are all nested in the tail model (13.1) albeit with different pairs of tail parameters (a, α).

Clearly, the tail likelihood in (13.1) is defined for a given time horizon of the loss series X and values of the crisis barrier or VaR level x_p. Alternatively, (13.1) can be inverted and solved for the tail quantile x as a function of p:

$$x_p \sim \left(\frac{p}{a}\right)^{-1/\alpha}. \tag{13.2}$$

Although VaR has become an extremely popular device for financial risk management and even a cornerstone of Basel II, financial economists also argue it is not a "coherent" risk measure; alternative risk measures have therefore been proposed, like, for example, the "expected shortfall" (i.e., the conditional expected loss on a firm's equity capital given a sharp decline in equity capital $(X > x_p)$). It can be easily shown that the expected shortfall is very closely related to the VaR:

$$E(X - x_p | X > x_p) = \frac{x_p}{\alpha - 1}. \tag{13.3}$$

Thus, within an EVT framework, the expected shortfall is a rescaled VaR. Notice that $E(X - x_p | X > x_p) < x_p$, provided the variance of the process exists ($\alpha > 2$). The conditional expected loss in (13.3) reflects how severe the violation of the VaR crisis level is. In the context of bank equity, it reflects the expected decline in equity capital once a critical threshold is exceeded.

13.2.2 "Extreme Systematic" Risk Indicator or Tail-β

Similar to the downside risk measures discussed in the previous section, the proposed indicator of systemic risk is also market-based in the sense that it requires the input of daily extreme stock price movements of an individual financial institution together with daily sharp fluctuations in a nondiversifiable risk factor. The aggregate (macro)factor is supposed to act as a propagation channel of the adverse aggregate shocks whose effects we want to assess on individual financial institutions.

Let us now define this so-called tail-β in more detail. Suppose one is interested in measuring the probability of a stock price collapse conditional on an adverse shock in a nondiversifiable macro factor. This probability reflects the dependence between the loss on an individual institution's stock and a macro factor during times of market stress. Assume these two losses are represented by X_1 and X_M, respectively. As in the univariate case, we take the negative of stock returns so as to study the joint losses in the upper-upper quadrant. Without loss of generality, we choose the tail quantiles Q_1 and Q_M such that the tail probabilities are the same across the two random variables, that is, $P\{X_1 > Q_1(p)\} = P\{X_2 > Q_2(p)\} = p$. The crisis barriers Q_1 and Q_M will generally differ because the marginal distribution functions for X_1 and X_M are unequal. However, a common significance level p makes the corresponding tail quantiles or extreme "VaR" levels of Q_1 and Q_M better comparable.

From elementary probability theory, we can simply write down a bivariate probability measure by using the notation introduced above:

$$\mathcal{T}_\beta \equiv P\{X_1 > Q_1(p) | X_M > Q_M(p)\} = \frac{P\{X_1 > Q_1(p),\, X_M > Q_M(p)\}}{P\{X_M > Q_M(p)\}}$$

$$= \frac{P\{X_1 > Q_1(p),\, X_M > Q_M(p)\}}{p}. \qquad (13.4)$$

The probability measure $\mathcal{T}_\beta$ reflects the strength of the interdependence for the loss pairs X_1 and X_M when both variables jointly exceed the crisis barriers Q_1 and Q_M. Under complete statistical independence, $\mathcal{T}_\beta$ reduces to $\frac{p^2}{p} = p$, which acts as a lower bound for the true value of extreme systematic risk.

This tail-β measure is inspired by portfolio theory, as it can be interpreted as a tail equivalent of a CAPM-β. Just as the CAPM-β, it relates individual stock return movements to movements in a market portfolio. However, and in contrast to CAPM-βs, the tail-β is neither a regression coefficient nor is it based on the entire sample. It is a probability that we evaluate on the tail area of the joint distribution.

Correlation-based measures such as ordinary βs can be quite misleading dependence measures for multiple reasons. First, CAPM or more general factor models reveal only linear relations, whereas the systemic risk spillovers we are interested in may well be nonlinear in nature. Also, correlations are often used in conjunction with the normality assumption. This is a rather dangerous cocktail because correlations tend to zero when truncated on the tail area and assuming multivariate normality. Thus, if tail co-movements are present in the data, they will not be revealed by multivariate normal models, and systemic risk will be severely underestimated as a consequence. For a more extensive discussion of the flaws of correlation-based measures, see, for example, the monograph by Embrechts et al. (1997).

Tail-βs have been previously implemented to measure the propensity towards tail co-movements between individual risky security returns and adverse market shocks. Straetmans et al. (2008) examine the intraday effects of the 9/11 terrorist attacks on U.S. stocks before and after the attacks took place; Hartmann et al. (2006) and Straetmans and Chaudhry (2015) make a cross-Atlantic comparison of tail-βs for U.S. and Eurozone banks using slightly different techniques and time periods. De Jonghe (2010) runs cross-sectional regressions of tail-βs on candidate-explanatory variables such as the size and sources of bank revenue to determine what drives banking system (in)stability. Conditional exceedance probabilities for higher dimensions are defined in the same manner. In this chapter, we select a Datastream-calculated U.S. banking market index as the conditioning macro factor X_M.

13.3   TAIL RISK AND SYSTEMIC RISK ESTIMATION

Imposing one and the same fully parametric distribution model for both the center of the distribution and the tail observations would greatly simplify the quantification of the considered downside risk indicators, and the tail-β for it would require only the maximum likelihood estimation of the distributional parameters. However, if one makes the wrong distributional assumptions, the tail risk and systemic risk estimates may be severely biased because of misspecification. As there is no evidence that stock returns are identically distributed – even less so for the crisis situations we are interested in – we want to avoid the model risk of making too restrictive distributional assumptions for bank stock returns. We will therefore employ semiparametric estimation procedures from statistical extreme value analysis. First, we introduce semiparametric estimators for extreme downside risk (tail indices, tail quantiles, and conditional expected shortfalls) before turning to estimation procedures for the systemic risk indicators.

13.3.1   Estimating Tail Risk Measures

Univariate tail risk estimation exploits the empirical stylized fact that financial return distributions exhibit fat tails, see (13.1) and (13.2). More specifically, we are interested in a sample counterpart of (13.1) – (13.3). Let the "tail cut-off point" $X_{n-m,n}$ (with $X_{n,n} \geq \cdots \geq X_{n-m,n} \geq \cdots \geq X_{1,n}$ representing the descending order statistics defined on the samples of return losses $X > 0$) stand for the lower bound of the set of upper-order extreme returns used to identify the tail probability (13.1) or tail quantile (13.2), with m being the number of extremes used in the estimation. The tail probability (13.1) could then be estimated as

$$P(X > x) \simeq \frac{m}{n}(X_{n-m,n})^{\alpha}x^{-\alpha}, \tag{13.5}$$

with $\frac{m}{n}(X_{n-m,n})^{\alpha}$ being an estimate of the scaling constant a in (13.1). In financial risk management, the tail quantile or crisis barrier x is usually referred to as the

"VaR," although it is often used in a reversed fashion: what is the value of x for a given level of the tail probability p? (alternatively, called the "p-value" or "marginal significance level"). Simply inverting the tail likelihood estimator (13.5) renders

$$\widehat{x}_p \simeq X_{n-m,n} \left(\frac{m}{np} \right)^{\frac{1}{\alpha}}. \tag{13.6}$$

The tail quantile estimator $\widehat{x}_p$ extends the empirical distribution function of the return loss data outside the historical sample boundary of X by means of the Pareto-law parametric assumption for the tail behavior in (13.1). The quantile estimator (13.6) still requires plugging in a value for the tail index α. In line with the bulk of empirical studies on nonnormality, power laws, and extreme events, we estimate the tail index with the popular Hill (1975) statistic

$$\widehat{\alpha} = \left(\frac{1}{m} \sum_{j=0}^{m-1} \ln \left(\frac{X_{n-j,n}}{X_{n-m,n}} \right) \right)^{-1}, \tag{13.7}$$

where m has the same value and interpretation as in (13.6). For $m/n \to 0$ as $m,n \to \infty$, it has been shown that the tail index and tail quantile exhibit consistency and asymptotic normality (see Haeusler and Teugels, 1985; De Haan et al., 1994). Further details on the Hill and quantile estimators above are provided in Jansen and De Vries (1991) and the monograph by Embrechts et al. (1997). An estimator for the expected shortfall (13.3) easily follows by plugging in the Hill statistic and the quantile estimator in the definition of the expected shortfall (13.3):

$$\widehat{E}(X - \widehat{x}_p | X > \widehat{x}_p) = \frac{\widehat{x}_p}{\widehat{\alpha} - 1}. \tag{13.8}$$

The Hill statistic and the accompanying quantile and expected shortfall estimators are still conditional on picking a value of the nuisance parameter m. Goldie and Smith (1987) suggest to select this threshold such as to minimize the asymptotic mean-squared error (AMSE) of the Hill statistic. Because of the bias–variance tradeoff of the Hill estimator, such a minimum should exist. This minimization criterion actually constitutes the starting point for most empirical techniques to determine m. We determine m by both considering the curvature of the so-called Hill plots $\widehat{\alpha} = \widehat{\alpha}(m)$ and implementing the Beirlant et al. (1999) algorithm that minimizes a sample equivalent of the AMSE.

13.3.2 Estimating the Systemic Risk Indicator (Tail-β)

In order to estimate the tail-β in (13.4), it suffices to calculate the joint probability in the numerator. Upon assuming a bivariate parametric distribution function for the return pair, the distributional parameters and the resulting co-exceedance probability could be easily estimated using maximum likelihood optimization. However, we want to avoid making very specific distributional assumptions about both the marginal return distributions and their (tail) dependence structure. We therefore opt for Ledford and Tawn's (1996) semiparametric approach. The latter authors first propose to transform the marginal distributions to unit Fréchet distributions, which leave the tail dependence structure unchanged. We opt for an alternative marginal transformation (to unit Pareto marginals), which renders comparable results. After such a transformation, differences in joint tail probabilities across asset return pairs should be solely attributed to differences in the tail dependence structure of the return pairs.

The unit Pareto transform is performed in a purely nonparametric manner by using the return's own empirical distribution:

$$\widetilde{X}_i = \frac{1}{1 - R_{X_i}/(n+1)}, \quad i = 1, 2 \tag{13.9}$$

where R_{X_i} stands for the (ascending) rank of the observation X_{it} for stock return i in the time series dimension.[1] Upon applying this unit Pareto marginal transformation, it can be easily shown that the bivariate numerator likelihood in (13.4) boils down to

$$P\{X_1 > Q_1(p), \ X_2 > Q_2(p)\} = P\{\widetilde{X}_1 > s, \widetilde{X}_2 > s\},$$

with $s = 1/p$, see, for example, also Hartmann et al. (2006). Consequently, the common quantile s enables one to reduce the estimation of the bivariate probability to a univariate probability by considering the cross-sectional minimum of the two return series:

$$P\{\widetilde{X}_1 > s, \widetilde{X}_2 > s\} = P\{\min(\widetilde{X}_1, \widetilde{X}_2) > s\} = P\{Z_{\min} > s\}, \tag{13.10}$$

where the auxiliary variable $Z \equiv \min(\widetilde{X}_1, \widetilde{X}_2)$. In order to identify the marginal tail probability at the right-hand side, we assume that the auxiliary variable's tail inherits the fat tail property of the original financial firm's returns:

$$P\{Z_{\min} > s\} \approx as^{-\alpha}, \quad \alpha \geq 1, \tag{13.11}$$

with large s ($p = 1/s$ small). Obviously, fatter (thinner) tails of the $Z_{\min}$ variable imply weaker (stronger) tail dependence.

Steps (13.9) – (13.11) show that the estimation of joint probabilities, like (13.10), can be mapped back to a univariate estimation problem. By using the inverse of the previously defined quantile estimator from De Haan et al. (1994), univariate excess probabilities can be estimated:

$$\hat{p}_s = \frac{m}{n}(Z_{n-m,n})^{\alpha} s^{-\alpha}, \tag{13.12}$$

---

[1] Division by $n + 1$ instead of n is performed in order to prevent division by zero for the largest observational rank.

where the "tail cut-off points" $Z_{n-m,n}$ is the $(n-m)$th ascending order statistic of the auxiliary variable $Z_{\min}$.

An estimator of the co-exceedance probability $\mathcal{T}_\beta$ in (13.4) easily follows by dividing (13.12) with p:

$$\mathcal{T}_\beta = \frac{p_s}{p} = \frac{m}{n}(Z_{n-m,n})^\alpha s^{1-\alpha}, \tag{13.13}$$

for large but finite $s = 1/p$.

Clearly, the tail index α plays a double role in the estimator for the tail-β: it drives both the tail thickness of the auxiliary variable Z and the degree of the tail dependence for the original return pair (X_1, X_2). We need to distinguish two polar cases in which the (X_1, X_2) pair, as well as the transformed pair $(\widetilde{X}_1, \widetilde{X}_2)$, either exhibits tail dependence ($\alpha = 1$) or tail independence ($\alpha > 1$). *Tail dependence* implies that $\alpha = 1$, or alternatively

$$\lim_{p\to 0} P\{X_1 > Q_1(p)|X_2 > Q_2(p)\} = \lim_{s\to\infty} P\{\widetilde{X}_1 > s|\widetilde{X}_2 > s\} = \frac{m}{n}Z_{n-m,n} > 0. \tag{13.14}$$

Stated differently, the conditional tail probability never vanishes regardless of how far one looks into the tail of the joint distribution, that is, how large s (how small p) is taken. On the other hand, *tail independence* ($\alpha > 1$) implies that

$$\lim_{p\to 0} P\{X_1 > Q_1(p)|X_2 > Q_2(p)\} = \lim_{s\to\infty} P\{\widetilde{X}_1 > s|\widetilde{X}_2 > s\} = 0. \tag{13.15}$$

For obvious reasons, the tail index of the auxiliary variable is also sometimes called the "tail dependence" parameter.[2] The bivariate normal distribution or the bivariate Morgenstern distribution constitutes popular examples of tail independent models, whereas the bivariate Student-t or the bivariate logistic model exhibits tail dependence. The bivariate normal distribution is characterized by both thin tailed and tail-independent marginal return distributions and may therefore lead to an underestimation of the true systemic risk when pairs of bank stock returns are tail dependent. To illustrate this, consider a pair of bank stock returns from our bank panel (Citigroup; Bank of America) and assume that the bivariate return process is driven by a bivariate normal distribution function. The estimated first and second moments (means, standard deviations, and correlation) completely determine the joint distribution. Next, we employ the bivariate normal model as a simulation vehicle to draw a sample of the same size as the raw data sample. Figure 13.1 shows both data clouds.

For sake of comparison, the axes are identical. One observes that the right-hand side (RHS) Gaussian data cloud does not reproduce the LHS joint downward bank stock crashes visible in the true data cloud (tail dependence). That there is so little tail dependence in the RHS graph may seem surprising because

---

[2]Many papers on multivariate extreme value analysis also talk about the tail dependence "coefficient," which is typically defined as the conditional asymptotic probability itself. The tail dependence parameter thus determines the tail decay of the tail dependence coefficient (either vanishing to zero or to a constant bounded away from zero).

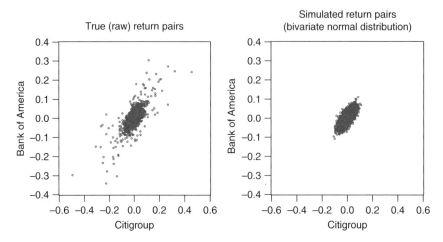

FIGURE 13.1 **Joint bank crashes: historical versus simulated (Gaussian) return pairs.**

correlation between the two bank stock returns seems quite high. However, the bivariate normal distribution is characterized by tail independence, which implies that statistical dependence (or nonzero correlation in case of a bivariate, normally distributed process) in the center of the distribution disappears in the tails, that is, condition (13.14). What this shows is that one has to either opt for parametric models that nest both data features of heavy tails and tail dependence or decide to work with purely nonparametric techniques that pick up these stylized facts in the data automatically.

In this paper we do not want to make a parametric choice for either the marginal distributions or the tail dependence structure. We nevertheless decide to impose tail dependence on pairs of bank stock returns, which implies the parameter restriction $\alpha = 1$. The economic intuition for this restriction goes as follows: if banks have common risky exposures either at the asset side or the liability side, and these common risk drivers are heavy tailed, bank stock returns should automatically be tail dependent. De Vries (2005) provides an analytic exposition of this argument. Form a statistical point of view, the restriction $\alpha = 1$ is convenient because it reduces the estimation risk (the Hill statistic does not need to be employed to estimate the tail dependence parameter α in (13.13)). Imposing tail dependence also imposes an upper bound on the systemic risk measure. From a regulatory point of view, a conservative assessment of systemic risk by means of an upper bound seems preferable to underestimating the potential of financial instability.

13.4   EMPIRICAL RESULTS

Our empirical analysis boils down to a *cross-industry comparison* of tail risk and systemic risk contributions of top U.S. financial firms based on daily data sampled from January 1, 1990 until September 1, 2011. We also consider two subsamples: January 1990 to August 2007 is the "pre-crisis sample"; and September 2007 to September 2011 is the "crisis" sample (the crisis sample is also partly post-crisis in nature). The considered top financial institutions fall within four industry groups, see Acharya et al. (2011) and Brownlees and Engle (2015). The "deposit banks" group mainly contains standard commercial banks and constitutes the benchmark group of financial institutions. The "B&D" group contains the top U.S. investment banks. Many of these firms were in severe distress in the crisis: Lehman Brothers declared bankruptcy, Bear Stearns was sold to J.P. Morgan, Merrill Lynch was sold to Bank of America, and Goldman Sachs and Morgan Stanley became commercial banks switching to a stricter regulatory regime. The group "other" contains real estate firms, most of which were also severely hit by the sub-prime crisis. However, compared to the "deposit group," they fall under looser financial regulations.

13.4.1 Tail Risk and Systemic Risk

Disaggregated (bank level) results in tail risk and systemic risk are reported in Appendix A: Table A1 (depositories), Table A2 (others), Table A3 (insurance companies), and Table A4 (B&Ds). Proxies for tail risk encompass the tail index α, VaR, and expected shortfalls. VaR levels are calculated for a p-value 0.1%, which implies an expected VaR violation every 1000 days ($=1000/260 \approx 3.85$ years). We calculate this extreme tail quantile using (13.6). We also report extreme and nonextreme expected shortfall estimates conditioned on a crisis barrier of 50% and on $p = 5\%$ VaR numbers, respectively. The former is estimated using Eq. (13.10), whereas the latter is determined via historical simulation, that is, by taking the $p = 5\%$ downside risk quantile from the empirical historical return distribution. As concerns estimates of systemic risk, we report nonextreme values for the MES via historical simulation and estimates of the tail-β in (13.13) using extreme value analysis. The MES is defined along the lines of Acharya et al. (2011) and Brownlees and Engle (2015) as the expected loss on an individual bank stock given a simultaneously sharp drop on the market index:

$$\text{MES}_i = E(R_i | R_M > Q_M(5\%)), \tag{13.16}$$

with (R_M, R_i) the pair of equity losses on the U.S. banking market index and bank i's capital, respectively. For sake of calculating MES, we condition on the (nonextreme) crisis barriers $Q_M(p)$ with a p-value of 5%. For sake of comparability, the MES and the tail-β are conditioned on the same banking market index. We estimate MES by historical simulation, that is, by calculating the conditional average based on the joint empirical distribution of (R_M, R_i). All tail risk and systemic risk indicators are estimated for full sample as well as pre-crisis and crisis samples. To make certain patterns in the appendix tables more easily visible, Table 13.1 summarizes Tables A1–A4 by considering means, medians, and standard deviations of all considered estimates per type of financial institution as well as for all financial institutions together.

TABLE 13.1 Tail risk and systemic risk for different types of financial institutions

		Full sample						Pre-crisis						Crisis				
	α	q (p=0.1%)	ES (X>50%)	ES (95%)	MES (95%)	Tail-β	α	q (p=0.1%)	ES (X>50%)	ES (95%)	MES (95%)	Tail-β	α	q (p=0.1%)	ES (X>50%)	ES (95%)	MES (95%)	Tail-β
Depositors																		
Mean	2.5	17.4	35.4	5.7	3.2	52.3	3.0	10.7	26.2	4.1	1.7	44.8	2.2	46.1	50.3	10.9	6.8	63.4
Median	2.4	16.5	35.6	5.7	3.4	54.5	2.9	10.1	25.9	4.0	1.8	44.9	2.1	38.9	47.0	9.7	7.1	64.1
Std. Dev.	0.3	4.1	7.8	0.8	0.9	10.2	0.4	2.1	4.8	0.7	0.5	8.5	0.6	33.6	21.1	5.3	1.3	8.0
Others																		
Mean	2.9	21.2	30.2	7.3	3.5	47.7	3.2	13.4	27.1	4.9	1.2	39.4	2.5	34.8	38.4	10.4	6.1	58.9
Median	2.9	18.4	26.6	6.5	3.4	46.7	3.2	10.7	22.5	4.5	1.1	37.1	2.4	27.8	35.4	8.8	6.4	58.5
Std. Dev.	0.8	12.8	12.3	3.1	1.0	7.8	0.9	7.1	15.9	1.4	0.4	6.0	0.7	22.3	16.0	5.8	1.7	5.3
Insurances																		
Mean	2.5	20.2	40.3	5.9	2.8	43.4	2.8	11.8	30.6	4.1	1.2	37.6	2.0	47.6	67.5	8.9	5.8	52.8
Median	2.4	16.5	36.4	5.3	2.8	42.5	2.6	11.2	31.4	3.9	1.3	38.2	1.9	37.3	56.7	8.0	5.8	54.8
Std. Dev.	0.5	10.7	17.9	2.1	1.0	8.8	0.6	4.1	7.8	1.2	0.4	5.6	0.6	37.9	39.8	4.2	1.1	7.9
B&Ds																		
Mean	2.9	19.8	29.4	7.2	2.6	46.2	3.1	14.5	25.2	5.6	1.7	45.5	2.2	53.8	55.2	13.1	4.9	58.2
Median	2.7	17.9	28.9	6.4	2.6	45.8	3.0	13.4	25.6	5.1	1.7	46.3	1.9	43.7	57.9	10.0	6.2	59.8
Std. Dev.	0.6	9.1	10.5	2.4	0.8	5.5	0.6	4.2	5.9	1.6	0.4	4.0	0.7	37.0	25.5	8.2	2.5	9.4
All																		
Mean	2.6	19.6	35.3	6.3	3.1	47.4	3.0	12.2	27.9	4.4	1.4	41.0	2.2	44.7	54.1	10.3	6.1	58.0
Median	2.5	17.0	33.7	5.9	3.0	46.7	2.9	10.8	26.5	4.2	1.4	41.2	2.1	33.5	47.6	8.6	6.5	58.5
Std. Dev.	0.6	9.8	14.1	2.3	1.0	9.5	0.6	4.8	9.9	1.3	0.5	7.4	0.6	33.9	30.9	5.6	1.6	8.7

Note: Sample means, medians, and standard deviations for tail risk measures (the tail index α; the tail quantile q; and the expected shortfall ES($X>50\%$), ES(95%)) and for systemic risk measures (MES(95%) and Tail-β) are reported across the time-series dimension (pre-crisis vs crisis) as well as for different financial industry groups. All estimates – except the tail indices – are expressed as percentages.

Before making any general inferences about Appendix Tables A1–A4 or the condensed version in Table 13.1, it is important to grasp the economic interpretation of the risk estimates in the table. For example, consider the subsample results for Bank of America in Table A1. The tail index of Bank of America dropped from 4 to 1.6, indicating that the probability mass in the tails enormously increased during the crisis period. Indeed, the crisis values of extreme quantiles and expected shortfalls climbed sharply as compared to their pre-crisis level. Bank of America's 0.1% tail-VaR increased from 13.7% to 82.5% since the outbreak of the crisis, whereas the tail-βs increased from 56.7% to 75.9%, but what do all these percentages actually mean in economic terms? A pre-crisis tail-VaR level of 13.7% implies that one expects on average a (daily) decline of 13.7% or more in the market value of Bank of America's equity capital every 3.8 years; but that crisis barrier has risen to 82.5% over the crisis period. However, a VaR crisis barrier does not tell how severe the violation of the VaR barrier may be. For that purpose, it is informative to calculate the so-called coherent risk measures, such as the expected shortfall. For example, the pre-crisis value $E(X - 50\%|X > 50\%) = 16.7\%$ for Bank of America implies that, if a VaR exceedance of 50% or more strikes, one expects an additional daily loss of 16.7%. Turning to the interpretations of the extreme systematic risk estimates (tail-βs), a crisis value of 75.9% for Bank of America's tail-β implies that, on average, a meltdown in the banking sector (proxied by a crash in the banking index) will go hand in hand with a meltdown in Bank of America's equity 3 out of 4 times! Notice that even before the crisis, the coincidence of a banking index collapse and a Bank of America collapse in common stock is more than 1 out of 2.

Let us now analyze the outcomes in Table 13.1 in somewhat more detail. In general, there is a large cross-sectional and time-series heterogeneity in bank risk. Going more systematically through Tables A1–A4 and Table 13.1, one can see that (i) all values of tail risk and systemic risk dramatically increase in the crisis period, and (ii) systemic risk estimates differ markedly across institutions but also across industry groups, see also the differences in cross-sectional standard deviations for different industry groups (we will later assess whether the cross-sectional averages are significantly different from each other). Tail risk seems highest for insurance companies, although this seems to be limited to the crisis period. For the full sample, insurance companies and the residual category "other institutions" dominate other types of financial institutions in terms of tail risk. As concerns systemic risk, deposit banks seem most vulnerable during the crisis period and the full sample, whereas deposit banks and B&Ds share the first place for the pre-crisis episode. The relatively high degree of systemic risk for deposit banks is somewhat surprising, given the important role investment banks supposedly played in triggering and propagating the financial crisis and resulting great recession. As the pre-crisis and crisis levels of bank risk in Table 13.1 also show, there is a spectacular surge in bank risk during the crisis period, which is hardly surprising. This confirms earlier outcomes, also based on EVT measures, by Straetmans and Chaudhry (2015).

To illustrate the bank risk dynamics even further, we also consider individual risk and systemic risk exposures over moving windows of 6 years, the first period covering the years 1990–1995. Since the sample period spans 21 years, we obtain

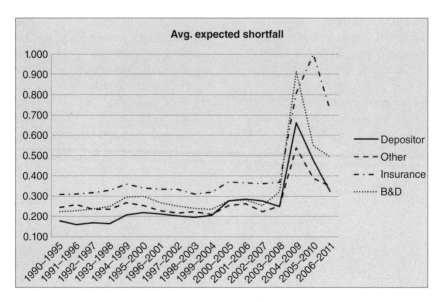

FIGURE 13.2   Expected shortfall E $(X - 50\%|X > 50\%)$: cross sectional averages over 1-year rolling window.

17 rolling subsamples. Rolling estimates for tail risk and systemic risk are included in Figures 13.2 and 13.3, respectively.

The figures further distinguish rolling estimates per type of financial institution. Figure 13.2 confirms that insurance companies dominate B&Ds in terms of tail risk, whereas B&Ds in turn dominate deposit banks and the residual category "other." Figure 13.2 also reveals that this hierarchy of tail risk already seems to hold for the pre-crisis rolling samples (although tail risk lies much closer to each other during pre-crisis). Overall, all groups exhibit a similar time series pattern, which can be associated with the general level of risk in the economy. Brownlees and Engle (2015) report comparable findings for the average daily volatility within a GARCH framework, but the rolling nature of our EVT estimates reduces sharp peaks and troughs. The relatively high levels of expected shortfall (ES) in the early 2000s correspond to the dot com bubble burst and the recession at the beginning of the 2000s. Next follows a period of lower tail risk, which lasts until mid-2007. Afterward, and similar to volatility, ES literally explodes in 2008 and peaks to the highest level measured over the considered sample. The degree of co-movement between the average values of ES across banking groups differs across time. Prior to the crisis, ES clusters together for all sectors, but when the financial crisis developed, ES of all industry groups jumps significantly and it shows a clearer spread between groups. On average, insurance group takes the lead in ES, followed by the B&D group. This contradicts Brownlees and Engle's (2015) findings, in which the insurance group stays consistently least risky in term of volatility as compared to the other industry groups.

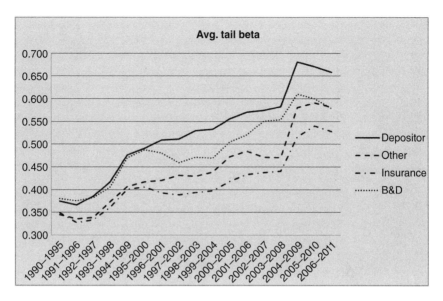

FIGURE 13.3 **Tail-β: cross-sectional average over 1-year rolling window.**

Figure 13.3 confirms that deposit banks seem systemically the most important followed by B&Ds, the residual category "other institutions" and "insurance companies." The relative ranking of different financial industry types according to their systemic risk contribution confirms the findings in Harrington (2009) and Acharya et al. (2011). Notice also that for both figures tail risk and systemic risk both started to decline again toward the end of the sample period.

Notice that Table 13.1 contains both mean and median estimates for each type of financial institution. We also report medians because the cross-sectional distributions of bank risk might be skewed. However, mean and median estimates generally lie close to each other. Moreover, upon applying mean–median equality tests, we could nearly never reject the null hypothesis of equal mean and median.[3] In order to assess whether the cross-sectional differences in bank risk are statistically significant, we limit ourselves to performing a simple t-test on cross-sectional averages to evaluate the equality of bank risk across different types of financial institutions. Equality tests are contained in Table 13.2. The table distinguishes between full sample (left panel), pre-crisis (middle panel), and crisis (right panel) cross-sectional comparisons. The cross-sectional equality test is performed for three tail risk measures and two systemic risk measures (panels A–F). Per subsample and risk measure, we make $C_4^2 = 6$ cross-sectional comparisons.

The vast increases in tail risk and systemic risk over the crisis sample – and thus apparent instability – raises the issue whether these measures have any value added toward predicting future systemic instability. If they only function as descriptive indicators that tell us what the current (over a given sample) state of systemic risk is, their value stays relatively limited. Acharya et al. (2011) and

---

[3]The test results are not reported in this chapter, but they are available from the authors upon request.

TABLE 13.2 Equality test for sample means across financial industry groups

	Full sample				Pre-crisis				Crisis			
	Depositories	Others	Insurance	Broker-dealers	Depositories	Others	Insurance	Broker-dealers	Depositories	Others	Insurance	Broker-dealers
Panel A: estimated α												
Depositors		2.58**	0.24	1.92*		1.41	1.65	0.74		2.05*	1.13	0.14
Others			2.55**	0.12			2.27**	0.47			3.09	1.13
Insurance				1.95*				1.61				0.75
B&Ds												
Panel B: q (p = 0.1%)												
Depositors		1.35	1.36	0.74		1.69	1.35	2.56**		1.42	0.16	0.56
Others			0.33	−0.37			0.92	0.52			1.57	1.44
Insurance				0.12				1.66				0.45
B&Ds												
Panel C: ES(X > 50%)												
Depositors		1.73*	1.43	1.57		0.23	2.64**	0.49		2.26**	2.14**	0.52
Others			2.49**	0.18			0.96	0.48			3.75***	1.83*
Insurance				2.32**				2.24**				1.12
B&Ds												
Panel D: ES(95%)												
Depositors		2.33**	0.53	1.88*		2.53**	0.25	2.81**		0.29	1.55	0.78
Others			1.81*	0.06			2.15**	1.1			1.01	0.91
Insurance				1.49				2.60**				1.48
B&Ds												

Panel E: MES(95%)

Depositors	1.19	1.61	1.71	3.88***	3.74***	0.11	1.82*	3.48***	2.23**
Others		2.60**	2.55**		0.52	3.38***		0.70	1.24
Insurance			0.43			3.18***			0.98
B&Ds									

Panel F: Tail-β

Depositors	1.79*	3.61***	2.28**	2.59**	3.82***	0.36	2.35**	5.20***	1.50
Others		1.92*	0.60		1.16	3.30***		3.46***	0.23
Insurance			1.20			4.85***			1.57
B&Ds									

Note: The table reports the *t*-test for equal sample means cross-industry groups for different measures of risk. The test is carried for the full sample, pre-crisis sample, and crisis sample separately. Two-side rejections at the 10%, 5%, and 1% significance level are denoted with *, **, and ***, respectively.

Brownlees and Engle (2015) already argued that their pre-crisis MES estimates exhibit some predictability toward adverse shocks in the banks' equity capital during the crisis. In order to judge whether the pre-crisis EVT-based measures exhibit predictive content toward their crisis counterparts, we take a slightly alternative route and scatter pre-crisis tail risk versus crisis tail risk and pre-crisis tail-βs versus crisis tail-βs. The scatter plots are summarized in Figure 13.4, and further distinguish between scatters containing all financial institutions or sectoral scatters. Ordinary least-squares (OLS) regression lines are also included in the scatters. The graphs already provide some casual evidence of a positive relationship that pre-crisis values of tail risk (systemic risk) indeed have something to say about their crisis counterparts.

In addition to the scatter plot analysis, we also calculate the (Spearman) rank correlations between the pre-crisis rank vector and the crisis rank vector of tail

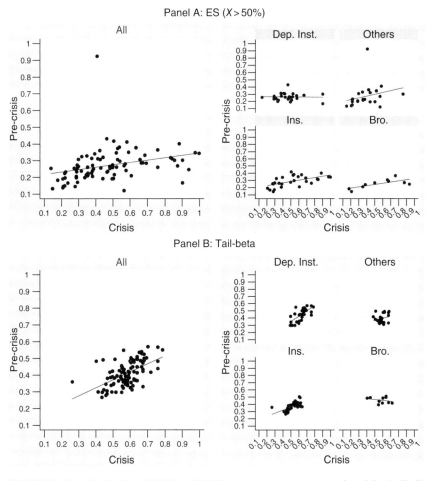

FIGURE 13.4 **Tail risk (ES($X > 50\%$)) and extreme systemic risk (tail-β)**
pre-crisis versus crisis for all institutions and for industry groups.

TABLE 13.3 Rank correlation (in %) of tail risk and extreme systemic risk measures pre-crisis versus crisis

	$q\ (p=0.1\%)$	ES($X>50\%$)	ES(95%)	MES(95%)	Tail-β
Depositories	−3.3	16.7	−18.6	60.8***	70.2***
Others	43.6**	44.6**	19.4	39.1*	16.8
Insurance	35.6**	69.2***	2.4	57.0***	63.0***
Broker-dealers	53.9	72.1**	24.9	44.8	−0.03
All	28.5***	58.4***	5.6	56.0***	56.8***

Note: The table reports Spearman's rank correlation coefficients between pre-crisis and crisis ranks for different risk measures and the independence *t*-test results. The test was carried across four industry groups separately and for all institution as a whole. The null-hypothesis rejections at the 10%, 5%, and 1% significance level are denoted with *, **, and ***, respectively.

risk and systemic risk proxies. Rank correlation estimates between pre-crisis and crisis ranks are reported in Table 13.3.

Also here, we can distinguish between rank correlations for the whole cross section of institutions as well as for rank correlations per financial industry sector. It is not because the bank risk measures nearly all doubled or tripled that the relative riskiness of institutions relative to each other has changed. The table clearly shows that the majority of rank correlations are statistically significant and quite high in most cases (economic significance). The expected shortfall measure ES(95%), though, is very unstable over time, which may be due to the fact that it is not an EVT-based measure capturing crises or distress events, that is, it is unsuited to capture the univariate tail behavior. Summarizing, pre-crisis EVT indicators of tail risk and systemic risk that produce stable ranks over time exhibit some predictive power toward their crisis counterparts and thus still represent useful information for regulators and supervisors. Thus, tail risk and systemic risk seem relatively persistent in that the riskiest (safest) financial institutions in the pre-crisis period seem to remain the riskiest ones (safest ones) once the crisis struck.

13.4.2 Size as a Potential Driver of Tail Risk and Systemic Risk

That there is a relation between the size of financial institutions and their systemic risk contribution seems to be taken for granted nowadays by governments or central banks. According to theory, systemic risk arises because of either "direct" channels via interbank market linkages or "indirect" channels such as similar portfolio holdings in bank balance sheets. However, bigger banks are not necessarily more interconnected with the rest of the financial system nor do they necessarily exhibit more diversified portfolio holdings. In the end, however, whether the size–systemic risk relation exists or not remains an empirical issue. Despite the consensus that seems to exist in the policy arena, the number of empirical studies that try to link some proxy of institutional size to systemic risk remains limited, see, for example, De Jonghe (2010) or Zhou (2010). One typically finds a positive size–systemic risk relation but the relation is often unstable across different time periods.

Downsizing financial institutions' balance sheets is generally considered as the corner stone of financial reforms nowadays, but one seems to forget that institutional size almost surely also impacts the diversification properties of financial institutions. In other words, it may well be that although the systemic contribution of banks is decreased by shrinking the balance sheet, the bank becomes less diversified and thus more unstable, that is, higher individual bank risk. Whereas the empirical work on the size–systemic risk relation is already pretty scant, empirical studies on the size–univariate bank tail risk relation are nearly nonexistent. This is somewhat remarkable because the "usual suspects" that are expected to trigger system instability and tail risk are probably partly overlapping, that is, a joint analysis of tail risk and systemic risk seems a natural way to proceed. We apply two types of empirical exercises on the triangle size–tail risk–systemic risk. First, we calculate rank correlations between tail risk and systemic risk. Second, we calculate rank correlations between tail risk and size and systemic risk and size. Rank correlations are calculated for different time-series samples (full sample, pre-crisis, and crisis samples) and different cross sections (all banks as well as the separate segments of the financial industry that we earlier considered). We decided to solely focus on the size variable because it is the most widely considered trigger of bank risk.

Rank correlations between individual tail risk and systemic risk are contained in Table 13.4 and Figure 13.5. Robust, statistically and economically significant correlations seem to exist only for the full sample. Thus, it is difficult to conclude that there is a positive relationship between tail risk and systemic risk in a robust manner because they do not seem to be related across the pre-crisis and crisis sample. Next, we try to correlate the ranks of tail risk and systemic risk with the size ranks of the respective institutions. Rank correlations between different size proxies, tail risk and systemic risk are contained in Table 13.6. For the sake of sensitivity analysis, we distinguish four different proxies for a financial institution's size: total market capitalization, total asset, total equity, and total debt (all

TABLE 13.4   **Rank correlation between extreme tail risk and tail-β**

	Full sample	Pre-crisis	Crisis
ES($X > 50\%$) versus tail-β			
Depositors	41.6 **	−25.8	46.6 **
Others	34.8	32.3	−5.2
Insurances	57.4 ***	11.0	42.9 **
B&Ds	16.4	73.0 **	−44.2
All	41.4 ***	−3.7	7.4

Note: The table reports Spearman's rank correlation coefficients between risk measures and the independence *t*-test results. The test is carried across four industry groups separately and for all institution as a whole. The test is also carried across time dimension over full-sample, pre-crisis, and crisis . The null-hypothesis rejections at the 10%, 5%, and 1% significance level are denoted with *,**,and ***, respectively.

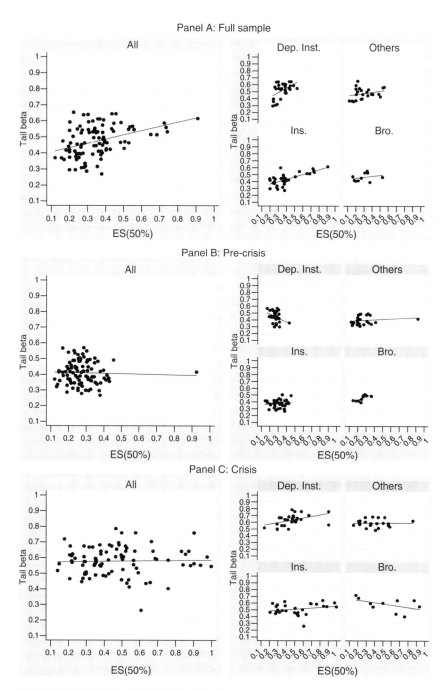

FIGURE 13.5 Tail risk ($\mathrm{ES}(X > 50\%)$) versus extreme systemic risk (tail-β) for full-sample, pre-crisis, and crisis.

TABLE 13.6 Rank correlation of tail risk and systemic risk with different proxies for size

	Total market capitalization			Total asset			Total equity			Total debt		
	Full sample	Pre crisis	crisis	Full sample	Pre crisis	Crisis	Full sample	Pre crisis	Crisis	Full sample	Pre crisis	Crisis
Panel A: q (p = 0.1%)												
Depositors	11.2	−1.1	−11.9	18.6	1.0	39.1 *	16.4	−1.6	35.2	19.2	−3.8	29.8
Others	2.6	0.3	−36.4	−4.8	−27.2	−3.2	−11.4	−23.7	−24.2	−9.9	−41.7 *	9.0
Insurances	−6.1	−20.6	−22.2	30.4 *	−7.4	42.9 **	10.2	−14.7	8.6	6.0	−20.4	8.8
B&Ds	32.1	28.5	−32.1	37.0	27.3	48.6	25.0	15.0	48.6	36.7	26.7	40.0
All	4.0	−1.9	−19.3 *	20.7 **	−3.1	43.8 ***	7.7	−10.0	18.5 *	9.1	−11.2	28.4 **
Panel B: ES(X > 50%)												
Depositors	20.3	−15.1	21.8	23.7	−17.1	51.5 ***	23.8	−22.6	41.1	29.4	−14.9	44.8
Others	11.3	16.2	−3.6	8.8	−1.2	17.0	14.8	13.3	−5.7	−1.4	−7.7	0.8
Insurances	15.0	−4.7	−4.0	42.3 **	19.5	35.4 *	19.9	3.8	12.7	10.6	−10.5	−1.2
B&Ds	47.9	62.4 *	−3.6	49.1	50.3	71.4	30.0	31.7	71.4	48.3	48.3	70.0
All	19.0 *	10.7	5.2	36.0 ***	14.5	41.2 ***	23.8 **	12.0	23.8 **	21.5 **	2.8	20.5 *
Panel C: Tail-β												
Depositors	68.7 ***	77.6 ***	67.2 ***	80.0 ***	81.4 ***	91.6 ***	78.9 ***	77.0 ***	88.6 ***	76.3 ***	76.9 ***	81.4 ***
Others	30.9	48.1 **	−3.8	20.8	53.6 **	10.3	28.9	48.5 **	8.5	29.7	45.0 **	20.7
Insurances	11.6	34.9 **	7.0	45.4 ***	47.6 ***	32.2 *	27.4	30.8 *	14.7	21.9	32.6 *	2.5
B&Ds	59.0 *	76.6 ***	39.3	67.5 **	55.3 *	−8.6	77.0 **	41.8	−8.6	64.4 *	47.7	60.0
All	36.1 ***	50.9 ***	23.4 **	50.7 ***	55.9 ***	41.7 ***	43.9 ***	44.6 ***	32.7 ***	48.7 ***	53.1 ***	42.4 ***

Note: The table reports Spearman's rank correlation coefficients between a risk measure and a size proxy and the independence *t*-test. The test is carried across four industry groups separately and for all institution as a whole. The test is also carried across time dimension over full-sample, pre-crisis, and crisis period. The null-hypothesis rejections at the 10%, 5%, and 1% significance level are denoted with *, **, and ***, respectively.

market values). We consider two tail risk proxies and the tail-β systemic risk measure. Conforming to previous tables, we distinguish different time-series samples (full sample, pre-crisis, and crisis outcomes) and different cross sections (results averaged across all institutions or across separate financial industry segments). Whereas size and tail risk seem to be rather independently evolving from each other (very few rank correlations are statistically significant), the size–systemic risk relationship appears to be significant in a majority of cases. However, notice that the significance is strongest for the full sample and the pre-crisis sample, whereas the relation seems severely weakened over the crisis sample. Total assets seem most strongly correlated with systemic risk. Our results generally confirm earlier findings on the size–systemic risk relationship.

13.5 CONCLUSIONS

The financial sector maintains a central role in every economy as creator of money and a transmitter of monetary policy, but they are also strongly involved in the multilateral payment system and finance investment and growth in the real sector. Thus, long-term financial stability, both for individual financial institutions (tail risk) and for the system as a whole (systemic risk), is of utmost importance for regulators and supervisors. In this study, we used techniques from statistical extreme value analysis to estimate a downside risk measure (per individual institution) and a systemwide risk measure (systemic risk). Both are market-based indicators: they use the loss tails of the market value of equity capital as an input. The downside risk is measured using an extreme tail quantile estimator, whereas the systemic risk is measured by the so-called co-crash probability of an individual bank stock together with a banking market index, that is, a so-called tail-β. Tail-βs are estimated by the so-called Ledford and Tawn approach.

We compare tail risk and systemic risk outcomes across four different industry groups containing 91 financial institutions as in Acharya et al. (2011) and Brownlees and Engle (2015): depositors, insurances, B&Ds, and others. This enables one to make cross-industry tail risk and systemic risk comparisons, which constitutes the main objective of this chapter. First, we find that different groups of financial institutions exhibit different levels of tail risk as well as systemic risk. Insurance companies exhibit the highest equity tail risk. Second, industry groups exhibiting the highest tail risk not necessarily contribute the most to the risk of the financial system as a whole. Somewhat surprisingly, deposit banks (and not B&Ds) seem to be most strongly exposed to adverse macro shocks. Third, both tail risk and systemic risk have increased over the crisis, which does not come as a surprise. However, the relative ranking of the financial institutions' riskiness is not changing dramatically over time: extreme systematic risk seems to exhibit some predictability toward future distress, as the rank correlations between pre-crisis and crisis tail-βs are found to be relatively high. Finally, institutional size proxies are not strongly correlated with tail risk (no diversification effect for larger institutions); but size seems to be correlated with our systemic risk measure. However, the size and ranking results vary considerably across industries and across time.

References

Acharya, V., Pedersen, L., Philippon, T., Richardson, M. Measuring Systemic Risk. Working Paper, New York University; 2011.

Adrian, T., Brunnermeier, M.K. CoVaR. NBER. Working Paper nr. 17454; 2011.

Allen, F., Gale, D. Financial contagion. J Polit Econ 2000;**108**(1):1–33.

Beirlant, J., Dierckx, G., Goegebeur, Y., Matthys, G. Tail index estimation and an exponential regression model. Extremes 1999;**2**(2):177–200.

Brownlees, C.T., Engle, R. SRISK: a conditional capital shortfall measure of systemic risk. Working Paper; 2015.

Demirgüc-Kunt, A., Detragiache, E. The determinants of banking crises in developing and developed countries. IMF Staff Pap 1998;**45**(1):81–109.

De Haan, L., Jansen, D.W., Koedijk, K., de Vries, C.G. Safety first portfolio selection, extreme value theory and long run asset risks. In: Galambos, J., Lechner, J., Simiu, E., editors. *Extreme Value Theory and Applications*. Dordrecht: Kluwer Academic Publishers; 1994. p 471–487.

De Jonghe, O. Back to basics in banking? A micro-analysis of banking system stability. J Financ Intermed 2010;**19**:387–417.

De Nicolo, G., Kwast, M. Systemic risk and financial consolidation: Are they related? J Bank Financ 2002;**26**:861–880.

De Vries, C.G. The simple economics of bank fragility. J Bank Financ 2005;**29**:803–825.

Embrechts, P., Klüppelberg, C., Mikosch, T. *Modelling Extremal Events*. Berlin: Springer-Verlag; 1997.

Goldie, C., Smith, R. Slow variation with remainder: theory and applications. Quart J Math 1987;**38**:45–71.

Gonzalez-Hermosillo, B., Pazarbasioglu, C., Billings, R. Banking system fragility: likelihood versus timing of failure – an application to the Mexican financial crisis'. IMF Staff Pap 1997;**44**(3):295–314.

Gorton, G. Banking panics and business cycles. Oxf Econ Pap 1988;**40**:751–781.

Gropp, R., Moerman, G. Measurement of contagion in banks' equity prices. In: Hasan, I., Tarkka, J., editors. *Banking, Development and Structural Change*, Special Issue of the J Int Money Financ; **23**(3): 2004. p 405–459.

Gropp, R., Vesala, J., 2004. Bank contagion in Europe. Paper presented at the Symposium of the ECB-CFS Research Network on 'Capital Markets and Financial Integration in Europe'; 10–11 May; Frankfurt am Main: European Central Bank.

Haeusler, E., Teugels, J. On asymptotic normality of Hill's estimator for the exponent of regular variation. Ann Stat 1985;**13**:743–756.

Harrington, S.E. *The Financial Crisis, Systemic Risk, and the Future of Insurance Regulation*, Public Policy Paper. National Association of Mutual Insurance Companies; 2009.

Hartmann, P., Straetmans, S., de Vries, C.G. Banking System stability: a cross-atlantic perspective. In: Carey, M., Stulz, R.M., editors. *The Risk of Financial Institutions*. Chicago and London: The University of Chicago Press; 2006. p 133–193.

Hellwig, M. Liquidity provision, banking, and the allocation of interest rate risk. Eur Econ Rev 1994;**38**(7):1363–1389.

Hill, B.M. A simple general approach to inference about the tail of a distribution. Ann Stat 1975;**3**(5):1163–1173.

Iori, G., Jafarey, S., Padilla, F. Systemic risk on the interbank market. J Behav Org 2006;**61**(4):525–542.

Jansen, D.W., de Vries, C.G. On the frequency of large stock returns: putting booms and busts into perspective. Rev Econ Stat 1991;**73**:19–24.

Kho, B.-C., Lee, D., Stulz, R. U.S. banks, crises, and bailouts: from Mexico to LTCM. Am Econ Rev Pap Proc 2000;**90**(2):28–31.

Ledford, A., Tawn, J. Statistics for near independence in multivariate extreme values. Biometrika 1996;**83**(1):169–187.

Mandelbrot, B. The variation of certain speculative prices. J Bus 1963;**36**:394–419.

Slovin, M., Sushka, M., Polonchek, J. An analysis of contagion and competitive effects at commercial banks. J Financ Econ 1999;**54**:197–225.

Smirlock, M., Kaufold, H. Bank foreign lending, mandatory disclosure rules, and the reaction of bank stock prices to the Mexican debt crisis. J Bus 1987;**60**(3):347–364.

Straetmans, S., Verschoor, W., Wolff, C. Extreme US stock market fluctuations in the wake of 9/11. J Appl Econ 2008;**23**(1):17–42.

Straetmans, S., Chaudhry, S. Tail risk and systemic risk for U.S. and Eurozone financial institutions in the wake of the global financial crisis. J Int Money Financ 2015;**58**:191–223.

Swary, I. Stock market reaction to regulatory action in the Continental Illinois crisis. J Bus 1986;**59**(3):451–473.

Tarashev, N., Borio, C., Tsatsaronis, K., 2010. Attributing systemic risk to individual institutions. BIS Working Paper nr. 308.

Wall, L., Peterson, D. The effect of Continental Illinois' failure on the financial performance of other banks. J Monetary Econ 1990;**26**:77–79.

Zhou, C. Are banks too big to fail? Measuring systemic importance of financial institutions. Int J Cent Bank 2010;**6**(4):205–250.

Appendix A

TABLE A1 Tail risk and systemic risk for deposit banks

	Full sample						Pre-crisis						Crisis					
	α	q (p = 0.1% > 50%)	ES (X > 50%)	ES (p = 5%)	MES (p = 5%)	Tail -β	α	q (p = 0.1% > 50%)	ES (X > 50%)	ES (95%)	MES (95%)	Tail -β	α	q (p = 0.1% > 50%)	ES (X > 50%)	ES (95%)	MES (95%)	Tail -β
Bank of America	2.1	22.9	45.8	6.5	4.0	64.5	4.0	13.7	16.7	4.3	2.2	56.7	1.6	82.5	90.2	13.2	8.3	75.9
BB&T	2.9	12.5	25.9	4.9	3.4	56.7	3.1	8.9	23.8	3.6	1.6	44.9	2.6	23.7	31.6	8.2	7.1	66.7
Bank of N.Y. MEL.	2.6	15.2	30.5	5.5	3.4	54.5	3.1	10.8	23.6	4.5	2.1	53.6	2.1	33.2	47.0	8.8	6.8	65.4
Citigroup	2.1	23.4	43.5	6.9	3.9	64.5	2.7	12.5	28.6	4.5	2.2	56.9	1.8	66.5	66.5	14.0	7.7	70.3
COM.BANC.	2.9	14.1	26.7	5.3	0.9	30.8	3.0	13.9	25.4	5.4	0.9	29.7	4.6	5.9	13.9	3.0	2.5	51.7
Comerica	2.4	16.5	36.7	5.3	3.8	61.2	3.0	9.1	25.4	3.6	2.2	52.4	2.0	38.9	48.3	9.7	7.6	68.1
HUNTINGTON BCSH.	2.2	25.2	43.4	7.2	3.3	55.1	3.3	9.2	21.6	3.9	1.8	44.1	2.0	59.9	50.8	15.1	6.8	60.6
HUDSON CITY BANC	2.3	14.3	39.4	4.4	3.8	47.9	2.2	10.0	43.1	2.7	1.2	35.5	2.1	24.6	46.4	6.4	6.6	60.6
JP Morgan C&CO.	2.8	15.1	27.8	5.7	3.9	63.9	3.2	11.5	23.1	4.8	2.2	55.1	2.1	33.9	46.5	8.9	8.2	78.6
KEYCORP	2.3	20.0	38.9	6.3	3.7	60.6	2.9	9.8	26.5	3.7	2.1	50.3	2.0	48.1	48.1	12.7	7.8	69.5
MARSHALL & ILSLEY	2.3	20.1	38.3	6.3	3.4	57.4	3.6	7.6	19.1	3.4	1.8	44.9	2.0	50.1	49.5	13.1	7.2	61.6
M&T BK.	2.3	13.4	38.4	4.1	3.5	52.8	2.8	7.0	27.2	2.7	1.6	41.3	2.3	25.6	38.1	7.5	7.3	64.1
NATIONAL CITY	1.9	20.9	52.9	5.9	2.8	54.8	2.7	10.0	30.3	3.5	2.0	54.9	1.6	124.6	90.2	23.8	7.6	56.3
NORTHERN TRUST	2.8	12.6	27.1	4.9	3.4	54.2	2.9	10.4	26.1	4.0	2.1	50.0	2.0	32.1	52.1	7.7	6.5	64.1

NY.CMTY.BANC.	3.1	12.1	24.0	4.8	2.7	39.5	3.1	9.7	23.3	4.0	1.2	34.5	2.7	18.7	28.9	6.8	6.1	57.4
PEOPLES UNITED FIN.	2.7	15.3	28.8	5.6	1.6	31.9	2.6	16.3	31.4	5.7	0.5	29.6	2.3	17.2	37.6	5.3	6.4	55.1
PNC FINL.SVS.GP.	2.6	14.4	30.6	5.2	3.6	59.4	3.0	10.1	25.6	4.0	2.0	50.0	2.2	31.4	42.9	9.0	7.2	68.1
REGIONS FINL.NEW	2.0	24.9	48.6	6.8	3.5	59.0	2.8	10.1	28.0	3.7	1.7	44.9	1.9	63.2	57.2	14.0	6.9	64.1
SYNOVUS FINL.	2.3	21.5	38.5	6.7	3.1	48.7	3.3	9.0	21.5	3.9	1.7	45.6	2.5	40.0	34.5	12.7	5.8	55.1
SOVEREIGN BANCORP	2.5	19.1	32.8	7.0	2.0	39.3	2.8	14.2	27.7	5.2	1.0	32.4	1.5	130.8	102.5	21.0	8.5	60.2
SUNTRUST BANKS	2.7	17.7	30.2	5.9	3.8	64.1	3.5	7.5	19.9	3.4	2.1	54.0	2.5	34.4	33.6	11.7	7.5	66.7
STATE STREET	2.5	17.0	33.9	6.0	3.3	54.5	2.6	12.8	30.7	4.5	2.0	48.6	1.9	40.3	52.7	10.8	6.9	66.1
UNIONBANCAL	3.1	11.3	24.0	4.6	1.6	35.9	2.8	12.0	27.3	4.6	1.3	34.4	2.7	14.4	29.2	4.9	4.1	50.2
US BANCORP	2.5	15.1	32.9	5.2	3.4	53.2	3.1	10.1	24.1	4.1	1.6	43.9	1.9	39.1	57.7	8.7	8.0	75.9
WACHOVIA	2.1	19.9	44.6	6.3	3.0	58.5	2.8	10.8	28.0	3.9	2.1	52.9	1.5	139.3	100.4	25.1	8.4	66.8
WELLS FARGO & CO	2.4	16.2	35.6	5.3	3.8	61.2	2.9	9.7	25.9	3.7	2.0	48.3	2.0	39.7	49.8	9.9	8.2	75.9
WASTE MAN.	3.1	12.0	23.3	5.1	1.2	29.5	3.0	12.9	25.3	5.2	0.6	29.8	2.7	11.8	29.2	4.2	4.6	49.3
WESTERN UNION	2.3	19.5	38.9	5.9	5.1	49.7	2.6	10.1	30.7	3.3	0.8	42.3	2.2	22.5	42.5	6.3	5.4	49.7
ZIONS BANCORP.	2.1	23.4	44.4	6.6	3.2	53.5	2.6	11.9	31.2	4.2	1.3	36.8	2.2	44.2	41.2	12.3	6.8	63.5

TABLE A2 Tail risk and systemic risk for category "others"

	Full sample						Pre-crisis						Crisis					
	α	q (p =0.1%)	ES(X >50%)	ES (95%)	MES (95%)	Tail-β	α	q (p =0.1%)	ES (X>50%)	ES (95%)	MES (95%)	Tail-β	α	q (p =0.1%)	ES (X>50%)	ES (95%)	MES (95%)	Tail-β
AMERICAN CAPITAL	2.2	30.4	40.8	9.2	3.4	46.3	2.4	15.7	36.1	5.0	1.0	33.8	2.2	52.4	42.3	15.3	5.7	58.5
AMERIPRISE FINL.	3.2	20.5	22.3	8.3	5.7	65.4	3.2	8.8	23.2	3.7	1.1	48.8	3.2	23.1	22.3	9.6	6.7	62.3
TD AMERITRADE HOLDING	3.5	21.2	20.1	9.3	2.3	37.3	3.6	21.6	19.3	9.7	1.2	39.4	2.0	29.4	50.3	7.5	6.9	59.0
AMERICAN EXPRESS	2.9	14.1	26.6	5.5	3.3	52.4	3.2	10.6	22.6	4.5	1.8	48.8	2.3	27.8	37.5	8.4	7.3	68.1
FRANKLIN RESOURCES	3.3	12.4	22.0	5.3	3.2	50.3	3.5	10.0	19.8	4.5	1.6	43.4	2.7	20.8	28.7	7.5	7.6	67.4
BLACKROCK	2.8	15.6	28.4	5.8	3.4	46.2	2.5	13.4	32.9	4.5	0.7	35.8	2.4	23.3	34.8	7.4	5.8	56.0
CB RICHARD ELLIS GP.	3.5	27.1	20.2	11.3	5.0	59.3	4.3	9.5	15.0	4.7	0.8	36.0	3.3	33.1	21.8	14.2	6.0	57.9
COMPASS BANCSHARES	5.1	6.9	12.1	3.7	1.5	37.0	5.1	6.9	12.1	3.7	1.5	36.9	1.9	17.0	56.5	2.9	-1.3	58.3
CIT GROUP	1.9	71.6	55.1	18.8	4.0	56.7	2.6	13.3	32.1	4.6	1.3	49.4	2.1	109.5	44.2	33.7	4.6	51.2
CME GROUP	3.4	15.8	20.6	6.5	4.1	46.2	3.5	9.4	19.7	4.3	0.6	37.1	3.3	19.7	22.0	8.3	5.8	56.9
CAPITAL ONE FINL	2.4	24.1	35.5	8.0	3.7	53.2	2.4	19.8	34.7	6.6	1.9	47.3	2.0	46.6	52.0	11.4	7.0	67.4

EATON VANCE NV.	2.9	14.3	26.4	5.5	2.5	39.4	3.6	9.7	19.2	4.5	0.8	33.0	2.1	32.9	44.1	8.8	7.1	67.4
FIDELITY NAT.INFO.SVS.	2.8	12.2	27.5	4.7	3.5	39.8	2.6	11.3	30.8	4.2	1.2	38.2	2.7	15.0	29.9	5.3	5.1	50.8
FIFTH THIRD BANCORP	1.9	25.4	53.6	6.7	3.5	56.2	2.7	10.6	30.3	3.6	1.9	47.8	1.6	76.7	85.5	14.8	7.2	62.3
INTER-CONTINENTAL EX	2.0	35.6	48.4	9.2	4.4	46.7	2.2	26.9	41.2	7.4	0.7	36.4	1.9	44.6	58.2	9.8	5.5	53.3
JANUS CAPITAL GP.	3.1	21.6	24.4	8.5	4.1	54.9	3.4	14.5	20.6	6.3	1.4	47.5	2.7	31.8	28.7	11.3	7.2	60.6
LEGG MASON	2.5	18.4	33.4	6.2	2.9	49.5	3.2	10.7	22.5	4.6	1.5	41.0	2.4	34.5	35.4	10.9	6.4	56.9
LEUCADIA NATIONAL	2.4	14.0	34.6	4.7	2.9	44.6	3.3	7.3	21.4	3.2	1.1	34.4	2.4	26.6	35.4	8.6	6.5	58.5
MASTERCARD	2.3	22.0	39.3	6.4	5.1	46.7	1.5	37.9	92.4	5.3	0.5	41.6	2.2	23.7	40.8	6.7	6.2	48.2
NYSE EURONEXT	3.5	18.1	20.1	7.7	4.7	54.0	4.6	9.7	13.8	5.2	0.5	33.6	3.4	21.5	20.7	9.2	6.8	61.7
SEI INVESTMENTS	3.9	13.0	17.1	5.8	2.4	35.9	3.2	13.1	22.4	5.4	1.2	31.1	3.3	16.6	21.8	7.0	6.6	61.2
SLM	2.0	25.9	50.4	6.9	2.6	42.9	2.8	10.9	27.0	4.2	1.0	33.3	1.9	63.1	56.5	14.4	5.9	55.5
UNION PACIFIC	4.2	8.3	15.6	4.0	2.4	36.9	4.8	6.3	13.3	3.3	1.0	32.2	4.4	11.5	14.8	6.0	6.4	56.0

TABLE A3 Tail risk and systemic risk for insurance companies

	Full sample						Pre-crisis						Crisis					
	α	q (p =0.1%)	ES(X >50%)	ES (95%)	MES (95%)	Tail-βa	α	q (p =0.1%)	ES(X >50%)	ES (95%)	MES (95%)	Tail-β	α	q (p =0.1%)	ES(X >50%)	ES (95%)	MES (95%)	Tail-β
AETNA	2.3	16.6	37.4	5.3	2.0	36.2	2.3	15.1	38.1	4.8	1.0	34.5	1.9	30.5	53.8	7.0	4.5	45.9
AFLAC	2.2	17.6	40.4	5.4	2.8	42.7	2.7	11.5	29.9	4.0	1.3	38.8	1.4	73.0	113.2	10.0	6.2	59.0
AMERICAN INTL.GP.	1.7	35.3	74.3	7.8	3.2	53.3	2.5	11.1	33.0	3.6	1.9	43.4	1.4	130.2	111.2	19.3	4.7	56.5
ASSURANT	1.7	31.5	73.6	6.4	4.9	56.0	2.2	9.3	40.1	2.7	0.8	37.6	1.6	51.4	88.3	8.4	6.8	55.1
ALLSTATE	2.2	17.3	42.6	5.1	2.9	42.3	2.5	12.4	34.4	4.0	1.5	38.4	1.5	54.3	99.7	8.1	6.6	54.6
AON	2.3	13.4	37.5	4.4	2.2	41.1	2.2	14.3	41.7	4.4	1.4	39.5	2.0	18.7	50.5	4.3	5.3	52.4
W R BERKLEY	3.5	8.9	20.0	3.9	1.9	29.5	3.6	7.8	19.1	3.6	0.9	28.7	3.4	11.7	20.7	5.1	5.7	46.5
BERKSHIRE HATHAWAY A'	2.7	9.5	28.6	3.5	1.9	33.5	2.5	9.5	32.5	3.2	0.8	30.5	2.6	12.8	31.9	4.4	5.2	46.5
BERKSHIRE HATHAWAY B'	3.0	8.9	25.3	3.5	2.6	37.1	2.9	7.8	26.1	3.0	1.0	33.8	2.4	14.1	35.2	4.4	5.8	48.9
CHUBB	3.6	8.9	19.6	3.8	2.8	44.1	4.0	7.0	16.6	3.4	1.7	41.3	3.1	14.5	23.7	5.7	6.6	59.5
COUNTRYWIDE FINL.	3.0	15.3	25.1	6.1	1.1	39.5	3.4	11.8	21.0	5.2	0.4	35.9	1.8	37.5	60.8	8.3	4.1	26.3
LOEWS	2.3	13.0	38.3	4.1	2.8	44.9	2.6	9.4	31.8	3.2	1.2	36.6	1.6	42.2	83.3	7.0	6.8	64.1
CIGNA	2.3	16.3	38.1	5.2	2.2	40.1	2.4	12.8	35.1	4.3	1.0	34.8	1.8	38.1	59.2	8.3	5.3	50.4
CINCINNATI FINL.	3.1	10.6	24.3	4.3	2.8	45.6	3.4	8.2	20.6	3.6	1.3	37.0	2.3	20.6	38.1	6.4	6.7	62.3
AMERICAN NAT	2.2	15.5	40.3	4.8	2.9	41.8	2.9	8.8	26.0	3.4	1.4	36.3	1.7	49.8	75.9	9.4	6.5	58.5
COVENTRY HEALTH CARE	2.3	26.6	37.8	8.7	1.1	27.0	2.3	27.0	37.8	8.6	0.4	26.6	1.8	37.2	63.5	8.6	4.1	43.5

Company																		
FIDELITY NAT.FINANCIAL	2.5	21.1	33.5	7.1	4.1	44.5	2.5	12.1	34.1	4.0	0.6	38.5	2.3	26.9	39.4	7.9	5.2	48.6
GENWORTH FINANCIAL	2.5	44.2	32.9	13.7	4.6	59.9	4.4	5.6	14.5	2.8	0.9	41.5	2.8	51.3	28.0	18.3	5.5	55.1
HARTFORD FINL.SVS.GP.	1.7	36.9	68.5	8.4	3.5	51.5	2.3	15.6	39.8	4.3	1.9	42.6	1.3	150.9	166.5	17.3	5.8	53.7
HEALTH NET	2.8	17.5	28.2	6.5	1.5	31.1	2.7	17.0	29.7	6.1	0.8	29.9	1.9	31.2	54.1	7.6	3.7	41.3
HUMANA	2.4	19.8	35.4	6.6	1.6	31.6	2.3	20.3	37.3	6.3	0.7	29.6	1.9	29.2	52.8	7.3	5.3	43.7
LINCOLN NAT.	1.8	29.7	65.1	6.9	3.1	51.6	2.3	13.4	37.9	3.9	1.7	41.9	1.3	157.0	185.0	15.4	7.0	62.3
MBIA	2.4	27.2	36.6	8.4	2.8	45.9	2.9	10.5	26.5	4.1	1.4	38.9	2.7	47.8	29.9	17.0	6.0	49.7
METLIFE	1.9	28.6	55.9	7.1	4.2	54.6	2.6	11.4	31.1	3.8	1.5	44.7	1.6	65.3	84.2	11.3	6.8	55.5
MARSH & MCLENNAN	2.9	10.2	26.4	4.0	2.6	43.7	3.0	9.3	25.0	3.8	1.6	42.2	2.3	16.1	38.7	4.8	5.8	56.0
PRINCIPAL FINL.GP.	1.7	41.5	72.6	8.6	4.6	58.7	2.4	10.7	34.8	3.3	1.5	50.3	1.5	89.0	97.5	13.2	7.3	60.6
PROGRESSIVE OHIO	2.4	13.5	36.0	4.4	2.6	41.1	2.5	11.5	33.3	3.9	1.3	38.3	1.7	32.7	68.6	6.0	6.9	59.5
PRUDENTIAL FINL.	1.5	45.9	91.0	8.3	4.7	61.6	2.1	12.7	45.5	3.2	1.7	49.1	1.4	105.4	133.8	12.9	6.9	61.7
SAFECO	3.1	8.9	23.6	3.7	1.5	37.7	3.0	9.2	24.9	3.7	1.3	38.0	2.8	11.1	28.1	3.9	2.8	46.8
TORCHMARK	2.4	13.8	36.3	4.5	3.0	49.4	2.8	9.5	28.5	3.5	1.6	42.1	1.7	40.5	69.4	8.0	6.4	59.0
TRAVELERS COS.	3.5	9.8	20.0	4.2	2.8	41.9	3.9	7.9	17.0	3.6	1.5	39.2	2.7	16.6	29.4	6.0	6.9	57.4
UNITEDHEALTH GP.	2.7	15.9	29.5	5.9	1.5	28.7	2.8	14.6	27.4	5.6	0.7	27.8	2.0	26.8	49.8	6.8	4.5	45.9
UNUM GROUP	2.0	23.1	50.8	6.3	2.9	47.1	2.2	17.2	42.7	5.3	1.4	37.6	1.5	67.2	101.9	9.4	7.0	62.3
WELLPOINT	3.0	12.7	25.4	5.1	2.9	39.6	3.0	10.7	25.4	4.2	0.8	31.1	2.8	15.6	27.4	6.1	4.9	44.6

TABLE A4 Tail risk and systemic risk measures for "Broker-dealers"

	Full sample						Pre-crisis						Crisis					
	α	q (p =0.1%)	ES (X >50%)	ES (95%)	MES (95%)	Tail-β	α	q (p =0.1%)	ES (X >50%)	ES (95%)	MES (95%)	Tail-β	α	q (p =0.1%)	ES (X >50%)	ES (95%)	MES (95%)	Tail-β
A G EDWARDS	3.7	9.4	18.2	4.4	1.6	41.7	3.7	9.4	18.3	4.4	1.6	41.6	3.8	4.1	17.8	1.9	1.2	71.9
BEAR STEARNS	2.9	13.3	26.7	5.9	2	45.2	3	11.8	24.6	4.7	1.8	44.2	1.5	85.2	93.8	28.7	2.6	55.3
E*TRADE FINANCIAL	3.2	27.2	23	11.3	2.6	41.2	3.1	24.2	24	9.7	1.1	39.2	2.3	46.5	38.1	14.9	6.1	54.6
GOLDMAN SACHS GP.	2.6	17	31	6	4	52.7	2.9	12.8	26.5	4.8	2	48.4	2	32.8	49.9	8	6.3	60.1
LEHMAN BROS.HDG.	1.9	42.7	53	12.2	2.3	46.4	2.4	19.2	36.5	5.9	2	48.3	1.7	117.2	75.9	26.3	3	40.3
MERRILL LYNCH & CO.	2.4	18.8	34.7	6.3	3	52.7	2.9	13.2	26.8	4.9	2	49.4	1.6	112.2	87.3	16.4	8	64.2
MORGAN STANLEY	2.5	21.3	34	7.2	3.7	55.4	2.7	15.2	28.7	5.5	2.1	51	1.7	56.4	67.4	11.7	7	64.1
NYMEX HOLDINGS	2.3	20.6	37.3	6.5	1.6	38.9	2.6	13.7	30.7	4	0.9	49.1	1.8	40.9	65.8	7.8	1.1	44.2
CHARLES SCHWAB	3.5	14.8	20	6.7	2.7	40.8	3.4	15	21	6.6	1.7	41.6	2.4	23.6	35.1	7.2	6.5	59.5
T ROWE PRICE GP.	4	12.3	16.4	5.9	3	47.4	4.4	10.1	14.6	5.2	1.5	42.2	3.4	19.2	21	8.3	7.3	67.4

Chapter Fourteen

Extreme Value Theory and Credit Spreads

Wesley Phoa

Capital Fixed Income Investors, The Capital Group Companies, Inc., Los Angeles, CA, USA

While the use of extreme value theory (EVT) in risk management for financial assets became well developed in the 1990s (Embrechts et al., 1997), its applications to modeling credit risk and credit spreads came somewhat later (e.g., Phoa, 1999; Campbell and Huisman, 2003). Interest in this area intensified because of the extraordinary behavior of debt securities during the global financial crisis of 2008, and the apparent breakdown of risk models that did not explicitly incorporate heavy tails (see Chavez-Demoulin and Embrechts, 2011).

This chapter is a practical introduction to the use of EVT in modeling and managing credit portfolios. It is aimed at investment professionals rather than researchers, so all technical details and proofs are omitted. Some knowledge of EVT, as described in the earlier chapters of this book, is assumed.

The focus of this chapter is on credit spreads for corporate bonds and for credit default swaps (CDS), which refer to corporate bonds. We also refer to spreads on index products based on a basket of issuers, such as the MarkIt CDX indices. We omit discussion of other credit markets such as bank loans (which are now frequently traded) and emerging market debt.

14.1 PRELIMINARIES

A cursory look at the data suggests that EVT should be of great utility in modeling the behavior of credit spreads. For example, Figure 14.1 shows the historical 5-year

Extreme Events in Finance: A Handbook of Extreme Value Theory and its Applications,
First Edition. Edited by François Longin.

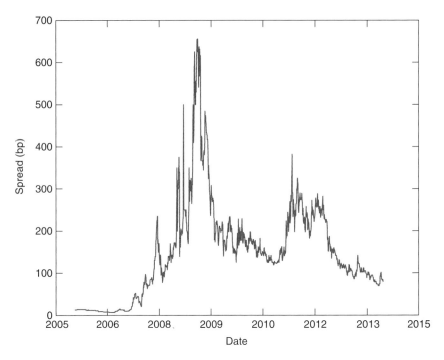

FIGURE 14.1 Citigroup 5-year CDS spread. Daily history of the 5-year CDS spread for Citigroup senior debt. For periods when CDS traded points upfront, trading levels have been translated into spread terms. Note the extreme volatility in spreads observed during the crisis period in late 2008/early 2009. *Source*: Data from Barclays.

CDS spread for Citigroup senior debt, and Figure 14.2 shows a quantile–quantile plot of daily changes in this CDS spread. There is ample evidence of fat tails. Virtually any other time series in credit markets tells a similar story.

However, when applying the theory, a number of practical problems present themselves. One is whether to model changes in spreads or changes in prices. Past work has tended to focus on the distribution of daily changes in observed credit spreads. While working directly with spreads is reasonable when analyzing swap spreads, it is inconvenient when studying the behavior of individual credits. The reason is that, when a credit experiences a sufficiently large adverse event, it ceases trading on a spread basis – instead, the bonds are quoted in terms of dollar price, and CDS trade points upfront (i.e., the buyer of default protection must make an upfront payment in addition to paying a running premium).

It is thus more convenient to work with total returns (for bonds/CDS of a fixed maturity) rather than spread changes. This is also consistent with how EVT is applied to other financial assets; this is an important consideration when analyzing how credit exposures interact with other risk factors, for example, via multivariate EVT.

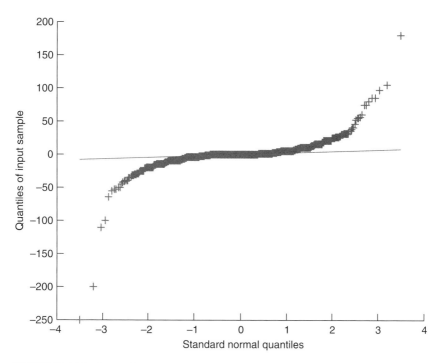

FIGURE 14.2 **Quantile–quantile plot of daily changes in Citigroup CDS spread. Quantile–quantile plot of observed daily changes in the 5-year CDS spread for Citigroup senior debt. The deviation from normality in both left and right tails is evident.**

A second problem is data quality. Most of the literature on EVT in finance is concerned with highly liquid markets, such as equities, currencies, or swap spreads, in which reliable daily data are readily available. By contrast, many corporate credits are thinly traded – cash bond transactions in less liquid credits may be spaced weeks or even months apart, and reported valuations in between transactions may be either unchanged or merely estimates based on the prices of related securities, rather than true observations. In either case, the use of the data for statistical estimation becomes problematic.

The practitioner is therefore forced into two compromises: (i) conduct estimation using data on more liquid credits with reliable daily data, and hope that the results can be carried over to less liquid credits, and (ii) analyze CDS pricing, which is generally "cleaner" than cash bond pricing, and hope that the results carry over to cash bonds.

Both assumptions are questionable, since in each case there is a valuation wedge: (i) the liquidity difference itself has a market price which fluctuates over time, and (ii) there is a cash-CDS basis in credit pricing, which is itself volatile. These difficulties can be partly overcome by treating credit-specific liquidity premia and cash-CDS bases as determined largely by two systematic risk factors (i.e., a generic liquidity premium and a generic cash-CDS basis) that can be modeled independently of issuer-specific liquid CDS credit spreads.

Bank loans are even more problematic than cash bonds, since their position higher in the capital structure means that there is a third valuation wedge, corresponding to the fluctuating market value of seniority, secured status, and implicit control (via covenants).

A third problem is the choice of historical data that should be used to estimate quantities of interest in EVT. The data will not be informative about tails of the return distribution unless it spans a period that includes some large market movements. But, should it include data from the period of the global financial crisis, that is, between September 2008 (the conservatorship of Fannie Mae and Freddie Mac, and the failure of Lehman Brothers) and May 2009 (the release of the US bank stress test results)?

The case against including crisis-period data is that credit markets were driven by extraordinary events that are unlikely to be repeated in our lifetimes. The case in favor is that these are precisely the kind of events that EVT is meant to inform us about. A complication is that the quality of daily data on individual credits is often quite poor before around 2006, so if the crisis period is included in the analysis, it turns out to have a rather high weight. The author's preferred approach is to rely primarily on post-crisis data, but where possible to compare the results with an analysis including crisis-period data.

14.2   TAIL BEHAVIOR OF CREDIT MARKETS

The use of the tail index to quantify the frequency of extreme asset price returns dates back to Jansen and de Vries (1991). The distribution of extreme returns was characterized in Longin (1996). As mentioned previously, initial applications focused on equity and currency markets.

We proceed to look at credit markets by taking a look at daily data on the MarkIt 5-year CDX high-grade and high-yield indices and selected 5-year single-name CDS. Tail index estimates are computed by applying a plateau-finding algorithm to the "alternative Hill plot" described in Vollmer (2003).

Table 14.1 shows tail index estimates for the 5-year CDS HG5 index and for 5-year Citigroup CDS, using daily return data from 2006 to 2013, and comparing the results obtained using different sub-periods. A couple of observations are worth making.

First, most of the tail index estimates are lower than 0.5, suggesting that the second moments of the return distributions exist, that is, it is meaningful to work with return volatilities. (This is fortunate; otherwise risk analysis would be extremely inconvenient.) Overall, assuming a tail index of around 0.3–0.4 seems reasonable for both the index product and the single-name CDS; it is unwise to assume much more precision than that.

Second, while the behavior of the credit index was fairly similar in the pre- and post-crisis periods, both Table 14.1 and Figure 14.1 suggest that the behavior

TABLE 14.1 **Tail index estimates for CDX HG5 and Citigroup 5-year CDS**

	CDX HG5			Citigroup		
	Left	Right	Volatility (%)	Left	Right	Volatility (%)
Full period	0.29	0.35	3.6	0.48	0.46	9.7
Post-crisis	0.38	0.32	2.5	0.30	0.26	6.3
Pre-crisis	0.47	0.42	2.8	0.55	0.31	3.4
Ex-crisis	0.43	0.25	2.6	0.31	0.30	6.2
Crisis	0.39	0.59	8.4	0.43	0.63	27.0

Based on daily total returns on the MarkIt CDX HG5 index and on Citigroup 5-year credit default swap. The full sample covers the period January 2, 2006 to February 24, 2014. The crisis sub-sample covers September 1, 2008 to May 29, 2009; that is, the full months spanning the GSE conservatorship and Lehman bankruptcy (marking the start of the crisis), and the release of the Federal Reserve's Comprehensive Capital Analysis and Review (marking its end).

of Citigroup CDS returns had experienced a regime change in volatility, though not in tail fatness. This is a first indication that tail indices, though harder to estimate than volatilities, may in some sense be more stable over time.

Table 14.2 shows post-crisis estimates for a number of selected credits, including some high-yield credits (marked with an asterisk). While there is considerable variation in return volatilities, the tail index estimates are more consistent, with

TABLE 14.2 **Tail index estimates for the post-crisis period**

	Left tail index	Right tail index	Volatility (%)
CDX HG5	0.38	0.32	2.5
CDX HY5*	0.62	0.46	27.8
General Electric	0.40	0.25	5.7
Bank of America	0.27	0.34	6.6
Citigroup	0.30	0.26	6.3
AT&T	1.11	1.13	0.6
Ford	0.50	0.61	15.0
Walmart	0.38	0.48	0.8
Hewlett-Packard	0.25	0.37	3.9
Dow Chemical	0.32	0.36	3.7
Prudential	0.43	0.35	6.3
HCA*	0.37	0.48	8.4
Tenet Healthcare*	0.42	0.44	9.1
Caesar's*	0.18	0.25	30.8
MGM Resorts*	0.51	0.25	19.1

Based on daily total returns on the two indicated MarkIt CDX contracts, and on 5-year credit default swaps for senior debt of the indicated issuers; an asterisk indicates a high-yield issuer. The sample covers the period June 1, 2009 to February 24, 2014. "Left tail" refers to negative total returns, that is, spread widening; "Right tail" refers to positive total returns.

two possible exceptions: (i) there is some evidence that high-yield credits may often have a tail index of around 0.4–0.5, and (ii) very high quality, stable credits such as AT&T can exhibit very low return volatility but with unusually fat tails, perhaps attributable to the disproportionate impact of event risk on returns.

(Since this is inconvenient for applications, in practice we may often treat such credits "as if they have significantly higher volatilities, but a more typical tail index." More precisely, the empirically observed tail index is used to scale up the empirically observed volatility, using a rule-of-thumb multiplier as shown in Table 14.5, explained later in this chapter. This process is of course purely heuristic.)

Figures 14.3 and 14.4, which use post-crisis CDS data on 64 individual high-grade and high-yield credits, present some cross-sectional evidence on the nature of return tails versus the nature of return volatility. Figure 14.3 plots realized return volatility against initial spreads, revealing a linear relationship consistent with the finding of Ben Dor et al. (2007) that, for fixed duration, volatility is generally proportional to initial spread.

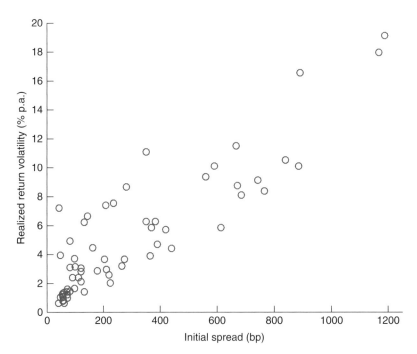

FIGURE 14.3 Return volatility versus initial spread for selected credits, post-crisis data. This chart shows, for 50 selected issuers, the relationship between the 5-year CDS spread on June 1, 2009 and the annualized volatility of daily returns for the period June 1, 2009 to February 24, 2014. Note that the initial spread was a good predictor of subsequent return volatility: the relationship was approximately linear.

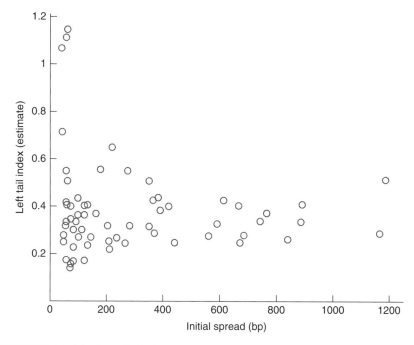

FIGURE 14.4 Left tail index versus initial spread for selected credits, post-crisis data. This chart shows, for the same 50 issuers shown in Figure 14.3, the relationship between the 5-year CDS spread on June 1, 2009 and the left tail index estimated using daily CDS total returns for the period June 1, 2009 to February 24, 2014. Except for a few high-quality issuers with low initial spread, the observations are distributed around a horizontal line. That is, the estimated tail index appears to be independent of the initial spread level.

By contrast, Figure 14.4 plots the estimated (left) tail indices against initial spreads. The tail index appears to be independent of spread, which is a very convenient empirical property of the tails. A possible exception is that at very low spread levels, some credits had very low realized volatilities but with fat tails, as exemplified by AT&T above.

Figure 14.5, which is a histogram of the above tail index estimates, shows that a value of 0.3 or somewhat higher appears to be fairly typical, and should be an appropriate generic assumption to make about credits for which data suitable for estimation are not available.

It was not obvious a priori that the tail index should be roughly the same for lower risk and higher risk issuers, and we currently have no structural model that explains this observation. One possible explanation is that extreme returns are generally triggered by events such as large exogenous shocks (e.g., banks during a financial crisis), scandals (e.g., Enron, Petrobras, Volkswagen), or other idiosyncratic events (e.g., Texaco, BP). Intuitively, the likelihood of such events may be

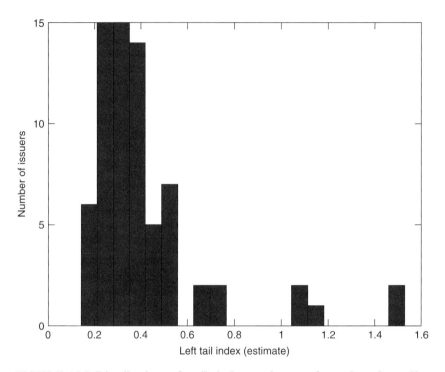

FIGURE 14.5 Distribution of tail index estimates for selected credits, post-crisis data. This histogram shows the distribution of left tail index estimates for the same 50 issuers shown in Figure 14.3. The left tail indices mostly fall in the range 0.3–0.4; the exceptions are a few high-quality issuers with low initial spread, as shown in Figure 14.4.

about equal across firms, and unrelated to an individual firm's leverage or other standard financial metrics.

14.3   SOME MULTIVARIATE ANALYSIS

Practitioners generally deal with a portfolio of credits rather than a single credit in isolation. Multivariate analysis, cf. Joe (1997), is therefore often useful.

For example, an investor with exposures to multiple credits may want to assess the likelihood of simultaneous extreme events. In the most general case, this would involve estimating the tail copula, cf. Schmidt and Stadtmüller (2006). In practice, much insight can be gained by estimating pairwise tail dependence coefficients, that is, the probability of an extreme return in one credit given an extreme return in another. We use a simple nonparametric estimator for the tail dependence coefficient, based on comparison of rank-order statistics, though more sophisticated methods exist.

TABLE 14.3 **Left tail dependence coefficients for selected credits, post-crisis data**

	GE	BAC	C	T	F	WMT	HPQ	DOW	PRU	HCA	THC	CZR
GE	1.00	0.34	0.36	0.09	0.34	0.25	0.05	0.30	0.25	0.31	0.29	0.14
BAC	0.34	1.00	0.60	0.09	0.28	0.12	0.06	0.26	0.27	0.31	0.25	0.18
C	0.36	0.60	1.00	0.09	0.36	0.15	0.04	0.38	0.30	0.34	0.27	0.21
T	0.09	0.09	0.09	1.00	0.15	0.06	0.00	0.10	0.12	0.12	0.10	0.03
F	0.34	0.28	0.36	0.15	1.00	0.15	0.00	0.36	0.39	0.32	0.28	0.12
WMT	0.25	0.12	0.15	0.06	0.15	1.00	0.11	0.17	0.11	0.16	0.16	0.05
HPQ	0.05	0.06	0.04	0.00	0.00	0.11	1.00	0.03	0.01	0.04	0.06	0.13
DOW	0.30	0.26	0.38	0.10	0.36	0.17	0.03	1.00	0.33	0.40	0.30	0.24
PRU	0.25	0.27	0.30	0.12	0.39	0.11	0.01	0.33	1.00	0.37	0.37	0.16
HCA	0.31	0.31	0.34	0.12	0.32	0.16	0.04	0.40	0.37	1.00	0.55	0.22
THC	0.29	0.25	0.27	0.10	0.28	0.16	0.06	0.30	0.37	0.55	1.00	0.23
CZR	0.14	0.18	0.21	0.03	0.12	0.05	0.13	0.24	0.16	0.22	0.23	1.00

Based on daily total returns on 5-year credit default swaps for the issuers shown in Table 14.2 (except for MGM resorts), using the same sample period. "Left tail" refers to negative total returns, that is, spread widening.

Table 14.3 shows left tail dependence coefficients for 12 selected individual credits, estimated using post-crisis CDS data. There is strong evidence of asymptotic dependence. The average probability of a joint extreme adverse event is about 21%, which is significant. However, note that there is considerable variation in estimates: the tail dependence between issuers in the financial sector is significantly higher, whereas tail dependence coefficients for high-grade industrial issuers tend to be significantly lower. This is intuitive if we think of financial issuers as sharing exposure to a common systemic financial risk factor, and it is mirrored by the observed return correlations, that is, the behavior of non-extreme returns.

Note that all these tail dependence estimates are significantly higher, by up to an order of magnitude, than reasonable estimates of the correlation of default events for these credits, for example, as computed via the method described in either Zhou (2001) or Jarrow and van Deventer (2005). In other words, left tail dependence seems to be influenced by additional market factors beyond fundamental default correlation.

One reason why the observed tail dependence coefficients are quite high is because tail events can be generated by systemic shocks, which affect market credit risk premia as well as default risk itself. Systemic financial shocks can have a very large impact on market liquidity spreads as well (notably during the 2008–2009 financial crisis); see, for example, Coro et al. (2013).

A less standard use of methods from multivariate EVT is to estimate correlations for use in "stressed" scenarios, as in Phoa (2015). The idea here is that in periods of market dislocation, correlations usually shift markedly, tending to rise across all classes of risky assets. Of course, this should be detected rapidly *ex post* by risk management systems that rely on multivariate GARCH correlation estimates, but for stress testing purposes it is useful to have *ex ante* estimates of what these "correlations under stress" might look like.

To do this, we can use a method originally developed in Dominicy et al. (2013). They propose the following definition of "outlier" for multivariate data. Suppose there are a total of N observations, and we want to pick out a subset of n outliers, where $n < N$; the smaller the n, the fewer and more extreme the outliers. We do this by finding the $N - n$ observations whose covariance matrix has smallest determinant – this can be done efficiently using the *FastMCD* algorithm described in Rousseeuw and van Driessen (1999) – and then simply picking the other n observations. This method can be used to estimate "correlations under stress" from multivariate return data as follows:

Step 1: For each n, pick the n outlier observations as above, and call these the "n-outlier returns." Then compute correlations using just the n-outlier returns instead of the full sample; call these the "n-outlier correlations" for n.

Step 2: We think of the n-outlier correlations as estimates of the outer correlation, with high variance for low values of n, but increasing bias as n gets higher. Then estimate the "limit as $n \to 0$" by combining the "alternative Hill plot" rescaling as in Vollmer (2003) with the linear regression method described in Huisman et al. (2001).

The resulting estimates can be regarded as "correlations under stress," and attempt to capture a different aspect of dependence in the tails. They are dubbed "outer correlations" in Phoa (2015), to which the reader is referred for further explanation and examples. This is intended to be a notion of conditional correlation that appears to get around the pitfalls described in Boyer et al. (1999) and Longin and Solnik (2001), though a rigorous mathematical analysis has not yet been conducted.

Table 14.4 compares the sample correlations of returns for selected credits (upper) with their outer correlations as estimated above. The outer correlations are, on average, about 0.14 higher than the corresponding sample correlations. These differences are most likely on the threshold of statistical significance (based on Monte Carlo analysis).

Therefore, these estimates should not be relied on too literally. Still, they are interesting because they temper the finding of relatively low tail dependence for industrial credits that was noted above. The outer correlations involving industrial credits show the greatest increase relative to the corresponding sample correlations, sometimes being around 0.3 higher. This suggests that in stressed markets, these correlations are similar to the (higher) correlations between financials in normal markets, and value at risk (VaR) scenario analysis should perhaps reflect that assumption.

The following remark may help provide some intuition. Note that the outer correlation of two credits depends not just on their returns alone but the returns on all the credits used in the estimation process, since it is this full set of multivariate returns that is used in the definition of n-outlier. The outer correlation should be thought of as measuring the dependence of returns when the market as a whole is

TABLE 14.4 Sample correlations and outer correlations for selected credits, post-crisis data

	GE	BAC	C	T	F	WMT	HPQ	DOW	PRU	HCA	THC	CZR
Sample correlations												
GE	1.00	0.66	0.69	0.17	0.44	0.30	0.22	0.46	0.49	0.53	0.51	0.44
BAC	0.66	1.00	0.84	0.17	0.43	0.24	0.31	0.46	0.49	0.55	0.52	0.51
C	0.69	0.84	1.00	0.19	0.45	0.26	0.29	0.48	0.52	0.54	0.53	0.49
T	0.17	0.17	0.19	1.00	0.24	0.20	0.08	0.23	0.16	0.20	0.17	0.15
F	0.44	0.43	0.45	0.24	1.00	0.20	0.16	0.41	0.48	0.48	0.43	0.41
WMT	0.30	0.24	0.26	0.20	0.20	1.00	0.21	0.29	0.23	0.28	0.26	0.22
HPQ	0.22	0.31	0.29	0.08	0.16	0.21	1.00	0.23	0.19	0.27	0.29	0.33
DOW	0.46	0.46	0.48	0.23	0.41	0.29	0.23	1.00	0.45	0.55	0.49	0.40
PRU	0.49	0.49	0.52	0.16	0.48	0.23	0.19	0.45	1.00	0.49	0.49	0.40
HCA	0.53	0.55	0.54	0.20	0.48	0.28	0.27	0.55	0.49	1.00	0.83	0.52
THC	0.51	0.52	0.53	0.17	0.43	0.26	0.29	0.49	0.49	0.83	1.00	0.54
CZR	0.44	0.51	0.49	0.15	0.41	0.22	0.33	0.40	0.40	0.52	0.54	1.00
Outer correlations												
GE	1.00	0.60	0.62	0.26	0.35	0.46	0.41	0.55	0.47	0.58	0.52	0.50
BAC	0.60	1.00	0.89	0.37	0.52	0.41	0.48	0.62	0.57	0.78	0.64	0.67
C	0.62	0.89	1.00	0.40	0.55	0.43	0.53	0.70	0.71	0.73	0.68	0.70
T	0.26	0.37	0.40	1.00	0.39	0.38	0.44	0.33	0.27	0.38	0.34	0.34
F	0.35	0.52	0.55	0.39	1.00	0.25	0.29	0.45	0.60	0.61	0.51	0.61
WMT	0.46	0.41	0.43	0.38	0.25	1.00	0.38	0.55	0.33	0.48	0.42	0.36
HPQ	0.41	0.48	0.53	0.44	0.29	0.38	1.00	0.52	0.36	0.39	0.45	0.44
DOW	0.55	0.62	0.70	0.33	0.45	0.55	0.52	1.00	0.57	0.74	0.61	0.56
PRU	0.47	0.57	0.71	0.27	0.60	0.33	0.36	0.57	1.00	0.66	0.67	0.64
HCA	0.58	0.78	0.73	0.38	0.61	0.48	0.39	0.74	0.66	1.00	0.88	0.68
THC	0.52	0.64	0.68	0.34	0.51	0.42	0.45	0.61	0.67	0.88	1.00	0.65
CZR	0.50	0.67	0.70	0.34	0.61	0.36	0.44	0.56	0.64	0.68	0.65	1.00

Based on daily total returns on 5-year credit default swaps for the issuers shown in Table 14.2 (except for MGM resorts), using the same sample period. A comparison of the sample and outer correlations shows how correlations are expected to change when credit markets become extremely dislocated. In nearly all cases, correlations rise sharply.

stressed, not just when one credit is (perhaps idiosyncratically) stressed. This may explain why, in regard to industrial credits, the outer correlations appear to tell a somewhat different story from the tail dependence coefficients.

14.4 APPROXIMATING VALUE AT RISK FOR CREDIT PORTFOLIOS

The best known application of EVT is in modifying the interpretation of VaR. Full-scale VaR engines, as used in middle office, involve drawing from

TABLE 14.5   Value-at-risk rule-of-thumb adjustments and the impact of 0.05 error in tail index estimate

Tail	95% Factor	95% Error (%)	98% Factor	98% Error (%)	99% Factor	99% Error (%)	99.9% Factor	99.9% Error (%)	99.99% Factor	99.99% Error (%)
0.10	1.2×	8	1.2×	11	1.3×	13	1.4×	21	1.6×	30
0.15	1.3×	8	1.4×	11	1.4×	14	1.7×	22	2.1×	33
0.20	1.4×	8	1.5×	12	1.6×	14	2.2×	24	2.9×	35
0.25	1.5×	9	1.7×	12	1.9×	15	2.7×	25	3.9×	37
0.30	1.6×	9	1.9×	12	2.2×	15	3.3×	26	5.3×	38
0.35	1.8×	9	2.1×	13	2.5×	16	4.2×	27	7.4×	40
0.40	1.9×	9	2.4×	13	2.9×	16	5.4×	28	10.5×	42
0.45	2.1×	9	2.7×	13	3.3×	16	6.9×	28	14.9×	43
0.50	2.3×	10	3.1×	14	3.9×	17	8.8×	29	21.4×	44
0.55	2.5×	10	3.5×	14	4.6×	17	11.5×	30	30.9×	45
0.60	2.8×	10	4.0×	14	5.4×	18	14.9×	31	45.1×	46
0.65	3.0×	10	4.6×	14	6.3×	18	19.6×	31	66.0×	47
0.70	3.4×	10	5.2×	15	7.4×	18	25.7×	32	97.3×	48
0.75	3.7×	10	6.0×	15	8.8×	19	34.0×	32	144.0×	48
0.80	4.1×	11	6.9×	15	10.5×	19	45.1×	33	214.0×	49
0.85	4.5×	11	8.0×	15	12.5×	19	60.0×	33	319.2×	49
0.90	5.0×	11	9.2×	16	14.9×	20	80.1×	34	477.9×	50
0.95	5.6×	11	10.7×	16	17.8×	20	107.3×	34	717.6×	50
1.00	6.2×	11	12.4×	16	21.4×	20	144.1×	34	1080.6×	51

The "factor" columns in this table show, for a given tail index and confidence level, how a naïve VaR estimate (based on a Gaussian return assumption) may be adjusted to obtain an improved estimate of VaR; for example, if the tail index is 0.35 and the confidence level is 99%, the naïve VaR estimate should be multiplied by 2.5. The "error" columns show the approximate error in the adjusted VaR estimate resulting from an error of 0.05 in the estimate of the tail index.

fat-tailed distributions, and EVT can be used to help estimate the parameters of those distributions, thus introducing the possibility of drawing returns more extreme than those that appear in the empirical distribution (albeit with very low probability).

Perhaps more useful to the front office practitioner is a more heuristic application of EVT. Naïve, quick-and-dirty estimates of VaR are often generated using the assumption that return distributions are multivariate normal. Since return distributions are nearly always fat-tailed, this will always underestimate VaR. However, if one is prepared to make an assumption about the tail index of the portfolio, it is possible to "scale up" the naïve figure to generate a somewhat less inaccurate VaR estimate.

Table 14.5 shows this rule-of-thumb adjustment to naïve VaR for a range of VaR confidence levels and assumed tail indices. It uses a parametric approach, which assumes that extreme observations are drawn from the generalized extreme value distribution, for example, see Section 14.4 of Bensalah (2000). For example, the table says that to obtain a 99.9% VaR estimate for a portfolio with an assumed tail index of 0.3, the naïve VaR estimate should be multiplied by 3.3, and if the tail index assumption is off by 0.05, the VaR estimate will be off by about 26%.

Conveniently, as noted earlier, we can often assume that credit exposures do have a common tail index of about 0.3–0.4. So for a portfolio of long-only credit exposures, it is possible to use the corresponding rows of Table 14.5 to derive rough VaR estimates from naïve VaR calculations, based on this generic assumption.

14.5 OTHER DIRECTIONS

This chapter closes by indicating some additional lines of investigation that cannot be pursued here. The first, of course, is to employ more sophisticated methods of estimation. However, in a practical setting, any technical advantage gained from these methods must be weighed against the increased difficulty of explaining them to the end users of the analysis – whereas simple plateau-finding algorithms or linear regressions can be presented visually in a much more intuitive way.

In most of the above discussion, we implicitly had long-only credit portfolios in mind. It is often important to analyze long–short positions, or single-name positions hedged with index products. In principle, the risks involved can be assessed in a relatively straightforward way by applying standard univariate methods to the returns on the hedged position. Practical difficulties arise when one leg of the position has poorer liquidity or a valuation lag relative to the other, so that reliable daily data are not available for use in the estimation process.

The above analysis also dealt with credit exposure for fixed maturity (5 years, in all the examples). In practice, the term structure of credit spreads is itself volatile, and in systematic ways: notably, an issuer's credit curve tends to become inverted when it becomes distressed. Unfortunately, attempts to apply EVT to fluctuations in this term structure tend to run into data quality problems rather rapidly.

Another common situation is when credit exposures must be analyzed as components of broader portfolio exposures, for example, alongside equity, rates, and currency exposures. For example, credit indices have fairly high tail dependence with equity indices, with estimated probabilities of joint extreme adverse events typically around 20% (compared to around 70% between equity indices).

Finally, it was noted earlier that tail dependence coefficients estimated for mark-to-market returns on credit exposures appear to differ greatly from estimates of the correlation of default events. This may have interesting implications for the valuation of collateralized loan obligations (CLOs). In Monte Carlo simulation of cashflows, it is default correlations that matter; but market-value-based estimates of dependency, which presumably incorporate systematic factors such as fluctuating credit market risk premia, may provide a better way to understand mark-to-market risk for CLOs – for example, the fact that CLO spreads widened so much during the financial crisis, despite the fact that CLO structures held up well from a fundamental perspective.

References

Ben Dor, A., Dynkin, L., Hyman, J., Houweling, P., van Leeuwen, E., Penninga, O. DTS (duration times spread). J Portfolio Management 2007;(Winter):77–100.

Bensalah, Y. Steps in applying extreme value theory to finance, Bank of Canada Working Paper 2000-20; 2000

Boyer, B., Gibson, M.S., Loretan, M. Pitfalls in tests for changes in correlations. Board of Governors of the Federal Reserve System, International Finance Discussion Papers, No. 597; 1999.

Campbell, R., Huisman, R. Measuring credit spread risk. J Portfolio Management 2003;(Summer):121–127.

Chavez-Demoulin, V., Embrechts, P. An EVT primer for credit risk. In: Lipton, A., Rennie, A., editors. *The Oxford Handbook of Credit Derivatives.* New York: Oxford University Press; 2011. p 500–532.

Coro, F., Dufour, A. and Varotto, S., Credit and liquidity components of corporate and CDS spreads. Working Paper, ICMA Centre, 31 May; University of Reading; 2013.

Dominicy, Y., Ilmonen, P., Veredas, D. A multivariate Hill estimator. ECARES Working Paper 2013-33; 2013.

Embrechts, P., Klüppelberg, C., Mikosch, T. *Modelling Extremal Events for Insurance and Finance.* New York: Springer; 1997.

Huisman, R., Koedijk, K., Kool, C., Palm, F. Tail-index estimates in small samples. Journal of Business and Economic Statistics 2001;**19**:208–216.

Jansen, D.W., de Vries, C.G. On the frequency of large stock returns: putting booms and busts into perspective. Rev. of Economics and Statistics 1991;**73**:18–24.

Jarrow, R., van Deventer, D. Estimating default correlations using a reduced-form model. Risk 2005;(January):83–88.

Joe, H. *Multivariate Models and Dependence Concepts.* New York: Chapman & Hall/CRC; 1997.

Longin, F. The asymptotic distribution of extreme stock market returns. Journal of Business 1996;**63**:383–408.

Longin, F., Solnik, B. Extreme correlation of international equity markets. Journal Finance 2001;(January):651–678.

Phoa, W. Estimating credit spread risk using extreme value theory. Journal Portfolio Management 1999;(Spring):69–73.

Phoa, W. Extreme correlations and optimizing for stress. Journal Portfolio Management 2015;(Winter):71–75.

Rousseeuw, P., van Driessen, K. A fast algorithm for the minimum covariance determinant estimator. Technometrics 1999;**41**(3):212–223.

Schmidt, R., Stadtmüller, U. Nonparametric estimation of tail dependence. Scand J Statist 2006;**33**:307–335.

Vollmer, J.H. (2003), A survey of Hill's estimator, M.Sc. Thesis, University of Georgia.

Zhou, C. An analysis of default correlations and multiple defaults. Rev. Financial Studies 2001;**14**:555–576.

Chapter Fifteen

Extreme Value Theory and Risk Management in Electricity Markets

Kam Fong Chan[1] and Philip Gray[2]

[1]*The University of Queensland Business School, University of Queensland, St Lucia, Queensland, Australia*
[2]*Department of Banking and Finance, Monash Business School, Monash University, Melbourne, Victoria, Australia*

15.1 INTRODUCTION

The last 40 years have seen a dramatic increase in the complexity of markets. This is true in relation to the types of assets, securities, and commodities traded, as well as the mechanisms for trading and the linkages between markets. Recent decades have also witnessed a series of notable shocks and episodes of extreme volatility in a variety of markets.[1] Consequently, while risk management has always been an essential function of market participants, its importance has reached unprecedented levels and is unlikely to abate.

Perhaps surprisingly, in light of recent attention on risk management, value at risk (VaR) remains the metric most popular in practice and often favored by regulators. Put simply, VaR is an estimate of the maximum loss that will occur over a given time period (τ) for a specified significance level (α). For example, if VaR is estimated to be \$X with $\alpha = 5\%$ and $\tau = 1$ day, there is a 95% chance

---

[1]Obvious examples include the 1973 oil embargo, the stock market crash in October 1987, the Asian currency crisis in 1997, the Russian Ruble crisis and the collapse of the Long Term Capital Management fund in 1998, the technology bubble burst and California electricity crisis in early of 2000s, the US subprime mortgage crisis in 2008 and beyond, and the Eurozone sovereign debt crisis during 2009–2013.

Extreme Events in Finance: A Handbook of Extreme Value Theory and its Applications,
First Edition. Edited by François Longin.
© 2017 John Wiley & Sons, Inc. Published 2017 by John Wiley & Sons, Inc.

that losses over a 1-day period will not exceed \$X. In practice, the choice of the significance level (α) and the time horizon (τ) will vary depending on the particular VaR application on hand and the risk manager's risk attitude.[2]

Implementing VaR also requires a forecast of the distribution of τ-day profit/loss. While, at face value, VaR is an elementary concept, it is the forecast of this distribution that has attracted increasingly sophisticated statistical and econometric techniques. This is likely attributable, at least in part, to advances in available econometric tools. However, the increased importance of nontraditional markets, as well as the distinctive nature and behavior of assets traded therein, is also relevant.

Financial economists have long recognized that the distribution of asset returns is nonnormal, exhibiting fat tails and skewness. Further, rather than being constant, volatility varies through time, with episodes of high volatility tending to cluster. While these stylized facts are derived predominantly from studies of traditional assets, they are also acutely prominent amongst nontraditional securities. Power markets are an interesting case in point. Unlike commodities, electricity cannot be stored in space and time. Demand for electricity is highly sensitive to extreme weather conditions, yet inelastic to price. As a consequence, electricity prices display a number of distinctive characteristics, including seasonality, mean-reversion toward an equilibrium level (equal to the marginal cost), occasional negative values, time-varying volatility, and volatility clustering. Of particular relevance to estimating VaR, electricity prices feature temporal spikes of magnitudes that are uncommon in traditional financial markets.[3]

Individually and collectively, these distinctive features present challenges for market participants involved in trading and hedging electricity price risk. Given that VaR is essentially an estimate of tail probabilities, extreme value theory (EVT) is potentially well suited to the task of risk management in power markets. Rather than attempting to model the entire distribution of interest, EVT is primarily concerned with modeling the tails of a probability distribution. A parametric model can be chosen to accommodate a range of distributional shapes. Further, as Marimoutou et al. (2009) note, EVT allows each tail to be modeled separately, thereby accommodating asymmetry and nonstandard distributions.

This chapter illustrates the application of EVT to risk management in electricity markets. Two variations of the EVT approach to forecasting VaR are

---

[2]In some cases, regulation dictates the choice of parameters. For example, under the Basel II regulatory framework, banks using internal risk models to assess their market risk capital requirement must measure VaR at $\alpha = 1\%$ (i.e., 99% confidence level) over a $\tau = 10$-day holding period.

[3]There are a number of distinctive features underlying electricity prices. Intuitively, when compared to weekends, electricity usage is higher during weekdays (and especially during on-peak periods). Demand for electricity is also significantly higher during summer (reflecting cooling needs) and winter (reflecting heating needs). On rare occasions, electricity prices can even be negative, which occurs when electricity generators are reluctant to incur the substantial costs to starting up and shutting down power generators. Finally, temporal but nontrivial price spikes arise from occasional outages, which are a consequence of severe and abrupt weather conditions, resulting in unexpected constraints and failures in generation and transmission units. Knittel and Roberts (2005) and Geman and Roncoroni (2006) provide further discussion on the properties governing electricity prices.

explored. The first is a vanilla application of EVT to raw electricity returns. Second, conscious that electricity returns are unlikely to be independent and identically distributed (IID), EVT is applied to the residuals of a parametric model that serves to filter the data of heteroskedasticity and intertemporal dependence. The VaR forecasting performance of these EVT-based approaches is compared with that of a number of more traditional approaches including bootstrapping from historical returns, autoregressive (AR), and generalized autoregressive conditional heteroskedasticity (GARCH)-style models. In particular, we utilize the nonlinear generalized autoregressive conditional heteroskedasticity (NGARCH) specification suggested by Christoffersen (2009) for volatility forecasting for risk management, with explicit application to electricity power markets. Our most sophisticated parametric model combines an AR process for the mean returns with NGARCH modeling of conditional volatility. The second EVT-based approach mentioned above is then applied to the standardized residuals of this model.

For each model considered, we tabulate the VaR forecasting performance in terms of the frequency with which VaR forecasts of a given model are violated by actual electricity returns. These violation ratios (VRs) are augmented with formal statistical testing of unconditional and conditional coverage. Further, VaR forecasting performance is analyzed separately for violations in the left and right tails. Given the nonstandard distribution of electricity returns and notable differences across power markets, it is likely that the optimal approach to forecasting will depend on the tail and the market of interest.

In addition to traders operating in power markets, the findings of this study are potentially of interest to utility firms who, as providers of electricity to end consumers, face constant exposure to high electricity prices. These market participants often impose optimal trading limits to prevent extreme price fluctuations from adversely impacting firm profitability and allocate capital covering potential losses should the trading limits be breached.

The rest of this chapter is structured as follows. Section 15.2 overviews the development of EVT and the range of assets (traditional and nontraditional) to which it has been applied in the extant literature. Section 15.3 presents technical details of all models for which VaR forecasting performance will be compared. Section 15.4 contains the empirical analysis, including description of the European and US power markets, an in-sample fit of the model of interest, and, most importantly, a detailed analysis of each model's out-of-sample forecasting accuracy. Section 15.5 makes some concluding remarks.

15.2 PRIOR LITERATURE

While the statistical distribution theory pertaining to EVT is well established (Gumbel, 1958; Galambos, 1978; Leadbetter et al., 1983), its application to finance is notably more contemporary. Longin (1996) demonstrates several parametric and nonparametric approaches to estimating the parameters of the extreme value distribution. In an application of EVT to extreme stock market movements, he demonstrates that minimal and maximal returns follow a heavy-tailed Fréchet distribution. A number of other early EVT applications in finance (such as foreign exchange and equities) and insurance settings include Embrechts et al. (1997), McNeil (1997), Daníelsson and de Vries (1997, 2000), and Embrechts et al. (1999).

Building on this early literature, Longin (2000) develops an approach to VaR measurement that utilizes EVT to model the relevant tail probabilities. First, maximum likelihood is utilized to estimate the parameters of the asymptotic distribution of extreme returns, where the notion of "extreme" is relative to a chosen threshold. Second, VaR metrics are constructed using probabilities from the distribution of extreme returns (as opposed to probabilities from the full distribution of returns, as is traditionally the case in VaR measurement).[4] With one important modification, this approach is the basis for most EVT applications to VaR measurement. Acknowledging that asset returns are often non-IID, McNeil and Frey (2000) advocate a conditional approach whereby the volatility of returns are modeled using a GARCH process, and then EVT is applied to the standardized model residuals. While this still allows EVT to model the tails of distribution that are of interest in VaR estimation, it conditions on the current volatility background and generates GARCH-filtered residuals that are likely to be closer to IID.

A growing empirical literature provides support for the conditional EVT (i.e., GARCH-EVT) approach of McNeil and Frey (2000) in a variety of scenarios for both traditional and nontraditional assets. Examining the US and Swedish stock markets, Byström (2004) documents that the conditional-EVT approach provides more accurate VaR forecasts than non-EVT approaches, especially for the extreme tails (i.e., the superiority is more noticeable for $\alpha = 1\%$ than for $\alpha = 5\%$). Neftci (2000) and Bali (2003) adopt a vanilla EVT approach to derive VaR for US Treasury yield changes, while Bali and Neftci (2003) find that the conditional-EVT specification provides more accurate VaR forecasts in short-term interest rates than those afforded by a non-EVT GARCH-only model. Gençay and Selçuk (2004) reach a similar conclusion when comparing the relative performance of various models in forecasting VaR for stock returns in emerging markets. Similarly, Kuster et al. (2006) compare alternate methods in predicting VaR for the NASDAQ composite index returns, showing that the conditional-EVT approach performs best in general.

Despite the suitability of EVT-based applications to energy risk management, existing studies are sparse. Byström (2005) provides cautious support for the conditional-EVT approach using NordPool electricity prices over the period 1996–2000. Similarly, Chan and Gray (2006) find that a conditional-EVT model generates more accurate forecasts of VaR for several electricity markets (Australia, USA, Canada, New Zealand, NordPool) over the period 1998–2004. Krehbiel and Adkins (2005) also show that a conditional-EVT specification is more accurate than conventional approaches for forecasting VaR in most of the energy futures markets traded on New York Mercantile Exchange, including

---

[4]Daníelsson and de Vries (1997) and Embrechts et al. (1998) follow a similar process to VaR estimation, with the exception that the extreme value distribution is fitted semiparametrically. Longin (2000) highlights the advantage of parametric estimation for out-of-sample VaR computation.

crude oil, heating oil, and natural gas. Marimoutou et al. (2009) study risk management relating to crude oil prices over a long-time horizon spanning 1983 and 2007. While the conditional-EVT approach performs strongly, a non-EVT approach that bootstraps the residuals from a GARCH model also performs well.

15.3 SPECIFICATION OF VaR ESTIMATION APPROACHES

15.3.1 Historical Simulation (HS)

As a starting point, we estimate VaR using the simple, yet popular, historical simulation (HS) approach. Rather than making an arbitrary parametric assumption about the true (but unknown) return distribution, HS draws on the distribution of historical returns. At any point in time t, the T most recent daily return observations represent the empirical distribution. The next-day estimate of VaR_{t+1} is given by the $q\%$ quantile of this empirical distribution:

$$\text{VaR}_{t+1} = \text{Quantile}\left\{\{r_t\}_{t-T}^t, q\right\}, \tag{15.1}$$

Consistent with Manganelli and Engle (2004), who note that it is common practice to utilize a rolling window of up to 2 years for HS approaches, we assume $T = 500$ days. If one requires the left-tail (downside) one-day VaR_{t+1} with $\alpha = 1\%$, one takes the $q = \alpha = 1\%$ quantile from the most recent 500 observed daily returns. Conversely, if the right-tail (upside) VaR_{t+1} is of special interest, one takes the $q = 1 - \alpha = 99\%$ quantile from the empirical distribution.

Naturally, the success of the HS approach to VaR estimation depends on the extent to which the prior distribution of returns is an adequate representation of future returns. Even though this assumption is reasonable, HS may still suffer from the fact that it is entirely unconditional – it makes no use of current information in the mean and volatility of the underlying process. The parametric approaches described next propose a variety of ways to incorporate conditioning information into the VaR forecast.

15.3.2 Autoregression with Constant Volatility (AR-ConVol)

Our first parametric approach to estimating VaR utilizes a first-order AR model for daily returns with constant volatility (hereafter denoted AR-ConVol):

$$r_t = \phi + \rho r_{t-1} + \varepsilon_t, \tag{15.2}$$

$$\varepsilon_t \sim N\left(0, \sigma^2\right), \tag{15.3}$$

where r_t is the daily returns and $|\rho| < 1$ controls the gradual convergence to price equilibrium. The AR-ConVol specification is sufficiently simple to be estimated using the ordinary least-squares method. At each point in time, a rolling window encompassing the previous 5 years' daily returns are utilized to fit the model.[5] The next-day VaR_{t+1} is computed as

$$\text{VaR}_{t+1} = \hat{\phi} + \hat{\rho} r_t + F^{-1}(q)\hat{\sigma}, \tag{15.4}$$

where $\hat{\Omega} = \{\hat{\phi}, \hat{\rho}, \hat{\sigma}\}$ are the parameter estimates from Eqs (15.2) and (15.3), and $F^{-1}(q)$ is the desired $q\%$ quantile of the standard normal distribution function.

15.3.3 Auto-regression with Time-Varying Volatility (AR-NGARCH)

In light of extensive empirical evidence refuting constant volatility in asset returns, the second parametric model relaxes the constant volatility assumption defined in Eq. (15.3). Denoted AR-NGARCH, the first-order autoregression is augmented by assuming that the return innovations follow a time-varying conditional variance process:

$$r_t = \phi + \rho r_{t-1} + \varepsilon_t, \tag{15.5}$$

$$\varepsilon_t | \Xi_{t-1} \sim N\left(0, h_t\right), \tag{15.6}$$

$$h_t = \beta_0 + \beta_1\left(\varepsilon_{t-1} - \theta\sqrt{h_{t-1}}\right)^2 + \beta_2 h_{t-1}, \tag{15.7}$$

where Ξ_{t-1} is the information set at time $t-1$ and h_t is the conditional variance process.[6]

The extant literature boasts many possible specifications for the conditional variance process. In modeling oil returns, Marimoutou et al. (2009) adopt a (symmetric) GARCH process. For electricity returns, however, a specification that captures positive leverage effects is desirable. Knittel and Roberts (2005) argue that the convex nature of the marginal costs of electricity generation causes positive demand shocks to have a greater impact on volatility than negative shocks. Accordingly, Eq. (15.7) represents the nonlinear, asymmetric GARCH process introduced by Engle and Ng (1993) and advocated by Christoffersen (2009) for the purpose

---

[5]In a similar vein, all parametric and semiparametric models described in this section are estimated using a rolling 5-year window.

[6]The unconditional (long-run) variance of h_t is given by

$$E\left(h_t\right) = \frac{\beta_0}{1 - \beta_1\left(1 + \theta^2\right) - \beta_2} \equiv \frac{\beta_0}{k},$$

where $k = 1 - \beta_1(1 + \theta^2) - \beta_2$ refers to the speed of mean reversion in the conditional variance process. Following Christoffersen (2009), we restrict $k > 0$ during the optimization procedure to ensure variance stationarity of the model.

of forecasting volatility for risk management. The parameter θ captures asymmetric, nonlinear volatility behavior. For $\theta < 0$, a positive shock on day $t-1$ increases current volatility by more than a negative shock of the same magnitude.

Given the normality assumption in (15.6), the AR-NGARCH model is estimated by the maximum likelihood approach. The next-day VaR_{t+1} is computed in a manner similar to Eq. (15.4), with the exception that the constant volatility $\hat{\sigma}$ is replaced with the time-varying estimate $\hat{h}_{t+1}$:

$$VaR_{t+1} = \hat{\phi} + \hat{\rho} r_t + F^{-1}(q)\sqrt{\hat{h}_{t+1}}, \tag{15.8}$$

$$\hat{h}_{t+1} = \hat{\beta}_0 + \hat{\beta}_1\left(\varepsilon_t - \hat{\theta}\sqrt{h_t}\right)^2 + \hat{\beta}_2 h_t. \tag{15.9}$$

15.3.4 AR-NGARCH with No Distributional Assumption (Filteredhs)

While the HS approach is appealing due to its nonparametric nature, it ignores potentially useful information in the volatility dynamics (Marimoutou et al., 2009). Following Hull and White (1998), Barone-Adesi et al. (1999), and Marimoutou et al. (2009), we attempt to capture the best of both worlds by combining the distribution-free flavor of the HS approach with the conditional variance dynamics in AR-NGARCH.

The AR-NGARCH model given by Eqs. (15.5)–(15.7) is estimated as described above. However, rather than relying on the normal distribution function $F^{-1}(q)$ as in Eq. (15.8), VaR estimation draws on the empirical distribution of filtered residuals (hence, the approach is denoted *filteredHS*). The residuals from (15.5) are standardized by the conditional volatility estimates $\sqrt{\hat{h}_t}$ from Eq. (15.7):

The next-day VaR_{t+1} is then computed as

$$VaR_{t+1} = \hat{\phi} + \hat{\rho} r_t + \sqrt{\hat{h}_{t+1}}\,\text{Quantile}\left\{\{\hat{z}_t\}_{t-500}^t, q\right\}, \tag{15.11}$$

where the residuals $\{\hat{z}_t\}_{t-500}^t$ are standardized residuals. While the AR-NGARCH parameters are estimated using a 5-year rolling window period, to maintain consistency with the HS approach, the tail quantiles are constructed by bootstrapping from the 500 most recent standardized residuals.

$$\hat{z}_t = \frac{r_t - \left(\hat{\phi} - \hat{\rho} r_{t-1}\right)}{\sqrt{\hat{h}_t}}, \tag{15.10}$$

15.3.5 EVT Approaches

Whereas the parametric AR-ConVol and AR-NGARCH approaches model the entire return distribution, EVT focuses on the part that is of primary interest in risk management (i.e., the tail). Explicitly modeling tail behavior seems natural in VaR applications. Following recent literature, the peak over threshold method is used to identify extreme observations that exceed a high threshold u (which is defined below). EVT is then used to specifically model these "exceedences."

Let x_i denote a sequence of IID random variables from an unknown distribution function. For a chosen threshold u, the magnitude of each exceedence is $y_i = x_i - u$ for $i = 1, \ldots, N_y$, where N_y is the total number of exceedences. The probability that x exceeds u by an amount no greater than y, given that $x > u$, is

$$F_u(y) = \Pr(x - u \leq y | x > u),$$

$$= \frac{F_x(y + u) - F_x(u)}{1 - F_x(u)}. \tag{15.12}$$

Balkema and de Haan (1974) and Pickands (1975) show that $F_u(y)$ can be approximated by the generalized Pareto distribution (GPD)

$$G(y) = \begin{cases} 1 - \left(1 + \dfrac{\xi y}{v}\right)^{-1/\xi} & \text{if } \xi \neq 0, \\ 1 - \exp(-y/v) & \text{if } \xi = 0, \end{cases} \tag{15.13}$$

where ξ and v are the shape and scale parameters, respectively. Interestingly, the GPD subsumes various distributions, with $\xi > 0$ corresponding to heavy-tailed distributions (such as Pareto, Cauchy, and Fréchet), $\xi = 0$ corresponding to thin-tailed distributions (such as Gumbel, normal, exponential, gamma, and lognormal), and $\xi < 0$ corresponding to finite distributions (such as uniform and beta distributions). By setting $x = y + u$ and rearranging Eq. (15.12), we obtain

$$F_x(x) = \left[1 - F_x(u)\right] F_u(y) + F_x(u). \tag{15.14}$$

Noting that the function $F_x(u)$ can be estimated by its empirical counterpart as $(T - N_y)/T$, where T refers to the total sample observations, and after substituting Eq. (15.14) into (15.12), we obtain

$$F_x(x) = 1 - \frac{N_y}{T}\left(1 + \frac{\xi(x - u)}{v}\right)^{-1/\xi}. \tag{15.15}$$

The next-day VaR_{t+1} for a given $\alpha\%$ is computed by inverting (15.15):

$$\text{VaR}_{t+1} = F_x^{-1}(q) = u + \frac{v}{\xi}\left[\left(\frac{T\alpha}{N_y}\right)^{-\xi} - 1\right]. \tag{15.16}$$

Critically, the EVT procedure depends on the threshold u chosen to define exceedences. The choice of u involves a tradeoff. On one hand, u must be set sufficiently high to maintain the asymptotic theory of EVT and generate unbiased estimates of the GPD parameters (particularly the shape variable ξ). On the other hand, if

u is set too high, there may be too few exceedences from which to estimate ξ and v. Guided by Hull (2010) and Christoffersen (2012), we set u such that the most positive (most negative) 5% of observations are used to estimate ξ and v in the right (left) tail of the distribution. Given u, the parameters (ξ, v) of the GPD equation (15.13) are estimated by maximum likelihood, and then substituted into (15.16) along with the known values of T, N_y, α, and u to calculate VAR.

Two variations of the EVT approach are explored. First, the approach described above is applied to the raw data. That is, x_t is simply the daily electricity return r_t. This vanilla application is simply denoted as "EVT." The second approach recognizes that raw electricity returns are unlikely to be IID. With this in mind, McNeil and Frey (2000) advocate applying EVT (as described above) to the "filtered" residuals from a parametric model. Specifically, we fit the AR-NGARCH model Eqs (15.5)–(15.7) as described in Section 15.3.3. Model residuals are then filtered as in Eq. (15.10) and EVT is applied to these standardized residuals. This approach is denoted condEVT. The corresponding next-day VaR$_{t+1}$ is computed in a manner to Eq. (15.11), with the exception that the normally distributed quantile $F^{-1}(q)$ is replaced by the EVT tail estimator $F_x^{-1}(q)$ defined in Eq. (15.16).

To summarize, the empirical analysis will explore the relative merits of a number of alternate approaches to estimating VaR for electricity markets. The approaches range from a simple, nonparametric, HS approach through to a sophisticated approach that applies EVT to the filtered residuals of a model that accommodates mean-reverting returns and nonlinear, asymmetric, time-varying volatility (i.e., the condEVT model).

15.4 EMPIRICAL ANALYSIS

15.4.1 Data

The empirical analysis features two prominent European power markets (European Energy Exchange EEX Phelix in Germany, and PowerNext PWX in France) and one of the major power markets operating in the United States (Pennsylvania, New Jersey, and Maryland; PJM). Daily peak load prices are sourced from DataStream over the period from January 3, 2006 to December 20, 2013 (2010 days). As such, this sample period represents a significant update on the time horizons utilized in prior work (e.g., Chan and Gray, 2006; Huisman et al., 2007; Klüppelberg et al., 2010; Lindström and Regland, 2012).

For each power market, Table 15.1 reports the basic summary statistics that depict daily continuously compounded returns, that is, $r_t = \ln\left(p_t/p_{t-1}\right) \times 100$. Figure 15.1 plots the time series of daily prices (left panels) and continuously compounded returns (right panels). Arguably, if one ignores the scale, the diagrams resemble those commonly observed for traditional assets (or, at least, traditional assets with stationary prices). Prices, while highly volatile, revert to mean. Each market exhibits a number of extreme price movements. Volatility clustering is readily apparent.

TABLE 15.1   Descriptive statistics

	EEX	PWX	PJM
Mean	0.00	−0.03	−0.03
Std. dev.	22.19	20.02	27.13
Skewness	−0.18	0.06	0.04
Excess kurtosis	7.54	13.30	3.37
Jacque–Bera statistic	4777***	14,805***	954***
$Q(1)$	247.78***	178.85***	145.11***
$Q^2(1)$	388.45***	281.19***	34.50***
Minimum	−138.31	−142.72	−133.36
Prctile 1%	−77.97	−65.39	−73.33
Prctile 5%	−31.51	−25.48	−43.43
Prctile 25%	−8.60	−6.86	−14.16
Prctile 50%	0.08	−0.06	0.00
Prctile 75%	8.61	6.43	14.76
Prctile 95%	31.81	27.62	41.94
Prctile 99%	69.46	60.48	72.85
Maximum	136.92	145.53	174.56

This table reports summary statistics for daily returns on the EEX, PWX, and PJM power markets over the period covering January 3, 2006 to December 20, 2013 (2010 days). From daily peak load prices, continuously compounded returns are calculated. All returns are stated on a daily basis in percentage (i.e., multiplied by 100). $Q(1)$ and $Q^2(1)$ are the respective Ljung–Box Q-statistics for first-order autocorrelation in returns and squared returns. *** indicates statistical significance at the 1% level.

In the VaR context of this study, the fundamental differences between electricity markets and traditional markets come to the fore when the scale of the diagrams is considered. The magnitude of price movements, and therefore resulting returns, are rarely seen in stock markets. In fact, the electricity movements dwarf even oil markets, despite oil prices being highly vulnerable to economic, political, and military events.[7] A case in point surrounds the unrelenting US heatwave of July 2013, when temperatures exceeded 100 °F. PJM peak load price jumped from $98/MW h on July 17, 2013 to $162/MW h the following day. After remaining around this level for a further day, price reverted to $47/MW h.

Figure 15.1 exhibits movements of this magnitude regularly throughout the sample, with obvious consequences for the distribution of returns. While the mean daily return is near zero in each market, the standard deviation is several orders of magnitude higher. The interquartile range and skewness statistics suggest that electricity returns have a near-symmetric distribution. However, the probability mass in each tail far exceeds a normal distribution, with the Jarque–Bera statistic overwhelmingly rejecting the null of normality.[8] Further, both positive and negative extreme returns are well represented in the distribution of returns. This is

---

[7]See, for instance, Figures 1 and 2 of Marimoutou et al. (2009) for examples of typical oil price movements.

[8]Chan and Gray (2006) utilize simple returns and document severe positive skewness in daily electricity returns. Here, the logarithmic transformation of continuous compounding serves to diminish the

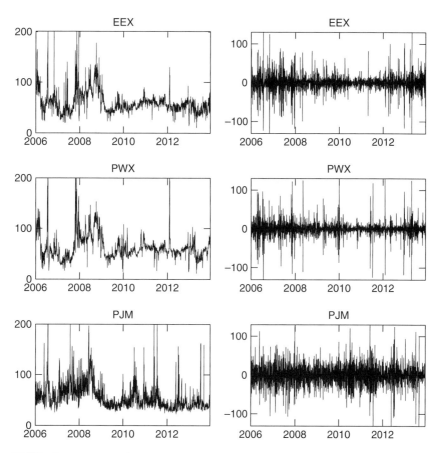

FIGURE 15.1 **Time Series Plots of Prices and Returns. Data are daily peak load prices for the EEX, PWX, and PJM power markets over the sample period covering January 3, 2006 and December 20, 2013. The left panel plots daily spot prices, while the right panel plots the corresponding daily continuously compounded returns (in %). For ease of comparison, the *y*-axis in the left and right panels are truncated between 0 and 200, and between −130% and +130%, respectively.**

relevant to our study of VaR in both left and right tails. Together, Table 15.1 and Figure 15.1 demonstrate the unique characteristics of the power markets: high volatility, volatility clustering, and infrequent extreme movements that result in a fat-tailed return distribution. This casual empiricism provides strong motivation to study various alternative model specifications, particularly the EVT-based models, to forecast VaR.

---

magnitude of (extreme positive) returns and reduce skewness. Even so, Table 15.1 and Figure 15.1 shown in the present study document extremely large returns.

15.4.2   Parameter Estimates

With the exception of the purely nonparametric HS approach, the alternate approaches to forecasting VaR require an estimate of the parameters of each model. While Section 15.4.3 describes a rolling estimation approach used to generate a series of VaR forecasts, we begin by simply fitting the main model of interest, the condEVT specification, over the entire sample between 2006 and 2013. Table 15.2 presents the parameter estimates and corresponding standard errors (in parentheses) that are computed using the quasi-maximum likelihood (QML) procedure of Bollerslev and Wooldridge (1992).

For each power market, returns are negatively autocorrelated ($\rho < 0$), suggesting that a large positive (negative) return on a given day is followed by a large negative (positive) return the next day. This is likely to be driven at least in part by the occurrence of large temporary spikes in electricity prices. Each market also exhibits clear GARCH effects (β_1 and β_2 significant). Curiously, the direction of the leverage effect in volatility shocks (θ) differs between markets. In PJM, a positive prior-day shock increases current volatility by more than a negative shock of the same magnitude ($\theta < 0$). For EEX and PWX, the reverse is true.

The final two rows in Panel A reports the corresponding statistics of the shape (ξ) and scale (v) parameters of the EVT framework, estimated by fitting the GPD distribution to the standardized residuals defined in Eq. (15.10). Estimates of ξ and v are calculated separately for the left and right tails of the distribution. The left tail is of primary concern to utility- and electricity-provider firms since they have a short position in electricity. On the other hand, when electricity prices increase, electricity buyers such as retailers incur losses because they have a long position with the providers and generators. As such, electricity buyers are more interested with the extreme right tail of the distribution.

Recall that values of $\xi > 0$ are indicative of heavy-tailed distributions. In the right tail, ξ is positive for all three power markets, corroborating the casual empiricism provided in Figure 15.1 that the distribution of standardized residuals follows a Fréchet distribution. In the left tail, EEX and PWR markets also exhibit fat tails, while ξ is negative for PJM.

Panel B provides an indication of how far the tail behavior deviates from normality. The condEVT model is fitted using a rolling in-sample period (the procedure is described in full in Section 15.4.3). For each day in the out-of-sample period, the right- and left-tail quantiles $F_x^{-1}(q)$, defined in Eq. (15.16), (in absolute values) are estimated for $\alpha = 5\%$, 1%, 0.5%. Panel B then reports the time-series mean of the daily quantile estimates.

For comparison, note that the tail quantiles $F^{-1}(q)$ (in absolute values) from a normal distribution for the respective q's are 1.645, 2.326, and 2.576, respectively. The estimates provided in Panel B reveal that the tail quantiles from the condEVT model are higher than those of the normal distribution especially when we move to more extreme quantiles at $q = 99\%$ and $q = 99.5\%$, with the empirical right-tail fatness even more apparent for the PJM power market.

TABLE 15.2   In-sample parameter estimates of condEVT model

	EEX	PWX	PJM
	Panel A		
ϕ	−0.826	−0.647	2.462
	(0.022)	(0.008)	(0.021)
ρ	−0.345	−0.304	−0.292
	(0.019)	(0.032)	(0.008)
β_0	24.063	31.839	42.991
	(0.605)	(1.205)	(0.395)
β_1	0.205	0.276	0.089
	(0.021)	(0.015)	(0.008)
β_2	0.761	0.681	0.715
	(0.022)	(0.012)	(0.007)
θ	0.149	0.065	−1.373
	(0.018)	(0.004)	(0.007)
ξ (right tail)	0.046	0.089	0.129
	(0.105)	(0.109)	(0.113)
v (right tail)	0.551	0.650	0.881
	(0.08)	(0.096)	(0.132)
ξ (left tail)	0.278	0.639	−0.038
	(0.128)	(0.164)	(0.096)
v (left tail)	0.769	0.530	0.796
	(0.123)	(0.096)	(0.11)
	Panel B		
$q = 95\%$ (right tail)	1.459	1.361	2.266
$q = 99\%$ (right tail)	2.421	2.384	3.724
$q = 99.5\%$ (right tail)	2.887	2.947	4.446
$q = 95\%$ (left tail)	1.591	1.496	2.232
$q = 99\%$ (left tail)	3.151	2.982	3.476
$q = 99.5\%$ (left tail)	4.069	4.271	3.988

Panel A reports QML parameter estimates and the corresponding standard errors (in parentheses) for the condEVT model for the EEX, PWX, and PJM markets. The model is estimated over the full sample period covering January 3, 2006 to December 20, 2013. Panel B reports the sample mean for the EVT right- and left-tail quantiles $F_x^{-1}(q)$ (in absolute values) of the standardized residuals; the sample mean is estimated based on a rolling series of 750 parameter estimates of the EVT corresponding right- and left-tail quantiles from January 4, 2011 to December 20, 2013. For comparison, the tail quantiles $F^{-1}(q)$ (in absolute values) of a normal distribution for $q = 95\%$, 99%, and 99.5% are equal to 1.645, 2.326, and 2.576, respectively.

15.4.3   VaR Forecasting

In order to compare the various approaches, we generate a series of VaR forecasts over an out-of-sample period. For each parametric approach, this requires an estimate of model parameters.[9] With a relatively modest time series available, it is a delicate tradeoff between the length of in-sample period used for parameter estimation and the length of the out-of-sample period used to compare performance. For each parametric approach, we employ a rolling in-sample estimation window of approximately 5 years. The initial in-sample period spans January 3, 2006 through December 31, 2010 (1260 days). Parameter estimates from each model are used to forecast next-day VaR_{t+1} (on January 3, 2011). Rolling forward one day, VaR on January 4, 2011 is based on parameters estimated over January 4, 2006 and January 3, 2011. This procedure is repeated to generate VaR forecasts for a total of 750 out-of-sample days spanning January 3, 2011 through December 20, 2013.

Out-of-sample VaR forecasting performance of the competing models is assessed using a VR. The VR for the right (left) tail is calculated as the percentage of positive (negative) realized returns that exceed (fall below) the VaR predicted by a particular model. If, for example, $\alpha = 1\%$ and given that there are a total of 750 observations in the out-of-sample period, violations are expected on approximately 7–8 days. The competing models are then ranked according to how close their actual VRs are to the expected rates.

Consistent with prior studies, we also utilize statistical metrics of forecasting accuracy. First, the unconditional coverage test statistic (LR_{uc}) assesses whether the actual VR is statistically different from the expected failure rate. The no-difference null is rejected if a model generates either too many or too few violations. Second, following Christoffersen (1998), we employ the conditional coverage test (LR_{cc}) that jointly tests unconditional coverage and whether VaR violations are independently distributed across time. Under this test, the null hypothesis that the VaR approach is accurate is rejected if the violations are too many, too few, or too clustered in time. A third test, which also follows from Christoffersen (1998), examines the independence property of VaR violations through time (LR_{ind}).[10] For each of the six competing models, Tables 15.3 and 15.4 report the respective out-of-sample performance relating to the right and left tails of the distribution. For each market, a range of significance levels is examined, that is, $\alpha = \{5\%, 1\%, 0.5\%\}$.

Table 15.3 provides strong support for the use of EVT-based approaches to VaR forecasting. The vanilla EVT and condEVT approaches rank in the top two in every case (rankings shown in brackets), with the exception of PJM and EEX for $\alpha = 5\%$ and $\alpha = 0.5\%$, respectively. For example, for EEX with $\alpha = 5\%$, VaR forecasts under the conditional EVT approach are violated on 5.47% of the out-of-sample days. Similarly, the vanilla EVT approach has an actual VR of 6.00%. In contrast, forecasts under the HS approach are violated in 8.67%

---

[9]As noted in Section 15.3.1, the purely nonparametric HS approach simply uses the 500 most recent returns to approximate the empirical distribution.

[10]Interested readers are referred to Christoffersen (1998, 2012) for technical details of the tests.

TABLE 15.3 Out-of-sample VaR forecasting accuracy (right tail)

	VR	Rank	LR$_{uc}$	LR$_{ind}$	LR$_{cc}$	VR	Rank	LR$_{uc}$	LR$_{ind}$	LR$_{cc}$	VR	Rank	LR$_{uc}$	LR$_{ind}$	LR$_{cc}$
			EEX					PWX					PJM		
α = 5%															
HS	8.67	(4)	**16.50**	0.42	**16.92**	5.73	(3)	0.83	**12.51**	**13.34**	4.93	(1)	0.01	0.49	0.49
AR-ConVol	4.53	(1)	0.34	**5.62**	**5.97**	3.47	(4)	**4.11**	**25.25**	**29.35**	5.07	(1)	0.01	0.00	0.01
AR-NGARCH	4.00	(2)	2.17	0.03	2.19	2.27	(6)	**14.63**	3.68	**18.31**	9.20	(4)	**22.65**	0.02	**22.68**
filteredHS	2.80	(3)	**8.98**	**9.73**	**18.71**	7.33	(5)	**6.81**	**19.69**	**26.50**	11.07	(5)	**42.28**	1.10	**43.37**
EVT	6.00	(2)	1.51	0.04	1.55	4.93	(1)	0.01	**4.32**	4.33	5.33	(2)	0.18	0.01	0.19
condEVT	5.47	(1)	0.18	0.89	1.07	4.53	(2)	0.58	1.31	1.89	6.40	(3)	2.88	2.10	4.98
α = 1%															
HS	1.87	(3)	**4.55**	0.53	5.08	1.87	(3)	**4.55**	0.53	5.08	1.33	(2)	0.77	0.27	1.04
AR-ConVol	2.53	(4)	**12.53**	**11.34**	**23.87**	1.87	(3)	**4.55**	**10.34**	**14.89**	2.00	(3)	**5.89**	1.07	**6.97**
AR-NGARCH	0.53	(2)	1.98	0.04	2.02	0.67	(2)	0.95	0.07	1.01	4.93	(5)	**60.37**	0.02	**60.39**
filteredHS	1.07	(1)	0.03	0.17	0.21	3.73	(4)	**33.40**	**28.15**	**61.55**	4.67	(4)	**53.94**	0.31	**54.25**
EVT	1.47	(2)	1.45	0.33	1.78	1.20	(1)	0.29	0.22	0.51	1.33	(2)	0.77	0.27	1.04
condEVT	0.53	(2)	1.98	0.04	2.02	0.67	(2)	0.95	0.07	1.01	1.20	(1)	0.29	0.22	0.51
α = 0.5%															
HS	1.20	(4)	**5.31**	0.22	5.53	0.80	(3)	1.15	0.10	1.25	0.93	(3)	2.26	0.13	2.39
AR-ConVol	1.60	(5)	**11.53**	**6.34**	**17.87**	1.47	(4)	**9.27**	**7.05**	**16.32**	1.60	(4)	**11.53**	1.80	**13.33**
AR-NGARCH	0.27	(1)	0.98	0.01	1.00	0.67	(1)	0.38	0.07	0.45	4.13	(6)	**77.54**	0.38	**77.92**
filteredHS	0.93	(3)	2.26	0.13	2.39	3.07	(5)	**45.49**	**17.87**	**63.35**	3.07	(5)	**45.49**	0.12	**45.60**
EVT	0.93	(3)	2.26	0.13	2.39	0.67	(1)	0.38	0.07	0.45	0.80	(2)	1.15	0.10	1.25
condEVT	0.13	(2)	2.86	0.00	2.86	0.27	(2)	0.98	0.01	1.00	0.67	(1)	0.38	0.07	0.45

The table reports the out-of-sample violation ratios (VR), the model rankings (in parentheses), as well as the likelihood ratio test statistics for unconditional coverage (LR$_{uc}$), independence (LR$_{ind}$), and conditional coverage (LR$_{cc}$) of the right tail of the distribution for all six competing models. Bold test statistics indicate statistical significance at the 5% level or below. The out-of-sample period covers January 3, 2011 to December 20, 2013 (750 days).

TABLE 15.4 Out-of-sample VaR forecasting accuracy (left tail)

	VR	Rank	LRuc	LRind	LRcc	VR	Rank	LRuc	LRind	LRcc	VR	Rank	LRuc	LRind	LRcc
			EEX					PWX					PJM		
α = 5%															
HS	7.33	(3)	**7.61**	0.34	**7.95**	6.00	(3)	1.51	0.04	1.55	3.87	(4)	2.17	0.61	2.78
AR-ConVol	4.80	(1)	0.06	0.04	0.10	2.93	(5)	**7.83**	**9.01**	**16.83**	3.73	(5)	2.74	2.71	5.45
AR-NGARCH	7.73	(4)	**10.24**	0.07	**10.31**	4.40	(2)	0.58	0.17	0.75	10.00	(6)	**31.09**	**10.28**	**41.36**
filteredHS	10.13	(6)	**32.60**	2.59	**35.19**	8.13	(6)	**13.21**	2.62	**15.83**	5.60	(3)	0.56	4.99	5.55
EVT	6.40	(2)	2.88	0.00	2.89	4.67	(1)	0.17	1.03	1.20	4.67	(2)	0.17	0.08	0.26
condEVT	8.93	(5)	**20.09**	0.89	**20.98**	6.67	(4)	**4.02**	2.50	**6.53**	5.07	(1)	0.01	4.06	4.07
α = 1%															
HS	1.60	(3)	2.32	1.80	4.12	1.20	(2)	0.29	2.85	3.14	1.07	(1)	0.03	3.31	3.35
AR-ConVol	2.80	(5)	**16.53**	1.21	**17.74**	1.73	(4)	3.36	**5.70**	**9.06**	1.33	(3)	0.77	2.45	3.22
AR-NGARCH	3.07	(6)	**20.92**	1.46	**22.37**	2.00	(5)	**5.89**	0.61	**6.50**	4.93	(4)	**60.37**	**3.85**	**64.22**
filteredHS	1.47	(2)	1.45	0.33	1.78	1.07	(1)	0.03	0.17	0.21	1.20	(2)	0.29	0.22	0.51
EVT	1.73	(4)	3.36	0.46	3.82	1.33	(3)	0.77	0.27	1.04	1.20	(2)	0.29	2.85	3.14
condEVT	1.20	(1)	0.29	0.22	0.51	1.07	(1)	0.03	0.17	0.21	1.20	(2)	0.29	0.22	0.51
α = 0.5%															
HS	0.80	(2)	1.15	0.10	1.25	0.53	(1)	0.02	0.04	0.06	0.67	(2)	0.38	0.07	0.45
AR-ConVol	2.53	(5)	**31.52**	0.99	**32.51**	1.60	(4)	**11.53**	**6.34**	**17.87**	1.20	(5)	**5.31**	2.85	**8.16**
AR-NGARCH	1.87	(4)	**16.55**	0.53	**17.09**	1.73	(5)	**13.96**	0.46	**14.42**	3.33	(6)	**53.02**	1.73	**54.75**
filteredHS	0.67	(1)	0.38	0.07	0.45	0.40	(2)	0.16	0.02	0.18	0.40	(1)	0.16	0.02	0.18
EVT	0.80	(2)	1.15	0.10	1.25	0.80	(3)	1.15	0.10	1.25	0.93	(4)	2.26	0.13	2.39
condEVT	1.07	(3)	3.66	0.17	3.83	0.80	(3)	1.15	0.10	1.25	0.80	(3)	1.15	0.10	1.25

The table reports the out-of-sample violation ratios (VR), the model rankings (in parentheses), as well as the likelihood ratio test statistics for unconditional coverage (LR_{uc}), independence (LR_{ind}), and conditional coverage (LR_{cc}) of the left tail of the distribution for all six competing models. Bold test statistics indicate statistical significance at the 5% level or below. The out-of-sample period covers January 3, 2011 to December 20, 2013 (750 days).

of cases. Comparing the two EVT-based approaches, no clear winner is evident across Table 15.3. Arguably, applying EVT to the distribution of raw returns is of comparable reliability to the more sophisticated condEVT approach that applies EVT to the filtered model residuals.

The success of EVT-based approaches is also evident in the statistical tests. Twenty-seven statistical tests are presented for each approach in Table 15.3 (rejections at the 5% level of significance are indicated in bold). The condEVT approach records no rejections, while the vanilla EVT approach records a single rejection (the independence test in PWX for $\alpha = 5\%$).

With respect to the non-EVT parametric approaches, it is not readily apparent that more sophisticated approaches to modeling volatility are justified. The relative rankings of AR-ConVol, AR-NGARCH, and filteredHS vary widely across Table 15.3. Curiously, the performance of the semiparametric filteredHS, which bootstraps from the filtered model residuals, is underwhelming. This is in sharp contrast to applications in oil markets, where Marimoutou et al. (2009) document that its performance rivals the condEVT approach.

Taken as a whole, the out-of-sample testing of competing approaches to VaR forecasting in the right tail provides strong support for the use of EVT-based approaches. Even a vanilla EVT application to raw (unfiltered) returns generates forecasts of risk exposures that are superior to traditional approaches to risk management.

Table 15.4 presents a similar analysis of left-tail performance, a result which is of particular interest to plant generators and electricity providers since they naturally have a short position in electricity. Examining the rankings of competing approaches, it is readily apparent that no single method dominates across all power markets and significance levels (α). This is in sharp contrast to the right-tail analysis of Table 15.3, where the EVT-based approaches ranked highly in most cases. With the exception of the AR-NGARCH approach, each method ranks first in at least one scenario. While the filteredHS approach performs poorly for $\alpha = 5\%$, it ranks consistently in the top two for higher levels of significance, that is, $\alpha = \{1\%, 0.5\%\}$. In terms of statistical inferences, the two EVT-based approaches generate no significant violations for $\alpha = \{0.5\%, 1\%\}$. However, the same is also true for the HS and filteredHS approaches.

To conclude, it is useful to compare and contrast the findings from Tables 15.3 and 15.4 across the three power markets. With respect to the right tail (Table 15.3), casual empiricism suggests that the PJM market is fundamentally different from EEX and PWX. To illustrate, for $\alpha = 5\%$ in EEX, some forecasting approaches underestimate the risk exposure (e.g., HS, 8.67%; EVT, 6.00%), while others overestimate risk (AR-NGARCH, 4.00%; filteredHS, 2.80%). Similar findings occur for the PWX market. In contrast, risk exposures in the PJM market are underestimated in nearly all cases (VR > α). This is true for all levels of α. The possible idiosyncrasies of PJM were highlighted in relation to Table 15.2, where the leverage effect (θ) for PJM differed notably from the other markets. Similarly, the fatness of the tail (ξ) of filtered model residuals was most pronounced for PJM.

In terms of statistical performance, several other idiosyncrasies are observed. The right tail analysis (Table 15.3) suggests that the PWX market behaves differently with respect to the assumption that VaR violations are distributed independently through time. Whereas the other markets display very few rejections of independence, LR_{ind} is significant for many combinations of forecasting model and α in the PWX market. Curiously, the lack of independence for PWX is confined to the right tail; there are very few significant LR_{ind} statistics in Table 15.4. Table 15.4 also flags EEX as a difficult market in which to forecast left tail violations. Although not attributable to lack of independence, EEX exhibits many rejections of unconditional coverage (LR_{uc}). Perhaps not surprisingly, EEX stands out in Table 15.2 as being the only market for which the distribution of returns is negatively skewed.

15.5   CONCLUSION

The importance of risk management is paramount for participants in a wide range of markets. The recent development of markets in nontraditional securities, coupled with prominent episodes of extreme volatility, only serves to heighten interest in risk management tools. Power markets are a prime example where recent deregulation in many countries has resulted in the rapid emergence of markets for electricity. While these markets share some features in common with traditional markets (e.g., volatility clustering and nonnormal return distributions), they are also are characterized by extreme jumps and levels of volatility rarely observed in traditional financial securities. Naturally, these distinctive features present unique challenges for market participants involved in trading and hedging electricity price risk.

Given that EVT explicitly models the tails of a distribution, as opposed to attempting to model the entire distribution, it is *ex ante* well suited to risk management practices such as VaR. This chapter explored the usefulness of EVT for risk management in electricity markets. The VaR forecasting accuracy of two EVT-based approaches was compared with those of a range of more traditional approaches (e.g., bootstrapping and AR-GARCH-style parametric models). The out-of-sample forecasting accuracy of each model was documented in terms of the frequency with which VaR forecasts are violated by actual daily returns, compared to expected violations rates for a given level of significance.

On the whole, out-of-sample testing provides cautious support for the potential usefulness of EVT in electricity risk management. This is particularly the case in the right-tail analysis, which is relevant to market participants (e.g., electricity retailers) engaged in buying electricity. Of the six competing VaR forecasting approaches examined, the two EVT-based approaches consistently rank highly. This is the case across the three markets examined and for all levels of significance considered. Curiously, a vanilla application of EVT to the distribution of raw returns appears to perform on par with a more sophisticated approach that applies EVT to the residuals of a parametric model. The empirical analysis is less emphatic when examining the left tail, where selecting an optimal approach to forecasting VaR proves to be a difficult task. The out-of-sample analysis fails to identify a method that performs consistently well. Rather, the optimal forecasting approach differs markedly, depending on the specific market under consideration and the level of significance chosen. This finding suggests that utility firms, power generators, and other traders who have long/short positions may need to carefully consider the idiosyncrasies of each power market to determine the approach best suited to risk management.

While EVT applications to risk management are still in their infancy, prior work has provided encouraging results that it is a potentially useful tool in both traditional financial markets and nontraditional markets (such as oil and electricity). This study lends further support to its application in power markets. In many circumstances, the practice of augmenting VaR with EVT generates forecasts that clearly outperform traditional forecasting approaches. However, the superiority of EVT-based approaches is not across the board, with the left tail of the distribution proving particularly challenging to model. Not only do electricity returns exhibit distinctive characteristics, but different power markets also appear to have idiosyncratic features. Risk management practice in these markets will benefit from future work that seeks to document and understand return behavior in each market, thereby further facilitating refinement of the approach chosen to forecast VaR.

Acknowledgment

We gratefully acknowledge Professor Longin (the Editor of this handbook) for his helpful suggestions.

References

Bali, T. An extreme value approach to estimating volatility and value at risk. Journal of Business 2003;**76**:83–107.

Bali, T., Neftci, S. Disturbing extremal behaviour of spot price dynamics. Journal of Empirical Finance 2003;**10**:455–477.

Balkema, A., de Haan, L. Residual lifetime at great age. Annals of Probability 1974;**2**:792–804.

Barone-Adesi, G., Giannopoulos, K., Vosper, L. VaR without correlations for portfolios of derivatives securities. Journal of Futures Markets 1999;**19**:583–602.

Bollerslev, T., Wooldridge, J. Quasi-maximum likelihood estimation and inference in dynamic models with time-varying covariances. Econometric Reviews 1992;**11**:143–172.

Byström, H. Managing extreme risks in tranquil and volatile markets using conditional extreme value theory. International Review of Economics and Finance 2004;**13**:133–152.

Byström, H. Extreme value theory and extremely large electricity price changes. International Review of Economics and Finance 2005;**14**:41–55.

Chan, K., Gray, P. Using extreme value theory to measure value-at-risk for daily electricity spot prices. International Journal of Forecasting 2006;**22**:283–300.

Christoffersen, P. Evaluating interval forecasts. Int Econ Rev 1998;**39**:841–862.

Christoffersen, P. Value-at-risk models. In: Andersen, T., Davis, R., Kreiss, J.-P., Mikosch, T., editors. *Handbook of Financial Time Series*. Berlin, Heidelberg: Springer-Verlag; 2009. p 753–766.

Christoffersen, P. *Elements of Financial Risk Management*. 2nd ed. Amsterdam: Academic Press; 2012.

Daníelsson, J., de Vries, C. Tail index and quantile estimation with very high frequency data. Journal of Empirical Finance 1997;**4**:241–257.

Daníelsson, J., de Vries, C. Value-at-risk and extreme returns. Annals of Economics and Statistics 2000;**60**:239–270.

Embrechts, P., Klüppelberg, C., Mikosch, T. *Modelling Extremal Events for Insurance and Finance*. Berlin: Springer; 1997.

Embrechts, P., Resnick, S., Samorodnitsky, G. Living on the edge. Risk 1998;**11**:96–100.

Embrechts, P., Resnick, S., Samorodnitsky, G. Extreme value theory as a risk management tool. North American Actuarial Journal 1999;**3**:30–41.

Engle, R., Ng, V. Measuring and testing the impact of news on volatility. Journal of Finance 1993;**48**:1749–1778.

Galambos, J. *The Asymptotic Theory of Extreme Order Statistics*. New York: Wiley; 1978.

Geman, H., Roncoroni, A. Understanding the fine structure of electricity prices. Journal of Business 2006;**79**:1225–1261.

Gençay, R., Selçuk, F. Extreme value theory and value-at-risk: relative performance in emerging markets. International Journal of Forecasting 2004;**20**:287–303.

Gumbel, E. *Statistics of Extremes*. New York: Columbia University Press; 1958.

Huisman, R., Huurman, C., Mahieu, R. Hourly electricity prices in day-ahead markets. Energy Economics 2007;**29**:240–248.

Hull, J. *Risk Management and Financial Institutions*. 2nd ed. New Jersey: Prentice-Hall; 2010.

Hull, J., White, A. Incorporating volatility updating into the historical simulation method for VaR. Journal of Risk 1998;**1**:5–19.

Klüppelberg, C., Meyer-Brandis, T., Schmidt, A. Electricity spot price modelling with a view towards extreme spike risk. Quantitative Finance 2010;**10**:963–974.

Knittel, C., Roberts, M. An empirical examination of restructured electricity prices. Energy Economics 2005;**27**:791–817.

Krehbiel, T., Adkins, L. Price risks in the NYMEX energy complex: an extreme value approach. Journal of Futures Markets 2005;**25**:309–337.

Kuster, K., Mittnik, S., Paolella, M. Value-at-risk prediction: a comparison of alternative strategies. Journal of Financial Econometrics 2006;**4**:53–89.

Leadbetter, M., Lindgren, G., Rootzèn, H. *Extremes and Related Properties of Random Sequences and Processes*. New York: Springer Verlag; 1983.

Lindström, E., Regland, F. Modeling extreme dependence between European electricity markets. Energy Economics 2012;**34**:899–904.

Longin, F. The asymptotic distribution of extreme stock market returns. Journal of Business 1996;**69**:383–408.

Longin, F. From value at risk to stress testing: the extreme value approach. Journal of Banking and Finance 2000;**24**:1097–1130.

Manganelli, S., Engle, R. A comparison of value-at-risk models in finance. In: Szegö G., editor. *Risk Measures for the 21st Century*. Chichester: Wiley; 2004. p 123–144.

Marimoutou, V., Raggad, B., Trabelsi, A. Extreme value theory and value at risk: application to oil market. Energy Economics 2009;**31**:519–530.

McNeil, A. Estimating the tails of loss severity distributions using extreme value theory. ASTIN Bull 1997;**27**:117–137.

McNeil, A., Frey, R. Estimation of tail-related risk measures for heteroscedasticity financial time series: an extreme value approach. Journal of Empirical Finance 2000;**7**:271–300.

Neftci, S. Value at risk calculations, extreme events, and tail estimation. Journal of Derivatives 2000;**7**:23–38.

Pickands, J. Statistical inference using extreme order statistics. Annals of Statistics 1975;**3**:119–131.

Chapter Sixteen

Margin Setting and Extreme Value Theory

John Cotter[1] and Kevin Dowd[2]

[1]*UCD School of Business, University College Dublin, Dublin, Ireland*
[2]*Economics and Finance, Durham University Business School, Durham, United Kingdom*

AMS 2000 subject classification. Primary 62G32, 62E20; Secondary 65C05.

16.1 INTRODUCTION

This chapter outlines some key issues in the modeling of futures margins using extreme value theory (EVT). We examine its application in the context of setting initial futures margins. There is a developing volume of literature that examines using EVT in setting margins, and this study provides an overview of the key issues that have been examined.[1] The chapter illustrates how EVT can be a useful approach in the setting of margins with examples for a set of stock index futures.

The successful operation of futures exchanges for the relevant stakeholders such as traders and the exchange necessitates that there be a tradeoff between optimizing liquidity and prudence.[2] The imposition of margins is the mechanism by which these objectives are met.[3] Margin requirements act as collateral that investors are required to pay to reduce default risk. Default risk is incurred if the effect of the futures price change is at such a level that the investor's margin does

---

[1]The chapter relies heavily on this previous literature, and in particular, on the work that we as authors have completed – see References.

[2]For a detailed discussion of the tradeoffs in setting prudent margins by clearinghouses, see Jackson and Manning (2007).

[3]Futures exchanges are not completely reliant on margins and also use capital requirements and price limits to protect against investor default.

Extreme Events in Finance: A Handbook of Extreme Value Theory and its Applications,
First Edition. Edited by François Longin.
© 2017 John Wiley & Sons, Inc. Published 2017 by John Wiley & Sons, Inc.

427

not cover it, leading to nonpayment by one of the parties to the contract.[4] Margin committees face a dilemma, however, in determining the magnitude of the margin requirement imposed on futures traders. On one hand, setting a high margin level reduces default risk. On the other hand, if the margin level is set too high, then the futures contracts will be less attractive for investors due to higher costs and decreased liquidity, and finally less profitable for the exchange itself. This quandary has forced margin committees to impose investor deposits, which represent a practical compromise between meeting the objectives of adequate prudence and liquidity of the futures contracts.

The clearinghouse sets initial margins so that this deposit protects against a vast range of possible price movements with a relatively low probability that actual price changes exceed the margin. This is equivalent to modeling the initial margin as a quantile or value at risk (VaR) estimate. Using this, the clearinghouse imposes margins based on a statistical analysis of price changes, and adjusts this to take account of other factors such open interest, volume of trade, concentration in futures positions, and the margins of competing exchanges. This chapter deals with the statistical modeling element of margin setting and examines different approaches in the context of using EVT and the application of nonparametric measures for the optimal margin level. Given the true distribution of futures price changes being nonnormal and, in fact, unknown (e.g., Cotter and McKillop, 2000; Hall et al., 1989), it is appropriate to examine margins from using a number of possible distributions. We do so in by comparing margins that are set using EVT, the normal distribution, and the Student-t distribution.

The chapter proceeds as follows. In the next section we provide details of margin setting. This is followed by a discussion of the methods, primarily EVT, that should be used for modeling margins. We then illustrate some empirical results for a selection of stock index futures. Finally, we provide some concluding comments.

16.2   MARGIN SETTING

We begin with a discussion of margin setting in futures markets. We outline the different elements of a margin account and provide examples of how margins are set in practice and in the literature.

Futures clearinghouses use margin requirement accounts to minimize default risk and act as counterparty to all trades that take place within its exchanges. This provides stability and encourages trading. Setting margins ensures that individual traders do not have to concern themselves with credit risk exposures to other traders, because the clearinghouse assumes all such risks itself. Margin requirements consist of an initial margin (deposit) and a variation or daily margin, assuming a minimum or maintenance margin is breached. The variation margin

---

[4]Defaults are pretty rare given the voluminous trading, but they have occurred in, for example, Paris, Kuala Lumpur, and Hong Kong. Further, individual high profile disasters including Barings affect investor confidence in futures markets.

will result in a margin call, where the broker asks the trader to top up their margin account. The focus of this chapter, the initial margin, represents the deposit a futures trader must give to a clearinghouse to initiate a trade.

The modeling approaches followed for initial and variation margins are usually quite distinct. Setting initial margins utilizes the unconditional distribution of returns. Typically, there is a focus on the tails of the distribution and modeling the asset price movements for extreme confidence levels for extraordinary market events so as to minimize the probability that the associated quantile is exceeded. Most of the previous literature has focused on this approach as we do in this chapter. The variation margin comes into play once the futures contract is trading, and can thought of as supporting the initial margin after it has been breached to help avoid trader default. Here, the focus is on the conditional distribution of returns where we would be interested in the levels of volatility during the lifetime of the futures contract.

We now provide an example of the way the initial margins are typically set by clearinghouses and the exchange on which the futures are traded.

Let us describe as an example the way margins are set on the London International Financial Futures and Options Exchange (LIFFE). For products traded on this exchange, margin requirements are set by the LCH.Clearnet Group (London Clearing House, LCH). The LCH risk committee is responsible for all decisions relating to margin requirements for LIFFE contracts. Margin committees generally involve experienced market participants who have widespread knowledge in dealing with margin setting and implementation, through their exposure to various market conditions and their ability to respond to changing environments. The LCH risk committee is independent of the commercial function of the Exchange. In order to measure and manage risk, the LCH uses the London systematic portfolio analysis of risk (SPAN) system, a specifically developed variation of the SPAN system originally introduced by the Chicago Mercantile Exchange (CME). The London SPAN system is a nonparametric, risk-based model that provides output of actual margin requirements that are sufficient to cover potential default losses in all but the most extreme circumstances.[5] The inputs to the system are a set of estimated margin requirements relying on price movements that are not expected to be exceeded over a day or a couple of days. These estimated values are based on diverse criteria incorporating a focus on a contract's price history, its close-to-close price movements, its liquidity, its seasonality, and forthcoming price sensitive events. Market volatility is especially a key factor to set margin levels. Most important, however, is the extent of the contract's price movements with a policy for a minimum margin requirement that covers three standard deviations of historic price volatility based on the higher of 1-day or 2-day price movements

---

[5]Alternative approaches to compute the margin requirement have been developed in the academic literature: Figlewski (1984), Kofman (1993), Hsieh (1993), Longin (1995), Booth et al. (1997), Longin (1999), and Cotter (2001) use different statistical distributions (normal, historical, or extreme value distribution) or processes (GARCH). In contrast, Brennan (1986) proposes an economic model for broker cost minimization in which the margin is endogenously determined, and Craine (1992) models the distributions of the payoffs to futures traders and the potential losses to the futures clearinghouse in terms of the payoffs to barrier options.

over the previous 60-day trading period. This is akin to using the normal distribution, where multiples of standard deviation covers certain price movements at various probability levels.[6]

In the literature, margins have been typically modeled as a quantile or VaR, and we interchange between these terms in this chapter. The clearinghouse then selects a particular confidence level, and sets the margin as the VaR at this confidence level.[7]

16.3   THEORY AND METHODS

We concentrate our discussion of setting margins using EVT. Here we will discuss two commonly used approaches: estimation assuming maximum domain of attraction (MDA), and fitting excesses (extremes) over a threshold. There is also a third approach, where one would estimate the parameters for an extreme value distribution. This is less applied in margin setting but an application is outlined in Longin (1999). We also provide a brief discussion of non-EVT approaches such as assuming alternative distributions, the most common being normality and nonparametric approaches, for example, historical simulation.

16.3.1   Maximum Domain of Attraction

The statistical properties of financial returns have interested many, and none more so than the modeling of tail returns and the fitting of candidate distributions. For initial margin setting and associated measures of violation probabilities, it is common to use the theoretical framework of EVT. Three alternative extreme value distributions are detailed, the Weibull, the Gumbell, and the fat-tailed Fréchet distribution.

The distributional assumptions of EVT are applicable through the MDA, allowing for approximation to certain distributional characteristics rather than being required to belong to a specific distribution (Leadbetter et al., 1983; Fraga Alves and Neves, 2017). Thus, financial returns do not have to exactly fit a particular set of distributional assumptions. Rather, our analysis assumes that the return series have extreme values that are approximated by a Fréchet-type distribution, and this implies that the series belong to the MDA of the Fréchet distribution. Advantageously, it avoids our having to ascertain the exact form of a, for example, fat-tailed distribution that matches the data we are analyzing. While there is a general agreement on the existence of fat tails for financial data, its exact form for all financial returns is unknown. For this reason, it is appropriate to deal with approximation of the Fréchet distribution in the sense of being in the

---

[6]For instance, under the hypothesis of normality for price movements, two standard deviations would cover 97.72% of price movements, and three standard deviations 99.87%.

[7]Note there has been extensive work on the properties of risk measures in the context of margin setting, and the VaR measure has been criticized as it does not satisfy the properties of coherence and, most particularly, because the VaR is not subadditive (Cotter and Dowd, 2006).

MDA. This property will lead to the use of nonparametric statistics in modeling tail returns.

The three extreme value distributions can be divided into three separate types depending on the value of their shape parameter α. The classification of a Weibull distribution ($\alpha < 0$) includes the uniform example where the tail is bounded by having a finite right end point and is a short-tailed distribution. The more commonly assumed class of distributions used for asset price changes includes the set of thin-tailed densities. This second classification of densities includes the normal and gamma distributions, and these belong to the Gumbell distribution, having a characteristic of tails decaying exponentially. Of primary concern to the analysis of fat-tailed distributions is the Fréchet classification, and examples of this type generated here are the Cauchy, Student-t, ordinary Fréchet, and the Pareto distributions. This important classification of distributions for extreme asset price movements has tail values that decay by a power function. A vast literature on asset returns has recognized the existence of fat-tailed characteristics, and thus we will focus on the Fréchet type of extreme value distribution.

Turning to the task of margin setting using futures, we examine a sequence of futures returns $\{R\}$ arranged in ascending order and expressed in terms of the maxima (M_n) of n random variables belonging to the true unknown cumulative probability density function F, where

$$M_n = \max \{R_1, R_2, \ldots, R_n\}. \tag{16.1}$$

The corresponding density function of M_n is obtained from the cumulative probability relationship, and this represents the probability of exceeding a margin level on a short position for n returns:

$$P_{\text{short}} = P\{M_n > r_{\text{short}}\} = P\{R_1 > r_{\text{short}}, \ldots, R_n > r_{\text{short}}\} = 1 - F_{\text{max}}{}^n(r_{\text{short}}), \tag{16.2}$$

where r_{short} represents the margin level on a short position.

With margin setting required for both long and short positions, we are interested in both the upper and lower tails of the distribution $F^n(r)$. We also can apply EVT to examine the associated lower order statistics where lower tail price movements are relevant for margin requirements of a long position in a futures contract. The theoretical framework for examining sample minima tail statistics can easily be converted by applying the identity $\text{Min}\{R_1, R_2, \ldots, R_n\} = -\text{Max}\{-R_1, -R_2, \ldots, -R_n\}$. The corresponding probability expression for exceeding a margin level on a long position for n returns is

$$P_{\text{long}} = P\{M_n < r_{\text{long}}\} = P\{R_1 < r_{\text{long}}, \ldots, R_n < r_{\text{long}}\} \stackrel{\sim}{=} F_{\text{min}}{}^n(r_{\text{long}}), \tag{16.3}$$

where r_{long} represents the margin level on a long position.

16.3.2   Tail and Probability Estimators

Because of the semiparametric specification of being in the MDA of the fat-tailed Fréchet distribution, it is appropriate to apply nonparametric measures of our tail estimates. We apply the commonly used nonparametric Hill index (1975) that determines the tail estimates of the stock index futures (see Beirlant et al., 2017). It is given as

$$\gamma h = \frac{1}{\alpha} = \left(\frac{1}{m}\right) \sum [\log r_{(n+1-i)} - \log r_{(n-m)}] \quad \text{for } i = 1, \ldots, m. \quad (16.4)$$

This tail estimator is asymptotically normal, that is, $(\gamma - E\{\gamma\})/(m)^{1/2} \approx (0, \gamma^2)$ (Hall, 1982).

As this study is examining the probability of a sequence of returns exceeding a particular margin level relying on expressions (16.2) and (16.3), an empirical issue arises in determining the number of returns entailed in the tail of a distribution. From a large number of methods of identifying the optimal tail threshold, we adopt the approach proposed by Phillips et al. (1996). The optimal threshold value M_n, which minimizes the mean square error of the tail estimate γ, is $m = M_n = \{\lambda n^{2/3}\}$, where λ is estimated adaptively by $\lambda = |\gamma_1/2^{1/2}(n/m_2(\gamma_1 - \gamma_2)|^{2/3}$.

In setting margins, futures exchanges and clearinghouses would be interested in variations in the upper and lower tail values. If these are invariant across tails, the clearinghouse can set similar margins for long and short trading positions. To investigate this, the tail index estimator is used to determine each tail individually, but it is also used to measure a common margin requirement encompassing the extreme price movements of both tails. The relative stability of the tail measures determines the optimal margin policy. Stability across the tails supports the hypothesis of having a common margin requirement regardless of trading position, and instability suggests the need for separate margin levels. Tail stability is tested using a statistic suggested by Loretan and Phillips (1994):

$$V(\gamma^+ - \gamma^-) = \frac{[\gamma^+ - \gamma^-]^2}{[\gamma^{+2}/m^+ + \gamma^{-2}/m^-]^{1/2}}, \quad (16.5)$$

where γ^+ (γ^-) is the estimate of the right (left) tail.

The application of EVT allows us produce different margin measures. We outline a measure that allows us to determine the probability of exceeding a certain price movement. From this, the setting of optimal margin requirements can be made based on an examination of the violation probability for a range of price movements in association with the tradeoff between optimizing liquidity and prudence for an exchange's contract. The nonparametric measure detailing the probability p of exceeding a certain large price change r_p for any tail measure is

$$r_p = r_t \left(\frac{M}{np}\right)^\gamma. \quad (16.6)$$

Using (16.6), a related nonparametric measure examines the margin level or quantile that would not be violated for particular extreme price movements r_p at different probabilities p:

$$p = \left(\frac{r_t}{r_p}\right)^{1/\gamma} \frac{M}{n}. \quad (16.7)$$

We can then compare these measures with alternative approaches such as using a Student-t distribution at similar confidence levels.

16.3.3   Peaks Over Threshold

An alternative extreme value approach is to use the peaks over threshold (POT) (generalized Pareto) distribution (see Cotter and Dowd, 2006). Here, the risks of extremely high losses can be modeled with the POT approach based on the generalized Pareto distribution (GPD).[8] This approach focuses on the realizations of a random variable R (in our case futures returns) over a high threshold u. More particularly, if R has the distribution function $F(r)$, we are interested in the distribution function $F_u(r)$ of exceedances of R over a high threshold u. As u gets large (as would be the case for the thresholds relevant to clearinghouses), the distribution of exceedances tends to a GPD. The shape ξ and scale $\beta > 0$ parameters of the GPD are estimated conditional on the threshold u (Embrechts et al., 1997, pp. 162–164). We have described a variant of the shape parameter before as the inverse of the tail index parameter, and which we are using the well-known Hill estimator. The GPD parameters can be estimated by maximum likelihood methods. Maximum likelihood estimates are then found by maximizing the log-likelihood function using suitable (e.g., numerical optimization) methods.

16.3.4   Further Models

We turn our attention briefly to some non-EVT approaches to setting margins. We provide a brief overview of different statistical models that have been used to compute the margin level for a given probability. Many of these, for example, the use of the normal distribution and historical simulation methods, are heavily relied upon in practice and also discussed extensively in the literature.

First, we discuss the normal distribution. It is commonly applied in risk management and in margin setting. For example, the SPAN margin system estimates normal margin requirements. It requires the estimation of two parameters only, the mean μ and the variance σ^2. For a given probability p, the margin level corresponds to the quantile or VaR where one is examining what margin level is sufficient to exceed futures price changes over a time-period of length T for the probability level p. Because of the fat-tailed phenomena of financial returns, it tends to underestimate tail behavior and the associated margins associated with futures price movements. An alternative distribution often suggested as overcoming this weakness but keeps its strong links with normality is the the Student-t distribution. Here, the number of moments of the distribution is detailed by the t parameter. A further approach not relying on distributions is the use of historical simulation. This is heavily used in practice, where margins are calculated as quantiles of the historical distribution of returns. As there is no model per se, it avoids model risk.

---

[8]Alternatively, extreme tail returns could be modeled by generalized extreme value (GEV) theory, which deals with the distribution of the sample maxima. The GEV and POT approaches are analogous in the limit (see Longin, 1999).

Returns of the historical distribution are ordered in an ascending manner and the margin is read of as a quantile of the distribution.

All the above approaches assume that we are modeling an unconditional distribution of futures returns. However, during the lifespan of a contract the inherent volatility that drives the level of deposit in the margin account may vary substantially. This would potentially involve an initial margin being breached and a margin call taking place requiring variation margin being posted. To model this, it is important to look at the conditional distribution of returns and look at time-varying approaches. The most commonly applied of these is the use of generalized autoregressive conditional heteroscedasticity (GARCH) models. For example, one study exclusively uses GARCH models in the setting of variation margins (see Cotter and Dowd, 2012). As the variation margins require modeling of returns as the contract trades, the modeling of the associated volatility is of paramount importance. As we have seen clearly before, during and after financial crises, market conditions may vary substantially over time, and a conditional model like a GARCH process would attempt to capture this variability.

Now we turn to the use of EVT in setting margins with an illustration of modeling margins in practice.

16.4 EMPIRICAL RESULTS

We are going to illustrate the use of EVT in setting initial margins. We will also show results for other approaches. First though, we will describe the types of preliminary analysis that would be followed in setting margin requirements. The analysis requires some futures returns data. This will be analyzed both as a full distribution of returns but also for break-outs of upper and lower distributions. The main focus of analysis is the tails of the distribution.

To set the scene, Figure 16.1 shows the distribution of asset returns where we have marked out the upper tail of the distribution. Going from the lower

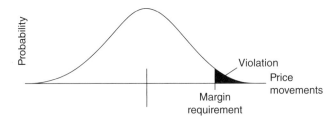

FIGURE 16.1 Margin requirements for a short position and a distribution of returns. This figure illustrates a distribution of futures returns with special emphasis on the short position. At the upper tail of the distribution, a certain margin requirement is identified. Any price movement in excess of this margin requirement, given by the shaded area, represents a violation of this by the investor.

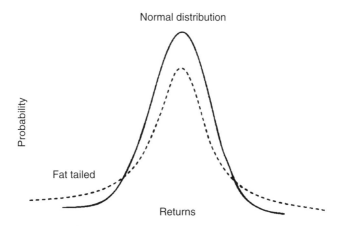

FIGURE 16.2 **Fat-tailed and normal distributions. This figure illustrates the tail distribution of futures returns with fat tails (dashed curve) and a normal distribution (solid curve). The fat tails ensure more probability mass in the tails than the normal distribution.**

distribution that would deal with the returns of a long position, the upper distribution focuses on a short position. Here, a quantile of the distribution is identified, and this represents an initial margin or margin requirement. Returns in excess of this would represent violations of the associated initial margins. These violations are large price movements and would be those that might result in investor default. It is these large returns that we will model using EVT, and we will determine whether a large movement is covered by an initial margin or whether it represents a violation of the size of the margin deposit.

Figure 16.1 is the well-known and heavily applied normal distribution. Financial returns, for example, those of futures, have relatively fat tails, and this characteristic is shown in Figure 16.2. Here, the probability mass for the fat-tailed distribution is greater around the tails vis-à-vis the normal distribution. This implies that volatility levels calculated assuming normality would be less (and incorrectly so) than that which reality dictates. This leads us to using EVT and the modeling of tail returns with the Fréchet distribution.

We now present some EVT statistics where we model the tail behavior for a selection of European stock index futures. We convert the price data into returns using the first difference of the natural logarithm of closing-day quotes. Some summary statistics for the series is given in Table 16.1. We report findings in common with those reported for financial returns. Returns do not belong to a normal distribution, and there is excess kurtosis and, in general, excess skewness. Note the excess kurtosis describes the fat-tailed characteristic of the data. The lack of normality also suggests that using this distribution to model margins is inappropriate. The lack of normality and how it relates to the tail returns can be clearly seen from a Q–Q plot. An example is given for the DAX index in Figure 16.3. Here it is clear that there is extensive deviation for this contract's returns from the normal distribution as given by the straight line.

TABLE 16.1   Summary statistics for stock index futures

Contract	Mean[a]	Minimum[a]	Maximum[a]	Skewness	Kurtosis	Normality
BEL20	0.06	−5.26	5.48	−0.11[b]	4.40	0.07
KFX	0.04	−7.80	6.65	−0.33	5.19	0.08
CAC40	0.04	−7.74	8.63	−0.08[b]	3.36	0.05
DAX	0.06	−12.85	8.38	−0.56	8.31	0.08
AEX	0.06	−7.70	7.28	−0.33	5.94	0.08
MIF30	0.08	−7.84	7.07	−0.06[b]	2.27	0.06
OBX	0.04	−19.55	21.00	0.32	97.69	0.18
PSI20	0.13	−11.55	6.96	−0.87	7.95	0.11
IBEX35	0.07	−10.84	7.25	−0.49	4.72	0.07
OMX	0.06	−11.92	10.81	−0.27	8.93	0.07
SWISS	0.08	−9.09	7.08	−0.50	9.30	0.06
FTSE100	0.05	−16.72	8.09	−1.18	18.78	0.05

The summary statistics are presented for each future's index returns. The mean, minimum, and maximum values represent the average, lowest, and highest returns, respectively. The skewness statistic is a measure of distribution asymmetry, with symmetric returns having a value of zero. The kurtosis statistic measures the shape of a distribution vis-à-vis a normal distribution, with a normal density function having a value of zero. Normality is formally examined with the Kolmogorov–Smirnov test, which indicates a normal distribution with a value of zero.

[a]Statistics are expressed in percentages.

[b]Represents insignificant at the 5% level, whereas all other skewness, kurtosis, and normality coefficients are significant different from zero.

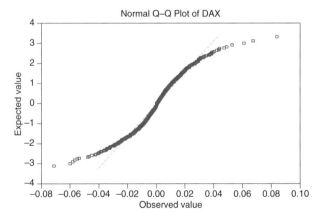

FIGURE 16.3 *Q–Q* plot of DAX log returns series. This figure plots the quantile of the empirical distribution of the DAX futures index returns against the normal distribution. The plot shows whether the distribution of the DAX returns matches a normal distribution. The straight line represents a normal quantile plot, whereas the curved line represents the quantile plot of the empirical distribution of the DAX contract. If the full set of DAX returns followed a normal distribution, then its quantile plot should match the normal plot and also be a straight line. The extent to which these DAX returns diverge from the straight line indicates the relative lack of normality.

We now turn to our explicit modeling of the futures returns using EVT. We start by showing the Hill index tail estimates in Table 16.2. The table shows the optimal number of tail returns and nonparametric Hill index estimates for the lower tail, the upper tail, and both tails, corresponding to the shape parameter used in the calculation of long, short, and common margin requirements. The optimal number of returns in each tail appears to be reasonably constant, hovering around the 5% mark for each contract.

All the tail estimates range between 2 and 4 with the exception of the lower tail estimate for the Portuguese PSI20 contract, indicating their fat-tailed characteristic. We find that all values are significantly positive, corresponding to the requirement that $\gamma = \alpha^{-1} > 0$. Testing the stability in tails from lower and upper values, findings indicate that while the right tail estimators are always greater than their left tail counterparts, a common margin requirement is sufficient based on

TABLE 16.2 **Optimal tail estimates for stock index futures**

Contract	m^-	γ^-	m^+	γ^+	m^*	γ^*	$\gamma^+ - \gamma^-$
BEL20	63	2.81	68	2.85	92	3.20	0.07
		(0.35)		(0.35)		(0.33)	
KFX	72	2.65	78	3.01	111	2.98	0.78
		(0.31)		(0.34)		(0.28)	
CAC40	100	2.97	103	3.33	137	3.89	0.83
		(0.30)		(0.33)		(0.33)	
AEX	95	2.72	95	2.93	141	2.95	0.51
		(0.28)		(0.30)		(0.25)	
DAX	83	2.92	83	3.07	116	3.30	0.33
		(0.32)		(0.34)		(0.31)	
MIF30	55	3.31	55	3.66	77	3.41	0.53
		(0.45)		(0.49)		(0.39)	
OBX	71	2.04	70	2.89	113	2.47	2.02•
		(0.24)		(0.35)		(0.23)	
PSI20	41	1.91	43	2.38	57	2.32	0.99
		(0.30)		(0.36)		(0.31)	
IBEX35	74	2.62	78	3.35	118	3.21	1.50
		(0.30)		(0.38)		(0.30)	
OMX	88	2.59	98	2.77	177	2.67	0.46
		(0.28)		(0.28)		(0.20)	
FTSE100	126	2.99	134	3.36	204	3.21	0.93
		(0.27)		(0.29)		(0.22)	
SWISS	72	2.81	84	2.89	103	3.12	0.17
		(0.33)		(0.32)		(0.31)	

Hill tail estimates γ are calculated for lower tail, the upper tail, and both tails for each stock index future. The symbols $-$, $+$, * represent the lower tail, upper tail, and both tails, respectively. The optimal number of values in the respective tails, m, is calculated following the method proposed by Phillips et al. (1996). Standard errors are presented in parentheses for each tail value. Tail stability is calculated in the last column, with the symbol • representing significant different upper and lower tail values at the 5% level.

a 5% significance level in each case with the exception of the OBX index. This implies that common initial margin for long and short traders would be sufficient based on the contracts analyzed.

We now look at the VaR or quantile, which would be of interest to the clearing-house in setting initial margins, and compare the results for different distributions. What are the margin levels, or quantiles, required to cover a range of extreme price changes under the assumptions of a normal and Fréchet distribution? The latter method explicitly assumes the existence of fat-tail returns for stock index futures. The results are presented in Table 16.3, which incorporate the common margin requirement, so 98% covers all eventualities with the exception of a 2% default, that is, 1% long and short, respectively.

TABLE 16.3 Common margin requirements to cover extreme price movements

Contract	Method	98%	99%	99.80%	99.90%	99.98%
BEL20	Normal	2.15	2.38	2.86	3.04	3.45
	Student-*t*	4.20	5.40	9.44	11.95	20.52
	Extreme	3.10	3.88	6.52	8.16	13.72
KFX	Normal	2.47	2.73	3.27	3.48	3.95
	Student-*t*	7.37	10.51	23.63	33.45	74.84
	Extreme	3.93	4.96	8.53	10.76	18.48
CAC40	Normal	2.93	3.25	3.89	4.14	4.70
	Student-*t*	5.72	7.36	12.86	16.28	27.96
	Extreme	3.92	4.69	7.09	8.48	12.83
AEX	Normal	2.61	2.89	3.46	3.69	4.18
	Student-*t*	7.80	11.12	25.01	35.40	79.20
	Extreme	3.95	5.00	8.62	10.91	18.82
DAX	Normal	2.97	3.28	3.93	4.19	4.75
	Student-*t*	5.78	7.44	13.00	16.45	28.26
	Extreme	4.20	5.19	8.45	10.43	16.98
MIF30	Normal	3.88	4.30	5.15	5.48	6.22
	Student-*t*	7.57	9.73	17.02	21.54	37.00
	Extreme	5.34	6.54	10.48	12.83	20.56
OBX	Normal	2.83	3.14	3.76	4.00	4.54
	Student-*t*	8.47	12.08	27.17	38.45	86.03
	Extreme	3.83	5.07	9.72	12.86	24.66
PSI20	Normal	3.78	4.19	5.02	5.34	6.06
	Student-*t*	11.31	16.11	36.25	51.31	114.80
	Extreme	6.55	8.83	17.68	23.85	47.74
IBEX35	Normal	3.46	3.83	4.58	4.88	5.53
	Student-*t*	6.73	8.66	15.15	19.17	32.93
	Extreme	4.79	5.94	9.81	12.17	20.09
OMX	Normal	3.67	4.07	4.87	5.19	5.88
	Student-*t*	10.53	15.00	33.74	47.76	106.86
	Extreme	5.35	6.93	12.65	16.40	29.95

TABLE 16.3 (*Continued*)

Contract	Method	98%	99%	99.80%	99.90%	99.98%
FTSE100	Normal	2.56	2.83	3.39	3.61	4.09
	Student-*t*	4.98	6.41	11.20	14.17	24.35
	Extreme	3.41	4.23	6.99	8.67	14.31
SWISS	Normal	2.13	2.36	2.83	3.01	3.42
	Student-*t*	4.16	5.35	9.36	11.84	20.34
	Extreme	2.99	3.73	6.24	7.79	13.04

The values in this table represent the margin requirements needed to cover a range of extreme price movements for each contract, for example, 98% of all movements. The associated margin requirements are calculated relying on extreme value theory, normal, and Student-*t* distributions. Student-*t* degrees of freedom are given by the Hill tail estimates γ^*, which are also incorporated in the extreme value estimates. Values are expressed in percentages.

Dealing with a normal and extreme value comparison, it is clear that the former method underestimates the true margin requirement for any price movement and that this becomes more pronounced as you try to cover the larger price movements. This indicates that the fat-tailed characteristic has greater implications for margin setting as you move to greater extremes. The inclusion of the Student-*t* distribution allows for some degree of fat tails (the respective Hill tail estimates are used to proxy for the degrees of freedom for the different futures). These Student-*t* results are larger than the other measures because of estimated degrees of freedom.

16.5 CONCLUSIONS

In this chapter, we provided an overview of margin setting for futures contracts using EVT. We discussed the margin account and its composition. We detailed how margins are set in practice. Margins are important. Each exchange's clearinghouse must impose margins given the relationship of securing the safety of the exchange against large price movements for contracts and encouraging investor participation in trading. Low margins discourage (encourage) the former (latter), whereas high margins discourage (encourage) the latter (former).

We examined the potential role of EVT in margin setting. Here, a statistical analysis was pursued to calculate margin levels focusing on extreme price movements of futures. These returns are located in the tails rather than the entire distribution, as it is the violation of these that margin requirements are meant to combat against. Given previous findings of futures price changes being associated with fat tails, EVT and the limiting Fréchet distribution were applied in the calculation of the risk characteristics for the futures analyzed. The tail indexes were measured using the nonparametric Hill estimates, and this is appropriate given the semiparametric nature of the relationship of a set of futures price changes and the Fréchet distribution.

We illustrated the use of the Hill tail index by estimating VaRs, that is, the margin requirement that would be imposed to protect investors from a range of extreme price movements for different confidence levels. For a selection of stock index futures, we found that common margin requirements are generally sufficient. We illustrated that assuming normality results in underestimation and smaller margins than using EVT, and this becomes more pronounced as you try to protect against returns further out in the tail of a distribution.

This is an area that is ripe for further work. Issues that might be considered include looking at setting margins for other assets such as options. Here you would have to take the nonlinear payoffs into account when modeling potential tail behavior. Further, the discussion here was focused on univariate modeling of individual contracts or for a collection of contracts. We have not commented on the potential for using EVT in a multivariate context where you would account for diversification effects in a portfolio context. Diversification allows for the netting-off of some of the individual contracts risk and would require assessing the modeling of dependence between tails of multiple assets.

Acknowledgment

Cotter acknowledges the support of the Science Foundation, Ireland, under Grant Number 08/SRC/FM1389. We thank the editor, Francois Longin, for helpful comments on this chapter.

References

Beirlant, J., Herrmann, K., Teugels, J.L. Estimation of the extreme value index. In: Longin, F., editor. *Extreme Events in Finance*. Wiley; 2017.

Brennan, M.J. A theory of price limits in futures markets. Journal of Financial Economics 1986;**16**:213–233.

Booth, G.G., Brousssard, J.P., Martikainen, T., Puttonen, V. Prudent margin levels in the Finnish stock index futures market. Management Science 1997;**43**:1177–1188.

Cotter, J., McKillop, D.G. The distributional characteristics of a selection of contracts traded on the London international financial futures exchange. Journal of Business Finance and Accounting 2000;**27**:487–510.

Cotter, J. Margin exceedances for European stock index futures using extreme value theory. Journal of Banking and Finance 2001;**25**:1475–1502.

Cotter, J., Dowd, K. An application to futures clearinghouse margin requirements. Journal of Banking and Finance 2006;**30**:3469–3485.

Cotter, J., Dowd, K. Estimating Variation Margins Using Conditional Risk Measures, UCD Working Paper; 2012.

Craine, R. Are Futures Margins Adequate? Working Paper. Berkley: University of California; 1992.

Embrechts, P., Kluppelberg, C., Mikosch, T. *Modelling Extremal Events for Insurance and Finance*. Berlin: Springer Verlag; 1997.

Figlewski, S. Margins and market integrity: margin setting for stock index futures and options. Journal of Futures Markets 1984;**4**:385–416.

Fraga Alves, I., Neves, C. Extreme value theory: an introductory overview. In: Longin, F., editor. *Extreme Events in Finance.* Wiley; 2017.

Hall, J.A., Brorsen, B.W., Irwin, S.H. The distribution of futures prices: a test of the stable Paretian and mixture of normals hypothesis. Journal of Financial and Quantitative Analysis 1989;**24**:105–116.

Hall, P. On some simple estimates of an exponent of regular variation. Journal of the Royal Statistical Society, Series B 1982;**44**:37–42.

Hill, B.M. A simple general approach to inference about the tail of a distribution. Annals of Statistics 1975;**3**:1163–1174.

Hsieh, D.A. Implications of nonlinear dynamics for financial risk management. Journal of Financial and Quantitative Analysis 1993;**28**:41–64.

Jackson, J., Manning, M.J. Comparing the Pre-Settlement Risk Implications of Alternative Clearing Arrangements, Bank of England Working Paper No. 321; 2007.

Kofman, P. Optimizing futures margins with distribution tails. Advances in Futures and Options Research 1993;**6**:263–278.

Leadbetter, M.R., Lindgren, G., Rootzen, H. *Extremes and Related Properties of Random Sequences and Processes.* New York: Springer Verlag; 1983.

Longin, F.M., 1995. Optimal margins in futures markets: a parametric extreme-based method. Proceedings of the Seventh Chicago Board of Trade Conference on Futures and Options; 1994 Sep; Bonn, Germany.

Longin, F.M. Optimal margin levels in futures markets: extreme price movements. Journal of Futures Markets 1999;**19**:127–152.

Loretan, M., Phillips, P.C.B. Testing the covariance stationarity of heavy-tailed time series. Journal of Empirical Finance 1994;**1**:211–248.

Phillips, P.C.B., McFarland, J.W., McMahon, P.C. Robust tests of forward exchange market efficiency with empirical evidence from the 1920s. Journal of Applied Econometrics 1996;**11**:1–22.

Chapter Seventeen

The Sortino Ratio and Extreme Value Theory: An Application to Asset Allocation

G. Geoffrey Booth[1] and John Paul Broussard[2]

[1]*Eli Broad Graduate School of Management, Michigan State University, East Lansing, MI, United States*
[2]*School of Business – Camden, Rutgers, The State University of New Jersey, Camden, NJ, United States*

17.1 INTRODUCTION

Modern portfolio theory has its genesis in the seminal works of Markowitz (1952) and Roy (1952).[1] Before their works, the notion of considering investments in the portfolio context was known by academicians and practitioners but lacked a coherent theory.[2] Combining stocks and other assets to create diversified portfolios with desired risk and return characteristics quickly caught on and was extended to describe the behavior of the stock market using the capital asset pricing model

---

[1]In 1990, Markowitz won the Nobel Prize for his work and Roy did not. Markowitz (1999) attributes this outcome to the difference in the visibility of their total work in this area. He subsequently published many articles derived from his initial insights. See in particular Markowitz (1959, 1987). Roy, however, appears to have stopped contributing to this area after his initial article.

[2]See, for example, Hicks (1935), Markschak (1938), and Williams (1938). Rubinstein (2002) suggests that Fisher (1906) may have been the first to suggest that variance be used as a measure of economic risk. Much earlier, Shakespeare (1600) alludes to diversification in the *Merchant of Venice* by having Antonio, who is involved in maritime trade, comment that his business is spread across different ships, locations, and time.

Extreme Events in Finance: A Handbook of Extreme Value Theory and its Applications,
First Edition. Edited by François Longin.
© 2017 John Wiley & Sons, Inc. Published 2017 by John Wiley & Sons, Inc.

(CAPM) (Sharpe, 1964; Lintner, 1965; Mossin, 1966). This model (often referred to simply as the CAPM), provides the theoretical basis for the Sharpe ratio (Sharpe, 1966, 1994), a performance measure that relates the return of a portfolio in excess of the risk-free rate to the risk of the portfolio as measured by its volatility, or more precisely, the standard deviation of its returns. This ratio has remained popular since its introduction and has proven to be robust in many environments.

Following the finance orthodoxy initiated by Bachelier (1900), the CAPM and the Sharpe ratio assume that the returns distribution is Gaussian, a distribution that is completely described by its mean and variance. This assumption is heroic, because the tails of the observed distributions are typically fatter (thicker) than those associated with a normal distribution (e.g., Mandelbrot, 1963; Fama, 1965a; Brock et al., 1991; Mandelbrot, 1997). Markowitz (1952) recognized that asset price distributions may not be normal and mentioned the possible need to consider the notion of left-tail skewness. Roy (1952) independently formalized this concept by promoting the safety-first criterion for portfolio construction. Following the influence of Mandelbrot (1963), Fama (1965b) considered the situation of portfolio selection when stock returns are described as a stable Paretian distribution. Arzac and Bawa (1977) and Harlow and Rao (1989) extended the safety-first notion of portfolio choice to asset pricing. Eventually, the label of "safety first" was replaced with the more general (and perhaps descriptive) term "downside risk."

Asset allocation is an aggregate version of portfolio construction. It involves the creation of an overall portfolio using instruments of different asset classes (e.g., bonds, stocks, real estate, commodities, money market instruments, and so forth) as inputs. Many researchers have explored the notion of downside risk in the asset allocation framework (e.g., Harlow, 1991; Lucas and Klaassen, 1998; Neftci, 2000; Booth and Broussard, 2002; and more recently Ornelas et al., 2012). Practitioners are also very concerned with the issue of downside risk, as can be witnessed by the recent development and usage of value-at-risk methods and stress testing (e.g., Longin, 2000; Berkowitz and O'Brien, 2002; Jorion, 2007). The concern of both groups is rooted in the notion that the typical remedies for diversification are inadequate in periods of stress and turmoil because large price swings appear to correspond to agents attempting to adjust their portfolios in the same manner.[3]

Brian Rom (Investment Technologies) created what is now known as the Sortino ratio in 1983.[4] He named it after Frank A. Sortino, who was an early promoter of using downside risk to measure performance. The Sortino ratio is a modification of the Sharpe ratio and requires as input minimum acceptable return (MAR) – often referred to as the target return (TR). Its numerator is the portfolio return in excess of the TR.[5] Its denominator is the square root of the

---

[3]This observation is supported by the empirical findings of Gabaix et al. (2003) and is consistent with the notion that agents learn from each other and behave accordingly. See, for example, Duffy and Feltovich (1999), Hong et al. (2005), and Booth et al. (in press). Using an agent-based model, Feng et al. (2012) show that this characteristic is consistent with the presence of fat-tailed return distributions.

[4]Examples of Sortino's work include Sortino and van der Meer (1991), Sortino and Price (1994), and Sortino (2001, 2010).

[5]In some early versions of the Sortino ratio, the target return is replaced by the risk-free rate.

lower second moment around the target rate. Like the Sharpe ratio, the Sortino ratio can be expressed in ex post and ex ante terms. The ex post version can be used as a performance measure, while the ex ante formulation can be employed to construct an expected optimal portfolio.

The purpose of this chapter is to apply extreme value theory (EVT) techniques when using the Sortino ratio for selecting optimal portfolio weights. We restrict our analysis to two assets for simplicity, with one of the assets being a portfolio of the U.S. real estate investment trusts (REIT) and the other a broad-based portfolio of U.S. equities represented by the S&P 500 stock index.[6] Both of these asset classes are well represented in the overall investment holdings of institutional investors such as foundations, pension funds, and insurance companies.

Our approach is threefold. First, we use an extensive daily dataset to calculate the Sortino ratio using various two-asset allocation weights. This requires calculating the second lower partial moment for selected MARs using discrete daily data. Second, we repeat the calculations after replacing the empirical data by a fitted generalized Pareto distribution (GPD). Third, we compare the Sortino ratio asset allocation results provided by the various scenarios to the portfolio suggested by the Sharpe ratio.

In our study period, we find that optimal asset allocation is strongly dependent on the risk tolerance of the investor. We also find that the choice of performance measure matters. Depending on the risk level and measure chosen, the appropriate portfolio allocation ranges from 100% S&P 500 to 81% REIT. Our allocation results differ markedly from those indicated by the Sharpe ratio, which does not explicitly consider downside risk. Our results also show, not surprisingly, that the recent financial crisis highlights the potential volatility embedded in real estate investments, and this volatility may have underpinned the long-held notion that real estate should only comprise a small part of an investor's investible assets.

The remainder of this chapter is divided into four sections. First, we describe and discuss the data, paying particular attention to its statistical properties. Second, we mathematically define the Sharpe ratio and Sortino ratio, and emphasize the specification of the second lower partial moment. In this section we also present our statistical methods, tools, and statistical considerations. Third, we present the results of our analyses, including a comparison of the allocation implications of the Sortino and Sharpe risk measures. Finally, we conclude by summarizing our findings, commenting on their relationships to previous work, and providing some suggestions for further research.

---

[6]REITs are functionally similar to closed-end mutual funds and are authorized and governed by the Real Estate investment Act of 1960. The purpose of this legislation is to increase real estate investment by institutions and wealthy individuals by creating an investment vehicle that is tax free at the corporate level but taxable to the investor when the generated income is distributed. REITs became a major investment category only after the enactment of the Tax Reform Act of 1986, which significantly reduced the financial advantages of real estate partnerships. A brief history of REITs is provided by Woolley et al. (1997). This chapter also summarizes some of the industry's major business strategies. See also Brock (1998).

17.2 DATA DEFINITIONS AND DESCRIPTION

We use daily observations of the S&P 500 index and a U.S. REIT index. Daily data are used because studies have shown that persistence is not present in empirical trading data (Menkhoff, 2010) and that fund managers put very little emphasis on intraday trading (Eisler and Kertèsz, 2007). Daily returns are expressed as the first difference of the natural logarithm of the ratio of successive index values. Natural logarithms convert the price indexes to a series that theoretically contains infinitely small and infinitely large values, and first differencing produces returns that are continuous and stationary in the mean.

The S&P 500 index is a capitalization-weighted index that consists of 500 large company stocks, which represent the leading stocks in major U.S. industries. Over $5 trillion in financial paper is benchmarked to this index, and this index itself accounts for approximately 80% of the capitalization of all U.S. stocks. Thus, academics and practitioners often consider this index to be a proxy for the U.S. market in general.

U.S. REITs account for roughly half of the global supply of these instruments.[7] We construct our REIT index from REIT stocks extracted from the daily CRSP files using "Share Code = 18" or "SICCD = 6798." These REITs, although real estate oriented, often differ in capital structure and investment strategy. For example, some REITs are funded by a mixture of debt and equity, while others are fully funded by equity. Additionally, some provide mortgage financing, other REITs concentrate on construction projects, and still others focus on real estate ownership. We calculate daily market values for all REITs by multiplying share price by shares outstanding. These market values are used to generate daily weightings for each REIT's returns. Summing the daily products of all REIT's weights and returns generates a daily weighted market value REIT return index.

Our data begin on January 2, 1987, which is the first full year following the 1986 Tax Reform Act (see footnote 6), and end on December 31, 2012. The sample contains 6555 daily observations. This 26-year span includes the October 1987 crash as well as the recent financial crisis that began in 2007. Figure 17.1 displays the time-series plots of the daily observations for both the return series. Figure 17.2 condenses these data and illustrates the nature of the left-hand tails of the two distributions. Table 17.1 presents some sample descriptive statistics for five portfolios: mean, variance, skewness, kurtosis, minimum value, maximum value, a measure of linear dependence (Ljung–Box statistic), and a measure of nonlinear dependence (Lagrange multiplier statistic). The five S&P/REIT portfolios are labeled 100%/0%, 75%/25%, 50%/50%, 25%/75%, and 0%/100%, with the first number being the S&P 500 weight and the second the REIT weight. The five portfolios are used to illustrate numerically our results throughout the remainder of this chapter. Figure 17.3 provides a scatter plot of the returns with the S&P 500 return on the x-axis and the REIT return on the y-axis.

---

[7]Over 40 countries have some type of tradable real estate security that is similar to the U.S. model. Major non-US players include the UK, France, Australia, and Japan. Smaller nations such as Finland, Singapore, and Turkey also have viable REIT markets.

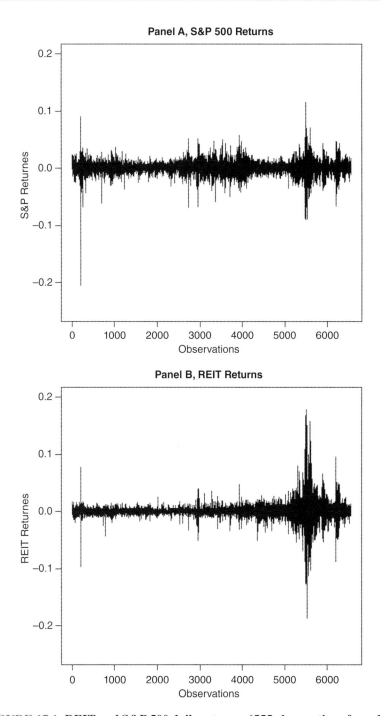

FIGURE 17.1 REIT and S&P 500 daily returns. 6555 observations from January 1987 to December 2012.

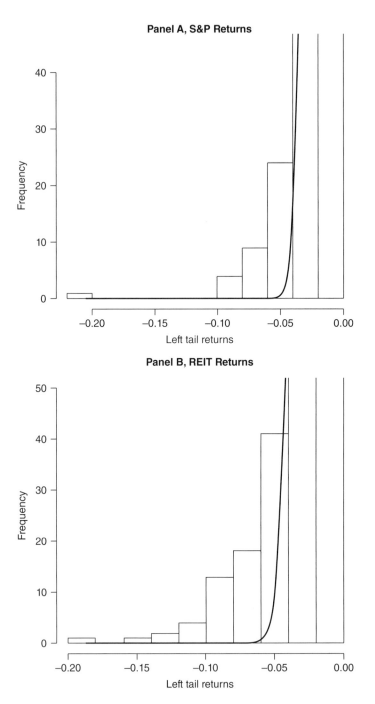

FIGURE 17.2 REIT and S&P 500 return left-tail histograms, as represented by bars, with normal distribution overlay, as represented by line.

TABLE 17.1 **Descriptive statistics for portfolios with various REIT weights**

	100/0 SP/REIT	75/25 SP/REIT	50/50 SP/REIT	25/75 SP/REIT	0/100 SP/REIT
Mean $\times 10^3$	0.343	0.374	0.405	0.435	0.466
Variance $\times 10^3$	0.144	0.136	0.146	0.173	0.217
Skewness	−0.829	−0.617	−0.243	0.137	0.413
Skewness t-stat.	−27.4	−20.4	−8.04	4.53	13.6
Kurtosis	17.8	17.4	19.7	23.7	26.8
Kurtosis t-stat.	294.	287.	325.	392.	442.
Min.	−0.205	−0.178	−0.151	−0.163	−0.189
Max.	0.116	0.123	0.138	0.153	0.179
Ljung–Box	14.7	36.4	78.1	128.	168.
Lagrange multiplier	169.	262.	520.	742.	835.

Headings correspond to portfolio weightings. The first number represents the weight of the S&P 500, while the second number represents the weight REITs. The individual null hypotheses that there is no skewness, no kurtosis, no linear dependence (Ljung–Box), and no GARCH effects (Lagrange multiplier) are rejected at least at the $p = 0.00015$ level. The correlation coefficient between the REIT and S&P 500 portfolios is 0.63.

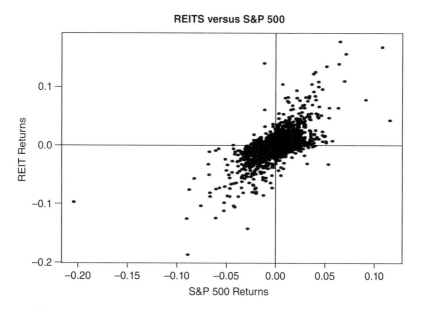

FIGURE 17.3 **REIT returns plotted against S&P 500 returns. Correlation coefficient between the REIT and S&P 500 is 0.63.**

A visual inspection of Figure 17.1 reveals that both the S&P 500 and REIT return series show volatility that changes over time and this phenomenon is aperiodically clustered. Both series also contain positive and negative spikes, that is, large abrupt changes. Particularly noticeable in both series is the October 1987 crash and its speedy recovery as well as the prolonged market turmoil associated with the 3-year financial crisis that began around 2007. This return behavior suggests that the unconditional distribution may have tails that are thicker than those associated with a Gaussian distribution. Figure 17.2 supports this observation and suggests that the left-tail probability mass of the REIT distribution is greater than that of the S&P 500 distribution. There also appears to be some asymmetric behavior leaning toward the presence of negative returns for the S&P 500 returns and of positive returns for the REIT returns.

These observations are supported by the statistics contained in Table 17.1. As indicated by the kurtosis statistics, both return series have fat tails, that is, they are thicker than those that characterize a Gaussian distribution, and they are skewed. The S&P 500 returns are negatively skewed, while the REIT returns are positively skewed. Both series have large negative spikes. Particularly noticeable is the 20% daily loss in 1987 for the S&P 500 returns and the 19% loss for the REIT series in the midst of the 2007–2009 financial crisis. The Ljung–Box and Lagrange multiplier tests indicate the strong presence of linear and nonlinear dependence, respectively, although both types of dependency appear stronger in the REIT series. Finally, not only is the REIT mean return higher than its S&P 500 counterpart, but also its standard deviation is higher. Nevertheless, the latter series yields more return per unit of volatility as measured by the standard deviation.

Asset allocation depends not only on the return and return volatility of the assets under consideration but also on the way in which the returns of these assets are related to each other. Figure 17.3, which plots the daily REIT returns against the corresponding S&P 500 returns, provides some insights into the co-movement of the returns of these two assets. The denser concentration of returns in the lower left and upper right quadrants as compared to the upper left and lower right suggests some sort of positive relationship between the two return series. Indeed, the linear correlation between the two return series is 0.63. This measure, however, is dominated by the majority of observations falling approximately between −0.03 and 0.03. For values that lie outside this fuzzy range, there are numerous instances of plots that fall far from this linear relationship. Again, the crash of October 1987 serves as an example. At this time, the REIT index experienced a 10% loss, or about one-half of that associated with the S&P 500.

The above statistics and visual patterns suggest that some performance enhancement may be possible through diversification. Comparing the descriptive statistics displayed in Table 17.1 for the five sample portfolios that contain different mixtures of the S&P 500 and REIT indexes as well as the indexes themselves supports this contention. For example, although the 100% REIT portfolio exhibits the most positive skew, the 75%/25% S&P/REIT portfolio has the thinnest tails. Further, The 100% REIT portfolio has the largest maximum return, but the smallest minimum return is associated with the 50%/50% S&P/REIT portfolio. Finally, the 50%/50% portfolio has the largest return per unit of volatility.

17.3 PERFORMANCE RATIOS AND THEIR ESTIMATIONS

We begin our formal analysis by specifying our performance ratios, which express the performance per unit of risk. As mentioned above, our benchmark is the Sharpe ratio, where the numerator is the mean portfolio return ($\bar{R}$) in excess of the risk-free rate (R_F), and the denominator is the square root of the variance (standard deviation) of the portfolio returns (Var). In other words

$$\text{Sharpe} = \frac{\left(\bar{R} - R_F\right)}{\left(\text{Var}\right)^{1/2}}. \tag{17.1}$$

According to the CAPM, the goal of the investor is to select the portfolio that generates the largest feasible Sharpe ratio value, which is equivalent to maximizing performance. Thus, portfolios can be ranked on the basis of the Sharpe ratio and their relative performances judged accordingly.

The Sortino ratio also measures portfolio performance, but it is structured to focus on downside risk, that is, the left tail of the distribution of returns. The numerator is the portfolio return that is in excess of a MAR (R_{MAR}), while the denominator is a measure of downside risk. The downside risk is defined as the square root of the second lower partial moment (LPM_2), which is the average sum of squares of the returns that are less than the MAR. In mathematical terms

$$\text{Sortino} = \frac{\left(\bar{R} - R_{MAR}\right)}{\left(LPM_2\right)^{1/2}} \tag{17.2}$$

and

$$LPM_2 = \frac{1}{n} \sum_{i=1}^{n} \left(R_{MAR} - R_i\right)^2, \quad \forall R_i \leq R_{MAR}, \tag{17.3}$$

where n is the number of observations in the left tail as defined by R_{MAR}.

One drawback of the definition depicted in Eq. (17.3) is that it depends heavily on the returns observed during a specific performance period. In other words, this discrete version LPM_2 measures only what is observed and not what might be observed. For ex post performance assessment, this is acceptable because it measures what actually happened. For deciding ex ante portfolio allocations, this formulation ignores the notion of what might happen. Following Harlow (1991), Booth and Broussard (2002), and Choffray and Mortanges (2017), among others, we remedy this drawback by recasting Eq. (17.3) in probabilistic terms.

Two possibilities are usually considered: the generalized extreme value distribution (GEV) and the GPD. The GEV is estimated using the block maxima method. This approach splits the time series in question to sequential segments. In each segment, the smallest value is selected to be included in the estimation process. The GEV is then fitted to the sample of sequential minimum observations.

The GPD is estimated using the threshold exceedance approach. The threshold defines the tail of the distribution to contain (i) all of the sample observations that fall at or below a predetermined value, or (ii) a specified number of observations beginning with the smallest. We use the threshold exceedance approach for two reasons. First, it intuitively mirrors the notion of a MAR. Second, it makes sure that all of the large negative return spikes are included in the analysis.

In particular, we assume that the left tail of the return distribution can be modeled as a GPD. The cumulative density function (F) of this distribution is given by

$$F(R) = 1 - \left[1 + \tau \left(\frac{R - \lambda}{\sigma}\right)\right]^{-1/\tau}, \tag{17.4}$$

where $\lambda = $ location and $\in (-\infty, \infty)$, $\sigma = $ scale and $\in (0, \infty)$, and $\tau = $ tail shape and $\in (-\infty, \infty)$.[8] Its accompanying probability distribution function is

$$f(R) = \frac{1}{\sigma}\left[1 + \tau \left(\frac{R - \lambda}{\sigma}\right)\right]^{-((1/\tau)+1)}. \tag{17.5}$$

Location represents the MAR and is determined exogenously by the investor. The other two parameters, τ and σ, are endogenously estimated. Increasing τ, given a value of σ, steepens the slope in the central part of the density function and increases the tail. Increasing σ, given a value of τ, flattens the slope in the central portion of the density function but also increases the tail. Various tail index estimation techniques are discussed in Beirlant et al. (2017).

To calculate the second lower partial moment, we numerically integrate the squared difference between MAR over a return multiplied by the GPD probability that the return occurs. The result is valued from R equals minus infinity to R_{MAR}, the minimum accepted return. More formally

$$\text{LPM}_2 = \int_{-\infty}^{R_{MAR}} (R_{MAR} - R)^2 f(R) \, dR. \tag{17.6}$$

This version of LPM$_2$ replaces its counterpart in (17.3).

Before proceeding with the analysis, it is useful to point out the difference between Eqs (17.3) and (17.6). In Eq. (17.3), $(R_{MAR} - R)^2$ is weighted by $1/n$. In other words, each exceedance in the calculation of LPM$_2$ is equally weighted. In contrast, if Eq. (17.6) is used, each exceedance is weighted by different probabilities. For large negative values, these probabilities are very small even if modeled by a GPD. Thus, the contribution to LPM$_2$ for a specific exceedance is typically less if Eq. (17.6) is used than if Eq. (17.3) is employed, which results in a larger Sortino ratio, *ceteris paribus*. This impact is mitigated by recalling that Eq. (17.6) uses an infinite instead of finite number of exceedances. Nevertheless, it is doubtful whether the calculated values of the Sortino ratio under both alternatives will

---

[8] The GPD and the GEV are closely related. Not only is the tail shape parameter the same for both distributions, but also the limiting distribution of the exceedances is GPD if and only if the corresponding distribution of the block maxima is GEV.

be of the same magnitude. Whether they provide similar optimal asset allocation information is an empirical question.

To estimate Eq. (17.5), we use **R** to estimate the GPD's probability density function associated with the left tail of the 101 return distributions.[9],[10] **R** is a readily available statistical package that is well suited to our task. There is no precise way to determine where the tail of a distribution ends and its body begins. We investigate this issue by examining the sensitivity of the GPD to different left tail demarcations by first following the empirical rule derived by Loretan and Philips (1994), that is, $k = n^{2/3}/\ln[\ln(n)]$, where k is the number of observations in the left tail and n is the sample size. This calculation suggests a tail size of the 161 most negative observations. We then halve, double, and quadruple this number and pick the n that provides the best coherence between the estimated GPD and its associated observed value as measured by the midpoint of the histogram generated by the return data.[11]

We report the parameter estimation results for the 100% S&P 500 and 100% REIT portfolios in Table 17.2 for the four different tail sizes. The threshold (λ) is the return associated with the accompanying exceedance number. The estimated probability density function for the two portfolios for each of the four exceedance sizes is plotted in Figure 17.4. Superimposed on these plots are the respective empirical distributions that are constructed by connecting the midpoints of the empirical histograms.

A review of the two figures indicates that the 644 observation sample, or approximately 10% of the total number of observations, appear to provide the best overall fit. This is equivalent to defining the distributions left tail to start at approximately -0.01. The tail shape and scale parameters are highly significant, and the fitted distributions closely follow their associated empirical ones. The main difference between the four distributions for each portfolio is that the samples with the larger number observations appear to better depict the sharp drop off in the number of observations around -0.025. The better fit is seen even for much larger losses, but the discrepancy is much smaller. This is the case even if this loss amount is contained within the sample observations used to estimate the model's parameters. These relationships hold for the other 99 return distributions as well,

---

[9]Sweeting and Fotiou (2011) and Scarrott and MacDonald (2012) provide excellent reviews of the use and estimation of the GPD. Nadarajah and Chan (2017) provide a listing of other software platforms useful when estimating extreme value distribution parameters.

[10]An alternate approach is to link the two GPDs using a copula. There are two ways of creating this link. One is to consider only those cases where both series exhibit exceedances, and the other is where at least one of the series exhibits an exceedance. Our analysis is in the spirit of the latter. See Rootsén and Tajvidi (2006) for more details concerning the second approach, which we believe is more appropriate for portfolio allocation applications. For finance applications using copulas to address portfolio risk management issues, see, for example, Hu (2006), Palaro and Hotta (2006), and Bhatti and Nguyen (2012).

[11]Other tail size selection rubrics include the 10% and $n^{1/2}$ rules (e.g., DuMouchel, 1983; Ferreira et al., 2003, respectively). For our data, the second rule suggests a tail size of 81, while the first rule indicates a tail containing the 656 smallest observations. These sizes compare favorably to our smallest and largest tail sizes.

TABLE 17.2   GPD estimates for S&P 500 and REIT portfolios.

Relationship estimated is from Eq. (17.4) $F(R) = 1 - \left[1 + \tau\left(\frac{R-\lambda}{\sigma}\right)\right]^{-(1/\tau)}$

Number of exceedances	Threshold (λ)	Tail shape (τ)	Scale (σ)
Panel A: S&P 500			
81	−0.03	0.3107	0.0112
		(1.97)	(5.38)
161	−0.0238	0.3542	0.0083
		(3.21)	(7.79)
322	−0.0179	0.2851	0.0075
		(4.09)	(11.89)
644	−0.0122	0.1887	0.0076
		(4.48)	(18.29)
Panel B: REIT			
81	−0.0397	-0.0584	0.029
		(0.60)	(6.79)
161	−0.0275	0.1507	0.0192
		(1.41)	(7.61)
322	−0.0169	0.2865	0.0135
		(3.52)	(10.4)
644	−0.0096	0.4022	0.009
		(6.68)	(14.64)

Note: *t*-values in parentheses.

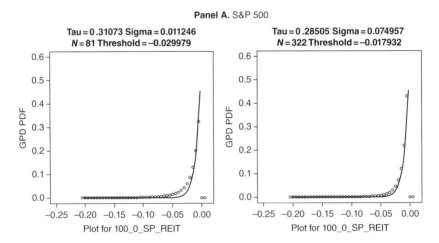

Panel A. S&P 500

FIGURE 17.4 Plots of S&P 500 and REIT portfolios with various exceedances used for GPD estimation. GPD PDF generated from (17.5) $f(R) = \frac{1}{\sigma}\left[1 + \tau\left(\frac{R-\lambda}{\sigma}\right)\right]^{-((1/\tau)+1)}$ **. Panel A: S&P 500 and Panel B: REIT.** Note: Circles indicate GPD fit. Line shows empirical fit using mid-point histogram plotting. *N* equals various exceedances used in the estimation. Threshold corresponds to the return associated with that exceedance observation.

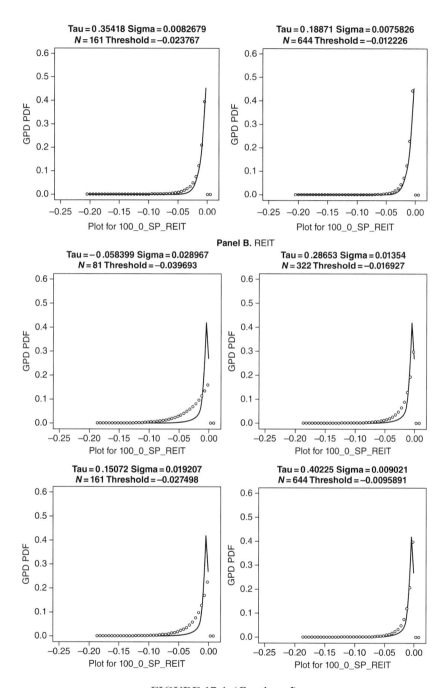

FIGURE 17.4 (*Continued*)

although we do not report their detail here. Because of the better fit, we proceed with our analysis using the GPD parameters provided by the 644 observation sample.

Before turning to the performance results, three points are worthy of note. First, although the 644 sample provides the best fit the S&P 500 and REIT returns, the physical nature of their left tails are not the same. The main difference is in the tail shape parameter (τ) of the REIT index, which is more than twice the size of the S&P 500's parameter while the scales (σ) of both extreme value distributions are similar, although the size of the REIT parameter is slightly larger. This indicates that the estimated return distribution of the former has longer tails but also a sharper bend in the middle of the distribution.

Second, the minimum acceptable rate of return is determined by the investor and reflects his/her risk–reward tradeoff. The rate, then, could be any real number that the investor deems to be minimally acceptable. However, we are interested in tail risk. Thus the maximum allowable target rate should be less than or approximately equal to the rate that separates the left tail from the rest of the distribution. If it is not, its use must involve the issues associated with out-of-sample prediction.

Third, for benchmark purposes we consider the entire 26-year period as a single unit. Over this span of time, the returns are stationary in the mean but not in the variance. This is typical of financial assets. Some have suggested that, before the stochastic process that determines the tail behavior of the series is estimated, the impact of the time-varying variance should be removed. Although it is possible to remove the conditional variance from the return series using generalized autoregressive conditional heteroskedastic (GARCH) methods, we do not do so for two related reasons. First, tail behavior and conditional variances are not independent. For example, in the GARCH setup, a large negative return will cause the next day's conditional variance to increase. Thus, removing the GARCH effects may inadvertently impact the magnitude of a future spike.[12] Second, we currently do not know when crashes or extended periods of turbulence caused by financial crises will occur. Along these lines, Booth and Broussard (2002) document that spikes are often statistically independent of each other. Nevertheless, recently some preliminary research has addressed the issue of whether financial stability can be predicted through the development of early warning systems. Some interesting examples of this ongoing research include Bussière and Fratzscher (2006), Alessi and Detken (2011), and Lo Duca and Peltonen (2013), to name but a few.

17.4   PERFORMANCE MEASUREMENT RESULTS AND IMPLICATIONS

Figure 17.5 depicts the Sortino ratio values, (17.2), which uses (17.3) to calculate its denominator, while Figure 17.6 also reports these performance values but

---

[12]Kozhan et al. (2013) suggest that the skew and variance premium are manifestations of the same underlying risk factor.

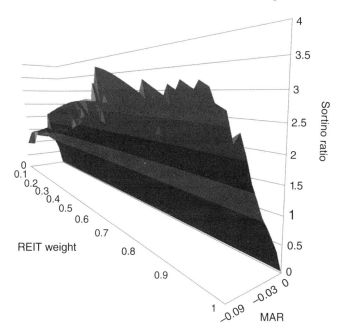

Panel B–Selected Sortino Ratios from Panel A					
	REIT Weights (boldface signifies largest row value)				
Minimum Acceptable Return	0	25	50	75	100
0.00	0.0271	0.0305	0.0321	**0.0322**	0.0315
−0.01	**0.6766**	0.6377	0.5526	0.4798	0.4149
−0.02	**1.0010**	0.9158	0.8129	0.7134	0.6535
−0.03	1.0747	**1.1021**	1.0631	0.9661	0.8777
−0.04	1.1788	1.2342	**1.2940**	1.2246	1.0778
−0.05	1.2824	1.4801	**1.5596**	1.4899	1.3797
−0.06	1.4406	1.5826	1.8772	**1.8787**	1.6668
−0.07	1.2357	1.7318	**2.2083**	2.0484	2.0823
−0.08	1.4290	1.7066	2.3336	2.3455	**2.4183**
−0.09	1.1142	1.7139	2.2687	**2.6422**	2.2647
−0.1	0.9587	1.7991	2.7168	**3.1551**	2.7191

FIGURE 17.5 Sortino ratio values using (17.3) versus various MAR and REIT weights. Panel A: Plots of 1111 Sortino ratio values. *X*-axis represents weight in REIT portfolio, *Z*-axis represents Minimal Acceptable Return (MAR), and *Y*-axis represents calculated Sortino ratio provided REIT weight and MAR. Panel B: Selected Sortino ratios from Panel A.

calculates the denominator of this ratio using (17.6). In both figures, Panel A visually illustrates the calculated performance results for 101 portfolios and numerous target rates. The portfolio weights run from 0.0 (100% S&P 500) to 1.0 (100% REIT) by 0.01, and the MARs run from −0.01 to −0.10 by −0.01, thereby creating 1111 data points. Panel B provides the numerical estimates for the aforementioned five S&P–REIT portfolios, that is, 100%/0%, 75%/25%, 50%/50%, 25%/75%, and 0%/100%.

Turning first to Figure 17.5, Panels A and B, we find that the Sortino ratio's value depends heavily on the choice of the MAR. Its value tends to increase as the investor increases his/her ability to tolerate risk but then decrease slightly if the target rate becomes too onerous. The same hoop-shaped pattern occurs as the portfolio changes from one that is 100% S&P 500 to one that is 100% REIT. The joint movement can be seen in Panel B, where the Sortino ratios for the listed minimal accepted returns and REIT weights are in boldface type. This pattern suggests that for the period being examined investors with a low tolerance for medium-large losses would have been better off on a risk–return basis if they had relatively more heavily allocated their investable resources to the S&P 500. In contrast, those individuals with a low tolerance for only very large losses would have been better off by investing more in the REIT portfolio.

As shown in Figure 17.6, Panels A and B, the results are markedly different if the GPD approach to calculate the Sortino ratio is used. In this case, the optimal portfolio appears to be 100% S&P 500 no matter what the choice of the minimum accepted return. We suspect that this difference in allocation involves the way in which the two versions of the Sortino ratio are calculated with the values in Figure 17.5 associated with the equal weighting of exceedances and those in Figure 17.6 with probability weighting. Our intuition is that the results associated with the GPD approach are a result of the REIT index having a longer left tail than the S&P 500 index as evinced by the tail shape and scale parameters (see Table 17.2) and the heavier probability mass in the left tail as documented in Figure 17.2.

Table 17.3 displays the specific optimal allocation weights for both versions of the Sortino ratio and the Sharpe ratio. The optimum REIT weight according to the Sortino ratio, that is, (17.3), ranges from 0.00 to 0.81, depending on the MAR chosen. The corresponding weights for the Sortino ratio, that is, (17.6), are always 0.00 at least to the precision of two decimal places. By way of comparison, the Sharpe ratio calculated the optimal REIT weight to be 0.56.[13] These results indicate that that performance measurement and asset allocation decisions to obtain future performance are extremely sensitive to the way in which risk is measured.

---

[13]The risk-free rate is assumed to be zero. Relaxing this assumption does not affect the performance ranking.

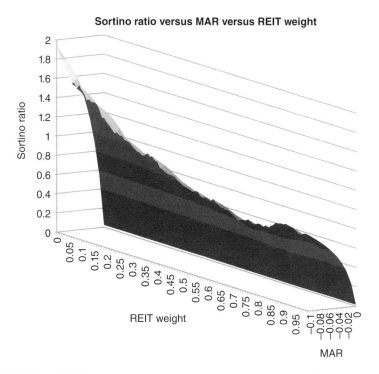

FIGURE 17.6 Sortino ratio values using (17.6) versus various MAR and REIT weights. Panel A: Plots of 1111 Sortino ratio values. *X*-axis represents weight in REIT portfolio, *Z*-axis represents Minimal Acceptable Return (MAR), and *Y*-axis represents calculated Sortino ratio provided REIT weight and MAR. Panel B: Selected Sortino ratios from Panel A.

Panel B–Selected Sortino Ratios from Panel A					
	REIT Weights (boldface signifies largest row value)				
Minimum Acceptable Return	0	25	50	75	100
0.00	**0.0227**	0.0211	0.0177	0.0149	0.0147
−0.01	**0.5505**	0.4204	0.3089	0.2382	0.2388
−0.02	**0.9025**	0.6430	0.4620	0.3566	0.3695
−0.03	**1.1543**	0.7872	0.5614	0.4363	0.4596
−0.04	**1.3435**	0.8899	0.6342	0.4970	0.5284
−0.05	**1.4911**	0.9683	0.6921	0.5472	0.5847
−0.06	**1.6096**	1.0313	0.7407	0.5909	0.6331
−0.07	**1.7072**	1.0840	0.7834	0.6303	0.6761
−0.08	**1.7891**	1.1296	0.8219	0.6668	0.7153
−0.09	**1.8591**	1.1701	0.8576	0.7012	0.7520
−0.1	**1.9198**	1.2069	0.8913	0.7341	0.7867

TABLE 17.3   **Optimal REIT portfolio weights**

Minimum acceptable return	Sortino ratio		Sharpe ratio
	Equation (17.3)	Equation (17.6)	
0.00	0.65	0.00	0.56
−0.01	0.01	0.00	0.56
−0.02	0.00	0.00	0.56
−0.03	0.18	0.00	0.56
−0.04	0.39	0.00	0.56
−0.05	0.63	0.00	0.56
−0.06	0.67	0.00	0.56
−0.07	0.46	0.00	0.56
−0.08	0.63	0.00	0.56
−0.09	0.81	0.00	0.56
−0.10	0.63	0.00	0.56

Notes: The Sharpe ratio is constant by construction, while the Sortino ratio calculated using (17.6) is constant, that is, 0.00 by calculation.

17.5   CONCLUDING REMARKS

Our study contributes to two strands of the performance and asset allocation literature. First, Ornelas et al. (2012) suggest that there may not be any material differences in the performance rankings between the Sharpe ratio and the Sortino ratio. In a study involving mutual funds and asset allocation, using monthly data, they find that the rankings of the Sharpe ratio and the Sortino ratio are highly correlated. The correlation is 0.998 if Spearman's rank correlation is used and 0.971 if Kendall's rank correlation is used. The correlation between the Sharpe ratio and conditional Sharpe ratio is 0.989 and 0.920, respectively. In contrast, our empirical results support the notion that the choice of the performance measure does matter.

Second, with respect to the performance of REITs, earlier studies such as Firstenberg and Ross (1988), Ennis and Burik (1991), and Kallberg et al. (1996) find that real estate is typically unrepresented in investor portfolios when compared to that suggested by modern portfolio theory. These and other studies find that investors should hold somewhere between 10% and 20% of their investible assets in real estate instead of the typical 3%. Wilshire (2012) using mean-variance optimization suggests no exposure to REITs for those investors who are retired or about to retire and around 15% for those just beginning their work-life. Booth and Broussard (2002) using the standard approach also find that the appropriate allocation is around 10%, but when they employ a downside risk framework using GEV probabilities they conclude that, depending on the target rate of return, investors should hold at least 40% of their investments in REITs and perhaps as much as 100% depending on their need to avoid substantial exposure to unwanted losses. These studies, however, with the exception of Wilshire (2012) and ours, do not consider the impact of the 2007–2009 financial crisis. It appears then that the old industry prescription of having no more than 3% of investible assets allocated to real estate may not be as out of line as has been recently thought.

We believe that future research should be directed in two directions. First, the implications of downside risk should be explored for asset allocation decisions involving more than two assets. This will better fit the needs of institutional investors that routinely deal with risk management decisions dealing with several or even more asset classes. It will also provide additional insights into the role of extant (especially REITs) and new asset classes that have been or yet to be proposed. Second, the notion of a conditional Sortino ratio should be fully explored. This suggests that whatever extreme value measure is used, it must not only be time dependent but also must discriminate between ordinary volatility caused by noise and the normal ebb and flow of business activity and extreme volatility caused by unpredictable financial crises. Such research can help the investment practitioner make better asset allocation decisions.

Acknowledgments

We thank Ishaq Bhatti for providing the initial version of the **R** code used to estimate the various GPDs. We also acknowledge the research help of Allison Braetzel and Ryan Timmer.

References

Alessi, I., Detken, C. Quasi real time early warning indicators for costly asset price boom/bust cycles: a role for global liquidity. European Journal of Political Economy 2011;**27**(3):520–533.

Arzac, E.R., Bawa, V.S. Portfolio choice and equilibrium in capital markets with safety-first investors. Journal of Financial Economics 1977;**4**:277–288.

Bachelier, L. *Théorie de la spéculation.* Paris: Gauthier-Villars; 1900.

Beirlant, J., Herrmann, K., Teugels, J.L. Estimation of the extreme value index. In: Longin, F., editor. *Extreme Events in Finance.* Wiley; 2017.

Berkowitz, J., O'Brien, J. How accurate are value-at-risk models at commercial banks. Journal of Finance 2002;**57**(3):1093–1111.

Bhatti, M.I., Nguyen, C.C. Diversification evidence from international equity markets using extreme values and stochastic copulas. Journal of International Financial Markets, Institutions & Money 2012;**22**:622–646.

Booth, G.G., Broussard, J.P. The role of REITs in asset allocation. Finance (Revue de l'Association Francaise de France) 2002;**23**(2):109–124.

Booth, G.G., Gurun, U.G., Zhang, H.H. Financial networks and trading in bond markets. Journal of Financial Markets 2014;**18**:126–157.

Brock, R.L. *Investing in REITs.* Princeton, NJ: Bloomberg Press; 1998.

Brock, W.A., Hsieh, D.A., LeBaron, B. *Nonlinear Dynamics, Chaos, and Instability: Statistical Theory and Economic Evidence.* Cambridge, MA: The MIT Press; 1991.

Bussière, M., Fratzscher, M. Towards a new early warning system of financial stress. Journal of International Money and Finance 2006;**25**(6):953–973.

Choffray, J.M., Pahud de Mortanges, C. Protecting assets under non-parametric market conditions. In: Longin, F., editor. *Extreme Events in Finance*. Wiley; 2017.

Duffy, J., Feltovich, N. Does observation of others affect learning in strategic environments? An experimental study. International Journal of Game Theory 1999;**28**: 131–152.

DuMouchel, W.H. Estimating the stable index α in order to measure tail thickness: a critique. Annals of Statistics 1983;**11**:1019–1031.

Eisler, Z., Kertèsz, J. Liquidity and the multiscaling properties of the volume traded on the stock market. Europhysics Letters 2007;**77**:28001.

Ennis, R.A., Burik, P. Pension fund real estate investment under a simple equilibrium pricing model. Financial Analysts Journal 1991;**47**(3):20–30.

Fama, E.F. The behavior of stock market prices. Journal of Business 1965a;**38**(1): 35–105.

Fama, E.F. Portfolio analysis in a stable Paretian market. Management Science 1965b;**11**(3):404–419.

Feng, L., Li, B., Podobnik, B., Preis, T., Stanley, H.E. Linking agent-based models and stochastic models of financial markets. Proceedings of the National Academy of Science (PNAS) 2012;**109**(22):8388–8393.

Ferreira, A., de Haan, L., Peng, L. On optimizing the estimation of high quantiles of a probability distribution. Statistics 2003;**37**:401–434.

Firstenberg, P.M., Ross, S.A. Real estate: the whole story. Journal of Portfolio Management 1988;**14**(3):22–34.

Fisher, I. *The Nature of Capital and Income*. London: Macmillan; 1906.

Fogler, H.R. 20% in real estate: can theory justify it? Journal of Portfolio Management 1984;**10**(2):6–13.

Gabaix, X., Gopikrishnan, P., Pierou, V., Stanley, H.E. A theory of power-law distributions in financial market fluctuations. Nature 2003;**423**:267–270.

Harlow, W.V. Asset allocation in a downside-risk framework. Financial Analysts Journal 1991;**47**(5):29–45.

Harlow, W.V., Rao, R.K.S. Asset pricing in a generalized mean – lower partial moment framework. Journal of Financial and Quantitative Analysis 1989;**24**(3):285–311.

Hicks, J.R. A suggestion for simplifying the theory of money. Economics 1935; (February):1–19.

Hong, H., Kubik, J.D., Stein, J.C. Thy neighbor's portfolio: word-of-mouth effects in the holdings and trades of money managers. Journal of Finance 2005;**60**:2801–2824.

Hu, L. Dependence patterns across financial markets: a mixed copula approach. Applied Financial Economics 2006;**16**:717–729.

Jorion, P. *Value at Risk: The New Benchmark for Managing Financial Risk*. 3rd ed. New York: Mc-Graw-Hill; 2007.

Kallberg, J.G., Liu, C.H., Greig, D.W. The role of real estate in the portfolio allocation process. Real Estate Economics 1996;**73**:18–24.

Kozhan, R., Neuberger, A., Schneider, P. The skew risk premium in the equity index market. Review of Financial Studies 2013;**26**(9):2174–2203.

Lintner, J. The valuation of risk assets and the selection of risky investments in stock portfolios and capital budgets. Review of Economics and Statistics 1965;**47**(1):13–37.

Lo Duca, M., Peltonen, T.A. Assessing systematic risks and predicting systematic events. Journal of Banking & Finance 2013;**37**(7):2183–2195.

Longin, F. From value at risk to stress testing: the extreme value approach. Journal of Banking & Finance 2000;**24**:1097–1130.

Loretan, M., Philips, P.C.B. Testing the covariance stationarity of heavy tailed time series: an overview of theory with applications to several financial datasets. Journal of the Royal Statistical Society D 1994;**1**:211–248.

Lucas, A., Klaassen, P. Extreme returns, downside risk, and optimal asset allocation. Journal of Portfolio Management 1998;(Fall):71–79.

Mandelbrot, B.B. *Fractals and Scaling in Finance: Discontinuity, Concentration, Risk.* New York: Springer-Verlag; 1997.

Mandelbrot, B.B. The variation of certain speculative prices. Journal of Business 1963;**36**(4):394–419.

Markowitz, H.M. The early history of portfolio theory: 1600–1960. Financial Analysts Journal 1999;**55**(4):5–16.

Markowitz, H.M. Portfolio selection. Journal Finance 1952;**7**:77–91.

Markowtiz, H.M. *Portfolio Selection: Efficient Diversification of Investments.* New York: John Wiley & Sons; 1959.

Markowitz, H.M. *Mean-Variance Analysis in Portfolio Choice and Capital Markets.* Oxford, UK: Basil Blackwell; 1987.

Markschak, J. Money and the theory of assets. Econometrica 1938;**6**:311–325.

Menkhoff, L. The use of technical analysis by fund managers: international evidence. Journal of Banking & Finance 2010;**34**:2573–2586.

Mossin, J. *Equilibrium in a capital asset market.* Econometrica 1966;**34**(4):768–783.

Nadarajah, S., Chan, S. Estimation methods for value at risk. In: Longin, F., editor. *Extreme Events in Finance.* Wiley; 2017.

Neftci, S.D. Value at risk calculations, extreme events, and tail estimation. Journal of Derivatives 2000;(Spring):23–37.

Ornelas, J.R.H., Silva, A.F. Jr, Fernandes, J.L.B. Yes, the choice of performance measure does matter for the ranking of US mutual funds. International Journal of Finance and Economics 2012;**17**(1):61–72.

Palaro, P., Hotta, L.K. Using copula to measure value at risk. J Data Sci 2006;**4**:93–115.

Rootsén, H., Tajvidi, N. The multivariate generalized Pareto distribution. Bernoulli 2006;**12**:917–930.

Roy, A.D. Safety first and the holding of assets. Econometrica 1952;**20**:431–449.

Rubinstein, M. Markowitz's "portfolio selection": a fifty-year retrospective. Journal of Finance 2002;**57**(3):1041–1045.

Scarrott, C., MacDonald, A. A review of extreme value threshold estimation and uncertainty quantification. REVSTAT – Statistical Journal 2012;**10**(1):33–66.

Shakespeare, W. circa 1600. *The Merchant of Venice*, Act I, Scene I. Available at http://www.online-literature.com/shakespeare/merchant.Accessed 2016 May 30.

Sharpe, W.F. Capital asset prices: a theory of market equilibrium under conditions of risk. Journal of Finance 1964;**19**(3):425–442.

Sharpe, W.F. Mutual fund performance. Journal of Business 1966;(January):119–138.

Sharpe, W.F. The Sharpe Ratio. Journal of Portfolio Management 1994;(Fall):49–58.

Sortino, F.A. *Managing Downside Risk in Financial Markets: Theory, Practice and Implementation*. Boston, MA: Butterworth-Heinemann; 2001.

Sortino, F.A. *The Sortino Framework for Constructing Portfolios: Focusing on the Desired Target Return to Optimize Upside Potential Relative to Downside Risk*. Amsterdam, NL: Elsevier; 2010.

Sortino, F.A., Price, L. Performance measurement in a downside risk framework. Journal of Investing 1994;(Fall):59–65.

Sortino, F.A., van der Meer, R. Downside risk: capturing what's at stake. Journal of Portfolio Management 1991;(Summer):27–31.

Sweeting, P.J., Fotiou, F., 2011, Calculating and communicating tail association and the risk of extreme loss: a discussion paper, presented to The Institute and Faculty of Actuaries, London, UK, September 26, pp. 1–66.

Williams, J.B. *The Theory of Investment Value*. Cambridge, MA: Harvard University Press; 1938.

Wilshire. *The Role of REITS and Listed Real Estate Equities in Target Date Fund Asset Allocations*. Washington, DC: Nation Association of Real Estate Investment TrustsMarch; 2012.

Woolley, S., Morris, K., Melcher, R.A., Forest, S.A. The new world of real estate. Business Week 1997;**22**:78–87.

Chapter Eighteen

Portfolio Insurance: The Extreme Value Approach Applied to the CPPI Method

Philippe Bertrand[1,2] and Jean-Luc Prigent[3]

[1] *CERGAM, Aix-Marseille University, Aix, France*
[2] *KEDGE Business School, Marseille, France*
[3] *THEMA and Labex MME-DII, University of Cergy-Pontoise, Cergy-Pontoise, France*

18.1 INTRODUCTION

Portfolio insurance is designed to give the investor the ability to limit downside risk while allowing some participation in upside markets. This return pattern has seemed attractive to many investors who have poured up to billions of dollars into various portfolio insurance products, based either on basic financial assets such as equity or bond indices or on more complex assets such as credit products and hedge funds. There exist several methods of portfolio insurance: stop-loss strategy, the option-based portfolio insurance (OBPI) introduced by Leland and Rubinstein (1976), the constant proportion portfolio insurance (CPPI), and so on (see Bertrand and Prigent, 2005 for a comparison of these methods).

Here, we are interested in a widely used one: the CPPI introduced by Black and Jones (1987) for equity instruments and by Perold (1986) and Perold and Sharpe (1988) for fixed-income instruments (see also Black and Perold, 1992). The standard CPPI method uses a simplified strategy to allocate assets dynamically over time. It requires that two assets are exchanged on the financial market: the riskless asset with a constant interest rate (usually treasury bills or other liquid money market instruments), and the risky one (usually a market index or a basket of market indices). The key assumption is that, at any time of the management period, the amount invested on the risky asset (usually called the *exposure*) is proportional to the difference (usually called the *cushion*) between the current

Extreme Events in Finance: A Handbook of Extreme Value Theory and its Applications,
First Edition. Edited by François Longin.

portfolio value and the floor, which corresponds to the guaranteed amount. In particular, such a method implies (theoretically) that the exposure is nil as soon as the cushion is nil. Advantages of this strategy over other approaches to portfolio insurance are its simplicity and its flexibility. The initial cushion and the floor can be chosen according to the own investor's objective, while the multiple can be derived from the maximization of the expected utility of the investor (see Prigent, 2001a). However, in that case, the optimal multiple may be a function of the risky asset, as shown in El Karoui et al. (2005). Usually, banks do not directly bear market risks on the asset portfolios they manage for their customers. This is not necessarily true when we consider management of insured portfolios. In that case, banks can use, for example, stress testing since they may suffer the consequences of sudden large market decreases, depending on their management method.[1] For instance, in the case of the CPPI method, banks must at least provision the difference on their own capital if the value of the portfolio drops below the floor. Therefore, one crucial question for the bank that promotes such funds is: what exposure to the risky asset or, equivalently, what level of the multiple to accept? On one hand, as portfolio expectation return is increasing with respect to the multiple, customers want the multiple as high as possible. On the other hand, due to market imperfections,[2] portfolio managers must impose an upper bound on the multiple m. First, if the portfolio manager anticipates that the maximum daily historical drop (e.g., -20%) will happen during the period, he chooses m smaller than 5, which leads to a low return expectation. Alternatively, he may think that the maximum daily drop during the period he manages the portfolio will never be higher than a given value (e.g., -10%). A straightforward implication is to choose m according to this new extreme value (e.g., $m \leq 10$). Another possibility is that, more accurately, he takes account of the occurrence probabilities of extreme events in the risky asset returns. Finally, he can adopt a quantile hedging strategy: choose the multiple as high as possible but so that the portfolio value will always be above the floor at a given probability level (typically 99%). However, he must take care of heavy tails in the return distribution, as emphasized in Longin (2000) and also in Hyung and De Vries (2007). The answer to the previous questions has important practical implications in the management process implementation. It is addressed in this chapter, using extreme value theory (EVT).

This chapter is organized as follows. Section 18.2 presents the model and its basic properties. In Section 18.3, we examine the gap risk of the CPPI method and provide upper bounds on the multiple, in particular when using a quantile hedging approach. EVT allows us to get approximation of these bounds. We provide an empirical illustration using S&P 500 data.

---

[1] Customers indirectly bear part of the risk in that they abandon part of the expected return when they invest in an insured portfolio.

[2] For example, portfolio managers cannot actually rebalance portfolios in continuous-time. Additionally, problems of asset liquidity may occur, especially during stock markets crashes (see Longin, 1996a, 1997; Jansen and de Vries, 1991).

18.2 THE CPPI METHOD

18.2.1 Illustrative Example

To illustrate the method (see Figure 18.1), consider, for example, an investor with initial amount to invest V_0 (=100). Assume the investor wants to recover a prespecified percentage α (= 95%) of her initial investment at a given date in the future, T (=1 year). Note that the insured terminal value αV_0 (=95) cannot be higher than the initial value capitalized at the risk-free rate (= 3%), $V_0 e^{rT}$ (= 103.04). Her portfolio manager starts by setting an initial floor $F_0 = \alpha V_0 e^{-rT}$ (=92.2). To get a portfolio value V_t at maturity t higher than the insured amount αV_0, he keeps the portfolio value V_t above the floor $F_t = \alpha V_0 e^{-r(T-t)}$ at any time t during the management period $[0, T]$. For this purpose, the amount e_t invested in the risky asset is a fixed proportion m of the excess C_t of the portfolio value over the floor. The constant m is usually called *the multiple*, e_t *the exposure*, and C_t *the cushion*. Since $C_t = V_t - F_t$, this insurance method consists in keeping C_t positive at any time t in the period. The remaining funds are invested in the riskless asset B_t.

Both the floor and the multiple are functions of the investor's risk tolerance. The higher the multiple, the more the investor will participate in a sustained increase in stock prices. Nevertheless, the higher the multiple, the faster the portfolio will approach the floor when there is a sustained decrease in stock prices. As the cushion approaches zero, exposure approaches zero, too. Normally, this keeps the portfolio value from falling below the floor. Nevertheless, during financial crises, a very sharp drop in the market may occur before the manager has a chance to trade. This implies that m must not be too high (e.g., if a fall of 10% occurs, m must not be higher than 10 in order to keep the cushion positive).

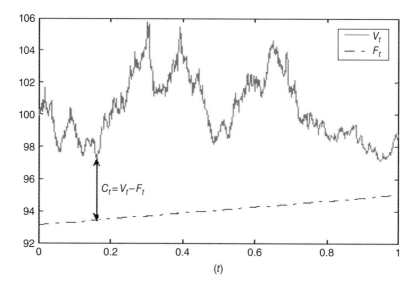

FIGURE 18.1 The CPPI method.

18.2.2   The CPPI Method (Continuous-Time Case)

The continuous-time framework is generally introduced to study the CPPI method as in Perold (1986). Recall that it is based on a dynamic portfolio strategy so that the portfolio value is above a floor F at any time t. The value of the floor gives the dynamical insured amount. It is assumed to evolve as a riskless asset, according to

$$dF_t = F_t r \, dt.$$

Obviously, the initial floor F_0 is smaller than the initial portfolio value V_0^{CPPI}. The difference $V_0^{CPPI} - F_0$ is called the cushion, denoted by C_0. Its value C_t at any time t in $[0, T]$ is given by

$$C_t = V_t^{CPPI} - F_t.$$

Denote by e_t the exposure, which is the total amount invested in the risky asset. The standard CPPI method consists of letting

$$e_t = mC_t,$$

where m is a constant called the multiple.

Note that the interesting case for portfolio insurance corresponds to $m > 1$. When the risky asset dynamics follows a geometric Brownian motion, it implies that the portfolio value at maturity is a convex function of the risky asset value. Such feature can provide significant percentage of the market rise.

Assume that the risky asset price process $(S_t)_t$ is a diffusion process with jumps:

$$dS_t = S_{t-}[\mu(t, S_t)dt + \sigma(t, S_t)dW_t + \delta(t, S_t)dN_P],$$

where $(W_t)_t$ is a standard Brownian motion, independent of the Poisson process N_P that models jumps. All coefficient functions satisfy usual assumptions to guarantee the existence and uniqueness of the previous stochastic differential equation. It means, in particular, that the sequence of random times $(T_n)_n$ corresponding to jumps satisfies the following properties: the inter-arrival times $T_{n+1} - T_n$ are independent and have the same exponential distribution with parameter denoted by λ.

The relative jumps of the risky asset $\frac{\Delta S_{T_n}}{S_{T_n}}$ are equal to $\delta(T_n, S_{T_n})$. They are supposed to be strictly higher than -1 (in order for the price S to be nonnegative). We deduce the portfolio value and its basic properties (see Prigent, 2007).

PROPOSITION 18.1 Portfolio and cushion values. *The value of the portfolio* V_t^{CPPI} *at any time* t *in the period* $[0, T]$ *is given by*

$$V_t^{CPPI} = F_0 \cdot e^{rt} + C_t,$$

where the cushion value C_t is equal to

$$C_t = C_0 \exp\left((1 - m)\, rt + m\left[\int_o^t \left(\mu - 1/2m\sigma^2\right)(s, S_s)ds + \int_o^t \sigma(s, S_s)dW_s\right]\right)$$

$$\times \prod_{0 \le T_n \le t} (1 + m\,\delta(T_n, S_{T_n})).$$

REMARK 18.2 *Consequently, the guarantee constraint is satisfied as soon as the relative jumps are such that*

$$\delta(T_n, S_{T_n}) \geq -1/m.$$

Thus, when the risky asset jumps are higher than a given constant, the condition $0 \leq m \leq -1/d$ allows us to get always the positivity of the cushion value. For example, if d is equal to -10%, we get $m \leq 10$, while if d is equal to -20%, we get $m \leq 5$. Additionally, in practice, the portfolio manager may need 2 or 3 days to sell his whole position on the risky asset in a bearish market. Therefore, he may face a cumulative drop equal, for example, to 33%. In that case, m *must be smaller than 3. Note that these upper bounds on the multiple do not depend on the probability distribution of the jump times T_n.*

Corollary 18.1 Geometric Brownian motion case. *When the risky asset price has no jump ($\delta = 0$) and the coefficients $\mu(\cdot, \cdot)$ and $\sigma(\cdot, \cdot)$ are constant, we deduce the following standard formula:*

$$V_t^{CPPI}(m, S_t) = F_0 \cdot e^{rt} + \alpha_t \cdot S_t^m,$$

where

$$\alpha_t = \left(\frac{C_0}{S_0^m}\right) \exp[\beta t] \quad \text{and} \quad \beta = \left(r - m\left(r - \frac{1}{2}\sigma^2\right) - m^2\frac{\sigma^2}{2}\right).$$

The cushion value is given by

$$C_t = C_0 e^{m\sigma W_t + \left[r + m(\mu - r) - \frac{m^2\sigma^2}{2}\right]t} \quad \text{with} \quad C_0 = V_0 - P_0.$$

REMARK 18.3 *For the geometric Brownian motion case, both the portfolio and cushion values are path-independent. They have lognormal distributions (up to the deterministic floor value F_T for the portfolio). The volatility is equal to $m\sigma$, and the instantaneous mean is given by $r + m(\mu - r)$. This illustrates the leverage effect of the multiple m: the higher the multiple, the higher the excess return but also the higher the volatility.*
Note also that, since we have $V_t^{CPPI}(m, S_t) = F_0 \cdot e^{rt} + \alpha_t S_t^m$, the portfolio profile is convex as soon as the multiple m is higher than 1.

Let us examine the Lévy process case. For this, we assume that $\delta(\cdot)$ is not equal to 0 but μ and σ are constant. Suppose also that the jumps are i.i.d. with probability distribution $K(dx)$, with finite mean $E[\delta(T_1, S_{T_1})]$ denoted by b and $E[\delta^2(T_1, S_{T_1})] < \infty$ equal to c. The logarithmic return of the risky asset S is a Lévy process. Then, we deduce the following:

PROPOSITION 18.4 *The first two moments of the portfolio value are given by*

$$
\begin{cases}
E\left[V_t\right] = (V_0 - P_0)e^{[r+m(\mu+b\lambda-r)]t} + P_0 e^{rt}, \\
\mathrm{Var}[V_t] = (V_0 - P_0)^2 e^{2[r+m(\mu+b\lambda-r)]t}\left[e^{m^2(\sigma^2+c\lambda)t} - 1\right].
\end{cases}
$$

REMARK 18.5 *From the mean-variance point of view, note that both the mean and the variance of the CPPI portfolio value are increasing functions of the multiple m. Thus there does not exist any multiple m allowing the mean-variance dominance over the other ones. In fact, the expectation of gains is not the first goal: the guarantee level is crucial, which means that there is no floor gap risk. When it has been determined, the multiple allows the adjustment of the percentage of anticipated profit when the financial market rises. But, as seen previously, the guarantee condition relies (only) on the risky asset jumps and, unfortunately, the multiple has a "leverage" effect on these latter ones.*

18.2.3   The CPPI Method (Discrete-Time Case)

Previous modeling is based on the continuous-time strategy. However, continuous-time processes are usually estimated from discrete-time observations. In that case, we have to decide whether a given return observation is due to a jump or to a relatively high fluctuation of the diffusion component (see the literature about statistical estimation of stochastic processes, and in particular, estimation of diffusion processes with jumps based on bi-power variations and its extensions). One solution is to consider that there exists a jump as soon as the observed arithmetic return lies in a given subset. However, in such a case, we have to take account of the inter-arrival time distribution.

Additionally, from the practical point of view, the discrete-time framework is more convenient since the actual CPPI strategy is based on discrete-time portfolio rebalancing. Additionally, transaction costs and/or illiquidity problems on some specific financial assets can induce discrete-time strategies.

18.2.3.1   The standard discrete-time case

Changes in asset prices are supposed to occur at discrete times along a whole time period $[0, T]$ (e.g., 10 years). Particular subperiods indexed by l, $[l\theta, (l+1)\theta]_{l\leq p}$ with $p\theta = T$, can be introduced. They may correspond to several standard portfolio management periods (e.g., 1 week, 1 month, 1 year, etc.). Finally, for each subperiod l, consider the sequence of deterministic prices variations times $(t_k^l)_k$ in $[l\theta, (l+1)\theta]$, which for simplicity, for each l, we denote by $(t_k)_k$ (e.g., daily variations).

In this framework, the CPPI portfolio value can be determined as follows. Denote by X_k the opposite of the arithmetical return of the risky asset between times t_{k-1} and t_k. We have

$$
X_k = -\frac{S_{t_k} - S_{t_{k-1}}}{S_{t_{k-1}}}.
$$

Consider the maximum of these values. For any l, define

$$M_l = \text{Max}(X_1, \ldots, X_l).$$

Denote by V_k the portfolio value at time t_k. The guarantee constraint is to keep the portfolio value V_k above the floor P_k. The exposure e_k invested in the risky asset S_k is equal to mC_k, where the cushion value C_k is equal to $V_k - P_k$. The remaining amount $(V_k - e_k)$ is invested on the riskless asset with return r_k for the time period $[t_k, t_{k+1}]$. Therefore, the dynamic evolution of the portfolio value is given by (similar to the continuous-time case)

$$V_{k+1} = V_k - e_k X_{k+1} + (V_k - e_k)r_{k+1},$$

where the cushion value is defined by

$$C_{k+1} = C_k[1 - m\, X_{k+1} + (1 - m)r_{k+1}].$$

Thus, we deduce both the cushion and the portfolio values.

PROPOSITION 18.6 *For the discrete-time case, the cushion and the portfolio values are given by*

$$C_k = C_0 \prod_{1 \le l \le k} [1 - m\, X_l + (1 - m)r_l] \quad \text{and} \quad V_k = C_k + F_k.$$

Since at any time t_k the cushion value must be positive, we get, for any $k \le n$

$$-mX_k + (1 - m)r_k \ge -1.$$

Since r_k is relatively small, the previous inequality can be approximated.

PROPOSITION 18.7 *The perfect guarantee condition is given by*

$$\forall k \le n, \quad X_k \le \frac{1}{m} \text{ or equivalently } M_n = \text{Max}(X_k)_{k \le n} \le \frac{1}{m}.$$

Assuming, as usual, that the right end point $-d$ of the common distribution F of the variables X_k is nonnegative, we deduce that the insurance is perfect along any period $[0, T]$ if and only if

$$m \le -\frac{1}{d}.$$

For example, if the maximum drop is equal to -20% (the "Black Monday" on October 1987), then $d = -0.2$. Thus m must be less than 5.

18.2.3.2 The "truncated" discrete-time case

Because of the discrete-time estimation of stochastic processes or of the possible anticipation of the portfolio manager concerning the relative jumps during a given period (e.g., X_k is considered as an actual jump if its value is higher than 3% or X_k will never be higher than 20%, corresponding to the market crash in October 1987), we introduce also the truncated jumps $X_k^{[a,b]}$ defined by

$$X_k^{[a,b]} = X_k 1_{a \leq X_k \leq b},$$

where $I_{a \leq X_k \leq b}$ is equal to 1 if $a \leq X_k \leq b$, and 0 otherwise.

In fact, when determining an upper bound on the multiple m, we have only to consider positive values of X_k (see Section 18.3). Therefore, it is sufficient to take $a = 0$ and b equal to the maximum relative drop anticipated for the management period. Since the portfolio manager may take account of the occurrence probabilities of some given values of the relative jumps (corresponding, e.g., to maximum drops), we must introduce their arrival times which are random variables. Denote by $(T_k^{[a,b]})_k$ the sequence of times at which X_k takes values in the interval $[a, b]$. The sequence $(T_k^{[a,b]}, X_k^{[a,b]})_k$ is called a *marked point process*.[3]

18.3 CPPI AND QUANTILE HEDGING

18.3.1 Upper Bounds on the Multiple

As seen in Proposition 18.4, there exists an upper bound on the multiple, which allows the perfect guarantee. However, this latter one is usually rather stringent and does not allow making significant benefit from market rises.

This strong condition can be modified if a quantile hedging approach is adopted, like the value at risk (see Föllmer and Leukert, 1999 for application of this notion in financial modeling). This gives the following relation for a time period $[0, T]$:

$$P[C_t \geq 0, \forall t \in [0, T]] \geq 1 - \varepsilon.$$

18.3.1.1 The standard discrete-time case

In our framework, the portfolio manager must keep the cushion positive for each trading day. Thus, we measure stock market price fluctuations by the daily rates of returns. More precisely, we use the opposite of the arithmetical rate X_k, which determines the conditions to impose on the multiple m, within the context of the CPPI method. If these variables are statistically independent and drawn from the same distribution, then the exact distribution of the maximum is equal to the power of the common distribution of X_k.

---

[3]For the basic definitions and properties about marked point processes, we refer, for example, to Bremaud (1981), Last and Brandt (1995) for marked point processes on the real line, and Jacod (1977) for more general multivariate point processes.

Assume that the random variables X_k are not truncated and the arrival times are the times t_k themselves. Let us consider M_T the maximum of the X_k for all times t_k in $[0, T]$. Then, the previous quantile condition is equivalent to

$$P\left[\forall t_k \in [0, T], X_k \leq \frac{1}{m}\right] = P\left[M_{T'} \leq \frac{1}{m}\right] \geq 1 - \varepsilon.$$

Note that, since m is nonnegative, the condition $X_k \leq \frac{1}{m}$ is equivalent to $X_k 1_{0 \leq X_k} \leq \frac{1}{m}$.

If the N random variables X_k are i.i.d. with cumulative distribution function (CDF) F, then we get the following result:

PROPOSITION 18.8 *Upper bound for the i.i.d. case with known CDF.*

$$m \leq \frac{1}{F^{-1}\left[(1 - \varepsilon)^{\frac{1}{N}}\right]}.$$

But, in most cases the CDF F is not exactly known, and some consecutive returns can be dependent. However, if block-maxima can be assumed to be independent by using a suitable length of the blocks, then the insurance condition on the multiple m can be analyzed by applying EVT.

Indeed, the fundamental result of EVT proves that there exists a normalization procedure of the maxima to get nondegenerate distributions at the limit (like the well-known central limit theorem for the sums of random variables).[4] This is the well-known Fisher–Tippett theorem (1928). Indeed, we know that there exist scale and location parameters ψ_N and μ_N such that $\frac{M_T - \mu_N}{\psi_N}$ converges in distribution to a generalized extreme distributions (GEV) defined by

$$H_\xi(x) = \begin{cases} \exp\left(-(1 + \xi x)^{\frac{-1}{\xi}}\right) & \text{if } \xi \neq 0, \text{ where } 1 + \xi x > 0 \\ \exp(-\exp(-x)) & \text{if } \xi = 0 \end{cases},$$

where the parameter ξ is called the tail index:

$$\begin{aligned} \xi &= \alpha^{-1} > 0 & \text{for the Fréchet distribution,} \\ \xi &= 0 & \text{for the Gumbel distribution,} \\ \xi &= -\alpha^{-1} < 0 & \text{for the Weibull distribution.} \end{aligned}$$

Consequently, from the condition $P\left[M_T \leq \frac{1}{m}\right] \geq 1 - \varepsilon$, and by applying EVT to M_T, we get $H_\xi\left(\frac{\frac{1}{m} - \mu_N}{\psi_N}\right) \geq 1 - \varepsilon$. This leads to the result. Indeed, we get the following approximation of the upper limit on multiple m.

---

[4]See, for instance, Gumbel (1958), Leadbetter et al. (1983), Embrechts et al. (1997), and several chapters in this book. .

PROPOSITION 18.9 *Upper bound for block-maxima.*

$$m \leq \frac{1}{\psi_N H_\xi^{-1}(1-\varepsilon) + \mu_N}.$$

The statistical problem is to find the correct distribution of extremes of returns from the data and, in particular, to estimate the normalizing constants μ_n, ψ_n, and the tail index ξ. For this purpose, when using a maximum likelihood method, we need the GEV distribution of a general, non-centered, non-reduced random variable, defined by

$$H_{\xi,\mu,\psi}(x) = \begin{cases} \exp\left(-\left(1+\xi\left(\frac{x-\mu}{\psi}\right)\right)^{\frac{-1}{\xi}}\right) & \text{if } \xi \neq 0, \text{ where } 1+\xi\left(\frac{x-\mu}{\psi}\right) > 0, \\ \exp\left(-\exp\left(-\left(\frac{x-\mu}{\psi}\right)\right)\right) & \text{if } \xi = 0. \end{cases}$$

When examining the sequence $X_{k+1} = \frac{S_{t_k} - S_{t_{k+1}}}{S_{t_k}}$, it is obvious that its distribution has a right end limit equal to 1. Therefore, the normalized maxima $\frac{Max(X_1,\dots,X_n) - \mu_n}{\psi_n}$ converge either to the Gumbel distribution Λ or to a Weibull distribution Ψ_α. For the sequence of the opposite of log-returns $R_{k+1} = Log\left[\frac{S_{t_{k+1}}}{S_{t_k}}\right]$, we get a Gumbel distribution or a Fréchet distribution.

For the determination of the limit, we can use the characterizations of Resnik (1987) for the maximum domains of attraction based on generalizations of the von Mises functions (see Embrechts et al., 1997).

18.3.1.2   The "truncated" discrete-time case

Consider now the truncated values $X_k^{[a,b]}$; denote the truncated jumps $(X_k 1_{a \leq X_k \leq b})$, and $(T_k^{[a,b]})_k$ the corresponding sequence of arrival times. As has been previously mentioned, the times $T_k^{[a,b]}$ are random variables and the range of their distributions can be the set of times $(t_k)_k$ or the whole management period $[0, T']$ if we consider jump-diffusion processes.

Define $M_T^{[a,b]}$ as the maximum of the $X_k^{[a,b]}$ in $[0, T]$. The quantile hedging condition leads to

$$P\left[\forall T_k^{[a,b]} \in [0,T], X_k^{[a,b]} \leq \frac{1}{m}\right] = P\left[M_T^{[a,b]} \leq \frac{1}{m}\right] \geq 1 - \varepsilon.$$

Denote by $N_T^{[a,b]}$ the random number of random variables $X_k^{[a,b]}$ during the period $[0, T]$.

Then, by conditioning with respect to the random number $N_T^{[a,b]}$, the quantile hedging condition becomes

$$P\left[\forall T_k^{[a,b]} \leq T, X_k \leq \frac{1}{m}\right] = \sum_k P\left[M_k^{[a,b]} \leq \frac{1}{m} \cap N_T^{[a,b]} = k\right] \geq 1 - \varepsilon,$$

which is equivalent to

$$\sum_k P\left[M_k^{[a,b]} \le \frac{1}{m}|N_T^{[a,b]} = k\right] P[N_T^{[a,b]} = k] \ge 1 - \varepsilon.$$

Introduce the function $L_T^{[a,b]}$

$$L_T^{[a,b]}(x) = \sum_k P\left[M_k^{[a,b]} \le x | N_T^{[a,b]} = k\right] P\left[N_T^{[a,b]} = k\right].$$

Since $F^{[a,b]}$ is increasing, $L_T^{[a,b]}$ has also the same property. Consider its inverse $L_T^{[a,b]-1}$.

Then we get the following result:

PROPOSITION 18.10 *Upper bound for a general marked point process. The general quantile hedging condition $P[C_t \ge 0, \forall t \le T] \ge 1 - \varepsilon$ is equivalent to*

$$m \le \frac{1}{L_T^{[a,b]-1}(1 - \varepsilon)}.$$

As can be seen, this condition involves the joint conditional distributions of the marked point process $(T_{k+1}^{[a,b]}, X_{k+1}^{[a,b]})_k$. In the independent marking case, where $(T_k^{[a,b]})_k$ and $(X_k^{[a,b]})_k$ are independent, the CDF $L_{T'}^{[a,b]}$ can be simplified as

$$L_T^{[a,b]}(x) = \sum_k P\left[M_k^{[a,b]} \le x\right] P\left[N_T^{[a,b]} = k\right].$$

Suppose, for example, that the number of times t_k is sufficiently high so that we can consider that the set of t_k seems like an interval (continuous time at the limit). Assume also that the sequence of inter-arrival times $(T_{k+1}^{[a,b]} - T_k^{[a,b]})_k$ is an i.i.d. sequence and is exponentially distributed with a parameter $\lambda^{[a,b]}$. This case corresponds to the special case of an independent marked Poisson process. $\lambda^{[a,b]}$ corresponds also to the parameter of the Poisson counting distribution. This implies that the expectation of the number of variations with values in $[a, b]$ during the period $[0, T]$ is equal to $T\lambda^{[a,b]}$. We get

$$L_T^{[a,b]}(x) = \sum_k P\left[M_k^{[a,b]} \le x\right] \frac{(\lambda^{[a,b]}T)^k}{k!} e^{-\lambda^{[a,b]}T}.$$

Furthermore, if $(X_k^{[a,b]})_k$ are also i.i.d., then we get (see Prigent, 2001b)

$$L_T^{[a,b]}(x) = e^{-\lambda^{[a,b]}T} \sum_{k=0}^{\infty} (F_T^{[a,b]})^k(x) \frac{(\lambda^{[a,b]}T)^k}{k!}.$$

This latter formula allows the explicit calculation of the upper bound.

PROPOSITION 18.11 *Upper bound for the independent marked Poisson process.*

$$m \leq \frac{1}{F^{[a,b]-1}\left(1 + \frac{Log(1-\varepsilon)}{\lambda T}\right)}.$$

This condition gives an upper limit on the multiple m, which is obviously greater than the standard limit $\frac{1}{b}$ (which is given in Proposition 18.4 with $b = d$ if the distribution is not truncated). It takes account of both the distribution of the variations and of the inter-arrival times. Note that, if the intensity $\lambda^{[a,b]}$ increases, then this upper limit decreases. So, as intuition suggests, if the frequency $\lambda^{[a,b]}$ increases, then the multiple has to be reduced and, if $\lambda^{[a,b]}$ goes to infinity, then the previous upper limit converges to the standard limit $\frac{1}{b}$.

REMARK 18.12 *Estimation of the function $L_T^{[a,b]}(x)$ in the independent case.*

Again, if the distribution of the opposite of arithmetic returns is not known, we can apply EVT to get approximation of the upper bound, provided that the management period T over which the risk is evaluated is sufficiently high and that the probabilities $P[N_T^{[a,b]} = k]$ are small, for small values of k. Under the previous conditions, we get

$$L_T^{[a,b]}(x) \simeq \sum_k H_\xi^{[a,b]}\left(\frac{x - \mu_k^{[a,b]}}{\psi_k^{[a,b]}}\right) P\left[N_T^{[a,b]} = k\right].$$

From the practical point of view, condition "$P[N_T^{[a,b]} = k]$ small, for small values of k" implies that the set $[a,b]$ is not too small. Thus, we have to carefully calibrate this set in order to get rational upper bounds.

18.3.2   Empirical Estimations

In what follows, we illustrate numerically the upper bound given in Proposition 18.9 when dealing with upper bound for block-maxima series.

18.3.2.1   Estimations of the variations X_k

We examine the variations of the opposite of the arithmetic returns, X_k, of the S&P 500 during both the period December 1983–December 2013 and the subperiod December 2003–December 2013. First we consider the whole support of X_k. We refer to Longin (1996b) for details about estimation procedures when dealing with EVT. We begin with some usual descriptive statistics about daily variations X_k (Table 18.1).

As expected, X_k is far from normally distributed and has fat tails. We find evidence for heteroskedasticity and autocorrelation in the series. More precisely, the original series should be replaced by the innovation of an AR(5).[5]

---

[5]We have used the Akaike's information criterion (AIC) to choose the appropriate model. In fact, an AR(6) has emerged but, due to the well-known problem of overparameterization of the AIC and to the fact that 5 days is a week of exchange, we select an AR(5) model.

TABLE 18.1 **Descriptive statistics of daily variations**

	S&P 500 (10 years)	S&P 500 (30 years)
Mean	−0.029057%	−0.038591%
Median	−0.078802%	−0.056489%
Maximum	0.0903	0.2047
Minimum	−0.1158	−0.1459
Standard deviation	0.0129	0.0116
Skewness	0.0762	0.5550
Kurtosis	14.3041	27.0027
Jarque-Bera	13409	18040

Nevertheless, the estimates on the raw data do not differ qualitatively from the ones on innovations.[6] As we need estimates on the raw data for the upper bound on the multiple, we conduct econometrics work on the original series.

We examine the behavior of maxima for various time periods. We first plot the maxima of X_k over 20 and 60 days for the two time periods (Figures 18.2 and 18.3).

Notice, first, that on our sample the maximum values of X_k are always positive. Knowing that we have to discriminate between the Weibull and the Gumbel distribution, the analysis confirms that the extremes of X_k seems to follow a Weibull distribution.

Equivalently, we can introduce the opposite of the log-returns:

$$-R_k = -Log\left(\frac{S_{t_k}}{S_{t_{k-1}}}\right).$$

In that case, we get a Fréchet distribution.

We consider the maximum likelihood estimation of GEV distribution of the non-normalized series (see Martins and Stedinger, 2000). The density is given

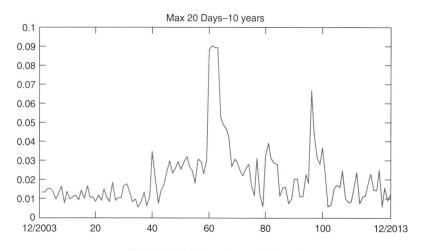

FIGURE 18.2 **Maxima (20 days).**

[6]The same kind of results can be found in Jondeau and Rockinger (1999).

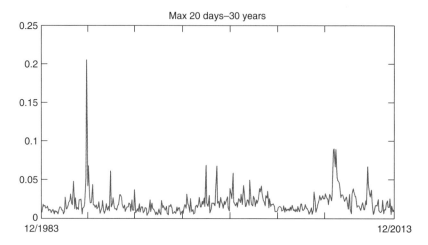

Max 20 days–30 years

FIGURE 18.2   (*Continued*)

by

$$
h_{\xi,\mu,\psi}(x) = \begin{cases} \frac{1}{\psi}\left(1+\xi\left(\frac{x-\mu}{\psi}\right)\right)^{\frac{-1}{\xi}-1}\exp\left(-\left(1+\xi\left(\frac{x-\mu}{\psi}\right)\right)^{\frac{-1}{\xi}}\right) & \text{if } 1+\xi\left(\frac{x-\mu}{\psi}\right)>0, \\ & \text{and } \xi \neq 0, \\ \frac{1}{\psi}\exp\left(-\frac{x-\mu}{\psi}-\exp\left(-\left(\frac{x-\mu}{\psi}\right)\right)\right) & \text{if } \xi = 0. \end{cases}
$$

The likelihood function to maximize is defined as follows:

$$
L(\xi,\mu,\psi) = \prod_{l=1}^{p} h_{\xi,\mu,\psi}(M^{(l)}) 1_{1+\xi\left(\frac{M^{(l)}-\mu}{\psi}\right)>0}.
$$

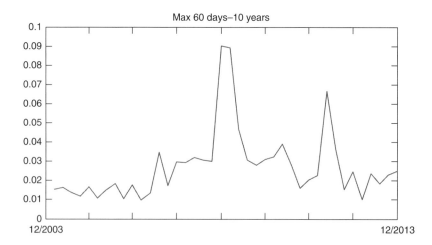

Max 60 days–10 years

FIGURE 18.3   Maxima (60 days).

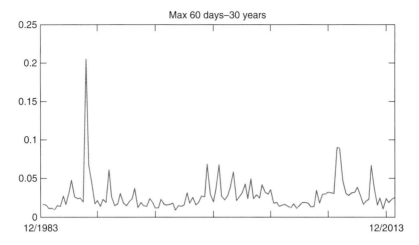

FIGURE 18.3 (*Continued*)

TABLE 18.2 Estimation results for a Fréchet distribution

Length of the selection period	Tail parameter ξ	Scale parameter ψ_θ	Location parameter μ_θ
Estimation over 10 years			
$\theta = 5$	0.3210	0.0062	0.0074
$\theta = 20$	0.4162	0.0071	0.0134
$\theta = 60$	0.3704	0.0086	0.0186
$\theta = 120$	0.4741	0.0081	0.0227
$\theta = 240$	0.5589	0.0108	0.0258
Estimation over 30 years			
$\theta = 5$	0.2296	0.0059	0.0071
$\theta = 20$	0.2936	0.0068	0.0130
$\theta = 60$	0.3816	0.0079	0.0186
$\theta = 120$	0.4614	0.0098	0.0221
$\theta = 240$	0.4978	0.0142	0.0287

The estimation results for a Fréchet distribution and for various lengths of the subperiod θ are reported in Table 18.2.

18.3.2.2 Estimations of the upper bound

We are now able to give an estimation of the upper bound on the multiple. From Proposition 18.9, the upper bound is given by $\dfrac{1}{\psi_\theta H_\xi^{-1}(1-\varepsilon)+\mu_\theta}$, where θ denotes the number of transaction dates during the management period. For the log-returns,

TABLE 18.3   **Numerical upper bounds on the multiple**

Length of the selection period	$\varepsilon = 5\%$	$\varepsilon = 1\%$	$\varepsilon = 0.1\%$
Estimation over 10 years			
$\theta = 5$	23.8	12.4	5.6
$\theta = 20$	18.6	9.4	3.9
$\theta = 60$	12.2	5.7	2.4
$\theta = 120$	7	3.1	1.4
$\theta = 240$	5.3	2.3	1.1
Estimation over 30 years			
$\theta = 5$	28.2	16.1	8.4
$\theta = 20$	22.6	13.1	6.5
$\theta = 60$	15.1	8	3.8
$\theta = 120$	7.1	3.3	1.5
$\theta = 240$	5.3	2.4	1.2

we get an analogous expression of the upper bound:

$$m \leq \frac{1}{1 - \exp\left[-\mu_\theta - \psi_\theta H_{R,\xi}^{-1}(1 - \varepsilon)\right]},$$

where $H_{R,\xi}^{-1}$ denotes the inverse of the extreme distribution of maxima of $(-R_k)_k$.

We illustrate numerically this upper bound in Table 18.3.

As expected, the upper bound on the multiple decreases when the probability level ε decreases, which corresponds to a more stringent gap risk control. It also decreases when the length of the selection period θ increases because at the same time the risk of significant drops increases. If bank "risk tolerance" to the probability level is very small, say $\varepsilon = 0.1\%$, while the length of the rebalancing period is short, or if the length of the rebalancing period is high with $\varepsilon = 1\%$, the upper bound on the multiple is in line with standard values of the multiple used by practitioners (between 4 and 8). As soon as bank risk tolerance is higher, $\varepsilon = 5\%$, the corresponding multiple is above its usual values except for long periods. Note also that the upper bounds on the multiple are smaller when dealing with data on the past 10 years due to the more important impact of the financial crisis than for the longer time period corresponding to 30 years. However, for long management period (e.g., 1 year corresponding to $\theta = 240$ trading days) and for $\varepsilon = 1\%$ (resp. $\varepsilon = 0.1\%$), the upper bound is small (resp. very small) compared to $m = 5$, which corresponds to the historical maximum daily drop of about 20%. In fact, when using the Fréchet distribution with parameter values in Table 18.3 for $\theta = 240$, we can check that the probability that the maximum daily drop is higher than 20% is about 25%, which is much higher. This is due to the weak convergence speed to the extreme distribution. On the contrary, using parameter values for the maximum on a week, this probability is much more in accordance with empirical frequency. Of course, it is possible to consider the dependence in the time series, such as the GARCH or stochastic volatility models. In that case, we can use results about the asymptotic of maxima. Note that, for example, using results of Davis and Mikosch (2009) for GARCH models, the upper bound involves the extremal index, which is the inverse of the mean cluster size of exceedances (see Ben Ameur et al., 2015). Another way to solve this problem is to introduce time-varying conditional multiples together with local quantile or expected shortfall risk measures to better take account of market fluctuations (see Ben Ameur and Prigent, 2014; Hamidi et al., 2014).

18.4 CONCLUSION

As expected, it is possible to choose higher multiples for the CPPI method than standard values if quantile hedging is used. The upper bounds can be calculated for each level of probability, according to the distributions of the marked point process, which indicates the variations of the underlying asset and its times of variations. EVT allows the approximation of these distributions in order to provide a numerical upper bound. We have illustrated this result on S&P 500 data. The difference with the standard multiple is significant, especially if we consider that the highest historical daily market decrease is unlikely to appear during the management period and when the probability level is not too small.

References

Ben Ameur, H., Prigent, J.-L. Portfolio insurance: gap risk under conditional multiples. European Journal of Operational Research 2014;**236**:238–253.

Ben Ameur, H., Bertrand, P., Prigent, J.-L. Extreme value theory for portfolio insurance with multiple assets. Working Paper Thema, University of Cergy-Pontoise, France; 2015.

Bertrand, P., Prigent, J.-L. Portfolio insurance strategies: OBPI versus CPPI. Finance 2005;**26**:5–32.

Black, F., Jones, R. Simplifying portfolio insurance. Journal of Portfolio Management 1987;**14**:48–51.

Black, F., Perold, A.R. Theory of constant proportion portfolio insurance. Journal of Economic Dynamics and Control 1992;**16**:403–426.

Bremaud, P. *Point Processes and Queues: Martingale Dynamics*. Berlin: Springer Verlag; 1981.

Davis, R.A., Mikosch, T. Extreme value theory for GARCH processes. In: Andersen, T.G., Davis, R.A., Kreiss, J.-P., Mikosch, T., editors. *Handbook of Financial Time Series*. New York: Springer; 2009. p 187–200.

El Karoui, N., Jeanblanc, M., Lacoste, V. Optimal portfolio management with American capital guarantees. Journal of Economic Dynamics and Control 2005;**29**: 449–468.

Embrechts, P., Kluppelberg, C., Mikosch, T. *Modelling Extremal Events*. Berlin: Springer-Verlag; 1997.

Fisher, R.A., Tippett, L.H.C. Limiting forms of the frequency distribution of the largest and smallest member of a sample. Proc Cambridge Philos Soc 1928;**24**:180–190.

Föllmer, H., Leukert, P. Quantile hedging. Finance and Stochastics 1999;**3**:251–273.

Gumbel, E.J. *Statistics of Extremes*. New York: Columbia University Press; 1958.

Hamidi, B., Maillet, B., Prigent, J.-L. A dynamic autoregressive expectile for time-invariant portfolio protection strategies. Journal of Economic Dynamics and Control 2014;**46**:1–29.

Hyung, N., De Vries, C.G. Portfolio selection with heavy tails. Journal of Empirical Finance 2007;**14**:383–400.

Jacod, J. A general theorem of representation for martingales. Proceedings of the Symposia in Pure Mathematics 1977;**31**:37–53.

Jansen, W.D., De Vries, C.G. On the frequency of large stock returns: putting booms and busts into perspective. The Review of Economics and Statistics 1991;**73**:18–24.

Jondeau, E., Rockinger, M. The tail behavior of stock returns: emerging versus mature markets. Proceedings of Seminar of the "Fondation Banque de France," Paris, June 1999; 1999.

Last, G., Brandt, A. *Marked Point Processes on the Real Line*. Berlin: Springer-Verlag; 1995.

Leadbetter, M.R., Lindgren, G., Rootzen, H. *Extremes and Related Properties of Random Sequences and Processes*. New York: Springer-Verlag; 1983.

Leland, H.E., Rubinstein, M. The evolution of portfolio insurance. In: Luskin, D.L., editor. *Portfolio Insurance: A Guide to Dynamic Hedging*. Wiley; 1976.

Longin, F. Boom and crash options: winning in the best and worst of times. In: *Proceedings of the Conference "Futures and Options" of the Chicago Board of Trade*. Tilburg, Netherlands: Journal of Business 1996a.

Longin, F. The asymptotic distribution of extreme stock market returns. Journal of Business 1996b;**69**:383–408.

Longin, F. Portfolio Insurance and Stock Market Crashes. Working Paper. ESSEC France; 1997.

Longin, F. From value at risk to stress testing: the extreme value approach. Journal of Banking and Finance 2000;**24**:1097–1130.

Martins, E.S., Stediger, J.R. Generalized maximum-likelihood generalized extreme-value quantile estimators for hydrologic data. Water Resources Research 2000;**36**(3):737–744.

Perold, A.R. Constant Proportion Portfolio Insurance. Working Paper. Harvard Business School; 1986.

Perold, A.R., Sharpe, W.F. Dynamic strategies for asset allocations. Financial Analysts Journal 1988;**44**:16–27.

Prigent, J.L. Assurance du portefeuille: analyse et extension de la méthode du coussin. Banque et Marchés 2001a;**51**:33–39.

Prigent, J.L. Option pricing with a general marked point process. Mathematics of Operation Research 2001b;**26**:50–66.

Prigent, J.-L. *Portfolio Optimization and Performance Analysis*. Chapman & Hall; 2007.

Resnik, S.I. *Extreme Values, Regular Variation and Point Processes*. New York: Springer-Verlag; 1987.

Chapter Nineteen

The Choice of the Distribution of Asset Returns: How Extreme Value Can Help?[1]

François Longin

Department of Finance, ESSEC Business School, Cergy-Pontoise Cedex, France

19.1 INTRODUCTION

The statistical distribution of asset returns plays a central role in financial modeling. Assumptions on the behavior of market prices are necessary to test asset pricing theories, to build optimal portfolios by computing risk/return-efficient frontiers, to value derivatives and define the hedging strategy over time, and to measure and manage financial risks. However, neither an economic theory nor a statistical theory exists to assess the exact distribution of returns. Distributions used in empirical and theoretical research are always the result of an assumption or estimation using data. The paradigm adopted in finance is the Gaussian distribution. In the 1950s and 1960s, Markowitz (1952) and Sharpe (1964) assumed normality for asset returns when studying portfolio selection and deriving the capital asset pricing model. In the beginning of the 1970s, Black and Scholes (1973) and Merton (1973) derived the price and the hedging strategy of

---

[1]This chapter is a revised version of the article "The choice of the distribution of asset returns: how extreme value can help?" initially published in the *Journal of Banking and Finance* (2005).

Extreme Events in Finance: A Handbook of Extreme Value Theory and its Applications,
First Edition. Edited by François Longin.
© 2017 John Wiley & Sons, Inc. Published 2017 by John Wiley & Sons, Inc.

an option by assuming a Brownian motion for the price of the underlying asset, implying a Gaussian distribution for returns. More recently, with the changes in the banking and financial regulation on risks and capital, value-at-risk models developed and implemented by financial institutions also rely intensively on the Gaussian distribution.[2]

Although normality is the paradigm in financial modeling, several alternatives have been considered. The main reason for looking at other models is that there is growing evidence that the Gaussian distribution tends to underestimate the weight of the extreme returns contained in the distribution tails. For example, the stock market crashes of 1929 and 1987, corresponding to daily market drops of more than 10% and 20%, respectively, are very unlikely in a world governed by normality. Several other candidates have been proposed in the academic literature and used with more or less success by practitioners: a mixture of Gaussian distributions, stable Pareto distributions, Student's-*t* distributions, and the class of ARCH processes.[3] One problem with these alternatives is that they are *not nested* and therefore not directly comparable (by carrying out a likelihood ratio test, for example).

In this chapter, I propose a method that allows one to discriminate between these different models. I look at the two extreme parts of the distribution: the left tail and the right tail. The form of the tails is different for the models cited above as the weight of the extremes varies. I use *extreme value theory*, which provides a measure of the importance of extremes in the distribution of returns.[4] This measure, called the *tail index*, is used to build a formal test to discriminate among the models commonly used. This chapter shows how extreme value theory can be useful to know more precisely the characteristics of the distribution of asset returns and finally help to choose a better model by focusing on the tails of the distribution. An empirical analysis using equity data of the U.S. market is provided to illustrate this point.

The remainder of the chapter is organized as follows: Section 19.2 presents extreme value theory, while Section 19.3 gives the different methods of estimation of the statistical distribution of the extremes. Section 19.4 describes the application of extreme value theory for discriminating among distributions of returns. The empirical analysis is then presented in Section 19.5. The last section concludes.

---

[2]See Nadarajah and Chan (2017) in this handbook for a presentation of value-at-risk models.

[3]See Walter (2017) in this handbook for a presentation of the alternatives to the paradigm in finance based on the Gaussian distribution. Bourguinat and Bryis (2017) also give a critical view of the paradigm in finance based on normality.

[4]Earlier work applying extreme value theory in finance can be found in Jansen and De Vries (1991), Longin (1993, 1996), and Loretan and Phillips (1994). These studies focus on the distribution tails of the U.S. stock market returns.

19.2   EXTREME VALUE THEORY

This section presents the main results of extreme value theory. Two approaches are usually considered to define extremes: the minimum/maximum approach and the negative/positive exceedance approach.[5]

19.2.1   The Distribution of Returns

Starting with the notations, R will stand for the (logarithmic) return of the asset, position, or portfolio computed over a given time interval, and f_R and F_R, respectively, the density probability and cumulative distribution functions of the random variable R. The support of the density function is noted as $[l, u]$, the lower and upper bounds, l and u, being possibly equal to infinity (it is the case for the Gaussian distribution). Let $R_1, R_2, \ldots, R_n$ be n returns observed at n time intervals of frequency f.

19.2.2   Extremes Defined as Minimal and Maximal Returns

Extremes can be defined as the minimum and the maximum of the n random variables $R_1, R_2, \ldots, R_n$. We note Y_n the highest return (the maximum) and Z_n the lowest return (the minimum) observed over n trading time intervals.[6]

The extreme value theorem (EVT) is interested in the statistical behavior of the minimum and maximum of random variables. It is analogous to the central limit theorem (CLT), which is interested in the statistical behavior of the sum of random variables.[7] Both theorems consider the asymptotic behavior of the variables in order to get results that are independent of the initial distribution. In the EVT framework, extremes will have to be selected from a very long time interval, whereas in the CLT framework the sum is computed over a very long time interval. In order to get nondegenerated limiting distributions, the variables of interest have to be standardized first. This is illustrated below in the EVT case.

If the variables $R_1, R_2, \ldots, R_n$ are statistically independent and drawn from the same distribution (hypothesis of the random walk for stock market prices), then the exact distribution of the maximum Y_n is simply given by

$$F_{Y_n}(r) = (F_R(r))^n. \tag{19.1}$$

The distribution of extremes depends mainly on the properties of F_R for large values of r. Indeed, for small values of r, the influence of $F_R(r)$ decreases rapidly with n. Hence, the most important information about the extremes is contained in

---

[5]See Fraga Alves and Neves (2017) in this handbook for an introductory overview of extreme value theory.

[6]In the remainder of the paper, theoretical results are presented for the maximum only, since the results for the minimum can be directly deduced from those of the maximum of the opposite variable using the following relation: $Z_n(R) \equiv Min(R_1, R_2, \ldots, R_n) = -Max(-R_1, -R_2, \ldots, -R_n) \equiv -Y_n(R)$.

[7]See Leadbetter (2017) in this handbook for a comparison between the EVT and the CLT.

the tails of the distribution of R. From Formula (19.1), it can be concluded that the limiting distribution of Y_n is null for r less than the upper bound u and equal to 1 for r greater than u. It is a degenerate distribution.

As explained in Longin (1996), the exact formula of the extremes and the limiting distribution are not, however, especially interesting. In practice, the distribution of the parent variable is not precisely known and, therefore, if this distribution is not known, neither is the exact distribution of the extremes. For this reason, the asymptotic behavior of the maximum Y_n is studied. Tiago de Oliveira (1973) argues, "As, in general, we deal with sufficiently large samples, it is natural and in general sufficient for practical uses to find limiting distributions for the maximum or the minimum conveniently reduced and use them." To find a limiting distribution of interest, the random variable Y_n is transformed such that the limiting distribution of the new variable is a nondegenerate one. The simplest transformation is the standardization operation. The variate Y_n is adjusted with a scaling parameter α_n (assumed to be positive) and a location parameter β_n. In the remainder of the paper, the existence of a sequence of such coefficients ($\alpha_n > 0$, β_n) is assumed. Extreme value theory specifies the possible nondegenerate limit distributions of extreme returns as the variable n tends to infinity.[8] In statistical terms, a limit cumulative distribution function denoted by G_{Y_n} satisfies the following condition: $\lim_{n \to +\infty} \sup_{l<y<u} |F_{Y_n}(y) - G_{Y_n}(y)| = 0$. Gnedenko (1943) showed that the extreme value distribution (EVD) is the only nondegenerate distribution that approximates the distribution of extreme returns F_{Y_n}. The limit distribution function G_{Y_n} is given by

$$G_{Y_n}(y) = \exp\left(-\left(1 + \xi \cdot \left(\frac{y - \beta_n}{\alpha_n}\right)\right)^{-\frac{1}{\xi}}\right). \tag{19.2}$$

The parameter ξ, called the tail index, gives a precise characterization of the tail of the distribution of returns. Distributions with a power-declining tail (fat-tailed distributions) correspond to the case $\xi > 0$, distributions with an exponentially declining tail (thin-tailed distributions) to the case $\xi = 0$, and distributions with no tail (finite distributions) to the case $\xi < 0$.[9] The EVD is called a Fréchet distribution, a Gumbel distribution, and a Weibull distribution. The Gumbel distribution can be regarded as a transitional limiting form between the Fréchet and the Weibull distribution.

EVT gives an interesting result: whatever the distribution of the parent variable R, the limiting distribution of the extremes always has the same form. The distribution of the extremes for two different parent processes is differentiated by the values of the standardizing coefficients α_n and β_n and the tail index ξ.

More interestingly, the same limiting distribution is obtained if the i.i.d. hypothesis is relaxed. Berman (1964) has shown that the same result stands if the

---

[8]Proofs of EVT and other claims can be found Gnedenko (1943) and in Gumbel's (1958, Chapters 5 and 7) and Galambos's (1978) text books. See also Embrechts et al. (1997) and Reiss and Thomas (1997).

[9]Note that a different convention is sometimes used for the sign of the tail index and that the recent standard letter ξ (instead of τ) is used to represent the tail index.

variables are correlated and if the series of the squared correlation coefficients is finite. A common model is a discrete mixture of Gaussian distributions. In this particular case, the Gumbel distribution is still the limiting distribution of the extremes (see Leadbetter et al., 1983). De Haan et al. (1989) show that, if the returns followed an ARCH(1) process, the variable Y_n would have a limiting Fréchet distribution. Following their research, I detail below the relationship between the parameters of the ARCH process and those of the distribution of the extremes. Recall that an ARCH(1) process is given by two equations:

$$R_t = E_{t-1}(R_t) + \varepsilon_t, \tag{19.3a}$$

$$h_t = E_{t-1}(R_t - E_{t-1}(R_t))^2 = a_0 + a_1 \cdot \varepsilon_{t-1}^2. \tag{19.3b}$$

The realized return R_t observed at time t is decomposed into an expected part noted as $E_{t-1}(R_t)$ computed one period before at time $t-1$, and an unexpected part noted as ε_t known at time t only. The expected variance h_t varies over time and is conditioned upon the past value of the innovation ε_{t-1}. The ARCH models reflect quite well the time-varying behavior of volatility and especially the clustering of extremes. After a big shock (i.e., a large value for ε_{t-1}), one expects a high level of variance and then more big shocks in the future. The coefficient a_1 reflects the persistence of volatility (or the correlation of absolute returns). A high value of a_1 implies a high level of persistence, many clusters of extremes, and finally a fat-tailed unconditional distribution of returns. The tail index ξ is related to the degree of persistence a_1 by the following formula:

$$E((a_1 \cdot \varepsilon^2)^{1/\xi}) = 1. \tag{19.4}$$

Assuming a conditional Gaussian distribution for the innovation ε, Eq. (19.4) becomes

$$\Gamma\left(\frac{1}{\xi} + 0.5\right) = \sqrt{\pi} \cdot (2a_1)^{-1/\tau}, \tag{19.5}$$

where Γ is the gamma function and π the constant pi. For a given value of the parameter a_1, a unique value of ξ is obtained by solving Eq. (19.5). For example, for a_1 equal to 0.5, the tail index ξ is equal to 0.42.

These results show that the assumption of independence is less important for extreme values than would seem at first sight. Let us note that the extremes are (asymptotically) drawn from an unconditional distribution, even if the parent variable is drawn from a conditional distribution.

19.2.3 Extremes Defined as Return Exceedances

Extremes can also be defined in terms of exceedances with reference to a threshold denoted by θ. For example, positive θ-exceedances correspond to all observations of R greater than the threshold θ. As results for negative exceedances can be deduced from those for positive exceedances by consideration of symmetry, I focus on the case $(R > \theta)$, which defines the right tail of the distribution of returns.

The probability that a return R is higher than θ, denoted by probability p_θ, is linked to the threshold θ and the distribution of returns F_R by the relation: $p = 1 - F_R(\theta)$.

As explained in Longin and Solnik (2001), the cumulative distribution of θ-exceedances, denoted by F_R^θ and equal to $(F_R(x) - F_R(\theta))/(1 - F_R(\theta))$ for $x > \theta$, is exactly known if the distribution of returns F_R is known. However, in most financial applications, the distribution of returns is not precisely known and, therefore, neither is the exact distribution of return exceedances. For empirical purposes, the *asymptotic* behavior of return exceedances needs to be studied. Extreme value theory addresses this issue by determining the possible nondegenerate limit distributions of exceedances as the threshold θ tends to the upper point u of the distribution. In statistical terms, a limit cumulative distribution function denoted by G_R^θ satisfies the following condition: $\lim_{\theta \to u} \sup_{\theta \leq x \leq u} \left| F_R^\theta(x) - G_R^\theta(x) \right| = 0$. Balkema and De Haan (1974) and Pickands (1975) show that the generalized Pareto distribution (GPD), G_R^θ, is the only non-degenerate distribution that approximates the distribution of return exceedances F_R^θ. The limit distribution function G_R^θ is given for $x > \theta$ by

$$G_R^\theta(x) = 1 - \left(1 + \xi \cdot \left(\frac{x - \theta}{\sigma} \right) \right)^{\frac{1}{\xi}}, \tag{19.6}$$

where σ, the dispersion parameter, depends on the threshold θ and the distribution of returns F_R, and ξ, the tail index, is intrinsic to the distribution of returns F_R.

19.3   ESTIMATION OF THE TAIL INDEX

This section deals with the statistical estimation of the tail index. Two approaches are considered. First, in the so-called parametric approach, the parametric form of the asymptotic distribution of extremes is assumed to hold even though the database contains a finite number of observations. The parameters of the distribution of extremes, including the tail index, are directly estimated by classical methods such as the maximum likelihood (ML) method. Second, in the so-called nonparametric approach, no parametric distribution is assumed for the extremes.[10]

19.3.1   The Parametric Approach

The parametric approach assumes that minimal returns and maximal returns selected over a given period are exactly drawn from the EVD given by Formula (19.2) or, alternatively, that negative and positive return exceedances under or above a given threshold are exactly drawn from the distribution given by Formula (19.6). With either definition of extremes, the asymptotic distribution contains three parameters: ξ, α_n, and β_n, or extremes defined as minimal or maximal

---

[10]See Beirlant et al. (2017) and Gomes et al. (2016) in this handbook for a presentation of tail index estimators.

returns selected from a period containing n returns, or alternatively, ξ, σ_θ, and p_θ for extremes defined as negative or positive return exceedances under or above a given threshold θ. Under the assumption that the limit distribution holds, the ML method gives unbiased and asymptotically normal estimators (see Tiago de Oliveira (1973) for the system of equations). The system of nonlinear equations can be solved numerically using the Newton–Raphson iterative method. Note that the regression method (see Gumbel (1958)) gives biased estimates of the parameters but may be used to get initial values for the ML algorithm.

In practice, EVDs can be estimated with different values of the number of returns contained in the selection period n (for minimal and maximal returns) or, alternatively, with different values of the threshold θ (for negative and positive return exceedances). A goodness-of-fit test such as a Sherman test can then be carried out in order to choose the most relevant values from a statistical point of view.

19.3.2 The Nonparametric Approach

The previous methods assume that the extremes are drawn exactly from the EVD. Estimators for the tail index ξ, which do not assume that the observations of extremes follow exactly the EVD, have been developed by Pickands (1975) and Hill (1975). These estimators are based on order statistics of the parent variable R.

Pickands's estimator for the right tail is given by

$$\xi_{\text{Pickands}} = -\frac{1}{\ln 2} \cdot \ln \frac{R'_{N-q+1} - R'_{N-2q+1}}{R'_{N-2q+1} - R'_{N-4q+1}}, \qquad (19.7)$$

where $(R'_t)_{t=1,N}$ is the series of returns ranked in an increasing order, and q is an integer depending on the total number of returns N contained in the database. Pickands's estimator is consistent if q increases at a suitably rapid pace with N (see Dekkers and De Haan (1989)). Pickands's statistic is asymptotically normally distributed with mean ξ and variance $\xi^2 \cdot (2^{-2\xi+1} + 1)/[2(2^{-\xi} - 1) \cdot \text{Log}2]^2$. Pickands's estiamtor is the most general estimator because it can be used for all types of distributions.

Hill's estimator for the right tail is given by

$$\xi_{\text{Hill}} = \frac{1}{q-1} \sum_{i=1}^{q-1} \ln R'_{N-i} - \ln R'_{N-q}. \qquad (19.8)$$

Hill's estimator can be used in the case of the Fréchet distribution only ($\xi > 0$). In this situation, Hill's estimator is a consistent and the most efficient estimator. Consistency is still obtained under weak dependence in the parent variable R. Hill's statistic is asymptotically normally distributed with mean ξ and variance ξ^2.

In practice, as the database contains a finite number of return observations, the number of extreme returns q used for the estimation of the model is finite. As largely discussed in the extreme value theory literature, the choice of its value is a critical issue (see Danielsson et al., 2001; Huisman et al., 2001 for a discussion). On one hand, choosing a high value for q leads to few observations of extreme returns and implies inefficient parameter estimates with large standard errors. On the other hand, choosing a low value for q leads to many observations of extreme returns but induces biased parameter estimates, as observations not belonging to the tails are included in the estimation process. To optimize this tradeoff between bias and inefficiency, I use a Monte Carlo simulation method inspired by Jansen and De Vries (1991). Return time series are simulated from a known distribution for which the tail index can be computed. For each time series, the tail index value is estimated with a different number of extreme returns. The choice of the optimal value is based on the mean-squared error (MSE) criterion, which allows one to take into account the tradeoff between bias and inefficiency. The procedure is detailed in the appendix.

19.4 APPLICATION OF EXTREME VALUE THEORY TO DISCRIMINATE AMONG DISTRIBUTIONS OF RETURNS

This section reviews the different models for the distribution of returns and shows how extreme value theory can be used to discriminate between these models by focusing on the distribution tails.

19.4.1 Distributions of Returns

Several distributions for stock returns have been proposed in the financial literature. Most of the empirical works in finance assume that continuously compounded rates of return on common stock or on a portfolio are normally distributed with a constant variance. The Gaussian distribution is consistent with the log-normal diffusion model made popular by the Black–Scholes–Merton option pricing formula. Moreover, most of the statistical tests lie on the hypothesis of normality. Unfortunately, there is now strong evidence that the distribution of the stock returns departs from normality. High kurtosis usually found in the data implies that the distribution is leptokurtic. The empirical distribution is fat-tailed; there are more extreme observations than predicted by the normal model. This is of great importance because the tails of the density function partly determine the level of the volatility. And volatility is certainly a most important variable in finance.

I review below the alternative models to the Gaussian distribution, and show how these models can be discriminated using the tail index.[11]

---

[11] See Le Courtois and Walter (2017) in this handbook for a discussion of the alternative models to the Gaussian distribution.

Mandelbrot (1963) first suggested that the variance of certain speculative price returns could not exist. Studying cotton prices, he concluded that the stable Pareto distributions fitted the data better than the Gaussian distribution. Fama (1965) extended this approach to stock market prices.

If stock returns usually present fat tails, this does not imply that the variance is infinite. The mixture of Gaussian distributions and the unconditional Student-t distributions presents an excess of kurtosis but still possesses finite variance. Such models were proposed for stock prices by Press (1967) and Praetz (1972). A mixed distribution models the heterogeneity of the random phenomenon. The returns are drawn from different Gaussian distributions. Such a model has been used to take into account extreme price movements, such as stock market crashes, that do not fit in a model with a single distribution. Such events are assumed to be drawn from a distribution with a negative mean and high variance. Anomalies in the stock market like the "day effect" can also motivate this model.

The volatility varies in fact much more over time. Mandelbrot (1963) first found a "clustering effect" in volatility and pointed out that large changes in prices tend to be followed by large changes of either sign, and, similarly, that small changes tend to be followed by small changes of either sign. The ARCH process proposed by Engle (1982) models this feature and tends to fit quite well the behavior of volatility.

19.4.2   Test Based on Extreme Value Theory

An extreme value investigation allows one to discriminate among these non-nested models. Although all processes of returns lead to the same form of distribution of extreme returns, the values of the parameters of the distribution of extremes are in general different for two different processes. Especially, the value of the tail index ξ allows the discrimination of these processes. A tail index value equal to 0 implies a Gumbel distribution obtained for thin-tailed distributions of returns. A negative value for the tail index implies a Weibull distribution obtained for distributions of returns with finite tails. A positive value for the tail index implies a Fréchet distribution obtained for fat-tailed distributions of returns. More precisely, a value of ξ greater than 0.5 is consistent with a stable Pareto distribution. The Cauchy distribution corresponds to the special case $\xi = 1$. A value of ξ less than 0.5 is consistent with the ARCH process or Student's distribution. An interesting feature of the tail index is that it is related to the highest existing moment of the distribution. The tail index ξ and the highest existing moment denoted by k are simply related by $k = 1/\xi$ (for ξ positive). When ξ is equal to 0, then all moments are defined ($k = +\infty$). This is the case of the Gaussian distribution and the mixture of Gaussian distributions. For the stable Pareto distribution, k is less than 2 (the variance is not defined) and equal to the characteristic exponent. For the Student-t distributions, k is more than 2 and equal to the number of degrees of freedom. Table 19.1 summarizes these results.

TABLE 19.1   Tail index and highest existing moment for different models for returns

Models of returns	Type	Tail index ξ	Highest existing moment k
Gaussian distribution	Gumbel	$\xi = 0$	$k = +\infty$
Mixture of Gaussian distributions	Gumbel	$\xi = 0$	$k = +\infty$
Stable Pareto distributions	Fréchet	$\xi > 0.5$	$k < 2$
Student's-t distributions	Fréchet	$0 < \xi < 0.5$	$k \geq 2$
ARCH processes	Fréchet	$0 < \xi < 0.5$	$k \geq 2$

Note: This table gives the type of extreme value distribution, the tail index value, and the highest existing moment for different models of returns commonly used in financial modeling. The tail index ξ and the highest existing moment k are related by: $k = 1/\xi$. The last two columns indicate the constraints on the coefficients ξ and k imposed by each model.

The tail index provides us with a straightforward test. Two particular unconditional distributions are considered below: the thin-tailed Gaussian distribution and the fat-tailed stable Pareto distribution.

19.4.2.1   The Gaussian distribution

As the Gaussian distribution for returns implies a Gumbel distribution for extreme returns, the tail index can be used for testing normality. The null hypothesis is stated as

$$H_0 : \quad \xi = 0.$$

If the tail index ξ is significantly different from 0, then the asymptotic distribution of extreme returns is not a Gumbel distribution. As a consequence, the Gaussian distribution for returns can be rejected. Alternatively, if the tail index ξ is not different from 0, then the asymptotic distribution is the Gumbel distribution. Such a result is not inconsistent with the normal model.

19.4.2.2   The stable Pareto distribution

As the Pareto distribution for returns implies a Fréchet distribution for extreme returns (with a constraint on the tail index value greater than 0.5), the tail index can also be used for testing the Pareto model. The null hypothesis is stated as

$$H_0 : \quad \xi > 0.5.$$

If the tail index ξ is significantly less than 0.5, then the asymptotic distribution of extreme returns is not a Fréchet one with a high tail index value. As a consequence, the stable Pareto distribution for returns can be rejected. Alternatively, if the tail index ξ is not significantly less than 0.5, then the asymptotic distribution is the Fréchet distribution with high tail index value. Such a result is not inconsistent with the stable Pareto model.

19.5 EMPIRICAL RESULTS

19.5.1 Data

I use logarithmic daily percentage returns of the S&P 500 index based on closing prices. Data are obtained from Yahoo Finance. The database covers the period January 1954–December 2015 and contains 16,606 observations of daily returns (Figures 19.1 and 19.2).

The daily returns have a slightly positive mean (0.029%) and a high standard deviation (0.946). The values of the skewness (−1.016) and the excess kurtosis (27.290) suggest departure from the Gaussian distribution. The first-order autocorrelation (generally attributed to a nontrading effect) is small (0.029) but significantly positive. Little serial correlation is found at higher lags. For the second moment, I find a strong positive serial correlation: 0.114 at lag 1. The correlation decreases slowly and remains significant even with a lag of 20 days (0.056), which suggests a strong persistence in volatility.

I now give some statistics about the extremes. Let us first consider the definition of extremes as the minimum and maximum returns selected over a given time period. Considering yearly extremes, I get 66 observations for each type of extreme over the period January 1950–December 2015. The top 20 yearly largest daily market falls and market rises are reported in Table 19.2. Both types of extreme are

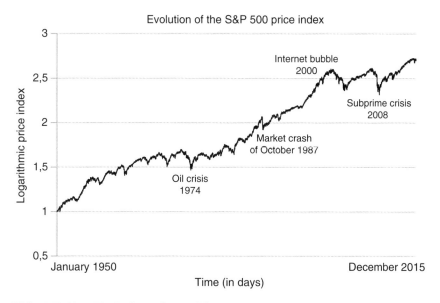

FIGURE 19.1 Evolution of the S&P 500 index over the period January 1950–December 2015.

Note: This figure represents the daily evolution of S&P 500 index over the period January 1950–December 2015. It represents the logarithmic standardized value (the value of the logarithmic price index is equal to one in January 1950).

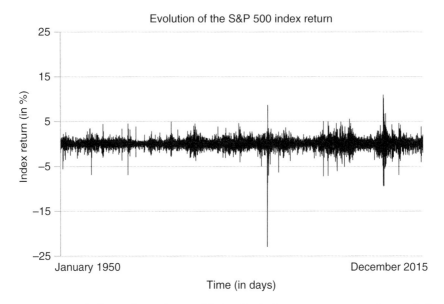

FIGURE 19.2 **Evolution of the S&P 500 index return over the period January 1950–December 2015.**

Note: This figure represents the daily evolution of S&P 500 index return over the period January 1950–December 2015. It represents the logarithmic return.

TABLE 19.2   **Top 20 yearly minimum and maximum daily returns in the S&P 500 index**

	Yearly largest daily market falls			Yearly largest daily market rises	
1	October 19, 1987	−22.90	1	October 13, 2008	10.96
2	October 10, 2008	−9.47	2	October 21, 1987	8.71
3	October 27, 1997	−7.11	3	March 23, 2009	6.84
4	August 31, 1998	−7.04	4	July 24, 2002	5.57
5	January 8, 1988	−7.01	5	October 28, 1997	4.99
6	May 28, 1962	−6.91	6	September 8, 1998	4.96
7	August 8, 2011	−6.90	7	May 27, 1970	4.90
8	September 26, 1955	−6.85	8	January 3, 2001	4.89
9	October 13, 1989	−6.31	9	March 16, 2000	4.65
10	April 14, 2000	−6.00	10	August 17, 1982	4.65
11	June 6, 1950	−5.53	11	August 9 2011	4.63
12	September 17, 2001	−5.05	12	May 29, 1962	4.54
13	September 11, 1986	−4.93	13	October 9, 1974	4.49
14	September 3, 2002	−4.24	14	October 23, 1957	4.39
15	October 25, 1982	−4.05	15	May 10, 2010	4.30
16	August 24, 2015	−4.02	16	November 30, 2011	4.24
17	May 20, 2010	−3.98	17	November 26, 1963	3.90

TABLE 19.2 (*continued*)

	Yearly largest daily market falls			Yearly largest daily market rises	
18	November 18, 1974	−3.74	18	November 1, 1978	3.90
19	November 9, 2011	−3.74	19	August 26, 2015	3.83
20	November 15, 1991	−3.73	20	January 17, 1991	3.66

Note: This table gives the 20 lowest yearly minimum daily returns and the 20 highest yearly maximum daily returns in the S&P 500 index over the period January 1954–December 2015. Yearly extreme returns are selected over nonoverlapping years (containing 260 trading days on average).

widely spread. For the largest declines, the minimum value (−22.90%) is obtained in October 1987, the second minimum values (−9.47%) during the subprime crisis in 2008, and the third minimum value (−7.11%) during the Asian crisis in 1997. The lowest yearly minimum daily returns (−1.33%) is observed in 1972. For the largest rises, the maximum value (+810.96%) is observed in October 2008 a few days after the market crash. Let us then consider the definition of extremes as negative and positive return exceedances under or above a given threshold. The top 20 largest daily market falls and market rises are reported in Table 19.3. As expected, the two definitions of extremes lead to similar sets of extreme observations. However, due to some clustering effect, extreme returns tend to appear around the same time.[12] This effect is especially severe for the stock market crash of October 1987 and the recent crisis. Among the top 20 largest daily market falls, the stock market crash of October 1987 appears twice: October 19 (−22.90%) and October 26 (−8.64%); the subprime crisis appears eight times: September 21 (−9.21%), October 7 (−5.91%), October 9 (−7.92%), October 15 (−9.47%), October 22 (−6.30%), November 19 (−6.31%), November 20 (−6.95%), and December 1 (−9.35%). The same remark applies to top 20 largest daily market rises. The period of extreme volatility following the stock market crash of October 19, 1987, contains three top positive return exceedances: October 21 (+8.71%), October 20 (+5.20%), and October 29 (+4.81%); the subprime crisis appears eight times: September 30 (+5.28%), October 13 (+10.96%), October 20 (+4.66%), October 28 (+10.25%), November 13 (+6.69%), November 21 (+6.13%), November 24 (+6.27%), and December 26 (+5.01%).

19.5.2 Tail Index Estimates

The approaches described in Section 19.4 are now used to estimate the tail index. The empirical results are reported in Table 19.4 for parametric estimates using minimum and maximum returns, in Table 19.5 for parametric estimates using negative and positive return exceedances, and in Table 19.6 for nonparametric estimates.

Let us begin to analyze the results for each estimation method as the tail index value tends to vary according to the method used and also to the parameter

---

[12]Note that this effect can be estimated by incorporating another parameter in the extreme value distribution called the extremal index (see Longin, 2000; Bertail et al., 2017 in this handbook).

TABLE 19.3   Top 20 negative and positive returns in the S&P 500 index

	Largest daily market falls			Largest daily market rises	
1	October 19, 1987	−22.90	1	October 13, 2008	10.96
2	October 15, 2008	−9.47	2	October 28, 2008	10.25
3	December 1, 2008	−9.35	3	October 21, 1987	8.71
4	September 29, 2008	−9.21	4	March 23, 2009	6.84
5	October 26, 1987	−8.64	5	November 13, 2008	6.69
6	October 9, 2008	−7.92	6	November 24, 2008	6.27
7	October 27, 1997	−7.11	7	March 13, 2009	6.17
8	August 31, 1998	−7.04	8	November 21, 2008	6.13
9	January 8, 1988	−7.01	9	July 24, 2002	5.57
10	November 20, 2008	−6.95	10	September 30, 2008	5.28
11	May 28, 1962	−6.91	11	July 29, 2002	5.27
12	August 8, 2011	−6.90	12	October 20, 1987	5.20
13	September 26, 1955	−6.85	13	December 26, 2008	5.01
14	October 13, 1989	−6.31	14	October 28, 1997	4.99
15	November 19, 2008	−6.31	15	September 8, 1998	4.96
16	October 22, 2008	−6.30	16	May 27, 1970	4.90
17	April 14, 2000	−6.00	17	January 3, 2001	4.89
18	October 7, 2008	−5.91	18	October 29, 1987	4.81
19	June 26, 1950	−5.53	19	October 20, 2008	4.66
20	January 20, 2009	−5.43	20	March 16, 2000	4.65

Note: This table gives the 20 lowest negative daily returns and the 20 highest positive daily returns in the S&P 500 index over the period January 1954–December 2015.

used to implement a particular method (i.e., the length of the selection period, the threshold value, and the number of tail observations). Let us consider the left tail, for example. For the left tail, the tail index estimate varies between 0.226 and 0.509 for the parametric method using minimum returns observed a given period, from 0.185 to 0.466 for the parametric method using negative return exceedances under a given threshold, and from 0.212 to 0.328 for the nonparametric methods. As the parametric approach assumes that the asymptotic distribution holds for finite samples, it is important to check the goodness of fit of the distribution to empirical data. For minimum returns, the Sherman test (reported in Table 19.4) shows that it seems cautious to select the extremes over a period longer than a semester. Similarly, for negative return exceedances, the Sherman test (reported in Table 19.5) shows that it seems cautious to select extremes under a threshold value lower than −3%. Looking at the nonparametric approach, Pickands's estimate is positive, suggesting that Hill's estimator can be used as it is restrained to the case of a positive tail index. Under this assumption, Hill's estimator is more precise than Pickands's estimator: the standard error of Hill's estimate is almost four times lower than the one of Pickands's estimate (see Table 19.6).

The first result is about the sign of the tail index, which determines the type of EVD. All tail index estimates are positive, implying that the distribution of extreme returns is a Fréchet distribution consistent with fat-tailed distribution of returns.

The second result is about the relative asymmetry between the left tail and the right tail. The tail index estimates for the left tail are systematically higher

TABLE 19.4   Parametric estimates of the tail index using minimum and maximum returns

Length of the selection period	Tail index estimate	
	Left tail	Right tail
One month	0.226	0.211
(792)	(0.027)	(0.030)
	[−0.040] {0.484}	[−0.190] {0.492}
One quarter	0.312	0.185
(264)	(0.049)	(0.049)
	[0.742] {0.229}	[0.981] {0.163}
One semester	0.412	0.172
(132)	(0.079)	(0.068)
	[−0.363] {0.358}	[0.502] {0.692}
One year	0.509	0.174
(66)	(0.137)	(0.095)
	[0.224] {0.589}	[0.582] {0.589}

Note: This table gives the tail index estimates using minimum and maximum returns observed over a given time period. Minimum and maximum returns are selected over different periods: from 1 month to 1 year. The number of minimum or maximum returns used in the estimation process is given below in parentheses in the first column. The parameters of the distributions of minimum and maximum returns are estimated by the maximum likelihood method (only the tail index estimates are reported). Asymptotic standard errors are given below in parentheses. The result of Sherman's goodness-of-fit test is given in brackets with the *p*-value (probability of exceeding the test-value) given next in curly brackets. The 5% confidence level at which the null hypothesis of adequacy (of the estimated asymptotic distribution of extreme returns to the empirical distribution of observed extreme returns) can be rejected is equal to 1.645.

than the one for the right tail. This statement can be formalized by testing the null hypothesis H_0: $\xi^{max} = \xi^{min}$. For the usual confidence level (say 5%), this hypothesis is sometimes rejected by the data, indicating that the left tail is heavier than the right tail.

19.5.3   Choice of a Distribution of Stock Market Returns

Two particular unconditional distributions are considered: the Gaussian distribution and the stable Pareto distribution by testing, respectively, the null hypotheses H_0: $\xi = 0$ and H_0: $\xi > 0.5$. Empirical results are reported in Table 19.7. Three confidence level are considered: 1%, 5%, and 10%. The lower the confidence level, the harder it is to reject the null hypothesis.

19.5.3.1   Gaussian distribution

Although the tail index estimates are always different from zero, they may not be significantly different from zero. Results reported in Table 19.7 show that the null

TABLE 19.5   **Parametric estimates of the tail index using negative and positive return exceedances**

Threshold used to select exceedances	Tail index estimate	
	Left tail	Right tail
±1%	0.185	0.159
(1.716) (1.614)	(0.029)	(0.029)
	[−0.051] {0.480}	[1.799] {0.964}
±2%	0.289	0.197
(373) (329)	(0.067)	(0.065)
	[0.157] {0.563}	[1.914] {0.972}
±3%	0.466	0.112
(112) (102)	(0.139)	(0.110)
	[0.233] {0.592}	[0.836] {0.798}
±4%	0.214	0.226
(46) (36)	(0.179)	(0.204)
	[0.362] {0.641}	[0.991] {0.839}
−2.60%, +3.27%	0.420	0.218
(168) (85)	(0.106)	(0.140)
	[0.183] {0.573}	[−0.045] {0.482}

Note: This table gives the tail index estimates using negative and positive return exceedances below or above a given threshold. Return exceedances are selected with fixed threshold values: ±1%, ±2%, ±3%, and ±4% (percentage point below or above the mean of returns). In the last row, return exceedances are selected with optimal threshold values: −2.60% for the left tail and +3.27% for the right tail (see Appendix for the description for obtaining optimal threshold). In the first column, the number of return exceedances used in the estimation process is given below in parentheses for both negative and positive return exceedances. The parameters of the distributions of negative and positive return exceedances are estimated by the maximum likelihood method (only the tail index estimates are reported). Asymptotic standard errors are given below in parentheses. The result of Sherman's goodness-of-fit test is given in brackets with the *p*-value (probability of exceeding the test value) given next in curly brackets. The 5% confidence level at which the null hypothesis of adequacy (of the estimated asymptotic distribution of extreme returns to the empirical distribution of observed extreme returns) can be rejected is equal to 1.645.

hypothesis is often rejected even at conservative confidence levels, such as 1%. The Gumbel distribution for extreme returns consistent with thin-tailed distributions for returns is then rejected. As the Gaussian distribution for returns implies a Gumbel distribution for extreme returns, this leads to the rejection of the Gaussian distribution.

19.5.3.2   Stable Pareto distribution

Although the tail index estimates are always lower than 0.5 (though positive), the null hypothesis H_0: $\xi > 0.5$ may not be significantly rejected. Results reported in Table 19.7 show that the null hypothesis is often rejected even at conservative

TABLE 19.6   Nonparametric estimates of the tail index

Estimator	Tail index estimate	
	Left tail	Right tail
Pickands	0.212	0.190
(left tail: 234) (right tail: 234)	(0.121)	(0.121)
Hill	0.328	0.253
(left tail: 168) (right tail: 85)	(0.025)	(0.027)

Note: This table gives the tail index estimates based on nonparametric methods developed by Pickands (1975) and Hill (1975). For each method, the optimum number of tail observations is computed by simulation (see Appendix and Table A1). The optimum number is given in parentheses for both the left and right tails below the method name in the first column. Asymptotic standard errors of the tail index estimates are given below in parentheses.

TABLE 19.7   Choice of the distribution of returns based on the tail index

Estimator	Test of the null hypothesis	
	Left tail	Right tail
A. Gaussian distribution		
Parametric (ML) (minimum and	1%: not rejected	1%: rejected
maximum returns)	5%: not rejected	5%: rejected
	10%: not rejected	10%: rejected
Parametric (ML) (return exceedances)	1%: not rejected	1%: rejected
	5%: not rejected	5%: rejected
	10%: not rejected	10%: rejected
Nonparametric Hill	1%: rejected	1%: rejected
	5%: rejected	5%: rejected
	10%: rejected	10%: rejected
B. Stable Pareto distribution		
Parametric (ML) (minimum and	1%: rejected	1%: not rejected
maximum returns)	5%: rejected	5%: not rejected
	10%: rejected	10%: not rejected
Parametric (ML) (return exceedances)	1%: rejected	1%: not rejected
	5%: rejected	5%: not rejected
	10%: rejected	10%: not rejected
Nonparametric Hill	1%: rejected	1%: rejected
	5%: rejected	5%: rejected
	10%: rejected	10%: rejected

Note: This table gives the result of the choice of a particular distribution for returns based on the tail index. Two particular distributions are considered: the Gaussian distribution characterized with a tail index value equal to 0 (Panel A) and the stable Pareto distribution characterized with a tail index value higher than 0.5 (Panel B). For the Gaussian distribution, the null hypothesis is $H_0: \xi = 0$. For the stable Pareto distribution, the null hypothesis is $H_0: \xi > 0.5$. Three estimators are used: the parametric maximum likelihood (ML) estimator based on minimum and maximum returns and return exceedances and the Hill nonparametric estimator. Three confidence levels are considered: 1%, 5%, and 10%.

confidence level such as 1%. The Fréchet distribution for extreme returns, with a tail index value higher than 0.5 consistent with heavy-tailed distributions for returns, is then rejected. As the stable Pareto distribution for returns implies a Fréchet distribution for extreme returns with a tail index value higher than 0.5, this leads to the rejection of the stable Pareto distribution.

Both the Gaussian distribution and the stable Pareto distribution seem rejected by the data. In terms of moments, the variance appears to be defined, although not all moments are defined. The highest existing moment is determined next.

19.5.4   Highest Existing Moment

The tail index can be used to compute the highest defined moment of the distribution of returns. Technically, it corresponds to the highest integer k such that $E(R^k)$ is finite. I proceed as follows: I consider a set of null hypotheses $H_0(k)$ defined by $\xi < 1/k$. If the null hypothesis $H_0(k)$ is rejected at a given confidence level, then the moment of order k is not defined at this level. The null hypothesis $H_0(+\infty)$ defined by $\xi \leq 0$ serves as a limiting case. If the null hypothesis $H_0(+\infty)$ is rejected, then not all moments are defined.

Table 19.8 gives the empirical results concerning the highest existing moment by looking at each tail independently. Three confidence levels are considered: 1%, 5%, and 10%. The lower the confidence level, the easier it is to accept the existence

TABLE 19.8   Maximum existing moment of the distribution of the S&P 500 index returns

Estimator	Maximum existing moment	
	Left tail	Right tail
Parametric (ML) (minimum and maximum returns)	1%: fifth	1%: all
	5%: third	5%: all
	10%: second	10%: tenth
Parametric (ML) (return exceedances)	1%: tenth	1%: all
	5%: seventh	5%: all
	10%: sixth	10%: all
Nonparametric Hill	1%: third	1%: fifth
	5%: third	5%: fourth
	10%: third	10%: fourth

Note: This table gives the highest existing moment of the distribution of stock market returns by investigating the weight of extreme price movements. For a given level of confidence, equal to 1%, 5%, and 10%, the null hypotheses $H_0(k)$ defined by: $\xi > 1/k$ where k is equal to $1, 2, 3, \ldots$ is studied. A t-test and its associated p-value are computed. The null hypothesis $H_0(+\infty)$: $\xi < 0$ serves as the limiting case. The highest integer k for which $H_0(k)$ is not rejected at the given level is reported in the table. If the null hypothesis $H_0(+\infty)$ is not rejected, then all the moments are defined. Three estimators are used: the parametric maximum likelihood (ML) estimator based on minimum and maximum returns and return exceedances and the Hill nonparametric estimator. Three confidence levels are considered: 1%, 5%, and 10%.

of lower moments. As expected, the conclusion of the test depends on the method used for estimating the tail index. However, general results emerged. The first result is that the second moment (the variance) seems to be always defined, as the null hypothesis $H_0(2)$ is never rejected. The fourth moment seems, however, not always defined. The second result is the relative asymmetry between the left tail and the right tail. The highest existing moment by considering the left tail is always lower than the highest existing moment by considering the right tail, suggesting that the left tail is heavier than the right tail. Moreover, by looking at the right tail, all moments seem defined in most of tests.

19.6 CONCLUSION

Extreme value theory gives a simple way to discriminate between the distributions of returns. The distributions commonly proposed in the literature can be differentiated by the tails: or, in other words, by the frequency of extreme price movements.

Empirical results for the U.S. stock market lead to the rejection of the Gaussian distribution and the stable Pareto distributions as well. The former contains too few extremes while the later too many. Although the distribution of stock market returns is fat-tailed, the variance appears to be well defined. Only the Student-t distribution and the class of ARCH processes are not rejected by the data. This suggests that for the U.S. stock market, a Student-t distribution could be used in an unconditional modeling of returns and that an ARCH process could be used in a conditional modeling of returns.

The French mathematician, physicist, and philosopher Henri Poincaré (1854–1912) once noted that "All the world believes it (the normal distribution) firmly, because the mathematicians imagine that it is a fact of observation and the observers that it is a theorem of mathematics." It seems that more than a century later, the world, especially of finance, has not changed much, as the Laplace–Gauss distribution is still considered as *normal*. This chapter showed that extreme value theory can be useful to choose a model for the distribution of returns. Empirical results for the U.S. market suggest that the Gaussian distribution should not be chosen because of its inappropriate fit of the tails.

References

Balkema A.A., De Haan L. Residual life time at great age. Annals of Probability 1974;**2**:792–804.

Beirlant J., Herrmann K., Teugels J.L. Estimation of the extreme value index. In: Longin F., editor. *Extreme Events in Finance: A Handbook of Extreme Value Theory and Its Applications*. Wiley; 2017.

Berman S.M. Limiting theorems for the maximum term in stationary sequences. Annals of Mathematical Statistics 1964;**35**:502–516.

Bertail P., Clémençon S., Tiller C. Extreme values statistics for Markov chains with applications to finance and insurance. In: Longin F., editor. *Extreme Events in Finance*. Wiley; 2017.

Black F., Scholes M. The pricing of options and corporate liabilities. Journal of Political Economy 1973;**81**:637–659.

Bourguinat H., Bryis E. Credo Ut Intelligam. In: Longin F., editor. *Extreme Events in Finance: A Handbook of Extreme Value Theory and its Applications*. Wiley; 2017.

Danielsson J., de Haan L., Peng L., de Vries C.G. Using a bootstrap method to choose the sample fraction in tail index estimation. Journal of Multivariate Analysis 2001;**76**:226–248.

Dekkers A.L.M., de Haan L. On the estimation of the extreme value index and large quantile estimation. Annals of Statistics 1989;**17**:1795–1832.

De Haan L., Resnick I.S., Rootzèn H., De Vries C.G. Extremal behavior of solutions to a stochastic difference equation with applications to ARCH process. Stochastic Processes and their Applications 1989;**32**:213–224.

Embrechts P., Klüppelberg C., Mikosch T. *Modelling Extremal Events for Insurance and Finance*. Berlin, Heidelberg: Springer Verlag; 1997.

Engle R.F. Auto-regressive conditional heteroskedasticity with estimates of the variance of United Kingdom inflation. Econometrica 1982;**50**:987–1007.

Fama E.F. The behavior of stock market prices. The Journal of Business 1965;**38**:34–105.

Fraga Alves I., Neves C. Extreme value theory: an introductory overview. In: Longin F., editor. *Extreme Events in Finance: A Handbook of Extreme Value Theory and Its Applications*. Wiley; 2017.

Galambos J. *The Asymptotic Theory of Extreme Order Statistics*. John Wiley & Sons; 1978.

Gomes M.I., Caeiro F., Henriques-Rodrigues L., Manjunath B.G. Bootstrap methods in statistics of extremes. In: Longin F., editor. *Extreme Events in Finance*. Wiley; 2016.

Gnedenko B.V. Sur la Distribution Limite du Terme Maximum d'une Série Aléatoire. Annals of Mathematics 1943;**44**:423–453.

Gumbel E.J. *Statistics of Extremes*. New York: Columbia University Press; 1958.

Hill B.M. A simple general approach to inference about the tail of a distribution. Annals of Statistics 1975;**46**:1163–1173.

Huisman R., Koedijk K., Kool C.J.M., Palm F. Tail index estimates in small samples. Journal of Business and Economic Statistics 2001;**19**:208–215.

Jansen D.W., De Vries C.G. On the frequency of large stock returns: putting booms and busts into perspectives. The Review of Economic and Statistics 1991;**73**:18–24.

Leadbetter M.R., Lindgren G., Rootzèn H. *Extremes and Related Properties of Random Sequences and Processes*. New York: Springer Verlag; 1983.

Leadbetter R. Extremes under dependence: historical development and parallels with central limit theory. In: Longin F., editor. *Extreme Events in Finance: A Handbook of Extreme Value Theory and Its Applications*. Wiley; 2017.

Le Courtois O., Walter C. Lévy processes and extreme value theory. In: Longin F., editor. *Extreme Events in Finance: A Handbook of Extreme Value Theory and Its Applications*. Wiley; 2017.

Longin F. Volatility and Extreme Movements in Financial Markets, PhD Thesis, HEC; 1993.

Longin F. The asymptotic distribution of extreme stock market returns. The Journal of Business 1996;**63**:383–408.

Longin F. From VaR to stress testing: the extreme value approach. Journal of Banking and Finance 2000;**24**:1097–1130.

Longin F., Solnik B. Extreme correlation of international equity markets. Journal of Finance 2001;**56**:651–678.

Longin F. The choice of the distribution of asset prices: how extreme value theory can help. Journal of Banking and Finance, 2005;**29**:1017–1035.

Loretan M., Phillips P.C.B. Testing for covariance stationarity of heavy-tailed time series: an overview of the theory with applications to several financial datasets. Journal of Empirical Finance 1994;**2**:211–248.

Mandelbrot B. The variation of certain speculative prices. The Journal of Business 1963;**36**:394–419.

Markowitz H. Portfolio selection. Journal of Finance 1952;**7**:77–91.

Merton R. Theory of rational option pricing. Bell Journal of Economics Management Science 1973;**4**:141–183.

Nadarajah S., Chan S. Estimation methods for value at risk. In: Longin F, editor. *Extreme Events in Finance: A Handbook of Extreme Value Theory and Its Applications*. Wiley; 2017.

Pickands J. Statistical inference using extreme order statistics. Annals of Statistics 1975;**3**:119–131.

Praetz P.D. The distribution of share price changes. The Journal of Business 1972;**45**:49–55.

Press S.J. A compound events model for security prices. The Journal of Business 1967;**40**:317–335.

Reiss R.-D., Thomas M. *Statistical Analysis of Extreme Values*. Basle, Switzerland: Birkhäuser Verlag; 1997.

Sharpe W. Capital asset prices: a theory of market equilibrium under conditions of risk. Journal of Finance 1964;**19**:425–442.

Theil H. *Applied Economic Forecasting*. Amsterdam: North Holland; 1971.

Tiago de Oliveira J. *Statistical Extremes – A Survey*. Lisbon: Center of Applied Mathematics; 1973.

Walter C. The extreme value problem in finance: comparing the pragmatic programme with the Mandelbrot programme. In: Longin F., editor. *Extreme Events in Finance: A Handbook of Extreme Value Theory and Its Applications*. Wiley; 2017.

Appendix A

Computation of the optimal value q for nonparametric estimators

I compute the optimal value of q by carrying out a Monte Carlo study as was done by Jansen and De Vries (1991). I proceed as follows: I simulate 16,606 return observations (the total number of daily returns in the database) drawn from different return distributions: a Cauchy distribution and Student's-t distributions with degrees of freedom equal to 2, 3, and 4. The fatness of these four distributions is different and corresponds to tail indices ξ equal to 1, 0.5, 0.33, and 0.25. The Cauchy distribution gives a lot of extreme values, while the Student's-t distribution with four degrees of freedom very few. Then I estimate the tail index using

TABLE A1 Optimal value for nonparametric estimators of the tail index

	$\alpha = 1\ (\xi = 1.00)$	$\alpha = 2\ (\xi = 0.50)$	$\alpha = 3\ (\xi = 0.33)$	$\alpha = 4\ (\xi = 0.25)$
A. Pickands's estimator				
$q = 632\ \alpha = 1\ (\xi = 1.00)$	$8.78 \times 10^{-3}\ [1.58.78 \times 10^{-3}]$	22.51×10^{-3}	33.51×10^{-3}	41.19×10^{-3}
$q = 358\ \alpha = 2\ (\xi = 0.50)$	13.29×10^{-3}	$15.01 \times 10^{-3}\ [0.70 \times 10^{-3}]$	21.45×10^{-3}	26.97×10^{-3}
$q = 259\ \alpha = 3\ (\xi = 0.33)$	18.09×10^{-3}	16.85×10^{-3}	$10.45 \times 10^{-3}\ [0.43 \times 10^{-3}]$	24.48×10^{-3}
$q = 234\ \alpha = 4\ (\xi = 0.25)$	20.03×10^{-3}	18.02×10^{-3}	20.66×10^{-3}	$24.04 \times 10^{-3}\ [0.27 \times 10^{-3}]$
B. Hill's estimator				
$q = 1396\ \alpha = 1\ (\xi = 1.00)$	$0.82 \times 10^{-3}\ [0.71 \times 10^{-3}]$	5.12×10^{-3}	13.22×10^{-3}	20.72×10^{-3}
$q = 400\ \alpha = 2\ (\xi = 0.50)$	2.59×10^{-3}	$0.77 \times 10^{-3}\ [0.62 \times 10^{-3}]$	1.72×10^{-3}	3.36×10^{-3}
$q = 168\ \alpha = 3\ (\xi = 0.33)$	6.28×10^{-3}	1.47×10^{-3}	$0.85 \times 10^{-3}\ [0.66 \times 10^{-3}]$	1.30×10^{-3}
$q = 85\ \alpha = 4\ (\xi = 0.25)$	13.07×10^{-3}	3.11×10^{-3}	1.25×10^{-3}	$0.92 \times 10^{-3}\ [0.74 \times 10^{-3}]$

Note: These tables indicate the mean-squared error (MSE) obtained from simulations for different values of q used to compute Pickands's estimate (Panel A) and Hill's estimate (Panel B) and for different values of the degrees of freedom α (or equivalently for different values of the tail index ξ). The case $\alpha = 1$ corresponds to a Cauchy distribution, and $\alpha = 2$, 3, and 4 correspond to Student's-t distributions. These values for the degree of freedom correspond to tail index values, respectively, equal to 1.00, 0.50, 0.33, and 0.25. The whole period is assumed to contain $16{,}606$ observations (corresponding to the number of observations in the historical database of SP& 500 index returns over the period January 1954–December 2015). For Pickands's estimate, values of q minimizing the MSE are 632 for $\xi = 1.00$; 358 for $\xi = 0.50$; 259 for $\xi = 0.33$; and 234 for $\xi = 0.25$. For Hill's estimate, values of q minimizing the MSE are 1396 for $\xi = 1.00$; 400 for $\xi = 0.50$; 168 for $\xi = 0.33$; and 85 for $\xi = 0.25$. Minimizing MSEs with the theoretical MSE below in brackets can be found in the diagonal of each table.

Pickands's or Hill's formula with different values of q ranging from 1 to 3.300 (about 20% of the observations). I repeat this simulation 10,000 times. For each distribution i (characterized by a tail index value ξ_i) and each value of q, I get a series of 10,000 observations of the tail index estimates. Then for each distribution i, I compute the MSE of this series and choose the value of q, written as q_i^{opt}, which minimizes the MSE. As explained by Theil (1971, pp. 26–32), the MSE criterion allows one to take explicitly into account the two effects of bias and inefficiency. The MSE of S simulated observations $\tilde{X}_s$ of the estimator of a parameter X can be decomposed as follows:

$$\text{MSE}\left(\left(\tilde{X}_s\right)_{s=1,S}, X\right) = \left(\overline{X} - X\right)^2 + \frac{1}{S}\sum_{s=1}^{S}\left(\tilde{X}_s - X\right)^2,$$

where $\overline{X}$ represents the mean of S simulated observations. The first part of the decomposition measures the bias and the second part the inefficiency.

Table A1 reports the minimizing q-levels and associated MSEs using Pickands's estimator and Hill's estimator. Along the diagonal are the minimal MSEs; the theoretical MSE value equal to ξ^2/q is also reported. As noted by Jansen and De Vries (1991), there is a U-shaped relationship between MSE and q. It reflects the tradeoff between inefficiency and bias: when few observations are used (q low), the bias in the estimation of ξ is negligible, as most of the observations are extreme but the variance of the estimator is high; when many observations are used (q high), a bias is introduced in the estimation of ξ because of the inclusion of more central values, but the variance of the estimator is low.

With real data I proceed as follows: I compute the tail index estimates with the four optimal values previously obtained given as $(q_i^{opt})_{i=1,4}$. These values correspond to the four chosen values of the tail index given as $(\xi_i)_{i=1,4}$. I retain the estimate that is closest to the chosen value ξ_i. To do this, I compute the statistics $(\xi^{Hill}(q_i^{opt}) - \xi_i)/\sigma_i$, where $\xi^{Hill}(q_i^{opt})$ is the Hill's estimate computed with q_i^{opt} extremes and σ_i is the standard error of this estimate, and the associated p-value noted p_i. I finally retain the estimate for which the lowest value of p_i is obtained. In my study, I keep 168 extreme returns to compute Hill's estimator for the left tail and 85 extreme returns for the right tails. Optimal value for Pickands's estimator is 234 for both the left and right tail.

Chapter Twenty

Protecting Assets Under Non-Parametric Market Conditions

Jean-Marie Choffray[1,2] and Charles Pahud de Mortanges[1]

[1]*Management Science Department, University of Liège, Liège, Belgium*
[2]*Marketing Science Department, ESSEC, Cergy-Pontoise, France*

Under non-parametric market conditions, investors usually become more concerned about the return of their money than about the return on their money. Protecting assets becomes the surest if not the only path to survival and growth. High frequency trading systems, over leveraged shadow entities, flash crashes, and stealth central bank actions, to name a few, contribute to create a "Rumsfeldian" type of world in which decision makers have to cope not only with "Known knowns" – things they know that they know – but also with "Unknown unknowns" – things they don't know that they don't know! The goal of this paper is to explore such a conceptual model of the "Unknown" and to derive from it a concise and coherent set of battle-tested heuristics aimed at designing effective investment strategies to protect assets.

> *The typical state or mankind is tyranny, servitude and misery.*
> –Friedman (1962).

The last 10 years have witnessed a major acceleration in the pace of change in the world of investing. The synthetic nature of the assets involved, the fragmented structure of the markets on which they are exchanged, and the virtual form of most Internet-based transactions, to name a few, contribute to the emergence of a new reality. These changes have fundamentally altered the core activity and the

Extreme Events in Finance: A Handbook of Extreme Value Theory and its Applications,
First Edition. Edited by François Longin.
© 2017 John Wiley & Sons, Inc. Published 2017 by John Wiley & Sons, Inc.

strategies of most investors – be it institutional or individual. They make today's markets more reactive, less understandable, and probably less manipulable – in two words, *less predictable*.

Our world usually evolves at the edge of *chaos*. The rule of the game is to avoid it. If not, the key to survival is to make the best possible use of available intelligence and of the situation at hand to create value, to grow assets, and to build capital. The Great Recession of 2008–2009 provides an excellent example of an exceptional environment, as one of the world's worst financial disasters and probably the most expensive of all. "Widespread failures in financial regulation, dramatic breakdowns in corporate governance, excessive borrowing and risk-taking, ill prepared policy makers, and systemic breaches in accountability," according to the *Financial Crisis Inquiry Commission* (2011), led to a tragedy whose final outcome will inevitably be a major shift in the international structure of power – financial and political. In the 12 months preceding March 2009, the world market capitalization experienced a nominal loss of the order of $30T (trillion, or thousands of billions): approximately twice as much as the USA or the European GDP!

Even a cursory knowledge of history reminds us that unpredictable, impossible, and unthinkable events happen and shape the future. When they happen, such events usually act as catalysts for the strategies investors deploy on the markets. Clews (1908), Kindleberger (1978), and Galbraith (1994) report that market participants – today: hedge funds buddies, institutional investor groups, individual investor crowds, and/or Internet-based flash hordes – tend to reproduce the same behaviors, misjudgments, and errors over time, leading to discontinuities and disruptions in market functioning. Some modesty, serious monitoring of market conditions, and a reasonable knowledge of economic history and financial theory might undoubtedly help prevent falling into such deadly traps. "Keep on dancing, as long as the music is playing" is definitely not the only, nor the surest, strategy to avoid blunders and generate regular asset growth.

We live in a world in which passenger planes disappear, buildings collapse, rockets explode, countries implode, and earthquakes, tsunamis, and floods occur. But, we live also in a world in which financial markets react in less than a few tens of a second on the basis of investors' perceptions of the incidence of these events on the behavior of others. In this chapter, by *nonparametric market conditions*, we mean market states and events that are not generated by continuous models – or probabilistic processes – that would render them amenable to mathematical analysis. For an alternate view on the integration of jumps in financial modeling, see Walter (2017).

To make it simple, we are not concerned so much about "tail events" or "black swans" – after all, aren't they still swans? – as we are about "charging rhinos," "dangling elephants," and other … "constrictor snakes!" The sheer complexity of the situations encountered on financial markets is such that they can only be dealt with through the development of a parsimonious and coherent set of empirically tested heuristics, aimed at conceptualizing response to the unknown, at connecting proven facts and at converting observed discrepancies into profitable investment opportunities.

Donald Rumsfeld, who served as Secretary of Defense under President Gerald Ford and under President George W. Bush, once said that things that haven't happened are as interesting as those that have happened, because if there are "known knowns" – things we know that we know – there are also "known unknowns" – things we know that we don't know – and "unknown unknowns" – things we don't know that we don't know! He also observed that it's wrong to believe that you can't do anything until you can do everything. To him, "First you crawl, then you walk, and then you run." So, let's face the *unknown*; stick some heuristics in the investing ground; and test, validate, and improve them gradually. And, most importantly, let us not pretend that this approach – at best, a tentative and incomplete theory – is the final word on investing under extreme circumstances.

It is a known fact that under nonparametric market conditions, investors usually become more concerned about the *return of* their money than about the *return on* their money. Protecting assets under management (AUM) becomes the surest, if not the only, path to survival and growth. High-frequency trading systems, over leveraged shadow entities, flash crashes, and stealth central bank actions, just to name a few, contribute to create a "Rumsfeldian" type of world in which decision makers have to cope with a whole spectrum of "unknowns." The goal of this chapter is to explore such a conceptual model and to derive from it a concise and coherent set of battle-tested heuristics aimed at designing effective investment strategies to protect assets.

20.1 INVESTORS' "KNOWN KNOWNS"

We all know that predicting the future is extremely hard, if not impossible. But, predicting the *past* is no easy task either! History, according to Napoleon Bonaparte, is a "succession of lies on which we all agree." We tend to take things that happened as truth, because they happened, or because we were told that they happened. But, most of the time, available facts constitute only the tip of the iceberg. If you add the fact that we are limited in the measurement and perception of what happened, what we call the past is usually nothing more than a representation – individual or collective – of a succession of events among alternative histories that we haven't observed, haven't measured, or haven't perceived.

As to financial markets, even if their current fragmentation renders this apparently easy task very difficult, we probably have access to reasonably valid and reliable estimates of prices, volumes, and intents: for the latter, through the derivatives market. The robustness of these estimates has probably increased over the last few years due to the overwhelming importance of institutional investors and to their reliance on synthetic types of assets: exchange traded funds (ETFs), exchange traded notes (ETNs), to name a few. Hence, if one assumes that the daily closing prices and volumes inevitably include some inaccuracies, these are sufficiently self-evident for their impact to be negligible over time.

World markets are extremely complex, creating a challenging environment especially for the individual investor. They rely on a structure of networks (and other electronic communication networks (ECNs), alternative trading systems (ATS), etc.), linking a diverse set of market platforms (including dark pools, and so on), to various participants and trading systems (and other market makers (MMs), supplemental liquidity providers (SLPs), high-frequency trading systems (HFTS), etc.) through the Internet. However, there is a certain rhythm (frequency and amplitude) in most human-engineered dynamic processes. Understanding the rhythm of such a complex system requires the use of at least one aggregate indicator of actual investment behavior – as characterized by the price and volume of a representative sample of assets or asset classes – and of another indicator of investors' anticipations – or aversion to risk – as characterized by their desire to hedge against the uncertainty surrounding the actual value and the lack of liquidity of their holdings.

Here, we suggest using as a basis for analysis a *market conditions matrix* (Choffray, 2012). This matrix is a two-dimensional typology of a reference market's observable stages of development. It is based on the MACD (moving average convergence divergence) analysis of a pair of indicators reflecting actual investment behavior (e.g., SPY) and the associated measure of fear or risk aversion (e.g., VIX), as depicted in Figure 20.1.

MACD is a descriptive time-series method aimed at specifying the underlying nature of a dynamic process – uptrend or downtrend – based on the difference between a short (e.g., 12 time periods) and a long (e.g., 26 time periods) exponential moving average (EMA). It also allows the identification of a possible acceleration or deceleration in trend by comparing this difference with its own

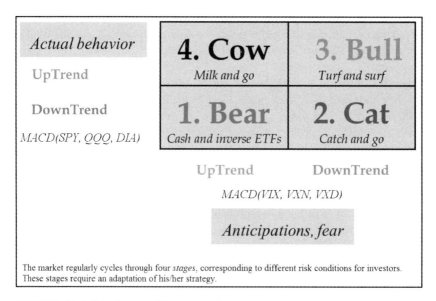

The market regularly cycles through four *stages*, corresponding to different risk conditions for investors. These stages require an adaptation of his/her strategy.

FIGURE 20.1 *Market conditions matrix*, **based on investors' actual behavior and anticipations.** (*Source*: Choffray (2012)).

short (e.g., nine time periods) EMA. If you are not familiar with this method, you may want to consult www.investopedia.com. SPY is an exchange traded fund, or synthetic asset, that provides investors with the exact performance of the Standard & Poor's 500 index (S&P 500). This index replicates the evolution of the market capitalization of the 500 largest American industrial and financial corporations (see: www.nyse.com, for more information). VIX is an index that reflects the performance of a portfolio of short-term put options on the S&P 500 (see: www.cme .com, for more information). It measures market volatility and can be interpreted as a fear index. Similar analyses should be run with two other pairs of indicators: DIA/VXD and QQQ/VXN to better understand the specific behavior of two key segments of the market: very large businesses (Dow Jones industrial average) and high-tech companies (Nasdaq 100).

It appears that the market regularly cycles through four stages, corresponding to different risk conditions for investors. These stages require an adaptation of his/her strategy: off-market position (Stage 1), gradual re-entry through selective buying (Stage 2), proactive portfolio management (Stage 3), and selective selling of mature positions (Stage 4). For risk-averse investors, a reasonable strategy might be to concentrate on Stage 3, when market conditions are close to ideal. To be successful, one doesn't have to be fully invested all the time. Quite the opposite! Staying out of the market, holding cash, may sometimes be the wisest strategy. In addition, staying liquid provides investors with an opportunity to prepare their next moves. "Fail to plan, plan to fail!"

If "the trend is definitely your friend," the duration and intensity of each of these market stages have to be empirically determined. They are influenced by the quarterly earnings of the underlying businesses (earnings surprises and guidance as to the future), as well as by the prevailing geopolitical, macroeconomic, and monetary conditions. To add robustness to your diagnosis, two parallel MACD analyses could be performed, based on daily and weekly data, in the latter case to gain perspective on the core evolution.

Heuristic No. 1. Never fight the market. Identify its current stage of development through the MACD analysis of the following pairs of descriptors: SPY/VIX, QQQ/VXN, and DIA/VXD.

The high level of internal correlation observed recently within and across asset classes – a byproduct of a historically accommodative monetary policy having led the Federal Reserve to quadruple the size of its balance sheet and to provide unlimited liquidity and risk coverage to financial institutions – makes it critical to monitor and respect markets bottoming- and topping-out processes. No flag will be posted when they end. The unstable nature of the correlation of international equity markets during crises is well documented (Longin and Solnik, 2001). Only a careful analysis of deceleration or acceleration in trend may help. Always keeping in mind that "Bull markets tend to climb a wall of worry" and "Bear markets tend to slide down a slope of hope!"

Over the years, ETFs and ETNs have become dominant investment vehicles. ETFs are synthetic or virtual assets that give investors direct access to the real-time performance of an underlying basket of assets (stocks, indices, etc.). Some of them – *Pro*Shares, Rydex*Funds, Velocity*Shares, and other Direxion*Fund* – are engineered to produce an inverse and/or structurally leveraged performance relative to their benchmark. Most of them have a high level of liquidity. And, as of now, the counterparty risk appears to be nonsignificant.

Today, an experienced investor could make intelligent use of any set or subset of available ETFs and ETNs – direct or inverse, with or without leverage, index-based, sector-based, commodity-based, treasury-based, or currency-based. If he/she so chooses, the key to success would be to identify as precisely as possible the current stage of development of the reference market and to choose his/her ETF investment vehicles accordingly. Special attention should be given to leveraged ETFs, however. If they not are used in the short run, they tend generate exponentially growing losses in case of error, mistakes that could significantly affect total return and/or destroy assets.

On the markets, as Gordon Gekko in the film *Wall Street* (1987) said: "Money itself isn't lost or made, it's simply transferred from one perception to another" When the markets collapsed in H2 of 2008, losing more than $20T in world capitalization, investors who positioned themselves on inverse – or inverse-leveraged – ETFs generated exceptional results. Acting intelligently, staying indifferent to the media buzz, and putting to work available investment technologies allowed them to focus on the single most important objective they might have had at that time: protecting assets under extreme market conditions!

Heuristic No. 2. Make intelligent use of available ETFs and ETNs. Monitor market dynamics and adjust investment strategies accordingly. Asset protection and survival stem from constant adaptation.

20.2   INVESTORS' "KNOWN UNKNOWNS"

Those who spend a significant amount of time reading quarterly reports, company press releases, and other message boards know that the world of investing has completely changed over the last two decades, particularly in terms of our access to financial information sources. Whatever your location on the surface of the earth, you are at the center of the world financial system if you have access to a high-speed Internet connection. But, this wealth of information has an unintended drawback. Too much information is as penalizing and paralyzing as a lack of information if you do not have the right conceptual framework and the appropriate tools to filter, validate, and analyze it. In addition, the level of accuracy of the information we have access to in the US, through the Securities and Exchange Commission's EDGAR database (https://www.sec.gov/edgar.shtml), does not compare with what is available in other parts of the world. Such a disparity of reliable and accurate access has far-reaching consequences and should incentivize Europe to establish a comparable public agency – to protect investors, maintain market integrity, and facilitate capital formation.

As most investors learn at their expense, "Accounting and finance reporting is more an art than a science!" If they decide to base some investments on the idiosyncratic or specific characteristics of individual businesses – a choice that would make sense if the goal were to try to exceed the reference market performance – investors have no other choice than to build and continuously improve their own information system. This system will aim at integrating today's almost infinite number of Internet sources – Yahoo/Finance, Investor, FinViz, Finra, Nasdaq, Bloomberg, and ZeroHedge – into a coherent structure capable of providing the right information – "right" meaning valid and reliable – at the right time, not an easy task even after having identified critical "known unknowns." The key is to carefully plan your investments and anticipate the consequences, organizing seemingly unrelated bits of information into hard facts, and waiting for the market to provide high-potential value discrepancies. To take full advantage of these discrepancies is what investors are paid for, namely making markets probably the most efficient mechanism to evaluate risky assets and to effectuate the transfer of their ownership.

20.2.1 Assessing Economic Value Added

The "science" of management can easily be summarized in two principles. (i) Never make any decision that could potentially have a negative impact on shareholders' equity. (ii) Never ever forget principle (i). "Equity" represents the financial resources that a company receives from its stockholders. It comprises nominal capital, retained earnings, and additional paid-in capital (capital premiums). Alternatively, it can be calculated as the firm's total assets or liabilities (total balance sheet) minus its debts.

Two measures of financial efficiency are commonly used to assess how effective management is in creating additional resources out of available funds: return on equity (roe) and return on assets (roa). roe is the ratio of the net income to stockholders' equity. roa is the ratio of net income to total assets or liabilities (total balance sheet). An estimate of leverage – that is, the importance of debt financing – is provided by the ratio: roe/roa.

As any investment strategy should take into consideration the opportunity cost associated with it, these measures of efficiency should be compared with the cost of capital (cc) and/or the weighted-average cost of capital (wacc). In simple terms, cc is the sum of the refinancing rate and of the risk premium. It corresponds to the rate of return that shareholders would receive if they invested available funds in a different business with a similar risk profile. The economic value added (eva) is the difference between roe and the cost of capital. If a company is consistently creating economic value, chances are that it is strategically independent and financially autonomous.

For a business, to create economic value is not a goal. It's a constraint. If a company's roe doesn't cover its cost of access to capital, its board should restructure it: adapt its strategy, free up assets, reduce debt, buy back shares, or any combination of them. Assuming you decided to invest, at least partially, in a portfolio of individual businesses during stage 2 and stage 3 of the market cycle, careful attention should be given to their performance on these dimensions. And, better cross-validate their estimates twice rather than once!

Heuristic No. 3. Investment candidates (businesses) should generate a recurrent level of return on equity greater that the cost of access to capital. Leverage should not threaten strategic independence and financial autonomy.

20.2.2 Assessing Earnings Growth

Like any other living organism, businesses adapt, grow, and multiply, or disappear. From an investment standpoint, the only measure of growth that matters is the fully diluted (stock options included) earnings per share (eps) growth. This measure is not necessarily related to the operational growth. The way management monitors costs, whatever their nature, is of utmost importance. Businesses should only concentrate on sales, market share, or any other operational criterion of growth, as long as it translates into earnings growth. Nonprofitable growth should be banned, even though in some parts of the world such a statement is "politically incorrect."

Stock splits are a natural consequence of a sustained level of earnings growth. Most high-tech, high-growth companies avoid paying dividends. They prefer keeping their financial resources internally – in the form of retained earnings – to finance future development (internal and/or external) and growth. Technically, the split rate is usually less than proportional to eps growth to prevent further dilution. Shareholders can take advantage of the greater liquidity of their investment and of its future valuation, assuming the earnings growth does not decelerate. Companies that pay dividends are usually those that cannot justify additional funding of their current activities or that are unable to grow earnings regularly.

Unfortunately, professional managers – as opposed to owners and shareholders – are mostly concerned about their next promotion or their next job than about working hard and growing their businesses. Some even tend to act as mercenaries, serving and obeying only those who pay them the most. That's why making sure that their personal future is intimately linked to profitable growth (e.g., through stock options) makes perfect sense!

Heuristic No. 4. Investment candidates (businesses) should generate a high level of earnings growth. To reduce the risk of future disappointment, earnings growth should be greater than operational growth and roe.

20.2.3 Assessing Value Discrepancies

"Buy low, sell high" is the key to success. But, to quote Oscar Wilde, "A cynic is a man who knows the price of everything and the value of nothing." The key difficulty when assessing the value of a business comes from the fact that the market price – assuming it is a valid and reliable estimate of the actual transaction price – is only the marginal price associated with a small fraction of ownership. It should never be mixed with the average price or with the actual economic value of an asset. In addition, as observed by so many over the course of history, "Markets can stay irrational longer than most investors can stay solvent," a condition that can become lethal for investors who use debt (leverage) to finance their purchases.

Assessing the fair value or the intrinsic value of an investment is a complex process requiring both expertise and experience. Expertise is needed to collect, validate, analyze, and extrapolate information from the Internet. Experience is required to put any estimate into perspective. Over a period of 15 years, the median price-to-sales ratio for the MSCI World Index has varied between 0.8 and 1.8, the price-to-earnings ratio (per) between 10 and 22, and the price-to-cash-flow ratio between 6 and 13. How a business scores along these criteria, and compares with today's market estimates (respectively, 1.8, 18, and 12), may help identify possible value discrepancies.

In the absence of a magic formula, one of the "best" measures of "value for the money" is provided by the price/earnings to growth ratio, or peg ratio ([per/100] / Δeps). This ratio balances the price an investor pays with the growth he gets. The next 5 years average earnings growth for S&P 500 Index being around 10% and the average P/E being around 19, the market forward peg ratio is approximately 1.9, suggesting that it is rather richly valued today.

Such an analysis is inevitably subjective. The choice of some valuation criteria, their combination, and/or ordering, reflect an investor's own biases as well as the specific nature and stage of development – in terms of its fundamentals – of the business at hand. If a valuation methodology is constantly updated as a result of the observed performance (or lack thereof) of the investments made through its implementation, it will gradually integrate the investor's cumulative experience. Such an iterative decision–evaluation process should help reduce both the frequency and the magnitude of future investment errors.

Heuristic No. 5. Focus on solid businesses that offer good value for the money (low peg) on historical terms, as well as on the basis of analysts' estimates. Stay put and emotionless when valuation ratios reach irrational levels.

All other things being equal, potentially interesting value gaps might hide behind three typical situations: (i) when price per share is significantly less than the book value per share – or net tangible assets per share, if there is a doubt as to the soundness of goodwill and intangibles; (ii) when the price to earnings ratio is considerably less than the trailing 12 months' fully diluted earnings per share growth – and is also less than the analysts' estimate of future eps growth; and (iii) when the price/earnings to growth ratio (peg) is noticeably less than the reference market equivalent. Such discrepancies – signaling potential investment opportunities – are as many invitations for deeper research.

20.3 INVESTORS' "UNKNOWN KNOWNS"

"Buy and hold" – and its corollary "Not sold ... not lost!" – is an investment principle that holds only for a diversified portfolio of assets invested in the long run: a strategy that can easily be deployed today if one makes intelligent use of the many market-based ETFs – and, if one assumes that brokers never rob their clients nor fall into bankruptcy! According to his last letter to Berkshire shareholders, Warren Buffett – a famous investor who perfectly understands that "Financing is … marketing!" – estimates the compounded annual gain for the period 1965–2013 of an investment made in the S&P 500 to be approximately 9.8%, while his company's performance is around 19.7%. Both percentages are subject to considerable annual variance. Assuming the average estimates are reliable and valid, why would anyone ever invest in a bond or keep money in cash? Need for liquidity, maybe; risk aversion, probably; ignorance, certainly!

Human beings are extremely complex systems. As noted by psychiatrists: "Desires are hypocritical." People usually do not really want what they say they want. They are expert at feigning, at feigning to feign, and at lying to others and to themselves! That's why "Performance" and "Success" are usually key obstacles on the road to actual performance and success. Knowing perfectly well – if not consciously! – that being successful would probably not solve any of their most critical problems. The same is true with investors who often behave as if they were more concerned about appearing as competent investors than about organizing themselves to become efficient and successful investors. They actually learn things, even important things, as to how markets behave and as to how others invest, but they prefer to ignore them for the benefit of seemingly more socially and morally acceptable concepts and principles. At other times, they prefer to ignore their intuition, based on apparently unrelated facts and observations, that constantly reminds them of the relevance of such key observations as: "Your first loss is your best loss!"; "It's never a bad decision to sell at a profit!"; and "Investments are like buses, when you miss one, just take the next one!" These last three are the simplest and most effective rules to protect assets and to avoid being trapped in chaos when the music stops. And, the music, as we all know, always stops!

It doesn't take much time, or require being an acute observer, to learn that "In a democracy you always get the opposite of what you voted for!" The same is true of financial markets. That's why it usually makes sense to "be fearful when others are greedy and greedy when others are fearful!" Investors are paid to identify and correct market discrepancies. Through their patient work and a wealth of seemingly unrelated investment decisions, they actually help markets tend toward efficiency.

On the markets, "Money doesn't get lost, it changes pockets!" That is during the period, which precedes what people call a crisis, a correction, or a recession, that the smartest investors design counterintuitive strategies that will lead, after the tragedy, to the desired change in the political, economic, or financial power structure. Associating that change to the observed event is always a mistake. The most important things are usually invisible and unknown to most. Businesses are playthings for bigger forces. The history of the world is a history of wars. Empires follow empires with surprising regularity. The causes of their collapse are well documented: among others, human beings' tendency to rest on their success, their innate taste for opulence, and their inclination to trust others for making a living and for their protection.

Sunzi et Sun Bin (2004), in *The Art of War* (476–221 B.C.), address the strategy of war in its broadest sense. Their theory stresses the necessity to understand the enemy, keep the initiative, adapt to the battlefield, engage only when sure of victory, act swiftly, win fast, be indifferent to any form of recognition, stay unpredictable, and avoid total destruction. It also stresses the importance of diplomacy and cultivating relationships with others. Each of these principles can readily be transposed to the world of investing.

Managers and board members, as probably university professors, tend to distinguish themselves more by their patience than by their competence. "Only invest in businesses that could be run by fools, one day they will" notes Warren Buffett. The incompetence and the irresponsibility of many leaders are well documented, particularly during periods of financial euphoria (Galbraith, 1994). If you let managers rest and destroy economic value, you will be surprised at how well they do it!

Today, investors have learned the hard way that to survive in the long run, they should better stay alive in the short run. Protecting assets becomes the surest path to growth. High-frequency trading systems, over leveraged shadow entities, flash crashes, and stealth central bank actions, to name a few, contribute to creating a "Rumsfeldian" world in which anything can happen anytime. But, every quarter, public companies publish their 10-Q and every year their 10-K (EDGAR database, www.sec.gov). The corresponding news releases usually cover the fact that they beat or missed analysts' estimates in terms of eps and revenues (over or underperformance). They also provide further guidance (upgrade or downgrade) as to future earnings and sales. Empirically, it appears that these quarterly results are impossible to forecast as, by the way, the resulting market reaction. Staying out of an investment when the company publishes its quarterly report is often a sound decision. It avoids being trapped in a possible brutal and significant market correction associated with profit taking and/or short selling by holders of stock options, call options, and other convertible bonds.

To protect assets and avoid being the "sucker", a reasonable strategy is to concentrate on a small number (focused diversification) of solid businesses (roe, Δeps, Δeps > roe, low peg, recurrent earnings beats), wait for and carefully analyze their quarterly results, and invest when the market ends its bottoming process (as depicted in Figure 20.2). An MACD analysis based on both daily and weekly data may help approach an "optimal" entry point. It usually happens between the second and third Option Expiration Friday (OEF) that follow the quarterly release. Option expiration (Witching day) occurs on the third Friday of every month. It is usually characterized by a high level of volatility, which may generate short-term value discrepancies and other asymmetric entry points.

Heuristic No. 6. Respect quarterly cycles. Invest in solid businesses (roe, Δeps, Δeps > roe, low peg, regular analysts' estimates beats) at the end of their consolidation (bottoming) process. Avoid being invested when quarterly reports are released.

Validating the soundness of individual investments on a quarterly basis makes perfect sense today, in a world where transaction costs are marginal compared to

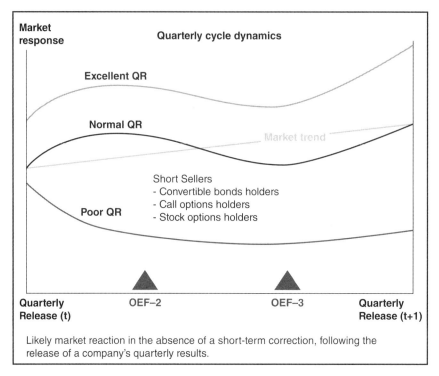

FIGURE 20.2 Usual market impact of a quarterly release. (*Source*: Choffray (2012)).

the potential losses induced by short-term volatility. More than ever, when protecting assets is a high priority, it is wise not to trade off "A good meal for a good night's sleep!"

To get hold of "unknown knowns," it is essential to keep track of your investment decisions, of the reasons why you made them, of the results they generated, and, most importantly, of what you learned from them. Intelligent investing requires accepting to learn patiently and stubbornly from past mistakes, from your misconceptions, and from your illusive and sometimes mythical "known knowns!" As a responsible investor, you are your sole enemy. And, the market is probably your only friend. Others' and experts' advice should be taken for what it is at best: *hypotheses*. They should never be trusted, but carefully investigated and tested!

20.4 INVESTORS' "UNKNOWN UNKNOWNS"

By definition, "unknown unknowns" are unknown! They cover "impossible," "unthinkable," and "unimaginable" events that can only be recognized after they have happened. They cannot be anticipated or forecasted. You can't connect them looking forward; you can only observe them, and sometimes connect them looking backwards. As they are as likely to affect assets under management positively or negatively, special attention and care should be devoted to the definition of a "flexible" investment strategy aimed at minimizing maximum losses and at preserving liquidity.

The starting point of an intelligent investment strategy should always be an assets growth objective. Based on the compounded annual gain for the period 1965–2013 that we discussed in the preceding section – 9.8% for the S&P 500 and 19.7% for Warren Buffett's Berkshire Hathaway – any goal greater than these could make sense. So, anytime an investment reaches this yardstick within its quarterly cycle – or within its annual cycle for an ETF – a rational investor should become wary and reach for the "return key."

There are essentially two strategies to protect assets from "unknown unknowns." The first one, discussed earlier, is to invest in a diversified portfolio of assets for the very long run. Market-based ETFs – or, better, sector-based ETFs, preferably without structural leverage – can be of considerable help here. Inverse ETFs can also be used when the reference market is in a confirmed downtrend. Second strategy: stay out of the market most of the time – after all, isn't cash king? – and invest very selectively only for short periods of time – inevitably less than 3 months! In this case, investors discover the wisdom and the pressure associated with "Sitting down, shutting up and thinking … hard!"

Henry Clews (1908), a well-respected investment banker and happy owner of a beautiful castle on the French Riviera, rightfully stressed the importance of experience in the design and execution of success-focused investment strategies:

> Few gain sufficient experience in Wall Street until they reach that period of life in which they have one foot in the grave. When this time comes these old veterans usually spend long intervals of repose at their comfortable homes, and in times of panic, which recur oftener than once a year, these old fellows will be seen in Wall Street, hobbling down on their canes to their brokers' offices. Then they always buy good stocks to the extent of their bank balances, which have been permitted to accumulate for just such an emergency. The panic usually rages until enough of these cash purchases of stock is made to afford a big 'rake in.' When the panic has spent its force, these old fellows, who have been resting judiciously on their oars in expectation of the inevitable event, quickly realize, deposit their profits with their bankers, or the over plus thereof, after purchasing more real estate that is on the upgrade, for permanent investment, and retire for another season to the quietude of their splendid homes and the bosom of their happy families.

This quote is a perfect illustration that the determinants of success have not changed fundamentally over the years. They were and still are primarily associated with the occurrence of market discontinuities and other value discrepancies that provide investors with short-term asymmetric investment opportunities. The only difference is that today, with the help of the Internet, anyone willing to invest seriously has the opportunity to take full advantage of the power of information, of analytics, and of the market dynamics.

Heuristic No. 7. *Sit down, shut up, and think*. Prepare investment decisions weeks and months in advance. Build watch lists of target companies with a stock screener. Contribute to God's work: *Buy despair, sell hope!*

As we all know or discover, *Life is a comedy* (Eramus, 1536). Periodically, however, it becomes a tragedy. At the end of the nineteenth century, Gustave le Bon produced his seminal work on the psychology of crowds (Le Bon, 1963). Technology aside, things haven't changed fundamentally since then. As markets behave like crowds, investors should spend time understanding how they function. Once formed, a crowd is not amenable to any form of rational thinking. It is, on purely psychological grounds, in a mental state resembling hypnosis. If well managed, crowd members can be influenced, and/or manipulated, with simple images and messages. They "wake up" and get back to normal life through a painful process that finally leads them to abruptly abandon their illusions. They literally surrender, "give up the ship," and, on the markets, swallow their losses – the capitulation, despondency, desperation stage! That's why crowds, if they are managed thoughtfully, are mostly efficient at destruction.

In his prescient novel *Money* which unfolds during the Second French Empire, Zola (1919) describes the terrible effects of fraudulent management, of the promotion of "concept" companies, of the negligence of board members, of the greed and corruption of investors, and of the chronic weakness of the law! More recently, in a short but insightful book on the history of financial euphoria, Galbraith (1994) effectively dissects investors' psychology and behavior. The regularity – every 7–10 years – with which financial markets fall into dementia is amazing, as is the conjunction of factors leading to it: a major financial innovation, the incompetence of market participants, the arrival of a new generation of investors, a tendency to self-delusion and self-righteousness, the excessive use of leverage, and the ignorance (or forgetting) of history. What we experienced over the last 5 years is probably nothing else than an additional example of what happens when people, and not only financial institutions, lose their sense of reality. This naturally leads to a search for culprits and other scapegoats (Girard, 1978), to the development of new myths and proscriptions, and, finally, to a new flight from reality.

When markets become irrational or show signs of dementia, as can be seen from the divergence between their valuation ratios and the corresponding range of historic variation, it is essential to stay put and emotionless. "Better get out a little bit too early than a little bit too late!" should inspire all your investment decisions. Use of an MACD analysis to identify signs of slowdown in a reference market trend – or to measure change in investment behavior for a specific business – coupled with close monitoring of the degree of achievement of your objectives, should help you protect effectively against "unknowns unknowns."

Independently of it being known or unknown, the incidence of an "unknown" on the performance of an investment or of a portfolio may be significant. As an example, consider the evolution of the price per share of Capstone Turbine Corp. for the period covering March through May 2014, as depicted in Figure 20.3.

As suggested by the MACD analysis, from a statistical standpoint, the company's uptrend started to decelerate from March 25 on, approaching downtrend territory on April 15. We have no idea of why it happened. Probably prevailing

Market capitalization impact of an unexpected action by management.

FIGURE 20.3 Capstone Turbine Corp.'s daily quote data for the period covering March through May 2014. (*Source*: BigCharts.com).

market conditions were the explanation at the time. But, in hindsight, wasn't something – a "known unknown" – brewing? On May 1, a press release informed the market that

> *Capstone Turbine Corporation (CPST) (the "Company") announced today that it has entered into an underwriting agreement to sell 18,825,000 shares of its common stock at a price to the public of $1.70 per share for gross proceeds of approximately $32.0 million. The shares were allocated to a single institutional investor. The net proceeds from the sale of the shares, after underwriting discounts and commissions, will be approximately $30.2 million. The offering is expected to close on or about May 6, 2014, subject to the satisfaction of customary closing conditions. The Company intends to use the proceeds from the offering to fund general working capital requirements and for other general corporate purposes.*

In less than a week, the price of Capstone's shares went down by more than 30% – representing a drop of essentially 50% in market capitalization since its last 52-week high (March 19, 2014) – while the share count increased only by 6%. So, an unexpected action designed to marginally fund general working capital requirements led to a drop in market capitalization … more than 10 times as big!

It is very difficult, if not impossible, to protect yourself against such "unknowns" except if you are out of the market at the time, as was discussed earlier.

But, for investors who have no other choice than to face the event, the right reaction should be – assuming the fundamentals of the business have not changed – to consider such extreme market conditions as offering an opportunistic, asymmetric entry point!

20.5   SYNTHESIS

> *The men who can manage men manage the men who can manage only things,*
> *and the men who can manage money manage all.*
>
> Durant and Durant (1968).

Under extreme market conditions – which we call here *nonparametric* to mean that they cannot easily be subjected to mathematical analysis – the surest way to grow *assets under management* (AUM) is, without any doubt, to avoid their loss in the first place! Under such conditions, investors face a whole range of unknowns: from "known unknowns" to "unknown unknowns." Analytic and/or probabilistic models cannot grasp the complexity of such a decision environment and can only be replaced by "battle-tested" heuristics.

The last 10 years have witnessed a major acceleration in the transformation of the world of investing. The synthetic nature of the assets involved, the fragmented structure of the markets on which they are exchanged, and the virtual form of most Internet-based transactions, all contribute to the emergence of a new reality. These changes have fundamentally altered the core activity and the strategies of most investors – be it institutional or individual. They make today's markets more reactive, less understandable, and probably less manipulable – in two words: less predictable.

We live in a world in which financial markets react in less than a few tens of a second on the basis of investors' perceptions of how unpredictable, impossible, and unthinkable events might affect the behavior of others. The sheer complexity of the situations encountered is such that they can only be dealt with through the development and use of empirically tested heuristics, aimed at conceptualizing a response to the unknown, at interpreting proven facts, and at converting observed discrepancies into profitable investment opportunities. That's why recent developments in the field of behavioral finance might lead to a renewed interest in heuristics-based intelligent systems – also called *expert systems*. Such systems express knowledge qualitatively, and make use of an inference engine to build a human-like mental process aimed at solving a problem or reducing decision risk (Choffray, 1992).

Under extreme conditions, investors naturally become more concerned about the return of their money than about the return on their money. Protecting assets becomes the path to survival and growth. High-frequency trading systems, over-leveraged shadow entities, flash crashes, and stealth central bank actions, all contribute to create a "Rumsfeldian" type of world in which decision makers have to learn to live with very few "knowns" and many "unknowns." This chapter explored such a conceptual framework and derived from it a concise and coherent set of battle-tested heuristics aimed at designing effective investment strategies to protect assets.

In a world where markets are, more than ever, battlefields for bigger forces, *We know you believe you understand what you think we wrote, but we are not sure you realize that what you read is not what we meant ! …*

References

Choffray, J.M. L'Art d'Investir Avec Internet. In: Longin, F., editor. *Gestion de Patrimoine*. Paris: The ESSEC Press; 2012; 124–153.

Choffray, J.M. *Systèmes Intelligents de Management*. Paris: Nathan; 1992.

Clews, H. *Fifty Years in Wall Street*. www.bnpublishing.net, 2009. 1908.

Durant, W., Durant, A. *The Lessons of History*. New York: Simon & Schuster; 1968.

Eramus, D. *The Praise of Folly*. New York: W. W. Norton Critical Edition, 1989; 1536.

Financial Crisis Inquiry Commission. 2011. *Report on the Causes of the Financial Crisis*. http://fcic.law.stanford.edu.

Friedman, M. *Capitalism and Freedom*. Chicago: The University of Chicago Press; 1962.

Galbraith, J.K. *A Short History of Financial Euphoria*. New York: Penguin Books; 1994.

Girard, R. *Des Choses Cachées depuis la Fondation du Monde*. Paris: Grasset; 1978.

Kindleberger, C. *Manias, Panics, and Crashes: A History of Financial Crises*. New York: Macmillan; 1978.

Le Bon, G. *Psychologie des Foules*. Paris: PUF; 1963.

Longin, F., Solnik, B. Extreme correlation of international equity markets. Journal of Finance 2001;**56**:651–678.

Sunzi et Sun Bin. *L'Art de la Guerre*. Paris: Payot & Rivages; 2004.

Wall Street, 1987, American Drama Film, directed by Oliver Stone, produced by Edward R. Pressman and distributed by 20th Century Fox.

Walter, C. The extreme value problem in finance: comparing the pragmatic program with the Mandelbrot program. In: Longin, F., editor. *Extreme Events in Finance*. New York: Wiley; 2017; 25–51.

Zola, E. *L'Argent*. Paris: E. Fasquelle; 1919.

Chapter Twenty One

EVT Seen by a Vet: A Practitioner's Experience on Extreme Value Theory

Jean-François Boulier
Aviva Investors, London, United Kingdom

21.1 WHAT HAS THE VET DONE?

I joined the financial industry in March 1987 with a quant background in engineering and scientific research experience in fluid mechanics. Six months later, the S&P 500 plunged 18% in what has come to be known as Black Monday and have seen long-term interest rate swings of more than 3% in a few days. The following year, I presented an empirical study on the French stock market daily movements – which crashed by an equivalent albeit lesser magnitude (15%) – at the French Finance Association (AFFI) conference, at a time when the stock market had more than rebounded. The French market index crashed by an equivalent albeit lesser magnitude (15%) on the same Black Monday. Sticking to the Gaussian distribution for the stock index variation leads to a roughly 15 standard deviation event, thus a highly unlikely event with an average waiting time period (1/probability) far exceeding the age of the universe … Our universe! This forced me into looking at other more realistic probability distributions.

We all experienced in the following decade a gold rush in quantitative finance stimulated by liberalization of markets, by access to technology and data, as well as by strong interactions between academics and practitioners. As an active member of the European Institute of Quantitative Investment Research, I had access to a large number of empirical studies on all financial markets and also presented my own. Heading a quant team at an innovative French Bank, Crédit Commercial de France, then acquired by HSBC, I looked at the possible use of a variety of these models to create new product and services for the clients of the bank. Our research

Extreme Events in Finance: A Handbook of Extreme Value Theory and its Applications,
First Edition. Edited by François Longin.

525

was partly shared with academics at conferences and also presented in a quarterly review, then called "Quants." The main applications at that time were pricing, investments, and risk management.

The main competitor to the Gaussian approach to stock price variation in the 1990s was the ARCH (autoregressive conditional heteroscedasticity) model and all its variations. But stable distributions, in particular the Levy stable model, were appealing. For all sorts of reasons, the Gaussian approach was still being used by practitioners in spite of the limitations of the model. As no obvious candidate prevailed at that time (does one today?), the pragmatic approach was to use different models under different circumstances. As the regulation forced the Bank into more accurate risk management and capital allocation, CCF put in place an internal model and had to select stress tests. That is where extreme value theory (EVT) came into play. In the following part, I will explain how and what kind of lessons I learned from that use. I then would like to highlight what I feel are the needs for future research and progress.

Later, during the new century, quant models came to be mainstream, and many people forgot about the inherent limitations of any kind of modeling. The overhang of sophisticated models created a too fuzzy and sometimes unchecked environment. In parallel, as the economy grew and debt developed to unprecedented levels, financial crisis erupted and devastated markets and institutions. It forced everyone to think twice about how to handle risk and modeling, and should one add the risk of modeling. This would lead to a humble conclusion.

21.2   WHY USE EVT?

The appetite for more formalized assessment of capital requests for financial institutions has grown dramatically in modern regulation. All started with the Basel 2 drafting, where the internal model concept appeared for the first time. Industry leaders, lured by the potential capital savings but also by the signaling effect attached to this innovative approach, made their best to build such models and to submit them to their regulators. The squadron by the French regulator was involved in the difficult task of checking and agreeing that the internal model was particularly shrewd and experienced. Needless to say, all applicants had their difficult moments. That regulation stipulated that, in addition to the normal model targeted at measuring the value at risk (VaR), there should be a comprehensive set of stress scenarios. VaR was meant to be on a typical horizon of 15 days and a probability of 99%, thus having an average waiting time period of approximately 4 years, an adverse but not a tough event. Stress scenarios, on the other hand, were meant at stressing – a very different game.

How to stress portfolios of mostly liquid assets has been the subject of debates. How to find the right level? Not too large a level that would have destroyed interest in holding any position and thus be a complete deterrent to engage in market activities; not too low because VaR was doing that job. The next question was to have a form of coherence between the shocks on equities, bonds, or currencies. Fairness is the key in people-intensive activities. Then come the difficulties related to the statistical estimation of these stress scenarios. Indeed, if one has the luxury of having data of more than a century, a question remains on the relevance of such old-time data to the present. But fortunately, or unfortunately, the lack of data is often what blocks efforts to estimate these rare quantiles with classic statistics.

The solution we came across at that time was to combine forward-looking stresses and a set of coherent stresses based on EVT. As an example of forward-looking stress, we ended naturally with the things we were afraid of during that period. I remember, for example, the exit from the nascent Euro, which was only used by institutions. Then the difficulty to have the Euro accepted by the general public could have triggered panic and therefore shocks, which we attempted to model with mostly guessed magnitudes. How to describe the perfect storms is indeed a never-ending exercise. Which can prove useful, not really to foster forecasting ability but more to enable a thorough preparation, in a disciplined manner? Let us now come to the historically based stresses.

Generally speaking, statistically the variation of a security price shows a distribution close to a normal one but not identical. The probability of little, almost nil, movements and the probability of sharp disruptions, especially on the downside, are much more important than in the Gaussian case. Instead, the "jaws" of the actual historical distribution are much less pronounced. Price hardly moves or moves hard! The relative difference for the tail of the distribution is the most acute because, as the Black Monday case showed, the probability of an event more than three standard deviations is negligible under the normal law, whereas history shows crises are quite frequent. As mentioned earlier, a stable law tends to offer a more realistic model for stock prices.

As the purpose was to design a coherent and flexible set of shocks, upwards and downwards, we really only cared about the modeling of the tails.

Modeling tails is not such a rare endeavor, and many practitioners use these models. This is particularly true in actuarial sciences, which are used in pricing insurance contracts of various sorts.

A number of empirical studies have been done on a large set of securities, stocks and bonds, indices, and currencies. The Fréchet distribution was the dominant outcome of these studies. Once the tail was modeled and the relevant parameters were estimated, we could come back to the leaders of the bank with a reliable and flexible representation of rare shocks. Depending on the management's appetite for risk, which varied over time and fluctuated with crisis or bank-specific concerns, we could adjust the magnitude of the stress scenarios. The language we used on these scenarios was related to the average waiting time. We talk about a 50-year shock, or a century shock, exactly like in hydrology for floods. All were on a 1-day period. But sometimes we considered longer periods to accommodate liquidity or execution time. The reference point, but not necessarily the one selected, was the probability assigned to the rating of the bank: historical corporate default distribution per rating (better known in the US than in other markets) gives an idea of the average waiting time attached to the rating. Part of the empirical findings were published and presented in many conferences at that time.

21.3   WHAT EVT COULD ADDITIONALLY BRING TO THE PARTY?

The first major finding highlighted by EVT was that extreme situations demanded another model. It seems to be true in human-related (prices are) and purely natural (e.g., seism) phenomena. There is a need to understand why it is so. Will this research come with results, hopefully yes; but in any case digging into what makes "extreme" different seems useful. Herding, force behavior, and non-rational behavior have to be better forecasted and, in my view, controlled. Regulation should take these behaviors into account, and the side effects of existing regulation in turbulent times should be better mastered. Is it a shame to change the rules in the middle of a crisis? Or, should we not positively think of the necessary changes in regulation in such times? By the way, modern central banking carries out such an experiment with quantitative ease, another word for unorthodox, unconventional, and improbable behavior, just suited to an extreme situation where the ordinary, conventional financing channel does not work. If the normal law does not work in critical situations, why do we try to tweak thing to cope with it? This leaves the unanswered question of what extreme is and how we measure it. Another area where EVT may help, at least in the description of phenomena, is liquidity. A great deal of the huge swings we have experienced during the last crisis was indeed related to liquidity – all sorts of liquidity by the way. My guess is that the many relations of financial agents change radically during a crisis. The consequences in trading and forced sales, like the so-called pro-cyclical capital rules, have been mentioned many times. But we should go beyond and look at many other aspects, such as the intensity in reporting and the widening gap in trust and behaviors, clearly highlighting a special period, like the phase approach in fluid mechanics! But this was another story, for me at least.

21.4   A FINAL THOUGHT

To a quant-minded professional, EVT is great but by no means a panacea. It has proven already very useful in modeling and managing extreme events. It has also the appeal to be different and exciting. In many topics, like option pricing or portfolio optimization, it becomes a challenge! And given the known benefits, it is worth trying to overcome the technical difficulties. Nevertheless, to damp the quant excitement, let us enjoy normal time and try not being obsessed more than needed by extreme and, thus, rare events. Fascination is no guide to a responsible realistic professional.

References

Boulier, J.-F., Dalaud, R., Longin, F. Application de la théorie des valeurs extrêmes aux marchés financiers. Paris Banque et Marchés 1998;**32**:5–14.

Boulier, J.-F., Gaussel, N., Legras, J. Crashes to crashes. Quants Review 1999;**33**, CCF.

Chapter Twenty Two

The Robotization of Financial Activities: A Cybernetic Perspective

Hubert Rodarie

Deputy CEO Groupe SMA (insurance), France

The purpose[1] of this chapter is to provide a practitioner's perspective of the ongoing developments in the organization of the financial world since the crisis of 2007.

Based on the commonly held observation of mounting complexity, we analyze the current situation in terms of the collective attempt to mechanize financial operations. This mechanization systemizes and generalizes the trend that began in the mid-1980s in asset management and banking portfolios, and in automated trading functions known as *program trading*.

Such mechanization, or robotization, is, in our opinion, indicative of what may be called the embedding of modern-day risk modeling within professional organizations. As such modeling produces a measure of risk considered to be accurate, this logically implies that future uncertainties, other than those calculated, are now attributed to human error. This point has been put forward in previous studies (Walter, 2010; Rodarie, 2012) as the main diagnosis of the 2007/2008 financial crisis.

---

[1] Article developed from the presentation delivered at the 30th International Conference of the French Finance Association (AFFI) on Thursday, May 30, 2013 during the "Global Stability and Systemic Risk" Day introduced by Professor Robert Engle, recipient of the Nobel Prize for economics in 2003, during the "New paradigms for risk in financial and insurance activities" round-table discussions. It was presented at the Third SMABTP Scientific Symposium in November 2013 and at the EHESS February 12, 2014, seminar of the Ethics and Finance Chair MSH, *Collège d'Etudes Mondiales*.

Extreme Events in Finance: A Handbook of Extreme Value Theory and its Applications,
First Edition. Edited by François Longin.
© 2017 John Wiley & Sons, Inc. Published 2017 by John Wiley & Sons, Inc.

Consequently, organizations are focusing on preventing human error by drawing on the efforts employed in other economic sectors to define and prevent it. We will thus show that organizations logically make use of the organizational frameworks used for industrial output, known as "quality assurance." Initially developed to control quality in the aeronautic and, then, nuclear sectors, these frameworks have gradually been extended to all industrial and service sectors, and are known as quality management systems. These measures have been subject to various and successive standardizations (ISO), and since the mid-1990s have been used to prevent the risks managed by, and inherent to, the banking and financial system.

To assess this process, we will employ the ideas put forward by Norbert Wiener, one of the founding fathers of cybernetics. We will identify the requirements for successfully implementing the process with respect to its ultimate goal of risk control. We will thus highlight the consequences of the choices currently employed in the financial system, which potentially reduce the number of limited-impact incidents, but which, on the other hand, create conditions favorable for the occurrence of extreme events.

22.1   AN INCREASINGLY COMPLEX SYSTEM

What is the most striking feature of financial activities today? It is their growing complexity. It is the main defining feature of the evolution of the financial system since the 2007–2008 North American banking crisis and its subsequent developments in Europe. Nothing is simple for anyone, be they professionals, customers, or regulators.[2] Everything has become complicated, and no sector has escaped – banking, market, asset management, and insurance activities have all been affected. Everything is becoming increasingly complex.

This complexity appears to have two main sources:

- *Creativity:* New calculation methods have facilitated the development of new products and new ways of entering into and trading commitments. From securitization, to derivatives, passing by high-frequency trading or alternative management, these new capabilities have led to the creation of new organizations that even today's finance professionals struggle to learn, and above all to master, both globally and in detail, immediately and over the long term.

- *Regulation:* Since the 2007–2008 crisis in particular, the desire to regulate activities has produced an impressive body of laws, rules, and specifications from various sources; the 2300-page Dodd–Frank Act in the United States is one such example. European output has not been left behind, and the same "risk control" trend is seen in the construction of an integrated European system. And to add further complexity, the European administrative, political,

---

[2]We use the term "regulators" to denote any entity or person who, whether they possess the regulatory capacity or not, regulates or controls activities.

and monetary framework, which is still under construction, is particularly multifaceted, imprecise, and slow, with the notable exception of the euro zone and its own institutions, the ECB in particular, which is naturally playing an ever greater role.

Overall, while the economic world is on the brink of recession and deflation, the regulatory world, on the other hand, is enjoying a period of enlargement and unfettered growth.

Is this complexity inevitable?

Has it arisen solely from the aforementioned creativity, or not? Does it derive from other sources?

We are not going to criticize creativity, because it is clear that all systems tend to expand. The multiplication of activities and services proposed by an economic sector is not, in itself, an undesirable symptom.

On the other hand, examining the origin and structure of the complexity generated by regulation, or more accurately by the standardization of activities, whether controlled by public supervision or not, is worthwhile.

To summarize, it could be argued that this increasing complexity principally arises from the desire of all actors, professionals, and regulators to *automate*. We are witnessing an attempt to organize financial activities as if they were a machine, or rather a collection of machines that must collectively be identifiable, predictable, controllable and reproducible, valid across all continents, in every corner of the world, and, finally, adapted to globalization.

Evidently, confronted with these developments, a professional who is familiar with other business sectors and who has, for example, worked in a manufacturing industry, is bound to recognize organizational frameworks that are very similar or analogous to those in the automotive or electronics industries. Given the views of the Basel Committee, it appears that the hope is for the Rhine Valley to become the new Silicon Valley, where a new way of working and producing will be invented.

Thus, concretely, we are trying to classify or reduce financial commitment activities, that is, contracts performed over time, to the production of reproducible objects that, with the exception of their aging, are only minimally time-dependent.

On this topic, it could be noted that the finance sector, in contrast to all manufacturing industries, never talks about its products aging, and even less about technical obsolescence. A bond will remain "fresh" as long as the issuer pays the interest; the financial sector speaks only in terms of default.

Why does this imitation exist, given that the objects in question are so different? Why is there a desire to replace people currently working in diverse organizations with quasi-robotized participants identically carrying out standardized procedures?

Is it the fascination with industrial efficiency? For many years, this efficiency has generated improvements in productivity, so, apparently, continuation of that seems to be a normal product of such activity. Yet, this does not appear to be especially decisive. In fact, if competition has driven industrial companies to continuously improve their techniques and products, in the financial domain the "risk" factor is not, evidently, a reproducible object likely to be treated by similar means to those used in manufacturing industries. This would effectively necessitate having resolved the quantification of risk.

We, therefore, need to consciously classify financial activities as issues that can be perfectly addressed by calculations, if not necessarily deterministically, at least stochastically. Accordingly, as expressed by André Gorz:

> *Using quantitative measures as a substitute for rational value judgements provides moral security and supreme intellectual comfort; the Good becomes measurable and calculable.*
>
> Gorz (1988)

And we could add to this citation that risk could be controlled and reduced to admissible bounds by employing adapted "metrics," to use the new terminology.

In such a context, there is an a priori refusal to consider the occurrence of all causes as fundamentally unexpected, or even as arising from the discontinuities that can compromise the organization's calculation model. All dysfunctions will thus be attributed to human error.

22.2   HUMAN ERROR

We now need to define human error and determine whether the robotization of activities is likely to prevent or reduce such human error.

Various university studies have been undertaken to characterize human error, and, at the request of professionals, to recognize and prevent its sources.[3] Drawing on the work of James Reason, we note that

> *The more predictable varieties of human fallibility are rooted in the essential and adaptive properties of human cognition. They are the penalties that must be paid for our remarkable ability to model the regularities of the world and then to use these stored representations to simplify complex information-handling tasks.*

Reason identifies two types of error in his study – slips and mistakes – which apply to two cognitive fields:

- The first is the *stack* or *working memory*, where the subject focuses his or her attention.
- The second is the *declarative knowledge base*, comprised of all of the information the subject possesses and the action plans, or schemas, that he or she is familiar with and which are likely to be suitable.

---

[3]A description of these studies and a bibliography can be found in Reason (1990).

He identifies three types of error, in accordance with the generic error modeling system (GEMS):

- SB slips (*skill-based slips*), occurring in activities based on automated practices well integrated into familiar plans, and which do not require conscious control;
- RB mistakes (*rule-based mistakes*), occurring in activities based on applying specific rules;
- KB mistakes (*knowledge-based mistakes*) occurring in activities requiring confirmed knowledge.

Two modes of control are employed to prevent these human errors:

- *The proactive mode:* Composed of a collection of control rules chosen a priori according to teams' goals and experience and according to well-known and detailed activity plans. The focus is on organization and discipline. The errors in this mode are at the SB or RB level.
- *The retroactive mode:* Control is attentional in this mode; there are no longer any rules applicable a priori, the subject acts on the basis of his or her knowledge, reacting to setbacks as quickly as possible, step by step. In this case, mistakes are at the KB level, generated by insufficient knowledge or inappropriate choices of action plan. Expertise and responsibility are the main tools used to deal with these mistakes.

We will illustrate these situations using the following examples:

For the driver of a car, the "changing gear" schema in general requires little attention. SB-level slips are quickly identified and corrected. RB-level mistakes may arise during schemas such as "driving out of a parking space" or "changing lanes." Controls are in place, taught, and often codified in law (use of indicator and rear-view mirror).

On the other hand, a KB-level mistake may arise if the driver needs to react to an unexpected event: for example, if another car goes through a stop sign, what should the driver do? Hit the breaks or swerve, etc.? We can easily find other examples related to driving or to operating other devices or installations.

This example also introduces, in very simplified manner, an indication of the limits between rules-based and knowledge-based modes of behavior. This point will be addressed later in this chapter.

In fact, based on this analysis, it is clear that, in companies, the organization will ensure that its overall activities take place as far as possible in a "knowledge-based" domain where all actions and behaviors are described and known by all the relevant participants. The organization will also clearly implement a "proactive mode of control," and will thus believe that it has reduced uncertainty regarding its results and increased confidence in its activities.

22.2.1 Quality Assurance

We thus find the origin of what is now known as "quality assurance." Giving rise to the Anglicism "*Assurance Qualité*" in French, the word "assurance" is used here to express certainty or confidence. The organization's goal is therefore to inspire confidence in the quality of the outputs generated by the production chain.

Thus, according to the definition extracted from the ISO 8402 standard, which has now been replaced, the Quality Assurance System is

> *All the pre-established and systematic activities implemented within the quality system framework, and proved when necessary, to give appropriate confidence that an entity will meet quality requirements.*

If we replace the word "quality" with "risk control," we find, almost word for word, the definition of risk management or risk control systems, the subject of various regulations and codes issued by European and U.S. legislators and regulators. To a certain extent, quality and risk have been likened to one another, which was tempting because both approaches strive to create confidence and certainty.

In the last 50 years, a number of practices and tools have therefore been developed, and are used to control quality: procedures manuals, identification, traceability, process diagrams, mapping, error modeling, recording of malfunctions, corrective and preventative actions, etc. All of these practices and tools have been standardized via the development of international standards (ISO standards). These standards are sometimes imposed by regulations, for example, in the case of dangerous activities, or health care activities. Finally, identical practices and controls already exist for asset management and risk control in the regulatory provisions currently in place for the financial sector.

We can therefore conclude that the organizational model currently in use has been designed and developed over several decades in order to prevent human error, and in particular the two first types of error (SB and RB).

However, the proforma model of this organization is the machine. Only with machines can all procedures be perfectly identified and recognized, and proactively controlled in a predefined manner.

Clearly, this type of organization has been shown to respond well to preventing human error, but only limited forms of error. Moreover, it has not been developed to address all the sources of deficiency or uncertainty that can arise in financial companies.

22.3   CONCRETELY, WHAT DO WE NEED TO DO TO TRANSFORM A COMPANY INTO A MACHINE?

First of all, in the interest of clarity, we set out the definition of a machine.

A machine is a device or a group of devices used to transform strictly defined inputs into planned outputs using controlled processes.

Techniques have been developed enabling an increasingly refined control of operations and their sequencing, limiting human intervention as far as possible, with the result that certain operations are referred to as *robotic* or *automated*.

This very same approach, applied to all financial company activities, is either in place, or in the process of being implemented by all participants, professionals, and regulators. It can be described as totalizing because it not only covers all actions, whether they are material services, often known as operational, or whether they relate to developing pricing, the counterpart to commitments and the assessment of the risk that they bring to the establishment, but also because its goal is to reduce risk to a single measure, for which the board of directors is responsible.

To do this, the large amounts of information that make up the inputs need to be gathered (the famous data). The focus will be on processes, data, internal control, and due diligence. Every effort needs to be made to make each activity as transparent as possible; no data can be missing. Each of these procedures is subject to laws and rules, and to the circulation of best practices with which, regardless of the theoretical legal force of the text, the professional needs to comply, either by conviction or out of inertia faced with the need to "comply or explain."[4]

Next, we need to develop the machine itself. It needs to process the data and produce meaningful results. What are the challenges for such a machine once the calculations have been made in accordance with the planned processes?

How can we judge whether the outputs are satisfactory? How can we continually improve the machine? Because, naturally, we would imagine that an a priori imperfect system must necessarily evolve and adapt to new developments.

The designers of such a machine thus face two main concerns:

- The first is detecting an error or a noncompliance compared to the expected results.
- The second is the ability to continually improve the quality of the results.

The overall framework to be implemented may thus be schematized as follows: it should comprise two stages, one producing the outputs, the other analyzing them. If a noncompliant result is obtained, this should trigger a so-called feedback effect, whose goal is ideally not just to reject the output but also to improve the first-stage processes.

We first simply introduce what is known in the manufacturing industry as *control*. According to the definition given in Larousse

"A control system is a subservient mode of operation in which the variable to be controlled tends towards a reference value."

It should be noted, somewhat ironically, that in a Francophone context, the word for control, "*régulation*," transposed from the English "regulation," which according to the Oxford Dictionary simply means "*Rule or directive made and maintained by an authority,*" in other words a regulation, has replaced the previously used terms of administrative control. By adopting this term for activities such as financial services, the Francophone legislator has perhaps involuntarily translated its search for an automated mode of operation that is physically regulated.

---

[4]Comply with the rules or explain noncompliance.

Control is the cornerstone of productivity and automation in the manufacturing sector. But the important technical word here is "*subservience*," which describes the relationships between processes. We can therefore identify two types of systems in a complex machine: the governed system and the governing system.

For example, the centrifugal "flyball" governor used in steam engines to simply control the speed of the engine is the governing system, and the vast boiler and the connecting rods are the governed system.

A considerable part of engineering sciences involves creating subservient mechanisms to make the particular machine as stable as possible: in other words, according to the textbook definition, to ensure "that the free response of the system tends towards zero at infinity" (Papanicola, 2010).

But this is not sufficient, because the aim, if possible, is to adapt the process to eliminate the source of the disparity, with the justified rationale that simple subservience will not suffice. This property is known by cyberneticians as *autoadaptivity*.

22.3.1   Cybernetics

Our research now needs to turn to cybernetics. We begin with a reminder of the purpose of cybernetics.

A definition: Cybernetics is the science of control and communication processes and their regulation in animals, machines, and in sociological and economic systems. Its main purpose is to study the interactions between "governing systems" (or control devices) and "governed systems" (operational devices) controlled by feedback processes.[5]

This is exactly the intellectual tool that a regulator would need in order to control a priori the quality of the devices that he or she wanted to implement to organize companies, individually and collectively, into a social machine.

A founder: The American mathematician Norbert Wiener is one of the founding fathers of cybernetics. He studied these issues, and popularized them through three main works: "*Cybernetics, or Control and Communication in the Animal and the Machine*" (1948)[6]; "*The Human Use of Human Beings*" (1950)[7]; and "*God & Golem, Inc.: A Comment on Certain Points where Cybernetics Impinges on Religion*" (1964).[8]

The analogy between the financial machine put in place to comply with prudential regulations and the automated translation processes that he studied appears entirely appropriate.

Effectively, for Wiener,[9] an automated translation machine is the textbook example of a machine in real need of autoadaptivity.

---

[5]Source: Wikipedia (French site).

[6]MIT Press (Cambridge, Mass.) and Wiley (New York).

[7]Boston: Houghton Mifflin (1952, re-ed. 1971).

[8]MIT Press and *L'éclat* 2000.

[9]In "God & Golem Inc."

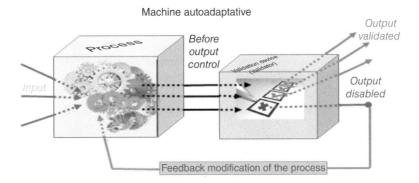

FIGURE 22.1 Self-learning mechanism.

In other words, a machine that needs to integrate a self-learning mechanism, which in the course of its operation should enable the machine to continually improve the quality of its output.

The mechanism can be schematized as follows (Figure 22.1).

One of the essential points is the design of the control device. However, according to Wiener,[10] this control device can be defined in two, and only two, ways:

This will involve one of two things:

- *either a complete set of objectively applicable rules determining when a translation is good,*
- *or some agency that is capable of applying a criterion of good performance apart from such rules.*[11]

We examine below various different devices:

An industrial machine: This falls into the first case. The mechanic-designer has a complete set of objective rules enabling him to manufacture his item. These rules are made up of technical specifications and plans. *Result: a control device is feasible.*

A translation machine: This is the example proposed by Wiener. It falls into the second case, as there is no complete set of objective rules for translating a text. Linguistic sciences are incomplete. We can, however, make use of an expert (a translator) who will apply a distinct criterion of the implementation rules (process) used by the translation machine, "The normal criterion of good translation is intelligibility,"[12] which means that the text must have the same meaning regardless of the reader. The expert can validate the translation, make

---

[10] In "God & Golem Inc." p. 78.

[11] Emphasis and bullet point added.

[12] Emphasis and bullet point added, pp. 97, 78.

corrections, and enhance the device. *Result: we can construct an autoadaptive translation machine.*

The financial machine is constantly evolving. Clearly, all participants want to use the most efficient and mechanized "control device" possible, in particular to be able to run increasingly large series of operations. It is therefore clear that effort is primarily focused on defining a body of objective rules, to be implemented via regulations, in order to control the models as effectively as the results.

However, financial science, like linguistic science, is incapable of producing such a body of objective rules.

Thus, to comply with the second criterion, we need to introduce a competent agent possessing a criterion separate from the output delivery rules.

Currently, risk is the main criterion used and imposed by western regulations. The acceptability of its level is left to the judgment of the expert or the person taking responsibility for it.[13]

Is it distinct from financial sector output delivery (or execution) rules? Is it measureable? These are the fundamental questions asked by the cybernetician to assess the suitability of the control device.

We thus come to the main subject of our study and research – risk measurement.

Precisely, and a genuine matter of reflection, the overall device[14] and its best execution criterion – risk and its measurement – are constructed and expressed based on the same elements that have enabled the activities to develop and lead to the current conglomeration of institutions: financial science and the powerful calculation methods provided by computer technology.

However, as highlighted in the quotation above, the criterion must be independent of the processes and the automatic execution rules.

Thus, intelligibility does not form part of the mechanics of translation; it merely allows the result to be judged.

In fact, financial science, which underpins the activities, also provides regulators with the means of constructing a regulatory framework considered as acceptable. It is developed from the same conceptual frameworks, paradigms, and models. The calculation tools used to create products (outputs) and fix prices are identical to those that calculate the risk and fix the limits for such products.

This tendency to reuse tools is even stronger, given that the professionals themselves have promoted auto-regulation. They have converted extremely senior figures such as Alan Greenspan in his time, or the Basel Committee. They have therefore favored this route themselves. Going even further, participants are no longer aware of the identity of these tools.

---

[13] In the insurance sector, for example, we can point to the forthcoming SOLVENCY II, which contains the requirement to identify processes, according to a breakdown by risks, or business line. Control and monitoring are concentrated in the risk department (expert), whose choices and limits are approved by the board of directors (responsibility).

[14] We are evidently not examining here those activities generally classified as operational, which are perfectly well described, and for which well-adapted quality management systems have already been used successfully for many years.

22.3.2 Cybernetician's Diagnosis of Financial Regulation

Result of this analysis: The financial structures device, intended to be autoadaptive by the regulators, does not meet either of the required criteria for cybernetic tools.

At the very least, the cybernetician will be tempted at this stage to consider that current regulation of the financial system must be suffering from an irremediable design error. This regulation, naturally and under such conditions, has every chance of non-satisfactorily achieving its objectives, and of generating potentially harmful, or even extreme, unexpected effects.

22.3.3 Observed Effects of the Dependency Between the Best Execution Criterion and Activity Process Design Rules

In fact, the dependency between the best execution criterion of the mechanized financial system and the design of the processes generates two principal distortions observable today, which would not have existed had there been independence:

- *The first distortion*, caused by using identical concepts, prevents the regulator-official from taking a global or organic approach to the financial system.

  In fact, the professional does not think in terms of system, but in terms of activities, while the regulator-official should give priority to the system, independently of activities.

  By using the professional's conceptual framework, the official is only able to visualize the financial system as an aggregation or addition of entities, and will therefore have a mainly aggregative vision, rather than an organic vision. The security of the overall system is thus reduced to ensuring the individual security of each entity. This immediately leads to an overwhelming tendency to favor an oligopolistic mode of organization, which facilitates "moral hazard" situations, the painful and costly consequences of which have been in evidence since 2008.

- *The second distortion* is that accepting devices for regulatory purposes enshrines paradigms, theories, and models for systemic uses in the social field, although they may not necessarily have been designed for this purpose.

  All models, including those relating to activity, thus become untouchable and beyond criticism, and worse, those who do not apply them are considered as unprofessional. This statement is not an exaggeration. Despite his colossal success, Warren Buffet is periodically criticized in this way. His method of financial management does not comply with financial theory standards, with his fund even being downgraded by S&P in May 2013.

22.3.4 What Thoughts Do We Have At This Stage?

In any case, is it not sensible to reliably automate certain tasks that we could, perhaps, consider as simple? This allows better control of the continuing growth and the market concentrations already achieved. Given that there is no point in seeking perfection, could we not accept, in cost-benefit analysis terms, the two distortions highlighted above? Could we not consider the subservience endured by teams as necessary evils for the benefit of all?

Perhaps, or why not?

Nevertheless, it is important to not only provide an answer in principle, but above all to analyze the system, both in its current form and as it develops, in order to come to a conclusion as to its quality.

22.3.5   An Increasingly Rigid System

And yet, the combined, and already visible, effect of the two distortions highlighted is to make activities increasingly rigid.

In fact, the first distortion, an aggregative vision, leads organizations, businesses, and regulators to concentrate on the device rather than the substance. It focuses attention on collecting information rather than on the relevance of the information. Professionals become more sensitive to the gadget nature of the device, as previously shown by Norbert Wiener. The loss of risk control becomes all the more likely given that this change in the focus of attention will reduce professionals' vigilance and ability to deal with actual risks.

This mechanization, and the standardization that frames it, thus create a series of devices that facilitate the abrogation of responsibility, or even the de-skilling, of the various actors in an often-described context where complying with the form quickly takes precedence over issues of substance.

In addition, standardization, whether it is regulatory or professional, forces imitation, which is always dangerous in periods of market shocks. Effectively, instead of being absorbed, the effects of even limited variations are at times amplified by reactions that have become identical. In the case of shocks, a so-called resonance phenomenon may arise, as was the case at a famous bridge on the River Maine in France, which on 16 April 1850 collapsed under the double marching of a regiment (Duban, 1896), although the bridge could easily bear the weight of the men and their equipment. In the elegant parlance of the statistician, we would in this case refer to *instabilities caused by the sudden appearance of unforeseen correlations.*

Pragmatically, we thus have every right to ask whether the system creates situations where extreme events can occur. This financial-system-wide reflection can already be confirmed by the misadventures that have befallen automated order placement mechanisms such as flash trading or high-frequency trading.

In terms of banking regulation, observers during the 2008 crisis, such as the FSB,[15] revealed the disastrous systemic effects of the synchronized generalization of practices judged to be appropriate on an individual level. The FSB thus showed that the mechanism for adjusting commitment guarantees in function of variations in default risk and the market price of collateral (*collaterization*), undertaken by all players at the same time, dramatically amplified the effects of market movements.

---

[15]The Financial Stability Board, which, at the time, was called the FSF, or Financial Stability Forum.

Overall, this mechanization, and the standardization that frames it, thus create a series of devices that make the structures rigid. It does reduce the frequency of limited-scope incidents, but by removing responsibility from the various actors and subjecting them to regulatory synchronization, the risk of extreme events, or even ruptures, increases substantially. We could therefore say that *this organization reduces daily volatility but increases the risk of serious disturbance.*

The **second distortion**, *the enshrining of rules*, facilitates what is known in cybernetics as the *homeostasis* of the financial system; in other words, scientific knowledge is part of the group of rules or ideas that are unaffected by external events. Thus, irrespective of the events encountered and of the results of the system, the paradigms, models, and conceptual frameworks are no longer called into question. On this aspect, which depends more particularly on the scientific community, we need only recall the words of Norbert Wiener in *God and Golem Inc.*:

> *The growing state of the arts and sciences means that we cannot be content to assume the all-wisdom of any single epoch. … In a period of relative stability, if not in the philosophy of life, then in the actual circumstances that we have produced in the world about us we can safely ignore new dangers such as have arisen … Nevertheless, in the course of time we must reconsider our old optimization, and a new and revised one will need to take these phenomena into account.*

> *Homeostasis, whether for the individual or the race, is something of which the very basis must sooner or later to be reconsidered. This means … that although science is an important contribution to the homeostasis of the community, it is a contribution the basis of which must be assessed anew every generation or so. … Permanent homeostasis of society cannot be made on a rigid assumption of a complete permanence of Marxianism, nor can it be made on a similar assumption concerning a standardized concept of free enterprise and the profit motive."*

And Wiener concludes:

> *It is not the form of rigidity that is particularly deadly so much as rigidity itself, whatever the form.*

22.3.6 A Degenerating and Increasingly Fragile System

The consequences of this increasing rigidity are obvious for the cybernetician: the risk of deadlock, reduced adaptability and, in the end, a weakened device that becomes increasingly unable to endure shocks. Rigidity should therefore clearly be proscribed as far as possible.

But, worse, after a certain point, degeneration may occur. How can this be defined? It is the situation in which the system produces the required effects on an increasingly infrequent basis, and where undesirable phenomena appear. Participants are thus increasingly unwilling to adhere to the system, which as a result becomes fragile.

This degeneration occurs rapidly, and the route is simple. In fact, the overall device inevitably shows flaws, certain of which may strengthen the demand for effective reforms. Where and how should attention be focused? Clearly not in the homeostasis validated by financial science; instead attention should be focused on data-collection devices and the technocratic framework of activities.

In fact, if the principles cannot be called into question, the error or the undesirable phenomenon can only be the result of a lack of data, an error in this data, or of a calculation considered too limited to measure risk. The authorities therefore seize the opportunity to impose new rules, interpretations, or additional monitoring.

Overall, the successive accumulation of rules means that they lose their relevance. They increasingly separate practices from concrete realities. The devices move further and further away from the initial principles. They maintain their initial form, but without their initial effectiveness.

My analysis is that, for financial activities, we have already entered this degeneration phase.[16] This analysis supports the identical diagnosis made by Niall Ferguson in his lecture series, initially presented for the BBC, and collected in the book, *The Great Degeneration: How Institutions Decay and Economies Die* (Ferguson, 2012) – quite a programme! He extends the same judgment to what he identifies as the pillars of the Western system, the free market and representative democracy.

22.3.7   So What Should be Done?

Faced with this situation, there is no question of giving in to such pessimism. On the contrary, it is a historic opportunity for researchers to make their mark by updating paradigms and models, and to combat the homeostasis of our system, the source of this dangerous degeneration. The crisis has weakened justifications, and facilitates questioning of the current situation.

This questioning evidently finds applications in extremely wide fields. It is likely to affect the three fields that form the basis of the financial system – business models, to begin with, but also prudential and accounting models.

- *Activity:* Because theoretical studies have a concrete impact. They have helped to create markets in, and the trading of, previously inaccessible subjects or concepts. As a result, traders, using the Black–Scholes formula, sell and trade volatility; managers have risk indicators that assist them in their decision making, and so on.

- *Prudential standards:* Because financial system activity forms part of general economic activity. It serves it as well as makes use of it. It offers services and puts amounts at stake, both of which are activities that need to be controlled at both the company level and socially, and especially so given that companies in this sector are not subject to that shared indicator of difficulties common to all other businesses, the cash-flow crisis.

- *Accounting:* Because the output of interventions always takes place in the context of a limited liability company. Although this legal form enables risk raking, its main constraint is that it is required to establish and respect rules

---

[16]This degeneration has also been presented in a previous study (Rodarie, 2013).

for sharing cash, the concrete product of its success, between shareholders, employees, and the company itself as legal entity.

The system will be even more solid when these three devices are structured by solid, homogenous, and mutually compatible concepts.

There is therefore no cause for concern, as this boldness is proportionate to the new scientific tools that are continuously under development. Furthermore, Norbert Wiener came to the same conclusion when he stated:

No, the future offers little hope for those who expect that our new mechanical slaves will offer us a world in which we may rest from thinking. Help us they may, but at the cost of supreme demands upon our honesty and our intelligence. The world of the future will be an ever more demanding struggle against the limitations of our intelligence, not a comfortable hammock in which we can lie down to be waited upon by our robot slaves.

Wiener (1966)

References

Duban, C. *Souvenirs Militaires d'un Officier Français, 1848–1887*. Second ed. 1896.

Ferguson, N. *The Great Degeneration*. Paris Penguin Books; 2012.

André Gorz, in *Métamorphoses du travail*, éd. Galilée; 1988.

Papanicola, R., editor. *Sciences industrielles pour l'ingénieur*. Ellipses; 2010.

Reason, J. *Human Error*. Cambridge University Press; 1990.

Rodarie, H. *Dettes et monnaies de Singe*. Second ed. Salvator; 2012.

Rodarie, H. Réformes financières, Progrès ou dégénérescence, July 2013 Policy Paper 286 Robert Schumann Foundation, and *Le Cercle des Echos;* July 2013

Walter, C. Proceedings of the First SMABTP Scientific Symposium, "*Nouvelles normes financiers,* organiser face à la crise," Springer; 2010.

Wiener, N. *God & Golem, Inc.: A comment on certain points where cybernetics impinges on religion*. MIT Press; 1966.

Chapter Twenty Three

Two Tales of Liquidity Stress

Jacques Ninet

Senior Research Advisor with La Française Group and Convictions AM. La Française, Paris

Liquidity is well known as one of the three risks inherent to any financial activity, together with market volatility (valuation) and solvency (credit) risk. However, it is not recognized as it should, in our opinion, as the most lethal risk. This misunderstanding has probably much to do with the fact that overall liquidity crisis occurs only under special systemic circumstances whereas market fluctuations are the common rule and credit risk is the essence of banking business. Market prices uncertainty has inspired thousands of academic researches and econometric pricing models in which the tails of return distributions are often discussed, as they are in this book, and professionals have built up hundreds of allocation tools. Debt solvency has for its part been the key issue for banks and rating agencies for more than one century. Comparatively, the channels of liquidity stress in the globalized financial world are not so richly documented. In this chapter, we present two stories of liquidity stress that occurred in the French Money Market Funds (MMF) universe. These stresses, which resulted from extreme events in credit and/or foreign exchange markets, fully demonstrate that the liquidity risk is indeed the worst of the trio, because once it bursts, insufficiently prepared financial companies will inevitably go belly up, unless they are bailed out.

These two tales show that extreme liquidity stress happens because of the vulnerability of the short-term segment of financial markets, a segment that can be described as complex system, in the theoretical sense, because of the intensity of its retroaction loops and spillover effects, in the face of an exogenous shock. This complexity and the following vulnerability stem from the sensitivity of the asset–liabilities relationship that frames the asset management industry and especially the MMF business. More precisely, this relationship can be severely upset by

Extreme Events in Finance: A Handbook of Extreme Value Theory and its Applications, First Edition. Edited by François Longin.

a shock, from both the investor and the fund manager standpoints, while prudential provisions that are designed to warrant the sustainability of the system under
normal conditions may suddenly trigger spillover effects across the broad market.

23.1   THE FRENCH MONEY MARKET FUND INDUSTRY. HOW HISTORY HAS SHAPED A POTENTIALLY VULNERABLE FRAMEWORK

Before starting our stories, let's first recall briefly how the MMF has become a
major segment of the French asset management industry in the 1980 and 1990.
This development owes much to three facts: (i) the legal restriction to the remu-
neration of sight deposits for nonfinancial corporations and households; (ii) the
high level of real short-term rates, because of the "*franc fort*" policy in the after-
math of the infamous devaluations in the early 1980. These rates would remain
high until the mid-1990 because of the Bundesbank's restrictive approach in the
wake of German reunification of the early 1990, in spite of a quickly decreasing
inflation; (iii) a very low taxation of income considered as long-term (LT) capital
gain for holdings of 2 years or more.

   MMF were first built as very short-term bond funds, the portfolio of which was
purchased and sold back on an overnight basis, thanks to a put option, under a provision of the French *Code Civil* called "*vente à réméré*" (Art 1659), to fill the lack
of repurchase agreement regulation. At the end of the 1980s, Certificate of deposits
(CD's), commercial paper ("*billets de trésorerie*"), and T-bills (BTF) had become
usual assets in MMF portfolios, between overnight repos and short maturities,
govies, and corporate-floating rate bonds. As fierce competition reigned among
banks[1] to retain investors, portfolio managers were eager to enhance their performance and especially to beat their mythic benchmark, the *TMP* (the money market
overnight rate average: today's EONIA). And here started the paradox.

   A large fraction of MMF was held by the treasurers of nonfinancial corporations, who used these funds as receipt for their cash positions, whatever their origin
and destination. One part of these positions resulted from daily movements, predictable or not, and the other represented short- to medium-term hoardings, which
back then were major contributors to firms' profitability, given the high level of
interest rates. Institutional investors (insurance and reinsurance companies, pension funds) would also invest in these funds according to their in/outflows cycles.
But from a strictly legal point of view, all these holdings had totally undefined
maturities and were indeed redeemable with "today's value," without any prior
notice.[2]

   Portfolio managers thus embarked in a nonclassical transformation business,
in which their mightiest and smartest customers were asking for the higher returns,

---

[1] Asset management companies became independent only in the late 1990.

[2] Subscription and repurchase orders could be given until 11 a.m. with today's value.

unavoidably involving assets with medium- or even long-term maturities, while retaining their instant exit opportunity. While this may look like a usual banking business, involving maturity transformation based on a statistical approach of depositors' outflows and sound liquidity ratio management, the major difference, however, is that the tradeoff between assets returns and balance-sheet soundness in commercial banks does not interfere with short-term (and especially sight) deposits collection.

MMF portfolio managers had, in fact, a limited number solutions to enhance their returns: (i) increase the average maturity of their assets, in order to get either higher fixed rates – provided that the yield curve will remain steep and that there won't be any rate hike by the Central Bank – or higher floating rates margins; (ii) downgrade the credit risk on short-term securities or medium- to long-term FRN for the reward of higher credit spreads; or (iii) build synthetic arbitrage positions through derivative strategies. Needless to say, except for the last one, any solution would surely weaken the sustainability of the fund in the face of massive outflows. Just for once, informational asymmetry would not be in favor of financial industry. Indeed, each party accepted a sort of moral hazard. But as far as markets cruised quietly with the comfortable cushion of an 8–10% risk-free rate, nobody worried.

23.2 THE 1992–1995 FOREX CRISIS

In the year 1992–1993, Western Europe experienced several monetary crises, stressing Forex and Euro and domestic money markets as well. European currencies had been pegged within the EMS, the pre-Euro system in which the fluctuation of each currency versus any other member should not exceed ±2.25% from the central parity. Because of severe economic performance decoupling (mainly on inflation), these quasi-fixed exchange rates quickly became unsustainable. After the devaluation of the Lira and the scathing defeat of the British Pound by G. Soros (September 1992), the French Franc was in turn attacked by international speculation (such attacks would be repeated in February/march 1995 for more specific French reasons, but the boundaries of the system had been widened to 15%, so the effects on money market were less severe). Unlike their English counterparts, the French authorities decided to defend the sacred FRF/DEM parity by withdrawing liquidity from the money market and sharply raising the overnight rate of interest, in order to cut back the funding of speculators selling borrowed French Francs and eventually to punish them (see the peak in Figure 23.1). As a consequence, the yield curve suddenly reversed, as the crisis was seen to last only a few weeks, everyone betting on either a devaluation of the Franc or the defeat of speculators.

Now, what happened to MMF? Tracking a benchmark suddenly jumping from 10% to 13.5%[3] was strictly impossible except for totally liquid funds (i.e., made only of overnight repos). For most funds, the "normal" rule dramatically reversed:

---

[3] And peaking at as high as 25% on the most epic days.

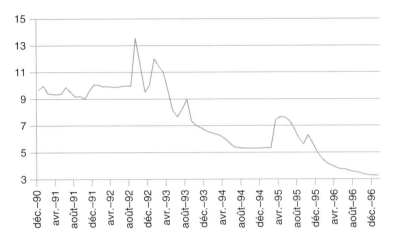

FIGURE 23.1   FRF overnight repo rate (T4M) 1990–1996.

the shorter the maturities of portfolio, the smaller their tracking error. Conversely, nonfinancial MMF holders, who were keen to browse MMF league tables day after day, didn't take long to exit from the laggards and invest in the best performing funds or, more often, directly purchase short-term securities. Such moves sparked the diabolical spiral of growing outflows striking the less liquid funds as their performance deviated from the benchmark.

As far as we know, no fund was shut down at this time, even though some were close to collapse. We guess the main reason was that banks who were at the same time promoting and managing the funds – independent asset management companies were still the exception – were eager to refund their MMF thanks to the cash they were collecting from the exiting companies by issuing Certificate of deposits.

This self-correcting mechanism notwithstanding, this crisis had shed light on the extreme vulnerability of the system in the face of a shock that was supposed to hurt only the benchmark yield and cause only performance disorder. Three years later, the author of the present chapter carried out an audit mission on the MMF recently launched by the Greek branch of a big international bank that comprised many medium-term debt securities among their assets. Unsurprisingly, the Greek colleagues listened politely to the above story, unbelieving it could ever strike Greece. What happened to their funds 10 years later, when the first Greek crisis burst, remains unknown. We guess, however, that like most fund managers in Europe, they had felt vindicated by the early success of the Euro, which was supposedly definitely dissipating the threat of monetary crisis within the Euro area – and had just kept purchasing medium-term private bonds, no matter the risk of liquidity.

With the introduction of the Euro, exchange rate fluctuations and therefore exchange risks within the Euro area have disappeared as expected, but as everyone is nowadays well aware, liquidity crisis stress may still spread across the banking and the MMF systems, and even faster. In fact, most self-corrective mitigations of the 1990s have receded, and several factors have aggravated the vulnerability of the credit market leading to the collapse of 2007–2008.

23.3 FOUR MUTATIONS PAVING THE WAY FOR ANOTHER MELTDOWN

The decade between the mid-1990s and 2006 saw one of major moves that would ultimately bring the greatest financial crisis since the 1930s. Among these, we retain as major determinants of the market stress four economic/financial evolutions:

- The promotion of home ownership, successively by Presidents Clinton and GW Bush, leading to a real-estate bubble in the US, thanks to the accommodative monetary policy of Greenspan/Bernanke and the easing of credit discipline, bottoming with the subprime boom;
- A regulation revival, in both the banking and the asset management industries, setting new requirements for banks capital (Cooke ratio) and severe assets and stockholders diversification ratios for mutual funds (notably in France);
- The progressive entry of the industrialized world into a low inflation/quasi-deflation era – due to globalization and new information technologies – implying ever lower interest rates, especially for "risk-free" assets. Unlike the Japanese nonfinancial corporations, institutional investors and savers across Western countries who had been used to comfortable nominal and real return on their fixed income portfolios were simply not ready to accept such declining yields and were thus be receptive to all kinds of strategies aimed to keep their passed returns alive;
- A bunch of financial innovation, especially in the field of debt, with derivative products and synthetic securities (CDS, collateralized debts obligation (CDO), collateralized loans obligation (CLO)) deeply modifying the origination/distribution/financing/refinancing production line for credit. Trying to assess the return distribution of such structured product implied also a real test of the fine line between risk and uncertainty.

Much has been written about the cascade of events that led from the burst of the American asset bubbles to the global credit crisis. Our contribution will thus only describe the case of dynamic MMF[4] and how some of them ultimately were locked to prevent bankruptcy, as they couldn't meet massive withdrawals. What is not known by the public is how some dynamics MMF had progressively became complex, long-term corporate bond funds, in order to satisfy the demand for high return from addict investors, in spite of the huge decrease of short-terms rates,

---

[4]Launched in the late 1980, Dynamic MMFs are aimed to outperform the overnight rate thanks to a pinch of risky strategies, as mentioned above (p. 3).

and how this transformation made them vulnerable to any freeze of the secondary market. Three special mentions must be made in this respect.

In the second half of the 1990, European banks were looking for equity or quasi-equity funding in order to match the requirements for capital (Cooke ratio, Bâle 1). As continental fixed income mutual funds, which were the richest, were not allowed to purchase equities, financial innovation was required to fill the gap. Having the same product construed differently (in terms of risk) by each party – and each party's supervisors – has always been a key mission of financial innovation, as a unique way to rebuild an otherwise broken confrontation of supply and demand. Infinite-duration subordinated debts (*TSDI*) were typically created under this rule. The trick to make them compatible with fixed-income funds regulation was the addition of a set-up provision, under which at a certain maturity (generally every other 5 years) the security would either be redeemed or see its coupon (or margin) increased by 75 or 100 bps. Although this construction was clearly a call option in the hand of the issuer, it was construed – and actively sold – as a put option in favor of the investor.[5] The underlying assumption was, of course, that the funding market will go on without any disruption for at least the next decade, making it cheaper for the banks to issue new bonds rather than bear additional costs on the existing ones. Such securities were thus considered as ordinary medium-term bonds, maturing at the first step-up date, and offering however a larger spread than genuine fixed maturity securities. What should have caught investors' attention was the growing number of banks issuing such securities, at the same time creating a sort of critical *rendez-vous* for the credit market 5 or 10 years later. Put in another way, the premise of easy refinancing should work as a binary option: for all or for none. Thanks to this singular application of the extreme correlation principle, the so-called diversification benefit was nil.

A second mention must be given to the world of securitization (asset-backed securities, CDOs) and the efforts made by financial scientists to model the credit risk for such instruments. As banks were less and less willing to retain the loans in their own balance sheet to match prudential constraints, securitization became the ultimate step of the disintermediation of financing the economy. But as the credit risk burden was only displaced, two unknowns remained when assessing the probability of default of such collateralized instruments. (i) Whereas one can correctly estimate the distribution law of one single default, anticipating the modification of correlations inside a cohort of similar primary loans in a spreading crisis remains highly uncertain, as mentioned above. (ii) For multi-tranch CDOs like those including subprime, it is therefore impossible to assess how the lack of guaranty will roll down toward the tranches with higher rating, once the defaults have started to burgeon.

Neither the financial institution packaging such securities nor the rating agencies paid sufficient attention to those underestimated risks, as the key hypothesis was that there would never be a real-estate crash in the US, even though recent Japanese history was a perfect counterexample.

---

[5]The same daring role reversal would occur a few years later when reverse-convertible bonds were sold as "protected bonds" whereas they were genuine "out of the money put options."

The third point deals with the regulation provisions that were supposed to warrant the sustainability of the financial system. In another version of the old debate about the reflexive effects of mandatory stop losses, diversification ratios may introduce a destabilizing effect in the market by forcing the portfolio manager and/or the investor to sell in an adverse market. Under French regulation, no investor may hold more than 10% of a fund. This rule creates real hurdles when launching a fund, but that is another story. Now, just consider that a rumor hits a certain issuer (bond, perpetual subordinated, CDO), the security of which is present in your portfolio. One of your fund holders, too cautious and/or too worried, decides to sell his shares, representing 9.5% of the fund. The next investor, with an initial holding of, say 9.2%, has now a 10.2% shares, exceeding in turn the limit and therefore forcing him to sell. Whereas he may sell only the exceeding fraction, he may also be tempted to sell more, and so engage the downsizing spiral for the fund. On the other hand, as the capital of the fund decreases, the manager has to sell liquid securities in order to pay the outflows. But as the total portfolio decreases, he must also, at some point of the process, sell private securities, which now represent more than 5% of the portfolio, which is the upper limit for private assets. This is the common way that causal chains of illiquidity start when fund managers suddenly facing self-reinforcing constraints are deprived of their ability to rationally decide.

23.4   THE SUBPRIME CRISIS SPILLOVER. HOW SOME MMFS WERE FORCED TO LOCK AND SOME OTHERS NOT

Now let us consider that this was not one single rumor, but real business crashes (Bear Stearns June 2007; IKB July 2007; Northern Rock Sept 2007) with many projections for similar companies, as the subprime meltdown suddenly appeared as a global affair. In fact, the credit market (corporate bonds, bank-subordinated and ABS) had been virtually illiquid since the beginning of January 2007. The author of this chapter had taken over, in September 2006, the management of a small dynamic fund (less 100 M Euros), the portfolio of which comprised more than 50% of subordinated and traditional corporate bonds. The decision was quickly taken to sell the totality as the only safeguard for this small independent asset management company against the lethal script described above. But, as the credit market collapse loomed, it actually took more than 6 months to sell the half-dozen subordinated banks securities and another eight BBB corporate bonds.[6]

On August 2, 2007, Oddo, France's largest independent asset manager, and BNP Paribas, one of Europe's largest bank, decided, with the agreement of French

---

[6]Those sales were executed with only a small discount for, as a clear second round effect, a straight sell-off would have produced a large set-back of NAV, triggering withdrawals, and again the diabolic spiral.

regulator AMF, to lock several dynamic MMFs because of severe NAV losses due to illiquid ABS linked to the US real-estate market.[7]

Locking an MMF is like closing a bank position in front of a bank run. Depositors' panic may spread and have dramatic consequences, as was seen in Iceland. In the 2007–2008 crisis, different scenarios emerged: pure bankruptcy (Lehman), total nationalization (Northern Rock; Dexia; AIG), public bail out (French banks), temporary lock-up of funds, etc. Although it was strongly discussed, the "too-big-to-fail" principle fully applied (except for Lehman, and most probably because of the apocalyptic reaction to Lehman's failure). But for smaller struggling companies (banks and asset management), the reputational effect of repurchase suspension would put a tragic end to their effort to survive, let alone grow.

At the other end of the risk–reward range of AM products, the multi-managers' alternative asset management segment (MMAAM: funds of hedge funds) took a death blow in 2009 from the "gates" it had to impose on subscribers. In their own style, MMAAM was another complex system, involving, between the final investor and the assets and derivative markets, two levels of interdependent fund managers.

23.5   CONCLUSION. WHAT LESSONS CAN BE DRAWN FROM THESE TWO TALES?

As a conclusion, we are not supposed to dispute in this pages the relevance of the official responses to the extreme events encountered during the 2007–2008 banking crisis, although there is some evidence that public interventions to avoid bankruptcies and the clemency of regulators when prosecuting professional misbehaviors have encouraged the astonishing revival of foolishness in financial industry after 2010. However, three essential lessons may be drawn from these short and sharp cold–hot cycles.

The first lesson is in fact a theoretical question: considering the last 30 years of market history, one can ask: what is the exact meaning of extreme? In other words, does "extreme" refer to the frequency of severe events or to the degree of severity of such events? From Bachelier, at the dawn of the twentieth century, to Mandelbrot, mathematicians have worked hard to assess the distribution laws of periodic returns and the size of their tails (thin or thick). But haven't we entered a new era, where extremely severe episodes burst with a sort of regularity, from the October 1987 daily crash to the 2010–2011 European debt crisis, the violence of which put

---

[7]*"L'Autorité des marchés financiers (AMF) a donné son feu vert mercredi à la fermeture des trois fonds d'Oddo Asset Management touchés par la crise des marchés du crédit américain, apprend-on auprès de l'AMF. Oddo AM a décidé de liquider trois fonds monétaires dynamiques exposés au "subprime" américain, représentant un encours total d'un milliard d'euros.". Le Point 02/08/2007. "Parvest Dynamics ABS, BNP Paribas ABS Euribor et BNP Paribas ABS Eonia ont perdu 23% de leur valeur totale entre les 27 juillet et 7 août." Les Echos 09/08/2007.*

the survival of short-sighted companies and mutual funds brutally at stake? A positive answer would introduce a major shift from stochastic to more deterministic binary approach of risk across all asset classes, with a new recognition of time and cycles.

This observation directly leads to our second operational lesson. Extreme situations, we think, are those in which certain categories of operators have no choice but to do things that rationally should not be done, thus contributing to strengthen the global irrationality of the situation. That's why, even though extreme risks may not be foreseeable, managers should always try to mitigate them by ensuring that a portfolio has kept a sufficient reserve of flexibility, albeit at the inescapable expense of return. What is obviously true for the diversification principle, which requires to remain totally efficient when correlations rises asset classes with low (or even no) risk premia but long time statistical independence, is all the more true for the liquidity risk, which can be covered, to a certain extent, thanks to securities that are permanently bought by the Central Bank and through a very careful management of short maturity asset roll-over.

The third lesson is a trivial one, although widely unlearnt: "things are not different this time" however sound the market looks. The American philosopher, George Santayana, once wrote: "Those who cannot remember the past are condemned to repeat it," a quote often transcribed as "Those who do not learn history are doomed to repeat it."

Further Reading

Galbraith, J.K. *A short story of financial euphoria*. USA: Viking Penguin; 1990.

Kindleberger, C. *Mania Panics and Crashes*. New York: Basic Books; 1978.

Longin, F., Solnik, B. Extreme correlation of international equity markets. The Journal of Finance 2001;**LVI**(2). p. 649–676

Minsky, H.P. The Modeling of Financial Instability: An introduction. *Modeling and Simulation*. Proceedings of the Fifth Annual Pittsburgh Conference **5**; 1974.

Minsky, H.P. The Financial Instability Hypothesis. Working Paper No. 74 ; May 1992.

Ninet, J. Les déterminants récurrents des bulles financières. Economie Appliquée. **T 57** 2 ; 2004.

Chapter Twenty Four

Managing Operational Risk in the Banking Business – An Internal Auditor Point of View

Maxime Laot
Banking Supervisor ECB

In 1999, the Basel Committee created sensation among the banking community by announcing its intention to include operational risks in its new regulatory capital requirements,[1] along with traditional credit and market risks. Although at that time banks were already well aware of the increase in operational risks caused by the deregulation, computerization, and sophistication of their activities, they initially met the bank supervisors' proposal with skepticism. On one hand, banks claimed that operational risks were an inescapable part of doing business in the financial sector, in contrast to credit and market risks, which are taken purposely and can be hedged against. On the other hand, banks argued that operational risks were difficult to identify and monitor and that large losses were often the results of events not previously recognized as risks.

Yet, facing the growing materialization of operational risks,[2] the Basel Committee persisted, and in 2006, asked the banks to develop better frameworks for managing operational risks while introducing capital requirements for those risks. Though most of the credit institutions finally accepted and agreed with this decision, questions remained on how to measure operational risks and what risks were

---

[1] Basel II.

[2] Losses incurred by institutions operational risk are indeed generally valued at more than € 200 billion over the 1980–2000 period, and the results for the 2002 Loss Data Collection Exercise realized by the Basel Committee showed that, over the 2001 FY, the 89 participating credit institutions experienced more 47,000 incidents for an aggregate amount of € 7.8 billion.

Extreme Events in Finance: A Handbook of Extreme Value Theory and its Applications, First Edition. Edited by François Longin.
© 2017 John Wiley & Sons, Inc. Published 2017 by John Wiley & Sons, Inc.

to be measured. Some of them will certainly remain unpredictable events against which banks can shield themselves only by building up predetermined capital buffers. But may not most operational risks be identified, measured, and controlled, as well as subject to optimal allocation of capital, such as credit and market risks? Besides, to what extent the internal audit function may help banks securing their operational risk management system and their evaluation of regulatory capital linked to operational risk?

The Basel Committee adopted, in 2001, a common industry definition of operational risk, different from the too broad "neither credit risk nor market risk" and the too narrow "risks arising only from operations" definitions. The first one encompasses, among others, strategic, commercial, and reputational risks, which are not, properly speaking, directly linked to operational risks. The second one is concerned only with incidents linked to processes such as making payments or securities settlements but does not take into account incidents related to people or external events, such as penalties for unfair dismissals, losses incurred by rogue traders, and natural disasters. The definition chosen for operational risks, namely "the risks of direct or indirect losses resulting from inadequate or failed internal processes, people and systems or from external events," focuses on the causes of operational risks, which is appropriate, according to the Basel Committee, for "both risk management, and, ultimately, measurement."

Bank supervisors therefore considered that operational risks could and should be measured. To do so, they offered the credit institutions three methodologies, each adapted to a specific risk's profile, to evaluate their regulatory capital. The first and simplest methodology is the *basic indicator approach* (BIA), where operational risk capital is set equal to 15% of the average gross income[3] for the whole bank over the previous 3 years. The *standardized approach* (STA) is based on the first methodology, but offers a more refined calculus of the operational risk capital. Banking activities are split between eight institutional business lines, and their average gross income over the past 3 years is multiplied by a "beta factor," fixed by the Basel Committee, and then summed up to determine the total capital.[4] This approach requires the bank to implement efficient risk management and loss-collecting systems in parallel. The *advanced measurement approach* (AMA) is based on internal models, validated by the local supervisor, used to produce a probability distribution of losses, relying on internal and external loss data, and analysis of scenarios, with a confidence level of 99.9% over 1 year. The estimation of this "value at risk" has to be done for each of the eight business lines combined with the seven categories of operational risks identified by the Basel Committee, which makes 56 combinations.[5] The operational risk capital is meant to cover either expected and unexpected loss, or only the latter, if a bank can prove that it already covers expected loss through its pricing policy, its reserves, or provisions. Besides, an AMA bank can reduce its operational capital requirements by entering into assurance contracts.

---

[3]Defined as the Net Banking Income, that is, the sum of the net interest and the net commissions margins.

[4]Table 24.1, Annexes.

[5]Table 24.2, Annexes.

The Basel Committee designed these three approaches with decreasing capital requirements depending on their level of sophistication, as incentives for banks to adopt the AMA for operational risks. In its "2008 Loss Data Collection Exercise," realized only 1 year after the official implementation of the Basel regulations in 2007, the Basel Committee found that, among the 119 participating credit institutions, 35% were already using the AMA, 43% the TSA, and only 22% the BIA. Moreover, it reported that operational risk capital for non-AMA banks was effectively higher than for AMA banks when reported to gross income: 15% for BIA banks, between 12% and 18% for TSA banks, and only 10.8% for AMA banks.

From an internal audit perspective, the choice of the approach is crucial and determines the nature and scope of our work when controlling an operational risk function.

For instance, for a BIA bank, internal auditors have only to make sure in the first place that the institution has defined and effectively implemented an "operational risks policy" compliant with local regulation. In France, it comes to the regulation "CRBF 97-02," which covers all the risk management topics for banking institutions, among others operational risk. It requires, for instance, that any fraud or loss exceeding 0.5% of the core capital should be declared to the regulatory authority. Besides, the BIA bank risk management organization has to be broadly consistent with the *Principles for the Sound Management of Operational Risk* published in 2003 by the Basel Committee.[6] Internal auditors therefore control the existence of a suitable environment for risk management (i.e., involvement of the hierarchy, regular and independent audit of the risk system) and the implementation of an effective operational risk management system, which has to be presented in the annual reports of the BIA bank.

The audit of an operational risk management function and determination of regulatory capital for STA and AMA banks are much more complicated and will be discussed more in detail later.

In its argument to convince banks to assign regulatory capital to operational risks, the Basel Committee listed more than 100 high-magnitude operational losses experienced by banks in the 1990s, each exceeding $100 million. Daiwa, Barings, and Allied Irish Bank were thus listed to have, respectively, lost $1.4 billion, $1 billion, and $ 700 million from fraudulent trading. Such scandals are still relevant today, with the Société Générale's € 4.9 billion loss in 2008 or the UBS's $ 2.3 billion loss in 2011, also from fraudulent trading. With these striking examples, one could be fallaciously led to believe that operational risks only concern major internal frauds and that the only way for a bank to create "robustness" against those "Black Swans" – to quote the best seller book of Taleb (2007) – is to build up large capital buffers. A this point, a distinction has to be made in terms of risks between the "unknown known" and the "unknown unknown," or between risk and uncertainty to refer to the famous distinction made by Knight (1921). The first concept refers to situations where the outcomes are unknown but governed by

---

[6]Strong operational risk management culture and adapted framework, effective governance and involved hierarchy, adequate risk management environment to promote the identification, assessment, monitoring, reporting, control and mitigation of operational risks, public disclosures of the operational risk management system.

probability distributions that are known (e.g., High-frequency but low-magnitude losses). It differs from the second one, where the outcomes are likewise unknown but governed by unknown probabilities (e.g., very low frequency but high magnitude losses).

In its "2008 Loss Data Collection Exercise," the Basel Committee reported results which undermine this "Black Swan" concept about operational risks. Even though high-magnitude losses remain a reality, most of the losses, both in number and value, concentrate on numerous minor risks that come in the "unknown known" situation and thus can be modeled. Indeed, the institutions participating to this loss collection exercise submitted a total of 10.6 million internal losses with an overall loss amount of € 59.6 billion for a minimum of 3 years of recorded loss data prior to 2008.[7] The losses of € 20,000 or more represented only 1.62% of the total number of losses but 89% of the overall loss amount, yet with the largest 20 losses accounting alone for € 17.6 billion, for example, 29.5% of the overall loss amount – this figure arguing for consideration of extreme values in operational risks loss models. Moreover, a typical bank[8] experienced 0.82 losses per year of € 20,000 or more for each billion Euros in consolidated assets, with a total loss amount of € 155,555 for each billion Euros in consolidated assets.[9] High-magnitude losses of more than $100 million at a typical bank accounted only for 0.02% of the number of loss and represented 41.79% of its total loss amount.[10]

Besides, the regulatory business line – as defined by the Basel Committee – with the highest loss frequency and total loss amount in the 2008 Loss Data Collection Exercise was retail banking.[11] It concentrated 55.8% of the number of losses, mostly due to external frauds, and also accounted for 32.0% of the total loss amount, mostly because of poor clients, products, and business practices, and to a much less extent to internal fraud. The second regulatory business line in loss amount reported was corporate finance, which accounted for 28% of the total loss amount, and again, but in a much larger way, because of poor clients, products, and business practices – and not all because of internal fraud.

From an internal audit point of view, the last two paragraphs are of high importance.

First, the minor operational losses, those lower than € 20,000, represent the majority of the incidents, especially in number but also in total value. So, there is a real issue in collecting all the operational losses. Indeed, the exhaustiveness and the quality of loss databases[12] are essential, on one hand, for AMA banks, which rely on them to estimate their regulatory operational capital, and, on the other hand, for STA banks, which should prove flawless on this topic if they are willing to be authorized to implement the AMA methodology. Internal auditors must therefore check with great attention the processes of gathering operational incidents and

---

[7] See Table 24.3, Annexes.

[8] In the "2008 Loss Data Collection Exercise" of the Basel Committee, the typical bank refers to the cross-banks medians.

[9] See Table 24.4, Annexes.

[10] See Table 24.5, Annexes.

[11] See Tables 24.6 and 24.7, Annexes.

[12] Databases that store the losses and incidents incurred by a credit institution.

their filling in loss databases, to make sure of their exhaustiveness and of the quality of the collected information.[13] But prior to that, internal auditors must ensure the existence, quality, and completeness of an updated and regularly back-tested operational risk mapping, which helps to identify and collect losses for an effective use thereafter, both in terms of capital calculation and risk management.[14]

Second, the prevalence of the risk related to poor practices in terms of clients, products, and business in retail banking and corporate finance is meaningful. This sort of operational risk could be defined as "unintentional or negligent failure to meet a professional obligation to clients and the use of inappropriate products of business practices.[15]" It covers, among other things, money laundering, insufficient advice, and abusive fees, three topics that are closely monitored by bank supervisor in the retail banking business line and often lead to lawsuits and regulatory fines. It covers also improper trading activities and the sale of unauthorized products, two major topics central for the corporate finance business line, where the activities of the front office are strictly framed by risk mandates, stating what is authorized from what is not, and setting relative and absolute limits to the operations. Internal auditors must therefore concentrate their efforts on those specific topics. In retail banking business lines, they could perform tests by sampling the treatment of suspected cases concerning anti-money laundering or check file of customer complaints or a list of sentences to identify any issue. In corporate finance business lines, internal auditors must ensure the existence and consistency of the risk mandates given to traders, check the observance of limits, and ensure that all products sold are actually part of the list of authorized products.

As viewed by most professionals, operational risk management is still in its infancy, even though the Basel Committee has succeeded in establishing an effective framework to identify, measure, and manage operational risk and allocate it regulatory capital. This incentive has made, indeed, the banks more aware of operational risk and led them to improve their processes and, more broadly, the way they are doing business. Yet, in this context as in many others, internal auditors are the rappel line that makes sure the regulatory prerequisites are met, for instance to evolve from one approach to another, and the main areas of risk are properly identified and controlled.

Further Reading

Basel Committee on Banking Supervision. *Consultative Document Operational Risk Supporting Document to the New Basel Capital Accord.* Bank for International Settlements; 2001

Basel Committee on Banking Supervision. 2011. *Principles for the Sound Management of Operational Risk.* Bank for International Settlements; 2011

Commission Bancaire. Le risque opérationnel, pratiques et perspectives réglementaires. *Rapport de la Commission bancaire pour l'année;* 2003.

---

[13]Date of detection and occurrence of the events, nature, and origin of the incidents, financial impacts, and potential recoveries.

[14]Reporting and action plans.

[15]Hull (2012).

References

Basel Committee on Banking Supervision. *Sound Practices for the Management and Supervision of Operational Risk*. Bank for International Settlements; 2003.

Basel Committee on Banking Supervision. *Results from the 2008 Loss Data Collection Exercise for Operational Risk*. Bank for International Settlements; 2009.

Hull, J.C. *Risk Management and Financial Institution*. 3rd ed. John Wiley & Sons, Inc.; 2012.

Knight, F.H. *Risk, Uncertainty and Profit*. Boston, MA: Hart, Schaffner & Marx; Houghton Mifflin Co.; 1921.

Taleb, N.N. *The Black Swan*. Random House; 2007.

Annexes

TABLE 24.1   **Beta factors in standardized approach**

Business line	Beta factor (%)
Corporate Finance	18
Trading and sales	18
Retail banking	12
Commercial banking	15
Payment and settlement	18
Agency services	15
Asset management	12
Retail brokerage	12

Source: Hull (2012).

TABLE 24.2   **Categorization of operational risks**

Operational risk	Examples
Internal fraud	Intentional misreporting of positions, employee theft, and insider trading on employee's own account
External fraud	Robbery, forgery, cheque kiting, and damage from computer hacking
Employment practices and workplace safety	Workers compensation claims, violation of employee health and safety rules, organized labor activities, discrimination claims, and general liability
Clients, products, and business practices	Fiduciary breaches, misuse of confidential customer information, improper trading activities on the bank's account, money laundering, and sale of unauthorized products

TABLE 24.2 (*Continued*)

Operational risk	Examples
Damages to physical assets	Terrorism, vandalism, earthquakes, fires, and floods
Business disruption and system failures	Hardware and software failures, telecommunication problems, and utility outages
Execution, delivery, and process management	Data entry errors, collateral management failures, incomplete legal documentation, unapproved access given to client accounts, non-client counterparty misperformance, and vendor disputes

Source: Basel Committee on Banking Supervision (2003).

TABLE 24.3 Number of internal losses and loss amount reported by the 2008 loss data collection exercise participants

	All losses		Losses≥ € 20,000		Average per Institution Losses ≥ € 20,000	
	Number	Amount (€M)	Number	Amount (€M)	Number	Amount (€M)
Participating institutions (119)	10,595,318	59,600	171,882	53,703	1444	451

Source: Basel Committee on Banking Supervision (2009).

TABLE 24.4 Annualized loss frequencies normalized per €billion of assets

All participants		Annualized number of losses ≥ €0	Annualized number of losses ≥ €20,000	Annualized number of losses ≥ €100,000	Annualized number of losses ≥ €1,000,000
Consolidated assets	Median	8.9	0.82	0.19	0.013
	(25–75th quartiles)	(3.2–47.1)	(0.36–1.66)	(0.07–0.33)	(0.000–0.032)

Source: Basel Committee on Banking Supervision (2009).

TABLE 24.5   Cross-bank median of distribution across severity brackets

Severity of loss	Number of losses (%)	Gross loss amount (%)
€0 ≤ X < €20,000	91.29	26.26
€20,000 ≤ X < €100,000	6.52	12.63
€100,000 ≤ X < €1 million	1.83	19.37
€1 million ≤ X < €2 million	0.15	5.48
€2 million ≤ X < €5 million	0.12	9.05
€5 million ≤ X < €10 million	0.04	6.87
€10 million ≤ X < €100 million	0.04	15.55
€100 million ≤ X	0.02	41.79

Note: the percentages represent medians.
Source: Basel Committee on Banking Supervision (2009).

TABLE 24.6   Sum and distribution of annualized loss frequencies and amounts by operational risk

Operational risk	Annualized loss frequencies (%)	Annualized loss amount (%)
Internal fraud	4	6
External fraud	26	8
Employment practices and workplace safety	18	6
Clients, products, and business practices	18	52
Damage to physical assets	1	1
Business disruption and system failures	2	1
Execution, delivery, and process management	31	25
All	100	100

Source: Basel Committee on Banking Supervision (2009).

TABLE 24.7   Sum and distribution of annualized loss frequencies and amounts by business line

Business line	Annualized loss frequencies (%)	Annualized loss amount (%)
Corporate finance	0.7	28.0
Trading and sales	9.6	13.6
Retail banking	558	32.0
Commercial banking	8.2	7.6
Payment and settlement	2.2	2.6
Agency services	2.7	2.7
Asset management	2.2	2.5
Retail brokerage	10.3	5.1
Unallocated	8.3	6.0
All	100.0	100.0

Source: Basel Committee on Banking Supervision (2009).

Chapter Twenty Five

Credo Ut Intelligam*

Henri Bourguinat[1] and Eric Briys[2]

[1]*Department of Economics, University of Bordeaux IV, Bordeaux, France*
[2]*Cyberlibris, Brussels, Belgium*

25.1 INTRODUCTION

During the tenth century, Saint Anselm of Aosta, Archbishop of Canterbury, pointed out in his address on the existence of God: "For I do not seek to understand in order to believe, but I believe in order to understand.[1]" In 1994, the French writer André Frossard, a friend of Pope Jean Paul II, aptly reformulated the famous saying: "Faith is what enables intelligence to live above its means." André Frossard surely did not imagine that one day his mischievous pirouette would be diverted and applied to the theory of finance: "Faith (in its models) is what enables the theory of finance to live beyond its means (disconnected from reality)."

25.2 "ANSELMIST" FINANCE

Just like their cousins the economists, practically all financial theorists have adopted an "Anselmist" posture; they believe in order to understand. They believe in their models, so they expend countless hours refining and mathematically schematizing. Their addiction to models would not be essential if the consequences remained confined to their ivory towers. Unfortunately, the academic word has been taken into ever greater account, and theoretical models feed into the thoughts and actions of our quotidian practitioners and governing

---

*This chapter draws on the authors' book (2010).
[1]"Neque enim quaero intelligere, ut credam; sed credo, ut intelligam."
http://remacle.org/bloodwolf/eglise/anselme/proslogion.htm.

Extreme Events in Finance: A Handbook of Extreme Value Theory and its Applications,
First Edition. Edited by François Longin.
© 2017 John Wiley & Sons, Inc. Published 2017 by John Wiley & Sons, Inc.

authorities. The situation is disconcertingly ironic. For once, theory and practice enjoy neighborly relations; we ought to jubilate over the exceptional proximity between the work of theorists and its practical application. Even so, wariness is in order; their proximity is hardly above suspicion. When all is said and told, financial theory is partially responsible for the crisis[2] that punctuated the end of the so-called aughties.

Such frequent adoption of a "credo ut intelligam" posture is all the more surprising given the profusion of financial data at our disposal today. Everything happens as if the experts had decided to shoehorn the data to conform to the models, even though a less flamboyant but more effective strategy would consist in teasing out the data by attempting to grasp them, and in questioning investors and savers so as to find sound reasons for intellectual inspiration. The repeatedly told story of a 20-Euro bill lying on the sidewalk untouched is, from this standpoint, distinctly revelatory. For the theorist who believes in market efficiency, there cannot possibly be any bill littering the ground; if there were an actual bank note, some pedestrian would surely have picked it up! But facts being facts, there is indeed a bill down on the ground. And so, what is to be done? Are we to believe in the model and pass for mental defectives by leaving the bill alone, or are we to pick it up and look into the possible reasons why it had yet to be put in anyone's pocket? Needless to say, the question posed in this anecdote is inoffensive, and the answers are inconsequential, but what happens when the stakes are incommensurably higher?

What's essentially at stake, of course, is our understanding of the behavior of the economic actors, which means producers, consumers, investors, and others. Financial theorists have developed heavy artillery designed to model the risk-related behavior of economic agents. In a nutshell, the latter are viewed as paragons of Homo Economicus, whose main characteristic is to privilege any actions that would maximize their expected utility with regard to future consumption. Expectation or hope for that matter is the watchword, for nothing could be less certain than the future, and it makes more sense to fall back on the ancient principle of mathematical expectation prized by Blaise Pascal. Utility is what matters, for it is not consumption per se that counts, but rather the greater or lesser satisfaction it brings. The financial theorist couldn't care less about Homo Sapiens; only Homo Economicus is of passionate interest. Homo Economicus is a methodical, unwavering, rational calculator whose company is appreciated by the theorist with his models. However, Amartya Sen, a Nobel Prize winner in economics and stalwart critic of all-purpose rationality, has observed that the cold calculator is devoid of nuance. His reckoning can produce adverse outcomes both as far as he's concerned and with respect to the general interest. The divorce between individual intention and individual or group-centered results is metaphorically and tragically typified when fire in a night club occasions mass movements of panic. The Belgian daily Le Soir published an article[3] on a conflagration in the "5–7" dancing hall of Saint-Laurent-du-Pont:

---

[2]For a detailed analysis, see Bourguinat and Brys (2009) and Bourguinat and Brys (2010).

[3]http://archives.lesoir.be/une-longue-liste-macabre-le-5-7-le-6-9-et-le-109-toujou_t-19900115-Z029KK.html.

"At Saint-Laurent-du-Pont, not far from Grenoble, France, hundreds of young people had come to the dancing hall known as 'le 5–7.' All of a sudden at 1:45 a.m., the lights went out. Flames had arisen from part of a ceiling. They had all but instantly wrought havoc on the sumptuous decor of the club, which was configured like a grotto with a multitude of plastic panels. The plastic caught fire and melted. The entire hall was engulfed in flames within a few seconds. Monstrously panic-stricken persons in the dozens crammed themselves in front of the three exits. All of them were too small, and two doors were sealed off (so as to keep free riders out), while a third was barred with a turnstile that was quickly blocked by the surge of the panicky crowd. In front of the three doors, in particular, and throughout the club, there were 146 lifeless bodies of young people grounded and pounded to death by human stupidity."

25.3 CASINO OR DANCE HALL?

Dance hall fire stories invariably follow the same plot: the outcome is fatal. Once the alarm resounds, panic pervades. All the customers converge simultaneously and savagely either toward the limited number of emergency exits or, more simply and reflexively, toward the door through which they had entered. The individual movements transformed into a hysteria-crazed human tide are unfortunately lethal. They tragically lengthen the number of victims. As each person desperately attempts to save his skin, he dooms himself and also condemns countless others. We wind up coming to a paradoxical conclusion: Emergency exits only function effectively when they are not needed. Conversely, they fail to fulfill their function when the fire alarm goes off and panic sets in.

So it goes with financial crises as well as dance halls, and one wishes that the theorists of finance had a more clinical approach to crises and were consequently better able to understand the risk of which they claim to be the specialists. Risk perceived from the ivory tower has nothing to do with the risk that blows billions of dollars away. Eminent researchers in the field of finance have nonetheless made risk and emergency exits the foundation on which the entire edifice has been erected. In the language of finance, the emergency exit is known and lauded as a well-diversified portfolio. To avoid breaking your eggs all at once, you must not put them in the same basket. This academic prescription came into being in the works of Harry Markowitz, professor at the City University of New York (and winner of the Nobel Prize in economics in 1990). Markowitz takes exception to Mark Twain, who humorously wrote: ≪ Put all your eggs in one basket – and watch that basket!! ≫ On the contrary, Markowitz urges investors to multiply their baskets, to diversify the composition of their portfolios. To sum up, an investor applying the prescriptions of the good Doctor Markowitz sleeps better than an investor following the advice of Mark Twain. Ownership of multiple shares in the same portfolio allows him not to worry about the highs and lows of any stock in particular. If one of them is falling, then he is bound to find another of which the rise will not fail to compensate for the attendant losses. Diversification is consequently the most efficient way to extinguish fires, and it is the cornerstone, the fundamental credo, of financial theory.

Such is the foundation that modern portfolio and asset assessment theory have built. Put to the test of fire, however, diversification is far from having fulfilled its promises. The 2008–2009 crisis is a patent example. The portfolios of investors all over the world underwent staggering monumental losses, far higher in any case than prudent diversification would have allowed them to imagine. Everything fell precipitately at the same time, entangling the portfolios in a devastating downward spiral. When crisis arose, the financial markets behaved like a gigantic night club with grossly under-dimensioned emergency exits. At the very moment when the need for diversification was of utmost urgency, it was nowhere to be found, and it became saddeningly obvious that diversification functions only when it is superfluous, that is to say, when stock market fluctuations remain reasonable. As soon as the fluctuations grow wild, panic and havoc ensue, as seemingly crazed investors run willy-nilly for their lives.[4] The instantaneous switch from mild randomness to wild randomness (to borrow the terminology of Benoît Mandelbrot) undermines the assumed benefits of diversification. The study of idiosyncratic and market risk in the long run delivers additional evidence that portfolio diversification is indeed much less effective than what it used to be at the beginning of the twentieth century (see Le Bris (2012) for instance on the French stock market). The consequent damage has several interconnected causes that financial theory, enveloped and consumed by its credo, has unfailingly omitted from its models.

25.4   SIMPLE-MINDED DIVERSIFICATION

The first of these causes is the "Black Swan" of Nassim Taleb (2010), the rare and unpredictable event, the improbable "outlier" with its drastic consequences that have not been factored into hypothesis-based theory. Theory is effective for mild risks highly concentrated around an average value, as is the case in Gauss's law. Of course fluctuations occur, but they show the good taste not to stray too far from the mean. Actual facts, however, belie the assumption that risks are mild. From 1916 through 2003, in accordance with the Gaussian hypothesis there should have been 58 days in which Dow Jones variations would have exceeded 3.4%, but in reality, they numbered 1001! Other salient examples would be easy to cite. For instance, François Longin (1996), again using extreme value theory, provides rich evidence that extreme values do matter and that the Gaussian assumption so frequently made is pure nonsense. It is worthwhile noting that Longin (1996) observes that "little attention has been given to extreme movements themselves." (p. 384). The stock market is wilder than theory assumes (or feigns to believe).

The worst is yet to come. Wildness cannot be dissociated from the peculiar herding behavior shown by investors. Risk is not some exogenous datum with which investors are confronted and that they try to rein in through diversification. It is only slightly a caricature to say that investors embody risk; they are their own

---

[4]For empirical evidence that equity market correlation does increase in bear markets, see, for instance, Longin and Solnik (2001). Interestingly enough, they use "extreme value theory" to reach their conclusions.

worst enemies. During tranquil periods they tend to ignore one another, which means that are not preoccupied with the impact their behavior will have on others. During a turbulent period, as happens when a dance hall catches fire, debacle calls for more debacle. Each investor has a pressing need for liquid funds at exactly the same time. Sell orders pile up and trigger a vicious circle, which gains additional traction through the regulations that require investors to recapitalize in proportion to their losses. While all the eggs may not be in the same basket, all the investors find themselves caught at the same time in the same trap.

Finally, a more subtle yet far from negligible effect is engendered by diversification. To be precise, it is derived from the double credo of diversification and from the principle according to which the financial market is efficient, and cannot be beaten. The consequences to be drawn from these duel tenets are potentially deleterious, insofar as theory converts them into the simplest of prescriptions: Since as a matter of principle you cannot beat the market and since it is imperative to shield yourself from risk as best you can, an investor should not only hold but also hold onto a diversified portfolio, that is to say he must refrain from buying or selling. In the long run, after all, it will pay off! It suffices to be patient, to leave time for time, and mutual funds (among other diversified stock market investments) will wind up reaping their fruits. All other things being equal, the underlying philosophy reminds us of the exhortations proffered by the Israeli Prime Minister Itzhak Shamir at the height of the First Gulf War at a time when SCUD missiles were targeting Israel, possibly with nerve agents such as sarin. A journalist asked him: "Mr. Prime Minister, what have you to say to your Israeli fellow citizens?" Shamir answered: "Be brave!" The journalist went on: "What have you to say to the Palestinians living in Israel?" His answer: "Keep calm!"

In the final analysis, what the portfolio theory requests from investors is that come what may, they be simultaneously Israeli and Palestinian, brave and sedate at the same time. Analogously, even when risk is indeed mild, the investing passivity recommended in theory is tantamount to our signing a blank check and addressing it to the institutions placed in charge of producing the mutual funds of which we patiently await the dividends. But who can assure us that these institutions have their pendulum synchronized with ours? The diversification advised by Markowitz has nothing to say on the subject, and it proceeds as though the institutions were neutral and transparent sails. But the role of financial institutions is not only primordial, but often massively destructive. The diversification recommended by theorists takes place in total financial asepsis; it is as though the institutions in charge of our money were not only transparent but also beneficent! Of course, there are a number of researchers who have made a specialty of analyzing the conflicts of interest inexorably brought about by institutions bringing together a wide variety of stakeholders. One may nonetheless regret that the loop has not been closed and that the theoretical precept of diversification is still placed on an uncontested pedestal. Whatever may occur, belief in passive diversification somehow remains essential to understanding. Given this, it is baffling to note the elevated frequency of market transactions; after all, the stock market is anything but passive. The Anselmist theorist is prone to brush aside this inconvenient fact:

Don't the transactions originate with investors showing excessive confidence in their financial capacities?

25.5 HOMO SAPIENS VERSUS HOMO ECONOMICUS

Such excessive confidence brings us back to the field of psychology, in which the subject to be studied is not Homo Economicus but rather Homo Sapiens. Andrew Lo, a Professor of Finance at MIT and one of the few iconoclasts of academic finance, excellently summarizes the different approaches separating psychology and economic science. Psychology is based mainly on observation and experimentation. Field studies are frequent, and empirical analysis leads to new theories. Psychology postulates several theories of behavior and its priority is not to achieve coherence between them. Contrastingly, economic science is founded on theory and abstraction. Field studies are few and far between. The theories lead to empirical analysis. There are not many theories on behavior, and coherence between theories is a key factor. To sum up, psychology is not Anselmist: It does not believe in order to understand. It tries to understand, and then may go on to believe. Economic science and financial theory are largely Anselmist: First they fervently believe, and only later (much later?) do they try to understand. And when they fail to understand, since the model has not been validated by the available data, they are by no means inclined to throw out the model. In economics as in finance, throwing things out is anathema!

Keynes had the habit of saying that many of us are "the slaves of some defunct economist." He did not realize how right he was! The "credo ut intelligam" can indeed be imputed to a famed and recently deceased economist, Paul Anthony Samuelson, whose manual in economics has sold millions of copies. A professor at MIT and the first Nobel Prize winner in economics, Samuelson stamped a lasting imprint on the discipline of economics and the researchers who have dedicated themselves to the field. The title of his 1947 thesis is anything but ambiguous: *Foundations of Economic Analysis.* His clearly enunciated ambition is to elaborate a coherent mathematical framework applicable to all sectors of the economy, starting with the area most propitious to such treatment: microeconomics. Samuelson seemed to be on fine terms with his inner physicist. As Andrew Lo[5] rather maliciously points out, economists in general, and financial theorists in particular, are prone to physics envy: "In physics, it takes three laws to explain 99% of the data; in finance, it takes more than 99 laws to explain about 3%."

The agenda put forward by Samuelson in 1947 bore the imprint of physics and was pervaded with the hope of discovering a few laws that would explain everything and create lasting foundations for a religion of economics and finance. Unfortunately and notwithstanding all the respect we may have for the numerous intellectual contributions of Samuelson, his agenda started off on the wrong track;

---

[5]Quoted in Martha E. Mangelsdorf, Overheard at MIT: Why Economics Isn't Like Physics, MITSLOAN Management Review, Fall 2010.

the analogy with physics is misleading. The economy and the financial markets are not physical systems; they function differently, and there is a good reason why. The economy is made up of human interactions that are in no way comparable to those of particles suspended in a fluid. Each morning on the radio station BFM, Marc Fiorentino[6] analyzes the "fundamentals" that shape and form the economy from one day to the next. But there's more to it than that. If that were just that, then Samuelson and his apostles would have had more success. In fact, what matters most is how agents consider the fundamentals, what they think of the reactions of the other agents with respect to the ABCs, and so on. Such complex human phenomena do not exist in physics, the laws of which are robust, and do not vary according to what happened on the financial markets over the previous month. Economic laws, which means those of economists, are constantly modified, and that is why a ≪ credo ut intelligam ≫ posture is at best fruitless, and at worst hazardous.

It is past time to adopt a new approach and to make ≪ intelligam ≫ the priority. This will be no easy task; the academic powers-that-be will not readily allow their PhD students to be iconoclasts. This is a shame, for they ought to be encouraging their students to constantly contest the established order; in so doing, of course, the mandarins would embrace the risk of seeing their own work taken to task and invalidated, from one day to the next.

Acknowledgement

We thank François Longin for his helpful comments and suggestions.

References

Bourguinat, H., Briys, E. *L'arrogance de la finance*. Paris: Editions de La Découverte; 2009.

Bourguinat, H., Briys, E. *Marchés de dupes: pourquoi la crise se prolonge*. Paris: Editions Maxima; 2010.

Le Bris, D. Is the Portfolio Effect Ending? Idiosyncratic risk and market risk over the long run, BEM Working Paper; 2012. Available at http://ssrn.com/abstract=1723162.

Longin, F. The asymptotic distribution of extreme stock market returns. Journal of Business 1996;**63**:383–408.

Longin, F., Solnik, B. Extreme correlation of international equity markets. The Journal of Finance 2001;**56**:651–678.

Taleb, N. *The Black Swan: The Impact of the Highly Improbable*. New York: Random House; 2010.

---

[6]A well-known French commentator who happens to be an ex-investment banker.

Chapter Twenty Six

Bounded Rationalities, Routines, and Practical as well as Theoretical Blindness: On the Discrepancy Between Markets and Corporations

Laurent Bibard

Management Department, ESSEC Business School, Cergy Pontoise, France

26.1 INTRODUCTION: EXPECTING THE UNEXPECTED

The 2008 subprime crisis abruptly awakened people as well as specialists about the dangers and vulnerability of the financial market. People had forgotten about the difference between risk and uncertainty as the economist Knight understood it. Knight posits that whereas risk may always be evaluated, even though most often only on the basis of probabilities, uncertainty cannot be evaluated and measured (Knight, 1921). Actually, nowadays, uncertain situations have become normal, and managing (in) the unexpected has become quite ordinary. Indeed, people need to learn again how to manage the unexpected (Weick and Sutcliffe, 2007). The real truth is nevertheless that the economic and financial world has never been only a risky world but always an uncertain one. The 2008 financial crisis surprise is not due to something that might have changed suddenly in the daily business life; on the other hand, people were quite naïve about it. The problem is in the human

Extreme Events in Finance: A Handbook of Extreme Value Theory and its Applications, First Edition. Edited by François Longin.

belief that the world can be totally measured, evaluated, and predicted. Such a belief favors potential crises, such as the 2008 one.

In his book *Risk, uncertainty, and profit*, Knight (1921) distinguishes between risk and uncertainty. Risk characterizes situations where the probability of every future event can be computed with a theoretical model or estimated with data. Uncertainty applies to situations where such a probability cannot be computed or estimated. Many chapters in this handbook (see Fraga Alves and Neves, 2017) tend to explain that the probability of extreme events in finance, such as stock market crashes, can be computed with extreme value theory, a statistical theory that is interested in the extremes of a random process (prices or returns of financial assets). As pointed out by Longin (1993) in his thesis and still discussed many years later during the First International Conference Extreme Events in Finance held in December 2014 at Royaumont Abbey (a peaceful place to discuss extreme events), such results seem to be at odds with Knight's view of risk and uncertainty. On one hand, extreme events in finance are associated with periods of extreme uncertainty, but, on the other, extreme value theory tells us that the statistical distribution of extreme returns is precisely known (even though we don't know the distribution of daily returns).

Some of the above "naïveté" has another kind of consequence. Introducing contradictory demands in corporations, it separates people from each other. As a matter of fact, shareholders wait for maximum profit-making on the basis of corporations' activities, and corporations are supposed to deliver the best, whatever happens. In doing so, corporations tend to become unilaterally short-term-oriented, whereas they should be medium- if not long-term-oriented if they are to be sustainable. They should invest, innovate, and adapt to a continuously changing if not chaotic environment.

It is possible to understand the tension between the short term and the long term as a tension related to power issues, and this is actually the case. But this is the case only to a certain extent. The potential divergence between shareholders' interests and those of companies depends on bounded rationalities, whose effects oppose each other. To deepen the understanding of the divergence between financial interests and economic and social ones, it is necessary to understand the discrepancy between a certain intellectual "naïveté," which conditions practices and reality.

We first make a bit clear the divergence between the financial and the economic and social spheres, and then we trace it back to some of its origins, particularly to a philosophical one related to the European Renaissance humanism. We finally briefly envisage some possible methods to get rid of the difficulty.

26.2 MARKETS AND CORPORATIONS: A STRUCTURAL AND SELF-DISRUPTIVE DIVERGENCE OF INTERESTS

Any organization, including networks and corporations, may be understood as not only involving but also being structured by a series of tensions, such as the tension between task division versus coordination, individuals versus collective interests, change versus stability, and so on. One of the most active tensions nowadays is the tension between the short and the long term. This tension may be described the following way:

On the short term, people are demanded to deliver the best they can, immediately, continuously, and on a visible way. People are never asked to deliver medium, later on, from time to time, and on a hidden way. No doubt, the most striking contemporaneous characteristic of the short term is nowadays related to visibility. Any sector, institution, corporation, organization, or structure is evaluated, rated, measured on the basis of its visible efficiency. Rating and ranking organizations, institutions, and even countries based on expectations about what they are supposed to deliver has become the norm and a normative behavior that conditions people's understanding of reality.

In the long term, expecting measurable and, thus, visible returns on investment is not as such possible. This is because nobody can really know what will happen in the long term. Particularly when remote, the future is not only risky but also undoubtedly uncertain and unpredictable – even on the basis of probabilities (cf Knight, above). According to Keynes, the only certainty people may claim about the long term is that they will die (Keynes, 1923).

This means that, in the long term, companies, organizations, and so on, cannot count on their knowledge, know-how, and skills to solve problems they still do not and cannot know. In the long term, organizations need to learn how to learn about their environment and to adapt to it. They need to prioritize learning processes, creativity, flexibility, and innovation versus immediately and constantly delivering the best, in a visible way.

Why is there a contradiction between delivering the best immediately, constantly, and on visible way on one hand, and adapting to a changing environment, innovating, and being creative on the other?

The most fundamental reason is that being innovative and creative involves uncertainty beyond usual risks. When people innovate, they do not yet know what they will actually produce, create, or invent. They consequently cannot evaluate the efficiency of their invention, creation, or innovation. They will know about it only afterward. And in the meantime, they will need to try and accept the risk of errors and search logic. When innovating, creating, or inventing, you can never rigorously evaluate in advance the return that you will get on the investment. You may wish such a return on investment, you may be scared about it, you may try to evaluate the probability of success of your project, but you can never be sure that it will work and produce exactly what you expect. Creating, innovating, and inventing are thus not compatible with short-term expectations. In the short term, particularly in the context of the capitalist system, people and par excellence shareholders wait for visible, immediate, constant – if not constantly increasing – and maximum profit and return on investment. They will spontaneously not tolerate errors, waste time, postponed benefit, and so on and so forth.

Added to the fact that such expectations are quite naïve, it is necessary to make clear how contradictory they are. No organization may survive on the medium and long term without adapting a minimum to its environment – for example, without innovating, inventing, creating, showing flexibility, and so on. Long- if not medium-term organizational sustainability depends on investments for the future without any kind of guarantee they will produce the expected return, whereas short-term expectations demand that organizations, institutions, and so on, deliver immediately, on the basis of previous taken-for-granted knowledge, know how, skills, and routines.

Complying with the short-term expectations of people and shareholders has the consequence that people will always privilege operations, actions, skills, know-how, and routines they *already* know. In other words, they will progressively become unilaterally short–term-oriented and forget about the future. They will endanger the sustainability of organizations and institutions, and potentially the shareholders' profits. This is what happened during the subprime crisis, as well as, for instance, to Enron.

26.3   MAKING A STEP BACK FROM A DREAM: ON PEOPLE EXPECTATIONS

"The social responsibility of business is to increase its profit." The difficulty we are tackling may be understood on the basis of this famous Milton Friedman's statement (Friedman, 1970). A more precise quotation is as follows: "There is one and only one social responsibility of business – to use it resources and engage in activities designed to increase its profits so long as it stays within the rules of the game, which is to say, engages in open and free competition without deception or fraud."

Friedman was of course right when stating that companies should increase their profit, because, added to the fact that profit is a relevant measure for companies' performance, this is a condition for their capacity to invest and to hire people. Making and increasing profit enables business to help society by increasing the general growth and welfare. But, on the other hand, everybody knows and admits that stating so Milton Friedman was wrong. When people make profit and are convinced that making profit suffices to help others, they are wrong. This is because making profit for the sake of making profit tends to separate people from each other and to provoke situations close to the situation prior to the subprime one.

Let us, nevertheless, not limit our caution against the Friedman statement to a moral argument. The reasons why Friedman was wrong are much more complex and subtle than the moral ones. These reasons are due to a theoretical focus on rationality first, and then to the way Milton Friedman, as a famous and respected scholar, stated his argument.

26.3.1   On Pure and Perfect Rationality

Milton Friedman's statement must be traced back to its most fundamental ground, which is the assumption that individuals behave rationally. Behaving rationally means, for economists, that when making decisions, people evaluate thoroughly the situation, depending, for instance, on what they know about the product they want to buy. They are supposed to be able to rank without ambiguity their possible choices, and consequently to make the best choice. Such a description is ultimately grounded on the hypothesis that people are purely and perfectly rational. Being purely and perfectly rational amount to knowing *everything* about a product or about any economic situation and, as a consequence, being able to systematically make the *best* choice of any considered transaction, by ranking systematically the possible choices and automatically choosing the best – for example, the best quality and the lowest price.

The hypothesis of "pure and perfect" rationality amounts to assuming that people *know everything* about any situation, and that they consequently can *do* everything. In other words, the dream is that people be *omnipotent* due to being *omniscient* – the dream is that people are like God: omnipotence and omniscience being the two theological characteristics of the Judeo-Christian god. It is an assumption based on total transparency and consequently on the total control of humans over their situations. Such a dream of total transparency and control is of course a mere dream. It is not realistic. People are actually always embedded in situations they do not know perfectly, because things are actually always somewhat dark. In other words, people's rationality is not "pure and perfect," to the contrary. It is bounded (March and Simon, 1993). And rationality being such bounded makes that organizations' rationality is also rooted on darkness and tacit skills and routines contrary to transparency, under control, and totally clear operations (Nelson and Winter, 1982).

Let us deepen the understanding of the issues related to the assumption of perfect and pure rationality.

Such an assumption is to be traced back to its very origin, which rests on the Renaissance humanism. Without arguing in detail, we may say that the European humanism consisted on a claim against "nature" as well as against the Judeo-Christian God. The core of the humanist intention may be described as the intention to take power over nature for the sake of humanity. Taking power over nature is to be done to the detriment of the Judeo-Christian God (Bibard, 2005). One of the most important consequences of humanism was that humans incorporated the dream as a reality. Among many, the mere efficiency of the modern sciences and technologies, which resulted from the humanist decision, to become, as the French philosopher Descartes (2005) states "masters and possessors of nature" was convincing enough to make people progressively develop on the belief that humans had reached the goal: the goal being that the whole world would be put under human control. Such a dream was radically criticized by some of the most famous philosophers of the twentieth century (see, e.g., Heidegger on technology, Heidegger, 1982). Nobody nowadays, indeed, thinks seriously that everything may be put under human control. The recent tsunamis – not only the Fukushima one, but some human tsunamis, such as the Arab spring, or precisely such as the subprime crisis one – show that humans do not control reality as they dream of. This is true *theoretically*. But observing humans and organizations *in practice* shows that people behave as if a total control of humans over their environment was possible, true, and the right way to operate reality. In other words, *in practice*, humans are quite naïve about their power on reality.

Before deepening the clarification of some huge consequences of such naïveté, it is necessary to remind ourselves a second origin of the economic notion of "pure and perfect rationality." This rests on the birth of modern political science. Modern political science was created by some philosophers during the Renaissance period, but it was made particularly clear by the philosopher Thomas Hobbes. Hobbes was the first in defining humans not as "political animals" – for example, as collective beings – but as free, equal-to-each-other, and rational individuals (Hobbes, 1968). With Hobbes, the new anthropology was born, created against the ancient anthropology coming from the Aristotelian understanding of humans.

The specificity of Hobbes's understanding of reality is that it became *a self-realizing prophecy*. Hobbes defined humans as free, equal-to-each-other, and rational individuals in order to ground a solid understanding of politics, able to help the governments' sustainability. But because of the way his thought was understood by his heirs, and particularly by the liberal philosopher John Locke (see Locke, 1980), the understanding of humans as being (selfish) free, equal-to-each-other, and rational individuals became the taken-for-granted anthropology. This means that people unconsciously believe that they *are* actually and legitimately (selfish) free, equal-to-each-other, and *rational* individuals.

It is now time to come back to our previous statement.

People's rationality is not "pure and perfect," but on the contrary, radically bounded. And people's rationality is bounded because of the organizations' and more generally life's *routines*. People need routines to do what they do in their daily lives. Otherwise, they cannot even live (Nelson and Winter, 1982; Polanyi, 2001). People's rationality being bounded means that people do not understand the whole as they should, in order to properly evaluate the consequences of their actions. People act and behave on the basis of their practices, which bound their understanding of reality. But they simultaneously as of now believe that they are endowed with "pure and perfect" rationality.

This is indeed the true root of the liberal understanding of reality. Liberal and neoliberal economists (Smith, Hayek, Friedman, and others) argue that the problems of economic life are not due to people's selfishness and individualistic behavior but to the institutional interferences with and into the markets. Should states and, generally speaking, institutions make room for individual initiatives and interactions, markets would by themselves operate the best. The famous Adam Smith's invisible hand would operate as a perfect regulation of the economic life.

Ironically enough, this understanding of reality is quite imperfect. It presupposes that a theoretical norm is (already) indeed real, which is not true. The problem is that such an understanding becomes the norm. In other words, the liberal understanding of reality became the normative or conventional taken-for-granted understanding of reality. And at the end of the day, people who do *not* think and question theoretically the world take for granted what they are told, without examining and taking any distance with what they are told.

What are they sometimes told? They are told that they are rational and that making profit ort increasing their profit suffices for them to comply with their social responsibility. "Be selfish, you will thus support society." Why should people doubt such a statement, particularly when it is written by such an important scholar as the Nobel Prize winner Milton Friedman? Here is the real problem of the Milton Friedman's statement: mixing reality and norms, and making public on the basis of this confusion a statement that people would just make theirs without further questions. Such a statement plays a real role in society and would certainly deserve more prudence for a scholar such as Friedman (see Strauss, 1952).

The consequences of such an understanding of reality, and of stating that a norm is indeed "already" real – the normative understanding of humans as "already" free, equal, and rational individuals – is the introduction of a hidden, invisible, and deeply deleterious complexity in reality. Because people behave *as if* they were purely and perfectly rational, free, and equal to each other, when this is absolutely *not* the case, they barely increase the spontaneous complexity of reality. People unconsciously *believe* that they are rational and that they have their environment under control – but they fight on this very basis against each other to impose their understandings of reality, which are actually bounded. Here we are with the deleterious naïveté we previously alluded to. This naïveté about themselves makes that people actually ignore a huge amount of aspects of reality, *and that they do not know that they do not know about this naïveté*. Indeed, ignorance is quite often, if not always, self-ignorance.

The way we put the issue may sound exaggerated. It is not. The High Reliability Organizations sociological studies (with scholars such as Karl Weick, Kathleen Sutcliffe, Charles Perrow) show that one of the main origins of catastrophes and organizational problems is that people do not know that they do not know many aspects of their environment including themselves. In other words, should people know about their *structural* ignorance, about themselves, and about their environment, they would be much more ready to learn and behave in an efficient way to help organizations and networks, if not society, to do their jobs the right way (see, e.g., the thorough analysis of the Bhopal case by Karl Weick for instance; Weick 1988, 2010). Because daily organizational life separates people, embedding them in bounded routines and skills, without being aware of it, people tend structurally to ignore their continuously changing environment and need to continuously relearn about it. But contrary to what they should know, due to the "control culture" we described above, they most often unconsciously believe that they know everything they should know and continue to behave out of date.

This happens when difficulties if not crises like the subprime one start looming ahead. It suffices to make even more clear that people *do not want* to imagine that they ignore their environment, because such an ignorance would endanger their capacities to comply with their partners' expectations – including the shareholders' – to make see how crises are prepared by the short-term and long-term tension described above. Accepting uncertainty, ignorance as a matter of fact, and continuously learning or being prepared to learn on such a basis would mean behaving on the basis of a structurally innovative, creative, and flexible attitude, which would favor real learning processes, through unlearning (skills, routines, know-how) and relearning.

Being short-term-oriented amounts to repeating already known procedures, operations, skills, and routines, on the basis of a radical compliance with others' expectations, and becoming more and more blind to oneself and the environment. Global crises or "tsunamis" are rooted on aggregated very local and apparently insignificant behaviors and attitudes.

Shareholders' expectations concerning the corporations' profitability are not automatically rooted on selfish and ill-intentioned behavior – far from it. But they certainly are the most often naïve. Should shareholders understand clearly their own best interest, they would support companies that do not systematically maximize their profit on the unique basis of the short term.

To finish this brief presentation of the reasons why there is a tension between financial markets and corporations, let us present some solutions to the contradictory dynamics between the short- and the medium- if not the long-term attitudes.

26.4 HOW TO DISENTANGLE PEOPLE FROM A UNILATERAL SHORT-TERM ORIENTATION?

Answers to this question are minimum two. They are both grounded on organizational theory and on political philosophy.

26.4.1 An Organizational Theory Perspective

The high-reliability organization trend makes clear that organizations that confront crises in contexts of complexity and uncertainty (at least, the unexpected) should favor the following:

– There should be awareness related to a lucid understanding that ignorance constantly looms ahead in organizations – *knowing* that people ignore a huge amount of data related to their own job, due to many interactions with others is to be understood as a competence: the capacity to learn continuously about what people are doing on the basis of their daily professional lives.

– Related to such a capacity, the capacity to *doubt* information, is consequently to question situations when they look abnormal. Such a capacity demands that people keep some distance from the daily tasks and operations. A while should be previewed on a regular basis to question the taken-for-granted activity.

– An example of this capacity to doubt consists in *debriefing* activities, whatever happens, good or bad. Making clear in teams why an operation went the right way or failed is deeply instructive for the future operations, and makes people used to take a step back from what they spontaneously consider as evident. Let us make clear that questioning and doubting are an aspect of people's daily work. Organizational life is much more ambivalent: because organizations need routines and taken-for-granted individual and collective skills. The method can consequently never consist in a unilateral choice for doubt or for taken-for-granted competences. Rather, it consists in *balancing the dynamics between routines and distance*, say between the short term and the long term. Managing organizations requires a kind of wisdom (Weick, 2001);

– Last but not least, organizations should favor that people *speak their minds*. Too often, due to short-term constraints and demands, the managerial culture provokes silence because people are scared of sanctions. The more people may feel able to trust their bosses and talk to them when doubting a process or an operation, and even when committing errors, the best it is for the organizational internal as well as external communication. When errors are made, it is crucial that people feel able to talk about – for example, that they will not be systematically sanctioned. In that case, they will feel to be able to tell the truth, and look for ways to prevent the same error in the future. Otherwise, they will keep silent and try to hide problems. In the first case, the organization has a chance to become genuinely a learning one. In the latter, it will sooner or later have problems if not break.

The above recommendations (Weick and Sutcliffe, 2007) concern the management of the *unexpected*. As a consequence, they concern par excellence the management of *financial markets*. Financial markets are not organizations, they are rather networks. Networks are much less vulnerable to constitutive ignorance as organizations are. But bounded rationality not only concerns people within organizations. It concerns everybody. And one may state that what happened, for instance, to the famous French trader Jérôme Kerviel "playing" with data on his computer screen may happen to anybody too much embedded in her/his job.

Anyway, another perspective should be of some help for people to get used to keeeping some distance with their jobs and short-term objectives and projects – including maximizing their profits. This second perspective depends on an understanding of some political philosophy issues.

26.4.2   A Political Philosophy Perspective

When tracing back the origin of Milton Friedman's statement on business social responsibility, we alluded to the theoretical revolution made by Thomas Hobbes. According to him, political philosophy was grounded on an Aristotelian understanding of politics, which takes for granted that political life is spontaneous to humans. As stated above, for Aristotle, humans are but "political animals" (Aristotle, 1995). Human lives are grounded on collective life, which starts with the family life. The radical difference between the ancient (e.g., Aristotelian) understanding of politics and the modern one (e.g., the Hobbes one) rests in considering or not considering humans as spontaneous "political" or living in collective structures.

By inaugurating the new anthropology, which will become the economic one, or by defining humans as free, equal to each other, and rational individuals, Hobbes makes room to the radical possibility of considering each human as equal to all the others. In other words, he potentially makes possible the abolition of slavery, the gender studies, and so on. This is the indomitably positive aspect of the modern understanding of politics. But on the other hand, this understanding potentially reduces humans to selfish and indifferent to the common good individuals, which is the dark side of modernity.

Taking distance with the short term amounts to taking distance with one's own interests, toward a consideration of the *common good* as well. A medium- and long-term attitude amounts to favoring open-mindedness and the capacity to balance one's own interests with the collective ones. In other words, a unilateral short-term attitude is structurally selfish, whereas a medium- or long-term one is collective and common-good-orientated. None of these perspectives is able to bring a solution by itself to the tension between the short term and long term, or between financial markets and corporations. Both are necessary. But a balance between short-term and long-term perspectives is necessary. In managerial terms, this means that neither the stakeholders theory nor the shareholders theory is true. *They are true together*.

Understanding how such knowledge may be of some help practically demands understanding a bit more on how the ancient political philosophy and the modern political science complete each other on the very basis of their initial difference if not contradiction. We discuss this issue in our book *Sexuality and Globalization, An Introduction to a Phenomenology of Sexuality* (Bibard, 2014).

References

Aristotle. *Politics*. New York: Oxford University Press; 1995.

Bibard, L. The ethics of capitalism. In: Djelic, M.-L., Vranceanu, R., editors. *Ethical Boundaries of Capitalism*. Aldershot, Great Britain: Ashgate; 2005. p 3–24.

Bibard, L. *Sexuality and Globalization, An Introduction to a Phenomenology of Sexuality*. Palgrave Macmillan; 2014.

Descartes, R. *Discourse on the Method of Rightly Conducting the Reason, and Seeking Truth in the Sciences*. UK: 1st World Library – Literary Society; 2005.

Fraga Alves, I., Neves, C. Extreme value theory: an introductory overview. In: Longin, F., editor. *Extreme events in finance*. Wiley; 2017.

Friedman, M. *The Social Responsibility of Business is to Increase its Profit*. NY: *New York Times*; 1970.

Heidegger, M. *The Question Concerning Technology and Other Essays*. Harper Collins; 1982.

Hobbes, T. *Leviathan*. Penguin Classics, Penguin Books: London; 1968.

Keynes, J.-M. *A Tract on Monetary Reform*. London: Macmillan; 1923.

Knight, F. *Risk Uncertainty and Profit*. Boston, MA: Shaffner & Marx; 1921.

Locke, J. *Second Treatise of Government*. Indianapolis and Cambridge: Hackett Publishing Company; 1980.

Longin, F. Volatlity and Extreme Movements in Financial Markets. PhD Thesis, HEC; 1993.

March, J.G., Simon, H.A. *Organizations*. Wiley; 1993.

Nelson, R.R., Winter, N.G. *An Evolutionary Theory of Economic Change*. Harvard University Press; 1982.

Polanyi, K. *The Great Transformation*. Bacon Press; 2001.

Strauss, L. *Persecution and the Art of Writing*. The Free Press; 1952.

Weick, K. Reflections on enacted sensemaking on the Bhopal disaster. Journal of Management 2010;**43**(7):537–550.

Weick, K. The attitude of wisdom : ambivalence as the optimal compromise. In: Weick, K.E., editor. *Making Sense of the Organization*. Malden, MA: Blackwell Publishing; 2001. p 361–379.

Weick, K. Enacted sensemaking in crises situations. Journal of Management Studies 1988;**25**:4.

Weick, K., Sutcliffe, K. *Managing the Unexpected, Resilient Performance in an Age of Uncertainty*. John Wiley & Sons; 2007.

Name Index

Extreme Events in Finance: A Handbook of Extreme Value Theory and its Applications,
First Edition. Edited by François Longin.
© 2017 John Wiley & Sons, Inc. Published 2017 by John Wiley & Sons, Inc.

Subject Index

A

aggregation, 240–244, 271, 276–277, 279
  high frequency, 240
  sample size, 241, 242, 245, 273, 276, 278
algorithms
  bootstrap, 118, 130–135
alternative Hill plot, 394
alpha-stable distributions, 190
analytical comparison, 242, 259, 272
annual maxima. *see* block maxima
anti-Leibnizian, 26
anything but Mandelbrot (ABM), 37
aperiodicity, 141
application-driven approach, 45
applications to finance, 161, 164–167
approximation
  Berry–Esséen bounds, 261
  Berry–Esséen inequality, 249, 261, 262, 264
  Edgeworth expansion, 249, 261
  Hermite polynomial, 249
  moments, 240
  normal approximation, 248–252, 254, 256–257, 259–260, 262, 265, 269, 277–278
  numerical approximation, 255, 259, 262, 265, 268, 269, 271–274, 276, 278
  Zaliapin method, 242, 247–248, 250–251, 266, 271–272
asset returns, 483–505
asymptotic independence, 89, 209
asymptotic mean-squared error (AMSE), 365
AT&T, 396

B

bank contagion, 358
banking market index, 381
bank loans, 394
bank run, 552
Barndorff–Nielsen, 46
Bessel function, 186
Basel Committee on Banking Supervision, 555–557, 559–562
Bernstein polynomials, 202, 207
beta distribution, 58, 59, 67, 69
bivariate extreme value distribution, 196, 198
bivariate normal distribution function, 367
Black Monday, 525–528
  crash, 220, 231
Black–Scholes model, 39
block maxima, 56, 70–72, 75, 76, 84
blocking techniques, 139
bootstrap methodology, 118, 127–135
bounded rationality, 7
BP, 397
breakout (fractal) signal, 226, 231
Brownian, 468, 469
Brownian motion, 31, 484
Brownian virus, 27

C

CAC40, 164–167
capital-guarantee, 5
central limit theorem, 485
CGMY model, 47

autoregression, 409–410
autoregressive conditional heteroscedasticity (ARCH) process, 217, 222, 484, 487, 491, 492, 526

Extreme Events in Finance: A Handbook of Extreme Value Theory and its Applications,
First Edition. Edited by François Longin.
© 2017 John Wiley & Sons, Inc. Published 2017 by John Wiley & Sons, Inc.

Wiley Handbooks in
FINANCIAL ENGINEERING AND ECONOMETRICS

Advisory Editor
Ruey S. Tsay
The University of Chicago Booth School of Business USA

The dynamic and interaction between financial markets around the world have changed dramatically under economic globalization. In addition, advances in communication and data collection have changed the way information is processed and used. In this new era, financial instruments have become increasingly sophisticated and their impacts are far-reaching. The recent financial (credit) crisis is a vivid example of the new challenges we face and continue to face in this information age. Analytical skills and ability to extract useful information from mass data, to comprehend the complexity of financial instruments, and to assess the financial risk involved become a necessity for economists, financial managers, and risk management professionals. To master such skills and ability, knowledge from computer science, economics, finance, mathematics and statistics is essential. As such, financial engineering is cross-disciplinary, and its theory and applications advance rapidly.

The goal of this Handbook Series is to provide a one-stop source for students, researchers, and practitioners to learn the knowledge and analytical skills they need to face today's challenges in financial markets. The Series intends to introduce systematically recent developments in different areas of financial engineering and econometrics. The coverage will be broad and thorough with balance in theory and applications. Each volume will be edited by leading researchers and practitioners in the area and covers state-of-the-art methods and theory of the selected topic.

Published Wiley Handbooks in Financial Engineering and Econometrics

Bauwens, Hafner, and Laurent · *Handbook of Volatility Models and Their Applications*

Brandimarte · *Handbook in Monte Carlo Simulation: Applications in Financial Engineering, Risk Management, and Economics*

Chan and Wong · *Handbook of Financial Risk Management: Simulations and Case Studies*

Cruz, Peters, and Shevchenko · *Fundamental Aspects of Operational Risk and Insurance Analytics: A Handbook of Operational Risk*

James, Marsh, and Sarno · *Handbook of Exchange Rates*

Peters and Shevchenko · *Advances in Heavy Tailed Risk Modeling: A Handbook of Operational Risk*

Viens, Mariani, and Florescu · *Handbook of Modeling High-Frequency Data in Finance*

Szylar · *Handbook of Market Risk*

Bali and Engle · *Handbook of Asset Pricing*

Veronesi · *Handbook of Fixed-Income Securities*

Longin · *Extreme Events in Finance: A Handbook of Extreme Value Theory and its Applications*

Forthcoming Wiley Handbooks in Financial Engineering and Econometrics

Chacko · *Handbook of Credit and Interest Rate Derivatives*

Florescu, Mariani, Stanley, and Viens · *Handbook of High-Frequency Trading and Modeling in Finance*

Jacquier · *Handbook of Econometric Methods for Finance: Bayesian and Classical Perspectives*

Starer · *Handbook of Equity Portfolio Management: Theory and Practice*

Szylar · *Handbook of Hedge Fund Risk Management and Performance: In a Challenging Regulatory Environment*

Szylar · *Handbook of Macroeconomic Investing*